This publication was prepared by U.S. Satellite Laboratory, Inc., in part under award NCC5433 from the National Aeronautics and Space Administration (NASA). The statements, findings, conclusions, and recommendations are those of the author(s) and do not necessarily reflect the views of the National Aeronautics and Space Administration (NASA).

This publication was prepared by U.S. Satellite Laboratory, Inc., in part under award NA06SEC4690006 from the National Oceanic and Atmospheric Administration (NOAA), U.S. Department of Commerce. The statements, findings, conclusions, and recommendations are those of the author(s) and do not necessarily reflect the views of the National Oceanic and Atmospheric Administration (NOAA) or the U.S. Department of Commerce.

Marine Science
The Dynamic Ocean

Meghan E. Marrero, Ed.D.

Glen Schuster, M.S.

U.S. Satellite
Laboratory
Rye, New York

Print Components

Student Edition
Teacher's Edition
Study Workbook

Technology Components

Marine Science website: www.us-satellite.net/marinescience
Classroom Resources: "*e-Tools*" DVD ROM
Signals of Spring website: www.signalsofspring.net
Examview® CD-ROM

Front Matter Acknowledgments **Front Cover:** NOAA, NDGC; NOAA National Marine Sanctuaries/Claire Fackler. **Back Cover:** photos.com. **xii:** NOAA, Cordell Bank NMS. **xiii:** photos.com. **xiv:** NOAA/Andy Bruckner. **xvii:** photos.com. **xviii:** NOAA Ocean Service Education, University of Hawaii/Dr. Craig Smith. **xix:** NOAA, NDGC; UC Santa Cruz; NOAA National Marine Sanctuaries Media Library/Claire Fackler. **xxii:** NOAA, NGDC; photos.com.

Additional acknowledgments appear on page 722, which constitutes an extension of this copyright page.

Student Edition ISBN: 978-0-13-319217-9

Teacher's Edition ISBN: 978-0-13-319208-7

U.S. Satellite Laboratory

1 2 3 4 5 6 7 8 9 10 V063 14 13 12

About the Authors

Meghan E. Marrero, Ed.D.

Dr. Meghan E. Marrero is Associate Professor of Secondary Education at Mercy College and Director of Research and Evaluation at U.S. Satellite Laboratory. She is President of the New York State Marine Education Association (NYSMEA) and is a true ocean lover. While studying biology and marine science as an undergraduate at Cornell University, Meghan spent a semester at sea, sailing the East Coast with her classmates on a wooden schooner. She later earned her master's and doctoral degrees in Science Education from Teachers College, Columbia University, where her theses focused on educating students about the ocean's importance in the Earth system.

As a high school teacher in the New York City public schools, Meghan initiated marine science programs to make ocean learning accessible to city students. Meghan's activities have also taken her far afield, most recently to Midway Atoll in the Pacific Ocean, with a group of other science educators to study the science and culture of the Northwest Hawaiian Islands.

While serving as Director of Curriculum for U.S. Satellite Laboratory from 2004–2011, she led curriculum development for large national projects from NASA, NOAA, and NSF awards. She led the instructional design and development of *Marine Science: The Dynamic Ocean*, building on her team's work in the earlier projects. Her research focus remains increasing ocean and environmental literacy of teachers and students. Meghan lives on Long Island Sound with her husband and her non-water-loving dog.

Glen Schuster, M.S.

Glen Schuster is a Scientist Educator and President of U.S. Satellite Laboratory, Inc. He attended public schools in his hometown of Peabody, Massachusetts, before earning a bachelor's degree in mathematics from the University of Pennsylvania. A NASA Fellowship paved the way to a master's degree in meteorology from the Florida State University, and an assignment as Chief On-Air Meteorologist for a New York state ABC-TV affiliate. In 1991, Glen founded U.S. Satellite Laboratory. Driven by his passion to make science engaging and user-friendly for all learners, Glen's organization has been designing and developing STEM (Science, Technology, Engineering, and Mathematics) classroom and professional development materials for over 20 years.

Glen's work as Principal Investigator and Project Director for NASA, NOAA, and NSF in various national projects has pioneered the integration of remote sensing and instructional technology assets and tools into core curriculum materials. He is a nationally recognized leader in STEM professional development for teachers, and is the Project Director of NASA's Endeavor Science Teaching Certificate Project. His collaborations in the Arctic and animal tracking work with wildlife biologists around the globe, combined with the time he spends in active instruction with students and teachers, helps him to keep U.S. Satellite focused on one goal: the improvement of teacher practice and student achievement in science and STEM.

As Chief Editor of *Marine Science: The Dynamic Ocean*, and creator of *Signals of Spring* from which this publication comes, he gratefully acknowledges his substantial debt to his co-author and the team at U.S. Satellite. He was elected to and currently serves on his local school board in Westchester County in New York. He lives with his devoted wife, Julie, and his amazing sons, Seth and Justin.

Special Contributors

Tara Alvarez, B.S.

Tara Alvarez is the Creative and Technical Director for U.S. Satellite Laboratory and began working on educational technology projects with *Signals of Spring* when it first launched in 1999. Her one-of-a-kind skill set has been applied to many exciting and innovative projects, which have included the complete print matter and book cover, plus the DVD, for *Marine Science: The Dynamic Ocean*. A mechanical engineer by training, Tara has used her computer and process skills to build database registration and tracking systems, stereo 3-D graphics and animations, simple-to-use interactive data tools, and over a dozen of the U.S. Satellite Laboratory project websites. Tara loves animals and enjoys the outdoors. She resides in rural Virginia with her family.

Karen Woodruff, M.A.

Karen Woodruff serves as U.S. Satellite Laboratory's Director of Curriculum and Instruction. She is dedicated to supporting teachers with effective pedagogy and meaningful content and expands upon her prior work with U.S. Satellite from 2005–2011 as both a curriculum developer and professional development instructor. As a former high school science teacher and naturalist, she has a diverse background in formal and informal education and a well-rooted enthusiasm for meaningful, inquiry-based, constructivist teaching and learning. Trained in environmental science, she is specifically interested in aquatic systems and ornithology, and her appreciation and love of nature pervade all aspects of her life and work. Karen deeply enjoys sharing her passion for science and the outdoors with her two young explorers and devoted husband.

Kathryn Taylor, Ed.D.

Dr. Kathryn Taylor has worked with U.S. Satellite Laboratory since its inception. A master curriculum designer who continues to craft authentic learning experiences with broad, contextual themes and instructional technologies for students, Kathryn pioneered truly integrated approaches to science education as a K–12 Science Supervisor in Northern New Jersey. A former college professor and teacher, Kathryn is a passionate, lifelong learner with diverse interests including the Native American Flute, natural nutrition, and photography. She has had a longtime love for the water since growing up along the Niagara River just upstream from Niagara Falls. Kathryn and her family live in Upstate South Carolina near the headwaters of many of the rivers of the Carolinas.

Special Acknowledgment

The authors wish to express deep appreciation and gratitude to **Dr. Shelley Canright**, of the National Aeronautics and Space Administration (NASA). With the initial NASA sponsorship for the *Signals of Spring* project in 1999, and over the years, Dr. Canright has been a supporter of the methodologies and learning strategies from which this course is built. Her professional development and guidance has motivated the project team to deliver the highest quality of education services, integrated with NASA assets, to schools around the nation. As part of the NASA education family, U.S. Satellite Laboratory has provided tens of thousands of students with the opportunity to be the beneficiaries of Dr. Canright's leadership. As dear parents, grandparents, family, teachers, and others in the personal lives of the authors have influenced this body of work, we acknowledge Dr. Shelley Canright as one who has championed it.

Contributing Writers

Amanda Bickerstaff, M.S.
The Graduate Center,
City University of New York
New York, NY

Shakira Castronovo, M.A.
Manhattan School for Children
New York, NY

Cris L. DeWolf, M.A.T.
Chippewa Hills High School
Remus, MI

Derek Dubossi, M.A.
Bronx High School of Letters
Bronx, NY

Jodi Duggan, M.A.
U.S. Satellite Laboratory, Inc.
Rye, NY

Marianne Goshorn, M.S. Ed.
Eastbrook Community Schools
Marion, IN

Amanda M. Gunning, Ph.D.
U.S. Satellite Laboratory, Inc.
Rye, NY

Amanda Jaksha, M.A.
University of Arizona
Tucson, AZ

Beth Jewell, M.Ed.
West Springfield High School
Springfield, VA

Linda B. Knight, Ed.D.
Science Education Consultant
Wylie, TX

Keira Lam, M.S.
Queens High School of Teaching
Bellerose, NY

Catherine Meechan, M.S.Ed.
Virginia Beach City Public Schools
Virginia Beach, VA

Jessica F. Riccio, Ed.D.
Teachers College,
Columbia University
New York, NY

Gina Schilling, B.A.
Hill Middle School
Novato, CA

Michelle Silk, M.S., M.L.I.S.
Mercy College
Dobbs Ferry, NY

Science Reviewers

Pranoti Asher, Ph.D.
Georgia Southern University
Statesboro, GA

Elizabeth Burton Burck, M.A.
Educational Consultant
Kasilof, AK

Amy Ellwein, M.S.
University of New Mexico
Albuquerque, NM

Kusali Gamage, Ph.D.
Integrated Ocean Drilling
Program, Texas A&M University
College Station, TX

Michelle Hester, B.A.
Oikonos Ecosystem Knowledge
Honolulu, HI

David Hyrenbach, Ph.D.
Hawaii Pacific University
Kaneohe, HI

Carol Keiper, M.S.
Oikonos Ecosystem Knowledge
Benicia, CA

Russanne Low, Ph.D.
University of Nebraska-Lincoln
Lincoln, NE

Julie Maxson, Ph.D.
Metropolitan State University
St. Paul, MN

Ross Nehm, Ph.D.
The Ohio State University
Columbus, OH

Linda Schubert, B.S.
Papahānaumokuākea Marine
National Monument
Hilo, HI

Jennifer Stock, M.S. Ed.
NOAA, Cordell Bank National
Marine Sanctuary
Point Reyes Station, CA

J. Michael Williamson, M.S.
Wheelock College
Boston, MA

Charles Yackulic, Ph.D.
Columbia University
New York, NY

Copy Editors

Renata Brunner Jass, M.S.
Edmonton, AB, Canada

Jacquelyn L. Goss
Newton, MA

Jennifer Jin
New York, NY

Proofreader

Elaine Caughlan
Scarsdale, NY

Project Coordinator

Sara Lou Wolter
U.S. Satellite Laboratory, Inc.
Rye, NY

Publishing Advisor

David Rust
Sandhill Consulting Group, LLC
New York, NY

Lesson 25: Animal Needs and Animal Tracking   486

Phase II: Research and Analysis— Interpreting Satellite Imagery and Analyzing Animal Movements   500

Lesson 26: Student Expert Research   502

Lesson 27: Student Expert Analysis   520

Sponsoring Agencies

U.S. Satellite Laboratory, Inc., gratefully acknowledges the National Aeronautics and Space Administration (NASA) and the National Oceanic and Atmospheric Administration (NOAA). These Federal Agencies provided financial support for the initial design, development, and implementation of the *Signals of Spring* project as well as the subsequent expansion of curriculum and teacher professional development to the marine animal component in *Signals of Spring – ACES (Animals in Curriculum-based Ecosystem Studies)*, from which this course is built.

Initial funding from NASA in FY2000–FY2002 was awarded with a Cooperative Agreement from the NASA LEARNERS (Leading Educators to Applications, Research, and NASA-related Educational Resources in Science) program, award number NCC5433. NASA LEARNERS, led by Dr. Shelley Canright and Dr. Robert Gabrys, was an educational technology initiative that promoted futuristic projects in their design and approach to learning. U.S. Satellite Laboratory's interactions and training sessions for educators at NASA centers, as well as relationships with NASA science teams and offices around the nation, have contributed to this body of work.

In 2006, NOAA awarded U.S. Satellite Laboratory, Inc., a three-year Environmental Literacy Grant (award number NA06SEC4690006) for funding for FY2006–FY2009. The authors wish to acknowledge NOAA's Office of Education and the collaborative work with Sarah Schoedinger and her team of esteemed educators. Additionally, U.S. Satellite is grateful for its work over the years with NOAA's National Marine Sanctuary Program, in particular with Cordell Bank National Marine Sanctuary and Jennifer Stock, Education and Outreach Coordinator. Jennifer's tireless efforts, dedication, and commitment to excellence for *Signals of Spring—ACES* raised the bar. U.S. Satellite Laboratory is honored to be affiliated with a number of divisions of NOAA.

Having successfully performed on the awards and sustained the operations of all of the project components, U.S. Satellite Laboratory expresses a desire to continue to offer NASA and NOAA a return on investment with the continued support of educators who have participated in the past and to broaden the scope of the projects in the coming years.

Overview and Introduction

Overview

Welcome to *Marine Science: The Dynamic Ocean*. Studying Earth's most visible feature—the ocean—is a great way to learn science, technology, engineering, and mathematics (STEM) content and processes. In the course, we will investigate the scientific world of ocean organisms and physical characteristics, use technological tools to access, interpret, and apply a wealth of data sets, use the Engineering Design Process to create a tool for cleaning up oil spills, and use mathematics to calculate the density of objects and depth of the seafloor. You will even get the opportunity to track real marine animals! *Marine Science: The Dynamic Ocean* is a truly integrated science course in which the science concepts are applied to authentic scientific settings, scenarios, and investigations. You will simultaneously learn about life, Earth, and physical sciences. As you explore real-world data, you get a unique and fresh perspective on the ocean, its inhabitants, and its processes. Science concepts such as plate tectonics, food and energy transfer, and the properties of water come to life as you participate in Student Expert teams that focus on the seafloor, marine food sources, and the sea's surface.

This curriculum program parallels other textbook programs, yet there are some notable distinctions in the way it was put together. Rather than chapters, the book is divided into 34 Lessons, each of which will help you to build your understanding about the ocean and its processes. *Marine Science: The Dynamic Ocean* gives you the opportunity to access and interpret data sets, including oceanographic, meteorological, and animal tracking observations. You will also participate in field work, assessing local water quality and your school's potential contribution to marine pollution.

e-Tools: The DVD and Website

The technology utilized in the course is very simple to use. You and your teacher will find that the technology visuals and tools are built right into the Lessons. Through the DVD, you will access data, videos, animations, and other tools through *Marine Science: The Dynamic Ocean e-Tools*. The course website (www.us-satellite.net/marinescience) has additional resources and links including the animal tracking piece. Animal tracking is performed through the *Signals of Spring* project website, available both on your school's computers and through the Internet.

As you use the classroom or online tools and the hands-on labs to engage in the process of scientific inquiry, you will come to better understand the nature of science, and how scientific ideas are established and refined. These tools will support and extend your learning both in class and at home.

See Appendix A on Page 694 for how to access *e-Tools*.

Phases

The course is divided into Three Phases:

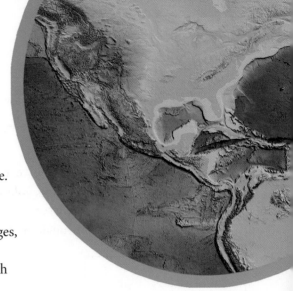

- **Phase I: Understanding the Ocean and Its Processes**

  Earth's last frontier, the ocean, is a vast and mysterious place. Explore features and processes of the ocean including: the seafloor and sea surface; tides, waves, and currents; marine populations and ecosystems; and food webs, seasonal changes, and weather. Learn how living and nonliving components of the ocean interact and the ocean's critical role in the Earth system and for human civilization.

- **Phase II: Research and Analysis – Interpreting Satellite Imagery and Analyzing Animal Movements**

  Study alongside wildlife biologists as you interpret authentic satellite data and explore the movements of animals, including penguins, sea turtles, whales, and sharks. Examine how marine animal movements are connected to physical and chemical properties of the ocean, and how environmental factors change over time. Create an optional Scientific Research Community Wall to tell the real-time story of your marine animal's movements over time.

- **Phase III: Understanding Human Impacts on the Ocean**

  It is the responsibility of each of us to protect the ocean and its many resources. Learn how humans affect the ocean— for better or for worse—as you examine issues such as coastal development, fishing, pollution, and climate change. Understand the importance of marine protected areas and how human activities on land affect the ocean, even when it is far away.

Each Phase will lead you toward understanding more about the ocean, its processes, and its significance in the functioning of our planet. You will collaborate with your peers to perform scientific investigations of real-world issues, building understandings that will help you make decisions about 21st Century environmental issues.

The 5 E Model

We will embark on a scientific journey in which we track live marine animals alongside scientists, using the skills and tools of scientific inquiry just as they do. In each Lesson, you will find five sections, which are described below:

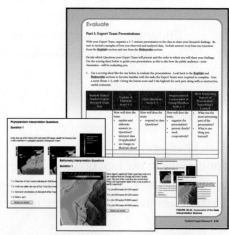

- The **Engage** section encourages you to think about what you already know about a topic; it will give you new things to consider as you embark upon and begin to work through the Lesson.

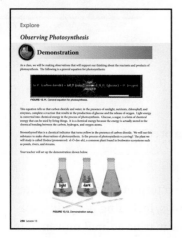

- In the **Explore** section, you may participate in fieldwork, conduct hands-on labs, or engage in Cyberlabs through which you formulate your ideas about a topic.

- The **Explain** section provides you the opportunity to relate what you found in the Explore section to what is known about the topic. You will read, answer questions, create charts and graphs, use online tools, and more to learn about the ocean system while you expand your understanding of powerful concepts.

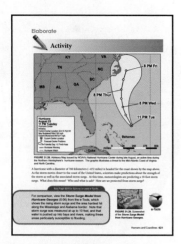

- In the **Elaborate** section of the Lesson you will extend your knowledge. You will conduct additional investigations, analyze case studies, or create projects.

- The **Evaluate** section invites you to demonstrate what you have learned by answering questions, applying ideas, creating work products, or completing online quizzes.

Discovery – Demonstration, (Hands-on) Labs, Cyberlabs

You will construct your knowledge of marine science through active participation in Teacher Demonstrations, hands-on Labs, Cyberlabs, and Activities.

- **Demonstrations** – Make careful observations as your teacher illustrates Marine Science concepts and ideas. Ask questions that you can further explore.

- **Labs** – Laboratory investigations allow you to explore properties of the ocean's waters and its inhabitants. In these hands-on activities, you will work directly with materials to make observations and inferences.

- **Cyberlabs** – Today's computer technologies permit us to learn even more about the ocean. Take advantage of these resources and tools as you collect, observe, and analyze authentic oceanographic data.

- **Activities** – Build and demonstrate your knowledge through dozens of diverse activities that include investigations of marine ecosystems, graphing tidal cycles, finding watersheds on topographic maps, and modeling international fishing practices.

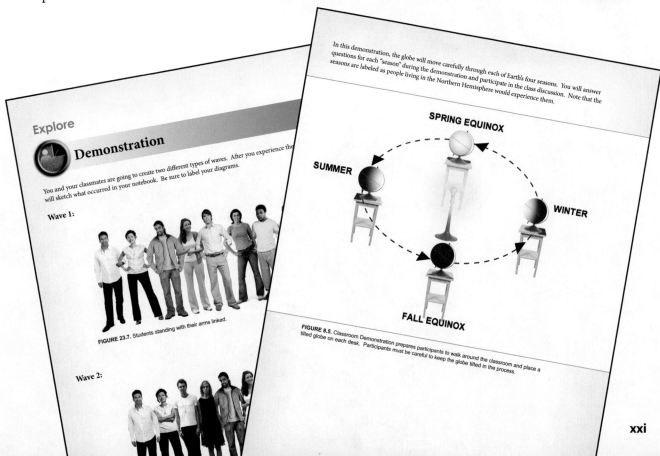

In this demonstration, the globe will move carefully through each of Earth's four seasons. You will answer questions for each "season" during the demonstration and participate in the class discussion. Note that the seasons are labeled as people living in the Northern Hemisphere would experience them.

SPRING EQUINOX

SUMMER

WINTER

FALL EQUINOX

FIGURE 8.5. Classroom Demonstration prepares participants to walk around the classroom and place a tilted globe on each desk. Participants must be careful to keep the globe tilted in the process.

Explore

Demonstration

You and your classmates are going to create two different types of waves. After you experience the will sketch what occurred in your notebook. Be sure to label your diagrams.

Wave 1:

FIGURE 23.7. Students standing with their arms linked.

Wave 2:

Satellite and Other Authentic Data

A unique component of *Marine Science: The Dynamic Ocean* is that you will be analyzing real data, collected by scientists. You'll have the opportunity to explore animal movement using the *Marine Science e-Tools* through the website in partnership with the *Signals of Spring* project (www.signalsofspring.net). You may look at animal tracks in real time or work with classic case studies and look at compelling archived animal movements. There are dozens of marine animal species, including Atlantic Bluefin Tuna, Polar Bears, Humpback Whales, Black-footed Albatross, and Loggerhead Sea Turtles, being tracked at any time. You will also study Earth data collected from satellites. These data include sea surface temperature, chlorophyll, ocean floor, and weather data, all of which affect the movements of marine animals.

In *Lesson 26: Student Expert Research* and *Lesson 27: Student Expert Analysis*, your work will be similar to that of wildlife biologists. You will have the opportunity to work with the *Signals of Spring* program. *Signals of Spring* is a project that, since 1999, has linked the work of research scientists with students. In addition to the *Marine Science e-Tools*, you will use the *Signals of Spring* website to use the simple-to-use Earth imagery to explain the animals' movements and record your findings in online Analysis Journals. There are many resources on the *Signals of Spring* website to complement your studies in the *Marine Science: The Dynamic Ocean* course.

You will also encounter data collected from ships, submersibles, and other vehicles used in the ocean. It is important to consider the characteristics of the ocean below the surface, including temperature, salinity, and light availability. There are also many interesting creatures inhabiting the ocean's depths.

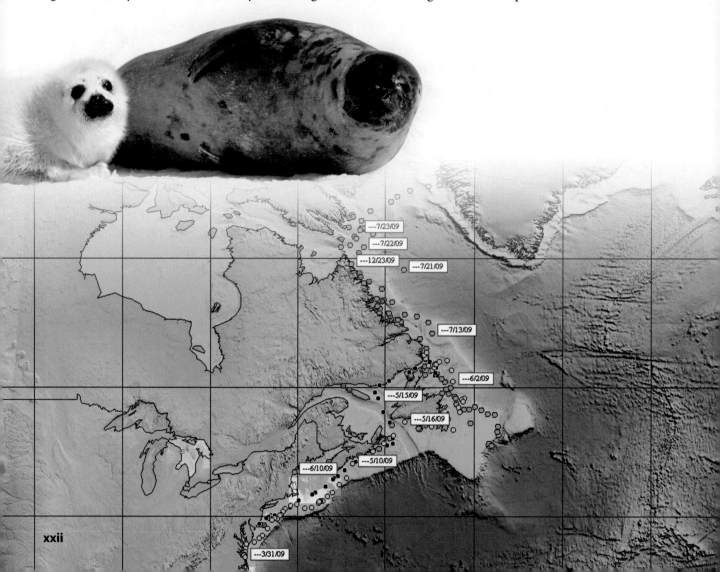

Fieldwork

Through the water cycle and our local watersheds, we are all connected to the ocean. By examining your local bodies of water, you will make connections to the ocean. In field investigations, you will collect plankton, assess water quality, and more. You will also make connections between litter on your school's campus and marine pollution.

Notebook

Good scientists have a system for keeping track of ideas, data, findings, understandings, hypotheses, and more. Like any scientist, keeping your notebook organized and complete will be important for your success in this course. Within a Lesson, when you see numbered Questions, answer those in your notebook. In addition, it is helpful to jot down important ideas as you read text and interpret diagrams and graphs. When you complete lab investigations or other worksheets, be sure to attach them to a page in your notebook so that you have everything in one place.

Study Spotlights

Many of the Lessons include Study Spotlights. These short articles are designed to give you insight into broad topics that relate to what you are learning, including Surfing, the Aquarius Underwater Research Laboratory, Scuba Diving, and a peek at a sediment core taken from the seafloor providing evidence of the huge impact from an asteroid 65 million years ago, the time when the dinosaurs became extinct on Earth.

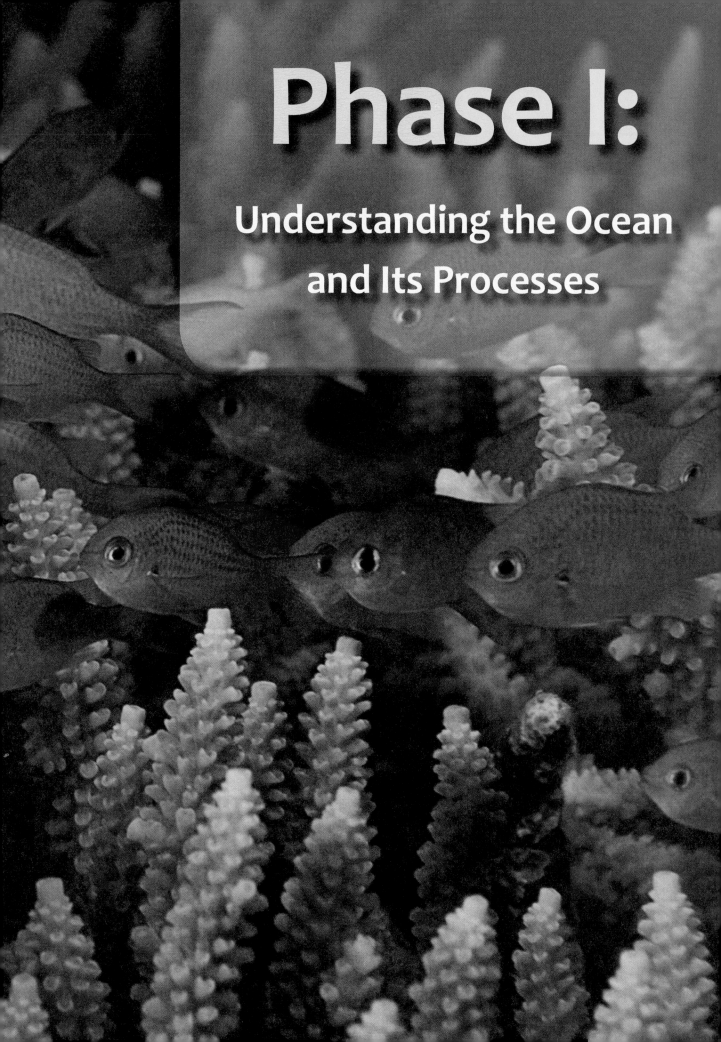

Phase I:

Understanding the Ocean and Its Processes

1

Diving Into Ocean Ecosystems

INSIDE:

Objectives

You will be able to:

✔ Recognize that while most of the planet is covered by ocean, it is not a uniform body of water.

✔ Give examples of diverse marine ecosystems and their locations on Earth.

✔ Characterize ecosystem components as abiotic and biotic factors and give examples of how they influence one another.

✔ Describe the process of biological succession, explaining that marine ecosystems undergo natural, gradual changes over time.

✔ Discuss how humans affect marine ecosystems both positively and negatively.

✔ Introduce wetlands as productive and highly diverse marine ecosystems.

Benchmarks

5e. The ocean is three-dimensional, offering vast living space and diverse habitats from the surface through the water column to the seafloor. Most of the living space on Earth is in the ocean.

5f. Ocean habitats are defined by environmental factors. Due to interactions of abiotic factors (e.g., salinity, temperature, oxygen, pH, light, nutrients, pressure, substrate, circulation), ocean life is not evenly distributed temporally or spatially (i.e., it is "patchy"). Some regions of the ocean support more diverse and abundant life than anywhere on Earth, while much of the ocean is considered a desert.

Engage

The ocean is a huge and mysterious place. Throughout human history, it has always been a source of inspiration. In this course, you will uncover many of the ocean's mysteries, and you will learn that there are many questions still unanswered.

As you proceed through your study of the ocean in *Marine Science: The Dynamic Ocean*, you will act as a scientist as you ask questions, make observations, and draw conclusions based on your observations. Scientists use many tools to learn about the ocean and different strategies to report their findings. You will learn about ocean and satellite technologies; you will see and work with pictures, animations, satellite imagery, and models. One important aspect of scientific work is keeping an accurate record of questions, observations,

FIGURE 1.1. The wide-open ocean holds many mysteries. Physics, chemistry, biology, and Earth science concepts and ideas help scientists solve them.

results of experiments, and new ideas to test. Most scientists use a *field notebook*, in which they record many of their activities and thinking. Peering into a scientist's field notebook, you would observe labeled sketches, measurements, mathematical calculations, and questions. Scientists keep their field notebooks very organized. As they work and evolve their thinking, they refer back to ideas they tried in the past, previous information, data sets, and their notes.

You will model the work that scientists do in your exploration of the ocean. Your notebook will hold your ideas, illustrate your thinking, and inspire new questions.

1. Think about what you already know about the ocean. What do you picture when you consider its waters? In your notebook, draw a sketch of what you think about when you picture the ocean.

2. Write 4–5 sentences about why you think the ocean is important.

3. Write at least 2 questions that you have about the ocean. Your questions can be about anything ocean related, including living things, the makeup of the water, how water flows, places in the ocean, etc.

In the *Marine Science: The Dynamic Ocean* course, you will observe the movements of many marine animals that are tracked by satellite. In most cases scientists attach a small satellite transmitter onto an animal so that they may observe its movements and learn more about its behavior. Life in the ocean is not easy. Marine animals face many challenges, both natural and as a result of human activities. Studying and understanding their movements is the first step in learning to protect them.

FIGURE 1.2. This Loggerhead Sea Turtle is outfitted with a satellite transmitter. Its release will provide scientists with data based on its movement through the sea.

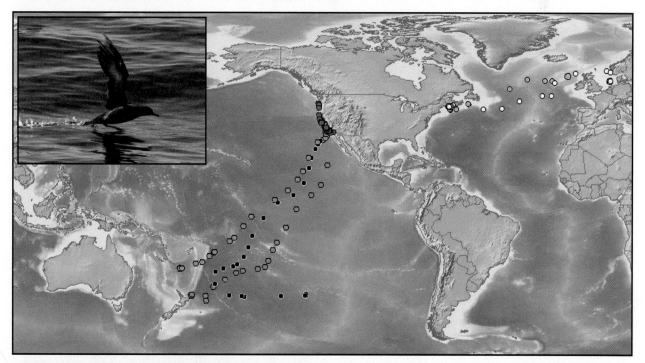

FIGURE 1.3. The map depicts the movements of six independent Sooty Shearwaters. A Sooty Shearwater is a type of seabird that migrates for thousands of miles.

Each color represents one individual animal and its movement over time. In this case, the animal is a seabird. The map shows the animals' travels over approximately two months. The movement of each animal over a period of time is observed to be thousands of miles.

4. Add at least one question you have about these animals' journeys to the list of questions in your notebook.

Explore

Marine Ecosystems Project

FIGURE 1.4. In *Marine Science: The Dynamic Ocean*, students study animal movements alongside scientist researchers.

In the *Marine Science: The Dynamic Ocean* curriculum program, you will actually study animals and their movements alongside scientists. Some animals will travel thousands of miles, others remain close to home. Regardless of how far each animal travels, it is important to learn about the environments through which they move. You will explore and report on some of the different ocean, or marine, habitats and relate the features of these environments to the needs of the animals.

The ocean covers more than 70% of our Blue Planet. The ocean includes many different ecosystems that range from the depths of the dark seafloor to the sunny surface, from close to shore to thousands of miles away from the coast. Each ocean ecosystem includes living, or **biotic**, and non-living, or **abiotic**, factors that characterize the ecosystem and make it unique. The relationships between interdependent biotic organisms and the physical abiotic factors is very important to the health of the ecosystem and the diversity of life that can exist. In fact, it is the abiotic factors that define marine habitats. In ocean ecosystems, important abiotic factors include temperature, pH, light and nutrient availability, and salt content. Another important abiotic factor is the availability of hard surfaces, or **substrates**, on which organisms can grow. Diverse ecosystems exist throughout the ocean with varying amounts of life. While much of the ocean has very little life, some marine ecosystems are incredibly productive and diverse.

The term, **wetland**, is used to describe a group of highly productive ecosystems found around the world that are home to a wide diversity of organisms. Wetlands include transitional areas between land and water where the soil is inundated with water either permanently or periodically. The biotic and abiotic factors in each type of wetland characterize it as unique from other types. In the following lesson activity, you will explore some examples of wetlands, including salt marshes and mangrove forests. In future lessons, you'll learn the importance of saltwater (marine) and freshwater wetland ecosystems.

 # Activity

Materials:

- *Classroom World Map*
- World map or atlas
- Internet access
- Various reference books, encyclopedias, and textbooks
- Poster paper or display boards
- Large sheet of paper (e.g., butcher paper)
- Markers, color pencils
- Chart paper

FIGURE 1.5. The ocean is home to a wide variety of marine ecosystems, some of which you will study in this Lesson. In every ecosystem, whether land or marine, there is interaction between biotic and abiotic factors.

1. Go to the **Marine Ecosystems Project** in the e-Tools and select the ecosystem you are assigned. Visit the accompanying website links and read the sources given. You should also use reference materials in the classroom. In your notebook, take notes <u>in your own words</u> that answer the following Questions:

e-Tools

- Describe your ecosystem. Which is it? What would it be like to live in your ecosystem?
- What are the major biotic factors in your ecosystem?
- What are the major abiotic factors in your ecosystem?
- Where in the world can your ecosystem be found? Include a map of the world indicating where your ecosystem can be found.
- What are the dominant (main) animals and plants in your ecosystem? Include pictures — draw them or print them out — to describe the animals and plants that live in your ecosystem.
- Describe the habitat in this ecosystem. Carefully consider the various components and determine what challenges an organism might face in your ecosystem (e.g., extreme cold water temperatures, amount of light, etc.).
- How do humans impact this ecosystem? What are some problems that this ecosystem might face in the future because of human activities?
- Identify interesting elements about your environment that you would like to share with the class.

2. Scientists write research papers and create posters to communicate their research, including their observations and findings, and present them at peer conferences and meetings. Other scientists will learn from their colleagues and ask additional research questions. They will often pursue additional research as they seek answers to these questions. This is an important part of the scientific process. Your poster on marine ecosystems will allow your peers to learn from your research and ask additional questions about your work.

   Once your research is complete, report your findings on a poster. The poster must answer all of the Questions above. Be creative. Use visuals to help illustrate important points whenever possible. Draw pictures, make charts and tables, and so on.

   Keep in mind that the poster you create will be the source for teaching your "classroom scientific community" about the ecosystem.

3. Hang the poster in the classroom.

4. On the **Classroom World Map**, illustrate the worldwide locations of the ecosystem your group has studied. Label the ecosystem by creating a key.

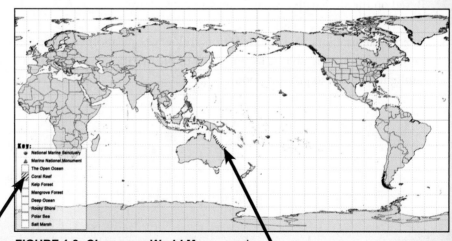

FIGURE 1.6. *Classroom World Map* example.

Explain

"Visiting" and Defining Ecosystems

5. You are attending a scientific conference on marine ecosystems. Your goal is to understand the characteristics of each marine ecosystem. Walk around the classroom to visit each poster. When visiting each ecosystem, fill in the information sheet or complete the chart in your notebook.

Marine Ecosystems Information Sheet

Ecosystem	Description of what it is like to live in this ecosystem	Examples of biotic factors in this ecosystem	Examples of abiotic factors in this ecosystem
Coral Reef			
Mangrove Forest			
Deep Sea			
Open Ocean			
Kelp Forest			
Polar Sea			
Salt Marsh			
Rocky Shore			

6. What common characteristics do you notice in all the marine ecosystems? What are some major differences?

7. Based on the similarities, what defines an ecosystem?

8. In ecosystems, biotic and abiotic factors influence one another. Give three examples of an interaction between a biotic and abiotic factor in any of the marine ecosystems you studied (e.g., plants [biotic] need sunlight [abiotic] to produce food).

Elaborate

Changing Ecosystems

All of the living things within an environment comprise a **biological community**. The interaction of the living things (biotic factors) with the non-living things (abiotic factors), along with an energy source, create an **ecosystem**. Ecosystems are dynamic—they constantly undergo change. Seasonal temperature fluctuations, changes in nutrient availability, the life cycles of organisms, and the rise and fall of the tides are just a few of the endless examples of natural changes that take place in marine ecosystems. Each living thing, or **organism**, and each molecule of water, source of nutrients, habitat, and so on, plays a role in the health and success of the ecosystem. When one of the abiotic or biotic factors changes, or a new factor is introduced, it can affect the rest of the ecosystem.

Case Study 1 - Whale Falls

See Page 694 for how to access e-Tools.

View the **Case Study 1 - Whale Falls Video** (2:30) from the e-Tools and consider what you are seeing.

e-Tools

FIGURE 1.7. Screenshot of **Case Study 1 - Whale Falls Video**.

9. What do you observe happening?

10. About how many different types of organisms did you see in the short video segment?

11. Do you think what you are observing is the result of a natural event or the result of human activity? Why?

Whales are a majestic and fascinating group of marine mammals with many interesting attributes. The Blue Whale, for instance, is the largest animal to have ever lived on Earth. Whales have the longest migration of all mammals; Humpback Whales, for example, migrate more than 8,000 kilometers (~5,000 miles). During their lifetimes, whales consume large amounts of krill, fish, crustaceans, and other organisms, and play an important role in ocean ecosystems. While the average life span of some species of whales is longer than that of humans and most other marine mammals, they too eventually die. When a whale dies, the carcass sinks to the seafloor, an event known as a *whale fall*.

A whale fall event introduces an abundance of nutrients to a specific area of the seafloor, and the result can be a change to the ecosystem over a period of time. Scientists estimate that a whale carcass weighing 40 tons can have approximately 2,000-3,000 kilograms of lipids in its skeleton. The rest of the animal's body provides even more nutrients to the wide diversity of organisms that will visit it. Scientists presently know of hundreds of species that feed on whale carcasses, and they suspect there are many more of which they are unaware.

To help understand the community of organisms that feed on whale carcasses, scientists observe whale fall sites with Remote Operated Vehicles (ROVs) fitted with high quality video cameras. With these tools they identify species feeding on whale carcasses over time. While scientists still have questions about how whale fall events impact marine ecosystems, they agree that whale falls are visited by a wide diversity of organisms that play a role in decomposing the whale carcass and moving the available nutrients into the marine food web. Scientists believe that factors such as depth, salinity, oxygen, and temperature play a role in the differences they observe in biological communities at each specific site they study.

To help identify the roles of the organisms that visit whale carcasses, scientists give groups of organisms descriptive names based on the task they perform. FIGURE 1.8 shows data from the observations of species visiting various whale carcasses approximately 1,000 meters below the sea surface, studied in Monterey Canyon, California. The photographs, shown with the figure were taken with an ROV camera. They show examples of organisms in three distinct groups: background specialists, bone specialists, and species with unclear connections. The background specialists include species of marine organisms that remove flesh or soft tissue from the whale's carcass. As the line graph shows, background specialists arrive early and remain present throughout the decomposition of the carcass. This important group may include hagfishes, sleeper sharks, slugs, worms, shrimp, crabs, and other scavengers that prefer the soft tissue of the whale. Some species visit to feed on the organisms that are attracted to the carcass, not the carcass itself.

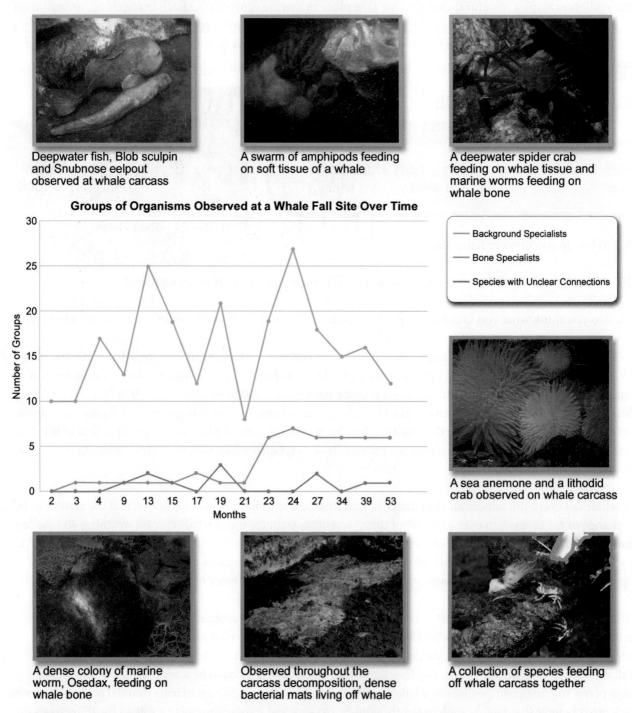

Deepwater fish, Blob sculpin and Snubnose eelpout observed at whale carcass

A swarm of amphipods feeding on soft tissue of a whale

A deepwater spider crab feeding on whale tissue and marine worms feeding on whale bone

Groups of Organisms Observed at a Whale Fall Site Over Time

Background Specialists

Bone Specialists

Species with Unclear Connections

A sea anemone and a lithodid crab observed on whale carcass

A dense colony of marine worm, Osedax, feeding on whale bone

Observed throughout the carcass decomposition, dense bacterial mats living off whale

A collection of species feeding off whale carcass together

FIGURE 1.8. Line graph illustrates the presence of three groups of organisms observed at a whale fall site off of the California Coast over time. Each group is classified by their role in the decomposition process.

Once the flesh is removed from the whale carcass, a group of organisms called bone specialists becomes more prevalent. These organisms are present for long periods, living off of the oil contained in whale bone. Osedax, a species of marine worms, is dominant at many whale fall sites off the California Coast.

The final group, the species with unclear connections, consists of another set of organisms. This group is not seemingly dependent on the whale fall.

Whale falls are one example of how, after a change occurs in an ecosystem, species progressively replace one another until they reach a stable community. This process is known as **succession**. In this specific example, the stable community is the seafloor, or **benthic**, ecosystem. The series of images below shows the progression of change as a whale carcass decomposes with the help of marine organisms that visit the carcass and take advantage of the influx of nutrients.

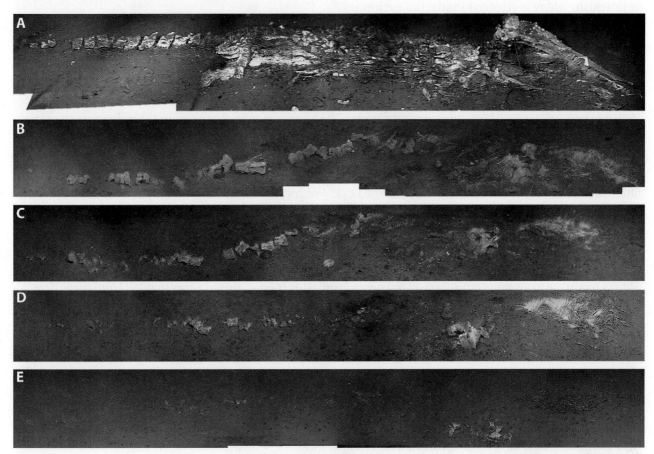

FIGURE 1.9. The series of images shows the decomposition of a whale carcass over a period of 7 years: (A) February 2002. Initial visit by scientists (~6 months after the whale fall event); (B) December 2004. 34 months since initial scientist visit; (C) November 2005. 45 months since initial scientist visit; (D) December 2007. 70 months since initial scientist visit; (E) March 2009. 85 months since initial scientist visit.

12. Study the line graph in FIGURE 1.8. What do you notice about the groups of organisms that are present at the whale carcass over time?

13. Can you explain the increase in bone specialists after Month 21?

14. How might you explain the increase in background specialists between Months 21 and 24?

15. How might you determine if your analysis in the questions above is accurate?

Case Study 2 - Mangrove Restoration

As you learned in your poster presentations of Marine Ecosystems, mangrove forests are an important ecosystem for species of fish, plants, birds, and other wildlife. Mangrove forests are found along the coast where fresh water from the land meets salt water from the ocean, in subtropical and tropical latitudes near the Equator in areas such as Florida, the Caribbean, Australia, and India. They cover less than 8% of the Earth's coastlines. The organisms that live in mangrove forests are able to survive in water that is slightly salty, or **brackish**. Many species rely on the unique biotic and abiotic factors in this environment for breeding, raising their young, and finding food. Mangrove forests are one of the most diverse marine ecosystems and serve many important functions.

FIGURE 1.10. Abiotic factors in mangrove forests include brackish, cloudy water, sediments, and warm temperatures. Common biotic components are mangrove trees, fish, and invertebrate species.

Very few tree species make up the mangrove forests. The species of trees that grow in the mangrove ecosystem, collectively called **mangroves**, include four main groups: red mangroves, black mangroves, white mangroves, and buttonwoods. The mangrove plant community provides a barrier between the ocean and the land. The plants stabilize the soil and reduce erosion from large storms and hurricanes. In addition, mangroves serve as filters for fresh water entering the ocean from the land. Freshwater runoff can contain pollutants and excessive amounts of sediment that can harm ocean ecosystems. Mangroves trap sediments that contain pollutants such as heavy metals (e.g., mercury, lead) and prevent them from being washed into the ocean. If the mangrove forests stay in place, the sediments and pollutants may remain undisturbed for hundreds of years or more.

Mangroves are also a significant source of nutrients for marine food chains. Leaves that fall from mangrove trees enter the water and become food for microorganisms. The underwater areas around mangrove roots are utilized by various species for breeding and protection from predators. They are grounds for many commercial species of fish.

FIGURE 1.11. The roots of mangrove trees prevent the movement of sediment. Mangrove forests, therefore, can prevent the erosion of coastlines that can damage homes and businesses.

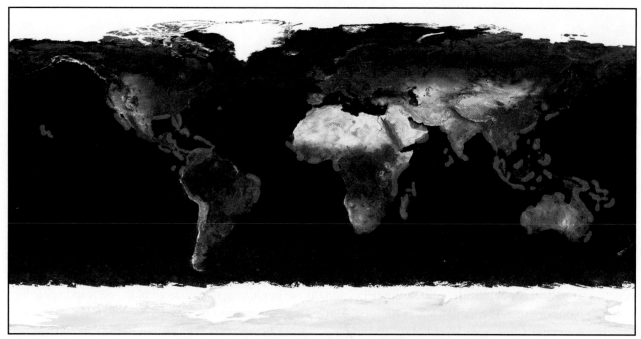

FIGURE 1.12. Global distribution of mangrove forests indicated in red on NASA Blue Marble image.

A: Before restoration   **B: After restoration**

FIGURE 1.13. Mangrove reestablishment at Cross Bayou, Florida.

16. Copy the chart into your notebook. Compare the biotic and abiotic factors in the photographs above.

Photograph	Biotic Factors	Abiotic Factors
A		
B		

17. How do the differences observed between Photographs A and B demonstrate succession?

FIGURE 1.14. Ecosystems on land, in the ocean, and in between can be restored in order to promote natural ecological succession. Here, volunteers in Maryland plant beach grasses to promote the healthy growth of a sandy beach ecosystem.

While the ocean seems very large, human activities on land affect large ocean ecosystems significantly. The ocean's resources are not infinite, and, fortunately, humans are beginning to realize all of us are responsible for protecting our oceans. The United States National Marine Sanctuaries and marine protected areas (MPAs) are illustrated on your *Classroom World Map*. During the *Marine Ecosystems Project*, some students "visited" the ecosystems that are found within the Sanctuaries. Now let's learn just what these special places are all about.

What Are National Marine Sanctuaries?

National Marine Sanctuaries are America's underwater treasures. They are a system of 14 marine protected areas that encompass nearly 250,000 square kilometers (more than 150,000 square miles) of marine and Great Lakes waters from Washington State to the Florida Keys and from Lake Huron to American Samoa. These areas have regulations that allow some human activities and do not allow others. Sanctuaries allow both commercial and recreational fishing unless these fishing activities become destructive to habitats. Each sanctuary has different regulations. The rules protect these special habitats. The habitat types are surprisingly quite varied.

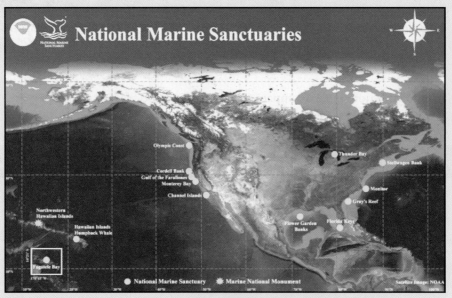

FIGURE 1.15. Map showing the locations of National Marine Sanctuaries.

Scientists conduct formal research in sanctuaries to learn more about the ecosystems and the organisms that make them their homes. You can't protect something you don't know about, so research is essential to understanding what lives in the sanctuaries and how marine ecosystems work.

Within their protected waters, giant Humpback Whales breed and calve their young, unique plants and animals flourish, and shipwrecks tell stories of our maritime history. Sanctuary habitats include beautiful rocky reefs, lush kelp forests, coral reefs, whale migration corridors, spectacular deepsea canyons,, and underwater archaeological sites. Our nation's sanctuaries also provide a safe habitat for endangered species, or they can protect historically significant shipwrecks. Ranging in size from less than 1 square kilometer (~0.4 square miles) to 362,074 square kilometers (~139,797 square miles), each United States National Marine Sanctuary site is a unique place needing special protections.

FIGURE 1.16. The Florida Keys National Marine Sanctuary is one of the most accessible sanctuaries to visitors, who visit the sanctuary to go boating, fishing, snorkeling, scuba diving, etc. It is located among the many islands, or "keys", in the southern part of the state.

You may notice from the map on Page 14 that the largest site within the National Marine Sanctuary system is actually the Papahānaumokuākea (pronounced: pah-pah-HAH-nō-mō-koo-ah-KAY-ah) Marine National Monument, located in the Northwest Hawaiian Islands. Marine National Monuments offer even more protections than National Marine Sanctuaries. For example, commercial fishing is not allowed in the Monument, and tourism is very limited. Papahānaumokuākea was created in 2006 during George W. Bush's term as U.S. President and is one of the largest MPAs in the world.

18. Why might the National Marine Sanctuaries be important when studying the paths of marine animals?

FIGURE 1.17. Humpback Whale mother and calf. The Hawaiian Humpback Whale National Marine Sanctuary was the first sanctuary designated to protect a specific species of organism. Some scientists in the area wish to see the sanctuary expanded to better protect other species.

Olympic Coast National Marine Sanctuary

The Olympic Coast National Marine Sanctuary was designated in 1994 by NOAA (National Oceanic and Atmospheric Administration) as the nation's twelfth marine sanctuary. Located off the coast of Washington State,

FIGURE 1.18. A map showing the location of the Olympic Coast National Marine Sanctuary.

the sanctuary spans 8,573 square kilometers (~3,310 square miles) and reaches 40–65 kilometers (25–40 miles) seaward. The protected area is the same size of the states of Delaware and Rhode Island combined. The sanctuary protects the shallow areas along the coast as well as its deep underwater canyons. There are 180 historical shipwrecks within its waters. One major ecosystem within the sanctuary is a lush kelp forest, in which a variety of invertebrates, seabirds, and marine mammals make their homes.

The sanctuary serves to protect all species and habitats, large, and small. NOAA and other research partners use Remote Operating Vehicle (ROVs) to search for and study corals and sponges. Researchers have confirmed deep water coral and sponge communities throughout the sanctuary, including a rare soft coral, *Lophelia pertusa* (pronounced: lō-FEE-lee-ay per-TUH-say). This was a deciding factor in designating 159 square nautical miles of the sanctuary, nearly one-third of its size, as a conservation area.

Extended tentacles of polyps (pronounced: PAW-lǐps) stem from the reef-building coral *Lophelia pertusa*, entwined with red arms of brittle stars, relatives of sea stars. These corals are soft and grow in cold water, unlike reef-building corals in the Tropics. In addition to corals, the Olympic Coast National Marine Sanctuary is home to many species of marine mammals, including Gray, Humpback, and Killer Whales, as well as seals, sea lions, and sea otters. A wide variety of seabirds, including Storm Petrels and Black-footed Albatross, are also observed soaring above the sanctuary's waters. Olympic Coast National Marine Sanctuary is just one of many of our nation's underwater treasures.

FIGURE 1.19. Gorgonian Soft Coral Polyps are in the range of deepwater corals off the Washington State Coast.

Kelp forests are characterized by clear water and thick growths of kelp, a long, fast-growing marine alga, also known as seaweed. There are many organisms, including sea otters and invertebrates such as crabs, sea urchins, sea stars, and mussels, that hide among the kelp's long blades. The kelp is also an important part of the food web in these ecosystems.

FIGURE 1.20. The Olympic Coast National Marine Sanctuary is home to a dense kelp forest. Other ecosystems within the sanctuary are sandy beaches, rocky shores, and salt marshes.

Evaluate

1. Name as many different marine ecosystems as you can.

2. Study the photograph to the right (FIGURE 1.21).

   a. Identify three biotic and three abiotic factors in the photograph.

   b. Choose one biotic and one abiotic factor and explain how they interact.

3. Study the images below (FIGURE 1.22) and answer the Question that follows.

FIGURE 1.21.

Before the Burn

One Year After Burn

Two Years After Burn

FIGURE 1.22. The Oak Creek area of the Fishlake National Forest, Utah, before and after a burn.

The whale fall data presented in the **Elaborate** section of the Lesson show the succession of organisms at whale fall sites. How do these photos taken before and after a forest fire demonstrate succession in the forest ecosystem?

4. Reflect on your personal interactions with your environment.

   a. Provide one example of something you choose to do that is positive for the environment.

   b. Provide one example of something you choose to do that is negative for the environment.

   c. How do these negative decisions affect marine ecosystems?

2

Water on Earth

INSIDE:

Objectives

You will be able to:

✔ Compare and contrast the heating and cooling of fresh water and salt water.

✔ Determine whether substances will float or sink in water, based on their densities.

✔ Give examples of how the properties of water affect marine organisms.

✔ Describe the structure of the water molecule and relate its structure to water's unique properties.

Benchmarks

1a. The ocean is the dominant physical feature on our planet Earth—covering approximately 70% of the planet's surface. There is one ocean with many ocean basins, such as the North Pacific, South Pacific, North Atlantic, South Atlantic, Indian, and Arctic.

1e. Most of Earth's water (97%) is in the ocean. Seawater has unique properties: it is saline; its freezing point is slightly lower than fresh water; its density is slightly higher; its electrical conductivity is much higher; and it is slightly basic. The salt in seawater comes from eroding land, volcanic emissions, reactions at the seafloor, and atmospheric deposition.

1f. The ocean is an integral part of the water cycle and is connected to all of the Earth's water reservoirs via evaporation and precipitation processes.

1h. Although the ocean is large, it is finite and resources are limited.

Engage

See Page 694 for how to access e-Tools.

View the **Blue Marble Animation** (0:25) from the e-Tools.

e-Tools

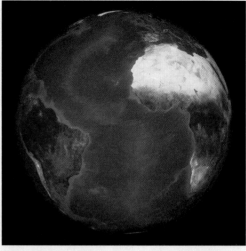

FIGURE 2.1. Screenshot of the **Blue Marble Animation**.

By viewing the animation of the Earth from Space, it is easy to observe that the planet's dominant feature is the ocean. The ocean covers approximately 71% of Earth's surface. The planet's ocean is often described as four oceans: the Pacific, Atlantic, Indian, and Arctic. These "oceans" are interconnected to form one ocean. The oceans we name are actually large, water-covered areas between continents, or **basins**. Earth's ocean contains 97% of the water on Earth, as salt water. That means that only 3% of the planet's water is fresh. About 1% of the fresh water is liquid and 2–3% is contained in ice in glaciers and sea ice caps in Earth's Polar Regions.

The Earth system is dynamic and its "spheres" are constantly changing. The spheres include the hydrosphere (water), biosphere (life), atmosphere (air), and lithosphere (land). Water plays an important role in influencing many Earth processes; this includes the distribution of water across the hydrosphere, which provides for life. As you studied in the last Lesson, Earth's ocean is full of diverse life forms and habitats. Contained within living organisms, water helps to maintain body structure, carries dissolved materials throughout the organism, and takes part in chemical reactions that carry out life processes. The bodies of marine animals are on average close to 80% water by mass.

The ocean is an important resource for humans—it is a source of food, transportation, energy, and more. Because the ocean is a resource that replenishes itself naturally over relatively short periods of time, it is considered to be a **renewable resource**. There is a constant influx of water into the ocean from rivers and precipitation. Water is involved in weathering, transport of sediments, weather activities, climate, and the storing and distribution of both heat energy and materials in the ocean.

Some resources, such as natural gas and minerals, are exhausted faster than they are naturally replaced; these are known as **nonrenewable resources**. Although the ocean is a renewable resource, humans must be careful about how we use ocean resources. For example, if we extract fish at rates faster than they can reproduce, this food source is no longer renewable. In many places around the world, **overfishing** has become a significant problem, threatening the well-being of ocean ecosystems as well as the livelihood of fishers.

Water is a unique substance with remarkable properties. The ocean's habitats are influenced by the physical properties of water. The distribution of marine ecosystems—where they are found on Earth—is also influenced by water's physical properties. In this Lesson, you will investigate some of these properties, which will support your further investigations of organisms in the sea.

1. Compare and contrast salt water and fresh water.

1. Your teacher will conduct *Demonstration 1*, allowing cold water to flow down the side of a beaker filled with very warm water.

   a. Record a hypothesis for what will happen in this demonstration.

   b. Draw and label the results that you observe for this demonstration.

FIGURE 2.2. Setup for *Demonstration 1*.

2. Your teacher will conduct *Demonstration 2*, placing ice cubes into cold water.

   a. Write a hypothesis for what will happen in this demonstration.

   b. Draw and label a beaker to illustrate the results of this demonstration.

FIGURE 2.3. Setup for *Demonstration 2*.

3. How can you relate these two demonstrations to what you know about the ocean?

Explore

Lab

Freezing, Melting, and Boiling

Water is a unique substance in that on Earth it naturally occurs in its solid (ice), liquid (water), and gaseous (water vapor) forms. You have experienced water in all three forms, and are aware that when the conditions are right, samples of water molecules change from one form to another. For instance, frozen water (i.e., ice) becomes liquid water by melting, and liquid water becomes a gas (i.e., water vapor) through evaporation. Water vapor becomes liquid through the process of condensation, and liquid water becomes solid through freezing.

Since 97% of Earth's water is contained in the ocean, as we study marine science it is important to consider water in its natural forms: as a solid, liquid, or gas. In this investigation, you will investigate phase changes of both fresh water and salt water.

FIGURE 2.4. Fresh water from our faucets and drinking fountains, or tap water, has been filtered and treated to make sure it is safe to drink.

Follow laboratory and safety procedures carefully. You will work with two types of water:

- *Tap water* is from a faucet and is safe to drink. Tap water is fresh water that has been filtered and treated to kill any bacteria and remove any harmful substances or organisms.
- *Salt water* is water that contains dissolved salts comparable to what would be found in the ocean.

Safety Notes: Observe the following safety procedures, as well as any other rules that are in place at your school.

- Dry ice must be handled with thick work gloves or tongs.
- Store the dry ice in a Styrofoam or other type of thermal container with a loose-fitting top to allow the carbon dioxide gas to escape.
- Safety glasses must be worn at all times for these laboratory exercises.
- Only tempered glassware should be heated and cooled. Heating and cooling must be done slowly.
- Do not use cracked glassware.
- Be very careful with thermometers, particularly when inserting them into rubber stoppers.
- Long hair and loose clothing must be tied back.

Safety Notes:

- Dry ice burns skin! Anyone handling dry ice <u>must</u> wear work gloves.
- Safety goggles must be worn for this investigation.
- Handle thermometers and rubber stoppers carefully to avoid injury.

Materials:

- Dry ice
- Work gloves
- Safety glasses
- Salt water
- Tap water
- Thermometers or temperature probes, ranging from below 0 °C to above 100 °C
- Test tubes
- Rubber stoppers (must fit test tubes and thermometers)
- Test tube labels or grease pencils
- Beakers
- Tongs
- Hot plates
- Stirring rods
- Stopwatches

FIGURE 2.5. Safety measures are a necessity in the lab. Chemical reactions from physical processes can be, at times, unpredictable.

Phase Changes of Water I: Freezing Point

Follow the procedures with your lab group. Have one group member read each step aloud.

1. a. Check to be sure your group has all of the necessary materials for this procedure. This experiment requires the use of solid carbon dioxide, referred to as **dry ice**. When the solid dry ice is heated above approximately -78 °C (~ -108 °F), it changes phase directly from a solid to a gas, bypassing the liquid state of matter. This process is called **sublimation**. Dry ice is commonly used as a cooling agent. It is often used to keep prepared meals or meats frozen during shipping.

   b. Prepare two test tubes each about ¾ full of the following liquids. Allow them to sit in a beaker:
      - 1 with tap water
      - 1 with salt water

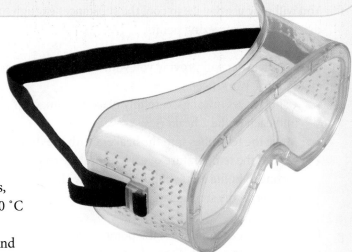

FIGURE 2.6. Setup for ***Phase Changes of Water I: Freezing Point***.

c. Label the tubes.

d. Place a rubber stopper and thermometer in each test tube. The thermometer bulb should be surrounded by liquid, not resting on the bottom.

Your team will be determining the **freezing points** of each of the tap and saltwater samples.

e. Make predictions: How will the freezing point compare between the samples?

f. You will now use dry ice to cool the substances enough to determine their freezing points.

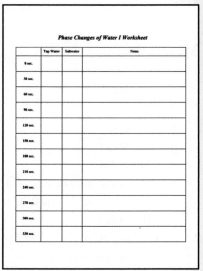

- Your teacher will provide you with the *Phase Changes of Water I Worksheet*.
- Using gloves or tongs, carefully place a chunk of dry ice into each of the 2 beakers.
- Move the test tubes into the beakers with the dry ice.
- Record the temperature of each test tube every 30 seconds. In the Notes column, note any changes you observe in the substances.

g. Recall that freezing indicates the point at which a liquid is changing into a solid. Once the substances are frozen, continue to record temperatures for 120 seconds.

FIGURE 2.7. Screenshot of the *Phase Changes of Water I Worksheet*.

h. Dispose of dry ice as directed by your teacher.

Phase Changes of Water II: Melting and Boiling Points

Now your team will determine the **melting** and **boiling points** of one water sample each of frozen tap water and frozen salt water.

Safety Note: Be very careful when heating substances—use gloves or tongs to handle the beaker and test tubes.

i. Your teacher will provide you with the *Phase Changes of Water II Worksheet* and two 250-mL beakers, each with approximately 150 mL of crushed ice. One sample is frozen salt water. The other is frozen tap water.

j. Put a thermometer in each beaker. After one minute, record the temperature of each substance in your data table.

k. Place each beaker on a hot plate and turn them on. Hold the beakers in place with tongs. Carefully stir each beaker every ½ minute with a stirring rod.

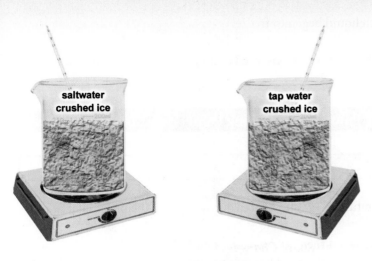

FIGURE 2.8. Setup for *Phase Changes of Water II: Melting and Boiling Points*.

Phase Changes of Water II Worksheet

	Tap Water	Saltwater	Notes
0 min.			
1 min.			
2 min.			
3 min.			
4 min.			
5 min.			
6 min.			
7 min.			
8 min.			
9 min.			
10 min.			
11 min.			
12 min.			
13 min.			
14 min.			
15 min.			
16 min.			
17 min.			

FIGURE 2.9. Screenshot of the *Phase Changes of Water II Worksheet*.

l. Record the temperature of the contents of each beaker in the data table every 1 minute. In the Notes column, note any changes you observe in the samples.

m. The substances are boiling when you notice rapid bubbling. Recall that boiling indicates that the water is changing from a liquid phase to a gaseous phase. Continue to record temperatures for 2 minutes after the substances begin to boil.

n. Clean up your laboratory station as directed by your teacher.

Follow-up Questions:

When conducting an investigation, we often take measurements of things that vary, or **variables**. There are two major types of variables: independent and dependent variables.

* Something that is not changed by the other variables being measured is the **independent variable**. In these experiments, the independent variable was time.

* Something that depends on other factors is called a **dependent variable**. In these experiments, the dependent variable was temperature. The temperature changed because of the other variable—the time the heat was added.

When drawing a graph, the independent variable should go on the bottom, or the *x*-axis. The dependent variable is plotted on the side, or the *y*-axis. After you plot the data, you can examine the relationship between the independent and dependent variables. Be sure to determine the appropriate units for each axis. Label the axes as well as the units.

Plot the results of your freezing, melting, and boiling point experiments on graph paper.

* Create one graph with the freezing point experiment data.
* Create one graph that has both the melting and boiling point experiment data.
* Add these to your notebook. Be sure each graph includes 1) a title, 2) labeled *x*- and *y*-axes, 3) units for each axis, and 4) a key.

2. Describe what you observed when each liquid began to freeze.

3. Draw the following chart in your notebook. List the observed boiling and freezing points of each substance in your chart.

Substance	Freezing Point	Boiling Point	Melting Point
Tap water			
Salt water			

4. Describe what happened to the temperature of the substances during each of the phase changes.

  a. How was the temperature changing when the liquid became solid?
  b. How was the temperature changing when the solid became liquid?
  c. How was the temperature changing when the liquid became a gas?
  d. How do the freezing and melting points compare for fresh water and salt water?

Explain

In your investigation in the **Explore** section, you have observed the phase changes of water. The chemical formula for water is H_2O. One oxygen atom bonds with two hydrogen atoms in each water molecule. Due to the chemical nature of the water molecule, when it forms, the structure looks something like FIGURE 2.10. The properties of water affect marine organisms. Let's review some basic chemistry, so we can better explore water's unique properties.

FIGURE 2.10. Structure of the water molecule with atoms of hydrogen and oxygen.

Atoms

The most basic particle of a unique element that has the properties of that element is called an **atom**. Atoms of each unique element have a nucleus made up of **neutrons**, with no electrical charge, and **protons**, each with a +1 ("positive 1") charge. Neutrons and protons have approximately the same mass. Around the dense nucleus of each unique atom is a "cloud" of very tiny, negatively charged **electrons**. There are approximately 90 different naturally occurring elements each with their own unique number of protons in their nucleus. The periodic table of the elements (Appendix B) describes their atomic structure and organizes these atoms relative to each other while also giving clues to their chemical nature.

Let's take a look at the structure of the atoms that make up water. In FIGURE 2.11 we see a neutral atom of hydrogen. The most common form of hydrogen atom has 1 positively charged proton and 0 neutral neutrons in the nucleus, and 1 negatively charged electron spinning in an electron cloud, or shell, around the nucleus. (The charge of the nucleus is +1, and the charge of the electron is -1.) Total charge of the entire hydrogen atom is 0. The diagrams illustrated here are models. Models are representations of something else. They are helpful to use in describing or visualizing the very basic structure and makeup of atoms, which are too tiny to observe, even under a common microscope.

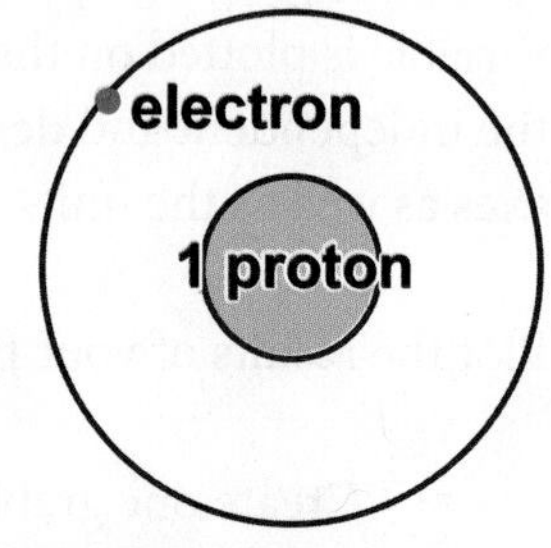

electron

1 proton

FIGURE 2.11. Shell model of the common hydrogen atom.

FIGURE 2.12 shows an atom of oxygen. The most common form of the oxygen atom has 8 positive protons and 8 neutral neutrons in the nucleus. The atom with complete outer shells of electrons has 2 negatively charged electrons spinning in the first electron cloud shell and 6 negatively charged electrons in the second shell around the nucleus. There is a total of 8 electrons. The electrons in the outer shell are called **valence electrons**. There are some heavier forms of oxygen that can have 1 or 2 more neutrons in the nucleus. These variations, or **isotopes**, of oxygen when discovered in ice core samples, sea shells, or cave formations help scientists to determine changes in Earth's temperature and climate over many years.

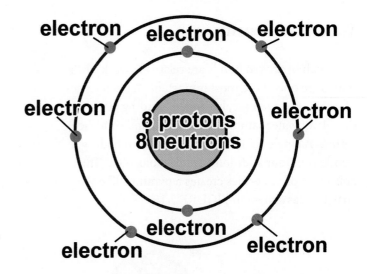

FIGURE 2.12. Shell model of common oxygen atom.

Molecules

Oxygen and hydrogen are usually not found alone as atoms in a natural state. Two or more atoms will naturally bond together to form molecules or a compound made of different types of atoms. They tend to become less chemically reactive, meaning they become more stable. Atoms in a compound or molecule are most stable when they have a complete outer shell of electrons. Both oxygen (O_2) and hydrogen (H_2) occur naturally as molecules with two atoms of the element chemically bonded together, and these molecules are called diatomic molecules. In the case of hydrogen and oxygen, the atoms attain complete outer shells, thus becoming more stable, or less reactive chemically, by sharing outer shell electrons. Diatomic hydrogen contains two hydrogen atoms that share one pair of electrons, one electron from each atom.

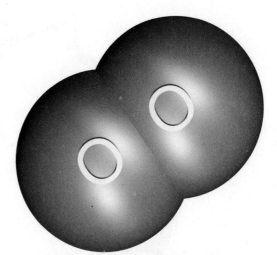

FIGURE 2.13. Oxygen gas naturally occurs when two atoms of oxygen bond together. Approximately 21% of Earth's atmosphere is oxygen gas. Concentrations of oxygen are much lower in the ocean.

In this diatomic hydrogen example, the two electrons, one from each atom, are shared and make a bond. Each pair of electrons that is shared between two atoms is called a covalent bond. Since neither positive hydrogen nucleus has any more pull for the negative electron than the other, the electrons are shared equally between the two atoms in an H_2 molecule. This is true for molecules that are made up of two of the same types of atom. Note that in some cases, two or more different atoms are combined such that the electrons may not be shared equally. These atomic bonds are **polar covalent bonds**.

Water

Water molecules are not quite symmetrical. The oxygen side of the molecule is slightly negatively charged, and the hydrogen side is slightly positively charged. Water is a polar covalent molecule because its electrons are not evenly distributed. Polar molecules will collectively attract one another, meaning that water molecules "stick" together. The attraction between water molecules is referred to as hydrogen bonding. The attraction is about one-tenth as strong as the covalent bond within the water molecule.

Water and Density

Although hydrogen bonds are relatively weak, these bonds are one of the most important characteristics of water. For example, hydrogen bonding affects the density of water samples in its liquid and solid (ice) forms. A single water molecule can form hydrogen bonds with four additional water molecules. This collection of molecules creates a pyramid-like shape, or structure, as shown in FIGURE 2.15.

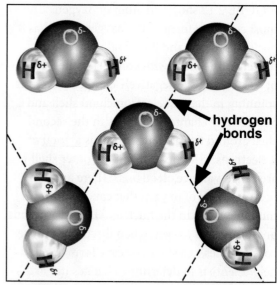

FIGURE 2.14. Notice the hydrogen bonds resulting from the slightly positively charged hydrogen part of one water molecule attracted to the slightly negatively charged oxygen part of another water molecule.

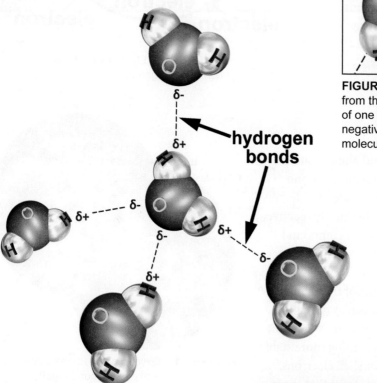

FIGURE 2.15.

In general, when most substances are cooled, their molecules move closer together. The substance becomes more compact. When cooled, the space its molecules occupy, or its volume, decreases. Its mass per unit of volume, density, increases. You might think of something very compact if it has a high density. A high amount of mass in a small volume means that something is more dense. Less mass in a large volume means that something is less dense. You will explore this idea further in the **Elaborate** section.

FIGURE 2.16. The structure of the water molecule gives in special characteristics. Note the iceberg in the background and chunky sea ice surrounding the scientists in the small boat in the foreground.

Due to the hydrogen bonding between water molecules, the molecules set up somewhat apart even as they are cooled. Water molecules in their liquid state are situated as closely as they can be at 4 °C. This is the temperature at which liquid water reaches its highest density. Below 4 °C, the hydrogen bonding tendency gets stronger and the water molecules move a bit farther apart, organizing into more of a "lattice" structure made up of ring shapes, as shown in FIGURE 2.17. When water freezes, of course, it becomes solid ice. The ice is made up of water molecules in a fixed crystal structure. Water actually expands as it freezes. This means that the same mass of water takes up more space, has a greater volume, in its solid form than its liquid form. Water in its solid form is less dense than its liquid form. This may seem counterintuitive since we usually think that solids, with their atoms packed closely together, are more dense than liquids. In fact, most substances are more dense in their solid form than in liquid form. Substances are least dense as a gas.

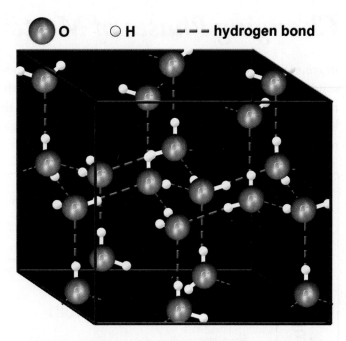

FIGURE 2.17. This "open lattice structure" of water molecules is shown for solid ice. Open space between the molecules illustrates why ice is less dense than liquid water. Hydrogen bonding orients the molecules so that each slightly negative "O" (shown in red) always lines up with a slightly positive "H" (shown in white). In ice, each water molecule is lined up to share four hydrogen bonds with other water molecules.

2. Distinguish between atoms and molecules.

3. What is density? How does the polarity of water molecules relate to the density of water?

FIGURE 2.18. Ice is less dense than water because the molecules form a lattice structure as the substance freezes. The small iceberg in the sea demonstrates this property as the it slowly melts and floats along the surface.

Changing Phases of Matter

In your laboratory investigation, you observed several phase changes—from liquid to solid, liquid to gas, and solid to gas. Water's hydrogen bonding ability also affects how it changes from solid, liquid, and gas. The figure below should resemble the graph you created from the data you collected when heating and cooling the water samples. This type of graph, which shows the changes a substance experiences as heat is added to or removed from a system, is called a **phase change diagram**.

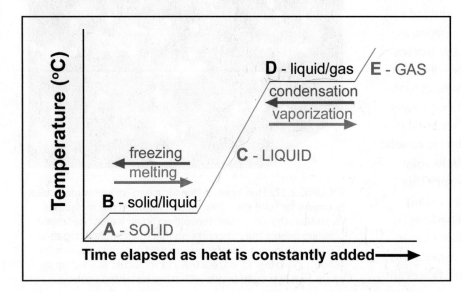

FIGURE 2.19. Phase change diagram showing water's state of matter in green. Changes in the states of matter are blue (cooling) and red (warming). Constant heat added over time illustrates how water absorbs energy.

The graph above gives a general picture of what happens with constant heating of a substance. The graphed data indicate that in general, as time passes and heat is constantly added, temperature increases. You'll notice, of course, that the temperature does not increase at a constant rate. The general direction, or **trend**, of the data indicates that the temperature is increasing. When analyzing plots or graphs, it is often helpful to consider the trend of the data.

The area labeled as A represents the range of time and temperature at which the substance is in solid form. Let's assume the graph is a plot of the phase changes of water, so the solid form, A, is ice.

FIGURE 2.20. Water occurs naturally in all three states of matter.

4. What happens to the temperature of the ice when heat is constantly added?

5. What happens to temperature as the melting of the ice occurs?

During an actual phase change (e.g., from solid to liquid), the measured temperature of the water remains constant. Heat energy continues to be added, but heat is being absorbed and used to melt the solid into a liquid. The same thing happens during the change from liquid to gas, a process called **vaporization** or **evaporation**. Heat energy continues to be added, but it is being absorbed and used to change the water's state of matter to gas. The heat absorbed during a phase change is called **latent heat**.

Water has a tremendous ability to take on energy without an increase in temperature. Because of its molecular structure, water has more ways of vibrating, rotating, and moving around faster internally; it can store more energy than nonpolar molecules. A small mass (e.g., 1 gram) of molecules larger than water usually has fewer molecules to absorb energy before the molecules break apart. The same mass of water (1 gram) contains more molecules to internally hold more energy. When liquid water is heated, the amount of heat needed to raise the temperature of 1 gram of liquid water 1 °C is 1 calorie.

FIGURE 2.21. When solids, such as the icebergs shown in this photograph, melt, they are absorbing energy from their surroundings. During the actual melting, energy is being used for the phase change.

When substances are cooled, the changes that occur are the opposite of the changes in vaporization. In the process of **cooling**, energy is taken away or given off. When you cooled your substances in the lab, heat energy was released into the classroom. When water changes from liquid to solid, the process called **freezing**, energy is released for a period of time and the temperature of the water does not change. The same process occurs when water in its gas form changes to a liquid, which is **condensation**.

During the processes of condensation and freezing, energy is released. Molecules with more average kinetic energy will end up having less in the process. When the top layer of the ocean freezes, forming sea ice, for example, energy is released into the atmosphere.

As noted earlier, the opposite occurs when water evaporates. Energy is absorbed by water molecules during evaporation. The molecules break away from liquid and become gaseous water vapor. Therefore, much of the energy in the ocean is transferred to the atmosphere through the process of evaporation. On Earth, water is one of the few substances that occurs naturally in all three states of matter—solid, liquid, and gas.

Pure, or distilled, water vaporizes at 100 °C (212 °F) and freezes at 0 °C (32 °F). This is observable at sea level. At higher altitudes, these temperatures are slightly different; they are lower. Why, for example, is the boiling point of water lower in the mountains? The pressure, or weight of the air above, is less. There are fewer molecules of air weighing down on a substance. Hence, the amount of energy needed to boil it, freeing the molecules from their bonds in the process, is less.

As observed during your laboratory experiment, salt water boils and becomes a gas at a slightly higher temperature than fresh water. It freezes at a slightly lower temperature than fresh water.

The reason for this is that liquids must form a very orderly structure during the process of freezing. Impurities in a substance—in the case of salt water, dissolved salts—make it more difficult for the liquid to form their crystalline structures and freeze. Therefore, freezing occurs at a lower temperature. Similarly, salts in water make it more difficult for water to evaporate or boil; this raises the temperature for vaporization.

6. Pure isopropyl alcohol (rubbing alcohol) freezes at -85.5 °C and boils at 82.3 °C. Sketch a phase change diagram for this substance. On the diagram, label the following:

- Solid, liquid, and gas
- Freezing, melting, condensation, and vaporization

Lab

Floating and Sinking

Have you ever seen a big ship, made of steel and other materials, and wondered how something so massive can possibly float? Do some of your friends seem to float better in the pool than you do? Of course, in the ocean, some things sink and some things will float. In fact, many living organisms rely on the ability to stay above the sea surface or not in order to propagate their species. For example, juvenile clams and lobsters float near the sea's surface for part of their life cycle and

FIGURE 2.22. We all know that with personal flotation devices, we are able to float. In this investigation, we will investigate items that float and sink.

then go through developmental changes that result in their sinking and finally settling on the seafloor. In this laboratory exercise, you will investigate the factors that allow some materials to sink through water and others to float in it.

Materials:

- Basins
- Tap water
- Triple-beam or electronic balance
- Graduated cylinders
- Rulers
- Calculators

- Various items to test floating and sinking
  - o Wood block
  - o Wood splint
  - o Vegetable shortening
  - o Pumice stone
  - o Rock
  - o Oil
  - o Seeds
  - o Nail
  - o Aluminum foil

Follow the procedures with your lab group. Have one group member read each step aloud.

1. a. Check to be sure your group has all of the necessary materials for this investigation.

    b. Draw a data table similar to the one below in your notebook.

1	2	3	4	5	6	7
Item	Prediction: Float or Sink?	Observation: Float or Sink?	Other Observations	Mass (g)	Volume (mL or cm³)	Density (g/cm³)

c. List the items to be tested in Column 1. Confer with your group and decide on a prediction for each item—do you predict that it will float or sink? List your predictions in Column 2.

Why do you think certain items float? What characteristics come into play in your decision?

d. Now, test your predictions for each item. List what you observe—whether the item floats or sinks—in Column 3. List any other observations you have in Column 4.

e. Measure the mass of each item and record the mass in Column 5.

f. Measure the volume of each item and record the volume in Column 6.

g. Do you see any patterns in mass or volume of floaters and sinkers? Explain.

h. Density is calculated by the following formula:

$$\text{density} = \frac{\text{mass}}{\text{volume}}$$

$$or$$

$$d = \frac{m}{v}$$

Calculate the density of each item. Record the density in Column 7.

i. Compare the densities of the floaters and sinkers.

j. Using the tools at hand, how could you determine the density of water? With your group, write down a procedure for finding the density of water. Be very detailed listing and explaining your steps.

k. Follow your procedure and calculate the water's density. Document your measurements along the way.

l. Now, knowing the correct formula, write and follow a similar procedure to find the density of ice. Follow your procedure and record your measurements along the way.

m. Clean up your lab station as directed by your teacher.

Follow-up Questions:

2. Compare the density of the floaters and sinkers to the density of water.

3. The density of fresh water is slightly less than that of salt water. Would salt water sink, float, or behave in some other fashion in fresh water? Why?

4. Explain what happens in an oil spill.

5. In the **Engage** section of this Lesson, your teacher conducted two demonstrations. You witnessed that very cold water sinks, yet ice floats. How can you explain this now based on what you know about density and the nature of the water molecule?

Density and Marine Organisms

In the laboratory activity, you observed that liquid water's density is approximately 1.00 g/mL. This measurement varies with the temperature of the water and other factors such as dissolved salts. You also should have observed that substances more dense than water will sink, and that substances less dense than water will float.

When considering why things float, one must also consider the upward force that keeps materials afloat in fluids, or **buoyancy**. Have you ever tried to lift something heavy, maybe a friend of yours, in water? That person or object felt lighter than usual, right? If so, you have experienced buoyancy.

FIGURE 2.23. Large ships have a very large volume and displace a lot of water. The buoyant force acting on them is therefore quite strong.

You are also familiar with the idea that when you add something to water, some water is displaced and the level of water in the container rises. For instance, if you were to fill your bathtub with water to nearly the top and climb in, you would expect it to overflow. Your body has displaced some water. The buoyancy, or upward force on an object, is equal to the weight of the water (or other fluid) that is displaced. That means that very voluminous things, like steel ships or large marine mammals, have tremendous buoyancy holding them up in the water. Much water is displaced by these giant objects and organisms.

Things seem to float even better, or higher up in the water column, in salt water than in fresh water. You might have experienced this if you have swum in both the ocean and a lake or pool. Salt water is slightly more dense than fresh water due to all of the substances dissolved within it. The density of fresh water is about 1.00 g/cm³, whereas the average density of salt water is 1.03 g/cm³. Therefore, an object floating in salt water displaces less water than one in fresh water. Ships used in both fresh water and salt water must account for this difference for optimum depth in the water. One way to do so is to add weight, often by taking water aboard, when in salt water. For instance, when ships cruise from the Atlantic Ocean, through the St. Lawrence Seaway, and into the Great Lakes, they often release this **ballast water** into the Lakes.

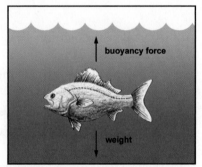

FIGURE 2.24. The buoyant force is what pushes upward on objects in water. This force opposes weight, the force that pulls objects downward, toward the center of the Earth.

FIGURE 2.25. The St. Lawrence Seaway is a series of locks and canals that connect the Atlantic Ocean with the Great Lakes. What states does the seaway connect?

As you know, some organisms float on top of the ocean, some live near its bottom, and others make their homes throughout the water column. Organisms have features that assist them with floating and sinking and with preventing themselves from moving up and down, which is called maintaining **neutral buoyancy**. For instance, some floating plant-like organisms called **phytoplankton** have oil deposits in their shells. The fact that oil is less dense than water enhances the organisms' floating ability.

Jellyfish are a unique group of marine animals that live all over the world. Not truly fish, these animals consist of more than 90% water. Many species of jellyfish float, whereas others rely on neutral buoyancy to remain suspended within the water column.

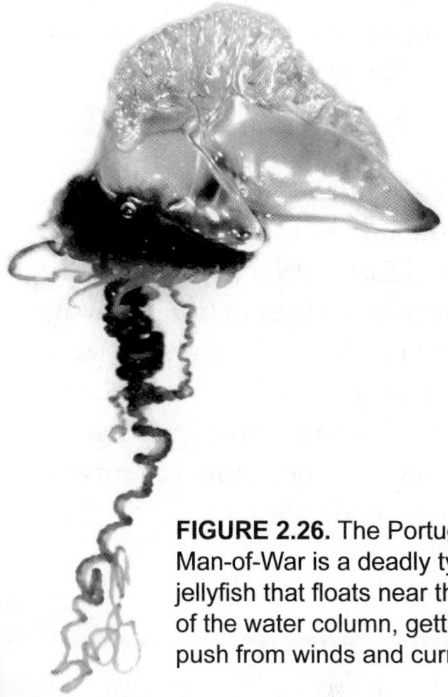

FIGURE 2.26. The Portuguese Man-of-War is a deadly type of jellyfish that floats near the top of the water column, getting a push from winds and currents.

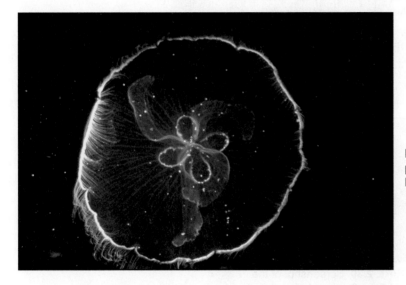

FIGURE 2.27. This Moon Jellyfish was photographed in the Florida Keys National Marine Sanctuary.

Sargassum is a seaweed that floats on the ocean's surface because of its very low density. Air sacs help to keep the seaweed's density low. View the image of *Sargassum* below in FIGURE 2.28.

FIGURE 2.28. Many seaweeds, including this *Sargassum*, have special air-filled sacs to help them float. Floating allows these algae to absorb ample sunlight for photosynthesis.

Marine organisms are also affected by the density of water's solid form, ice. As you know, ice is less dense than water and therefore floats on top of liquid water.

By tracking animals and monitoring ice concentrations, we can see that marine animals in Earth's Polar Regions are very dependent on the layer of frozen seawater called **sea ice**. Sea ice insulates the water below, keeping it relatively warm. Sea ice reflects much of the Sun's energy that hits it. Fish and other organisms can survive in the water under the ice.

FIGURE 2.29. Penguins walking on the edge of ice in the Antarctic take advantage of the fact that ice is less dense than water.

See Page 694 for how to access e-Tools.

View the *Polar Bear Sea Ice Animation* from the e-Tools and consider the relationship between the sea ice and Istas the Polar Bear's movements.

e-Tools

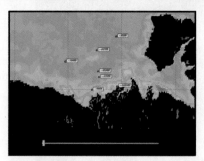

FIGURE 2.30. Screenshot of the *Polar Bear Sea Ice Animation*.

FIGURE 2.31. Polar Bears need ice for stalking prey, building dens, and caring for their young. Ice is a critical element in the animal's habitat.

When looking at the sea ice concentration imagery (FIGURE 2.32), the white areas indicate open ocean water locations, and blue indicates areas where the sea ice almost completely covers the surface. The brighter colors (i.e., red, orange, and yellow) indicate that ice is chunky and the sea surface is not completely ice-covered. As you view this animation, note that Istas moves northward in the spring and summer as the sea ice retreats. When the ice expands southward once more in the fall, Istas heads south again, and, in November, the bear is observed very close to Alaska's Northern Coast.

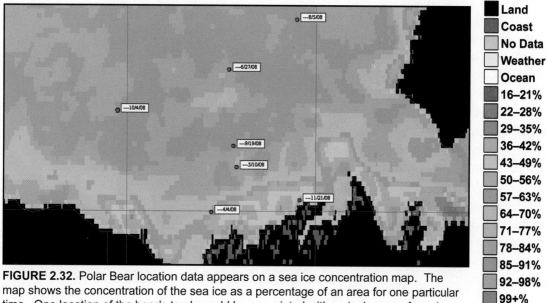

FIGURE 2.32. Polar Bear location data appears on a sea ice concentration map. The map shows the concentration of the sea ice as a percentage of an area for one particular time. One location of the bear's track would be associated with a single map of sea ice concentrations.

Polar Bears hunt primarily seals. One strategy for doing so is to lie on the ice near air holes and wait for seals to surface to take a breath. Polar Bears also prey on seals that are stretched out and resting on the ice. While Polar Bears are marine mammals and adept swimmers, seals are actually faster in the water. Therefore, Polar Bears must catch their prey on the ice. Female Polar Bears also build dens on the ice to birth and care for their cubs. Therefore, it is not surprising that Istas' movements followed the ice.

FIGURE 2.33. Bearded Seal on the ice in the Arctic. When underwater, these seals use their claws to dig holes in the ice in order to surface for air.

7. What is buoyancy? How does it allow large objects like massive whales to float?

8. Describe how the structure of the *Sargassum* helps it to float on water.

9. How does the fact that ice floats affect marine animals?

10. Describe the relationship between the movements of the Polar Bear and the seasonal changes in sea ice. How can you explain this relationship?

Thunder Bay National Marine Sanctuary

The Thunder Bay National Marine Sanctuary was designated in October of 2000 by NOAA (National Oceanic and Atmospheric Administration) as the thirteenth marine sanctuary designation. The designation of National Marine Sanctuary took approximately 17 years to come to fruition. It was established thanks to the hard work of NOAA and the State of Michigan. The Thunder Bay National Marine Sanctuary encompasses 448 square miles of Northwest Lake Huron, off the northeast coast of Michigan's Lower Peninsula. Its designation marks many firsts for marine sanctuaries: it is the first Great Lakes sanctuary, it is the first to completely be located within the confines of U.S. waters, and it is the first to focus completely on the large collection of underwater cultural resources.

Thunder Bay has a vast collection of shipwrecks that encompasses the maritime history of Thunder Bay. The wrecks include wooden schooners to steel-hulled steamers. More than 200 shipwrecks can be found in water as shallow as 12 feet deep or as deep as 180 feet. They date from 1825 to 1925, a span of time known as the "Shipwreck Century." Some shipwrecks are completely intact while others are composed of remnants such as boilers, anchors, or rudders. Believe it or not there are still more shipwrecks to be found in Thunder Bay. The focus of the work in the sanctuary is to document all shipwrecks and place buoys to identify the sites as well as develop a public maritime education program.

FIGURE 2.34. Map showing location of Thunder Bay Marine Sanctuary.

Thunder Bay has such a large collection of pristine shipwrecks because of Lake Huron's cold, fresh waters. It is just like keeping the shipwrecks in a giant refrigerator. Fresh water preserves these giant artifacts better than salt water would. Salt water is an excellent electrolyte, which means it can conduct an electrical current and will eventually corrode most metals down to nothing. The relative absence of salt in fresh water allows for the spectacular underwater preservation of artifacts.

FIGURE 2.36. A close-up view of the wheel from the shipwreck of the schooner *FT Barney* in Thunder Bay.

FIGURE 2.35. NOAA archaeologist documents the lower deck of the Great Lakes wooden freighter, the *SS Florida*, a shipwreck located in Thunder Bay Marine Sanctuary.

Evaluate

1. Give one example of how the polar covalent nature of water molecules leads to a characteristic of water.

2. The chart below gives the density of some common substances.

Substance	Density (g/cm³)
Gasoline	0.710–0.770
Antifreeze (Ethylene Glycol)	1.02
Gold	19.2
Magnesium	1.79
Benzene	0.879

   a. Which substances will sink in fresh water?

   b. Which will float in fresh water?

   c. The density of seawater is about 1.03 g/cm³. Which substance above would float in salt water but not in fresh water?

3. Describe one example of how the density of water, in any of its phases, affects marine organisms.

4. Identify the phase or process represented by A–G in the diagram below.

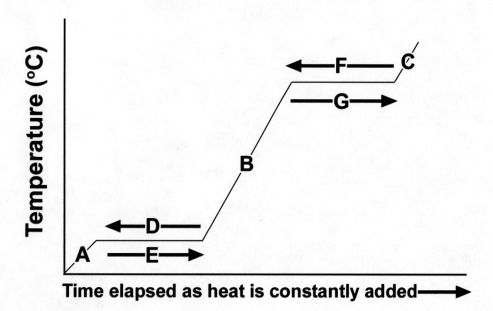

FIGURE 2.37. Phase Diagram.

3

More About Water

INSIDE:

Objectives

You will be able to:

✔ Describe water's unique properties and relate these properties to its chemical structure.

✔ Explain the sources of salt in seawater.

✔ Give examples of how the properties of water affect marine organisms.

Benchmarks

1e. Most of Earth's water (97%) is in the ocean. Seawater has unique properties: it is saline; its freezing point is slightly lower than fresh water; its density is slightly higher; its electrical conductivity is much higher; and it is slightly basic. The salt in seawater comes from eroding land, volcanic emissions, reactions at the seafloor, and atmospheric deposition.

1g. The ocean is connected to major lakes, watersheds, and waterways because all major watersheds on Earth drain to the ocean. Rivers and streams transport nutrients, salts, sediments, and pollutants from watersheds to estuaries and to the ocean.

5f. Ocean habitats are defined by environmental factors. Due to interactions of abiotic factors (e.g., salinity, temperature, oxygen, pH, light, nutrients, pressure, substrate, circulation), ocean life is not evenly distributed temporally or spatially (i.e., it is "patchy"). Some regions of the ocean support more diverse and abundant life than anywhere on Earth, while much of the ocean is considered a desert.

5i. Estuaries provide important and productive nursery areas for many marine and aquatic species.

7d. New technologies, sensors, and tools are expanding our ability to explore the ocean. Ocean scientists are relying more and more on satellites, drifters, buoys, subsea observatories, and unmanned submersibles.

Engage

In the last Lesson, you explored some of the properties of water, including how water's structure is less dense when in the solid form than the liquid form. We will continue this exploration of the water molecule here. The nature of the water molecule actually allows water to dissolve salt and other substances. Everyone knows that the ocean is salty, but how much do you know about salt water?

Answer the following questions using what you already know. Don't worry if you are not sure about your answers.

1. Where does the salt in the ocean come from?

2. Does the ocean have the same "saltiness" everywhere? Why or why not? Do you have any evidence to support you answer (e.g., visits to different parts of the ocean, readings)?

3. How might salt affect marine organisms?

FIGURE 3.1. Ninety-seven percent of the water on Earth is salty. Consider what you know about salt water.

FIGURE 3.2. Sea salt can be a flavorful addition to food. What do you know about the salt in our ocean?

 Lab

Solutions

FIGURE 3.3. Lemonade is an example of a solution, being made up of juice, water and sugar.

If you have ever dissolved sugar in coffee or tea, you have experience with this next topic that we will explore. In addition to salts, there are other substances dissolved in the ocean, as many substances dissolve in water; hence, water is a **solvent**. The substance that dissolves is the **solute**. A uniform mixture of two or more substances is called a **solution**. Lemonade is a solution; it contains lemon juice, water, and sugar. When you stir sugar into your coffee or tea, it dissolves, and the drink becomes a solution. The **solubility** of a substance is its ability to be dissolved in a solvent. Your team will be investigating the solubility of salt in water at different temperatures. You will determine the amount of salt that can dissolve in cold tap water, hot tap water, and heated water.

Safety Notes: Observe the following safety procedures, as well as any other rules that are in place at your school.

- Safety glasses must be worn at all times for these laboratory exercises.
- Only tempered glassware should be heated and cooled. Heating and cooling must be done slowly.
- Do not use cracked glassware.
- Be very careful with thermometers, particularly when inserting them into rubber stoppers.
- Long hair and loose clothing must be tied back.

Materials:

- Hot plates
- Beakers
- Triple-beam or electronic balance
- Table salt or seawater mix
- Tap water
- Stirring rods
- Thermometers
- Safety glasses
- Paper towels

In this experiment you will determine how the solubility of salt in water is affected by the temperature of the water, using tap water at three different temperatures. Follow the procedures with your lab group. Have one group member read each step aloud.

1. a. Check to be sure your group has all of the necessary materials for this experiment.

   b. Copy the data table below into your notebook.

1.	2.	3.	4.	5.
Temperature (˚C)	Water Volume (mL)	Starting Mass of Salt (g)	Ending Mass of Salt (g)	Mass of Salt Used (g)

   c. Choose the volume of water you will use for your experiment based on your beaker size. Write this volume in each row of the data table in Column 2. You will use the same measured volume of water for each part of this activity in order to have only one dependent variable—the temperature of the water.

   d. Fill a beaker with water and begin heating it on a hot plate. Use the same amount of cool and warm tap water when you get to Step f.

   e. Pour some salt onto a paper towel. Measure the mass of the salt. Record the mass in the first row of Column 3.

   f. Fill another beaker with the chosen volume of cold tap water.

   - Record the temperature of the water in Column 1.
   - Begin adding a little bit of salt at a time, stirring the water as you go.
   - The salt should dissolve into the water.
   - When no more salt will dissolve, the water is saturated. Measure the mass of salt left on the paper towel and record in Column 4.
   - Find the difference between Columns 3 and 4, and record in Column 5. This is the amount of salt that was added to the water.

   g. Make a prediction: Will you be able to dissolve more or less salt into warmer water? Why?

   h. Repeat steps e–f with both warm tap water and the water heated on the hot plate.

   i. Clean up your station as directed by your teacher.

FIGURE 3.4. Soda pop is a solution of water, carbon dioxide gas, corn syrup and coloring.

Follow-up Questions:

2. Plot the amount of salt added versus temperature on graph paper. Add it to your notebook. Be sure that your graph includes 1) a title, 2) labeled *x*- and *y*-axes, 3) units for each axis, and 4) a key.

3. Describe how solubility changes as temperature increases.

4. What would happen if you added more solvent to a saturated solution?

5. Based on your results, think about Earth's ocean. Which part or parts of the ocean would you expect to be more salty?

Explain

Water: The Universal Solvent

It is the polarity of water molecules and their uneven distribution of shared electrons that contribute to water's characterization as the "universal solvent". Many of the salts in the ocean easily dissolve in water. Interestingly, salts do not share electrons in their bonds like water or covalent compounds. Salts are usually made of *metals*, which have one or two electrons in the outer shell, and *nonmetals*, which need one or two electrons to complete an outer shell. So when they react, the *metals* transfer their outer shell electrons to the *nonmetals* in the compound. This process results in the *metal* becoming a positively charged atom (positive ion) and the *nonmetal* becoming a negatively charged atom (negative ion). When compounds consist of atoms that each have an electrical charge, called ions, the compound is **ionic**. The positive and negative ions are highly attracted to each other and form strong bonds.

FIGURE 3.5. Most salts in the ocean are ions of common table salt, NaCl.

Consider common table salt. This compound, NaCl, is made up of two elements, sodium (Na) and chloride (Cl). Table salt can be dissolved in water. NaCl by itself is held together by **ionic bond**. However, when water comes into contact with a compound such as this one, the polar nature of the water molecule pulls the compound apart. The Na⁺ ion is attracted to the negative side of the water molecule. The Cl⁻ ion is attracted to the positive side.

Salts and ionic compounds are usually solid at room temperature because it takes a great deal of energy to separate the ions. For example the melting point of table salt, sodium chloride, is 801 °C.

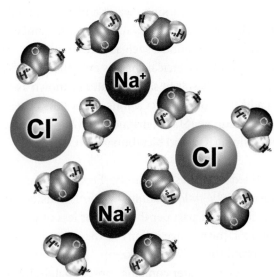

FIGURE 3.6. Table salt (NaCl) dissolved as ions in water. Smaller water molecules align themselves around positively and negatively charged sodium and chloride ions.

Water molecules have just the right polarity and size to be able to collect around the ions in salts and pull them apart from each other as shown in FIGURE 3.6. Since water can dissolve salts and polar covalent compounds it is considered the "universal solvent".

Oils are hydrocarbons that share electrons symmetrically in their molecules so they are nonpolar. Nonpolar molecules do not dissolve in water since there is no polar attraction.

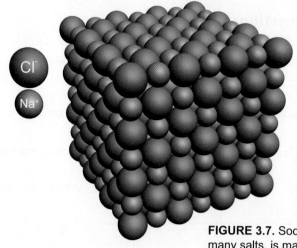

FIGURE 3.7. Sodium chloride, like many salts, is made up of very tightly bound ions that form a very regular crystalline structure like the one shown.

Properties of Compounds and Molecules

Properties	Ionic Compounds	Polar Covalent	Nonpolar Covalent
Bonding type	Ionic bonding	Sharing electrons unevenly	Sharing electrons evenly
States at room temperature	Solid	Solid, liquid, or gas	Mostly gases and some liquids
Examples	NaCl, KCl, KI, $CaCO_3$, $CuSO_4$, $MgSO_4$	H_2O, H_2S, alcohol, sugar, NH_3	O_2, H_2, CO_2, CH_4, N_2, CCl_4, oils and fats

The dissolved salts in water allow it to conduct electricity, as the solution can carry an electrical charge. This ability to carry an electrical charge is known as **conductivity**. Pure water, or distilled water, does not contain electrically charged ions so it does not conduct electricity. Water is not acidic or basic. It has a neutral pH balance of 7. The ocean, in contrast, is slightly basic, due to materials dissolved within the water.

The ocean is a solution of water and many dissolved materials, including gases such as oxygen and carbon dioxide. Compounds, such as NaCl, with elements that have opposite electrical charges are called salts. The measure of dissolved salts in water is known as **salinity**. In addition to Na^+ and Cl^- ions, other ions in seawater include sulfate $(SO_4)^{-2}$, magnesium (Mg^{+2}), calcium (Ca^{+2}), potassium (K^+), and bicarbonate $(HCO_3)^{-1}$.

Distilled water has no salinity. Fresh water and tap water have very low salinity. Water is considered fresh if it contains 1 part per thousand or less of salts. In contrast, the average salinity of the ocean is 35 parts per thousand (or 3.5% salt make-up). At this salinity, every liter of ocean water contains approximately 1.2 ounces of dissolved salts. Salinity is expressed in practical salinity units, or PSU. One PSU is equivalent to one part per thousand.

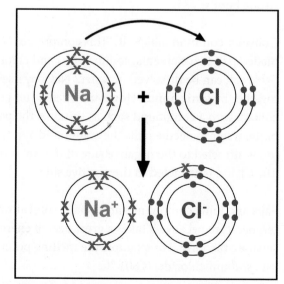

FIGURE 3.8. Table salt (NaCl) is illustrated as ions and as a molecule with its electron shells and electrons.

The image below shows average ocean surface salinity. Dark areas in the ocean indicate regions of lower-than-average salinity; white areas show higher-than-average salinity.

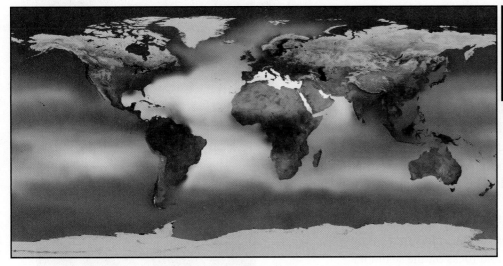

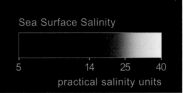
Sea Surface Salinity

5   14   25   40
practical salinity units

FIGURE 3.9. Global map of average sea surface salinity.

4. Copy the data table below into your notebook. Complete the table using the information provided on the previous page.

Type of Water	Average Salinity (PSU)
Distilled	
Tap	
Fresh	
Salt	

5. Explain how the polar nature of the water molecule contributes to its ability to act as a solvent.

Why Is the Sea Salty?

Water's excellent ability to act as a solvent implies that wherever water exists on Earth, it is carrying materials with it. This is true for water even in the human body, where water in the blood helps to carry oxygen, vitamins, minerals, and nutrients to the body's cells.

So, ocean water carries a lot of materials—but from where do the materials, including salt, come? There are several sources.

From land: Fresh water in streams and rivers contains salts. Rivers flow into the ocean. It is estimated that about 4 billion tons of salts are carried by rivers into the ocean each year. Over time, more and more salts are added to the ocean. In essence, salts are constantly entering the ocean because rivers and streams carry

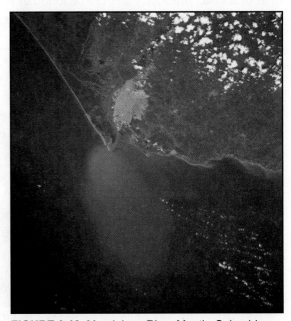

FIGURE 3.10. Magdalena River Mouth, Colombia. Water from land carries salts along with sediments into the ocean.

them there. Also, through evaporation, water leaves the ocean and goes into the atmosphere. When water evaporates, salts are left behind.

From inside the Earth: Volcanoes, vents, and other processes at the seafloor spew minerals from below Earth's crust into the ocean. FIGURE 3.11 shows an undersea volcano and a hydrothermal vent.

From the atmosphere: Particles, including minerals, can be carried by wind and deposited into the ocean. There are both natural and human-made substances in the atmosphere. FIGURE 3.12 shows volcanic ash entering the atmosphere. Minerals transported by the atmosphere can be deposited from the atmosphere directly into the ocean.

Salts remain dissolved in ocean water unless they become incorporated into sediments and rocks on the seafloor.

FIGURE 3.11. Processes at the seafloor spew salts from below Earth's crust into the ocean.

FIGURE 3.12. Particles, including minerals, can be carried by wind and deposited into the ocean.

Salinity and Marine Organisms

Water and its properties, which you have investigated, support life in the ocean and on Earth. Scientists infer that life on this planet began in the ocean. Marine organisms are well suited to living in salt water. Their body structures are equipped to handle the water's density, salinity, conductivity, cohesion, and other properties.

We generally consider water to be salty or fresh. Water that is somewhere in between salty and fresh is referred to as **brackish**. Brackish water can be found in some of the ecosystems you studied in Lesson 1: Diving Into Ocean Ecosystems, including mangrove forests and salt marshes. Both of these ecosystems occur where rivers meet the sea, areas called **estuaries**.

Estuaries are incredibly important to the ocean. They are sometimes called the "nurseries of the sea", because estuaries are places where the young of many seabirds, fish, shellfish, and other organisms can develop in a protected area. In other words, estuaries are home to many juvenile organisms. Many commercial fish species rely on estuaries as habitats for some portion of their life cycle. Migrating bird species often use estuaries as a resting place. Estuaries also protect coastlines by preventing **erosion**, the movement of sediment.

FIGURE 3.13. This estuary in Northern Florida is home to many organisms well suited to life in brackish water. Estuaries are also important habitats for juvenile organisms.

FIGURE 3.14. Coastal wetlands provide food for a variety of species including this Blue Heron. Estuaries are home to many juvenile organisms and help to protect both land and sea.

See Page 694 for how to access e-Tools.

View *NOAA Estuary Video* 1 (1:55) and *NOAA Estuary Video 2* (5:45) from the e-Tools to learn more about estuaries.

e-Tools

The first video introduces estuaries and their uses for humans and other organisms. In the second video, Dr. Jane Lubchenco discusses the importance of estuaries and introduces the National Estuarine Research Reserve System. The video shows how scientists study estuaries and how they are used by scientists and citizens.

FIGURE 3.15. Screenshot of the *NOAA Estuary Video 1*.

FIGURE 3.16. Screenshot of the *NOAA Estuary Video 2*.

Most aquatic organisms can tolerate either fresh water or salt water. Plants and animals that live in estuaries must endure wide ranges in salinity because estuaries are always changing. Salinity in estuaries can vary from 1 to 40 PSU depending on current conditions. Estuarine organisms have unique strategies for coping with differing conditions. Some mangrove trees, for example, release excess salt through their leaves. Blue crabs prefer different salinity at different parts of their life cycle.

6. Based on the videos and the above passage, describe three important roles of estuaries.

7. Based on what you know about density from the last Lesson, describe how the fresh water and salt water in an estuary would form layers.

Osmoregulation: A Balancing Act

Have you ever wondered why your hands look wrinkled when you are in the bath or a pool for a long time? You might think that your skin shrinks, causing wrinkles, but this is not true. The better explanation is that your skin actually swells. Water moves from the surroundings into your skin, but the swelling is uneven, causing your skin to appear wrinkled. Another explanation for the 'pruning' is that your blood vessels are shrinking when submerged in water.

The liquid or water in your cells has a higher salinity than the fresh water in which you take a bath. Water will move across membranes, in this case the cell membranes of your skin cells, from areas of lower salinity to areas of higher salinity. This process is called **osmosis**. The same process that is responsible for your wrinkled fingers, osmosis, is an important process for marine organisms. In the ocean and in brackish environments with a mix of fresh and salty water, many marine organisms must be able to survive with high salt concentrations. As shrinking or swelling of cells can be dangerous for animals, organisms have ways of balancing the amount of water that enters and leaves their cells.

Individual cells can control the balance of water, a process called **osmoregulation**. Most marine organisms have specialized ways of osmoregulating. Sea turtles have specialized salt-secreting glands that eliminate excess salts that the animals do not need when they drink seawater. Because of the process of osmosis, many bony fish in the ocean lose water to their highly saline environment. In order to stay hydrated, they drink a lot of seawater and secrete the salts through specialized cells and excrete concentrated urine.

Marine mammals, including seals, sea lions, walruses, whales, dolphins, manatees, and sea otters, do not drink seawater. They get their water from the food they eat, and the metabolic processes within their cells keep them healthy. They also produce urine that has a greater salt concentration than the surrounding seawater.

FIGURE 3.17. Because of the process of osmosis, many bony fish in the ocean lose water to their highly saline environment. In order to stay hydrated, they drink a lot of seawater and secrete the salts through specialized cells and excrete concentrated urine.

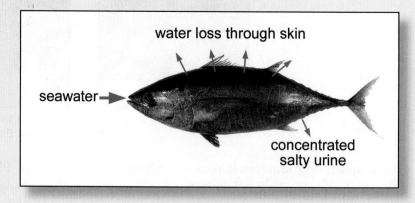

FIGURE 3.18. Freshwater fish experience the opposite problem. If it was not for osmoregulation, their cells would be constantly taking on water, like your skin cells in the bath. Instead, freshwater fish produce a lot of dilute urine, which gets rid of excess water in their systems.

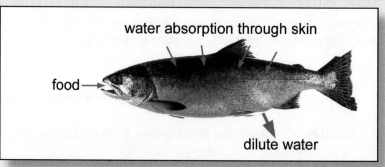

 **Lab**

Investigating Surface Tension

Have you ever seen or heard of insects that can walk on water? While these animals, including the water strider, may surprise you, the properties of water itself contribute to the insects' abilities. In this experiment, you will investigate some of these properties.

Materials:

- Tap water
- Pennies
- Dish detergent
- Plastic cups
- Spices

Follow the procedures with your lab group. Have one group member read each step aloud.

FIGURE 3.19. One example of an insect that can walk on water is a water strider. Water striders take advantage of water's unique properties.

1. a. Place a cup right side up on a paper towel. Fill it to the top with water.

    b. Make a prediction: How many pennies can you add to the cup before it overflows?

    c. Draw the following chart in your notebook. Now, test your prediction three times and calculate the average number of pennies added to the cup before overflowing occurred. Record your observations.

	Trial 1	Trial 2	Trial 3	Average
Number of Pennies Added Before Overflow				

    d. Was the average number of pennies you were able to add more or less than expected? Describe what happened.

    e. Remove the pennies from the cup and start over. Fill the water to the brim, at the same level as last time, but this time add two drops of dish detergent.

        Make a prediction: Will adding liquid dish liquid alter the number of pennies that can be added to the cup before it overflows? Why or why not?

f. Draw the following chart in your notebook. Repeat the experiment with the water and detergent combination. Record your observations.

	Trial 1	Trial 2	Trial 3	Average
Number of Pennies Added Before Overflow				

g. Did your results support your prediction? Explain.

h. Remove the pennies from the cup and start over. Fill the water to the brim, at the same level as last time, but this time add a few shakes of a spice.

Make a prediction: Will adding spices alter the number of pennies that can be added to the cup before it overflows? Why or why not?

i. Draw the following chart in your notebook. Repeat the experiment with a water and spice solution. Record your observations.

	Trial 1	Trial 2	Trial 3	Average
Number of Pennies Added Before Overflow				

j. Did your results support your prediction? Explain.

k. Clean up your laboratory station as directed by your teacher.

Follow-up Questions:

2. Plot the results of your three tests on graph paper and add this to your notebook. Be sure that your graph includes 1) a title, 2) labeled *x*- and *y*-axes, 3) units for each axis, and 4) a key.

3. Draw what the top of the cup looked like after you added the pennies in each scenario. Label each diagram.

FIGURE 3.20. A simple investigation using pennies will help you to learn about another important property of water.

Cohesion

The property of water making it attracted to other molecules of water via hydrogen bonding is called **cohesion**. When they "stick", as oxygen and hydrogen atoms from one molecule tend to attract opposite atoms of another water molecule, they look something like the image below.

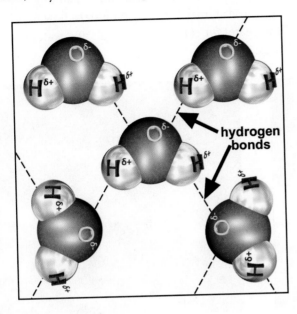

FIGURE 3.21. Notice the hydrogen bonds resulting from the slightly positively charged hydrogen part of one water molecule attracted to the slightly negatively charged oxygen part of another water molecule.

Cohesion leads to some of the phenomena that you investigated in the lab activity. You observed that at the top of the cup, cohesion caused the surface of the water to behave almost like a skin or membrane. The attraction between molecules at a liquid's surface is called its **surface tension**. Liquids such as water with high surface tension "bead up" at the top of a container. The images of water droplets onboard the International Space Station show water as "beads". The attraction of the water molecules between each other is strong. It all allows the molecules to bulge in a shape that appears somewhat spherical. It is cohesion that allows water to form drops. Water droplets are spherical.

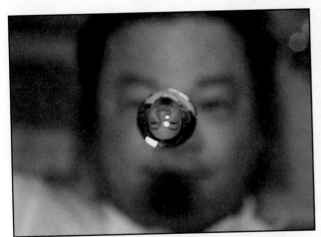

FIGURE 3.22. Astronaut Leroy Chiao watches a water bubble float between him and the camera on the International Space Station. Materials onboard are exposed to microgravity, allowing the properties of water to be understood more clearly.

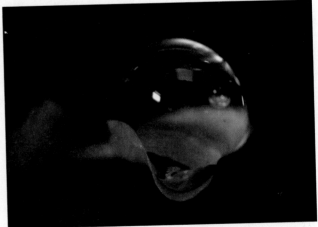

FIGURE 3.23. Water droplet on a leaf onboard the International Space Station. The spherical nature of water is shown in an environment with virtually no gravity.

Cohesion is important to other organisms besides the water striders you read about before your investigation. The fact that water molecules "stick" to one another allows them to travel together. Picture what travels through your blood vessels, or through the roots of plants. Picture your bloodstream, which is mostly water and has many of the properties of water. Its molecules stick to one another. If they didn't, water wouldn't flow very effectively. Like humans, many marine animals, including fish, birds, sea turtles, and marine mammals, have a circulatory system to bring materials to and from the cells. Other organisms, including clams and sponges, feed by filtering water through their tissues. These animals also rely on water's flow to bring them food and to rid their bodies of waste. Similarly, if it were not for cohesion, materials and water could not be carried from the roots of plants to the stems and leaves.

FIGURE 3.24. Mangrove trees in the U.S. Virgin Islands showing off their roots. Water's property of cohesion allows materials to be distributed through the bodies of living things like plants and animals.

FIGURE 3.25. Sponges, such as this large one with a Rock Hind hiding inside, are filter feeders. They pump water in through their pores and remove food particles.

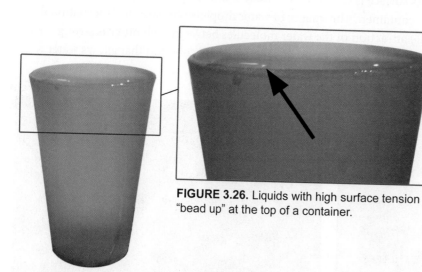

FIGURE 3.26. Liquids with high surface tension "bead up" at the top of a container.

FIGURE 3.27. The property of water that makes it attracted to other molecules of water is called cohesion.

8. Based on FIGURE 3.26 and FIGURE 3.27, sketch how the property of cohesion at the molecular level allows water to creep above the edge of a cup without overflowing.

9. In ***Investigating Surface Tension***, you experimented with detergent and spices. Explain how the detergent and spices affected the surface tension of the water.

Evaluate

1. List the following types of water in order of increasing salinity:

    *   Brackish water
    *   Distilled water
    *   Salt water
    *   Fresh water

2. Explain how the chemical structure of water is related to:

    a. Cohesion

    b. Salinity

3. Give two examples of how marine organisms are affected by the properties of water such as density, ability to exist in all three states of matter, ability to dissolve materials, high heat capacity, and cohesion.

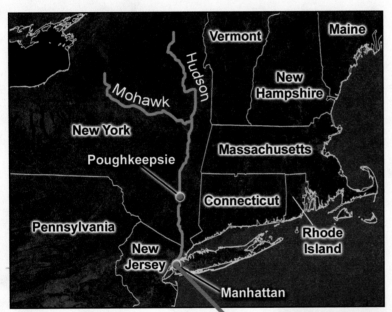

FIGURE 3.28. The Hudson River borders New York and New Jersey and is an interesting study in salinity. The river begins high in the mountains of New York State and runs fresh for hundreds of miles, even as far south as Manhattan during spring rainstorms and snowmelt. Salty water from the Atlantic Ocean pushes upriver due to the tides. During drought conditions when fresh water is scarce, salt water extends as far north as Poughkeepsie.

4

The Ocean Over Time

INSIDE:

Objectives

You will be able to:

✓ Identify how humans have relied upon and utilized the ocean for thousands of years.

✓ Construct a timeline of ocean events to scale.

✓ Observe that scientific inquiry is a cyclical process, and describe the value of differing perspectives about the process of science.

✓ Investigate the many technologies and tools that scientists use to make observations about ocean processes.

Benchmarks

5c. Some major groups are found exclusively in the ocean. The diversity of major groups of organisms is much greater in the ocean than on land.

6b. From the ocean we get foods, medicines and mineral and energy resources. In addition, it provides jobs, supports our nation's economy, serves as a highway for transportation of goods and people and plays a role in national security.

6c. The ocean is a source of inspiration, recreation, rejuvenation and discovery. It is also an important element in the heritage of many cultures.

6d. Much of the world's population lives in coastal areas.

6e. Humans affect the ocean in a variety of ways. Laws, regulations and resource management affect what is taken out and put into the ocean. Human development and activity leads to pollution (e.g., point source, nonpoint source, noise pollution) and physical modifications (e.g., changes to beaches, shores and rivers). In addition, humans have removed most of the large vertebrates from the ocean.

6g. Everyone is responsible for caring for the ocean. The ocean sustains life on Earth, and humans must live in ways that sustain the ocean. Individual and collective actions are needed to effectively manage ocean resources for all.

(continued on next page)

7a. The ocean is the last and largest unexplored place on Earth; less than 5% of it has been explored. This is the great frontier for the next generation's explorers and researchers, where they will find great opportunities for inquiry and investigation.

7b. Understanding the ocean is more than a matter of curiosity. Exploration, inquiry and study are required to better understand ocean systems and processes.

7f. Ocean exploration is truly interdisciplinary. It requires close collaboration among biologists, chemists, climatologists, computer programmers, engineers, geologists, meteorologists and physicists, and new ways of thinking.

Engage

Marine algae—including tiny photosynthetic organisms called **phytoplankton**, as well as seaweeds—are found in the ocean all over the world. In addition to being an important biotic factor in many marine ecosystems, seaweeds are used by humans for food and other reasons. In this Lesson, you will examine many ways in which humans have used the vast resource of the ocean and relied upon it for millennia. People around the world depend on the ocean for food, medicine, recreation, trade, scientific exploration, and even national security. There are thousands of important scientific discoveries throughout history that have led to our current understanding of the ocean and its important assets.

FIGURE 4.1. Red algae include some of the oldest seaweed groups. Some species are important in coral reef ecosystems.

FIGURE 4.2. A close-up of Maine seaweed. Scientists believe that true plants evolved from this group of algae, which is classified into Kingdom Protista.

Over the past few centuries, each new discovery about the ocean employed a scientific process. During today's activity, you will get a glimpse at some of those interesting ocean-centered events, the technologies available to scientists throughout history, and the processes that scientists still currently use to make discoveries about the ocean.

FIGURE 4.3. Brown algae, such as the seaweed shown here, are very common in a variety of ocean ecosystems. Kelp, such as those species that make up kelp forests, are brown algae.

Explore

The Ocean in History – An Ocean Timeline

Activity

In this activity, you will create an ***Ocean Timeline***. Each group will analyze and display one segment of the class timeline, representing one period of time. Work as a class to develop an appropriate scale for displaying your ***Ocean Timeline*** in the classroom. The entire timeline needs to span from 4000 B.C.E. (Before Common Era) to the present. You will display the timeline along the wall (e.g., around the room, in the hallway). Before planning to plot the events on the timeline, calculate an appropriate scale for the project using the instructions and measuring tools your teacher provides.

The time periods are as follows:

Group 1: B.C.E. (Before Common Era)
Group 2: 0–1500
Group 3: 1501–1799
Group 4: 1800–1850
Group 5: 1851–1899
Group 6: 1900–1950
Group 7: 1951–1999
Group 8: 2000–present

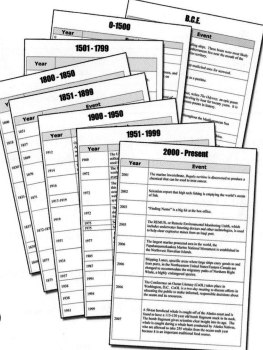

FIGURE 4.4. *Ocean Timeline* handouts.

Materials:

- ***Ocean Timeline*** handout
- Atlases (to identify locations of events)
- Meter sticks (to create an appropriate scale)
- Multicolor highlighters or crayons
- Encyclopedias (optional)
- Copy or construction paper
- Masking tape
- Scissors
- Butcher paper (to create the Ocean Timeline)
- ***Classroom World Map*** from Lesson 1: Diving Into Ocean Ecosystems

1. Your group has received an ***Ocean Timeline*** handout with a list of events related to the ocean. Each event relates to one or more of the following categories:

- *Food*
- *Products from the Sea*
- *Recreation*
- *Trade and Navigation*
- *Scientific Exploration and Research*
- *National Security*
- *Marine Technologies*
- *Ecosystem Protection and Management*

2. In your groups, read each event. For each event decide which category or categories it belongs to.

3. Using the color scheme below, or a variation to match your group's available colors, create a key for your group's part of the *Ocean Timeline*. Then use a highlighter or crayon to color or shade each event. *Note: Events may fall into several categories. If so, highlight them in multiple colors.*

- Food (RED)
- Products from the Sea (ORANGE)
- **Recreation (YELLOW)**
- Trade and Navigation (GREEN)
- Scientific Exploration and Research (BLUE)
- National Security (PURPLE)
- Marine Technologies (GRAY)
- Ecosystem Protection and Management (BROWN)

Example:

Year	Event
2007	Scientists and students track albatross across the Pacific.

The group would highlight this event in BLUE to indicate that it relates to Scientific Exploration and Research and GRAY to show the use of Marine Technologies .

4. Determine how much space your group will have for your portion of the timeline. Follow the steps below:

a. How many years are in your portion of the timeline span?

b. What is the scale you will use? What is the scenario for your piece of the class *Ocean Timeline*?

Example:

There are 20 total feet of wall space for the *Ocean Timeline*:

The timeline spans over 6,000 years. In this case, each foot of the timeline could represent approximately 300 years. More realistically, it makes better sense to create a "zoomed-in" section for *1800 to Present*, as illustrated on the next page, since there are many events in more recent years.

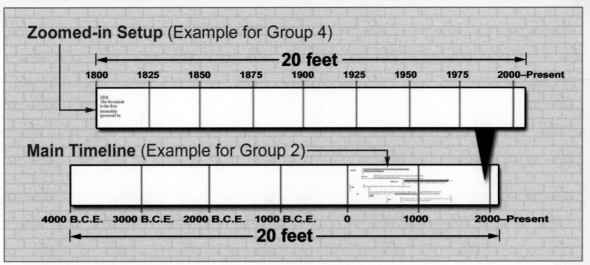

FIGURE 4.5. Main *Ocean Timeline* and Zoomed-in Setup illustration.

Example for Group 2:

Your group has years 0–1500, which is a span of 1,500 years. Therefore, you would use the main timeline, as illustrated above, not the zoomed-in one.

To fit about 6,000 years (from 4000 B.C.E. to 2000) over a 20-foot span, each foot represents 300 years.

Set up the proportion as follows:

$$\frac{6,000 \text{ years}}{20 \text{ feet}} = \frac{300 \text{ years}}{1 \text{ foot}}$$

$$1,500 \text{ years [from 0-1500]} \times \frac{1 \text{ foot}}{300 \text{ years}} = \textbf{5 feet of space}$$

Therefore, Group 2 has 5 feet of space with which to work on the main timeline.

Example for Group 4:

Your group has years 1800–1850. Therefore, you will use the zoomed-in section of the timeline.

To fit about 200 years (1800–2000) over the 20-foot span (shown in the zoomed-in illustration), each foot needs to represent 10 years.

Set up the proportion as follows:

$$\frac{200 \text{ years}}{20 \text{ feet}} = \frac{10 \text{ years}}{1 \text{ foot}}$$

$$50 \text{ years [from 1800-1850]} \times \frac{1 \text{ foot}}{10 \text{ years}} = \textbf{5 feet of space}$$

Therefore, Group 4 has 5 feet of space with which to work on the zoomed-in timeline.

5. Use paper to represent the correct length for your group's timeline. In the examples above, the two groups would each cut a 5-foot piece of paper. When the required length is greater than one piece of paper, tape several pieces of paper together as necessary.

6. Cut out the events you have colored or highlighted.

7. Label the dates of your events on your group's portion of the timeline. Attach the events to the appropriate spot on the timeline with tape. Your events might not fit on the timeline. If this is the case, simply draw a line to the correct date and allow the event to be posted off of the paper.

8. Work with your teacher and the other groups to paste all of the groups' timelines on the wall in order to form one giant timeline.

Explain

Human Reliance on the Ocean in the Past and Today

The ocean has been important to people around the world throughout history and today. Traveling via the ocean has allowed for trade of goods and knowledge, as well as cultural exchanges. Today, humans continue to benefit from new oceanic discoveries, including those that have advanced the pharmaceutical industry and energy resources.

FIGURE 4.6. The *Minnesota* is shown here in Puget Sound, the large sea inlet of Washington State. This vessel was once the largest United States merchant vessel. She launched in 1904.

1. With your group, choose two or three events from your time period that are geographically diverse (i.e., they happened in different parts of the world). For example, do not choose all of your events from North America. If you are unsure of an event's location, use atlases, online resources, or encyclopedias to help you choose the events. Note the events you choose and their locations.

FIGURE 4.7. Recreational activities that include surfing are increasingly popular in areas that generate ample waves.

2. Send a group member up to the *Classroom World Map*. The group member will carefully add the events to the map by making a dot at the location and carefully labeling it in as few words as possible. If your events are trade routes, voyages, etc., use a dotted line to show the approximate route.

Example:

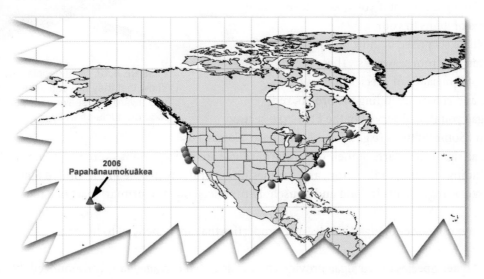

FIGURE 4.8. Example of dots representing locations on *Classroom World Map*.

3. Move around the room and read the events on the *Ocean Timeline*. After you review the timeline, answer the following Questions.

4. Compare how people in ancient times used the ocean with how we use the ocean today. Give specific examples.

5. Which are the three most interesting events on the entire timeline? Explain.

6. In your opinion, what are two of the most significant events presented on the timeline?

7. Describe the importance of marine technologies in the *Ocean Timeline*.

FIGURE 4.9. Fishing is a way of life for many. As a source of food, humans have been dependent on the sea for millennia.

If you are a fan of sushi, you know that you have eaten seaweed, which is typically used to wrap rice and fish together. Or maybe you have enjoyed seaweed salad, complete with sesame seeds sprinkled on top—yum!

But did you know that there is probably seaweed in your ice cream? What about your cake mix or shampoo? It may not be obvious at first glance, but if you take a close look at the ingredients of items in your home, you will be surprised by how many contain ingredients derived from seaweeds. These marine algae consist of thousands of species in many shapes, sizes, and colors, including the brown, red, and green algae you first observed in the **Engage** section of this Lesson. Some cultures (e.g., Chinese, Japanese, Korean) use marine algae as significant parts of their diet. Marine algae are an important source of Vitamins B and C and minerals including calcium, iodine, iron, and magnesium. For many people in the United States, marine algae are mainly used as ingredients in food and household products, not as a primary part of a meal.

FIGURE 4.10. Most people who eat sushi know that they are eating seaweed, but are you aware that seaweed is used in many other food products as well?

Each of the main categories of algae has distinct properties that are beneficial to humans.

- **Red Algae:** Species of red algae provide chemicals called carrageenans (pronounced: kǎr-eh-GEE-nens), which are used to thicken products such as jellies, yogurts, and ice cream. Carrageenans comprise a long strand of carbohydrates that when added to foods, help create a gel-like texture. For example, in chocolate milk, carrageenans help keep the chocolate well mixed throughout the milk. They are also used in cosmetics, pharmaceuticals, and industrial products.

- **Brown Algae:** Brown algae provide alginates (pronounced: AL-juh-nates), used as thickeners in foods such as ice cream and in products such as moisturizers and hair conditioners. Alginates allow the fats in foods to blend with water, while absorbing water quickly. Brown algae are also used to develop strong fibers that can be woven into fabrics and bandages for protecting wounds. They are part of rubber tires, paper, and asphalt.

- **Green Algae:** From green algae we are able to extract beta-carotene (pronounced: bay-tah KǍR-eh-teen), a yellow pigment, and xanthophylls (pronounced: ZAN-thuh-fills), which are yellowish or brownish pigments. Both pigments provide yellowish-orange food coloring.

It is apparent that there are many uses for marine algae, which is just one more good reason to protect the ocean.

FIGURE 4.11. Algae can be large, such as the seaweeds you observed, or tiny one-celled organisms. Some algae have a special relationship with corals and provide energy to them.

Activity

Investigating Marine Algae

Marine algae are found in many of our food and household products. Your assignment is to identify at least 5 items that have marine algae in them by looking at the ingredients.

When looking at the ingredients, be sure to consult the May Also Be Called row of the chart to notice alternate product names.

1. List the products you find in the first column of the chart below. Use a check or *x* to note which type of chemicals are found in each product.

	Red Algae – Carageenan	Brown Algae – Alginate	Green Algae – Beta-carotene
	May Also Be Called: Gigartina, eucheuma, chondrus, Algas, Carrageen, Carrageenin, Carragheenan, Chondrus crispus, Chondrus Extract, dulse, agar, gelidium cartilagineum, porphyra, ogo, limu Euchema species, Gigartina chamissoi, Gigartina mamillosa, Gigartina skottsbergii, Irish Moss Algae, Irish Moss Extract, Mousse D'Irlande, Red Marine Algae	*May Also Be Called:* algin, sodium polymannuronate, Calcium alginate, Sodium alginate, E400, E401, E402, E403, E404, E405, Kaltostat, Ropes, fucoidan, fucoxantin, vraic, kombu, algenate	*May Also Be Called:* A-Caro-25, Lumitene, Aphanizomenon, Spirulina, chlorella
Food Items			
Non-food Items			

Elaborate

Part 1: The Nature of Science

Have you ever watched fireworks and wondered how people have figured out how to create beautiful colors and patterns in the sky? Have you considered why the sky is blue or how a sea turtle, only minutes old, knows which way to crawl across the sand to reach the ocean? If you have ever asked questions like these, then you know what it is like to be curious about the natural world. Scientists ask questions, or inquire, all the time and begin a process of investigation that leads to discoveries, answers to their questions, and opportunities to ask additional questions. This process is known as **scientific inquiry**.

FIGURE 4.12. A Hawksbill Turtle hatchling heads for the ocean.

Scientific inquiry is a cyclical process. All scientists, students, and citizens use their senses (i.e., touch, taste, smell, sight, and hearing) to collect information, or **observations**, about the natural world. Observations are based on what our senses tell us. When scientists collect and record their observations they create **data**. One single observation is a *datum*, the plural is *data*. Data are presented in many different forms, including graphs, charts, tables, pictures, maps, and other ways of communicating information such as multimedia presentations, animations, and technology tools.

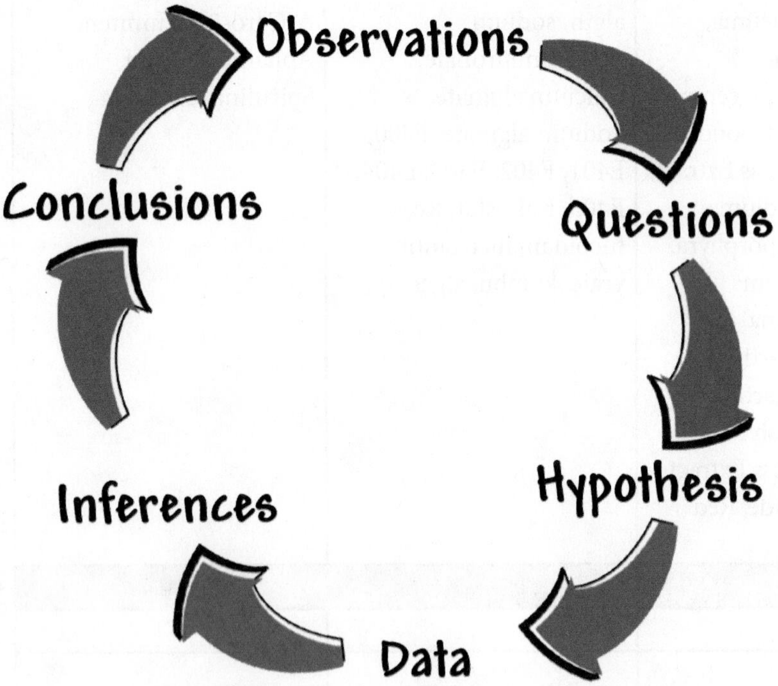

Observations → Questions → Hypothesis → Data → Inferences → Conclusions

FIGURE 4.13. The process of scientific inquiry is a circular process. Scientists are constantly searching for the answers to new questions that arise in the course of scientific study.

Scientific tools help scientists collect data, as an extension of human senses. For example, a microscope extends our ability to see small organisms and a telescope gives us the ability to see farther away. Without these tools we would not be able to make astute observations and collect detailed data about materials that are very small or very far away.

Data usually fit into one of two categories, depending on how they are collected. Data recorded as measurements are called **quantitative data**. Scientists use the internationally recognized metric system to record quantitative data. For example, instruments such as thermometers, temperature probes, or satellites can measure the kinetic energy of molecules to quantitatively derive temperature. Satellites and tools allow scientists and students to identify the distance that migrating marine mammals travel over time.

FIGURE 4.14. Tiger Sharks are found in Earth's Equatorial Regions. One of the world's largest sharks, these dangerous scavengers can grow to be more than 7 meters (~23 feet) in length.

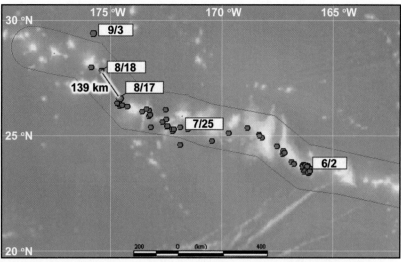

FIGURE 4.15. One individual Tiger Shark track over several months is presented at the *Signals of Spring* website.

The Tiger Shark tracked in the map on the right traveled 139 kilometers (~86 miles) in one day between August 17 and 18.

Data recorded as descriptions are referred to as **qualitative data**. A qualitative observation of the same data is: "The Tiger Shark generally moved in a westward direction during the summer". This is a statement based on the data, but it does not involve measurement. Other qualitative data could be a description of the habitat of the animal at a particular time or what the animal looks like. Quantitative and qualitative observations are both useful and are used together by scientists.

Qualitative data: **Quality** means property (e.g., appearance, taste, smell, texture).

Quantitative data: **Quantity** means measurement (e.g., temperature, length, height, cost, levels).

Let's practice to help clarify the difference.

8. Indicate whether each statement is qualitative or quantitative.

    a. The summer forest fire burned a kilometer of forest in several days.
    b. The shell of a diatom looks like shattered glass when observed under a precise microscope.
    c. The leaves on the tree, from top to bottom, are bright red.
    d. Our graduating class has over 700 students, and 60% of them are on the honor roll.
    e. The room is 6 meters x 9 meters.
    f. The sky gets darker over a period of time.
    g. This new yogurt I tried earlier today has a flavor that I find tastes sweet.
    h. More than two feet of snow fell in Washington, D.C., on February 10, 2010.
    i. The Loggerhead Sea Turtle traveled north northeast on Thursday.
    j. The Northern Elephant Seal dove 50 meters on its last dive.

Once scientists collect data they try to find a logical explanation to a question or situation based on their past knowledge and experience. This kind of explanation is an **inference**. A scientist might analyze the Tiger Shark data discussed above along with some observation data illustrating current fish movements. She may infer that the Tiger Shark traveled northeast because it was following its food supply. Inferences help scientists draw conclusions and form questions about data that can become the focus of scientific inquiry.

It is important not to confuse an observation with an inference. For example, when you observe your neighbor's car parked in the driveway, you infer that your neighbor is in the house. This inference is based on your prior experience and may well be correct. However, the owners of the home may have gone for a walk, driven in a different car, or taken public transportation somewhere. Your inference is not fact. Therefore it is not an observation and cannot be considered data. Most often in the *Marine Science: The Dynamic Ocean* animal tracking activities you will perform, your observations will be right on track. Then you will analyze all of your data. You will draw inferences about why your animal is responding the way it is to its environment at the time and moving in a certain direction. Then you will use this information, combining your observations and prior knowledge to support your ideas. Acting like a scientist in the *Marine Science: The Dynamic Ocean* program will give you practice in the process of scientific inquiry.

FIGURE 4.16. A car in the driveway suggests someone is home. This statement is an inference.

9. Look at the picture (FIGURE 4.17) and indicate whether each statement below is an observation or an inference.

FIGURE 4.17.

a. The boy jumped.
b. The boy is above the water.
c. It is a warm day.
d. He jumped out of a helicopter.
e. The water is a greenish color.
f. There is someone else in the water.
g. It will hurt when he hits the water.
h. The boy is having fun.
i. The boy is scared.
j. He has red hair.
k. The boy was pushed off a diving board.
l. The water is deep.
m. The other person jumped into the water.

10. Write an example of an inference not listed.

11. Write an example of an observation not listed.

Observations and inferences help scientists formulate a testable idea about their scientific question, called a **hypothesis**. To test a hypothesis, scientists set up a procedure or an **experiment**. They must clearly record their procedures, so that other scientists or researchers can repeat them exactly. Experiments result in more data, which scientists will analyze to help form **conclusions** that support, fail to support, or contradict their hypothesis. Inevitably, every time a scientist investigates something, it leads to more questions. Even a hypothesis that is not supported is valuable in science because it sparks additional questions.

You learned in Lesson 1: Diving Into Ocean Ecosystems that scientists use satellite tracking to learn about marine organisms and ecosystems. In the Lessons that follow, you will view various data sets and make observations. You will use your knowledge of marine ecosystems and ocean processes to analyze data and draw conclusions to potentially support or refute your hypothesis. These experiences will model how scientists engage in scientific inquiry to make discoveries about the ocean.

Many people believe that science is made up of boring facts that are set in stone. In fact, science is a very imaginative process. It can be creative as well. For example, scientific concepts may be applied to a new problem for designing solutions and systems, a process called **engineering**.

Science and engineering constantly require new ideas to learn about our world. Science is also always changing—there are plenty of ideas that were once believed to be true but those ideas have changed. Consider, for example, that scientists of the past used to believe that the Sun revolved around the Earth, or that nothing could live in the deep sea. Through investigation and exploration, data collection and inference, scientists have collected evidence that refute *these* hypotheses, but new questions about the solar system and deep oceans are being studied. It is important that scientists share recent and accurate findings with the public and with government agencies. From scientific results, we are then able to make informed decisions that protect the ocean and its resources.

The following statements describe the nature of science:

- Science is based on observations and inferences about the natural world.
- Science is creative.
- There is a relationship between science and culture.
- Scientific ideas are subject to change.

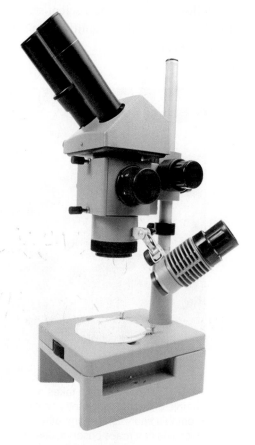

Marine scientists come from all different backgrounds and cultures and work in every country across the globe. They come from small villages to large cities, and, with their unique perspective on the world, each individual provides a valuable point of view and perhaps a creative way of thinking about a scientific question. In other words, they bring their culture, beliefs, and expertise into a scientific discussion or exploration at the onset. Their unique perspectives take a more creative and complete look at a world that is totally integrated on many levels. Scientists from around the globe gather at conferences and meetings to discuss the conclusions of specific investigations. They share new ideas about finding the answers to problems and the technologies needed to collect data. Although anyone can pursue a career in the ocean sciences, these careers take commitment, hard work, and years of study.

FIGURE 4.18. A microscope is an iconic tool scientists use to make compelling observations.

Western scientific knowledge and indigenous scientific knowledge are examples of perspectives that drive science. Groups of people that are native to a certain place for thousands of years are known as **indigenous** peoples. Other indigenous groups in the United States are Alaska Natives (such as Athabascan and Inuit), Native Hawaiian, and Native American (such as Sioux, Shinnecock, and Navajo). Indigenous peoples around the world understand changes in their environments through many generations of careful observation. Indigenous scientific knowledge is practical knowledge passed on from generation to generation. Most indigenous cultures dictate reverence for Earth's natural environments, and have lived sustainably within specific environments for thousands of years. Indigenous ways of knowing are an important perspective within the scientific community.

FIGURE 4.19. Alaska Native students assist Western scientists with bird banding.

Today's understandings about the ocean are the result of scientists from diverse backgrounds working together or valuing others' work, engaged in scientific inquiry. Because there is one ocean, it is natural that scientists from all over the world study its features and processes. In recent years, more people from diverse races, cultures, genders, and backgrounds have become scientists. The scientific community will benefit from the diversity of scientists and our understanding of the natural world will continue to grow as this trend continues.

The following images show scientists of different backgrounds working together on the same expedition. This NOAA expedition, entitled *Lophelia II: Deepwater Coral Expedition: Reefs, Rigs, and Wrecks*, took place in 2009.

FIGURE 4.20. A scientist takes a tissue sample of a coral for genetic analysis. From this analysis, she and other scientists can make observations and inferences.

FIGURE 4.21. Scientists on a ship work together and watch as seafloor imagery appears on the monitor in the research vessel's main lab.

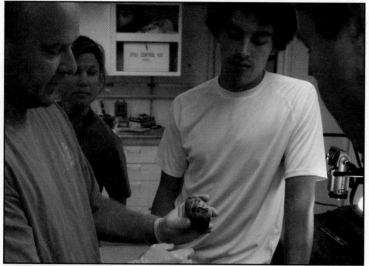

FIGURE 4.22. The team of scientists observes and discusses a biological sample.

FIGURE 4.23. Sediment traps are deployed from the stern of the ship. These tools will capture samples of the seafloor for analysis.

Part 2: Innovative Ocean Technologies

See Page 694 for how to access e-Tools.

View the **Ocean Technologies Videos** from the e-Tools.

Video 1 (0:53)   Video 2 (1:08)   Video 3 (1:04)   Video 4 (0:31)   Video 5 (0:39)   e-Tools

FIGURE 4.24. Screenshots of **Ocean Technolgies Videos**.

View several of the videos from the *Lophelia II* and other expeditions. Pay close attention to the remarkable technologies used by the scientists. Note that some of the underwater videos may appear a bit dark and grainy.

12. Give at least two examples of how scientists from different perspectives and disciplines work together.

The types of ocean exploration technologies shown in the videos were the dream of marine scientists and explorers for centuries. It is only over the past 50 years that explorers' fantasies have become reality, yet scientists estimate that 95% of the ocean has still not been explored in any great detail. Current technology allows scientists to explore depths and distances that were never before accessible. The technologies now available to an ocean technician or researcher include huge oceangoing vessels that serve as research stations and floating homes for scientists who embark on expeditions lasting for a few days to several months at a time. These ships carry computer systems, navigation and communication systems, research equipment, and full laboratories where scientists can conduct their research, and technicians and staff can assure safe voyages.

Modern diving equipment plays a major role in research. It gives scientists the freedom to move in and explore marine. Diving technology now enables humans to reach deeper than 40 meters (>130 feet) beneath the surface. When investigating beyond the safe depths for diving equipment, scientists use pressure-controlled chambers called **submersibles**. Submersibles are now widely used to allow humans or data collection tools, such as cameras or sensors, to explore deep ocean ecosystems. Submersibles in which humans travel are called human occupied vehicles, or **HOVs**. Some of the most famous oceanic discoveries, including life seen in hydrothermal vent communities, are a result of work in HOVs. These vehicles, however, are not as versatile as unmanned vehicles. The United States also maintains an

FIGURE 4.25. Scientists prepare to launch an ROV. Advantages of ROVs over submersibles are that there is less risk to humans, less cost, and much more time can be spent at the bottom. ROVs have been used to conduct research in a wide range of environments—from the tropics to the poles.

undersea laboratory located off the coast in the Florida Keys National Marine Sanctuary about 20 meters (~66 feet) below the surface. From the decks of ships or from shore, other scientist teams can send out unmanned equipment called remotely operated vehicles (**ROVs**), or autonomous underwater vehicles (**AUVs**). ROVs are connected to ships through a cable, or **tether,** whereas AUVs are not limited in this way. AUVs are self-guided by computers, allowing them to reach extremely deep water and wider geographic areas than ROVs. They can even be used during bad weather. Both ROVs and AUVs are equipped with a variety of sensors that allow them to observe physical and biological features of the ocean.

See Page 694 for how to access e-Tools.

View the *Aquarius Video* (3:14) from the e-Tools.

FIGURE 4.26 Screenshot of the *Aquarius Video*.

e-Tools

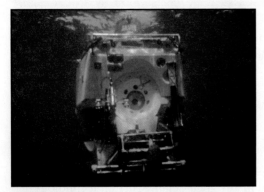

FIGURE 4.27. *Alvin*, arguably the most successful research submersible, can dive up to 4,500 meters (~14,764 feet). For many years it has performed underwater tasks and taken extensive photographs. It can stay underwater for up to 3 days.

In addition to these fascinating technologies, scientists use a wide range of observational tools to monitor Earth's processes. Many of these devices are used onboard research vessels and submersibles, while others collect data from thousands of miles above the surface of the ocean. Satellites house instruments that provide remote-sensing data, helping scientists to understand sea surface temperatures, currents, changes in food availability, pollution, flooding, the location of animals, and more of the activities on the planet. Ocean-observing systems (OOSs) combine satellite data along with observations from land, air, and ocean-based sensors such as those on ships, buoys, and aircrafts. These systems provide us with a great deal of data, which are processed by computers in laboratories onshore. Satellites are an extremely important tool for understanding ocean ecosystems, which you will discover in the Lessons to follow.

FIGURE 4.28. The tether on the right is connected to a ship or other support vessel closer to the surface. There, a pilot can control the ROV's movements and data collection activities.

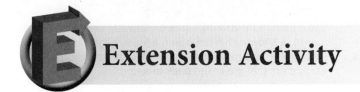 # Extension Activity

When compared to the ocean exploration tools used today, it is remarkable to consider what scientists were able to learn using the very limited technologies of the past. The NOAA Ocean Explorer website contains information on the history, development, and current applications of research equipment organized into four main categories: vessels, submersibles, diving, and remote-sensing. Choose a specific technology within one of these categories and create a brochure to educate others.

Access ***NOAA's Ocean Explorer Technology*** page through the *Marine Science: The Dynamic Ocean* website.

Include the following in your informational brochure:

1. An introduction to the technology and how it is used.

2. An explanation of the history of the ocean technology (e.g., when it was first developed, who came up with the initial ideas and plans). For example:

    One example of a useful technology is the diving suit. The designs of diving suits have progressed significantly since they were first used about 300 years ago. What did they look like then? How deep could people dive with the first suits? How has the technology progressed to today's diving suits?

3. The names of at least 2 research expeditions or initiatives where the technology has been featured during the past 10 years.

4. Possible future uses of the technology.

5. A title for your brochure.

6. Pictures, graphs, diagrams, or any other appropriate visual to help inform the reader.

Aquarius

The *Aquarius Underwater Habitat* is the sole underwater habitat on Earth. Its purpose is to study marine science. *Aquarius* is located about 20 meters (~66 feet) underwater in the Florida Keys National Marine Sanctuary at the base of a coral reef. The habitat is owned by the National Oceanic and Atmospheric Administration (NOAA) and operated by the National Undersea Research Center (NURC) at the University of North Carolina Wilmington.

Aquarius began underwater operations in 1988 when it was deployed in the U.S. Virgin Islands. After Hurricane Hugo hit the South Atlantic Coast in 1989, *Aquarius* moved to Wilmington, North Carolina to be repaired. It resumed work at its present location in 1992.

The habitat houses four marine scientists and two technicians and enables them to study the surrounding underwater environment in missions lasting about ten days. Due to the amount of time spent underwater, *Aquarius* scientists are called aquanauts. They are able to dive for nine hours at a time, whereas most divers are generally able to be underwater for up to two hours. The longer dives allow scientists to have time for specific and detail-oriented observations.

FIGURE 4.29. NOAA's *Aquarius Underwater Habitat.* Inside the 81-ton, 43 x 20 x 16.5-foot underwater laboratory are six bunks, a shower with hot water, a toilet, a microwave, trash compactor, and refrigerator, as well as air conditioning and computers that are linked back to shore.

Aquarius consists of three different sections. Scientists enter the water through what is referred to as the "wet porch", a safe area that allows for passing people and instruments into the water. The chamber keeps the pressure on the inside the same as the outside. The main compartment is divided into two pressurized compartments that are strong enough to support normal atmospheric pressure. This section houses the kitchen, workspace and sleeping quarters. The last compartment is an entryway with a large workspace.

NASA's Extreme Environment Mission Operations (NEEMO) program has utilized *Aquarius* since 2001. The NEEMO project simulates space in order for scientists to research and understand human spaceflight. By creating a place with properties as close to the International Space Station as possible, the close living quarters and daily logistical operations can be more easily modeled.

FIGURE 4.30. The *NEEMO* 13 crew watching the launch of the Space Shuttle *Endeavour* from the *Aquarius* bunkroom.

FIGURE 4.31. Astronaut/ Aquanaut Nicole P. Stott takes a moment to pose for a picture beside a habitat window during her stay inside the *Aquarius Underwater Laboratory*.

Evaluate

1. The ocean is an integral part of human life. You explored many examples of this from history and in our everyday lives during this Lesson.

   Review the classroom *Ocean Timeline* to help you identify one example for each category of how the ocean was important in the past. Then, use your knowledge of how humans rely on the ocean in our daily lives to provide a specific current example and how it is accomplished for each category.

	Example in history	Current example and how it is accomplished
• Food (RED)		
• Products from the Sea (ORANGE)		
• **Recreation (YELLOW)**		
• Trade and Navigation (GREEN)		
• Scientific Exploration and Research (BLUE)		
• National Security (PURPLE)		
• **Marine Technologies (GRAY)**		
• Ecosystem Protection and Management (BROWN)		

2. In your own words, describe why the process of scientific inquiry is cyclical.

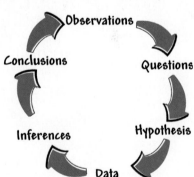

   FIGURE 4.32. Scientific Inquiry Process.

3. Match the part of the scientific inquiry process with its description:

   A. Scientists collect information from their surroundings using their senses and tools to extend their senses.   Observations

   B. Collection of observations and information.   Conclusion

   C. A testable idea related to a scientific question.   Hypothesis

   D. An explanation based on past experience but not necessarily fact.   Data

   E. Scientists make these statements based on data analysis. The result is further questioning.   Inference

5

Migrations in the Sea

INSIDE:

Objectives

You will be able to:

✔ Compare and contrast migratory movements of different marine animals.

✔ Utilize mapping and plotting skills by plotting sample animal movement data.

✔ Relate satellite tagging of marine animals to principles of the Nature of Science.

Benchmarks

7a. The ocean is the last and largest unexplored place on Earth; less than 5% of it has been explored. This is the great frontier for the next generation's explorers and researchers, where they will find great opportunities for inquiry and investigation.

7b. Understanding the ocean is more than a matter of curiosity. Exploration, inquiry, and study are required to better understand ocean systems and processes.

7d. New technologies, sensors, and tools are expanding our ability to explore the ocean. Ocean scientists are relying more and more on satellites, drifters, buoys, subsea observatories, and unmanned submersibles.

7f. Ocean exploration is truly interdisciplinary. It requires close collaboration among biologists, chemists, climatologists, computer programmers, engineers, geologists, meteorologists, and physicists and new ways of thinking.

Engage

In this Lesson, you will begin to investigate the movements of marine animals. Later in the course, you will get the opportunity to conduct a more in-depth study of a particular marine animal's movements.

The ocean covers more than 70% of the Earth's surface, and it is the habitat for a tremendous variety of living things. Some of these organisms travel great distances; others move on a much smaller scale. Humpback Whales, such as those shown to the right, are found in both the Northern and Southern Hemispheres, and in all major ocean basins. The

FIGURE 5.1. A Humpback Whale and her calf migrate north in search of food. Animal tracking is an effective way to learn science. The ocean is an excellent context in which to study the interactions between Life and Earth Sciences.

females are slightly larger than the males, growing up to about 13 meters (~43 feet). Humpback Whales travel great distances during their seasonal migration, one of the longest migrations of any mammal. The longest recorded migration was 8,300 kilometers (more than 5,100 miles). This trek from Costa Rica to Antarctica was completed by seven animals, including a calf. Humpback Whales feed at the surface, preferring small, shrimp-like animals called krill as their favorite food.

Gray Whales also undertake long migrations, traveling alone or in groups. They grow to about 15 meters (~50 feet) long and travel more than 16,000 kilometers (~10,000 miles) during a year's round-trip migration. Unlike Humpback Whales, Gray Whales are bottom feeders. To eat, they roll onto their side and filter mud from the seafloor through their broom-like **baleen** plates, straining out organisms and leaving a trail of mud as they go. Gray Whales are mainly found in shallow coastal waters of the Pacific Ocean.

FIGURE 5.2. Gray Whales seen from above off the coast of Alaska migrate along the North American West Coast to meet their survival needs.

FIGURE 5.3. Humpback Whale in the Pacific takes a dive. Scientists use patterns on the animals' tails to identify individuals.

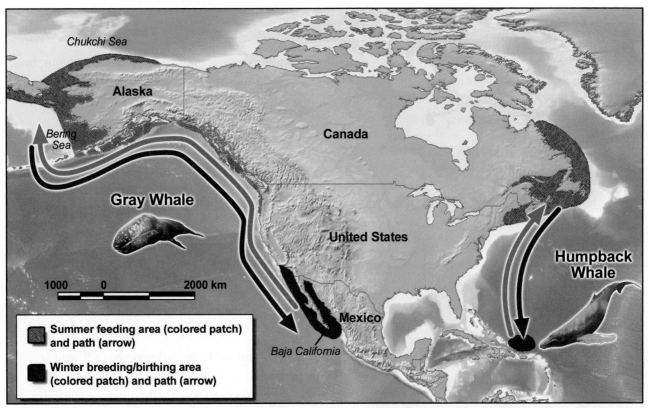

FIGURE 5.4. Migration pathways of the Gray Whale and Humpback Whale. Humpback Whales are found in both the Atlantic and Pacific Oceans. These pathways are just two examples of the migratory behavior of whales along each coast of the United States.

1. After studying the map above in FIGURE 5.4, answer the following Questions about the general patterns of migratory behavior for Humpback and Gray Whales.

   a. Describe the journeys of the two whale species.

   b. What are the differences in activities at winter and summer sites?

   c. What is the general direction of travel?

   d. Use the scale to determine the maximum total distance traveled during the migration.

FIGURE 5.5. A juvenile Gray Whale looks up off the Southern California Coast. Calves and their mothers will normally bask in relatively warm, shallow waters of Mexico and Southern California during the winter.

Explore

Scientists compiled the tracking data represented in the migration pathways of the Gray Whale and Humpback Whale map in FIGURE 5.4 with satellite location data from tagging and from whale sighting observations of many whales over many seasons. During this section of the Lesson, you will plot the actual migration data of one Leatherback Sea Turtle named Jamur.

See Page 694 for how to access e-Tools.

View the **Leatherback Sea Turtle Tagging Video** (2:28) from the e-Tools, of scientists tagging a Leatherback Sea Turtle in the Solomon Islands, located in the South Pacific.

e-Tools

FIGURE 5.6. Screenshot of the **Leatherback Sea Turtle Tagging Video**.

FIGURE 5.7. Map showing Solomon Islands.

The video was filmed in the Solomon Islands, which comprises more than 1,000 islands, making up 27,556 square kilometers (~10,639 square miles) of land. The scientists discuss and show how they attach a harness to these large reptiles. They also note the importance of working with local scientists and sharing information with them. The tags are attached to different animal species in different ways, sometimes on land, sometimes at sea. In the case of sea turtles, it is much easier to have access to tag female turtles, which crawl up on the beach to lay their eggs, as you can see in the video.

FIGURE 5.8. Leatherback hatchling on a beach in Indonesia may grow to be approximately 2 meters (~7 feet) and weigh 900 kilograms (~2,000 pounds). The Leatherbacks' paddle-like flippers make the sea turtle uniquely equipped for long-distance migrations for feeding.

The Leatherback Sea Turtle is one of the largest reptiles on Earth. Adult turtles can grow to 2 meters (~6½ feet) long and weigh up to 900 kilograms (~2,000 pounds). Unlike other turtles, Leatherback Sea Turtles do not have a hard shell. Instead, they have leathery skin that covers a series of bony plates. Very large front flippers help them swim faster and migrate farther than any other sea turtle.

Leatherbacks live in a wide variety of locations across the ocean. In fact, they are the most far-ranging of the sea turtles. Leatherbacks swim from tropical areas, where they nest, all the way to cooler temperate seas. When in the open ocean, they feed on jellyfish and other floating

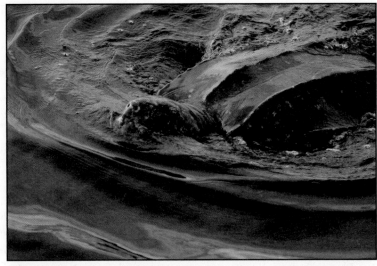

FIGURE 5.9. The Leatherback Sea Turtle is unique among marine turtles. This species has a soft shell, which allows them to dive much deeper than other sea turtles.

organisms. When they are feeding along the coast, Leatherbacks eat crustaceans such as shrimp, mollusks (e.g., clams, mussels), and other high-protein foods. Female Leatherbacks return to coastal beaches to build their nests and lay eggs every 2–3 years. During this time they lay about 100 eggs in each nest and build a new nest about every 10 days. After about 65 days, the hatchling Leatherbacks crawl out of their nests and find their way to the ocean.

Leatherbacks are an endangered species. Scientists estimate that there are just over 35,000 nesting females worldwide. Males do not come to shore, making it difficult to estimate the male population. Scientists are tagging Leatherback Sea Turtles in locations around the world including Africa, Central America, and the South Pacific.

FIGURE 5.10. Leatherbacks are the largest and most far-ranging of all sea turtles.

Activity

Plotting Animal Movements

Materials:

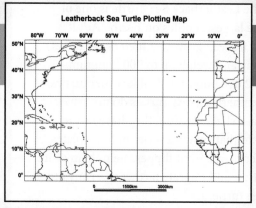

FIGURE 5.11. The *Leatherback Sea Turtle Plotting Map*.

- *Leatherback Sea Turtle Plotting Map*
- Atlases (*optional*)

1. Plot each date's location on your copy of the map by approximating it from the given latitude and longitude coordinates on the *Leatherback Sea Turtle Plotting Map*.

Location Data for Jamur, the Leatherback Sea Turtle

Date	Latitude	Longitude	Date	Latitude	Longitude
May 29, 2007	9.01° N	81.71° W	December 25, 2007	44.99° N	14.62° W
June 7, 2007	8.87° N	81.58° W	December 30, 2007	43.66° N	13.13° W
June 27, 2007	13.20° N	79.59° W	January 4, 2008	42.82° N	12.46° W
July 15, 2007	17.88° N	71.80° W	January 20, 2008	43.37° N	10.57° W
August 13, 2007	26.49° N	61.75° W	February 4, 2008	43.18° N	9.79° W
September 9, 2007	34.27° N	56.27° W	February 12, 2008	41.93° N	10.44° W
September 30, 2007	41.17° N	46.41° W	February 21, 2008	40.85° N	12.10° W
October 22, 2007	42.30° N	35.78° W	February 25, 2008	39.99° N	13.26° W
November 13, 2007	44.89° N	29.30° W	March 7, 2008	37.88° N	15.54° W
November 27, 2007	45.58° N	26.72° W	March 16, 2008	35.39° N	16.74° W
December 2, 2007	46.03° N	25.61° W	March 26, 2008	33.05° N	17.81° W
December 6, 2007	45.87° N	23.13° W	April 4, 2008	31.28° N	18.95° W
December 8, 2007	45.80° N	22.00° W	April 22, 2008	28.01° N	19.46° W
December 11, 2007	45.77° N	20.34° W	April 27, 2008	26.73° N	20.27° W
December 15, 2007	45.73° N	17.97° W	May 17, 2008	23.73° N	20.00° W
December 19, 2007	46.02° N	16.57° W	June 11, 2008	20.43° N	21.22° W

2. Describe Jamur's overall path and calculate his approximate distance traveled. What is the average movement of the animal in kilometers per week?

3. Why do you think scientists track animals such as the Leatherback Sea Turtle? What do they want to learn?

See Page 694 for how to access e-Tools.

View the **Leatherback Sea Turtle Observations Video** (3:51) from the e-Tools.

e-Tools

FIGURE 5.12. Screenshot of the **Leatherback Sea Turtle Observations Video**.

In this video, the marine biologists discuss some examples of observations they have made and questions that they have about Leatherback Sea Turtles. The two scientists share information as a turtle makes her way back out to sea. Notice that the scientists from both the United States and the Solomon Islands are sharing their different ideas, perspectives, and data. One scientist shares a hypothesis, and the other shares data that he has collected that support the first scientist's explanation. As diverse people work together, our scientific understanding is strengthened.

2. As you watch the video, list two types of observations or data that the scientists collect, and two questions that they still have.

Explain

Tracking with Signals of Spring

Using satellites to track animals is a ground-breaking technology. In fact, you are part of a special group of students helping research scientists as they track and learn about animals on their travels as they migrate across the vast oceans. The *Signals of Spring* classroom project was initiated with NASA sponsorship in 2000 to afford educators and students the ability to use various types of Earth imagery to explain the movement of animals that are tracked by satellite. Since then, hundreds of animals have been followed and studied. Wildlife biologists have gained a tremendous amount of information from dozens of species' tracks as *Signals of Spring* collaborates with and helps to sponsor researching scientists across the globe. Note that some traveling animals do not make regular seasonal migratory movements. This makes the study of behaviors of a large, diverse set of animals even more fascinating.

Scientists must travel across the globe to remote islands and rugged coastlines to attach satellite transmitters, or tags, onto animals. These tags relay a signal of the animal's location to a satellite orbiting Earth from pole to pole. The satellite in turn relays the animal's location to computers at tracking ground stations. In addition, the instrumentation may also provide animal dive depth, water temperature, light level information, and other data. The data are then analyzed by scientists and may be shared with students. As scientists track the movements of marine animals, they consider many of the factors that students analyze—food, temperature, landforms, and human influences. Students learn the content using authentic data in the context of animal behavior on land and in the ocean.

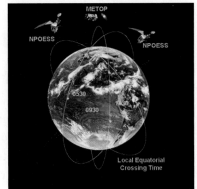

FIGURE 5.13. Polar orbiting satellites, including those from NOAA and the European Space Agency's MetOp satellite, house the Argos instrument.

Transmitters and Satellites

For years, scientists have used receivers to track *radio* signals attached to animals on land and at sea. This technology works in a similar way to radios at home or in your car. The animal wears a transmitter, and the VHF (very high frequency) signals are picked up by receivers. However, once an animal is out of range of the radio receiver, the scientist can no longer pick up a signal, limiting the amount of location data that can be collected. Satellite transmitter technology has evolved, and now animals can be tracked much farther as they migrate all over the Earth. Transmitters have become lighter and more efficient.

Tracking animals by satellite begins with scientists first trapping and then tagging an animal with the transmitter. At regular intervals, the device, which has stored information about the animal, transmits a higher-frequency radio signal to the Argos instrument (which is part of a data collection relay system) onboard NOAA polar orbiting satellites that orbit from pole to pole overhead. A transmitting signal (the communications connection) sent up to a satellite is called an **uplink**, and the connecting signal sent down from a satellite to a ground station is called a **downlink**. As the satellite passes over a ground or receiving station, the Argos data collection system relays the information.

Natural and Human-made Satellites

An object that orbits, or goes around, another object is a satellite. There are two types of satellites—natural satellites and human-made satellites. A planet or moon that orbits around another celestial body is called a **natural satellite**. The Moon is a natural satellite orbiting the Earth, just as the Earth is a natural satellite orbiting the Sun. The second kind of satellite is created by humans and is called an **artificial satellite**.

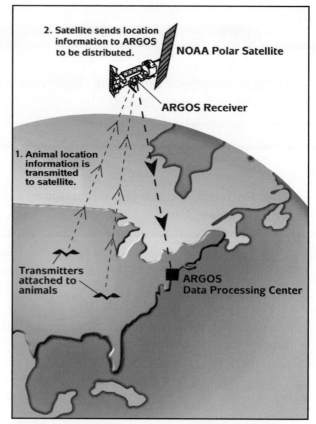

FIGURE 5.14. Illustration of how satellite signals are received. The process shows an animal's transmitter sending a signal, the Argos instrument receiving the signal, and the satellite sending the signal to a data processing center.

FIGURE 5.15. *Delta II Rocket* lifts off in 2009 to carry *NOAA-N Prime* satellite into orbit with Argos instrument onboard.

Artificial satellites are used to gather many types of data—scientific, weather, communications, navigation, and military. You are probably most aware of communication satellites that are used to transmit and receive high-speed television, radio, and telephone signals; this is radio wave energy. Some of these satellites are arranged in a network, working together to relay information to each other and to users on the ground.

The satellites that provide the data we require to track and study marine animals are called **remote sensing satellites**. These satellites carry many different tools, which measure, survey, and map our global environment. The system converts this data into visual information that scientists and students use to follow animals. Below is an image that shows a map with location data used by students to track a specific animal.

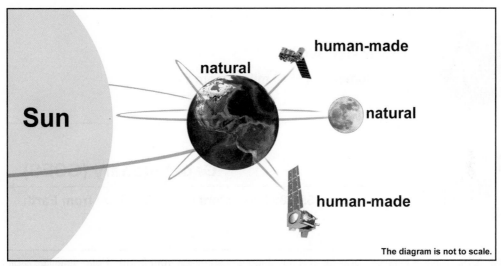

FIGURE 5.16. There are natural and artificial, human-made satellites. Each type of satellite orbits other objects in Space.

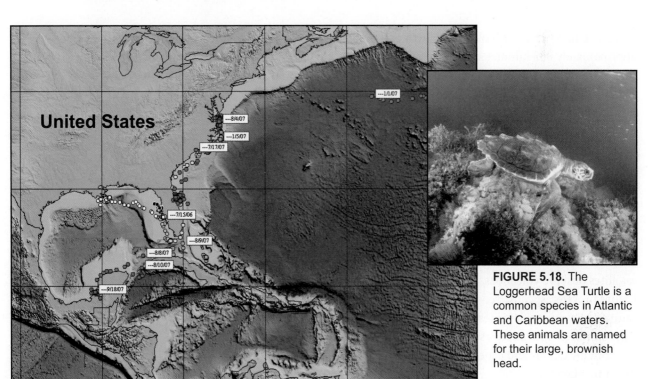

FIGURE 5.18. The Loggerhead Sea Turtle is a common species in Atlantic and Caribbean waters. These animals are named for their large, brownish head.

FIGURE 5.17. Map showing Loggerhead Sea Turtle location data. Scientists use satellite tagging data to learn and understand different species' behavior, about where they travel and the habitats that they use, and more.

Polar and Geostationary Satellites

Different remote sensing satellites take different paths as they orbit the Earth. Those that orbit from pole to pole and help track animals are called **polar satellites**. Others that remain fixed above one specific location and orbit the Earth at a speed in tandem with the rotating Earth are called **geostationary satellites**. The paths these satellites take are dictated by the specific information scientists need. Remote sensing satellites have various instrumentation onboard including meteorological instruments that provide weather satellite imagery and other visualizations of Earth.

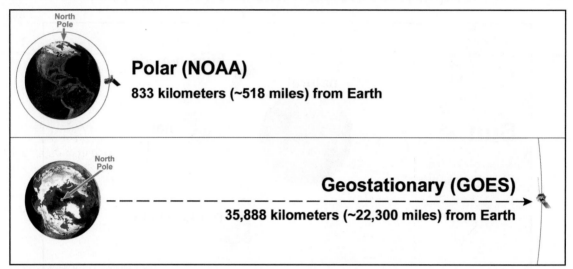

FIGURE 5.19. Relative locations of polar and geostationary satellites from Earth. Polar satellites orbit from pole to pole. Geostationary satellites orbit over the same location over the Equator.

Polar satellites orbit Earth over the North and South Polar Regions. Low-orbiting polar satellites stay approximately 833 kilometers (~518 miles) above the Earth. These satellites and the instruments performing their continuous functions collect detailed views of the Earth's surface over time. A full orbit around the Earth takes slightly more than 100 minutes to go from the vicinity of the North Pole to the South Pole and back again. Each polar satellite will do this approximately 14 times each day. As polar satellites orbit Earth's poles, the Earth spins from east to west. Over the course of a day, polar orbiting satellites will collect data from all over Earth's surface. These satellites observe volcanoes, polar ice, bodies of water, specific ecosystems, rainfall, and more. Satellites monitor various wavelength energies to learn about many details and aspects of our dynamic planet.

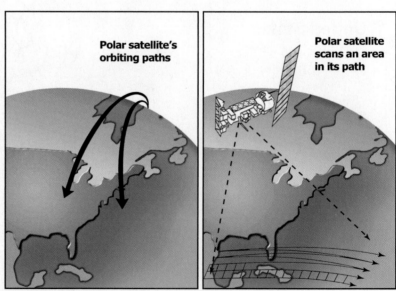

FIGURE 5.20. Polar satellites orbit the Earth from pole to pole.

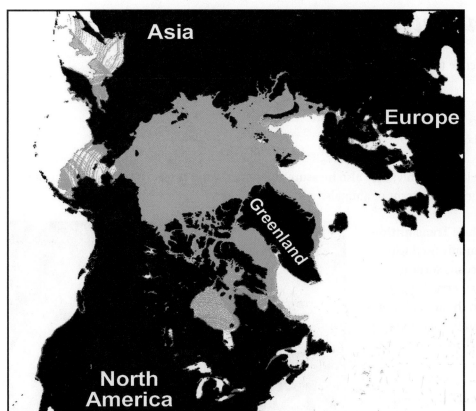

■	Land
■	Coast
■	No Data
□	Weather
□	Ocean
■	16–21%
■	22–28%
■	29–35%
■	36–42%
■	43–49%
■	50–56%
■	57–63%
■	64–70%
■	71–77%
■	78–84%
■	85–91%
■	92–98%
■	99+%

FIGURE 5.21. Sea ice concentration imagery is derived from data collected from polar orbiting satellites. Argos instruments onboard the satellites provide the locations of tagged animals so scientists and students may learn how animals interact with their habitats.

Geostationary satellites orbit the Earth above the Equator. As the Earth rotates east, the satellite remains above the same location. These satellites are designed to monitor Earth's changes over time from 50° N to 50° S (e.g., changes in ocean temperatures, cloud cover). They stay in orbit about 36,000 kilometers (~22,300 miles) from the Earth's surface, and they move at a constant rate as the Earth spins. The advantage of high-altitude geostationary satellites over low-orbiting polar satellites is that they can record Earth images more often; so, scientists can view these images with more frequency. Geostationary satellites are so far above the surface of Earth, they can collect data from an entire hemisphere at a time. However, the data collected by geostationary satellites from Earth's Polar Regions are not very useful since the satellite observes these areas at an angle instead of from directly above. Geostationary satellites help scientists track weather systems, which allow the careful tracking of approaching storms like hurricanes.

FIGURE 5.22. Geostationary satellites help scientists track weather systems like Hurricane Isabel, which approached North Carolina in 2003.

3. Compare and contrast polar and geostationary satellites.

Satellite Transmitters

There are several types of satellite transmitters used with animals, including:

- Smart Position or Temperature Transmitting Tags (SPOTs)
- Pop-up Archival Tags
- Satellite Relay Data Loggers (SRDLs)

Transmitters do not measure location only; they also measure and record various factors that may contribute to and be responsible for migratory patterns of animals.

Smart Position or Temperature Transmitting Tags (SPOTs) are most commonly used with animals that breathe at the ocean's surface. A SPOT only uplinks when its antenna is out of the water, which occurs when the animal comes up to breathe. SPOTs are used on large, air-breathing marine animals such as sea turtles, seals, and whales.

For large marine animals that do not spend much time at the ocean surface, scientists use a **Pop-up Archival Tag**, or pop-up tag, which is programmed to be released from the animal at a specific time. Pop-up tags are most often pre-set to detach one to three months after being attached to an animal. When it is released the tag floats up to the ocean surface. The tag then transmits its data to a satellite, and the data is relayed to the scientists. Pop-up tags are most often used on fish, such as tuna and sharks. Scientists sometimes offer rewards to fishers who return pop-up tags.

FIGURE 5.23. Scientists epoxy a SPOT onto the shell of a sea turtle. These tags are most useful for tracking animals that are air-breathing, because the tags uplink only when their antennae break the water's surface.

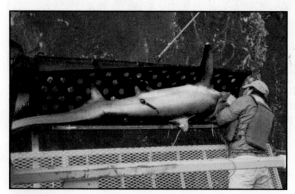

FIGURE 5.24. Rolling a shark onto its back puts the animal in a relaxed state. At that point, scientists can attach a pop-up tag.

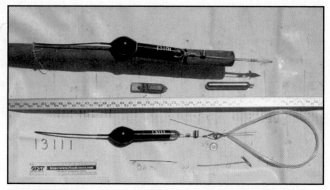

FIGURE 5.25. A pop-up archival tag on a tagging pole, two small pop-up tags beneath it, and a tag rigged for a shark harness.

FIGURE 5.26. A Tiger Shark wears a pop-up tag. Pop-up tags archive data for weeks or months at a time, and then detach from the animal and float to the surface. At that time, the data are transmitted to a satellite and are available to scientists and students.

FIGURE 5.27. Marine biologists attach various satellite transmitters, including an SRDL, to a sleeping Northern Elephant Seal. In addition to tracking the location of the animal, these tags collect salinity, depth, light, temperature, and other data so that we can learn more about the physical conditions of the ocean in the areas frequented by the seals.

A bulky, box-shaped tag that compresses more data than any other tag is called the **Satellite Relay Data Logger**, or **SRDL**. Oceanographers use these tags to measure salinity, temperature, and depth to better understand how ocean conditions affect animal movement. SRDLs are used on large marine animals that dive such as Southern Elephant Seals, California Sea Lions, and Leatherback Sea Turtles.

Satellite Imagery

Remote sensing satellites sense our Earth in a manner similar to the ways our eyes sense our environment. An orbiting satellite is equipped with digital imaging sensors that scan the Earth's surface twenty-four hours a day. Instruments onboard the satellites record radiation reflected from Earth's surface. Each satellite transmits large quantities of acquired numerical digital data to receivers and computers on Earth. The numbers are translated into digital displays and visualizations that scientists can use. The science of gathering and interpreting data from human-made satellites is called **remote sensing**. Via remote sensing we may not see an animal moving but we can see Earth's image together with an animal's location point and any associated information. Using remote sensing data brings together scientists from diverse fields. In addition to computer scientists, geologists, meteorologists, and biologists can share their perspectives and interpretations of data. These interpretations can be used to explain the movements of animals that are tracked by satellite.

FIGURE 5.28. One type of sea bird sometimes tracked by satellites is the Sooty Shearwater.

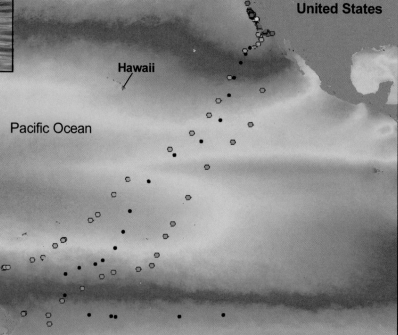

FIGURE 5.29. Using scientific data, researchers from various backgrounds can study and draw conclusions about the movements of marine animals that are tracked by satellite on a temperature map.

Areas covered by satellite images are much larger than images produced by an ordinary digital camera or computer. In fact, instruments from satellites produce images of areas thousands of kilometers in length. These images must be cut into more manageable sections and distributed to scientists for analysis. Processing large computer files from huge satellite databases in order to create imagery is a time-consuming task.

Remote sensing satellite technologies create high-resolution imagery because satellite sensors have the extraordinary ability to effectively capture and represent a portion of the Earth's surface as a single data point. This data point on a digital image is called a **pixel**. The word *pixel* is the combination of two words, *picture* and *element*. Computers display images by dividing the display screen into thousands of pixels arranged in rows and columns that appear to be connected. The more pixels an image displays, the higher its resolution and the closer the resulting image resembles detail in the originally sensed area. Also, the more data points and detail the image contains, the more variation in colors that can be used in the visual.

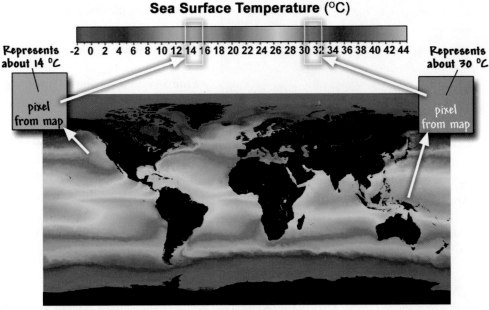

FIGURE 5.30. Example of pixels on an SST map.

The digital images below illustrate the difference between lower and higher resolution. The image to the left has a higher resolution (4 kilometers by 4 kilometers) than the image on the right (16 kilometers by 16 kilometers).

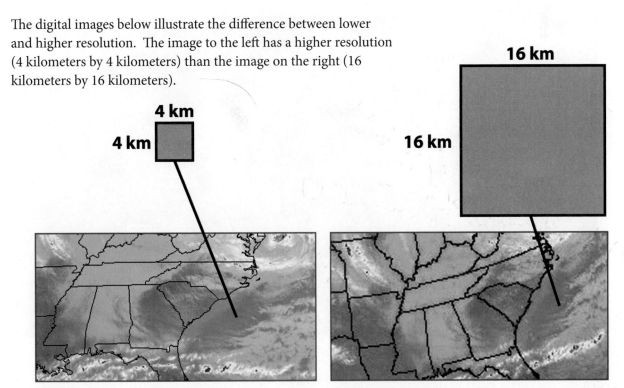

FIGURE 5.31. Sample of satellite imagery demonstrates that 4-kilometer resolution (km) imagery, where each pixel in the image represents an area of 4 km x 4 km, is more detailed than 16-kilometer resolution.

Scientific Discoveries

FIGURE 5.32. Dr. David Hyrenbach, surrounded by penguins in Antarctica.

Scientists have made many important discoveries through their pioneering efforts in using satellites and marine animal tagging. Scientists now have more access to information on the diversity of ocean organisms through data collected by satellites. This is helpful in establishing marine protected areas (MPAs) and other ways to conserve species and ecosystems.

One *Signals of Spring* scientist, Dr. David Hyrenbach, studies the Black-footed Albatross. Although it was thought until recently that these birds simply migrate to California from Hawaii, Dr. Hyrenbach made a surprising discovery. As seen in FIGURE 5.34 below, he learned that these birds were not traveling only to Hawaii as was expected, but they were also flying all around the Pacific Ocean—to faraway areas such as Canada, Alaska, and even Japan.

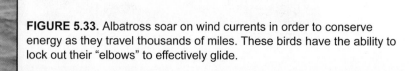

FIGURE 5.33. Albatross soar on wind currents in order to conserve energy as they travel thousands of miles. These birds have the ability to lock out their "elbows" to effectively glide.

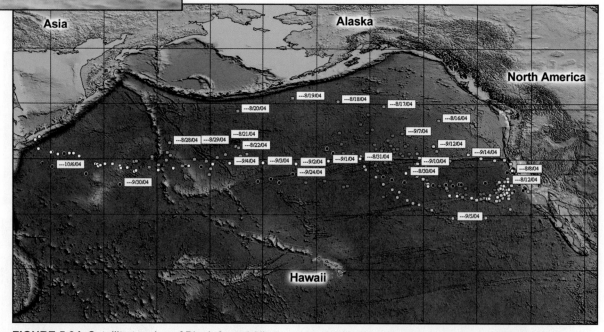

FIGURE 5.34. Satellite tagging of Black-footed Albatross resulted in the discovery that these animals travel throughout the North Pacific.

FIGURE 5.35. It was thought that Great White Sharks in the Pacific Ocean wandered aimlessly, never venturing into the San Francisco Bay. However, scientists recently followed over 100 tagged sharks and found that five sharks swam under the Golden Gate Bridge and into the San Francisco Bay on several visits.

Elaborate

4. Using the map below and the map you plotted in the **Explore** section, contrast distance and duration of the route of the Leatherback Sea Turtle with the route traveled by Zubenelgenubi, the Black-footed Albatross.

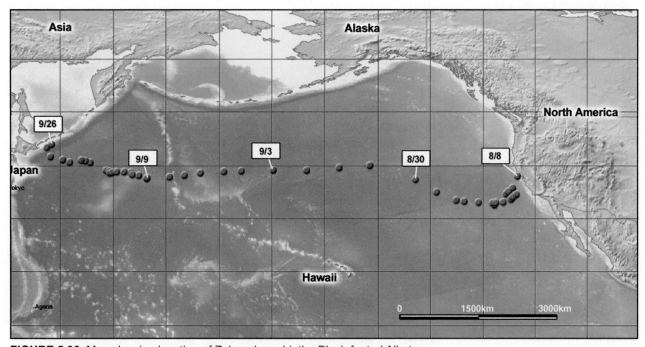

FIGURE 5.36. Map showing location of Zubenelgenubi, the Black-footed Albatross.

5. Identify the essentials that turtles, albatross, and whales need to survive. Discuss how they fulfill their needs, and how their movement may contribute to meeting them.

6. How do humans affect sea turtles, seabirds, and other marine animals?

7. In your groups, work to fill out a chart of factors needed for marine animals to survive, like the one below. Answer the following Question for each factor: *How could each factor influence where the animals move?* As you do this, make a list of questions that would be interesting to answer.

FIGURE 5.37. Humans have positive and negative effects on marine animals. In this photograph, a Hawaiian Green Sea Turtle rests on the beach in close proximity to a sunbather.

Factors	Effects on Marine Animal Movements	Questions We Have
Landforms (above or below the ocean surface, shorelines)		
Food (types, location)		
Temperature (water, air)		

8. Animals are continuously coping with environmental factors. How do you think each of these factors changes over time in the ocean?

FIGURE 5.38. As humans are finding new ways to study and understand these species, animals must cope with changing environmental conditions Note the satellite tag on this Spotted Seal's rear flipper.

Evaluate

In the last Lesson, we studied the Nature of Science. Some of the ideas we read about that are characteristic of science are:

- Science is based on *observations*, which lead to *inferences*. Observations include both *qualitative* and *quantitative* data. Scientific tools help scientists to make observations.

- Science is a cyclical process. New findings always lead to more questions.

- Science is a creative process. Scientists and engineers are constantly coming up with new ideas about how to study and learn more.

- Science is subject to change—new ideas are constantly helping us to refine what is already known.

- There is a relationship between science and culture. Scientists from around the world, and from many different backgrounds, are needed. Sharing ideas results in increased scientific knowledge.

The concepts in this Lesson reiterated and expanded many of these ideas about what science is.

Your task is to teach others about the Nature of Science. In an essay, poster, presentation, or other "product" (check with your teacher), further explain the characteristics of science in your own words, referring to the sentences above. Use several examples from this Lesson to illustrate the Nature of Science.

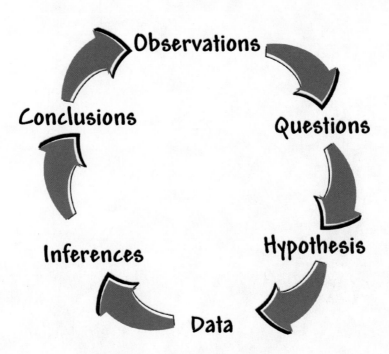

FIGURE 5.39. The Scientific Inquiry Process.

6

Explore the Seafloor

INSIDE:

Objectives

You will be able to:

✔ **Analyze bathymetric images and identify seafloor features.**

✔ **Describe how scientists map the ocean floor.**

✔ **Create a model of seafloor features.**

Benchmarks

1b. An ocean basin's size, shape, and features (e.g., islands, trenches, mid-ocean ridges, rift valleys) vary due to the movement of Earth's lithospheric plates. Earth's highest peaks, deepest valleys, and flattest vast plains are all in the ocean.

2b. Sea level changes over time have expanded and contracted continental shelves, created and destroyed inland seas, and shaped the surface of land.

7a. The ocean is the last and largest unexplored place on Earth; less than 5% of it has been explored. This is the great frontier for the next generation's explorers and researchers, where they will find great opportunities for inquiry and investigation.

7b. Understanding the ocean is more than a matter of curiosity. Exploration, inquiry, and study are required to better understand ocean systems and processes.

7d. New technologies, sensors, and tools are expanding our ability to explore the ocean. Ocean scientists are relying more and more on satellites, drifters, buoys, subsea observatories, and unmanned submersibles.

Engage

View the image below, which depicts the land features, or topography, of a selected region.

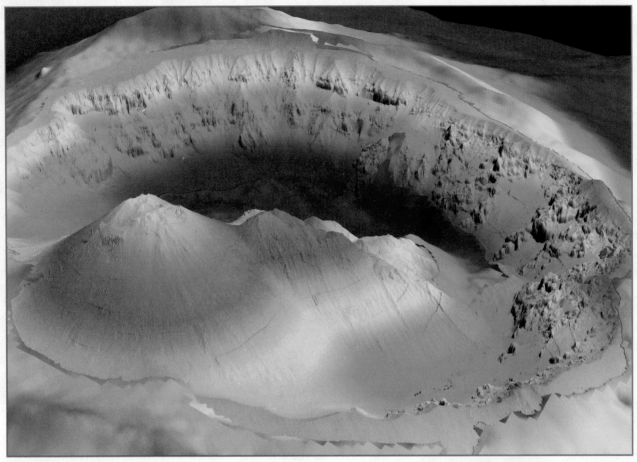

FIGURE 6.1.

1. What features can you identify in this image? What do you think it is?

2. Where do you think this place is located?

See Page 694 for how to access e-Tools.

View the ***Ring of Fire Expedition "Fly Through" Animation*** (1:00) from the e-Tools.

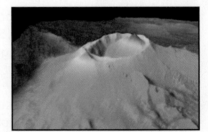

FIGURE 6.2. Screenshot of the ***Ring of Fire Expedition "Fly Through" Animation***.

e-Tools

Below are two mountains—one is Mauna Kea, and one is Mt. Everest.

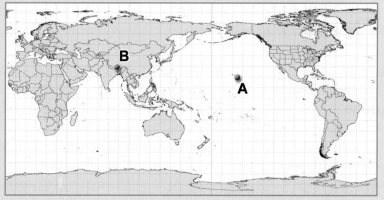

FIGURE 6.3.

Which of these mountains is Mt. Everest?

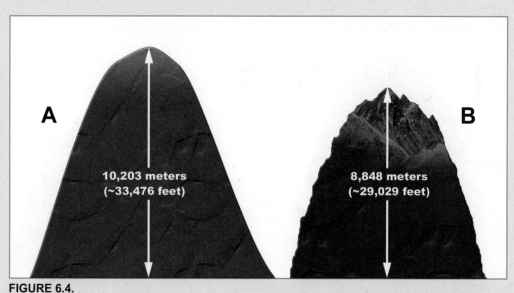

A — 10,203 meters (~33,476 feet)

B — 8,848 meters (~29,029 feet)

FIGURE 6.4.

See Page 694 for how to access e-Tools.

View the **Earth Animation** (0:15) and **Earth Map** from the e-Tools.

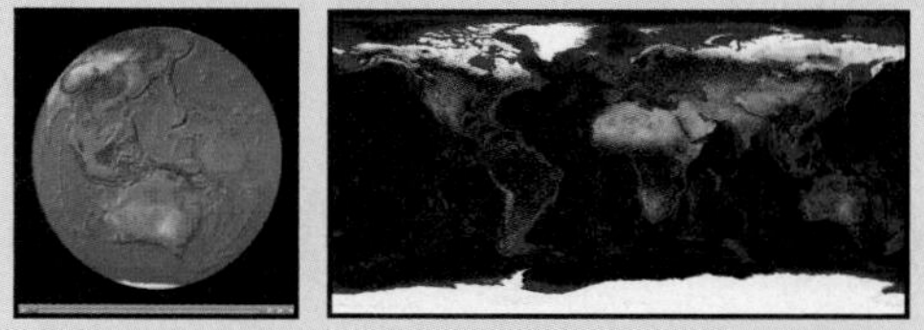

FIGURE 6.5. Screenshots of the **Earth Animation** and **Earth Map**.

e-Tools

The green and brown areas indicate land; white areas are ice. Everything else is ocean. Note that on the map you can zoom in to examine areas of the globe in more detail as you answer the Questions below.

3. List at least three observations or possible land features that you see on the seafloor.

4. Now, look at the **Earth Map**. Look closely at the area near Florida and describe the shape of the seafloor around the state.

5. How would you describe details of the seafloor off of the Florida Coast?

Explore

Features of the Ocean Floor

Looking at the ocean's surface, things look fairly uniform. There are waves, specks of white foam, birds swooping down to catch fish. What about the ocean floor? Most people believe that it is flat and lifeless. In reality, as you observed in the **Engage** section, the ocean floor is as varied as the land's surface. Earth's tallest mountain is not Mount Everest; it is actually Mauna Kea of Hawaii. Most of Mauna Kea is underwater. Less than half of its height, about 4,205 meters (~13,796 feet) of the mountain, is above **sea level**. Sea level is the ocean's average height relative to the land. Throughout Earth's history, sea level has changed because of shifts in climate, which results in melting or growing ice caps. During Ice Ages, when a tremendous amount of water is contained in ice, sea levels decrease. In warm periods, ice caps melt and the volume of liquid water expands, leading to higher sea levels.

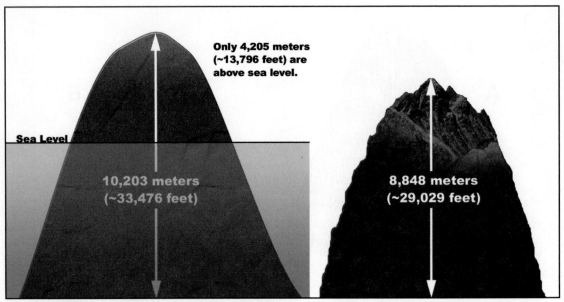

FIGURE 6.6. Earth's tallest mountain is not Mount Everest; it is actually Mauna Kea of Hawaii.

The average ocean depth is about 3,682 meters (~12,081 feet). The deepest part of the ocean is in the Mariana Trench, 11,033 meters (~36,200 feet) deep, in the Western Pacific Ocean. Just like on land, the ocean floor has hills, plains, volcanoes, valleys, river deltas, mountains, and canyons. The seafloor is home to Earth's tallest mountains, widest plains, and deepest valleys.

See Page 694 for how to access e-Tools.

View the *"Fly Through" of the Mariana Trench Animation* (0:41) from the e-Tools.

FIGURE 6.7. Screenshot of the *"Fly Through" of the Mariana Trench Animation*.

e-Tools

6. In this activity, you will read descriptions of some seafloor features. Copy the diagrams below into your notebook. Use the descriptions in the table below to label the features in your copy of the diagrams.

Description of Feature	Name of Feature
Gently sloping land area along the edges of continents	Continental Shelf
Underwater mountain range	Mid-ocean Ridge
Flat, featureless plain making up a large part of the seafloor	Abyssal Plain
Deepest feature of the ocean, plunging deep below the seafloor	Trench
Steep slope leading from the edge of a continent down to the seafloor	Continental Slope
Underwater mountain with a peak or flat top	Seamount
Hill of sediment at the bottom of the steep slope near the edges of continents	Continental Rise
Steep-sided underwater valley near the edge of a continent	Submarine Canyon

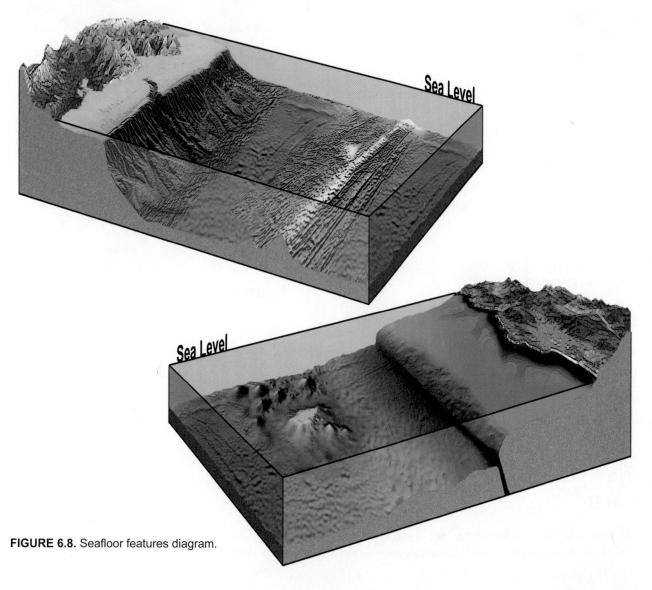

FIGURE 6.8. Seafloor features diagram.

A Classroom Model of the Ocean Floor

Now that you are familiar with the major seafloor features, you will create your own model of the ocean floor. Models are used often in science for many purposes. One purpose of a model is to study topics and features that are too large or too small to work with in real life, like the solar system or atoms. The seafloor is one such topic.

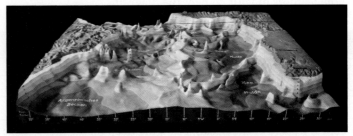

FIGURE 6.9. This 1920s model of the Atlantic Basin was created in Germany. The model was destroyed in World War II, but this image remains.

In your model, you will create at least three seafloor features out of corrugated cardboard inside a shoebox "ocean basin". As you create your model, try to make it as interesting and diverse as possible while still modeling actual seafloor features.

Lab

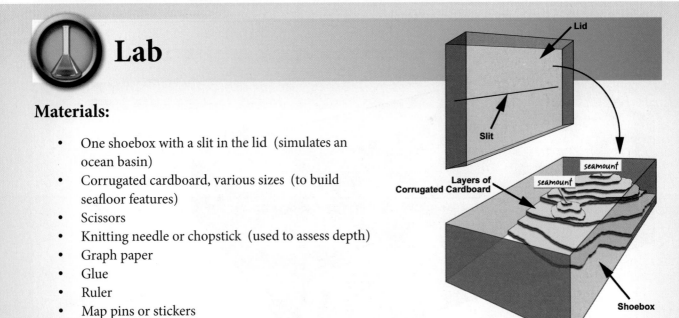

FIGURE 6.10. Sample model.

Materials:

- One shoebox with a slit in the lid (simulates an ocean basin)
- Corrugated cardboard, various sizes (to build seafloor features)
- Scissors
- Knitting needle or chopstick (used to assess depth)
- Graph paper
- Glue
- Ruler
- Map pins or stickers
- Masking tape

Part I:

1. Check to be sure your group has all of the necessary materials for this project.

2. Begin creating layers of cardboard to build your own "seafloor" in your box, as illustrated in the diagram. Be sure to create at least three distinct seafloor features in your box.

3. Use the map pins or stickers to label each of the seafloor features that you have modeled in your box.

4. Put the lid on the box and tape the box shut.

Part II:

1. Switch boxes with another group. <u>Do not look in the new box.</u> You are going to try to determine the seafloor features that your classmates have modeled in this box without opening it.

2. Place the ruler along the center line (slit) of your new box.

Make a mark every centimeter along the slit. Label one end of the line "0".

These marks represent where you will take your depth measurements.

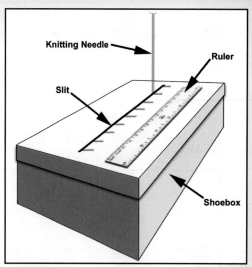

FIGURE 6.11.

3. Copy the data table below in your notebook.

Marker Distance (cm)	Depth (cm)
0	
1	
2	
3	
etc.	

4. Insert a knitting needle or chopstick straight into the slit at the zero mark. You should push the knitting needle in gently until you feel that you have reached something.

5. Pinch the needle with your fingers at the top of the box. Remove the needle and measure the distance from your fingers to the bottom of the needle.

You are measuring the modeled difference from sea level to the underlying seafloor feature.

6. Record this depth in the data table. Then repeat the process at each centimeter mark along the length of the box.

7. Since this is a model of the seafloor, you will need to convert it to a real-life scale. For marker distance, you may choose to use the scale of 1 centimeter = 100 kilometers, depending on your project. For depth, you may choose to use the scale of 1 centimeter = 300 meters.

Copy the table below into your notebook and record your converted data.

Distance (meters)	Depth (meters)
0	
100	
200	
etc.	

8. Using your converted data, create a plot on graph paper profiling Distance versus Depth.

Remember that you are measuring the depths below the zero line, the top of the shoebox. The zero line represents the ocean's surface on your profile. *Hint: The "zero" depth line is at the top of the scale.*

Example:

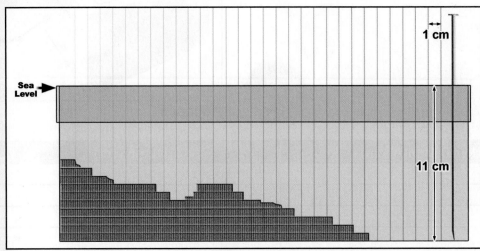

FIGURE 6.12. View of inside the shoebox from the side.

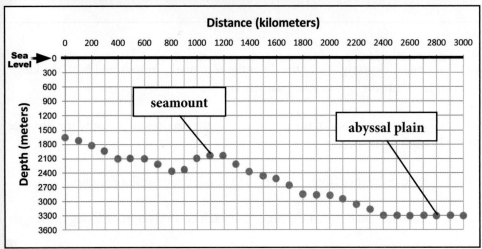

FIGURE 6.13. Sample graph for shoebox shown above.

9. Relate the profile that you created and drew to features that you might see in the ocean. If this were an actual ocean floor profile, what features would you be detecting or seeing?

Label these features on the graph.

10. Now, open the box. How well does your profile reflect the features modeled within the box?

11. How could your profile have been made more accurate?

12. How would you create an island with your shoebox model?

Explain

We know more about our Moon and the planet Mars than we do about Earth's ocean. Humans have only mapped 10% of the ocean. Why? Unlike the Moon and Mars, which are observed from Earth through telescopes, and in Space with rovers, landers, and satellites, the seafloor is covered by an incredible amount of water. Since it is hard to make observations of it, most of the seafloor has not been explored. Throughout history, what lies beneath the ocean's surface has always been something humans are interested in uncovering. Understanding the seafloor is very important for many reasons such as creating shipping routes, maintaining national security, and even understanding the movements of marine animals. There is much to learn about the ocean—it is Earth's final frontier, with many existing and future opportunities for careers in exploration.

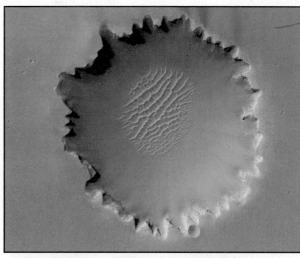

FIGURE 6.14. Observing striking details of topographic features on Mars, such as impact craters, is now commonplace with instrumentation and sensors onboard satellite orbiters on current Mars missions.

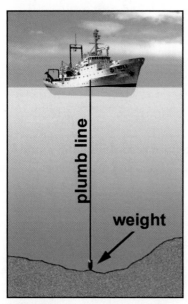

FIGURE 6.15. Plumb lines were one of the first technologies used to measure the depth of the seafloor.

Seafarers used to measure the depth of the ocean using a simple line with a weight on the end. Knots would be spaced at measured distances along the line. Crew members would simply throw the line, with a weight attached, over the side of their ship while holding on to the end of it. Once the weight hit bottom, the sailors would use the measured knots to tell the ocean's depth. These lines were called **plumb lines**. From these plumb line measurements, sailors began to create maps of the ocean floor.

Following World War I, scientists began to measure ocean depth a second way, using sound waves. The navigational technique or technology, **sonar**, is really just using echoes to learn about a surrounding environment. The word *sonar* was originally an acronym (SONAR) meaning <u>So</u>und <u>Na</u>vigation and <u>R</u>anging. When you shout in a large empty room, your sound bounces off the walls and returns; you hear the echo. To use sonar on ships, for example, crew members direct a pulse of sound, or a "ping", into the water below. The sound bounces off of the seafloor, and instruments record how long it takes the sound to return. Knowing how fast sound waves travel in water leads to knowing the ocean depth.

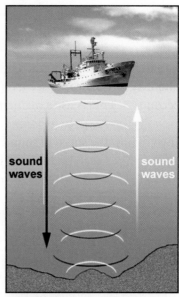

FIGURE 6.16. Sound bounces off the seafloor, and instruments record how long it takes the sound to return.

As a ship is moving, the instruments create a profile, like a picture, of the seafloor beneath the ship. Observe the 1967 plot (FIGURE 6.17) created by instruments on a ship in the Red Sea. The profile below shows the shape of the ocean floor. It is easy to note that the floor of the Red Sea is not a flat plain. It has hills and canyons.

FIGURE 6.18.

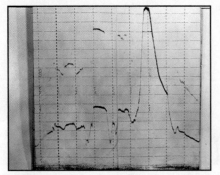

FIGURE 6.17. 1967 plot created by instruments on a ship in the Red Sea. Note how this plot resembles those created by your classmates in the **Explore** section.

See Page 694 for how to access e-Tools.

Listen to the **Sonar "Ping" Audio Clip** from the e-Tools.

e-Tools

7. Two ships send out a pulse, or ping, at the same time. Instrumentation on Ship A records that the sound returns in 22 seconds. Instruments on Ship B detect the echo in 10 seconds. Which ship is in deeper water? Use words and/or drawings to explain your answer.

Sound in water travels much faster than sound in the air travels. The average speed of sound in the ocean is about 1,500 meters per second (more than 3,000 miles per hour). Sound in the air travels at 340 meters per second. Scientists use a mathematical formula to calculate the depth of water.

If you know the speed of sound in water (1,500 meters/second), you can measure the time for sound waves to move to the ocean bottom and then to return. Therefore:

$$\text{Sea Depth} = \frac{1}{2} \times \text{Time} \times \text{Velocity}$$

or

$$D = \frac{1}{2}\,TV$$

The time it takes for the sound wave to travel from the surface of the ship to the ocean floor and return is T. That means the time the sound takes to travel the distance from the surface to the ocean floor is: ½(T).

8. If it takes 15 seconds for sound sent from a ship to return to the ship, what is the sea depth at the ship's location?

Today, NOAA researchers use very sophisticated sonar technology to map the ocean floor and also to locate shipwrecks, downed planes, and even schools of fish. The two major types of sonar used today are side scan and multibeam. Viewing the animation illustrating both types of sonar will help you understand how they work.

See Page 694 for how to access e-Tools.

View *Sonar Animation 1* and *Sonar Animation 2* from the e-Tools.

e-Tools

FIGURE 6.19. Side scan sonar is used to create a detailed image of the ocean floor. This image shows a shipwreck on the seafloor.

FIGURE 6.20. Screenshot of *Sonar Animation 1*. A ship uses a multibeam sonar to measure depth and side scan sonar to identify items on the seafloor.

FIGURE 6.21. Screenshot of *Sonar Animation 2*. A ship uses a multibeam sonar to measure the depth of the seafloor.

With side scan sonar, an instrument called a towfish is normally dragged behind a ship or attached to a submersible. A computer then generates an image that shows gray scale imagery, relating to the intensity of echoes received back at the ship. Hard objects, like metal ships and rocks, send back intense echoes. Black areas are acoustic shadows. Softer areas, such as those covered in mud and sand, result in less intense echoes and appear lighter. These side scan patterns give a useful image of the seafloor in an area but not specific depth information because it is the intensity of the echo, not the time it takes to return, that is being recorded. Side scan sonar is very useful for locating things like shipwrecks.

Multibeam sonar instruments attain the depth measurements. They also emit a pulse of sound, but normally do it from the ship's hull rather than from a towfish. Data are generally recorded over a wider area than with sidescan sonar. Multibeam sonar instruments record the time it takes for the sound waves to return, thus calculating depth just as you did in the exercise above. From multibeam sonar, therefore, new images with depth measurements are created. Differing depths are normally indicated by different colors. Reds and oranges represent shallow areas, and the dark blues and purples signify deep areas.

FIGURE 6.22. In side scan sonar, an instrument called a towfish is normally dragged behind a ship or attached to a submersible.

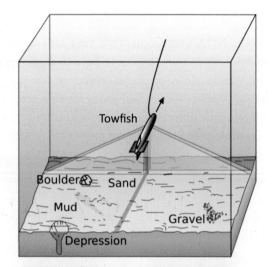

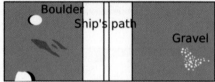

FIGURE 6.23. A side scan sonar towfish and the computer-generated sonar image.

FIGURE 6.24. Multibeam image of the Denson Seamount off the coast of Alaska accentuates the height of the bathymetric feature in vivid color.

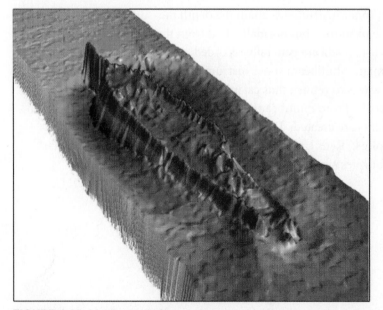

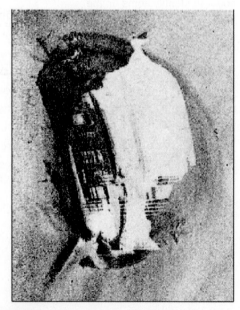

FIGURE 6.25. Multibeam (left) and side scan (right) sonar images show comparative, striking images of a 1910 shipwreck off the coast of Maryland. Multiple sources of data help researchers to construct ideas about bathymetric features and events related to the seafloor.

Echolocation

Animals that are unable to see in the dark use sound to determine the distance and direction of objects around them through a process called **echolocation**. Some animals, like bats, echolocate in order to find food or navigate through obstacles in caves. Toothed whales also have a weak sense of vision and smell. Toothed whales belong to the suborder *Odontocetes*, which also include dolphins, porpoises, Orcas, Belugas, and Sperm Whales. Scientists think that most toothed whales use echolocation to navigate and hunt for food in the dark or turbid waters of the ocean.

Toothed whales send out clicks and listen to the echoes of those clicks that bounce off different objects in their marine environment. Since sound travels more efficiently in water than on land, echolocation works well for these animals. While hunting, the time between the emission of their click and the return of the echo indicates the distance from their prey as well as its shape and size.

Toothed whales have a large fatty organ in front of their skull called a **melon**. The whales emit a series of clicks through the melon, which focuses the sounds so that they are projected out in front of the whale. Returning echoes are detected in a cavity in the lower jaw. The echoes then move through fat tissues in the lower jawbone and into their inner ear.

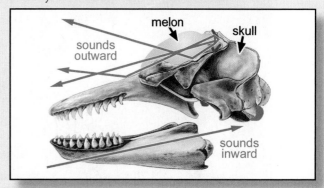

FIGURE 6.26. Diagram of sound generation in a toothed whale.

Unfortunately, echolocation does not help toothed whales avoid problems in the ocean. Sperm Whales have been struck by boats, and dolphins have become entangled in drift nets. This may suggest that toothed whales do not use echolocation when they are traveling.

FIGURE 6.27. Beluga Whales, found in the Arctic, have a well-developed sense of hearing and echolocation, and can also see quite well. They are generally found in shallow coastal waters.

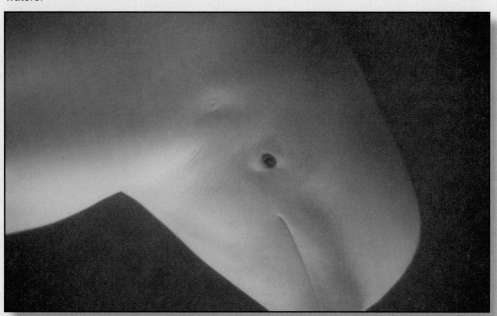

Mapping the ocean bottom with plumb lines or sonar is a very slow process. Since the ocean is so immense, it would be very difficult and expensive to accurately cover the entire seafloor. It turns out that there is another way to map it—one that you might not expect.

The third way of mapping the ocean floor is by utilizing data from orbiting satellites. This mapping technique is over 20 years old and continues today. Satellite measurements initially show something remarkable. The ocean's surface is not smooth. It is "lumpy".

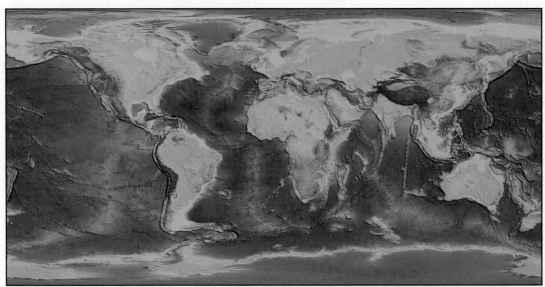

FIGURE 6.28. Global bathymetric image shows land and seafloor features. Shades of blue indicate depths of the ocean, measured below sea level.

The highs and lows of the sea surface actually mirror the seafloor features, the mountains and valleys beneath it. Therefore, scientists can use satellites to examine underwater topography, or **bathymetry.** Due to gravity, water molecules actually are attracted to and "pile up" over underwater mountains. The water sinks lower in valleys and canyons. As a result, higher sea levels indicate underwater mountains.

Lower sea levels indicate underwater valleys. Of course, the sea levels do not rise as high as the mountains on the floor. A sea surface rise of a few meters may indicate an elevation of hundreds of meters on the seafloor. These highs and lows of the sea surface are not visible from boats or beaches—it was not until the use of satellites that scientists saw the height differences attributed to bathymetry. In fact, satellite measurements allowed us to learn about bathymetry in remote areas of the ocean for the first time.

Satellite measurements of sea depth are compared with ship-based sonar measurements and are indeed accurate. Today, the best bathymetry maps are made from a combination of satellite and sonar data.

9. Which type of seafloor mapping (plumb lines, sonar, or satellite) did your mapping of your classmates' shoebox most resemble? Explain.

When tracking marine animals, you will examine the characteristics of the ocean floor along the animal migration route. In this exercise, you will identify specific seafloor features in a bathymetric image. When looking at any type of Earth imagery, it is important to look at the color bar. In this example, each color represents a different depth in meters.

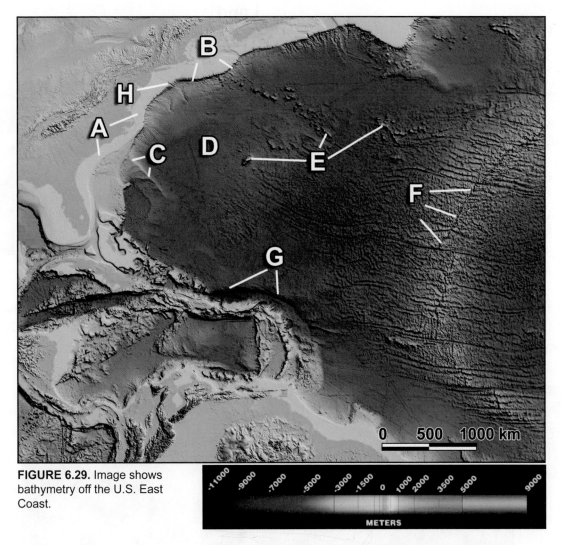

FIGURE 6.29. Image shows bathymetry off the U.S. East Coast.

10. Identify the seafloor features represented by the letters, A–H, in FIGURE 6.29.

It is important to note the connections between topographic features on land and at sea. For example, the following image gives a more detailed view of the Hudson Canyon, located on the continental shelf off the coast of New York State.

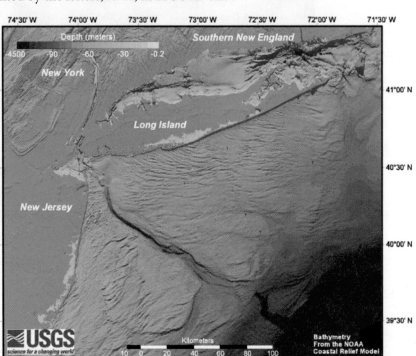

FIGURE 6.30. The New York submarine canyon likely shows an old extension to the Hudson River in the continental shelf off the U.S. East Coast.

Another example of topographic features of the seafloor is near river deltas. Observe the image of the Mississippi River Delta.

11. Describe the topography of the seafloor near the Mississippi River Delta in the Gulf of Mexico.

Land

FIGURE 6.31. Bathymetry image of the Mississippi River Delta.

Sea level changes throughout Earth's history have resulted in changes to the geographic area and shapes of our continents and continental shelves. For example, much of North America was once covered by the sea, as evidenced by the fossils of coral animals being uncovered in states including Tennessee and Utah. Sea levels have been much higher in the past than they are currently. Changes in sea level have contributed to the shaping of Earth's surface.

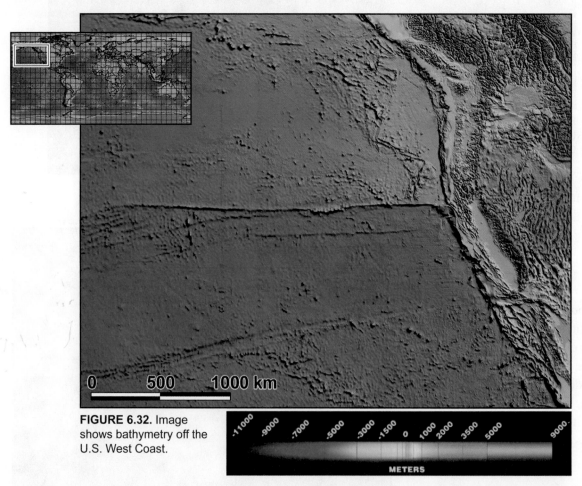

FIGURE 6.32. Image shows bathymetry off the U.S. West Coast.

12. The image above illustrates the bathymetry near the West Coast of the United States. Name two seafloor features that are evident in this image.

13. Use FIGURES 6.29 on Page 111 and 6.32 above to compare and contrast the bathymetry near the West and East Coasts of the United States. Give at least one similarity and two differences.

Seafloor Sediments

For centuries scientists have wondered about the specific details of the seafloor. With the use of modern technology and research methods humans have a greater understanding of the amazing features that exist beneath the ocean surface than ever before. Scientists study enormous undersea mountains and extensive abyssal plains, for example. They can map the location and determine the composition of tiny particles of rock called sediments. Sand, clay, and gravel are all sediments. Seafloor sediments are as diverse and complex as the ocean's bathymetric features.

Sediments consist of a variety of biotic and abiotic components. They differ depending on the type of material from which they originate. The two major sources of sediments are those that come primarily from land, **terrigenous** sediments (pronounced: ter-RIJ-in-us), and those from living organisms, **biogenous** sediments (pronounced: by-AW-jen-us). A smaller portion of sediments also come from chemical reactions in the water column just above the ocean floor and from materials that enter the Earth system from Outer Space.

FIGURE 6.33. Hawaii's famous black sand beaches are a result of sediment weathered from volcanic rock. Black sand beaches are found in other volcanic areas including Central America and some Caribbean islands.

Terrigenous sediments are primarily abiotic materials such as rock and debris that originate on land and are broken down, or weathered, into small particles. These particles are then carried by the action of water, wind, or ice, a process known as erosion. Erosion carries particles downstream to the ocean. As fragments move downstream via water, or are carried over land by wind, they knock against other fragments and larger materials, causing the edges to become smooth and uniquely shaped. The composition of terrigenous sediment is not the same everywhere and depends on the type of rock from which it originated, or the parent material. For example, many Hawaiian Island beaches have black sand from the erosion of volcanic rocks. Lighter colored sands along United States coasts are typically formed from the weathering and erosion of quartz. Terrigenous sediments may also originate from volcanic ash.

FIGURE 6.34. Foraminifera, a type of zooplankton that lives on the surface, are abundant throughout the world's oceans. By observing biogenous sediment under a powerful microscope, one can often identify the shells of foraminifera like these.

Biogenous sediment results from the shells of marine organisms. A common source of biogenous sediment is from tiny photosynthetic organisms called phytoplankton that live near the ocean's surface. Organisms that float along the top of the water column at the mercy of the ocean's processes are known collectively as plankton. Phytoplankton are plant-like plankton. In highly productive areas where there is an abundance of plankton, the seafloor sediment is largely composed of shells of organisms. Some white sand beaches are composed primarily of particles from the shells of plankton that were made of carbonate and silica. Other biogenous sediment results primarily from the weathering and erosion of coral reefs. Plankton in the open ocean die and fall to the seafloor, where their shells make up a large part of the sediment composition. The amount of quartz and terrestrial materials is lower in open ocean sediments because of the distance from the coast.

Scientists collect samples of seafloor sediments that accumulate over time and map their location and composition. Sediment surveys provide information about physical ocean science processes, biological health, and even past climates. The map to the right shows the general location of terrigenous and biogenous samples throughout the ocean.

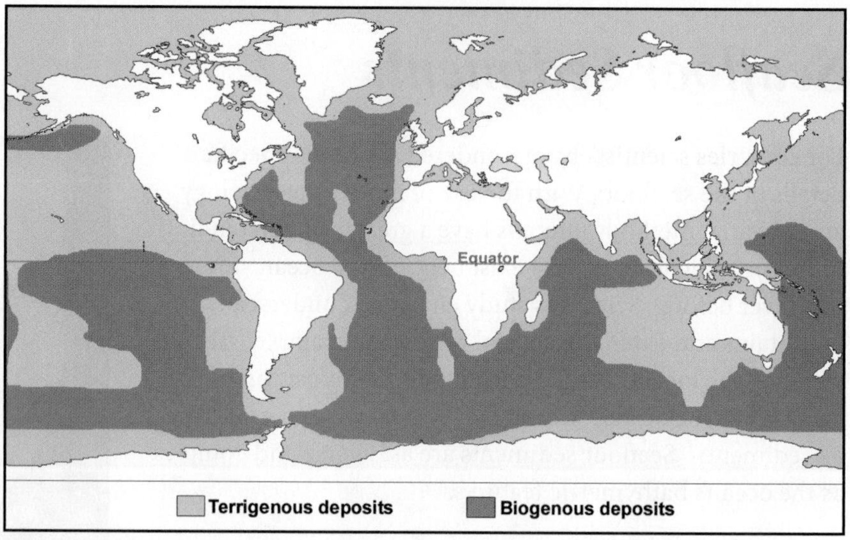

| Terrigenous deposits | Biogenous deposits |

FIGURE 6.35. Scientists have mapped the distribution of sediments throughout the seafloor. The map indicates the general location of terrigenous and biogenous sediments.

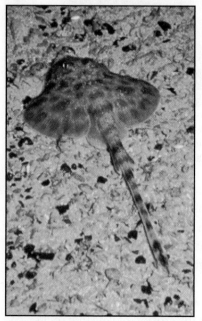

FIGURE 6.36. A skate swims along a field of manganese nodules. These are hydrogenous sediments.

Some seafloor sediments are formed when they precipitate out of the seawater itself. These are called **hydrogenous** (pronounced: hi-DRAW-jen-us) sediments. These sediments are very mineral-rich, containing elements in ionic form such as iron and manganese. Iron, manganese, and other metallic ions, such as nickel and cobalt, are found combined in rock-like formations known as polymetallic ("many metals") nodules. These nodules are often found in clusters on the seafloor. Some scientists have studied the possibility of mining polymetallic nodules for use of the metals on land.

The final major source of seafloor sediments is from Space; these are known as **cosmogenous** (pronounced: koz-MAW-jen-us) sediments. Earth is constantly being bombarded with dust and large particles from Space. Some of these particles reach the ocean, and may eventually settle to the seafloor. Cosmogenous sediments represent a very tiny fraction of seafloor sediments.

FIGURE 6.37. A large meteorite. Meteorites and smaller particles from Space that are not burned up in the atmosphere may reach the ocean and become cosmogenous sediments.

14. What are the major types of seafloor sediments? Where does each type originate?

Elaborate

Bathymetry and Marine Animals

Stephanie, the Gray Seal

The shape and physical characteristics of the seafloor often affect the paths of marine animals. Gray Seals, for example, are marine mammals that tend to travel and stick close to land. They haul out and take rest on rocks or beaches. Look at the track of the Gray Seal (FIGURE 6.39).

During March, notice that Stephanie, the Gray Seal, spent a lot of time very close to shore. She moved along the coastline, and then ventured out toward the edge of the continental shelf, near the continental slope. Notice, though, that this seal never left the continental shelf's shallow waters.

Gray Seals eat a varied diet that includes fish, such as herring and capelin, as well as invertebrates such as shrimp, squid, and octopus. All of these food sources can be found in the waters along the continental shelf. This information helps to explain Stephanie's movements.

FIGURE 6.38. Gray Seals lack external ear flaps and characteristically have large snouts. They are opportunistic feeders that consume between 4 and 6% of their bodyweight per day. Males can weigh up to 400 hundred kilograms (~880 pounds).

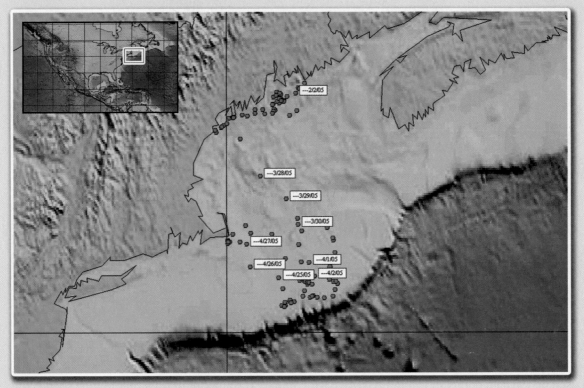

FIGURE 6.39. Locations of Stephanie, the Gray Seal.

Miguel, the Southern Elephant Seal

Southern Elephant Seals, native to the coastal waters of Antarctica, take a different approach to feeding and movement than do Gray Seals. The largest seals on Earth, male Southern Elephant Seals average more than 3,000 kilograms (~6,600 pounds). Many weigh in even more. To sustain their heft, Southern Elephant Seals spend a lot of time at sea searching for food, or **foraging**. These seals eat primarily fish and squid, but unlike Gray Seals, are known to dive to impressive depths for their prey, up to 1,500 meters (~4,900 feet). The depth of most dives is in the range of 300–800 meters (~984–2,625 feet), and dives can last 2 hours. Scientists estimate that Southern Elephant Seals spend about 90% of their time underwater.

FIGURE 6.40. Scientists in Antarctica pose with a Southern Elephant Seal. These seals are the Earth's largest seals and devote most of their time to foraging for food.

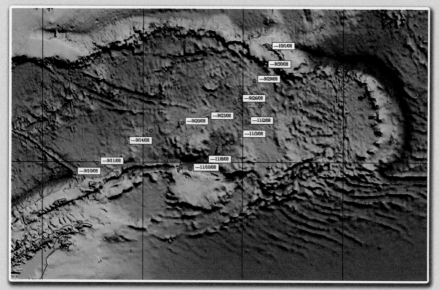

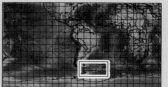

FIGURE 6.41. Locations of Miguel, the Southern Elephant Seal. Unlike Gray Seals, which remain on the continental shelf where depths rarely reach 150 meters, Southern Elephant Seals head to deeper waters to forage.

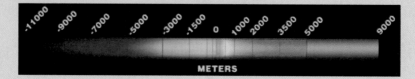

15. What was the approximate water depth of Miguel's location on 11/8/08, based on FIGURE 6.41?

16. Based on the data points shown in FIGURE 6.41, compare the amount of time that Miguel spends on continental shelves versus deeper waters.

How Deep Do They Go?

Satellite transmitters on marine animals can tell us just how deep they go. Using these and other instruments, scientists have gathered evidence that some animals go very deep to look for food, while others go deeper for protection from predators lurking above. Keep in mind that when you look at a point along an animal track, it just means that the animal passed that point on the date indicated. When considering the depth of water at a particular point, remember that it is likely that the animal did not even dive close to the seafloor, especially in deep areas. Many of the animals that *Signals of Spring* scientists and students track, including seals, whales, and sea turtles, must come to the surface to breathe. This limits their ability to dive to the ocean's deepest waters.

FIGURE 6.42. Emperor Penguins and Killer Whales are two air-breathing animals that dive for their food. Killer Whales are one of the top predators in the polar seas of the Antarctic.

FIGURE 6.43. A Weddell Seal pup takes a breath through an air hole in the ice near Ross Island in the Antarctic. Scientists think that Weddell Seals use their teeth to crack breathing holes in the ice.

FIGURE 6.44. A Southern Elephant Seal rests at the surface between dives. The need to breathe air prevents marine mammals from diving to the ocean's deepest depths.

The diagram below indicates the approximate maximum depths to which some air-breathing species can dive. Of course, scientists are always learning, and new findings may change what we know and strengthen our understandings about marine animal behavior. There are whole ecosystems in the deep sea. Organisms in these ecosystems, however, do not have to go to the ocean's surface to breathe.

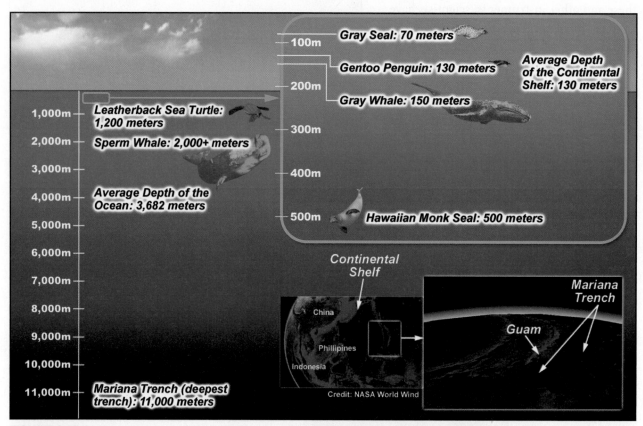

FIGURE 6.45. Marine animals characteristically take deep dives to varying depths. Scientists study behaviors including the search for food.

FIGURE 6.46. A Sperm Whale gets ready for a deep dive in the Gulf of Alaska. Male Sperm Whales are believed to range from the Equator to the polar seas, whereas females remain in tropical and subtropical waters.

Evaluate

1. The image below depicts the bathymetry of part of the Indian Ocean. Identify the seafloor features represented by letters A through D. Give a brief description in your own words of each feature.

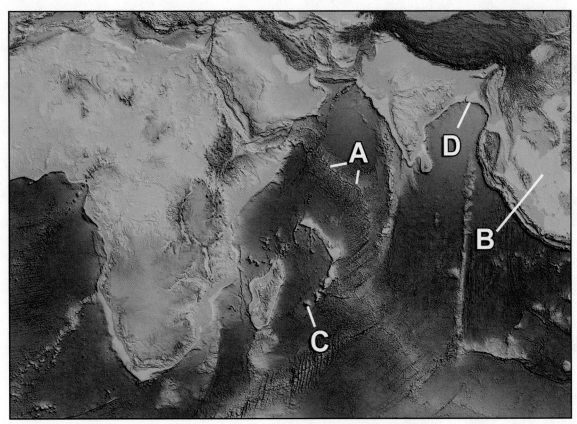

FIGURE 6.47. Bathymetric image of the Indian Ocean and surrounding landmasses.

2. Choose one of the methods by which scientists map the seafloor. Create a magazine advertisement in which you introduce others to the mapping method, and tell why it is useful in helping to learn about the seafloor. Your ad should include visuals as well as words.

7

The Formation of the Ocean

INSIDE:

Objectives

You will be able to:

✔ **Explain the Theory of Plate Tectonics by describing the processes involved, the geologic features used as supporting evidence, and the major changes in Earth's crust that have occurred as a result of crustal movement.**

✔ **Use the development of the Theory of Plate Tectonics to discuss how scientific ideas and research evolve into a unified theory.**

✔ **Identify the major layers of the Earth.**

Benchmarks

1a. The ocean is the dominant physical feature on our planet Earth—covering approximately 70% of the planet's surface. There is one ocean with many ocean basins, such as the North Pacific, South Pacific, North Atlantic, South Atlantic, Indian, and Arctic.

1b. An ocean basin's size, shape, and features (e.g., islands, trenches, mid-ocean ridges, rift valleys) vary due to the movement of Earth's lithospheric plates. Earth's highest peaks, deepest valleys, and flattest vast plains are all in the ocean.

1d. Sea level is the average height of the ocean relative to the land, taking into account the differences caused by tides. Sea level changes as plate tectonics cause the volume of ocean basins and the height of the land to change. It changes as ice caps on land melt or grow. It also changes as seawater expands and contracts when ocean water warms and cools.

2b. Sea level changes over time have expanded and contracted continental shelves, created and destroyed inland seas, and shaped the surface of land.

2e. Tectonic activity, sea level changes, and force of waves influence the physical structure and landforms of the coast.

7b. Understanding the ocean is more than a matter of curiosity. Exploration, inquiry, and study are required to better understand ocean systems and processes.

7e. Use of mathematical models is now an essential part of ocean sciences. Models help us understand the complexity of the ocean and of its interaction with Earth's climate. They process observations and help describe the interactions among systems.

7f. Ocean exploration is truly interdisciplinary. It requires close collaboration among biologists, chemists, climatologists, computer programmers, engineers, geologists, meteorologists, and physicists and new ways of thinking.

Engage

In the last Lesson, we identified diverse features of the seafloor, including trenches, mid-ocean ridges, and abyssal plains. But how did the ocean floor come to be? How did the features form? To find the answers to these questions, we will investigate the formation of the Earth and its ocean and how our dynamic planet continues to change.

First, we will review what you already know about Earth's crustal changes.

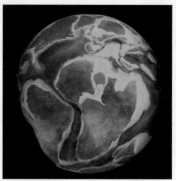

e-Tools

FIGURE 7.1. Screenshot of the *Pangaea Breakup Animation*.

See Page 694 for how to access e-Tools.

View the *Pangaea Breakup Animation* (0:30) in the e-Tools about the breakup of the Supercontinent of Pangaea.

1. Using what you know about Plate Tectonics, describe what is happening in the animation.

Explore

We will explore how the ocean has changed over Earth's history. First, however, let's explore how scientists infer the Earth and its ocean originally formed.

Nebula (cloud of ice, dust and gas-mostly hydrogen and helium) is left over from the Big Bang.

◀ previous   1 of 12   next ▶

e-Tools

View the *Earth Formation Animation* in the e-Tools.

2. *Briefly* describe the steps of Earth's formation as seen in the animation. Include how the ocean initially formed.

FIGURE 7.2. Screenshot of the *Earth Formation Animation*.

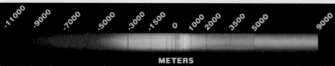

FIGURE 7.3. The ocean floor's features give many clues about changes our planet has experienced in its history.

METERS

As we consider the Earth's beginning with the physical development of the ocean, we next explore the development of the ocean's details. How has the ocean with its basins developed over time? How do Earth's crustal plates serve our ocean? Now we will examine a series of maps that simulate the position of Earth's continents through geologic time. The maps were constructed by compiling data from many scientific research reports. These maps serve as models that represent the interpretation of the massive amount of data gathered by scientists about Earth's features and changes over time.

See Page 694 for how to access e-Tools.

View the **Earth's Continents Through Time Tool** in the e-Tools.

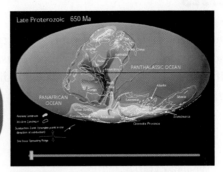

e-Tools

FIGURE 7.4. Screenshot of the **Earth's Continents Through Time Tool**.

3. Copy the following table or use the **e-Tools Worksheet: Crustal Changes Through Geologic Time Chart**. Observe each of the maps and their captions. Describe the geological changes that occur during each time period. Use scientific terms and focus on the development of the oceans whenever possible.

Crustal Changes Through Geologic Time		
Time of Animation (examples from slide-bar animation)	**Geologic Period**	**Event or Description**
Present	Modern World: Holocene	
18,000	Last Ice Age: Holocene	
14 million	Miocene	
50.2 million	Eocene	
66 million	end Cretaceous/start Tertiary	
94 million	late Cretaceous	
152 million	late Jurassic	
195 million	early Jurassic	
237 million	early Triassic	
255 million	late Permian	
306 million	late Carboniferous	
356 million	early Carboniferous	
390 million	early Devonian	
425 million	middle Silurian	
458 million	middle Ordovician	
514 million	late Cambrian	
650 million	Proterozoic	
–	4.6 billion years ago	

Explain

Toward a Unified Theory of Crustal Movements

FIGURE 7.5. Alfred Wegener first shared his Theory of Continental Drift in 1912. At the time, his ideas rocked the scientific community.

When Alfred Wegener published *The Origin of Continents and Oceans* in 1915, he upended all of science with his assertions. Wegener asserted in his Theory of Continental Drift that over time the continents, including the ocean, move around Earth's surface.

In his introduction, Wegener stated:

"The BACKGROUND to this book may not be wholly without interest. The first conception of continental drift first came to me as far back as 1910, when considering the map of the world, under the direct impression produced by the congruence of the coastlines on either side of the Atlantic. At first I did not pay attention to the idea because I regarded it as improbable. In the fall of 1911, I came quite accidentally upon a synoptic report in which I learned for the first time of paleontological evidence for a land bridge between Brazil and Africa. As a result I undertook a cursory examination of relevant research in the fields of geology and paleontology, and this provided immediately such weighty corroboration that a conviction of the fundamental soundness of the idea took root in my mind. On the 6th of January 1912 I put forward the idea for the first time in an address to the Geological Association in Frankfurt am Main, entitled 'The Geophysical Basis of the Evolution of the Large-scale Features of the Earth's Crust (Continents and Oceans)'."

Synoptic – giving a summary or overview

Paleontological – having to do with prehistoric life

Cursory – brief, not detailed

Corroboration – confirmation

4. Describe in your own words or sketch what Wegener is saying above.

It was shortly after this speech to the Geological Association that Wegener published his book about the theory of Continental Drift. As evidence supporting his theory, Wegener cited research done by different geologists and paleontologists, including the similarities of fossil species on different continents, the matching shapes of continental margins, the positions of mountain ranges on various continents, and other undisputed findings. Using this evidence he concluded:

"The continents must have shifted. South America must have lain alongside Africa and formed a unified block which was split in two in the Cretaceous; the two parts must then have become increasingly separated over a period of millions of years like pieces of a cracked ice floe in water. The edges of these two blocks are even today strikingly congruent. Not only does the large rectangular bend formed by the Brazilian coast at Cape Sao Roque mate exactly with the bend in the African coast at the Cameroons, but also south of these two corresponding points every projection on the Brazilian side matches a congruent bay on the African, and conversely. A pair of compasses and a globe will show that the sizes are precisely commensurate... It is easy to see that the whole idea of drift theory starts out from the supposition that deep-sea floors and continents consist of different materials and are, as it were, different layers of the earth's structure. The outermost layer, represented by the continental blocks, does not cover the whole earth's surface, or it may be truer to say that it no longer does so. The ocean floors represent the free surface of the next layer inwards, which is also assumed to run under the blocks. This is the geophysical aspect of drift theory."

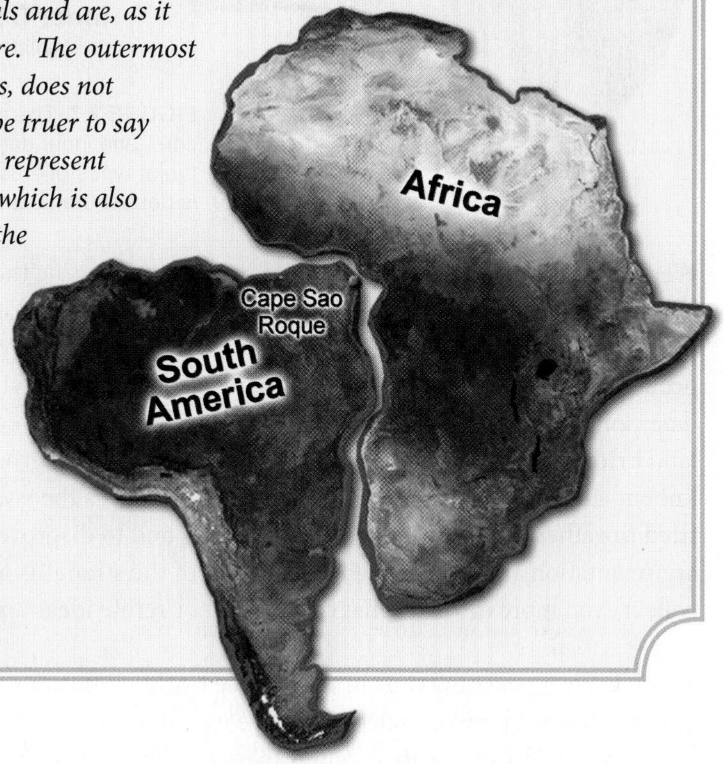

FIGURE 7.6. South America and Africa fit together like a puzzle. Hypothesizing, finding evidence, and analyzing information over time helps scientists to learn and begin to draw conclusions.

Wegener tried to combine all the known evidence into a unifying theory. He called it Continental Drift. In science, the term **theory** describes the culmination of many scientific investigations, drawing together all the current evidence on a specific topic. A scientific theory represents the most powerful explanation scientists have to offer about a topic. In science, theories are not taken lightly.

The idea of continents moving together and apart over time seemed wildly impossible to most people, and greatly stirred the scientific community to gather evidence to disprove Wegener's idea. His thinking "outside the box" is an example of creative thinking within science. Wegener's theory, however, suffered from the fact that he did not have an explanation for why the continents moved. He only proposed that there was observed fossil and landmass evidence that they had moved. Wegener also did not have knowledge of the ocean basins. He said that the continents and ocean were different layers of the Earth. In fact, they are both crust, just different types of crust.

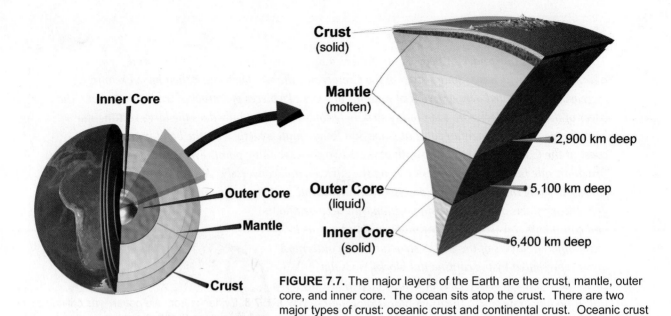

FIGURE 7.7. The major layers of the Earth are the crust, mantle, outer core, and inner core. The ocean sits atop the crust. There are two major types of crust: oceanic crust and continental crust. Oceanic crust is denser than continental crust.

Wegener's theory was at odds with contemporary scientific thought. In the early 1900s, many geologists believed that the features of the Earth were the result of the Earth going through cycles of heating and cooling, which caused expansion and contraction of landmasses. They were busy trying to explain why mountains occurred in some places and not in others, among other questions. Other scientists, ignoring landmass data, sought to explain the similarities of fossils on different continents by proposing that there had been land bridges that connected landmasses. Even though no group had a unifying theory to explain all the known facts, they were not willing to accept Wegener's theory. The battle raged as all the scientific groups tried to gather data to support their own ideas and to disprove the Theory of Continental Drift. Scientific argumentation and competing ideas are two of the strengths of science—they encourage diverse scientists to collect even more evidence that can support or refute ideas and lead to new, testable hypotheses.

This was a very exciting time in the science world. Emotions boiled over about conflicting ideas, but without critical dialogue between scientists, there would be far fewer scientific discoveries. John Harrington, in his *Dance of the Continents*, captures these tensions in his description of how a "scientific idea" becomes a "unifying theory":

> Here we see the link between scientific research and scientific reasoning. Conclusions that are too astonishing to be accepted, yet too interesting to be forgotten, serve to stimulate an ongoing hunt for more facts... Scientific reasoning is a major part of good fieldwork. It represents the culmination of the entire effort. It's the level where conclusions are drawn and learning takes place. Scientists learn by recognizing the probable truth of each conclusion as they are forced to admit that there is no other more reasonable way to assemble the facts at hand. (Harrington, John W. *Dance of the Continents*, 1983, pp. 25-26)

The more scientists tried to find evidence to disprove Wegener's theory, the more facts they found that supported his idea of crustal movement. Eventually, Wegener's hypothesis of continents drifting over an ocean basin crust was shown to be incorrect. Harrington noted, however, that the idea of crustal movement was "too interesting to be forgotten", and, in fact, the ocean data were the key to deciphering the puzzle of continental drift.

It was not until scientists discovered new seafloor features that the missing evidence needed to modify Wegener's original theory fell into place. These new observations provided the mechanism for crustal movement and explained the formation of the ocean basins. With every new discovery about ocean basins, scientists further refined the Theory of Continental Drift to include large pieces of Earth's crust, called **plates**. These plates include both continents and ocean basins. As more was learned about the ocean basins, scientists refined the idea of continents "drifting" to include larger sections or plates of the crust composed of continents and the ocean basins.

A key piece of evidence supporting the theory was discovered after World War I. In 1925, Germany outfitted a research boat and set out on a two-year expedition to systematically look for natural resources in the oceans. Using sonar, this expedition revealed new information about the previously unexplored seafloor. One of the

FIGURE 7.8. Evidence from the ocean was critical to explaining how Earth's continents move.

findings of the expedition was a continuous mountain-like ridge slicing through the Atlantic Ocean to the southwest coast of Africa. It is now known as the **Mid-Atlantic Ridge**. Scientists later discovered the Mid-Atlantic Ridge was part of a continuous feature that snakes through all of the ocean basins. This ridge is a mountain range on the seafloor. Its seamounts tower up to 3 kilometers (~2 miles) above the flat abyssal plains. The ridges are broken into segments by a number of features called fracture zones; the rocks in these zones slide past each other with a side-to-side movement. These fractures are called **transform faults**. Picture a fracture or transform fault like the seams of a baseball; the edges coming together are touching. The plates slide past each other at this "seam".

Details on the dynamic processes in the Earth's crust continued to be revealed. In the 1950s, geologists mapped a deep canyon, now called the **Great Global Rift**, which runs the length of the Mid-Atlantic Ridge. The average depth of the very elongated canyon, or rift valley, is approximately 1.6 kilometers (~1 mile) and its width ranges from 37 to 48 kilometers (~23–30 miles) wide. The Great Global Rift is a break in Earth's crust where frequent volcanic activity pushes new magma up through the seafloor as the divergent boundary pulls apart two plates. Ultimately this discovery led to the scientific knowledge that these ridges are sites of seafloor spreading, which are creating new oceanic basins. The forces pulling the crust apart are driven by heat rising from the molten mantle layer below the Earth's crust, in a heat distribution process known as **convection**.

FIGURE 7.9. The discovery of mid-ocean ridges was critical evidence to support Alfred Wegener's Theory of Continental Drift.

View the **Convection Animation** in the e-Tools.

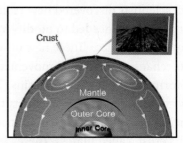

FIGURE 7.10. Screenshot of the *Convection Animation*.

At about the same time, scientists on a British survey ship called the *Challenger II* found extremely deep areas in the ocean, which are now called trenches. Trenches exist along the margins of some of the continents and encircle most of the rim of the Pacific. Trenches form when two plates collide and one plate plunges under the other. This region is called a **convergent plate boundary**. The stresses that can build up along these boundaries often cause deepsea earthquakes. High-energy waves called **tsunamis** are sparked when a particularly strong earthquake's energy is distributed through the ocean waters as shown in the animation. Tsunamis can also occur due to landslides, volcanoes, and other natural occurrences.

FIGURE 7.11. Screenshot of the *Tsunami Animation*.

View the **Tsunami Animation** (0:25) in the e-Tools.

The discovery of rift valleys, mid-ocean ridges, and trenches provided an explosion of new geologic data stemming from advances in technology. By the late 1960s and early 1970s, the evidence supporting the theory of crustal movement, known now as Plate Tectonics, was overwhelming. After more than a half century, the theory that started with Wegener was finally accepted by both the scientific community and the general public. The story of how the theories of Continental Drift and Plate Tectonics became a widely accepted unified theory is an example of how the scientific community builds broad and useful understandings of natural phenomena by starting with careful observations, evidence, and scientific dialogue.

Plate Tectonics and Volcanoes

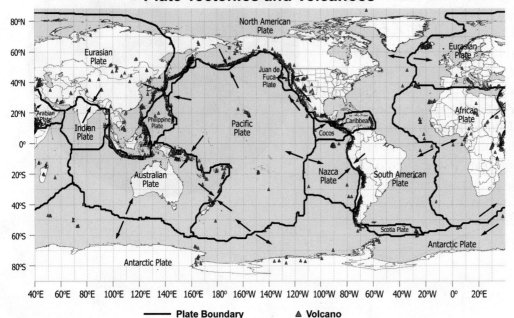

FIGURE 7.12. This map of Earth's major plates and boundaries represents what is currently inferred about our planet's crust. Scientific evidence for the locations of plate boundaries includes earthquake, volcano, and seafloor spreading data.

—— Plate Boundary   ▲ Volcano

We now know that six large and several smaller plates make up Earth's surface. Most of the world's earthquakes and volcanoes occur at the edges of these plates. The Theory of Plate Tectonics also provides evidence for locating buried mineral and energy resources, predicting natural disasters, and anticipating future changes on Earth. The growing knowledge of the history and characteristics of the ocean basins facilitates efforts to plan more ocean research.

Seafloor features and coastlines are constantly changing because of the movements of crustal plates. Some changes are rapid, such as when an earthquake or volcano occurs. Other changes take place over thousands or millions of years. The size of ocean basins and the sea level along continents varies with these changes. Sea level is also affected by changes in climate.

This story is an excellent illustration of the Nature of Science. Science involves much collection of data, testing of ideas, and making inferences. Scientific ideas are constantly being re-examined. In contrast, some ideas and topics are presented like science, but are not correctly characterized as science. A common example is the study of heavenly bodies and their influence on human activities—**astrology**. You are probably familiar with horoscopes, or your "sign". Perhaps you have read your horoscope in newspapers or magazines. Among the ideas that characterize astrology is the notion that the time of your birth influences everyday happenings in your life. If this idea were an accepted scientific idea, it would be testable and measurable. There would be many scientific studies generating evidence to support astrological ideas. There simply is not scientific evidence to support astrology, or the usefulness of horoscopes.

5. Why were Wegener's ideas about Continental Drift considered a theory?

6. How did the scientific discoveries in the 1950s and 1960s affect the debate about Wegener's theory?

FIGURE 7.13. Astrology is the idea that stars, planets, comets, and other bodies in Space influence events in human lives. Astrology is not considered to be science because there is not enough scientific evidence to support its assertions.

Elaborate

When most people think about how Earth's lithospheric plates affect the Earth, they think about the continents. The oceans, however, are also a major part of the story. Scientists use the Theory of Plate Tectonics as an organizing model to study geologic features and forces on Earth. These maps are predictions of Earth changes that have been extrapolated from evidence of past and present crustal plate movement. They are a model demonstrating what some scientists believe may happen in the future. Scientists, mathematicians, and map makers work together to come up with calculations and predictions, and then create a visual model to illustrate those ideas. Modeling is an important part of science and engineering. Models help us to better understand the processes of the ocean, the Earth in general, and the interactions between these systems.

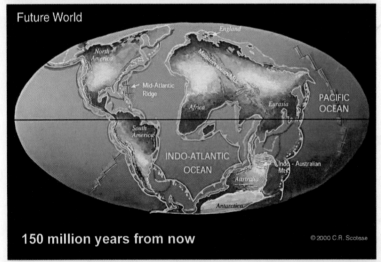

FIGURE 7.14. Scientists in diverse disciplines of Earth Science, including physicists, biologists, chemists, and geologists, continue to collect data to learn more about Earth's crust. The lithospheric data are used to make predictions about future changes. Projections of the movements of Earth's continents in the future look like the images on the left.

Activity

Part I: Exploring Oceanic Evidence for Plate Tectonics

You will work in research teams and review a topic related to the ocean and to the Theory of Plate Tectonics. Take "field notes" on your topic, which should include diagrams, drawings, and text that record details about what you observe and discover. Make a copy of the chart below, or use the *e-Tools Worksheet: Exploring Oceanic Evidence for Plate Tectonics*, to help organize your notes.

Exploring Oceanic Evidence Field Notes

Topic: _____

Important Ideas	Relationship to Plate Tectonics

Team 1: Plate Tectonics and Ocean Chemistry

Since the late 1960s, scientists have discussed the idea that convection currents in the mantle drive crustal plate motion. This process includes hot molten magma that rises along mid-ocean ridges where the crustal plates pull apart at divergent plate boundaries. Scientists are still gathering evidence on whether the plates pull apart and the magma rises through the weakened fractured crust, or whether the force of the rising magma forces the crust apart. It is also possible that the sinking of dense, usually oceanic, crustal plates in subduction zones drags the rest of the plate down into the mantle. This is an active area of research as scientists gather evidence to support these explanations.

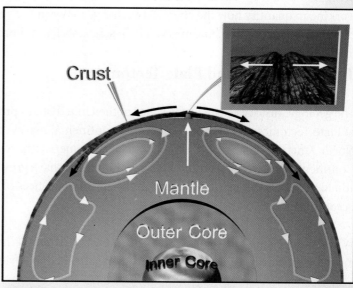

FIGURE 7.15. Plate motion is driven by convection currents in the mantle. Heated molten rock rises at the diverging mid-ocean ridges.

Another area of active research involves the interaction of seawater with liquid magma along the mid-ocean ridges. Scientists have long known that water in rivers and lakes slowly dissolves minerals in rocks and soil; the water transports the solutes (dissolved substances) to the ocean. It was thought that transport from land was the sole source of the ions that make seawater salty. Now that scientists have started to study mid-ocean ridges they have discovered another water cycle—one that they believe plays a key role in maintaining the chemical balance in seawater, including the concentration of salt.

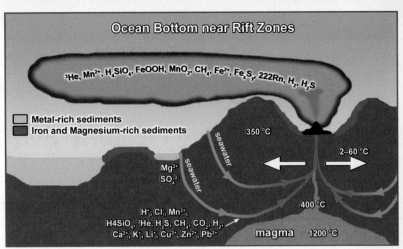

FIGURE 7.16. Studying ocean chemistry in undersea rift zones provides evidence for the Theory of Plate Tectonics. Notice the ions from seawater seeping into the crust, and the elements that are returned to the water from the undersea volcano.

Seawater soaks through the fractures and pores in the seafloor. As the water nears the magma in these fractures and pores, it is heated. Since heated water is less dense than cold water, the heated water rises toward the sea surface. Just as it does on the continental surface, the water chemically interacts with the molten rock and dissolves minerals, and the cyclical movement of the water circulates minerals from the mantle. These minerals include important metals such as copper (Cu), zinc (Zn), manganese (Mn), magnesium (Mg), and iron (Fe). The chemical-enriched water also includes gases such as hydrogen sulfide (H_2S), carbon dioxide (CO_2), helium (He), hydrogen (H_2), and methane (CH_4). Living marine organisms in the ocean also need these minerals. For example, photosynthetic organisms take in iron, which makes it available for animals that eat the phytoplankton. Marine animals use the iron to produce hemoglobin, which carries oxygen in the blood to the cells where respiration takes place.

The ocean is so vast that the chemical exchanges between the magma and the seawater are difficult to measure and quantify. Scientists are designing computer models to allow them to infer how much heat is being removed from the interior of Earth through these mid-ocean ridges and other seafloor vents. They are working to quantify how the chemical exchange between the vents and the seawater affects the ocean's overall chemical balance. These findings will help scientists learn more about the mechanisms of plate tectonics.

Team 2: Florida and Plate Tectonics

The geologic history of one of the states of the United States provides an interesting example in the study of Plate Tectonics. Like a number of other continental margin areas, Florida did not start out as a part of North America. Instead, it was added to North America through a process known as **continental accretion**. Continental accretion has resulted in continents that have grown as new land was "pasted" to their edges. The added materials can be gained through the addition of slices of other continents or by the pushing up of the oceanic crust.

What is today known as Florida was once a part of Africa. When Pangaea broke apart, the Florida peninsula moved with North America instead of staying attached to Africa.

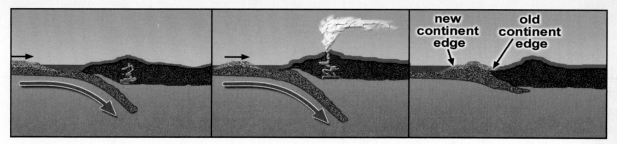

FIGURE 7.17. Continents "grow" as sediments are incorporated along their edges. This process is called continental accretion.

During the early Cenozoic (65 to 35 million years ago), Florida was underwater. Thick layers of marine invertebrate skeletons piled up, ultimately forming the familiar Florida limestone that today underlies much of the state. Over millennia, sea levels rose and fell, alternately depositing marine shells and sediment and then eroding the material away. In many places, the erosion created sinkholes, springs, and caves, which are still found throughout Florida.

Florida's position, projecting into the Atlantic Ocean and Gulf of Mexico, made it a natural connection between North and South America during periods of retreating seas. During the Pliocene Epoch (pronounced: PLĪ-ĭ-sēn Ē-pawk), about 2.3 million years ago, great diversity of land animals preserved as fossils in Florida rocks and sinkholes provides evidence that animals traveled freely across this temporary connection.

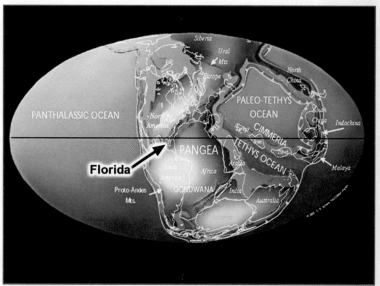

FIGURE 7.18. After the breakup of Pangaea, Florida remained with North America and moved with the continent to the northwest.

FIGURE 7.19. 50–100 million years ago, much of North America, including what is now the Florida peninsula, was underwater. Remains of living organisms in the area formed a very thick foundation of limestone. Today, this limestone layer sits beneath the state.

The most recent event in Florida's evolution occurred near the end of the Pleistocene Epoch (pronounced: PLĪS-tĭ-sēn Ē-pawk), when an Ice Age ravaged the globe, forming thick sheets of ice on the continents. The trapping of water in ice resulted in very low sea levels. At this time, the exposed landmass around Florida increased until it was nearly three times its current size. Near the end of the Ice Age, paleo-Indians colonized Florida, as did an extensive population of large terrestrial animals. Although much of the evidence of these early Floridians now lies buried offshore because they were most active along the ancient coastline, scientists have been able to piece together parts of the archaeological record with the marine excavation of animal bones and human artifacts.

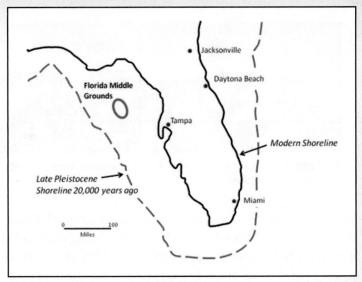

FIGURE 7.20. During the Late Pleistocene Epoch, Florida's shoreline extended much farther offshore than the present coast. The Florida Middle ground is an area, now underwater, in which human settlement artifacts have been found.

Team 3: Marine Animals and Black Smokers

In 1977, the use of submersibles allowed scientists to discover whole new ecosystems on the seafloor. They discovered that seawater seeps through cracks in the seafloor and becomes heated by Earth's mantle underneath. The water then spews out in chimneys called hydrothermal vents. Hydrothermal vents are essentially geysers on the seafloor. Very little is known about them since they are relatively small features appearing in a vast ocean basin. Frequently called black smokers, the water-spewing chimneys are composed of iron sulfides, copper, zinc, and other metals from the mantle. The superheated seawater cycling through the crust dissolves minerals from the oceanic crust or upper mantle layer. The minerals build up on the sides of the chimney, making the vent water look black as the minerals escape into the cooler ocean water. The vents indicate close interactions between the mantle and the crust, supporting the idea that there is convection underneath that is affecting crustal plates.

Hydrothermal Vent Ecosystems are one of the most interesting and strange ecosystems. Scientists continue to identify new species of clams, snails, worms, and fish every time a research vessel explores one of these locations. No light reaches these depths, so gathering data about these creatures is difficult. Marine biologists have

FIGURE 7.21. These small venting spires are built on top of a 7-meter-tall (~23 foot) chimney in the Black Forest vent field. The spires, approximately 30 centimeters tall (~11.8 inches), are releasing into the ocean "black smoke" composed of very hot fluids (~240 °C) and tiny chunks of black minerals.

discovered that the base of the food chain in these ecosystems are bacteria that utilize hydrogen sulfide and other inorganic compounds that are pumped out of the black smokers. Bacteria are able to obtain energy from chemicals such as iron, sulfur, and manganese. These bacteria serve the role of producers, similar to the role that photosynthesizing plants do in the more familiar food chains.

Researchers have begun only recently to learn a little about how these unique ecosystems work. There are animals that can thrive in total darkness, extreme temperatures ranging from freezing to 400 °C (~750 °F), and tremendous pressure. As researchers discover new vents and chimneys, they learn more

FIGURE 7.22. This mound of bacteria on top of a chimney is approximately 1 meter (~3 feet) across.

about the biological, physical, chemical, and geological variations of these amazing deep sea communities. Some scientists are proposing that life on Earth began at these hydrothermal vents. They believe the intense heat and abundant chemicals may have fueled the chemical reactions necessary to create living things.

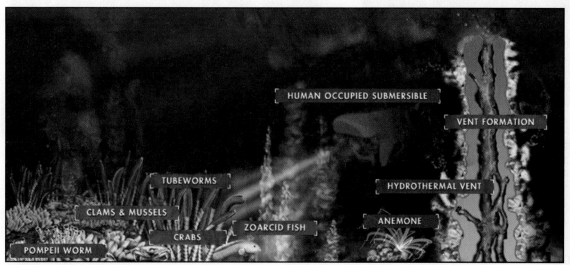

FIGURE 7.23. Hydrothermal vents support unique ecosystems of organisms that include tubeworms, crabs, anemones, and much more.

Team 4: African Rift Zone

When looking at the geography of water bodies, volcanoes and earthquakes around the Red Sea, scientists see evidence of rift zones. The Red Sea is strangely elongated, and its eastern edges connect to the Gulf of Aden as well as a canyon in Eastern Africa. This canyon is a string of extremely deep lakes, high volcanic mountains, including Mt. Kilimanjaro, and frequent earthquakes. Scientists have concluded that the Afar Triangle located at the southern end of the Red Sea is the site where three tectonic plates, the Arabian, Nubian, and Somalian Plates, meet.

Scientists and geographers find this rift zone to be significant. They believe that the area may be in the early stages of a seafloor spreading event, where intense heating begins under a spot in the continental crust. In seafloor spreading, the rocks in the area become more pliable and less dense. The area then bulges up and forms a dome because it is less dense than surrounding rock. Bending of the crust causes it to crack and fracture, eventually forming long breaks called rifts. These tears in Earth's crust radiate away from a central spot and will form three rift arms at approximately 120 degrees apart. These three angles form a "triple junction". The Red Sea-East Africa Rift is an example of a triple junction, which is visible from Space as a large crack in Earth's surface. If the movement continues along Eastern Africa and opens into the existing ocean, the rift system will flood with seawater. This would become a new sea, splitting Africa into two landmasses.

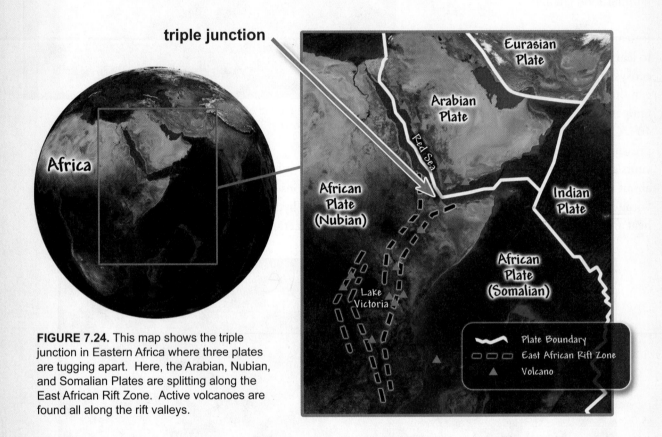

FIGURE 7.24. This map shows the triple junction in Eastern Africa where three plates are tugging apart. Here, the Arabian, Nubian, and Somalian Plates are splitting along the East African Rift Zone. Active volcanoes are found all along the rift valleys.

Team 5: Tsunamis

Activities such as subduction and rifting along Earth's plate boundaries are violent processes that often will result in earthquakes. When an undersea earthquake occurs, the energy travels through the seawater and may cause a tsunami, resulting in great waves washing suddenly onto shores both near and far from the epicenter of the quake. Tsunamis are more frequent in the Pacific and Indian Oceans than in the Atlantic, supporting the idea that there are more subduction zones in the Pacific Ocean basins. The map on the next page, FIGURE 7.27, shows global tsunami incidents that occurred between 1650 and 2008.

See Page 694 for how to access e-Tools.

View 2004 *Tsunami Animation 1* (0:30) and 2004 *Tsunami Animation 2* (0:42) in the e-Tools.

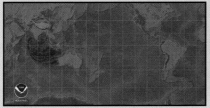

FIGURE 7.25. Screenshot of the *2004 Tsunami Animation 1*.

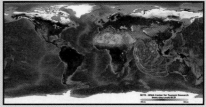

FIGURE 7.26. Screenshot of the *2004 Tsunami Animation 2*.

e-Tools

In 2004, an earthquake beneath the Indian Ocean along a subduction zone off the west coast of Sumatra, Indonesia, spawned a tsunami. It killed nearly 230,000 people in fourteen countries. In some places the waves were as high as 30 meters (~100 feet). Waves blasted onto shore with no advance warning, catching people off guard with devastating results. Indonesia, Sri Lanka, India, and Thailand were the hardest hit, but the waves' energy traveled around the world, as shown in the animations.

FIGURE 7.27. Data collected from around the world for hundreds of years allow scientists to create a map of tsunami events that have occurred.

FIGURE 7.28. Shown is the north end of Resurrection Bay after a tsunami struck at Seward, Alaska, about 75 kilometers (~47 miles) from the epicenter of the 1964 Alaska earthquake.

Scientists around the world have been working to reduce tsunami hazards and to protect lives by setting up advance warning systems. The work being done includes setting up buoys in the ocean to record violent seawater activity. This system is a real-time tsunami monitoring program called DART (Deep-ocean Assessment and Reporting of Tsunamis). Scientists are also developing computer models of wave propagation through the ocean. They are projecting how waves can strike coastal communities. With these models, scientists will be better equipped to predict the magnitude and speed of tsunamis headed toward vulnerable coastal areas. This will improve tsunami forecasting and warning abilities.

Tsunami Strikes with No Warning

On December 26, 2004, an earthquake struck off the coast of Sumatra in Indonesia, an island chain that separates the Pacific and Indian Oceans. The earthquake occurred deep below the surface of the ocean, within the Earth's crust. The energy from the earthquake sparked a series of high-energy ocean waves called tsunamis, which is Japanese for "harbor waves". Although the earthquake itself occurred near Sumatra, the waves quickly spread throughout the Indian Ocean, to places as far away as Somalia in Africa. In Sumatra, the wave was more than 10 meters (~33 feet) high. In Thailand, the tsunami measured about 4 meters (~13 feet).

An Indian Ocean warning system has been developed as a result of the huge loss of life from the 2004 tsunami event. The tsunami warning system monitors earthquake activity and sea levels throughout the world's oceans. If there is evidence that a tsunami might occur, the scientists issue a tsunami warning for certain geographic regions. The warning is then broadcast to the public through radio, television, cell phones, computer messages, and other means. In Hawaii, for example, coastal areas are equipped with loud sirens. If a siren sounds, citizens know to evacuate to higher ground. Such warnings might have saved lives in 2004.

See Page 694 for how to access e-Tools.

View the **Sumatra Animation** (0:24), which shows the propagation of tsunami waves in the 3 hours following the magnitude 9.0 earthquake.

e-Tools

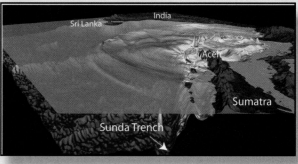

FIGURE 7.29. Screenshot of the **Sumatra Animation**.

People working and living near the coast often do not know when a tsunami is coming toward them. When they see the wave, it is too late to move away from the shore. When the wave's trough, the lower part of the wave, advances toward the shore first, water will be sucked out to sea and as many as several miles of seabed are exposed to the open air. With a very long wavelength, people have a bit of time to become inquisitive and walk out onto the exposed shoreline. After the trough passes, the wall of water comes ashore. Many have no chance to escape and are often drowned. Many troughs and crests of water can come ashore over a period of several hours, and simply because a person escapes the first wave, does not mean they are safe. One must always evacuate to higher ground and not return to the beach area until authorities sound the "all clear".

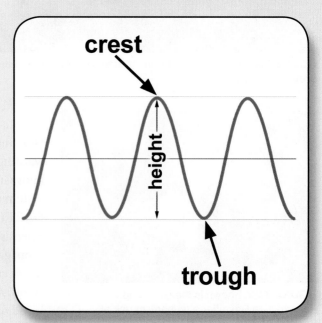

FIGURE 7.30. Any wave can be described by its height, the distance between its crest and trough.

Part II: Bringing It Together – Oceanic Evidence for Plate Tectonics

Each research team will now present their oceanic evidence findings that support the Theory of Plate Tectonics. Using the *Evidence for Plate Tectonics Graphic Organizer*, take notes on each group's findings about their topic, as well as how the topic relates to plate tectonics.

Now that you have a basic understanding of each group's topic, go back and read the information that was prepared by each of the other teams. Add details to your graphic organizer as necessary.

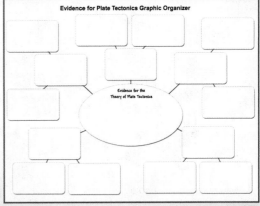

FIGURE 7.31. Screenshot of the *Evidence for Plate Tectonics Graphic Organizer*.

Evaluate

Using ideas learned in this Lesson and available online resources, propose a marine science research mission to study an aspect of plate tectonics in one of the ocean basins. Your proposal must include the following:

- A description of your research questions

- What you would study

- Where you would go

- Need for funding—that is, include how the research study would significantly contribute to the knowledge of oceans and benefit humanity

8

Seasons of Change

INSIDE:

Objectives

You will be able to:

✔ **Explain seasonal changes on Earth in terms of the intensity of solar radiation energy and the Earth's tilt, and understand that Earth's slightly varying distance from the Sun has nothing to do with the cause of the seasons.**

✔ **Illustrate how the angle of insolation relates to differential heating of the Earth's surface.**

✔ **Differentiate between types of incoming solar radiation.**

✔ **Give examples of how marine mammals respond to seasonal cues.**

Benchmarks

1a. The ocean is the dominant physical feature on our planet Earth—covering approximately 70% of the planet's surface. There is one ocean with many ocean basins, such as the North Pacific, South Pacific, North Atlantic, South Atlantic, Indian, and Arctic.

1f. The ocean is an integral part of the water cycle and is connected to all of the Earth's water reservoirs via evaporation and precipitation processes.

3b. The ocean absorbs much of the solar radiation reaching Earth. The ocean loses heat by evaporation. This heat loss drives atmospheric circulation when, after it is released into the atmosphere as water vapor, it condenses and forms rain. Condensation of water evaporated from warm seas provides the energy for hurricanes and cyclones.

7d. New technologies, sensors, and tools are expanding our ability to explore the ocean. Ocean scientists are relying more and more on satellites, drifters, buoys, subsea observatories, and unmanned submersibles.

Engage

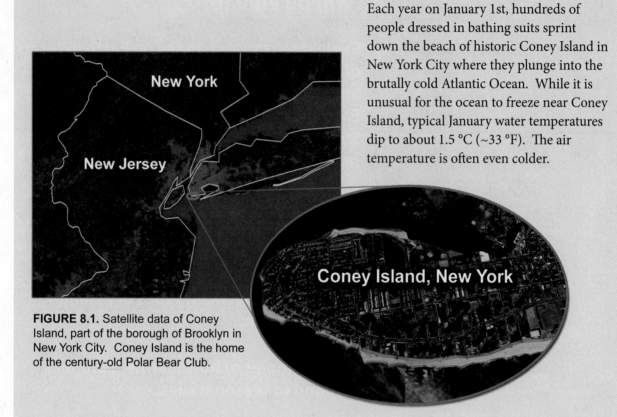

Each year on January 1st, hundreds of people dressed in bathing suits sprint down the beach of historic Coney Island in New York City where they plunge into the brutally cold Atlantic Ocean. While it is unusual for the ocean to freeze near Coney Island, typical January water temperatures dip to about 1.5 °C (~33 °F). The air temperature is often even colder.

FIGURE 8.1. Satellite data of Coney Island, part of the borough of Brooklyn in New York City. Coney Island is the home of the century-old Polar Bear Club.

These people are members of the Coney Island Polar Bear Club, which was established back in 1903. Today, there are many Polar Bear Clubs in diverse cities around the world. Some people join Polar Bear Clubs because they believe that the cold water provides health benefits, although scientific evidence for this hypothesis is lacking. Others use their daring plunge as a way to raise money for charity.

FIGURE 8.2. Polar Bear swimming in its icy Arctic Ocean habitat. Sea ice is utilized as a base from which to hunt prey.

1. If these same swimmers were also planning to jump into Coney Island's waters on July 1st, what would be a better name for the club? Why?

2. Would San Juan, Puerto Rico, be a good place for a new Polar Bear Club? Why?

FIGURE 8.3. Map of the Caribbean.

Explore

 **Demonstration**

Part 1: Modeling the Seasons

During the following activity you will model the Earth's revolution around the Sun. You will investigate what happens to the Earth during its revolution that might contribute to, or result in, Earth's changing seasons. As you know, Earth's revolution around the Sun takes approximately 365.25 days. Recall that the Earth is tilted at approximately 23.5° on its axis.

FIGURE 8.4. Earth tilted on its axis in this diagram represents the Northern Hemisphere summer, when during the Summer Solstice, the Sun's direct rays hit the Tropic of Cancer.

In this demonstration, the globe will move carefully through each of Earth's four seasons. You will answer questions for each "season" during the demonstration and participate in the class discussion. Note that the seasons are labeled as people living in the Northern Hemisphere would experience them.

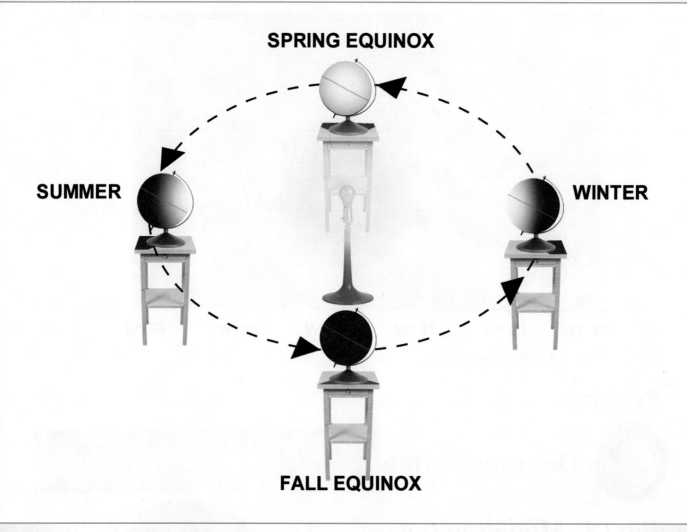

FIGURE 8.5. Classroom Demonstration prepares participants to walk around the classroom and place a tilted globe on each desk. Participants must be careful to keep the globe tilted in the process.

WINTER:

3. How does the "incoming solar radiation" in the Northern Hemisphere compare to that of the Southern Hemisphere in this position of the Earth in Space?

4. What season is it in the Southern Hemisphere?

SPRING:

5. Identify the main or center area the Sun's rays are hitting now.

6. Where is the distribution of light energy? Where on Earth is there a place receiving 24 hours of sunlight at this time?

SUMMER:

7. What changes have taken place for the Northern Hemisphere since the spring position?

8. What do you expect will happen over time to the amount of solar energy for areas in the Northern Hemisphere as the Earth revolves and moves toward fall?

FALL:

9. How do your observations compare to your predictions for fall?

The demonstration activity modeled each of the seasons. It showed that different latitudes are "favored" and the amount of solar radiation received at different latitudes differs with the time of year. The sunlight is most intense when the Sun is directly overhead. Twice each year the strongest solar radiation lines up over the Equator directly. These two dates are the **Autumnal Equinox**, which falls each year on September 22nd or 23rd, and the **Vernal Equinox**, which falls on March 20th or 21st. *Equi-* means equal; everyone on Earth experiences the same 12 hours of day and 12 hours of night.

On June 20th or 21st, the strongest amount of solar radiation is received over the Northern Hemisphere. This day is known as the **Summer Solstice**. It is defined by the Sun being directly overhead at the imaginary line of latitude, the Tropic of Cancer. The Northern Hemisphere receives stronger solar radiation and more hours of daylight. At this time, the Southern Hemisphere is experiencing their winter.

The **Winter Solstice** is on December 20th or 21st. This is when the highest amount of solar radiation hits the Southern Hemisphere, resulting in summer in the Southern Hemisphere. The Sun is directly overhead at the Tropic of Capricorn. This is the time of year when the Northern Hemisphere experiences winter.

The activity also simulated the rotation of the Earth on its axis as it revolved around the Sun. By spinning the globe, different parts of the Earth experienced sunlight and darkness over a 24-hour period. This daily cycle is called the **diurnal cycle**.

The Long and Short of It

The word *solstice* is derived from the Latin terms *sol* "sun" and *sistere* "stand still". It refers to the two special times of the year, when each of Earth's hemispheres experiences the least and most number of hours of daylight. The Winter Solstice offers the least amount of daylight in the Northern Hemisphere; the Summer Solstice offers the most.

In ancient times people were fascinated with the "stand still" aspect. For several consecutive days, at the time of the solstices, the Sun appeared to rise and set at the same points over the horizon. It slowed in its movement around the noon hour. Marking the end of a trend to longer or short days has always been a notable occurrence.

The Winter Solstice in the Northern Hemisphere has long been recognized as the "rebirth of the Sun", after which each day becomes gradually longer until the Summer Solstice. Winter Solstice is celebrated by the Chinese during the *Dong Zhi* festival when they recognize the turning point from the dark and cold (yin) of winter to the light and warmth (yang) that will come. In India, *Makar Sankranti* is a large festival celebrating the beginning of the harvest season. In Japan, people celebrate *Hari Kuyo*, in Pakistan, *Chaomas*, and in Tibet, *Dosmoche*.

Many Native American tribes continue to celebrate Solstice with prayer sticks, purification rituals, or a number of meaningful custom activities.

Many of the ways of the ancient Germanic *Yule* Solstice celebration continue today in Christmas traditions. Yule logs originally lit to keep away evil spirits are burned as a holiday tradition, and many of the plants associated with winter holidays today were used to honor the Solstice, including evergreens, ivy, mistletoe, and myrrh.

In addition to feasts and celebrations, ancient peoples constructed monuments to honor the Sun's rebirth. One of the most famous is Ireland's Newgrange Tomb, constructed in 3200 B.C.E. to capture the first rays of sunrise on the Winter Solstice. Tens of thousands of people apply each year to experience the Winter Solstice at Newgrange.

The Summer Solstice is welcomed as the longest day of the year, the official start of summer, and the mid-point of the growing season for many European countries. For people living in northern latitudes, the burst of life during the short summer growing season is welcomed and widely celebrated. The famous structure *Stonehenge*, in England, is visited by thousands of people each year at the Summer Solstice to celebrate the arrival of summer as the ancient people did.

FIGURE 8.6. Thousands of people visit Stonehenge, a famous structure constructed of stones, to commemorate the Summer Solstice. The orientation of the stones with respect to sunrises and sunsets throughout the year has captured imaginations for centuries.

Having modeled what happens during Earth's revolution around the Sun, you will now apply what you know about seasons to a new diagram.

10. Copy the diagram into your notebook and follow the directions below.

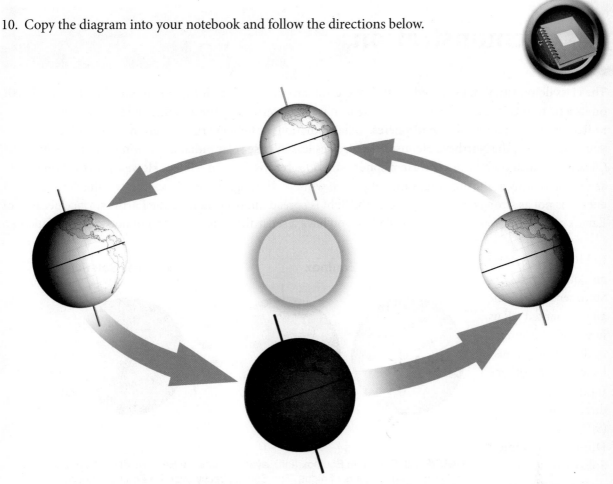

FIGURE 8.7. Earth rotating around the Sun. Note: The Sun is actually much larger compared to Earth, and Earth is much farther away, than shown.

a. Label the globes in the diagram with the appropriate season in the Northern Hemisphere—winter, spring, summer, and fall.

b. On the winter, summer, and fall globes in the diagram, label an "X" on the line of latitude where the Sun's rays are more concentrated on the Earth.

c. Why can't we place an "X" on the globe labeled *spring*?

d. Where are the Sun's rays most concentrated, or hitting most intensely, in the spring and fall illustrations?

e. Why does the Northern Hemisphere receive less concentrated solar radiation in winter?

11. Think back to the discussion of the Polar Bear Club, and explain why New York City's waters are so much colder in the winter than in the summer.

Part 2: It's All About the Rays

Demonstration

The class demonstration exhibited Earth's revolution around the Sun. It explained how the tilt of the Earth on its axis results in Earth's seasons. Each season is characterized by the amount and intensity of solar radiation received on Earth's hemispheres. Solar radiation, or light energy, travels in waves or "rays". As you determined, the Northern Hemisphere receives less intense solar radiation in winter than in summer. Of course, much of the Northern Hemisphere still does receive light in winter. However, as the Sun is not as high in the sky as during other times of year in winter—the angle of incidence is low—the Sun's light energy is not as strong over a given area. The light is spread out over more of the Earth's surface because of Earth's curvature. You may realize this when you have a sense that it is not as bright outside as it could be.

In FIGURE 8.8, for an Equinox and the Summer Solstice, the angles marked tell us how high the Sun is in the sky at various locations. At either Equinox, the Sun is directly overhead (90°) at the Equator. During the Summer Solstice the Sun is directly overhead at the Tropic of Cancer. Notice the angle of the Sun above the

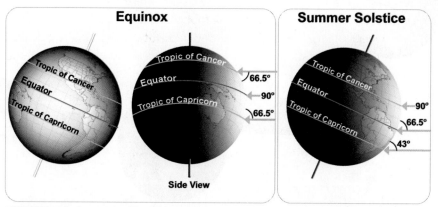

FIGURE 8.8. During an Equinox (left), every location on Earth receives 12 hours of daylight and 12 hours of night. The Sun is directly over the Equator. Notice the angle of incidence at the other locations. Because Earth is tilted, during a Northern Hemisphere Summer Solstice (right), the locations that have the greater angle of incidence are farther north.

horizon in various locations at each of these times. The higher the Sun is above the horizon, the higher the angle of incidence, the more solar energy reaches a location.

In this activity, you will analyze data that show how different latitudes receive different amounts of radiation. Following this activity, you will explore how the Sun's rays—the sun's radiative energy—travel to Earth, and how the Earth's atmosphere and surface absorb and reflect radiation. Your teacher will use a flashlight to model the Sun to demonstrate how the rays of the Sun hit the Earth's surface.

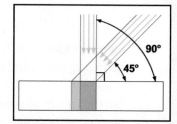

FIGURE 8.9. Notice how the same amount of energy is spread out over a given area when the Sun is not directly overhead.

12. The light is shining perpendicularly to the globe. Carefully observe where the light shines on the globe. Describe what you see.

13. Now observe the Sun's rays. Compare the light that hits the globe to when it was directly overhead at the Tropic of Cancer.

14. If you were on Earth at 60° N and looked directly up around noon, what would you see?

Activity

Materials:

*   *Surface Area Measuring Tools*

Now let's take a quantitative look at what the Sun's rays mean in terms of net energy received for Earth. Study the *Diagram of the Sun's Rays*. Notice that parallel lines are used to symbolize the rays or light of the Sun.

FIGURE 8.10. *Surface Area Measuring Tool*.

Consider how the curvature of the Earth and the tilt of the Earth affect the amount of solar energy received on Earth's surface. Using a simple measuring tool, a model to represent solar energy, you can quantify and compare the concentration of rays received over different latitudes. This tool, the *Surface Area Measuring Tool*, allows you to compare segments on the Earth's curved surface that are of the same length.

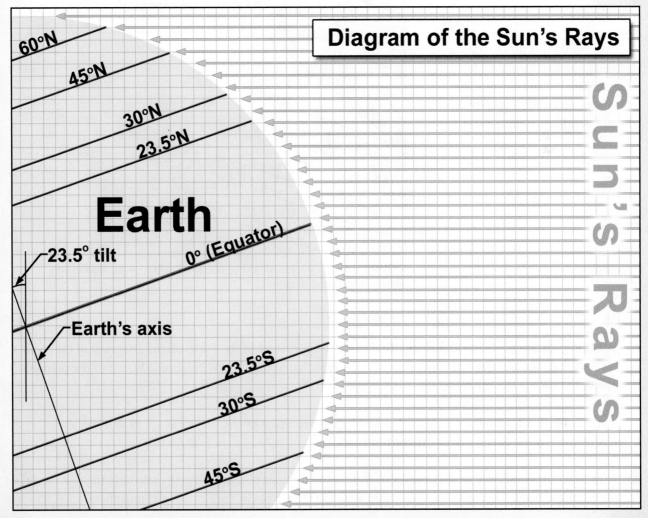

FIGURE 8.11. Diagram of the Sun's Rays.

By positioning the tool on areas at comparable northern and southern latitudes, you can see that the amount of solar energy received at a selected area of Earth is different.

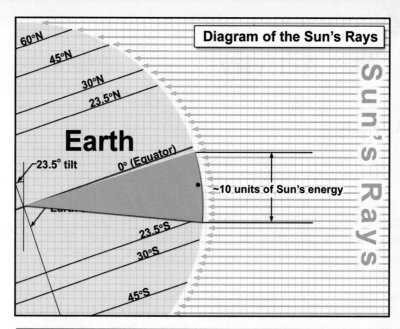

You can do this for other areas along the Earth's surface to compare the amount of solar energy received in the Northern and Southern Hemispheres.

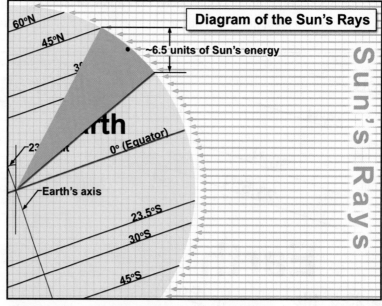

FIGURE 8.12. Examples of how to use the **Surface Area Measuring Tool** (pie tool) and diagram.

1. Position your **Surface Area Measuring Tool** along the curvature of the Earth on the **Diagram of the Sun's Rays** so that the dot on the curved portion of the tool aligns with the 45° N latitude line. Put the pointed end of the slice at the Earth's center.

    Approximately how many units of the Sun's energy are received by the surface at 45° N latitude, as represented by the **Surface Area Measuring Tool**?

2. Now, position the slice centered near 45° S. Count the number of units of energy reaching the tool along the Earth's surface. This represents the same land surface area as in the Northern Hemisphere.

3. Draw the following table in your notebook. Record the number of units of light that "hit" the tool, centered at each latitude.

Latitude	Number of Units
30° N	
0°	
30° S	

4. Why does the amount of energy received vary for different places on Earth?

5. Latitudes in Florida range from about 25° to 30° N. Why would seasonal differences in Florida be less pronounced than in New York, where latitudes range from about 40° to 45° N?

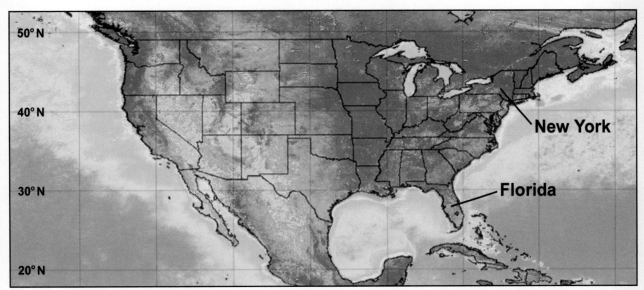

FIGURE 8.13. Map showing New York and Florida.

FIGURE 8.14. Niagara Falls, New York, during winter. New York receives far less of the Sun's radiation at this time of year. This results in frozen waters (and striking photographs).

Explain

Part 1: Differential Heating

During the Rays activity, you successfully compared the amounts of solar energy reaching the Earth at different latitudes. This demonstrated that different latitudes receive different amounts of solar radiation. The Sun's energy entering Earth's atmosphere is incoming solar radiation, or **insolation**. The angle at which the Sun's rays reach the Earth is the **angle of insolation**. As you determined, all places on Earth do not receive the same amount of energy from the Sun at all times of the year, a phenomenon known as **differential heating**.

The following data set, derived by sensors on a satellite, displays the average solar radiation that the *surface* of the Earth receives over the course of a year. Notice the color bar. These values indicate the amount of radiation, measured in watts per meter squared. Watts per meter squared may be explained as the amount of energy, measured in watts, received within an area of one square meter. Recall that the amount of energy output of a light bulb is measured in watts.

Red represents the greater amounts and green represents the lesser amounts of solar radiation.

Net Surface Solar Radiation

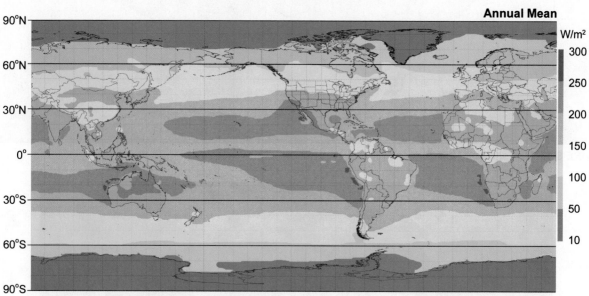

FIGURE 8.15. Display illustrates the net surface (positive) amounts of solar radiation in watts per meter squared. The image approximates the amount of energy that ultimately reaches the surface after considering the radiation reflected back to Space, effects of clouds, etc. Differences across Earth are evident.

3. What do you observe in this image?

4. Compare the solar radiation received in the Tropics to that of Earth's Polar Regions. Explain the difference.

5. Explain why two places on Earth in opposite hemispheres have a similar average amount of absorbed solar radiation.

The following animation demonstrates how the amount of solar radiation absorbed at different latitudes changes over a 12-month period.

See Page 694 for how to access e-Tools.

View the *Global Net Solar Radiation Animation* (0:10) from the e-Tools.

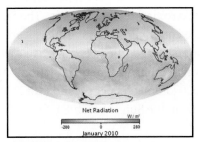

e-Tools

FIGURE 8.16. Screenshot of the *Global Net Solar Radiation Animation*.

Differential heating is responsible for the weather and climate patterns on Earth. Solar radiation is absorbed by clouds, water, and land by and at Earth's surface. Most of the energy reaching the Earth's surface is absorbed by the ocean. The ocean loses heat through evaporation. The energy is transferred to air molecules close to the surface. When excited by heat, air molecules move, resulting in wind and weather conditions. We will explore these concepts as they relate to weather and climate in future *Marine Science: The Dynamic Ocean* Lessons. Now we will take a closer look at how solar radiation reaches the Earth and what happens to it at the Earth's surface.

FIGURE 8.17. Earth's weather and climate patterns are caused by differential heating. Wind is one way that heat energy in the Earth system is redistributed.

Part 2: Solar Radiation

Solar radiation is a general term for the many different types of energy emitted by the Sun in the form of waves, also called **electromagnetic radiation**. The Sun's radiation travels to Earth through Space in the form of waves. These continuous waves of energy are generated by the Sun, from deep within it where high-energy, thermonuclear reactions continue to fuel the process. Energy is emitted or released from the surface of the Sun as electromagnetic radiation. All electromagnetic radiation travels to Earth at the speed of light, 300,000 kilometers per second (186,000 miles per second). That means it takes only about 8 minutes for energy from the Sun to reach Earth.

The **electromagnetic spectrum** represents the range of energy types in the universe. The spectrum can be divided into seven different types. The spectrum is a continuum, which means differently named types of energy have slightly different properties. The various types of energy can be thought about using a scale, from higher energy sources or types to lower. The spectrum includes, from highest to lowest energy types: gamma rays, X-rays, ultraviolet light, visible light, infrared waves, microwaves, and radio waves. The wavelength of each type of electromagnetic radiation is measured as the distance one complete wave travels. The shorter the wavelength, the higher the energy type.

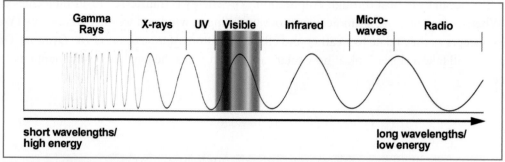

FIGURE 8.18. The electromagnetic spectrum is a tool to conceptualize all types of energy. We call the range of energy our retinas sense "visible light". All energy on the spectrum is light energy.

Various technology tools and sensors will sense and examine different portions of the electromagnetic spectrum. These processes help humans to learn about the physical and natural world. Instruments onboard satellites, for example, have sensors to detect energy types. The sensor we are most familiar with is the human eye. The retina of our eye senses energy in a small range of the spectrum; we call this visible light. Slight differences in the wavelengths allow the eye to detect different colors. You can sense heat, which is infrared energy, using your hands. The retina is unable to observe heat energy. Scientists use satellites with unique orbits and special telescopes to observe the various types of radiation that come from the Sun.

See Page 694 for how to access e-Tools.

View the *Electromagnetic Spectrum Tool* from the e-Tools.

Click on each type of radiation in the tool for an example of each as they appear to us on Earth. Copy the chart on the next page. Use the information in the tool to complete the chart.

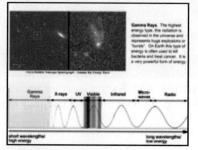

e-Tools

FIGURE 8.19. Screenshot of the *Electromagnetic Spectrum Tool*.

Type of Electromagnetic Radiation	Types of Electromagnetic Radiation in Order from Shortest (1) to Longest (7) Wavelength	Natural Sources and Interactions with Earth's Atmosphere	Human Uses and Sources
Gamma Rays			
Infrared			
Microwaves			
Radio			
UV			
Visible			
X-rays			

Electromagnetic radiation is necessary for life on Earth, providing visible light energy for photosynthetic organisms in the ocean, plants on land, and other organisms that drive Earth's food webs. However, too much of the Sun's radiation can be harmful to life. Earth's atmosphere protects the Earth's surface from much of the solar incoming radiation.

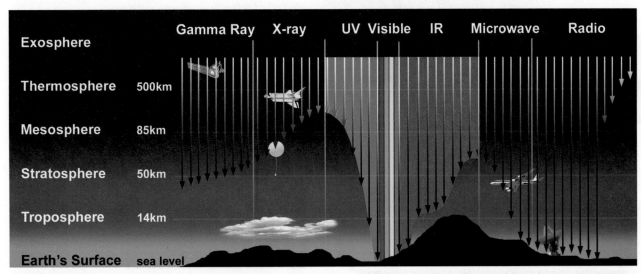

FIGURE 8.20. Solar energy reaching various levels of the Earth's atmosphere and including Earth's surface is displayed in a view of the electromagnetic spectrum.

Earth's protective atmosphere consists of 78% nitrogen, 21% oxygen, 1% argon, and trace gases such as water vapor, ozone, and carbon dioxide. These gases are distributed among four distinct layers. The layers have various compositions, temperatures, and densities. The layers are responsible for substantially absorbing and reflecting radiative energies from the Sun.

Each layer of the atmosphere helps protect Earth's surface by absorbing or reflecting incoming solar radiation. What about solar radiation that reaches the Earth's surface? Different surfaces and materials have varying capacities to absorb or reflect solar radiation. Think about the following: Have you ever tried to walk barefoot across hot dark pavement in the summer? Why do you need to wear sunglasses or tinted goggles on a ski slope? Pavement and snow are two surfaces with different abilities to absorb and reflect radiation. Scientists quantify or measure the reflectivity of different surfaces on Earth. This measure is called **albedo**.

FIGURE 8.21. Not all of Earth's surfaces reflect light in the same quantity. Light colored surfaces, such as sea ice covering the ocean in Earth's Polar Regions, reflect a higher percentage of light energy. Dark surfaces, including ocean water and pavement, are efficient at absorbing light energy.

FIGURE 8.22. Tinted ski goggles filter light off of reflective surfaces such as snow and ice, making the field of view appear less bright.

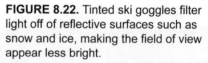

See Page 694 for how to access e-Tools.

View the *Light Absorption and Reflection Animation* (0:15) from the e-Tools.

e-Tools

FIGURE 8.23. Screenshot of the *Light Absorption and Reflection Animation*.

6. Which surface has a higher albedo: frozen water or liquid water? Which would absorb more radiation?

As you know, about 70% of Earth's surface is covered by ocean. The ocean plays an important role in absorbing solar energy on the planet. The top several meters of the ocean is the largest absorber of solar radiation on Earth. Review the *Net Surface Solar Radiation* data on Page 152. Notice that the greatest net amount of radiation is absorbed by the ocean in the Tropics. When land, water, and air molecules absorb light energy, the energy is converted into heat, or infrared energy. The wavelength changes as the energy moves from air to land. As you noted with the *Electromagnetic Spectrum Tool*, infrared radiation has a longer wavelength than visible or UV light. Energy in the ocean is redistributed around the globe, a process you will learn more about in Lesson 9: The Sea Surface: The Great Energy Distributor.

The data below show the global albedo for March 2000.

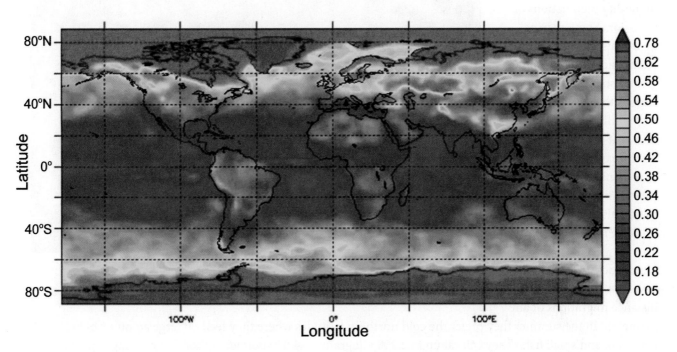

FIGURE 8.24. Albedo reflectivities display a range of values during March, the month of the Vernal Equinox. Red and yellow areas indicate high albedo, whereas blue and purple areas are good absorbers of solar radiation, or light energy.

In order for Earth to maintain a stable climate, the amount of the Sun's energy that is absorbed by the ocean, land, and other materials on Earth must be balanced by the amount of outgoing radiation from Earth back into Space. What about some of the energy that is emitted by the ocean or land? More heat energy is absorbed as water changes from a liquid to a gas, the process known as **evaporation**. This occurs in the water cycle. Energy is also transferred back to the atmosphere from land as air molecules closest to the land are warmed by energy radiated from the Earth's surface. Warm air rises away from the surface of Earth. Some is absorbed by the atmosphere.

7.   Which latitudes on Earth show the highest albedo? The lowest albedo? Why?

8.   Compare the albedo data with the Net Surface Solar Radiation from **Explore** Part 2. Do they support or refute one another?

Elaborate

Marine Mammals' Responses to Seasonal Change

Marine mammals are acutely in tune with their environment. They use cues such as changing seasons to indicate when to modify their actions or behavior. Some marine mammals, such as the Humpback Whale, migrate great distances. Others, such as the Harbor Seal, stay within a general area year round. Let's briefly explore the effect of seasonal changes on two species of marine mammals, using satellite tracking data.

FIGURE 8.25. Humpback Whales travel thousands of miles on their seasonal migrations. They birth their calves in warm waters, and travel to the polar seas in summer.

Humpback Whales have one of the longest distance migrations of any mammal. In the summer they prefer the cold northern latitudes where they feed on large amounts of krill, plankton, and small fish. They can eat up to 2,200 kilograms (~4,850 pounds) of food in one day. The food they consume in the summer helps build up a fat supply that they rely on in the winter. During the winter months, Humpbacks live in the warm shallow waters close to the Equator. This is where Humpback calves are born and raised.

FIGURE 8.26. Krill, small shrimp-like organisms, are an important food source for Humpback Whales and are abundant in polar seas.

Humpback Whales live in several oceanic regions. The map on the following page shows a track of an individual whale that migrates from the Dominican Republic in the Caribbean to off the coast of Nova Scotia.

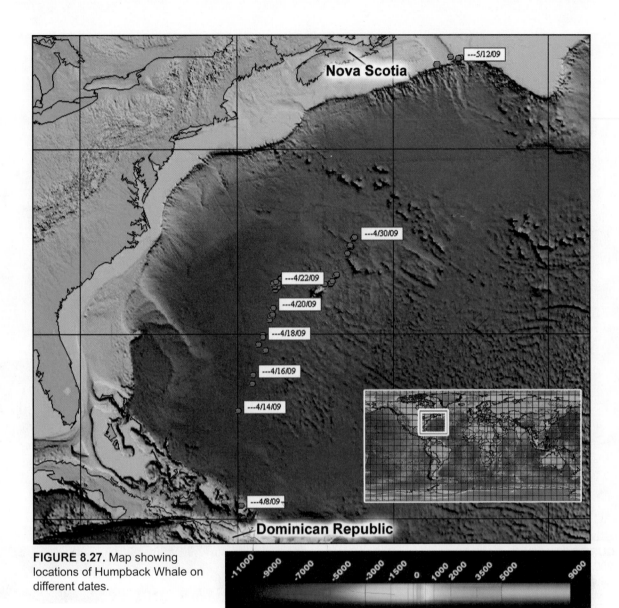

FIGURE 8.27. Map showing locations of Humpback Whale on different dates.

9. How long did it take for the whale to migrate north from the Dominican Republic to Nova Scotia?

10. Describe the changes in solar radiation that occur in these areas during this time period.

FIGURE 8.28. Harbor Seal rests on the beach. Many species of seals and sea lions use sandy and rocky shorelines for resting, mating, and birthing their pups.

Harbor Seals are the most common species of seal found along the East Coast of the United States. They are non-migratory, living year round in the reefs and along the beaches where they hunt for fish and crustaceans. The Harbor Seals indicated on the map in FIGURE 8.29 live on the continental shelf off the U.S. East Coast. The individual seal represented by the red markers stays off the coast of New England all year long. The seal shown with black markers remains off the coast of New Jersey. Harbor Seals begin pupping, or giving birth to young seals, from March to as late as June. Scientists infer that the exact timing of pup arrival depends on the latitude where the seal lives.

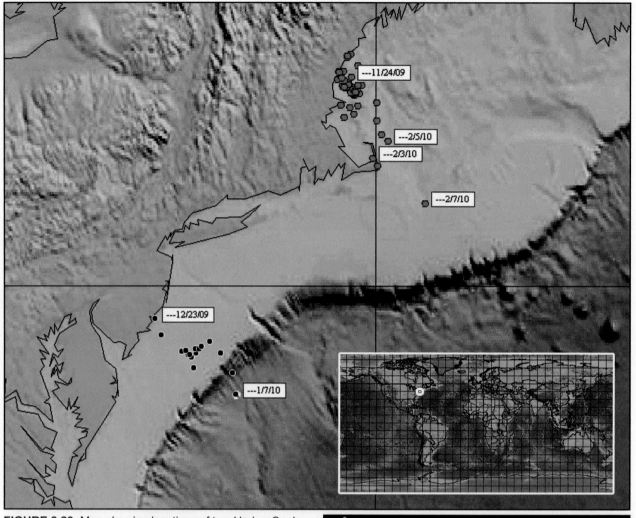

FIGURE 8.29. Map showing locations of two Harbor Seals in 2009 and 2010. The data indicate that the animals spent most of their time on the continental shelf.

11. Based on your knowledge of seasons, why do you think latitude has an impact on the time of the year when Harbor Seals have their pups?

12. If it is true that Harbor Seals use longer days and warmer temperatures as cues to begin pupping, which seal would have its pups first?

13. How might the following ecosystems be affected by seasonal change? Explain your answers in terms of changes in insolation.
    a. The Polar Seas
    b. Coral Reefs
    c. Kelp Forests

Evaluate

FIGURE 8.30. Sun's rays heading toward Earth.

1. Complete the following using a copy of the diagram of the Earth.

   a. Draw the Sun's rays hitting the Earth at 1) the Equator, 2) Florida, 3) Greenland, and 4) a location in South America.

   b. Label each location. Considering that the Sun's rays are reaching the Earth, describe how the angle of the Sun's rays differs at each location.

   c. Label the Northern and Southern Hemispheres, Tropics of Cancer and Capricorn and indicate the season.

2. Match the type of electromagnetic radiation with the appropriate description:

Infrared	A. Longest wavelength
Radio waves	B. The spectrum seen by human eyes
Gamma rays	C. Radiation blocked by ozone layer in the stratosphere
Visible light	D. Used to treat cancer
Ultraviolet radiation	E. Reradiates energy from Earth back into Space

3. Give an example of a surface on Earth that has a high albedo and one that has a low albedo. Explain why each example is considered high or low albedo.

4. Describe an example of how seasonal changes affect a type of marine organism.

9

The Sea Surface: The Great Energy Distributor

INSIDE:

Objectives

You will be able to:

✔ Indicate that energy in the ocean is distributed through currents.

✔ Identify sea surface temperature (SST) and ocean currents from satellite imagery.

✔ Explain how Earth's ocean basins are interconnected through the flow of currents.

✔ Define terms including *current*, *gyre*, and *Coriolis Effect*.

✔ Relate changes in SSTs to changes in animal movements.

Benchmarks

1c. Throughout the ocean there is one interconnected circulation system powered by wind, tides, the force of the Earth's rotation (i.e., Coriolis Effect), the Sun, and water density differences. The shape of ocean basins and adjacent land masses influence the path of circulation.

3f. The ocean has had, and will continue to have, a significant influence on climate change by absorbing, storing, and moving heat, carbon, and water.

7d. New technologies, sensors, and tools are expanding our ability to explore the ocean. Ocean scientists are relying more and more on satellites, drifters, buoys, subsea observatories, and unmanned submersibles.

7e. Use of mathematical models is now an essential part of ocean sciences. Models help us understand the complexity of the ocean and of its interaction with Earth's climate. They process observations and help describe the interactions among systems.

Engage

Investigating Distribution of Energy in the Ocean

In the last Lesson, we discussed Earth's seasons and how they affect broad and local environments and marine organisms. Earth's major source of energy is the Sun. The Sun's energy reaches the Earth, where it enters the atmosphere and is absorbed by Earth materials, including air, land, and the ocean. In fact, much of the solar radiation that enters Earth's atmosphere is absorbed by the top layers of the ocean.

This Lesson will give you the opportunity to explore patterns of energy in the ocean, and how that energy is transferred.

It used to be that the only way to measure temperature in the ocean was directly using a thermometer. Because the ocean is so immense, it was very difficult to learn about patterns of temperature across such a huge area.

Satellites, however, carry instruments onboard that can now detect the temperature of the ocean's surface. Instruments measure the infrared energy or microwaves emitted from the sea surface. The energy measurement provides the temperature of the very top layer of water. This measurement is known as the **sea surface temperature**, or **SST**. Global SSTs are recorded every day.

Once a remote sensing satellite makes its measurement, a computer can assign a color to each temperature. The computer then creates a complete image that can be examined. The following activity will simulate how these types of images are created.

FIGURE 9.1. Global SSTs are recorded every day from instruments onboard polar orbiting satellites. Often the imagery presented for analysis is a mean composite (a combination of other images collected over time) where data values are averaged and given false color.

Activity

SST Maps

Materials:

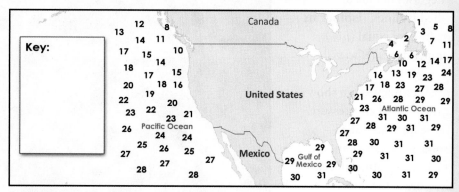

FIGURE 9.2. Map of SSTs indicating SST in °C.

- *SSTs Map*
- Crayons or markers

1. Your teacher will give you a map of sea surface temperatures (SSTs) similar to the one above. Shade all of the SSTs that are in the 30s as one color. Shade the 20s another color, 10s, and so on. Create a key with your colors.

2. Make at least two observations about the map you have created.

3. Now draw lines that separate each color. These lines now correspond with 10 °, 20 °, and 30 °C. The "10-50 Rule" is a simple way to derive a quick temperature conversion table between degrees Celsius and degrees Fahrenheit.

   a. Recall that 10 °C = 50 °F.
   b. Recall conversion formulas that have a varied 5/9 or 9/5 factor.
   c. ADD 5 ° to the 10 °C. ADD 9 ° to the 50 °F, which means 15 °C = 59 °F.
   d. ADD to each again and again—or subtract the 5 ° and 9 ° from each—to derive a simple table:

Celsius	Fahrenheit
...	...
...	...
0	32
5	41
10	50
15	59
20	68
25	77
30	86
...	...
...	...

The Sea Surface: The Great Energy Distributor **165**

Lines that separate the categories of data are called **isolines**. **Isotherms** are lines of equal (*iso-*) temperatures (*-therms*).

Weather maps often show lines of equal air pressure. These lines are called **isobars**. At any point on the line, the atmospheric pressure is the same.

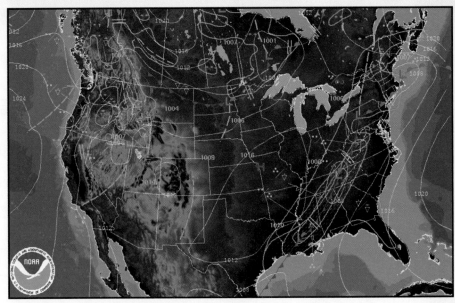

FIGURE 9.3. Isobars are lines of equal pressure. A barometer placed at any location on the line shows the same pressure reading on a barometer.

4. Using your constructed map that now shows isotherms, compare the temperature patterns off the East and West Coasts of the United States.

The image below is a false color satellite image. Each of the colors represents a specific temperature range, similar to what you did with the map you were coloring. By convention, higher temperatures are shown in reds and oranges, while lower temperatures are indicated by blues and purples.

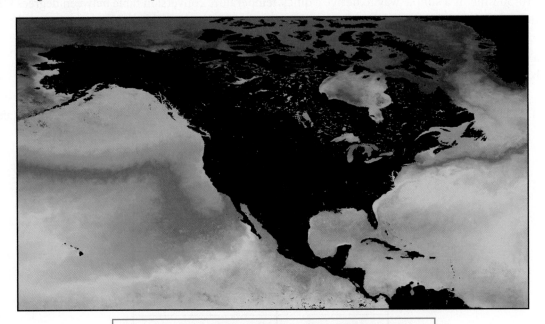

Sea Surface Temperature (°C)

-2 0 2 4 6 8 10 12 14 16 18 20 22 24 26 28 30 32 34 36 38 40 42 44

FIGURE 9.4. A false color satellite image gives meaning to scientific data.

SST measurements are averaged over time to create images such as this one. On the *Marine Science: The Dynamic Ocean* website, you can view SST maps that show weekly or monthly means of SST.

Use the color bar to help interpret the image and understand the temperatures at different places for the specific date on the map.

5. How does this map compare with the one you created?

6. Describe the locations of the warmest and coldest SSTs in this image.

7. Compare the SSTs off of the West and East Coasts of the United States.

8. What do you notice about the warm water along and off the East Coast?

Oh, Buoy!

The image that you have been interpreting is a false color image. It was generated from data collected by microwave energy sensors from an instrument called a **radiometer** flying in Space onboard a satellite. Another tool that scientists use to study physical characteristics of the ocean is a floating device called a **buoy**. There are many different types of buoys. Some indicate the presence of a lobster pot; others help boaters to navigate through channels.

Scientific buoys are anchored all over the world and collect many types of oceanic and atmospheric data, including air and sea temperatures, wave height, salinity, wind speed, and much more. The map on the next page shows the locations of major scientific buoys around the world in 2010. More buoys are always being added to a network of data collectors. One important role of buoys is to provide in-water data that are compared with satellite data to improve accuracy.

Buoys can give very accurate information for a very specific location, whereas satellites are better for understanding broader patterns of parameters such as sea surface temperature. Scientists and resource managers use satellite and buoy data for many reasons, including to study water quality and climate issues. The information also assists in the design and scope of marine protected areas (MPAs). Both satellite and buoy data are a part of ocean-observing systems (OOSs), which give scientists extensive information about the ocean and its processes.

FIGURE 9.5. In addition to collecting scientific data, buoys are used to indicate the presence of fishing gear on the seafloor. This lobster pot is one such example. The trap sits on the bottom, with a line connecting it to a buoy at the surface. The buoy helps fishers easily find their traps to check for lobsters.

FIGURE 9.6. NOAA scientists deploy a buoy from a research vessel.

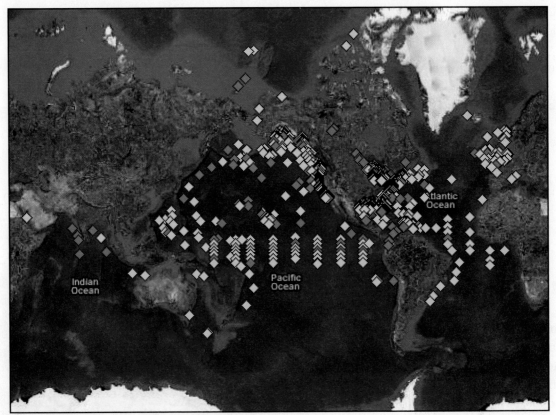

FIGURE 9.7. Scientific buoys are found around the world. Yellow points are recently updated. Red points represent data >8 hours old.

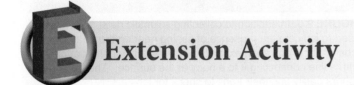

Extension Activity

1. Access the **National Data Buoy Center** from the *Marine Science: The Dynamic Ocean* website.

2. Zoom in to your local area, or the coastline nearest you.

3. Locate the buoy that is nearest to your school. Click on it.

4. You will see many different parameters, including SST, wind speed, air pressure, and so on. Create a data table in which you record (a) the name of your buoy, (b) the buoy's latitude and longitude, and (c) the measurements for three different parameters. If you are not sure what the parameters mean, try using a search engine to find the explanation.

5. Now choose two other buoys in other locations anywhere in the world. Record their names, latitudes, and longitudes. Record the data for the same parameters as in your data table.

6. Are there major differences in your three locations? Why or why not?

7. List at least one question you have about the buoy data you have observed.

Demonstration

Investigating Warm and Cold Water

Your teacher will now present a demonstration using the materials below.

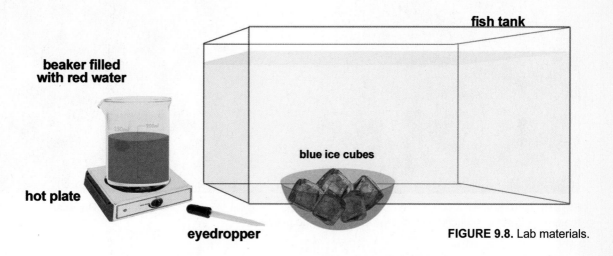

FIGURE 9.8. Lab materials.

1. Draw what is happening in the fish tank. Draw the tank, ice cubes, water, and so on. Use color.

See Page 694 for how to access e-Tools.

View the **Sea Surface Temperature Animation** from the e-Tools. Then answer the Questions that follow.

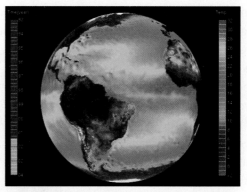

e-Tools

FIGURE 9.9. Screenshot of SST animation.

2. Make at least three observations about this animation.

3. Write at least one question about SSTs that you have, based on this animation and the demonstration using red and blue water.

FIGURE 9.10. Sun shining over the ocean affects SSTs as energy is reflected and absorbed. The ocean is a feature on Earth distributing heat energy throughout the planet.

Explain

In the demonstration, you saw how warm and cold water interact. In the ocean, there are also masses of moving warm and cold water; ocean water is constantly moving. Currents transport heat through the ocean. The large water masses move in a certain direction and at a certain speed. These moving water masses are called **currents**. Currents are sometimes described as warm or cold "rivers" within the ocean. Wind patterns and density differences result in the circulation of water throughout the world's ocean basins. In this Lesson, we are focusing on currents within the top 400 meters (~1,300 feet) or so of the ocean. These currents are called **surface currents**. You will learn more about deep water currents in a later Lesson.

FIGURE 9.11. A Hawaiian Green Sea Turtle soaks up energy from the Sun. Most of the Sun's energy entering Earth's atmosphere is absorbed by the ocean.

Ocean Currents

In liquids and gases, such as the water and air that make up Earth's ocean and atmosphere, energy is transferred through the circulation of heated molecules. Warmer areas transfer energy and become cooler; cooler areas become warmer. This method of energy transfer is called **convection**. As you learned when studying plate tectonics, convection currents are driven by density differences between two materials. When air or water is heated, the molecules gain kinetic energy and move apart; the substance becomes less dense. The less dense fluid will tend to rise.

Cooler air or water is more dense; the molecules have less energy. More dense fluids sink until they reach a layer of the same density. The fluid moves in the direction of equilibrium, at which point layers will appear. It is these density differences that begin to drive convection.

Surface currents are like seasons in that they are caused in part by the unequal heating of the Earth and Earth's tilt at different times of year. Due to the curvature of the Earth, there is more energy in areas of the ocean closer to the Equator than nearer the Poles. Currents are a mechanism for distributing some of that energy. Because of the Earth's rotation, and in line with Earth's prevailing winds, massive amounts of warmer water inch northward and southward, away from the Equator. Warm water currents carry energy from warmer to cooler areas, just as you saw with the red dye in the demonstration. Earth's prevailing winds help to push the top layer of water, resulting in currents.

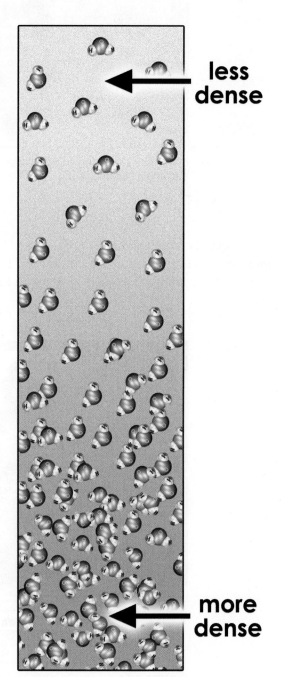

less dense

more dense

FIGURE 9.12. More dense fluids sink until they reach a layer of the same density.

If there were no currents, a SST image might look something like this:

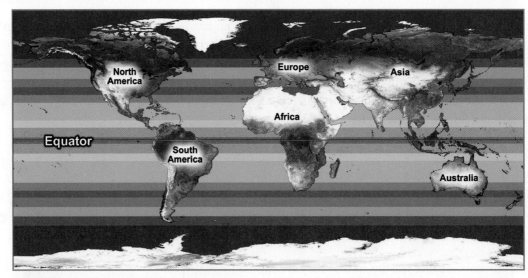

FIGURE 9.13. Portrayed SST image without currents doesn't take into account Earth's rotation, tilt, and effect from the Sun.

Instead, ocean currents carry some of the heat from the warmer waters to the Polar Regions. Colder water from the poles flows back toward the Equator. Refer to this in the diagram on the next page, *Selected Surface Currents Map*. Some of the major currents on Earth are labeled.

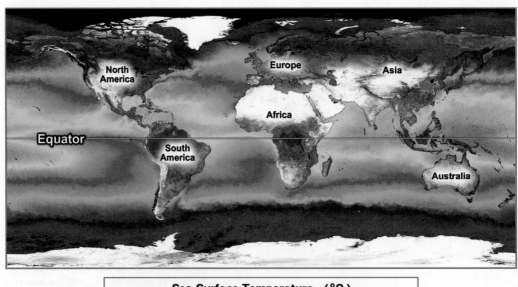

FIGURE 9.14. False color SST image derived from satellites provides scientists with data to analyze. Color representations demonstrate colder waters near Earth's poles.

Selected Surface Currents Map

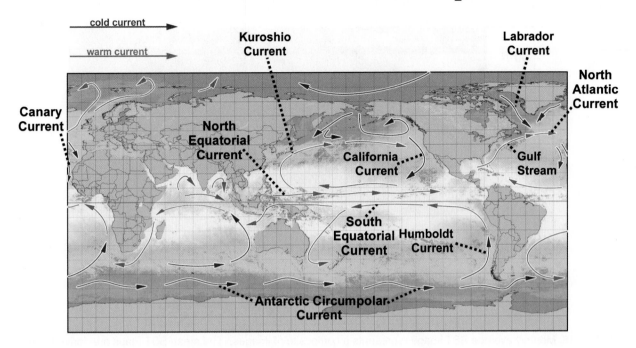

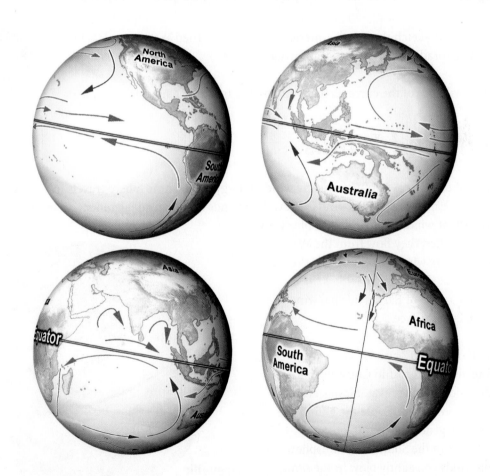

FIGURE 9.15. Selected major ocean currents illustrate the transport of surface waters.

Currents are evident in SST images. They can be seen as areas where cold or warm waters extend into waters of differing temperature.

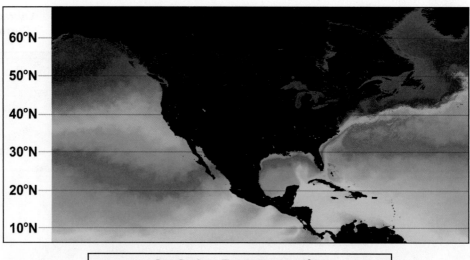

FIGURE 9.16. Monthly average SST image represents a composite of images. The mean SST maps are derived from dozens of images collected during the month. They are often used to compare temperatures from month to month, and year to year.

1. In your notebook, sketch the North American Continent. Then sketch and label the Gulf Stream, Labrador Current, and California Current.

2. Explain the evidence of the currents that you observe in the SST image.

Currents and Winds

In Earth's atmosphere, energy is transferred by wind. Energy in the atmosphere travels in wind currents. On the whole these are called **prevailing winds**. Prevailing winds affect ocean currents. Easterlies and westerlies represent a persistent wind in Earth's troposphere. If the winds are westerlies, they flow from the West to the East. Easterlies are winds that hail from the East.

To the right is a diagram of Earth's normal wind patterns at the Earth's surface.

Compare on FIGURES 9.17 and 9.18 how the warm Gulf Stream and Kuroshio Currents follow the general direction of the prevailing westerlies in the Northern Hemisphere. Note the Humboldt Current follows the general direction of the prevailing easterlies in the Southern Hemisphere. The prevailing winds constantly blow in the same direction, pushing the top layers of ocean water, leading to the formation of surface currents.

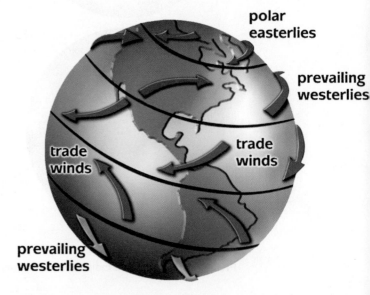

FIGURE 9.17. Earth's prevailing winds.

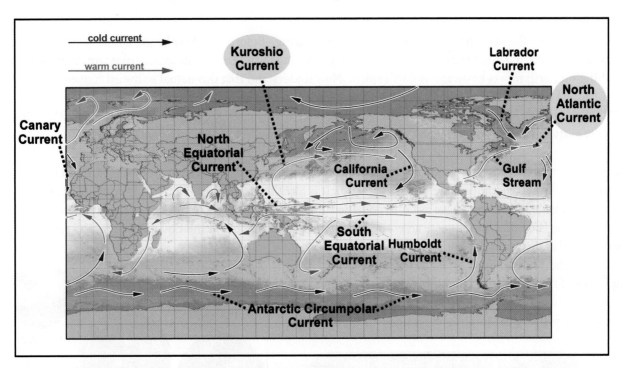

FIGURE 9.18. Selected ocean currents distribute heat across the globe in all directions.

The winds and currents are not completely parallel. Winds and currents are affected by the Earth's rotation. This causes winds and currents to curve. In the Northern Hemisphere winds and currents are pulled toward the right. In the Southern Hemisphere the opposite is true; the flow is toward the left. The farther the distance from the Equator, the greater the pull toward the right or the left. If the Earth did not rotate, fluids on the planet, including air and water, would tend to flow in straight lines. Instead, winds, currents, and even moving objects, such as airplanes and bullets, appear to be deflected to the right in the Northern Hemisphere, and to the left in the Southern Hemisphere.

This effect can be seen in the currents in computer animations of satellite imagery over time. Currents in the Northern Hemisphere will ultimately appear to almost become circular as evidenced in the map on Page 174. This phenomenon, the deflection of a mass moving over Earth's surface due to rotation, is called the **Coriolis Effect**. A "force" is put on the mass of water due to Earth's rotation.

FIGURE 9.19. Airplane flies in a straight line over both a non-rotating and rotating Earth.

To fully support the concept of the Coriolis Effect, "the effect of Earth's rotation on objects", and to realize for sure that winds (or air) or currents (or seawater) are deflected right or left, consider a flying airplane. Pretend the Earth is not rotating, and an airplane is flying north. It will get to its destination. Now pretend the plane is making the same trip north, but the Earth *is* rotating. Before the plane begins to move north, it is already actually moving quickly eastward, since Earth is rotating to the East on its axis…true? Anything and everything on Earth moves eastward as Earth spins. Now understand that this actual eastward movement is greater (faster) at the Equator. A place on Earth at a higher latitude toward the North Pole is literally closer to the actual axis line running through the Earth; anything on Earth farther north than the Equator is not moving as quickly eastward.

Objects on Earth that sit far from the Equator don't have as far to move in Space when rotating around the axis, so those objects will move more slowly eastward. It is like the inside lane of a track. The runner (or object) in an inside lane doesn't have as far to go. The runner doesn't have to run as fast as the runner on the outside lane (Equator) to complete an entire lap. So, when the plane is at the Equator, the Earth's eastern rotation speed at the ground is greater than the rotation speed at the plane's destination. It is the greater eastern component of the plane's movement that causes the plane to veer to the right and miss its destination. It ends up farther east when the plane itself simply goes straight.

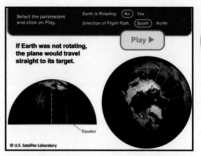

See Page 694 for how to access e-Tools.

View the **Coriolis Effect Animation** from the e-Tools.

FIGURE 9.20. Screenshot of the *Coriolis Effect Animation*.

As warm currents, such as the Gulf Stream in the Atlantic, flow away from the Equator, they eventually hit landmasses. In this example, warm currents hit the European Continent. In fact, landmasses and the shape of ocean basins affect the direction, flow, and speed of ocean currents. For example, on the image below, note that the Gulf Stream roughly follows the shape of the Continental shelf off the East Coast of the United States.

View the **Bathymetry and SST Animation** from the e-Tools.

Use the slider to observe changes over one year.

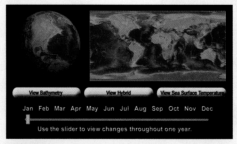

FIGURE 9.21. Screenshot of the *Bathymetry and SST Animation*.

Warm water that leaves the Tropics has to be replaced. Cold water near the poles that moves toward the Equator in the form of cold currents fills that role. The currents, curving because of the wind's push and the shape of continents, result in a loop of currents. The circular nature of the flow is called a **gyre**.

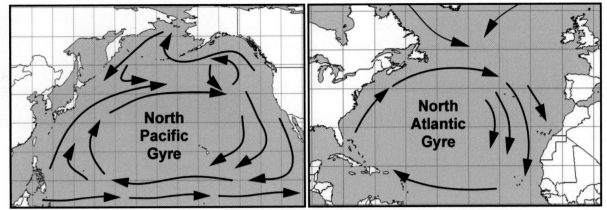

FIGURE 9.22. Loops of currents in ocean basins result in a circular flow of water called a **gyre**.

3. Using the **Selected Surface Currents Map** on Page 173, list the names of the currents that make up the North Atlantic Gyre.

The illustrations we have seen provide general information and help people better understand scientific processes. Think of these as averages of the environmental ocean currents and winds over time. The dynamic Earth is never exactly represented by a drawing. If you want to visualize ocean currents and winds for one particular time, utilize satellite imagery. Studying scientific data, including Earth satellite imagery, helps scientists understand how SSTs are affected by ocean currents and winds.

The two images below are from the same day. The image on the left shows ocean currents' speed and direction. The image on the right indicates the speed and direction for winds above the ocean's surface. Arrows indicate the direction of the water or air flow, whereas the background colors indicate speed.

Note that you can see similar patterns of currents and wind flow in the two maps, illustrating surface currents and winds for a particular day.

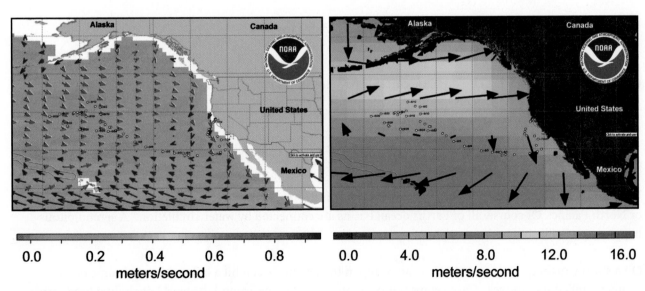

FIGURE 9.23. Ocean surface current image shows eastward (red) and westward (blue) surface water movement.

FIGURE 9.24. Wind speed and directions illustrate air movement over the ocean.

Remember that a Surface Currents Map will show wide-scale, average patterns of moving surface water. If you look more closely at a velocity map of currents for a particular time, you will be able to see more detail about how the water is moving.

Observe the Ocean Currents image below and answer the Questions that follow.

FIGURE 9.25. Seabirds such as the Laysan Albatross rely on wind currents for soaring many miles over the sea.

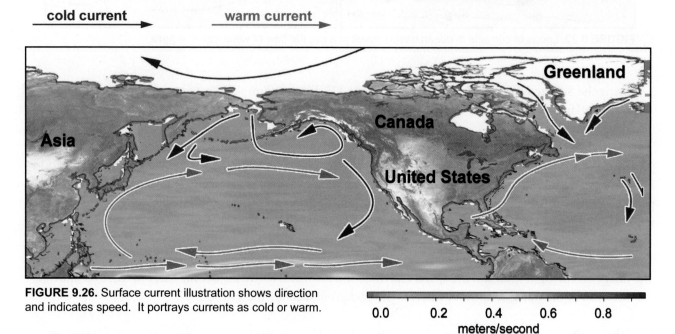

FIGURE 9.26. Surface current illustration shows direction and indicates speed. It portrays currents as cold or warm.

4. In this image, in which area(s) are currents moving the fastest?

5. Using the *Selected Surface Currents Map* on Page 173, list the names of the three fastest moving currents in the image.

6. Other than speed, what else do these currents have in common?

An Accidental Current Study

Until this point, your studies of currents have focused on distinct ocean basins, such as the North Atlantic or North Pacific. Of course, all of Earth's ocean basins are connected by water circulation. A serendipitous happening can illustrate this concept.

On a stormy night in January of 1992, a cargo ship in the Pacific Ocean hit a large wave, and some of its contents spilled into the sea. Cargo ships transport all sorts of items around the world, including food, cars, furniture and, in this case, toys! The ship was carrying toys from China to the United States. The storm resulted in the ship spilling 29,000 plastic ducks, turtles, frogs, and beavers into the sea. These toys have become a source of data for scientists studying surface currents.

Within ten months of the spill, by November of 1992, dozens of these toys washed up on the shores of Sitka, Alaska, having traveled about 3,500 kilometers (~2,100 miles). The toy company name was still legible, although the bright colors had begun to fade. In total, about 400 of the toys were found in the Sitka area.

By 1995, plastic ducks and turtles from the same spill were found in Hawaii and Japan, and others were reported in the Bering Sea. In 2000, ducks were found on the East Coast of the United States, in Maine and Massachusetts. Fifteen years after the original spill, in 2007, toys began to arrive on the beaches of England.

7. Your teacher will give you a map similar to the one below. Sketch the possible paths taken by the toys and where in the Pacific they could have been released, taking surface currents into account.

8. Complex interactions between the ocean currents, winds, sea ice, and landforms can lead to some surprises. Describe specifically how the lost toys could have made it all the way to England.

9. Could these toys take a journey around the world? Why or why not?

FIGURE 9.27. Cargo ships travel on the ocean and can sometimes experience accidents in which cargo is lost.

FIGURE 9.28. Cargo Ships are used to transport goods all over the world. This photograph shows cargo containers being transferred to a truck in Antarctica.

FIGURE 9.29. Toys spilled into the Pacific Ocean and later traveled to some faraway places.

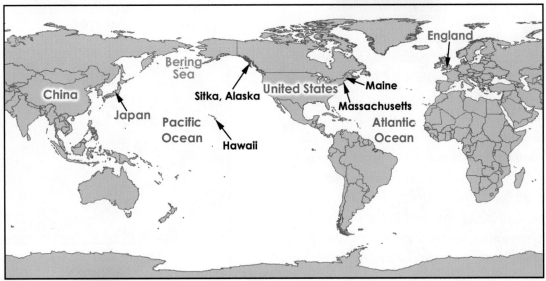

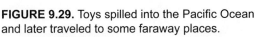

The Gulf Stream

The Gulf Stream, which originates in the Caribbean Sea and extends into the North Atlantic Ocean, is one of the most highly studied surface ocean currents. Benjamin Franklin, in the 1770s, was one of the first scientists to study the Gulf Stream, although explorers and fishers had known about its existence for centuries. The current flows northward along Florida's Atlantic Coast, and then makes an eastward turn off of North Carolina and begins to flow northeast, traveling across the ocean. In the middle of the ocean, the flow slows down and becomes the North Atlantic Current, carrying energy across to Europe.

In a 1785 letter to a fellow scientist, Benjamin Franklin wrote:

> This stream is probably generated by the great accumulation of water on the eastern coast of America between the tropics, by the trade winds which constantly blow there. It is known that a large piece of water ten miles broad and generally only three feet deep, has by a strong wind had its waters driven to one side and sustained so as to become six feet deep, while the windward side was laid dry. This may give some idea of the quantity heaped up on the American coast, and the reason of its running down in a strong current through the islands into the Bay of Mexico, and from thence issuing through the gulph [gulf] of Florida, and proceeding along the coast to the banks of Newfoundland, where it turns off towards and runs down through the western islands.

Although formed without the benefit of satellites and other marine technologies, Franklin's hypotheses about the current were quite accurate. His ideas were later supported by much scientific evidence. Scientists have determined that the Gulf Stream transports more than one billion cubic feet of water per second, an amount 1,800 times that of the Mississippi River. The average speed of the Gulf Stream is about 4 knots, or 4.6 miles per hour. Flow is fastest in the fall and slowest in the spring.

FIGURE 9.30. The Gulf Stream, as drawn by Benjamin Franklin (circa 1785).

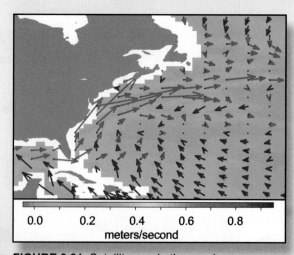

FIGURE 9.31. Satellites and other marine technologies allow scientists to learn more about currents such as the Gulf Stream. This image shows ocean current velocities.

Elaborate

The ocean stores an incredible amount of energy. In fact, there is as much energy stored in the top layer of the ocean (two to three meters) as the Earth's atmosphere. If the ocean did not store energy, people could not live on Earth; the planet would not be habitable. Ocean currents and winds transport energy around the Earth. The alternative would be that all of the energy from the Sun would stay in the Tropics, and the Polar Regions would be even colder.

Satellite imagery informs scientists how this energy is distributed in the ocean and helps us to monitor winds and currents. These environmental factors may help to explain the movements of marine animals.

FIGURE 9.32. The ocean stores a tremendous amount of energy, carrying it from the Equatorial to the Polar Regions.

The Sea Surface and Marine Animals

Sea surface temperatures and currents influence the movements of marine animals. For some animals, warming temperatures in the spring and cooling temperatures in the fall can signal a time to migrate. For example, as you saw in Lesson 5: Migrations in the Sea, Humpback Whales in the Atlantic migrate each winter and have their calves near the Dominican Republic. When water temperatures warm in the spring in the Northern Hemisphere, these whales begin their long journey northward to Canadian waters.

See Page 694 for how to access e-Tools.

View the **Marine Animals and SST Animation** from the e-Tools.

e-Tools

Observe the movement of the animals as sea surface temperatures change.

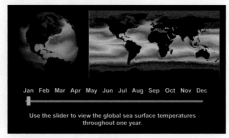

FIGURE 9.33. Screenshot of the **Marine Animals and SST Animation**.

Some animals take advantage of the fast currents on the ocean's surface. Sometimes sea turtles or other animals follow a current's path during their journeys. Look at this example of Jazz, the Loggerhead Sea Turtle's, movements.

FIGURE 9.34. Loggerhead Sea Turtles are one sea turtle species common in United States waters. Their diet consists primarily of invertebrate animals, including sponges and crabs.

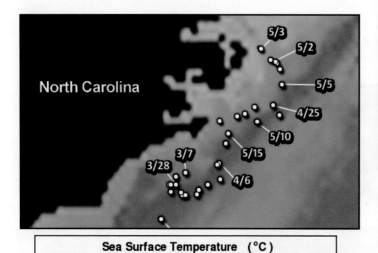

FIGURE 9.35. Jazz, the Loggerhead Sea Turtle, locations on a given SST map.

Loggerhead Sea Turtles such as Jazz can live within all of these temperature ranges—they do not require the warmer waters to survive. It is possible that the fast current gave Jazz a needed boost on her northward journey. You can use an image of "ocean current velocities" to gather evidence to support or refute that hypothesis.

It is also notable that Jazz spends a lot of time on the edge of the current. The boundary between water masses, in this case the coastal waters and the Gulf Stream, is called a front. In meteorology, a front is a boundary between air masses. In the ocean, fronts are often places where food collects—this might explain why Jazz stays near the current's edge.

Perhaps there are other factors that drive marine animal movements that we can learn about. Stay tuned: there is a lot more that the ocean provides for marine animals so they can thrive and maintain their life functions.

FIGURE 9.36. Studying the movements of sea turtles has taught scientists a lot about the behavior of these reptiles.

Evaluate

1. What are surface ocean currents? Explain how they contribute to the redistribution of heat on Earth.

2. Sketch the image below in your notebook and label the following:
   a. The area of highest SST
   b. The area of lowest SST
   c. A cold current
   d. A warm current

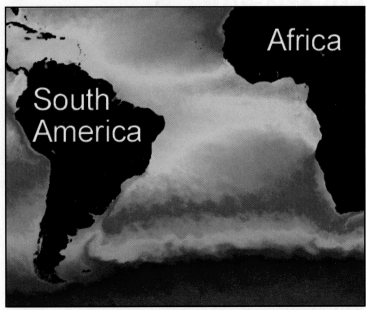

FIGURE 9.37. SST monthly mean image of the South Atlantic Ocean.

3. Describe what is meant by the Coriolis Effect. How does it relate to ocean currents?

4. Explain how heat from the Sun results in convection currents in the ocean.

5. Describe the relationship between wind and surface currents.

10

Energy and the Ocean

INSIDE:

Objectives

You will be able to:

✔ Explain the concept of heat capacity and the role of the ocean in moderating Earth's climate.

✔ Differentiate between open, closed, and isolated systems.

✔ Demonstrate the Law of Conservation of Energy in various scenarios of energy transformation.

Benchmarks

3f. The ocean has had, and will continue to have, a significant influence on climate change by absorbing, storing, and moving heat, carbon, and water.

7c. Over the last 40 years, use of ocean resources has increased significantly, therefore the future sustainability of ocean resources depends on our understanding of those resources and their potential and limitations.

7d. New technologies, sensors, and tools are expanding our ability to explore the ocean. Ocean scientists are relying more and more on satellites, drifters, buoys, subsea observatories, and unmanned submersibles.

7e. Use of mathematical models is now an essential part of ocean sciences. Models help us understand the complexity of the ocean and of its interaction with Earth's climate. They process observations and help describe the interactions among systems.

Engage

Imagine that you attend summer camp in New Jersey and the camp director decides to have an "end of summer" Labor Day party at the beach before everyone returns to school. The weather has been hot in New Jersey all summer, but when September begins it starts to feel a bit like fall. You and your friends are excited for good food, beach volleyball, and swimming in the ocean to celebrate the end of camp.

The day arrives and the weather is comfortable with a cool breeze blowing along the shore. The fresh wind makes you wonder if you might skip swimming and stick with just volleyball and soccer. It is a beautiful day with an air temperature of 20 °C (68 °F).

FIGURE 10.1. In areas of the Northeastern U.S. such as Fire Island, New York, the fall generally brings cooler temperatures.

After a long game of volleyball, you and your friends decide to brave the water. You run toward the waves and brace for the cold. You hop over the shallow breaking waves and dive in, expecting to come up shivering and running back to the beach for your warm sweatshirt. You are surprised to find that the temperature of the water is warmer than the air. The ocean feels like a giant bathtub and you and your friends decide to spend the rest of your time at the party playing in the waves.

Explore

Part 1: Human Thermometer Simulation

Thermometers are a common tool used to measure temperature. A doctor uses a thermometer to measure the temperature of someone's body when they feel ill. Meteorologists measure the temperature of the air and water to study the atmosphere and make predictions about weather. Car engines have thermometers connected to a dial in the dashboard that tells the driver when the engine is overheating. Scientists use sensors on satellites in Space to measure the temperature of Earth's surface and the different layers of the atmosphere. Instruments onboard satellites, as well as on stationary and drifting buoys, are used to assess temperatures of the sea surface. Other tools are used to measure temperatures at depth. Day-to-day conversations usually include a discussion of temperature, but what exactly is temperature?

FIGURE 10.2. When you've had your temperature taken, have you ever thought about what temperature actually is, or how the thermometer works?

Matter, which includes everything around you including air, is made up of atoms and groups of atoms or molecules. When atoms and molecules absorb energy from the Sun or another energy source, they move around, bumping into each other, and vibrate, exchanging energy with other matter. The vibration and movement of particles is **thermal energy**. All matter has thermal energy in varying quantities. In matter that is cold, molecules move slowly. Matter with no thermal energy has reached absolute zero, -273.15 °C (~ -459.67 °F), or 0 °Kelvin. **Temperature** is a measure of the average movement of all the atoms, molecules, or ions in the substance being measured. A thermometer is a tool that quantifies temperature on a calibrated scale.

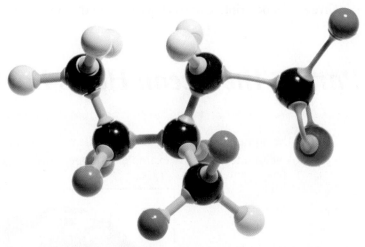

FIGURE 10.3. Atoms and molecules are constantly vibrating or moving due to thermal energy.

 # Demonstration

In the following activity, you and your classmates will behave as molecules to demonstrate how a thermometer works. Imagine the classroom is a beaker. In the beaker there is water and a thermometer. You will demonstrate what happens to the water at room temperature and after the water has been heated.

FIGURE 10.4. This classroom demonstration will model water inside a beaker, with a thermometer measuring its temperature.

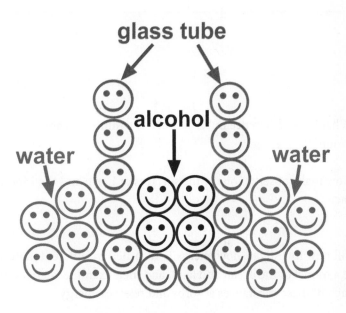

FIGURE 10.5. Demonstration setup.

1. Give a brief description of what occurred in the Human Thermometer Demonstration.

Part 2: The Ocean Helps Earth Support Life

Earth is the home to an amazing variety of life partly because our planet's temperatures are very stable. Let's look at an interplanetary example of temperature ranges.

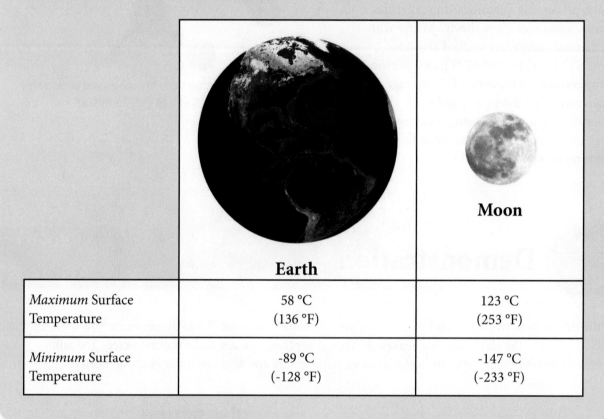

	Earth	Moon
Maximum Surface Temperature	58 °C (136 °F)	123 °C (253 °F)
Minimum Surface Temperature	-89 °C (-128 °F)	-147 °C (-233 °F)

2. What is the difference in °C between the minimum and maximum surface temperatures on Earth? On the Moon?

3. Now make observations of the surfaces of Earth and the Moon. What do you observe when you look at each?

We will now investigate how energy is absorbed by different materials. In this investigation, your group will create a model of the ocean and land, and then examine changes in temperature. Your task is to compare how fast each of these substances absorbs and releases energy.

Lab

Materials:

- Two pie pans
- Water
- Sand
- Two thermometers
- Incandescent light source

Procedure:

Make sure you read and follow the directions carefully as a group. Your teacher **must** approve your procedure before you begin setting up the experiment.

1. One pie pan will represent the ocean. One will represent land.

   a. Discuss with your group how you will examine changes in temperature of the ocean and land with the provided materials.

   b. Draw your proposed setup representing the ocean and land. Label the illustrations.

2. The purpose of the experiment is to investigate temperature changes of the modeled ocean and land.

FIGURE 10.6. Lab materials.

   a. Discuss with your group how you can use the provided materials to observe temperature changes.

   b. Describe how you will conduct the experiment to compare temperatures of the model land and water.

   c. Draw how you will set up your experiment.

3. Now it is time to create a procedure for the experiment.

   a. Discuss with the group exactly how you will conduct your experiment.

   b. Write the exact steps of your group's procedure below. Hint: Your procedure should be so clear that another group could follow it without asking you any questions.

4. Your group will record data using a table like the one below in your notebook. Make sure to label the data clearly. Your data table will need to extend to 20–30 minutes.

Time	Pie Plate 1: Land	Pie Plate 2: Ocean
1		
2		
3		
4		
...		

 Show your procedure and data table to your teacher. Do not begin setting up your investigation until your teacher gives his or her approval.

5. Once you are approved, it's time to follow your procedure. Make sure to record data in the data table.

6. After gathering your data, create a double line graph by plotting each set of data on the same graph.

7. Discuss the results of your experiment with your group. Describe your findings in words.

8. Why are the temperature ranges in the model ocean and model land so different?

Explain

Part 1: Heat Capacity of Water

See Page 694 for how to access e-Tools.

View the *Heat Capacity Video* (2:47), in which two scientists discuss a major difference between water and air, using a simple demonstration.

FIGURE 10.7. Screenshot of the *Heat Capacity Video*.

e-Tools

As you observed in the video demonstration, water absorbs a lot of heat. In the land and ocean lab activity, you demonstrated the same concept—water requires a lot of heat to increase its temperature. In fact, the ocean is a major storage place, or **sink**, for heat on Earth. The amount of energy it takes to increase or decrease a unit of temperature of a substance is its **heat capacity**. Water has a high heat capacity. It requires a large input of energy to increase temperature and a large loss of energy to decrease temperature. This property means that water is excellent for storing heat energy. It does not lose heat easily. The ocean plays a central role in Earth's climate and climate changes because it absorbs, stores, and moves heat and water.

The heat capacity of water is one reason that Earth can support life forms, or is a **habitable** planet. Because approximately 71% of the Earth's surface is covered in water, which is very effective for retaining heat, the ocean is able to moderate the planet's temperature changes. This prevents Earth from experiencing extreme temperature fluctuations. The daily fluctuation of the temperature on the Moon is very high compared to Earth because the Moon does not have an ocean or atmosphere.

The image below is a Day and Night Difference Map. Difference maps are created by taking, for a month, the daily mean high temperature and then subtracting the daily mean low temperature, for areas across the globe. Areas shown in dark reds and oranges indicate the greatest differences between high and low temperatures. White areas indicate no change in temperature between day and night.

Difference Map

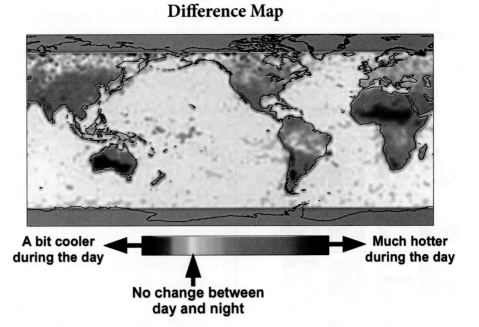

FIGURE 10.8. Differences in average, maximum, and minimum temperatures for January of a specific year. Areas of dark red are much warmer during the day than at night. White areas have little change in observed day and night surface temperatures.

A bit cooler during the day ← → Much hotter during the day

No change between day and night

4. Which surface in the lab activity had a higher heat capacity, the land or the ocean? Explain.

5. Describe the patterns you see on the Difference Map.

6. Note the large, dark areas in Africa and Australia. How can you explain these data?

7. For a given month, differences between the daily high and low temperatures in Nebraska were much greater than the differences observed in Florida. How might you explain observations like this?

8. How does the high heat capacity of water help to explain why the scenario presented in the **Engage** Section (the camp "end of summer" party) occurs?

Part 2: Energy in the Earth system

Have you ever sat down on a metal park bench or slide in the middle of a warm spring day? Were you surprised by how much hotter it was than the air temperature? If so, you got to experience first-hand the ability of metal to absorb energy. The metal of the park bench or slide has a low heat capacity so its temperature rises quickly. Electromagnetic energy from the Sun caused the atoms and molecules that make up the bench to move around more quickly. **Energy** is defined as the ability of an object or a system to do work on another object or system. Work is done on the molecules in the bench as they receive energy and move faster. You demonstrated this concept in the Human Thermometer Simulation.

FIGURE 10.9. A metal slide feels hot on a sunny day because electromagnetic energy from the Sun causes the atoms and molecules that make up the slide to vibrate more quickly.

Thermal energy is one of many forms of energy. You have heard of others: chemical, mechanical, electrical, nuclear, gravitational, sound, and radiant energy. These are all forms of energy we encounter every day.

Energy regularly changes from one form to another through **energy transformations**. For example, radiant or electromagnetic energy is transformed into chemical energy by photosynthesizing plants in the ocean. Chemical energy is transformed into mechanical energy by the engine of a car. Nuclear energy is transformed into electrical energy at nuclear power plants. The examples of energy transformations in the Earth system are endless.

Examples of energy transformations and their uses:

	A television changes electrical energy into sound and light energy.
	A toaster changes electrical energy into thermal and light energy.
	A car changes chemical energy from fuel into thermal energy and mechanical energy.
	A flashlight changes stored chemical energy from batteries into light energy.
	Light energy is converted into electrical energy using solar panels.
	Campfires convert chemical energy stored in wood into thermal energy, which is useful for cooking food and staying warm.
	A person moving a wheelbarrow changes their stored chemical energy to mechanical energy.

When you touch the metal bench, you perceive it as hot because energy is flowing from the bench to your hand. If the bench is at a lower temperature than your hand you would perceive the bench as cold. This flow of energy occurs because of the difference in temperature between the two objects, the bench and your hand. If your hand touches an object that feels cold, this indicates that your hand has a higher temperature than the object does.

The natural and spontaneous flow of energy from an object of higher temperature to one of lower temperature is the **Second Law of Thermodynamics**. This heat transfer will continue until both objects reach the same temperature, which is known as **thermal equilibrium**. Thermal equilibrium is reached when there is no longer a net exchange of energy. Energy may still flow between the objects, but at that point the amount of energy going into an object equals the amount of energy flowing out of the object.

Let's explore the movement or transfer of energy from one part of the universe and Earth system to another. **Thermal energy transfer** occurs in three main ways: conduction, convection, and radiation.

See Page 694 for how to access e-Tools.

View the **Heat Transfer Tool** from the e-Tools.

e-Tools

9. Copy the following chart into your notebook. Use the **Heat Transfer Tool** to describe the methods of energy transfer.

FIGURE 10.10. Screenshot of the **Heat Transfer Tool**.

Method of Transfer	Characteristics
Conduction	
Convection	
Radiation	

The animation showed examples of how energy transfer occurs on Earth. **Conduction** requires the direct contact of two materials for heat exchange. The warm Earth transfers energy to the air molecules above the Earth's surface by way of conduction. Here, air molecules in the lower troposphere are in direct contact with the ground. In the example of a pot on a stove, heat transfer occurs between the metal in the pot directly touching the metal handle. In fact, some cooking pots are designed to reduce the heat transfer between the pot and the handle. Take a look at your pots at home. Are the handles made of a different type of material than the metal pot? Different materials have different abilities to conduct thermal energy. A good conductor of thermal energy transfers energy efficiently, with little energy loss. If something is a poor conductor, it is considered a good insulator and prevents energy from being transferred. Materials that are better insulators may be used to prevent heat transfer, such as the new, modern handles of a pot.

FIGURE 10.11. When you touch a hot pot on the stove, energy is transferred to your hand by conduction. In order for energy exchange to occur by conduction, two materials must be in direct contact with one another.

Heat transfer also occurs by convection, the flow of energy through a liquid or gas. The water in the pot was heated by convection. As warm water at the bottom rises, cooler water takes its place. In the Earth system, air molecules receive energy from the Earth's surface by conduction; the warmed air rises into the atmosphere and cooler air replaces it. This cycle continues as Earth receives radiant, or electromagnetic, energy from the Sun. **Radiation** is the movement of energy through Space, such as light moving from the Sun to Earth. All wavelengths of the electromagnetic spectrum are transferred via radiation.

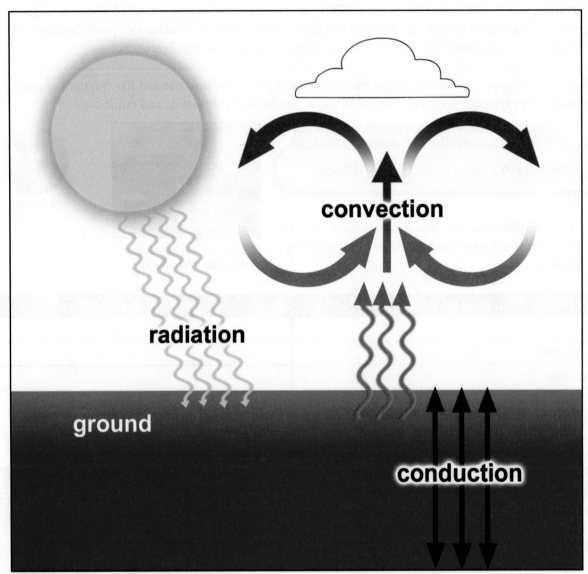

FIGURE 10.12. The Sun's energy is transmitted to Earth through radiation. In a liquid or a gas, energy is transferred by convection. As warm fluids (liquids or gases) rise, cooler fluids (liquids or gases) take their place.

10. Using your knowledge of heat transfer and ocean currents, describe the type of heat transfer that occurs in ocean waters. Use a diagram to communicate your ideas.

Elaborate

Lab

Part 1: Investigating Heat Flow

Scientists measure and predict energy flow to understand how the Earth absorbs, reflects, and distributes energy. Since most energy is invisible, this type of observation often requires special equipment, and scientists must study heat by how it affects matter. Thermal energy is heat. With the materials in this lab you will study the transfer of heat from one substance to another.

Materials:

- Graduated cylinder
- Aluminum transfer bar
- Boiling water
- Two thermometers
- Styrofoam containers
- Lids with slots to fit Styrofoam containers
- Triple beam balance or scale
- Graph paper

In this laboratory investigation, you will measure heat flow between equal amounts of water at different temperatures. You will use insulated plastic containers in this investigation because they are poor conductors and good insulators of heat, which will allow you to control the variables in the experiment.

Procedure:

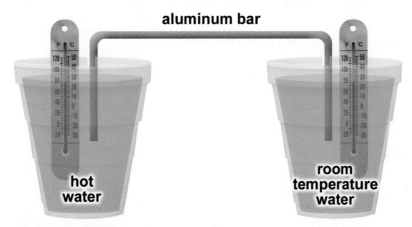

FIGURE 10.13. Example of setup.

1. Prepare 100 mL of boiling water using a hot plate, and take 100 mL of the prepared room temperature water.

2. While waiting for the water to boil, insert the thermometers and the heat transfer bar into the lids of the containers.

3. Fill one Styrofoam cup with room temperature water.

4. Record the temperature and the weight of the room temperature water.

5. Pour the boiling water into one of the Styrofoam cups and quickly cover it with the lid to prevent heat loss.

Safety Note: Be extremely careful when pouring boiling water. Pour it slowly, as Styrofoam containers have the tendency to tip over.

6. Record the temperature of both the room temperature and boiling water every two minutes for a period of 20 minutes. Also, create a data table like the one below. Your data table will need to extend to 20 minutes.

Time (minutes)	Hot Water (°C)	Room Temperature Water (°C)
0		
2		
4		
...		

7. Create a line graph of your temperature data. Plot two lines, one for the Hot Water and one line for the Room Temperature Water.

8. Answer the Questions below:

   a. What happens to the temperature of the liquids in the two containers?

   b. How does the energy travel from one cup to the other?

   c. What kind of heat transfer does this illustrate?

   d. Which direction does the energy flow?

   e. Will the plotted lines ever cross?

   f. When is the slope of the graph the greatest?

   g. What do the slopes of the plots on the graphs illustrate about the speed of heat flow compared to the amount of temperature difference?

   h. How does the amount of heat loss compare to the amount of heat gain? Is the amount equivalent? If not, why?

Part 2: The Law of Conservation of Energy

One of the most important understandings about the universe is the **Law of Conservation of Energy**, also known as the First Law of Thermodynamics. Simply stated, this law states that energy cannot be created nor destroyed, only transferred or transformed. Energy can be transferred—and measured—from one body of matter to another or transformed from one energy type to another energy type. Ocean waves carrying and transferring energy is an excellent illustration of the Law of Conservation of Energy in action.

FIGURE 10.14. The energy transferred in an ocean wave can be traced back to nuclear reactions in the Sun. Wave energy is a tremendous source of electrical power.

Most ocean waves are created from wind pushing the water. Wind is a result of the differences in pressure at the Earth's surface, due to differential heating. Different landforms and geographic locations have different measured temperatures depending on latitude, time of the year, and altitude. The Sun is responsible for much of the energy at the Earth's surface. The Sun's rays consist of electromagnetic radiation, or light. The Sun is able to continuously produce light because of the mass-to-energy conversion that occurs within the Sun. The Sun converts infinitesimal amounts of mass to huge amounts of energy through the nuclear reaction of fusion. This nuclear energy is converted to thermal energy and electromagnetic energy. The electromagnetic energy from the Sun travels to Earth. The energy is absorbed by Earth materials, including the land and ocean.

FIGURE 10.15. When wind is created, thermal energy is converted to mechanical energy. This mechanical energy can be converted into electrical energy using turbines such as the ones shown in this photograph.

Differences in air temperatures on the Earth's surface cause differences in air pressure. Areas of higher pressure—as measured by a barometer—flow toward areas of lower pressure. This flow of air is wind, an example of a conversion of thermal energy to mechanical energy. When wind moves across the ocean water, the air molecules physically push the water molecules, and this forms waves. You will see a similar movement if you blow air over a bowl of water.

The ocean wave example illustrates that nuclear energy from the Sun goes through many transformations and transfers before resulting in the mechanical energy of ocean waves. Along the way, energy is absorbed during each transfer and used by other systems; not all of the energy from the nuclear reactions on the Sun is used to make ocean waves, but the energy is conserved as it is transferred. At each conversion, some energy escapes as heat. This is true for all energy conversions; no conversion achieves 100% of energy converted into a new form, or 100% **efficiency**. However, no energy is ever "lost"—it is simply used elsewhere, ready to be transformed and transferred again.

A very familiar example of efficiency occurs when you flip on a light switch. The electrical energy is converted to light energy. But have you ever touched a light bulb? It gets hot. That's because much of the electrical energy is not creating light—it is escaping as thermal energy. In fact, most incandescent light bulbs are only about 10% efficient. That means approximately 90% of the electrical energy is being converted to thermal energy, not light. The Lab Activity earlier in the Lesson featured an "inefficient" light bulb. We capitalized on this inefficiency, using the thermal energy to warm our land and water materials. Compact fluorescent light bulbs (CFLs), sometimes called "energy efficient bulbs", are more efficient, operating at about 20% efficiency.

Now let's get back to the ocean example. Study the diagram below (FIGURE 10.17):

FIGURE 10.16. Traditional incandescent light bulbs convert only about 10% of the electrical energy they use into light; the rest escapes as thermal energy.

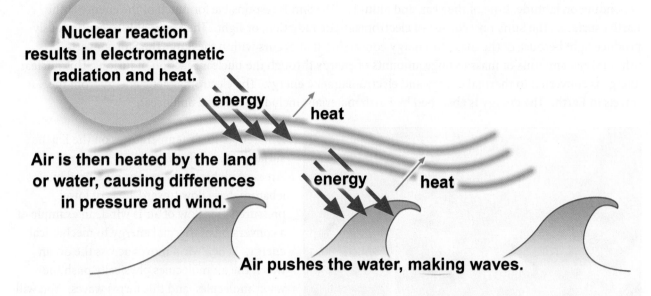

FIGURE 10.17. The diagram shows the transfers and transformations of energy from the Sun. Land or water is heated by the Sun. As a result the differences in pressure cause wind, which in turn causes waves.

The energy transformations look like this:

Let's consider another example, one within a biological system. Every time a living organism digests, breathes, moves, or does just about anything, energy transformations are involved. Picture a Green Sea Turtle swimming through the ocean searching for its next tasty seagrass bed.

FIGURE 10.18. As a Green Sea Turtle swims beneath the waves, the animal is converting chemical energy in its cells to the mechanical energy of motion. Perhaps this turtle is foraging for one of its favorite foods—seagrass. Green Sea Turtles, unlike most other sea turtle species, eat a vegetarian diet as adults.

FIGURE 10.19. A Jack Fish swims along a seagrass bed in the Florida Keys. The fish will obtain chemical energy from the plants. These plants convert light energy into chemical energy through the process of photosynthesis.

Sea Turtle Foraging: An Energy Conversion Story

Think back to the heat transfer lab, which demonstrated that even though energy was transferred across the metal bar by conduction, the total amount of energy in the hot water sample did not transfer to the room temperature water sample. Some of the energy from the hot water sample was transferred to the air. As stated above, the energy was not lost, simply transferred to another place, the air. This occurs with all types of heat transfer, not just conduction.

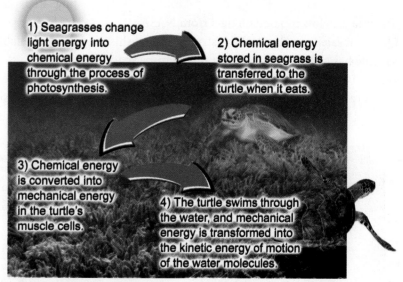

1) Seagrasses change light energy into chemical energy through the process of photosynthesis.

2) Chemical energy stored in seagrass is transferred to the turtle when it eats.

3) Chemical energy is converted into mechanical energy in the turtle's muscle cells.

4) The turtle swims through the water, and mechanical energy is transformed into the kinetic energy of motion of the water molecules.

FIGURE 10.20. Energy transformation illustration shows the transfer of energy over time.

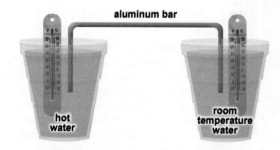

FIGURE 10.21. During the heat transfer lab, energy was transferred across the aluminum bar by conduction. Some energy, however, escaped. That energy was not "lost"; it was transferred to the air.

Wind Power

The same energy source that Europeans tapped to power their exploration of the New World may soon be used to provide the power you use to text your best friend. This power source arises because of differences in heating of our planet at different latitudes.

Wind-filled sails pushed the westward expansion of the colonial powers—England, France, Portugal, and Spain—across the Atlantic and back. Soon, wind-spun turbines will be generating more of the electrical power needed in our technological world. Already some countries, including Denmark, have established wind farms off their coasts. Currently, Denmark produces approximately 20% of its electricity from wind power. According to the World Wind Energy Association, the small percentage of global electricity production by wind power is increasing quickly.

The image below is based on data from NASA's QuikScat satellite. One of the instruments that this satellite has onboard to study our planet from Space is called SeaWinds. This instrument uses radar to measure wind speed and direction across the globe.

FIGURE 10.22. These wind turbines were erected in Antarctica to power research stations for scientists from the United States and New Zealand. By examining the Wind Speed image, one will note that areas near Antarctica are ideal for harnessing wind power.

The image shows wind power density for January and July. Red, pink, and white colors indicate where there are higher sustained winds. Blue areas are regions of lower available wind energy.

As can be seen in this image of wind density, there are areas close to our coasts here in the United States that are very suitable for the development of wind power to help meet our growing energy needs. What are the potential environmental effects of wind farms in our coastal waters? Could there be unexpected effects on tourism at our public beaches? What about communities near the wind farm? Are the turbines noisy? All of these issues need to be further addressed before we can effectively harness clean electrical power from the wind.

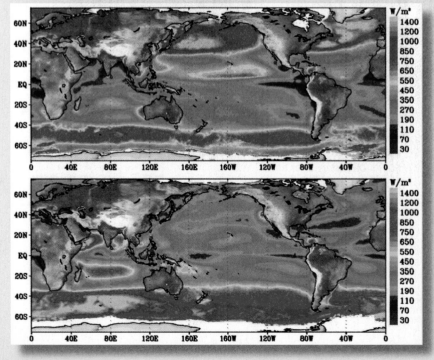

FIGURE 10.23. This satellite image illustrates measurements of wind speed throughout the globe in January (top) and July (bottom). Whites and reds indicate the highest wind speeds. Scientists and policy makers can use these data as they decide whether wind power is a viable option for powering homes and businesses in specific areas.

It is impossible in everyday life to create a system where heat transfer is 100% efficient. A system that would be completely efficient with no exchange of energy or matter with the outside world is an **isolated system**. If the results of the heat transfer lab had indicated that the total amount of energy removed from the hot water sample was transferred to the room temperature water sample, you would have made an isolated system. This ideal, however, has never been accomplished in any laboratory.

The Earth system is similar to the heat transfer lab setup because there is an exchange of energy with an outside system. The Earth system receives electromagnetic energy from the Sun and **reradiates** energy back into Space. Very little to no matter enters or leaves the Earth system, with the exception of scattered meteors entering, and tiny amounts of matter escaping from the upper atmosphere. Both the Earth system and the system created in the lab exchange only energy, not matter, with an outside system; they are each, essentially, then, **closed systems**. An **open system** exchanges both matter and energy with an external system. The human body is an example of an open system.

Longwave Flux (W/m²)

0   175   350

FIGURE 10.24. This image illustrates energy leaving the Earth system and reradiating back into Space. The blue areas represent clouds, which insulate the planet and help prevent energy from escaping to space. Earth is a closed system, exchanging only energy, not matter, with the Solar System.

11. Why did net energy loss not equal net energy gain in the heat transfer lab?

12. How might you alter the lab setup to increase the amount of energy that is transferred?

Evaluate

1. Is the ocean an open, closed, or isolated system? Explain. How does it differ from the other types of systems?

2. When an earthquake occurs within Earth's crust and sparks a tsunami, energy is transformed. Describe the transformations that occur in this example.

3. What is heat capacity? Describe how the high heat capacity of the ocean supports life on Earth.

11

Weather, Climate, and the Ocean

INSIDE:

Objectives

You will be able to:

✔ **Explain how energy and water are transferred from the ocean to the atmosphere through the formation of air masses and tropical weather systems.**

✔ **Describe how air masses, the water cycle, air pressure, and wind contribute to hurricane formation.**

✔ **Give examples of the ocean's influence on weather and climate.**

✔ **Describe how seabirds can be affected by wind patterns.**

Benchmarks

3a. The ocean controls weather and climate by dominating the Earth's energy, water, and carbon systems.

3b. The ocean absorbs much of the solar radiation reaching Earth. The ocean loses heat by evaporation. This heat loss drives atmospheric circulation when, after it is released into the atmosphere as water vapor, it condenses and forms rain. Condensation of water evaporated from warm seas provides the energy for hurricanes and cyclones.

3d. Most rain that falls on land originally evaporated from the tropical ocean.

3f. The ocean has had, and will continue to have, a significant influence on climate change by absorbing, storing, and moving heat, carbon, and water.

6a. The ocean affects every human life. It supplies fresh water—most rain comes from the ocean—and nearly all Earth's oxygen. It moderates the Earth's climate, influences our weather, and affects human health.

7d. New technologies, sensors, and tools are expanding our ability to explore the ocean. Ocean scientists are relying more and more on satellites, drifters, buoys, subsea observatories, and unmanned submersibles.

7f. Ocean exploration is truly interdisciplinary. It requires close collaboration among biologists, chemists, climatologists, computer programmers, engineers, geologists, meteorologists, and physicists and new ways of thinking.

Engage

See Page 694 for how to access e-Tools.

View the *Hurricane Wilma Animation* (0:13) from the e-Tools, which shows the storm's movements over SST imagery. Of note are water temperatures of greater than 28 °C (~82 °F), shown in orange.

e-Tools

FIGURE 11.1. Screenshot of the *Hurricane Wilma Animation*. Hurricane Wilma, the fourth Category 5 hurricane of the 2005 season, had sustained winds of 295 kilometers per hour (~185 miles per hour). The video shows its rapid development.

Observe the image from late August 2009. This imagery shows anomalies in SST. Deep blues are markedly cooler than what we would expect; deep reds are much warmer.

1. Describe your observations of the image below.

2. Explain what you are observing in the Atlantic Ocean.

Anomalies in SSTs, Late August 2009

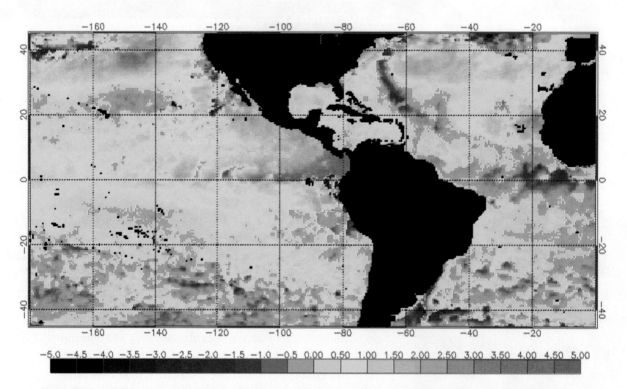

FIGURE 11.2. SST image of August 27, 2009, the same time Hurricane Bill steered through the Atlantic Ocean. The image shows that the storm had just completed moving through the North Atlantic. Can you track its path?

FIGURE 11.3. The area of disturbed water behind a moving boat is called a wake. Wakes are the water's response to forces that propel a boat.

Hurricanes are massive and energetic storms. Their high winds and heavy rains cause destruction in their paths. You might not have realized that their energy and moisture come from the ocean. In this Lesson, we will explore the characteristics and behavior of hurricanes.

Explore

Introducing Tropical Cyclones

Hurricane Andrew is shown below during its onslaught of the south Florida peninsula. Violent winds, heavy rain, and high **storm surges** walloped the state. Storm surge is the movement of ocean water onto land during a storm as a result of wind and changes in air pressure. It is often what causes the most damage to homes and businesses along the coast when a hurricane makes landfall. You will study storm surge further in Lesson 31: Humans and Coastlines. Hurricane Andrew itself caused approximately $25 billion in damage in 1992 dollars. In current dollars, this would equal more than $45 billion.

These same types of tropical storms are called typhoons or cyclones in other parts of the world. These large circulations are generally 500 kilometers, or around 300 miles, in diameter, although they can vary considerably in size. The eye at a hurricane's center, its eye, is a relatively calm, clear area approximately 20–40 miles across. Intense winds, swirling around the eye, are the hallmark of a hurricane.

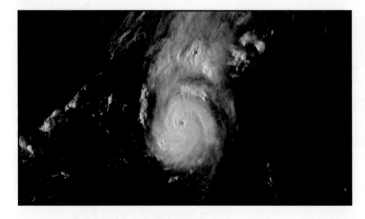

FIGURE 11.4. Hurricane Andrew made landfall over Florida in 1992. Areas just south of Miami, in particular Homestead, were hit the worst, causing billions of dollars in damage. Dozens lost their lives from the serious storm.

Across the globe, there are seven ocean basins over which tropical cyclones tend to develop. Tropical cyclones are called different names around the world. They are:

- **Hurricanes** in the Atlantic and Eastern Pacific Oceans
- **Typhoons** in the Western Pacific
- **Cyclones** in the Indian Ocean

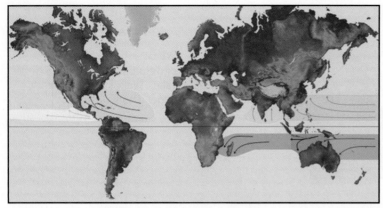

FIGURE 11.5. Tropical cyclones develop in areas north and south of the Equator around the globe, but are given different names in different parts of the world. Tropical storms do not form along the Equator because the Coriolis Effect is too weak to initiate large-scale rotation. Tropical cyclones have somewhat different characteristics than storms that develop in the mid-latitudes. Energy in tropical systems comes from warm tropical waters.

Common Locations of Tropical Cyclones

Tropical Location	Storm Activity
Atlantic Basin (North Atlantic Ocean, Gulf of Mexico, Caribbean Sea)	June 1 to November 30 (peak: early September)
Northeast Pacific Basin (Mexico to near the International Dateline)	Late May to early November (peak: early September)
Northwest Pacific Basin (International Dateline to Asia, including the South China Sea)	July to November (or anytime) (peak: early September)
North Indian Basin (Bay of Bengal and Arabian Sea)	April to December (peak: May and November)
Southwest Indian Basin (100° E [Southeast Asia] to eastern Africa)	Late October to mid-May (peak: January and February)
Southeast Indian/Australian Basin (North of Australia ~100° E to 142° E)	Late October to May (peak: January and February)
Australian/Southwest Pacific Basin (including southeast Pacific) (East of Australia ~142° E to 120° E)	Late October to early May (peak: early March)

3. Describe three patterns shown in the tropical cyclone data presented in the map and the table above.

Cyberlab

Investigating Hurricane Data

Part I: Using the Hurricane Tracks Data Tool

Materials:

- *Hurricane Tracks Data Tool Help Sheet*

See Page 694 for how to access e-Tools.

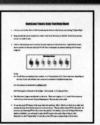

FIGURE 11.6. Screenshot of the *Hurricane Tracks Data Tool Help Sheet*.

www

View the *Hurricane Tracks Data Tool* from the *Marine Science: The Dynamic Ocean* website.

1. Once you are viewing the map, use the *Hurricane Tracks Data Tool Help Sheet* to practice navigating the tool.

Part II: Investigating Hurricane Data

2. Select Hurricane Isabel in 2003. Uncheck all of the other storms from that year.

3. a. Create a data table like the one below. Analyze Isabel's track by filling in the table. To do so, you will need to click on Isabel's locations that correspond to the Categories given in the first column. Then, complete the chart for the rest of the data. **Do not forget to change the date to get the correct SST for the locations and times you select!** If the storm is on land, write N/A, for "not applicable".

Storm Classification	Dates	Wind Speed Range (kts)	Atmospheric Pressure Range (mb)	SST
Category 5				
Category 4				
Category 3				
Category 2				
Category 1				
Tropical Storm				
Tropical Depression				

   b. Hurricanes are classified into Categories by maximum sustained wind speeds. Based on the data you collected:
   - Which classification corresponds to the highest wind speeds? The lowest?
   - What relationship is there between wind speed and atmospheric pressure?

   c. Give a general comparison of atmospheric pressure of tropical storms and depressions with that of Category 4 and 5 hurricanes.

4. Now look at storms in 2005, the busiest hurricane season in the Atlantic Ocean in recorded history. In order to answer the parts below, you may need to remove some of the storm tracks to better view the map.

   a. What patterns do you observe in terms of where storms move?

   b. What patterns do you observe as storms change between lower and higher storm classifications?

5. a. From either the 2003 or 2005 Map, choose 3 instances of storms at the time they were in the Category 4 or 5 range. Create a data table in which you record the name of the storm, the date, the storm classification, and the SST.

   b. Choose 3 instances in which storms were below Category 1 (i.e., tropical depression or tropical storm). Add these instances to your data table.

   c. Based on your data, what patterns do you observe between SST and storm classification?

   d. How can you explain your observations?

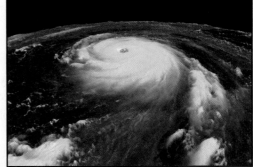

FIGURE 11.7. Hurricanes, like Hurricane Katrina shown here, are huge storms that form in the tropical ocean. Note the storm's eye, which is a calm area at the center of the storm.

Explain

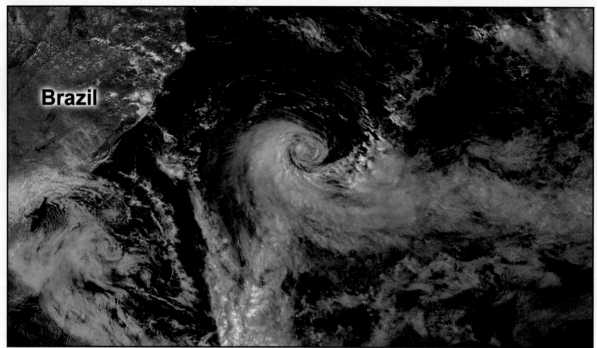

FIGURE 11.8. During March 2010, this storm in the South Atlantic Ocean, off of the coast of Brazil, was classified as a tropical cyclone by NOAA's Hydrological Prediction Center. This occurred 6 years after Cyclone Catarina, the first hurricane-intensity tropical cyclone ever recorded in the Southern Atlantic Ocean, in 2004.

See Page 694 for how to access e-Tools.

View the *27 Storms: Arlene to Zeta Video* (4:55) from the e-Tools.

e-Tools

FIGURE 11.9. Screenshot of the *27 Storms: Arlene to Zeta Video*.

The video illustrates a very unusual year for hurricane formation, 2005. The video includes a lot of information about hurricane formation. Use the Question below to help you focus as you listen to the speaker and watch the visuals.

4. Based on the *27 Storms: Arlene to Zeta Video*, describe at least two attributes of the climate that made 2005 a favorable year for hurricane formation.

Air Masses

Hurricane formation is a complex process. In order to better understand how hurricanes form, let's explore some basic weather principles and the connection between the ocean and the atmosphere. The study of the atmosphere, **meteorology**, is a science discipline that has a lot in common with oceanography.

In earlier Lessons, you studied several properties of liquid water, including its high heat capacity. Notably, whether water is in the ocean or the atmosphere, as a liquid or a gas, its properties hold true. Understanding the properties of water and the concepts of density in air masses and energy transfer will help to make important connections to weather and climate.

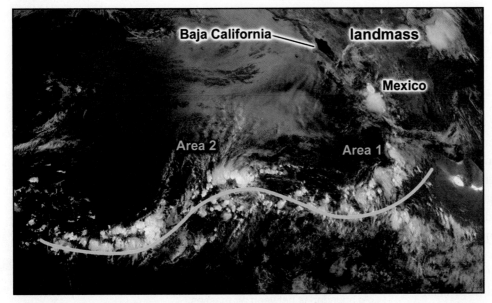

FIGURE 11.10. Looking carefully at this GOES-11 satellite image, one notices "waves" that appear to pass through areas of clouds. These areas are often the impetus for tropical storm (cyclonic) development.

Meteorologists classify large areas of air that have uniform properties of temperature and humidity as **air masses**. An air mass develops when a part of the lower atmosphere stays in contact with Earth's land or sea surfaces for an extended period of time. The time allows for the section of the atmosphere to take on similar temperature and moisture properties. Air masses can be very large in volume and cover hundreds or thousands of miles. Vertically, an air mass can extend to the top of Earth's troposphere. We will be focusing on the air masses over the Tropics to help explain hurricane formation and, to some extent, the formation of thunderstorms.

Let's back up for a moment. Air masses may be classified and named using two letters (e.g., **mT**) that indicate the characteristics of their source regions. The first letter indicates the moisture properties, using a **c** for dry, continental air and a maritime **m** for moisture-rich air. The second letter designates the temperature characteristics of the source area: **T** for Tropical, **P** for Polar, **A** for Arctic. Polar air is considered any area from Earth's mid-latitudes to the Poles, but it is distinguished from Earth's coldest winter air, Arctic air, which forms over snow and ice and is often thicker than a layer of polar air.

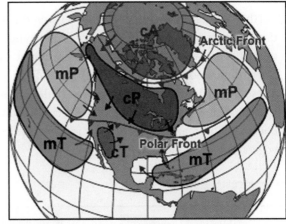

FIGURE 11.11. Air masses develop their characteristics from the area over which they develop.

Of course, air masses that form over the ocean contain a lot of moisture. Most of the rain that falls on land comes from **mT** air masses, which originate over tropical ocean basins.

Air Mass Classification		
Name (symbol)	Source Area	Characteristics
Continental Arctic (cA)	Originates over Earth's Polar Regions	Very cold and dry
Continental Polar (cP)	Originates over high-latitude continents (at least 60° N or 60° S)	Cold and dry
Maritime Polar (mP)	Originates over mid- to high-latitude ocean	Cool and moist
Continental Tropical (cT)	Originates over tropical continents	Hot and dry
Maritime Tropical (mT)	Originates over tropical ocean	Warm and moist

These air masses are useful classifications for describing weather conditions over a broad area over long time periods, which is **climate**. Climate not only includes the patterns of temperature, precipitation, and wind but also considers the range or extremes of these weather variables. Other factors contribute to climate, including latitude, **altitude** (height above sea level), and topographic features such as mountains and large bodies of water. For example, central Canada's temperatures are dependably cool. The middle latitudes (30° N to 60° N) are especially subject to weather variations much of the year because of the clashing of Polar and tropical air masses. Boundaries between air masses are called **fronts**. Fronts, separating air masses with different characteristics and represented by red and blue symbols along the Earth's surface in FIGURE 11.12, are often the locations of dramatic weather.

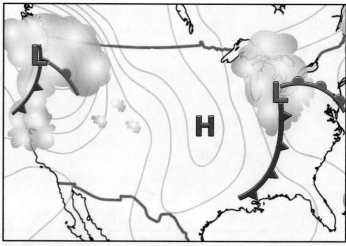

FIGURE 11.12. On weather maps, air pressure systems are indicated by Highs and Lows. Weather systems generally move from west to east in the continental U.S. Fronts illustrate the boundaries between air masses.

When you analyzed SST images in Lesson 9, it was easy to note that the cooler temperatures were found in the higher latitudes. You also observed a band of warmer temperatures around the Equator. These conditions are predictable and are evidence of the climate of these regions. The climate of Earth's Tropical Regions includes extreme amounts of water evaporation from the ocean, contributing to thunderstorms and tropical storms.

Earth's climates may also be classified using the Koppen (pronounced: KIR-pen) classification system, which uses average monthly values of temperature and precipitation to distinguish the different climates, which in turn affects the ecosystems found in the climatic regions. There are five primary climate types based upon the latitude and temperature: A) tropical; B) dry; C) mild, mid-latitude; D) cold, mid-latitude; and E) Polar. These five primary climate types are divided into sub-classifications characterized by the amount and type of precipitation or temperature. These include monsoon, tropical savanna, rainforest, humid subtropical, humid continental, oceanic climate, polar ice cap, tundra, and desert. Overall, a region's climate indicates a region's vegetation or biome.

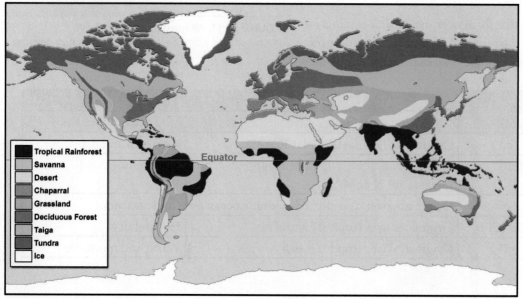

FIGURE 11.13. Earth's climatic regions, with their influences from temperature and precipitation, can be studied by biomes. Biomes are a good indication of climate.

The ocean is a major part of the climate story. The ocean's water holds on to heat because of its high heat capacity, and it distributes the heat around the globe via surface currents. Surface currents can influence climate on land. For example, Reykjavik, Iceland, located at 64° N latitude, has essentially the same average January winter temperature as New York City, located at about 41° N latitude, likely due to the influence of the warm Gulf Stream and North Atlantic Currents.

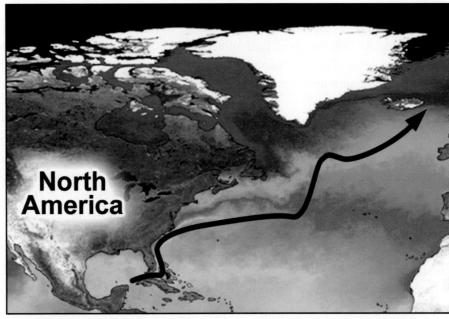

FIGURE 11.14. Heat is transferred from the ocean to the air above the North Atlantic Current through conduction and evaporation. This suggests the ocean's Gulf Stream and North Atlantic Currents affect temperatures.

5. How do air masses develop?

Density, Air Pressure, and the Water Cycle

One of the properties of an air mass is defined by the relative weight of air molecules pressing down on the Earth's surface, or **air pressure**. Visualize a "column" of air molecules that are stacked up above a point on the ground. The denser this stack of molecules is, the higher the pressure or weight of air that is measured at the surface of the Earth. Cold air masses are dense and heavy. Cold air has molecules with low kinetic energy. If air molecules are heated, their motion increases; they have more kinetic energy. In strict comparison, warm air masses contain air molecules that are farther apart. The space between the molecules increases, making the air less dense. Warm air takes up more space. It has a larger volume for a given number of molecules than cold air does.

Think about the properties of the air that sit over warm water. As the Sun increases the kinetic energy of water molecules, more liquid water will evaporate into the air. There is a balance, or **equilibrium**, between the amount of water molecules as a liquid and the amount of water molecules as a gas. This balance can be changed by the temperature. In warm air, the equilibrium point consists of a higher density of water vapor than it does in cooler air.

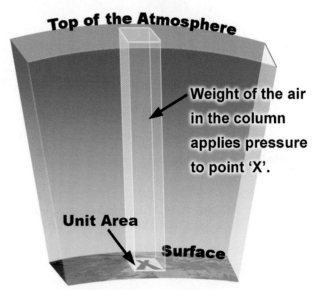

FIGURE 11.15. To understand air pressure, consider the weight of the gas molecules in the atmosphere above a specific point on Earth's surface.

Let's explore air pressure and moisture in the air. Recall, just as an example, that our atmosphere is composed of approximately 78% nitrogen. Each molecule within a volume of air has a molecular weight, calculated by adding the weights of its protons and neutrons in all atoms within the molecule. Let's consider the nitrogen molecules for the moment then, and compare them to the many fewer water molecules in the air.

As air molecules go, compared to the other most predominant gases in the atmosphere (i.e., oxygen, argon, carbon dioxide), nitrogen, with a molecular weight of 28, is pretty light. The nitrogen molecule (N_2) is made up of two nitrogen atoms, each with a molecular weight of 14. 14 + 14 = 28. Water molecules are even lighter and have a molecular weight of 18. Therefore, the more water molecules there are in the air compared to nitrogen molecules, for example, the lower is the air's "mass per volume" (M/V), or density. The pressure of air with *more* water in it is *less* than the pressure of air with *less* water in it.

The reason for this is that for any gas, including the air in the column, at a given temperature and pressure, the amount of molecules in the gas is the same. So, if lighter molecules (water) are added in the column displacing nitrogen for instance, the air pressure decreases.

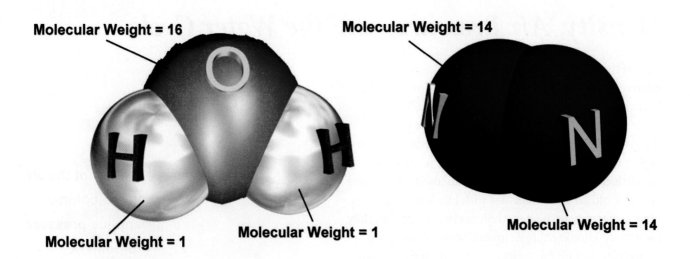

FIGURE 11.16. Water molecule and representative air molecule, nitrogen, illustrations show the molecules' atoms and respective molecular weights.

To understand the connections between density, air pressure, and the water cycle, let's explore air temperature. How do warm SSTs contribute to the amount of water in the atmosphere, precipitation, and even the development of hurricanes? We know that when it feels warm and humid, there is more water in the air than when it is cold. The animation in the following Cyberlab will help you to visualize the amount of water that warm air will contain.

Cyberlab

Air Temperature and Water Vapor

To understand the connections between air density and pressure and the water cycle, let's explore water vapor in the air at different air temperatures.

Part I:

First, how do warm SSTs contribute to the water in the atmosphere, precipitation, and even the development of hurricanes? We know that when it feels warm and humid, there is more water in the air than when it is cold. The animation will help you to visualize an important air–sea interaction.

See Page 694 for how to access e-Tools.

View the **Water Vapor and Thunderstorm Animation** from the e-Tools.

1. Describe what you observe in the animation.

2. What does this process have to do with hurricane formation?

e-Tools

FIGURE 11.17. Screenshot of the **Water Vapor and Thunderstorm Animation**.

Part II:

The amount of water in a parcel of air varies with temperature. Let's explore this concept further.

3. Copy the data table below, which shows the g/m³ of water vapor that can be supported by air at the different temperatures (in °C), into your notebook

Temperature (°C)	Temperature (°F)	Maximum Water Vapor (g/m³)
-10	14	2.36
0	32	4.85
5	41	6.80
10	50	9.40
15	59	12.83
20	68	17.30
25	77	23.00
30	86	30.40
40	104	51.10

4. Now, graph the data.

5. What is the relationship between air temperature and the amount of water vapor in the air?

6. Precipitation falls as snow when the air temperature is freezing or below (0 °C/32 °F). Why might less snow be measured in a snowstorm having temperatures well below 0 °C compared to a storm with an air temperature near 0 °C?

7. How much more water can air at 100 °F (~38 °C) hold than at 30 °F (~0 °C)?

8. Describe why thunderstorms or hurricanes are most likely to form in the Tropics.

Pressure Systems and Wind

Air molecules flow from areas of higher pressure to areas of lower pressure; understanding the characteristics of pressure leads to the ability to describe air flow. The movement of air molecules is known as **wind**. The greater the pressure difference between a high and a low, the stronger the wind. Large-scale weather features on Earth are often classified with low pressure or high pressure. A low-pressure system has an area of relatively low air pressure at its center. The air in the system's center is lighter than in the surrounding areas. The air will rise and cool, and clouds and precipitation will form. The center of this low-pressure area, if it is north of the Equator (i.e., ~5° N or more), will begin to experience a counterclockwise flow of air, called a circulation.

FIGURE 11.18. This thunderstorm forming over land is a result of converging air, forced upward. Rising air cools and condenses.

Let's say the area of lower pressure is in the Tropics (e.g., the Gulf of Mexico, the Caribbean); the air here is lighter compared to air from some distance away. The warm, moist light air will rise; heavier air from all around it will naturally flow toward the area of lower pressure. When the air converges from all directions, the only place it can go is up. Rising warm air and the process of evaporation help to cool the surface waters because energy is transferred from the ocean to the atmosphere. This helps to explain the cold wake you observed in the **Engage** section.

FIGURE 11.19. The center, or eye, of a hurricane has the lowest pressure of the storm. The fast winds reflect the large differences between high and low pressure.

The moist air rises into the atmosphere and cools. The water vapor (gas) condenses into liquid water to form clouds. When water vapor cools and condenses, energy is released, warming the surrounding atmosphere. This energy warms the parcel of air which is now warmer than its environment, so it rises farther. Water keeps condensing higher in the sky as energy is released. The colder air will contain less total moisture.

Thermal energy released along the way provides more energy to the system. As the pattern continues, great amounts of evaporated water are fed into the atmosphere from the ocean. If other conditions are favorable (e.g., winds above the storm are light or calm), a full-blown thunderstorm or tropical cyclone may form. tropical cyclones have an organized circulation around a core of low pressure, called the eye.

Hurricanes are huge low-pressure systems with embedded thunderstorms. In a hurricane, winds blow counterclockwise along the Earth's surface, and bands of rain form in the thick clouds swirling around the eye. When upper level winds above the storm are light, a hurricane is apt to intensify. If upper level winds are blowing over a hurricane, or the hurricane runs into a jet stream, a river of winds in the upper atmosphere, it will tend to lessen the strength of the hurricane. Upper level wind directions also contribute to the movement of the hurricane. The air flow blows or guides the entire tropical system and affects the direction of movement. Tropical meteorologists look at wind data in the upper troposphere when forecasting hurricane tracks.

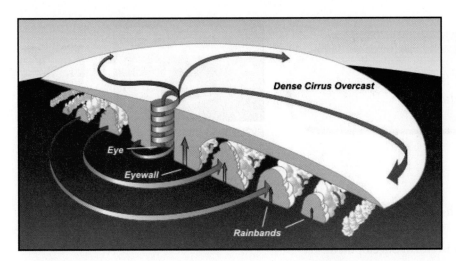

FIGURE 11.20. Cross-sectional view of a hurricane illustrates:
- counterclockwise wind flow at the surface
- calm winds, clear sky in the center
- wind flow along the edge of the eye, or "eye wall"
- outflow at the top of the storm
- thick clouds throughout the system with high cirrus clouds at the top
- rain banding (the areas of rain in bands at the surface)

FIGURE 11.21. A cross section of a hurricane shows converging air at the surface. This results in rising air. There is some sinking air (drying) at the eye, resulting in clear skies and light or no winds. At the top of the storm, there is an outflow of air.

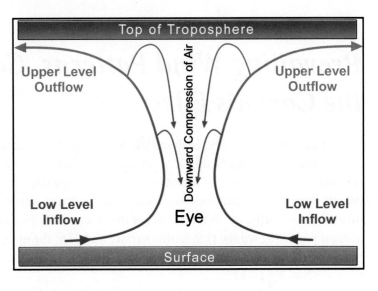

The more one understands about our amazing watery planet, the more one will understand that the water cycle is as much about energy transfer as it is about water transfer. The ocean loses heat by evaporation—that heat of course is not "lost" but is transferred to the atmosphere. We have seen when this happens over the tropical ocean, when the gaseous water vapor condenses, providing energy to power a hurricane.

Water cycles between each of the planet's spheres: the Atmosphere ("air sphere"), the Biosphere ("life sphere"), the Hydrosphere ("water sphere"), and the Lithosphere ("land sphere"). Because it cycles through all of Earth's spheres, it is known as a **biogeochemical cycle**. Other biogeochemical cycles include the carbon and nitrogen cycles.

FIGURE 11.22. A simple view of the water cycle includes evaporation, condensation, and precipitation. The water cycle, like all of Earth's material cycles, involves the transfer of energy.

See Page 694 for how to access e-Tools.

Review the basic processes of the water cycle by viewing the *Water Cycle Animation*.

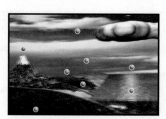

FIGURE 11.23. Screenshot of the *Water Cycle Animation*.

e-Tools

6.   Give a brief description of each of the processes described in the *Water Cycle Animation*.

7.   Describe the role of the ocean in storm development.

Prevailing Wind Patterns, Convection Cells, and the Coriolis Effect

In the **Explore** section, you analyzed the paths of past hurricanes. One of the most important jobs of scientists who study hurricanes is to predict where hurricanes will move to. Perhaps you have heard talk by weather forecasters about a hurricane "turning" as they track a hurricane's path. Have you wondered why Atlantic hurricanes often track westward from the West Coast of Africa toward the Caribbean and why they turn north or northeast? A major part of the explanation involves prevailing global winds. This section will address prevailing winds: 1) at Earth's surface and 2) in the upper troposphere, which contribute to steering hurricanes.

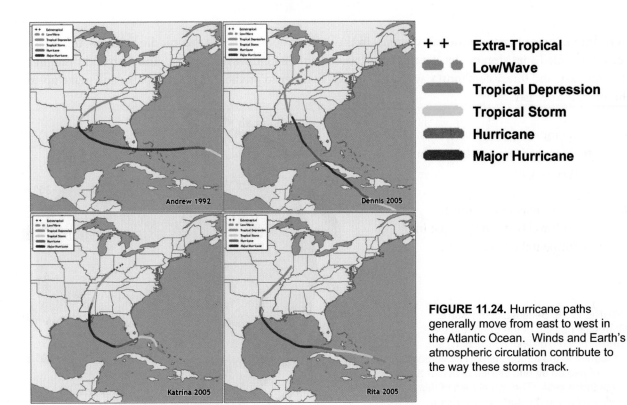

Extra-Tropical ++

Low/Wave

Tropical Depression

Tropical Storm

Hurricane

Major Hurricane

FIGURE 11.24. Hurricane paths generally move from east to west in the Atlantic Ocean. Winds and Earth's atmospheric circulation contribute to the way these storms track.

To make predictions on the paths of hurricanes, we need to understand prevailing wind patterns. In a model of the movement of air on Earth, air that is heated at the Equator rises straight up from Earth's surface. When the air reaches the top of the troposphere, it will flow outward toward the Poles. The air movement acts as a big convection cell, transporting heat to Earth's Polar Regions with the cooler air traveling back to the Equator along Earth's surface. In reality, the convection cells are more complicated than the simple Equator-to-Pole model in FIGURE 11.25. Examine FIGURE 11.26. Note that there are several convection cells moving the air molecules in the atmosphere. One convection cell begins at the Equator. Warm, moist air is lifted and carried northward (in the Northern Hemisphere) to about 30° N. At 30° N the air sinks as a higher pressure air mass. Some of this cooler air, now back at Earth's surface, moves south toward the Equator, thus completing the convective loop. Some of the air moves northward, warming the surface as it goes, until it rises again, forming a second loop as it approaches the 60° N latitude line. The path of this moving air along the surface is diverted from a true north-south path due to the Coriolis Effect.

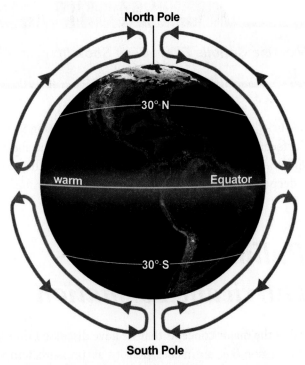

FIGURE 11.25. In this too-simple model, heated air rises at the Equator, cools as it travels away from the Equator, and sinks at the Poles. As it moves along the ground toward the Equator, it warms and completes the simple convection cell. In reality, the cooling air moving away from the Equator sinks at about the 30° latitude line.

In addition, there are narrow, fast air currents in the upper troposphere. In the middle latitudes, this air current is called a **jet stream**. Jet streams steer large storms, including hurricanes. The path and strength of jet streams vary, and forecasters must pay close attention in order to predict hurricanes' paths and make up-to-the-minute forecasts.

8. Why do most Atlantic hurricanes initially move from east to west but then turn north?

9. Why do air masses and storm systems travel from west to east in the continental United States?

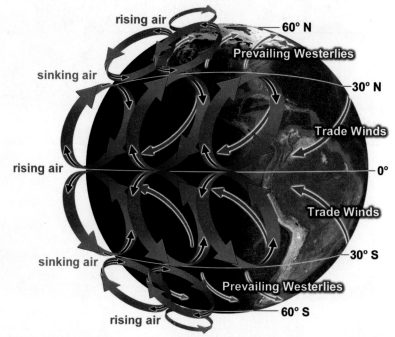

FIGURE 11.26. Because of the Sun's differential heating of the Earth and the Earth's rotation, distinct convection cells are formed in the atmosphere. The vertical rising of heated air and sinking of cooler air drives these cells. The actual path of this moving air along the surface is diverted from a true north-south path because of the Coriolis Effect.

See Page 694 for how to access e-Tools.

View the *Coriolis Effect Slide Show* from the e-Tools.

e-Tools

We briefly discussed the Coriolis Effect in Lesson 9: The Sea Surface: The Great Energy Distributor. View the short *Coriolis Effect Animation* from that Lesson again. Use the slider bar to gain a deeper understanding of this concept.

FIGURE 11.27. Screenshot of the *Coriolis Effect Slide Show*.

Pulling It Together – Hurricane Formation

All of the major concepts that we have discussed thus far in this Lesson (i.e., air masses, density, air pressure, temperature, wind, cloud formation, the Water Cycle, prevailing winds) relate to one another and to hurricane formation.

Tropical Storm force winds
Hurricane force winds

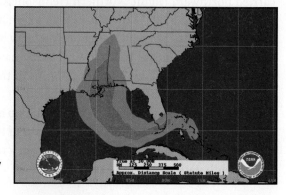

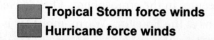

FIGURE 11.28. This map of Hurricane Katrina's path notes areas affected by both tropical storm and hurricane-force winds. Katrina devastated the Gulf Coast, including the City of New Orleans in Louisiana.

10. Consider how each of the following factors contribute to the development of hurricanes:
   - Air masses and air pressure
   - The Water Cycle and energy transfer
   - Prevailing winds

   Create a labeled comic strip in which you illustrate and describe how each of the above conditions result in and affect hurricanes.

Migrating Seabirds and Wind

All living things respond to their environments, which include weather and climate patterns. Seabirds rely on the ocean to meet their needs but are affected by weather and climate. For instance, Pink-footed Shearwaters migrate from the Northern Hemisphere to the Southern Hemisphere in order to always experience a warm summer climate. Black-footed Albatross are affected by wind patterns, both prevailing winds and more fleeting, localized air movements.

FIGURE 11.29. Seabirds such as albatross use wind currents to their advantage. These birds can lock out their "elbows" and soar with the winds.

The figure below features the actual location of a Black-footed Albatross named Oski. The bird's location is shown for August 24, 2008. Oski appears on a monthly mean wind speed and direction map on the left, and on an infrared satellite image on the right. The average winds for the month were westerly (to the East). On the infrared satellite image for August 24th, clouds are shown as white areas that reflect energy to satellite sensors. The whiter the area, the less heat the satellite senses. The light gray area near Oski on the date indicates generally fair, warm weather, perhaps some low level stratus clouds.

The "trail" of light gray suggests Oski may take advantage of a cold front during the time period to fly. Oski did, in fact, fly toward the East from this point, about 350 kilometers (~215 miles) in one day.

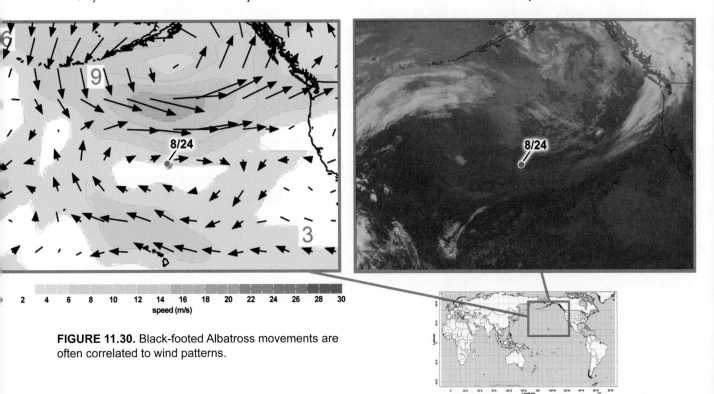

FIGURE 11.30. Black-footed Albatross movements are often correlated to wind patterns.

Watching an albatross fly is a breathtaking sight. These giant seabirds have the largest wingspan of any known bird on the planet. Wingspan is a measurement of the distance from the tip of one wing across the body of the bird to the tip of the other wing, with the wings fully extended. The wingspan of the Black-footed Albatross, one of the two dozen different species of albatross, measures about the distance of Michael Jordan's arm span, approximately 2.1 meters (~6.9 feet). The formidable wingspan of these giant birds allows them to ride the wind currents above the ocean for hours at a time, without landing or even flapping their wings. This process, in which seabirds use the wind currents to their advantage, thus conserving energy, is called **dynamic soaring**.

Seabirds migrate farther on clear days than on stormy days. The stormy conditions that result from low-pressure systems create conditions that are unfavorable for travel. Seabirds do take advantage of moving masses of air to help power their flight.

Elaborate

In addition to storms, air pressure also affects simply daily weather conditions. Let's explore one such example.

See Page 694 for how to access e-Tools.

View the *Sea Breeze Animation* from the e-Tools.

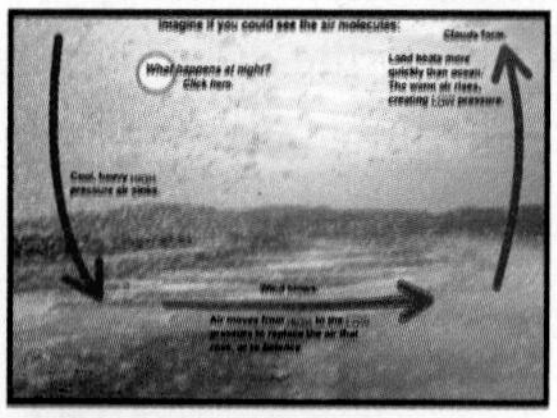

e-Tools

FIGURE 11.31.
Screenshot of the *Sea Breeze Animation*.

11. Compare and contrast what happens, in terms of wind, at the shoreline during a hot summer day and at night.

Intense heating of land causes air to rise and clouds to form. This is why many regions of the country, particularly the South and the Southwest, experience afternoon thunderstorms during the summer.

The shape of the land sometimes contributes to cloud formation. For example, when a humid air mass encounters mountains, flowing air is forced to rise. As temperatures cool, the water vapor condenses and clouds form. Precipitation occurs. The sinking air that actually flows past and over the mountain is therefore very dry. This is one reason that deserts are commonly found on the **leeward**, or downwind, sides of mountains.

Activity

Analyzing Weather and Climate Data

Next we will use the ideas that we have been studying to analyze weather and climate data from various United States cities.

SAVANNAH, GEORGIA

	Jan	Feb	Mar	Apr	May	Jun	Jul	Aug	Sep	Oct	Nov	Dec	Annual
Average Max. Temperature (°F)	60.40	64.10	71.00	77.70	84.30	89.50	92.30	90.30	86.00	78.10	70.50	62.60	77.20
Average Min. Temperature (°F)	38.00	40.90	47.50	52.90	61.30	68.10	71.80	71.30	67.30	56.10	46.90	40.10	55.20
Average Total Precipitation (in.)	3.95	2.92	3.64	3.32	3.61	5.49	6.04	7.20	5.08	3.12	2.40	2.81	49.58

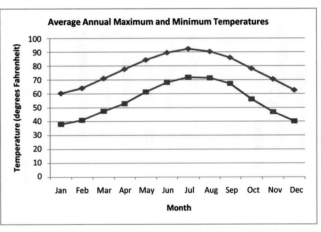

FIGURE 11.32. Graphs showing Average Annual Maximum and Minimum Temperatures and Average Annual Total Rainfall for **Savannah, Georgia**.

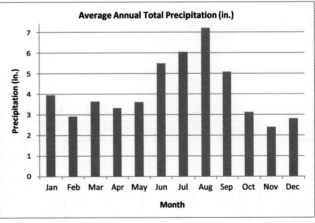

PHOENIX, ARIZONA

	Jan	Feb	Mar	Apr	May	Jun	Jul	Aug	Sep	Oct	Nov	Dec	Annual
Average Max. Temperature (°F)	65.00	69.40	74.30	83.00	91.90	102.00	104.20	102.40	87.40	86.40	73.30	65.00	84.50
Average Min. Temperature (°F)	43.40	47.00	51.10	57.50	66.30	75.20	81.40	80.40	74.50	62.90	50.00	43.50	61.10
Average Total Precipitation (in.)	0.83	0.77	1.07	0.25	0.16	0.09	0.99	0.94	0.75	0.79	0.73	0.92	8.29

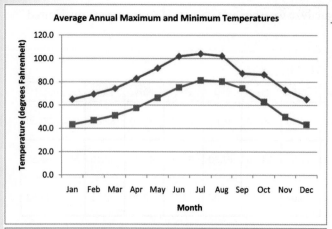

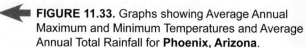

FIGURE 11.33. Graphs showing Average Annual Maximum and Minimum Temperatures and Average Annual Total Rainfall for **Phoenix, Arizona**.

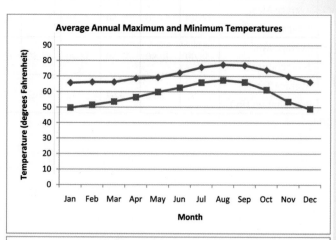

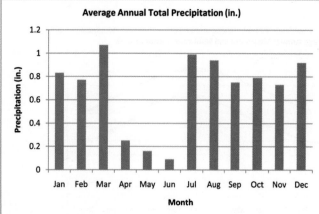

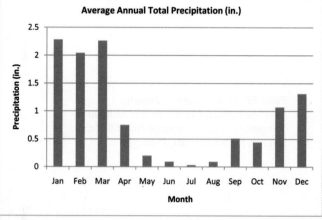

FIGURE 11.34. Graphs showing Average Annual Maximum and Minimum Temperatures and Average Annual Total Rainfall for **San Diego, California**.

SAN DIEGO, CALIFORNIA

	Jan	Feb	Mar	Apr	May	Jun	Jul	Aug	Sep	Oct	Nov	Dec	Annual
Average Max. Temperature (°F)	65.80	66.30	66.30	68.70	69.30	72.20	75.80	77.50	77.00	74.00	69.90	66.30	70.80
Average Min. Temperature (°F)	49.70	51.50	53.60	56.40	59.80	62.60	65.90	67.40	66.10	61.20	53.60	48.90	58.10
Average Total Precipitation (in.)	2.28	2.04	2.26	0.75	0.20	0.09	0.03	0.09	0.51	0.44	1.07	1.31	10.77

City Comparison			
City	Latitude	Longitude	Elevation
Savannah, GA	32.1° N	81.1° W	13 meters (~42 feet)
Phoenix, AZ	33.5° N	112.1° W	330 meters (~1,083 feet)
San Diego, CA	32.7° N	117.2° W	4 meters (~13 feet)

1. Would it be more accurate to refer to the data in these tables as climate data or weather data? What evidence did you use to reach your conclusion?

2. Using the data for these cities, compare the range from highest high temperature to lowest low temperature for the three cities. Explain your findings. Hint: Recall what you have learned about prevailing winds.

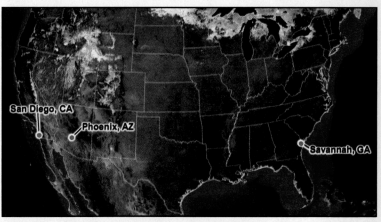

FIGURE 11.35. Map showing the location of the cities in the activity.

3. Why does Savannah experience so much precipitation in summer?

4. In terms of what you know about air masses, how can you explain the differences in temperature experienced in the three cities?

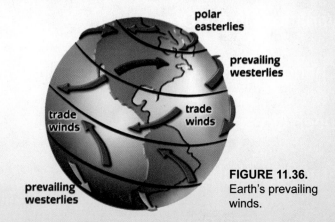

FIGURE 11.36. Earth's prevailing winds.

Evaluate

1. Describe two ways in which the ocean influences climate.

2. Give two examples of how the ocean influences weather.

3. Describe the general structure of hurricanes, how they form, and their typical movements. Be as detailed as possible in your answer and be sure to include the ocean's role in the process. Appropriately include at least 5 of the following vocabulary words from this Lesson:

- Pressure
- Wind
- Air mass
- Eye
- Jet stream
- Water cycle (or related words, such as evaporation, condensation, precipitation, cloud formation)
- Thermal energy

12

Voyage to the Deep

INSIDE:

Objectives

You will be able to:

✔ Explain how pressure, temperature, density, salinity, and light change with increasing depth.

✔ Describe the characteristics of some animals that allow them to cope with changes in pressure, temperature, density, salinity, and light.

✔ Analyze and interpret plots of density, salinity, pressure, and temperature with respect to depth at various locations.

 Benchmarks

1c. Throughout the ocean there is one interconnected circulation system powered by wind, tides, the force of the Earth's rotation (i.e., Coriolis Effect), the Sun, and water density differences. The shape of ocean basins and adjacent land masses influence the path of circulation.

3f. The ocean has had, and will continue to have, a significant influence on climate change by absorbing, storing, and moving heat, carbon, and water.

3g. Changes in the ocean's circulation have produced large, abrupt changes in climate during the last 50,000 years.

5d. Ocean biology provides many unique examples of life cycles, adaptations, and important relationships among organisms (e.g., symbiosis, predator-prey dynamics, energy transfer) that do not occur on land.

5e. The ocean is three-dimensional, offering vast living space and diverse habitats from the surface through the water column to the seafloor. Most of the living space on Earth is in the ocean.

7b. Understanding the ocean is more than a matter of curiosity. Exploration, inquiry, and study are required to better understand ocean systems and processes.

Engage

Starting out from sea level, the ocean is deeper than the land is high. Think about it. If you are standing right on the coast, the depth of the ocean in some locations is greater than the height of the highest mountains. In fact, the average depth of the ocean is approximately 3,800 meters (~12,500 feet) below sea level, and the average elevation of our continents is 840 meters (~2,756 feet). This means, the ocean is 4.52 times deeper than the continents are high.

FIGURE 12.1. Sea level is where the ocean surface meets land. The illustration demonstrates that the ocean is overall very deep.

$$\frac{\text{Average ocean depth}}{\text{Average continental height}} \quad \frac{3,800 \text{ m}}{840 \text{ m}} = 4.52$$

The maximum ocean depth, in the Challenger Deep, part of the great Mariana Trench in the Western Pacific Ocean, is 10,924 meters (~35,840 feet) below sea level. The maximum land elevation is 8,850 meters (~29,035 feet) above sea level at Mt. Everest.

FIGURE 12.2. Dr. Erika Raymond inside the *Johnson-Sea-Link* submersible.

Have you ever dreamed of going to the bottom of the ocean? As you learned in Lesson 4: The Ocean Over Time, submersibles make it possible. While satellites and ships allow scientists to study all of the ocean's surface, they do not let them observe the environmental conditions far beneath the ocean's waves. Submersibles protect people from the harsh conditions deep in the ocean. These vehicles allow scientists to make discoveries in the deep sea—including hydrothermal vent and other communities that thrive without sunlight.

Picture yourself sitting in a submersible craft that is lowered from a ship. Your journey starts at the surface as you are slowly sinking toward the seafloor. There are thick porthole windows, which allow you to see outside.

See Page 694 for how to access e-Tools.

e-Tools

View **Submersible Video Clip 1** (0:42) and **Submersible Video Clip 2** (0:34) from the e-Tools.

Each of the videos shows a unique aspect of the deployment and use of submersibles.

- The video clips are of different submersibles being deployed and show subsequent communication with scientists in ships at the surface.

FIGURE 12.3. Screenshot of **Submersible Video Clip 1**.

FIGURE 12.4. Screenshot of **Submersible Video Clip 2**.

See Page 694 for how to access e-Tools.

View **Submersible Video Clip 3** (0:30) and **Submersible Video Clip 4** (0:45) from the e-Tools.

e-Tools

- In Video 3, a scientist discusses some of the sampling techniques used by submersibles at the seafloor.

- Video 4 shows scientists descending into the depths and focuses on fish species they observe through their windows.

FIGURE 12.5. Screenshot of **Submersible Video Clip 3**.

FIGURE 12.6. Screenshot of **Submersible Video Clip 4**.

1. If you were to travel in a submersible, how would the ocean change as you went deeper?

2. Looking at pictures, what are some of the features you observe with respect to the construction of the submersibles?

3. What do you think are the purposes of each of the above features you observe?

FIGURE 12.7. *Mir* submersible is hoisted into the water via a cable connected to the ship's winch system. This front view shows the versatile manipulator arms and the huge viewing port.

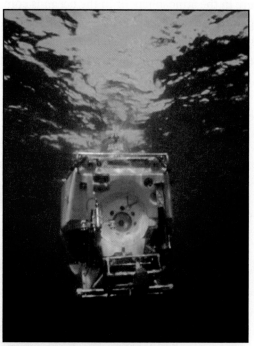

FIGURE 12.8. Submersibles are used to take humans to depths they cannot reach by any other means. Scientists are increasingly using ROVs, AUVs, and other unmanned systems to explore the deep sea.

There are tremendous differences in the various measurements of water, particularly with depth. Just as many have experienced jumping into a pool and getting a chilly shock when the *temperature* at the bottom of the pool is not quite as warm as the surface or the air, the temperature outside the submersible changes as it sinks down toward the ocean floor. The *pressure* you feel at the bottom of a pool is the weight of the water above pushing down on you. Most people know from experience that water is a very heavy substance. Consider, for example, how tough it is to lift a 5-gallon bottle of water—those are the ones typically used in a water cooler in an office or school. Going back to the pool, we know the amount of water and its weight, from the surface down to about 5 meters (~16 feet) deep, is greater than the weight of the water from the surface down to 2.5 meters (~8 feet) deep. The weight of the water creates a force per unit area, the measured **pressure**, on the diver. At 5 meters (~16 feet) deep, the pressure is great.

FIGURE 12.9. A full 5-gallon water bottle reminds us just how heavy water actually is. Marine organisms underwater have to function under great pressure.

Pressure in the atmosphere or in the ocean is commonly measured in pounds per square inch (psi). The average pressure of the air at sea level on Earth is 14.7 psi. This average pressure is simply referred to as *1 atmosphere*. Because water is so heavy, pressure increases rapidly with depth. Just 10 meters (~33 feet) below the surface, the pressure underwater is already 2 atmospheres, or 29.4 psi.

Later we will look at a data sample to investigate this further. You will look at a plot of how the pressure and temperature on the outside of our submersible changes as the submersible sinks to a greater ocean depth.

FIGURE 12.10. Girl swimming underwater acclimates to the environment, not conscious of the heavy water weighing upon her.

Explore

Modeling Changes in Water Temperature

 Lab

Let's model how water temperature changes as water depth increases. Be sure to follow the procedure carefully.

Your teacher will get the station ready just prior to beginning the procedure below. Be sure to follow each step with your lab group. It may be best for one person to read each step out loud to the rest of the group. To see results, be extremely careful not to stir the water with the thermometer. Avoid mixing.

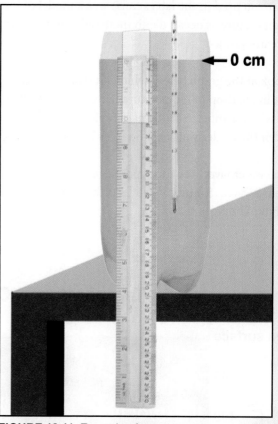

FIGURE 12.11. Example of setup.

Procedure:

1. **Do not disturb the contents of the container.** Hold the ruler against the outside of your container. The 0 cm mark should be level with the top of the water. Tape the ruler to the container if you wish. Using the marker, make a line to denote each centimeter of depth.

2. Copy the data table with the appropriate number of centimeters (see sample below) into your notebook:

Depth (cm)	0	1	2	3	4	5	6	7	8	9	10	11	12	13	14
Temperature (°C)															

3. Using the marks on the beaker that you made as reference points, very carefully measure the temperature of the water in 1-cm intervals (1 cm, 2 cm, 3 cm, etc.) by aligning the thermometer bulb with the centimeter marks all the way down to the bottom of your container. Wait 35–45 seconds at each interval for the thermometer to get an accurate read.

4. Create a line graph of the data from above. The 0 cm mark should be at the top of your graph. Label the axes and provide a title for the graph.

5. Describe the pattern you see in your graph.

Explain

Variations in the Ocean

Temperature Variations with Depth

As you have thought about with the lake example, when the water is not mixed, the deeper you descend, the colder the water becomes. In other words, as depth increases, temperature decreases. The container of water that you used in the lab exercise was a model of the ocean. Just as you observed in your model, the change in temperature as ocean depth increases is not uniform. The main impact from the Sun is primarily felt near the ocean's surface.

Look at the graph below, which illustrates a temperature pattern for the temperate ocean. Note that there is a dramatic drop in temperature between about 200 meters (~650 feet) and 1,000 meters (~3,300 feet). The layer in which temperature changes rapidly actually creates a boundary that separates the warmer surface water from the colder water below. This boundary layer is called the **thermocline**.

The water layers remain separate because the warmer water is less dense and "sits" on top of the colder, more dense water. Salinity also affects the density of water. You discussed this relationship in Lesson 3: More About Water.

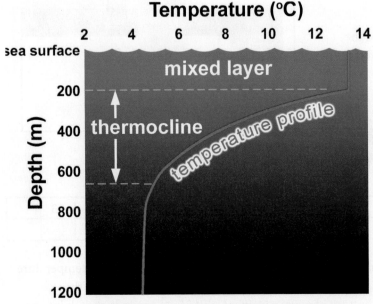

FIGURE 12.12. The graph shows that the change in temperature as ocean depth increases is not a linear relationship. A layer of water called the thermocline separates the warmer surface waters from the deeper, consistently cold ocean waters.

FIGURE 12.13. Scientists launch a CTD (conductivity, temperature, depth) device over the side of the research vessel *Thompson* to take ocean measurements.

4. On the graph you created during your lab activity, at what depth was a thermocline present? Label the thermocline on your graph.

5. The layer of warm water near the ocean's surface is sometimes called the *mixed layer*. What factors might cause water to mix in this layer?

In some locations on Earth, the mixed layer differs between the winter and summer months. Look at the graphs below.

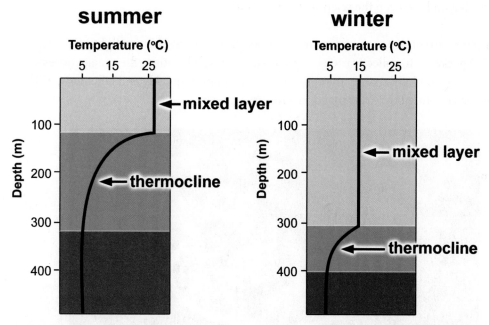

FIGURE 12.14. Seasonal differences in the position of the thermocline can present a shallow, warm mixed layer in summer. In winter the seasonal thermocline is located deeper in the water column, producing a more uniform upper layer.

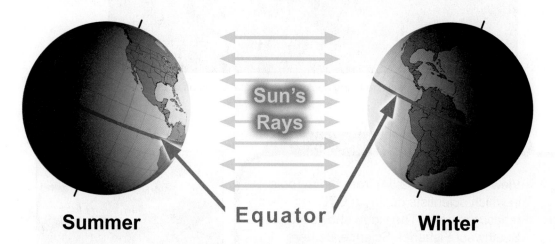

FIGURE 12.15. The globes illustrate that the Northern Hemisphere receives higher amounts of solar radiation in summer than in winter. This seasonal effect is caused by Earth's tilt on its axis. Notice the locations of the higher concentrations of rays and the more diffuse rays due to Earth's curvature.

6. How might you account for the difference in depth of the thermocline between summer and winter?

Scientists use a variety of tools to learn about the physical and biological conditions of the environment at different water depths. The data can tell us a lot about the conditions with which organisms must cope. These data are collected by instrument packages with various sensors. Collected data include conductivity, temperature, and density measurements. A **CTD device**, or CTD for short, is hoisted over the side of the ship to take measurements. While the CTD is still underwater it reports electronic messages through a cable back to the onboard computer lab. While the CTD is gathering data underwater, computers on the ship are constantly reading that data and creating charts and line graphs. This helps the scientists understand right away the changes in the water column as the CTD goes deeper and deeper. A typical CTD drop can take 5 to 15 minutes depending on how deep the scientists want to go.

Today, these sampling instruments measure other parameters, including salinity, light intensity, and pH. Scientists use CTD packages to collect various depth data at a single location, then make observations at many locations. This technology enables them to gather information quickly and efficiently. CTDs are often deployed with water sampling bottles arranged in a rosette pattern.

FIGURE 12.16. CTD package being deployed in the Bahamas off of the research vessel *Knorr*.

See Page 694 for how to access e-Tools.

e-Tools

View *CTD Video* (2:54) from the e-Tools in which scientists deploy a CTD to collect measurements. The video shows NOAA's Southwest Fisheries Science Center biologists launching CTDs to collect data of various parameters.

2006 Sardine Survey
Aboard the NOAA FRV *Oscar Dyson*

FIGURE 12.17. Screenshot of *CTD Video*.

Activity

Changes with Depth

Materials:

- Graph paper
- Pencils
- Rulers

Procedure:

1. Look at the illustration of the submersible. Note that the picture shows the temperature, pressure, salinity, and density readings outside the submersible at different depths. These data represent typical values in the temperate ocean.

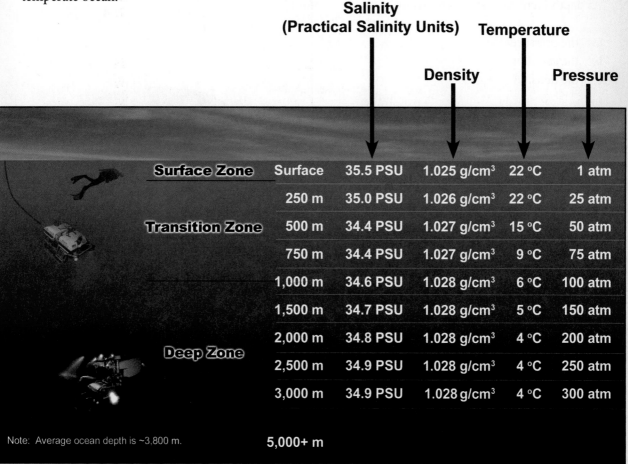

		Salinity (Practical Salinity Units)	Density	Temperature	Pressure
Surface Zone	Surface	35.5 PSU	1.025 g/cm³	22 °C	1 atm
	250 m	35.0 PSU	1.026 g/cm³	22 °C	25 atm
Transition Zone	500 m	34.4 PSU	1.027 g/cm³	15 °C	50 atm
	750 m	34.4 PSU	1.027 g/cm³	9 °C	75 atm
	1,000 m	34.6 PSU	1.028 g/cm³	6 °C	100 atm
	1,500 m	34.7 PSU	1.028 g/cm³	5 °C	150 atm
	2,000 m	34.8 PSU	1.028 g/cm³	4 °C	200 atm
Deep Zone	2,500 m	34.9 PSU	1.028 g/cm³	4 °C	250 atm
	3,000 m	34.9 PSU	1.028 g/cm³	4 °C	300 atm
	5,000+ m				

Note: Average ocean depth is ~3,800 m.

FIGURE 12.18. Illustration showing salinity, density, temperature, and pressure readings outside the submersible at different depths.

2. Create a data table to organize the data in your notebook.

Now you will create 4 graphs, with plots for each parameter (salinity, density, temperature, pressure) versus depth.

For each graph:

- Make an appropriate scale for the x and y axes. Depth will be on the y-axis for this plot, although it is the independent variable. Plotting the data in this way better allows one to visualize changes with depth.
- Label the axes with both the parameter and its units.
- Give the graph a title.

3. Create a plot of the depth versus temperature data.

4. Create a plot of the depth versus pressure data.

5. Create a plot of the depth versus salinity data.

6. Create a plot of the depth versus density data.

7. As depth increases, what happens to:

   a. the pressure?
   b. the salinity?
   c. the density?

8. If you were to hold your breath and dive deep into the ocean without a submersible, what might happen to you because of the increased pressure?

9. If you start at sea level, perhaps along the coast, and move up or rise in elevation into the atmosphere, how does the pressure you are experiencing change? How does air pressure differ when you are on a beach compared to when you are on a hot air balloon, up a mountain, or on an airplane?

10. If you are in a submersible sinking slowly down toward the seafloor, how does the amount of light change?

FIGURE 12.19. Pressure in the water and air pressure on land or in a balloon each measure the weight of a column of water or air above an object. Pressure can be measured in various units including pounds per square inch (psi) or atmospheres.

Deep Ocean Circulation

There is a driving force, running thousands of meters below the ocean's surface, that moves a tremendous amount of water. It is a system of deep water currents that connects all of the world's ocean basins, called the **Global Conveyor Belt**.

See Page 694 for how to access e-Tools.

View the *Global Conveyor Belt Animation* from the e-Tools to learn more about this system.

e-Tools

FIGURE 12.20. Screenshot of the *Global Conveyor Belt Animation*.

FIGURE 12.21. Globe showing the location of Greenland and Iceland.

The density of water is controlled by both the temperature and salinity of the water. As temperature decreases and salinity increases, the density of the water increases. Both factors drive the Global Conveyor Belt. Deep water circulation driven by density is known as **thermohaline circulation** (*therme* = heat, *halos* = salt). Let's begin by studying the process in the Polar Regions, where the water is extremely cold. Specifically, let's consider what happens near Greenland and Iceland.

In this region during fall and winter, the water cools rapidly. At the surface, some of that water freezes, trapping a few salt crystals in the ice. Much of the salt is left in the remaining water. As a result, the remaining liquid ocean water becomes saltier. The resulting cold and salty water is more dense than the surrounding water; therefore, it sinks. As the water moves downward, it must be replaced. Warmer surface water moves in. In time, this water also will become cold and salty, and it will sink, too. The cycle continues.

From the animation or illustration, note that once the water sinks, it travels near and along the Atlantic seafloor toward Antarctic waters. The current travels around Antarctica. More cold, salty water sinks in this Southern Ocean. The deep, cold water current splits into two sections—one moving into the Indian Ocean and one heading through the Western Pacific. Both of these currents travel in a northerly direction toward the Equator. It is here that the water begins to warm, decreasing its density, causing it to rise. This rising, called **upwelling**, is extremely important to ocean ecosystems. As water rises to the surface, it carries with it nutrients from the deep sea. The nutrients are used by marine organisms and are critical to ocean food webs. Upwelling is particularly prevalent when currents, driven by prevailing winds and the Coriolis Effect, move water offshore. This process results in the initial water being replaced with the cold, nutrient-rich water from below.

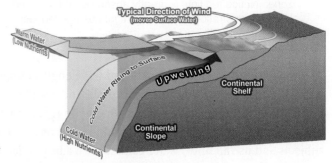

FIGURE 12.22. Upwelling diagram illustrates a scenario in which cooler surface waters are exposed. Winds moving water offshore set the stage for this typical environmental condition. In the process, nutrient-rich waters rise to the top of the water column.

The currents continue to travel until they reach the Arctic, and the cycle continues. The movement of water in deep currents is an extremely slow process. The Global Conveyor Belt moves much more slowly, just a few centimeters per second, than wind-driven surface currents, which move at tens of centimeters to meters per second. It is believed to take approximately 1,000 years to complete one Global Conveyor Belt cycle. The Global Conveyor Belt also allows mixing between the ocean basins. Substances such as sediments, salt ions, and dissolved gases, as well as heat, are also transported. Organisms can travel or be carried to different basins. The Global Conveyor Belt has important effects on climate. For instance, if its flow in the Atlantic Ocean were disrupted, some scientists predict that Europe would experience ice-age conditions. Both land and marine ecosystems would change across the globe. There is scientific evidence that rapid changes in the deep sea current have occurred within the past 20,000 years.

Another characteristic of the deep sea is the lack of visible light. Sunlight does not easily penetrate the ocean's waters. Near the surface, light is absorbed when water molecules vibrate, and light energy is converted into thermal energy. Some visible light and the various colors of the electromagnetic spectrum are absorbed closer to the surface than others. In fact, the reason that the ocean appears blue is that the red visible light is absorbed quickly by water, whereas the blue light is absorbed more slowly, allowing the color to be scattered back to our eyes. The layer of ocean surface water in which light is able to penetrate is referred to as the **photic zone**. The thickness of the photic zone depends on Earth's curvature and the directness or intensity of the Sun's rays, the season, and the turbidity (the cloudiness or haziness) of the seawater.

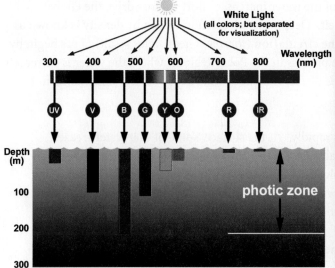

FIGURE 12.23. The depths to which various light energy will penetrate the ocean's surface, or photic zone. Notice red light is greatly absorbed. It has a very shallow penetration depth. Blue light has the deepest penetration depth.

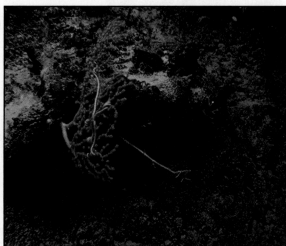

FIGURE 12.24. This Red Coral at more than 1,100 meters (~3,609 feet) deep would appear gray without the use of a camera flash.

As shown in the graphic above, the red wavelengths of light are absorbed within the ocean's very top few meters. Red objects, including fish, corals, and even blood, appear gray below the depth where red light has been absorbed. There is no red light energy to reflect back to your eye. To take vivid pictures of brightly colored organisms, such as those found in coral reefs, scientists and recreational scuba divers get close to their subjects and use an underwater camera with a bright flash. The flash is white light, which contains all of the visible light wavelengths—including red.

See Page 694 for how to access e-Tools.

View the **Deep Sea Jellyfish Video** (0:56) and the **Deep Sea Coral Video** (0:24) from the e-Tools.

e-Tools

- The videos show different examples of how ocean organisms produce their own light. The first video shows brilliant displays by a deep sea jellyfish. Jellyfish and other invertebrates show amazing displays of light.

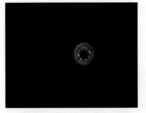

FIGURE 12.25. Screenshot of the **Deep Sea Jellyfish Video**.

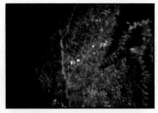

FIGURE 12.26. Screenshot of the **Deep Sea Coral Video**.

- The next video was taken from the *Johnson-Sea-Link-II* submersible during a deepsea dive off the coast of Florida. Although the video is black and white, you can see a deep sea Coral flashing, possibly in response to being agitated by the submersible.

Most light is absorbed by approximately 200 meters (~650 feet). By this depth, the ocean is essentially dark—there certainly is not enough light for human eyes to see. Most marine organisms live within the top, lighted areas of the ocean, but there are organisms that do live in this poorly lit area, sometimes called the "twilight zone". They often have big eyes to assist them in capturing as much light as possible, including light produced by other organisms. Toward the seafloor, below about 800 meters (~2,600 feet), the ocean is indeed pitch black. However, many living organisms overcome the lack of light in this zone by producing their *own* light through biochemical reactions. Light that is generated from biological processes is called **bioluminescence**.

The images below are examples of bioluminescence in the ocean:

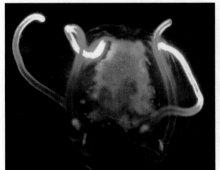

FIGURE 12.27.

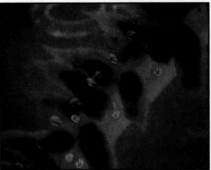

FIGURE 12.28.

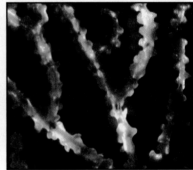

FIGURE 12.29.

FIGURE 12.30.

Bioluminescence is rare on land but extremely common in many groups of marine organisms. Some of these organisms use this ability to attract prey. Others use it as a distraction—emitting a flash of light so that they can escape quickly. Bioluminescence can also be used to attract a potential mate during reproductive season. Scientists believe that some species display "light shows" to be more attractive to the opposite sex. Because the deep ocean is so difficult to access, bioluminescence is a topic that remains quite mysterious—scientists are eager to study it and learn more.

In the last section we discovered that there are factors that dramatically change as the water depth increases. Have you ever wondered how organisms can survive in the ocean under the changing or extreme conditions? In this section we will explain how animals that dive deep are able to cope with the changes that occur.

When humans travel deep into the ocean in a submersible, they are protected from the immense pressure and cold temperatures by its thick metal walls. To overcome the dark waters, the submersible is also equipped with powerful lights. From the thick, acrylic windows of a submersible, scientists can view underwater structures and organisms.

FIGURE 12.31. A scientist peers out the window of a submersible.

FIGURE 12.32. An exploring submersible is a science research vessel for the deep ocean. Well equipped for high-pressure environments, much of what scientists learn about deep water comes from data collected by submersibles and ROVs.

FIGURE 12.33. A Sperm Whale moves up the water column after a dive.

A Sperm Whale's average dive depth is between 500 and 1,000 meters (~1,600 to ~3,300 feet). The deepest recorded dive of a Sperm Whale was approximately 2,000 meters (~6,600 feet), where there is no light and very low temperatures occur. Imagine how difficult it would be to find food where there is no light. Luckily, Sperm Whales do not need light to locate their prey. They use sound waves in a similar manner to scientists mapping the seafloor. The whale emits sounds, which bounce off the prey and return to the animal's highly sensitive ears. This process is called echolocation. Scientists believe that sound waves also stun a whale's prey, giving the slow-moving mammal time to find it.

Sperm Whales spend most of their time—as much as 90% of their life—diving to great depths in search of food. Their diet consists mostly of squid, including giant and colossal squid, and fish that live in the deep sea. When a whale surfaces from a dive, it expels leftover carbon dioxide and air from its lungs. Recall that in mammals, the blood carries oxygen from the lungs to the cells and carbon dioxide (a waste product) from the cells to the lungs. The whale will spend 10–15 minutes taking deep breaths, exhaling carbon dioxide from its lungs and then filling them up with fresh air. Immediately before the Sperm Whale takes its plunge into the depths, it will take a few more gulps of air, and then dive straight down toward the seafloor. As they dive, Sperm Whales are able to slow their heart rate down to just a few beats per minute. Blood may also be directed only to the heart, brain, and essential organs. Sperm Whales also have a flexible rib cage that, under extreme pressure, can squeeze inward and collapse the lungs. Both the redirection of blood and the collapsing of lungs preserve oxygen during a 45–60-minute dive—quite a long time for a mammal to hold its breath.

The Leatherback Sea Turtle is another example of an animal that has the ability to make deep dives. These turtles are different from all other sea turtles because they do not have a hard shell. Instead, their shell is soft and leathery (they are named for that leathery shell). The Leatherback's soft body can adjust to increasing water pressure by squeezing or compressing. This allows Leatherbacks to dive deeper than other sea turtles, which have hard outer shells and would be crushed by the pressure.

FIGURE 12.34. The soft shell of the Leatherback Sea Turtle allows it to dive much deeper than other sea turtle species.

See Page 694 for how to access e-Tools.

e-Tools

View the *Leatherback Sea Turtle Transmitter Video* (3:03) from the e-Tools to learn how scientists attach suction cup transmitters to Leatherback Sea Turtles in order to observe their behavior below the ocean surface.

FIGURE 12.35. Screenshot of the *Leatherback Sea Turtle Transmitter Video*. Researchers employ miniature depth recorders and transmitters using a suction cup on Leatherback Sea Turtles to gain new behavioral insights.

Leatherbacks do not dive as deep as Sperm Whales because most jellyfish, their main food source, are found at depths of 150 to 600 meters (~500 to ~2,000 feet). Scientists believe that the deepest dives recorded for Leatherbacks, more than 1,000 meters (~3,300 feet), are in response to a large predator, such as a shark, or being startled by a boat.

Some Leatherback Sea Turtles spend their entire lives in the deep sea. They are adapted to handle the extreme cold, lack of light, and crushing pressure at these depths. These factors are a problem for deep sea fish when they are caught in fishing nets or lines. When fish are brought up to the surface too quickly they cannot adjust to the quick decrease in pressure. The unfortunate result is that the animals' internal organs will explode, sometimes spilling out of their mouths or anuses.

FIGURE 12.36. Close-up of a tripod fish at 1,960 m (~6,430 ft) depth near the Bahamas. Deep sea fish have very interesting characteristics, but cannot withstand the pressure change of being brought to the surface.

Scuba Diving

Scuba diving is an activity and technique used by scientists and citizens alike to learn about the world beneath the ocean's surface. The term *scuba* is an acronym for Self-Contained Underwater Breathing Apparatus. Unlike other diving techniques, scuba allows divers the freedom to explore as they carry all the tools they need to remain underwater for a period of time. Scientists can reach sensitive coral reefs, observe organisms in their habitat, and collect important data about the marine environment with little, if any, impact to the ecosystem.

As you know, there is oxygen dissolved in seawater. However, unlike marine organisms, humans cannot take the oxygen out of water to breathe. Scuba divers breathe from air tanks they wear on their backs. The tanks are filled with compressed air (78% nitrogen, 21% oxygen) or nitrox (which has a slightly higher percentage of oxygen). Compressed air if breathed directly out of the tank can be harmful to human lungs. To account for this, the air passes through a **regulator** that reduces the pressure, which changes depending on the diver's depth. The regulator is a very important part of the diver's equipment. While underwater and at greater pressure, a diver's body absorbs more oxygen and nitrogen in the bloodstream than normal.

An important part of scuba diving training includes how to resurface safely after having been a number of meters below the sea surface on a dive. Divers ascend slowly, allowing nitrogen that has built up in their body to be slowly released. If a diver comes to the surface too quickly, bubbles of nitrogen gas build up in the bloodstream and cause decompression sickness, commonly known as "the bends". When this condition occurs, bubbles of nitrogen gas block blood vessels, causing life-threatening conditions such as paralysis, strokes, and heart attacks. NOAA and diving organizations supply divers with guidelines for decompression after diving to various depths.

FIGURE 12.37. NOAA scientist investigating changes to corals in the Florida Keys National Marine Sanctuary. Many marine biologists scuba dive to conduct their research.

FIGURE 12.38. Scuba diving allows divers greater freedom of movement underwater. One disadvantage is that there is no communication means between the diver and the surface.

Elaborate

Activity

Studying CTD Data

Now that you have investigated the relationships between water depth, temperature, salinity, and density, we are going to apply that knowledge to real station data gathered in May 2004 off the coast of California. The data include temperature, salinity, density, and a measure of light availability, or **fluorescence**.

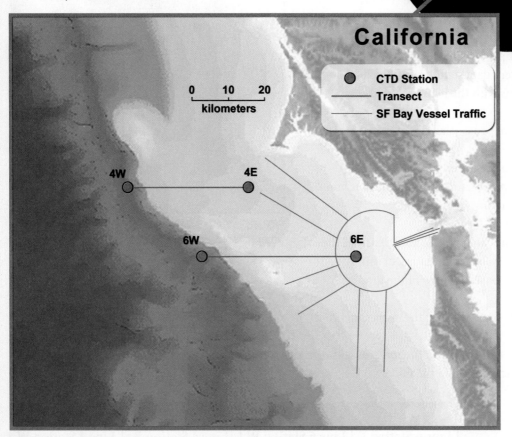

FIGURE 12.39. CTD Stations off of the California Coast are locations at which CTDs were deployed. Authentic measurements are presented for better understanding of the relationship between water parameters with depth.

1. Looking at the map above, you will notice 4 CTD stations. Each pair is along the same line of latitude. Using the scale, determine the distance between each of the following data stations:

    a. Stations 4W and 4E.

    b. Stations 6W and 6E.

2. Which data stations are on the continental shelf? Which are beyond the shelf break?

3. *Prediction:* What differences, if any, do you think you might observe in the data from the water samples collected at each of the CTD stations? Be specific for each of the parameters with respect to depth (density, temperature, salinity, and fluorescence—the availability of light). Be sure to explain your reasoning.

As you read in the **Explain** section, CTDs are equipped to gather data about multiple parameters at the same time. This technique helps scientists to look at relationships between the parameters and to get a better understanding of the conditions at a certain depth. Earlier in the Lesson, you plotted different parameters with respect to depth. These graphs show the same type of information, except each will now have several lines on it.

The graphs on the next page display the information gathered at the 4 different data stations in May 2004. Carefully study the plots with the help of these hints:

- Each colored line is associated with the same colored scale.
- The depth scales are different.
- Consider each parameter separately, just as you did with your graphs.

FIGURE 12.40. Scientists retrieve and document water samples from a CTD.

4. What generalizations can be made about each of the parameters, a) density, b) temperature, c) salinity, and d) fluorescence, based on all 4 of the graphs?

5. Which plot or plots show water at the *deepest* depths?

6. Draw the following table in your notebook. Use the graphs to record the highest and lowest values for each station in the table.

	Station			
	Line 6 Station E	**Line 6 Station W**	**Line 4 Station E**	**Line 4 Station W**
High Temp (°C)				
Low Temp (°C)				
High Salinity (PSU)				
Low Salinity (PSU)				
High Fluorescence (mg/m³)				
Low Fluorescence (mg/m³)				

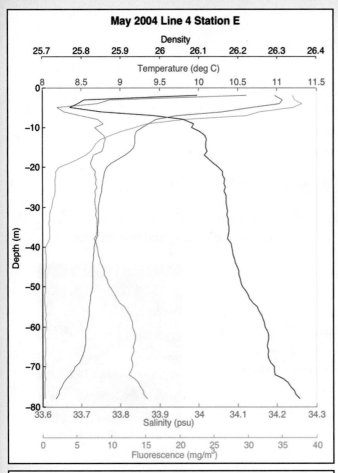

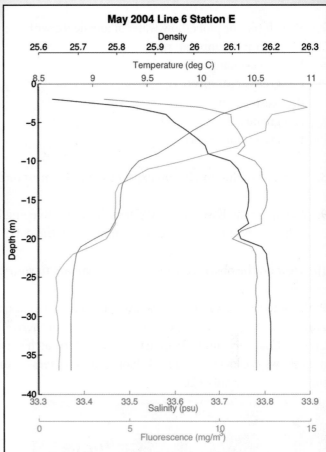

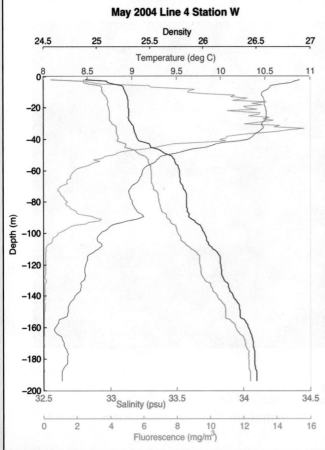

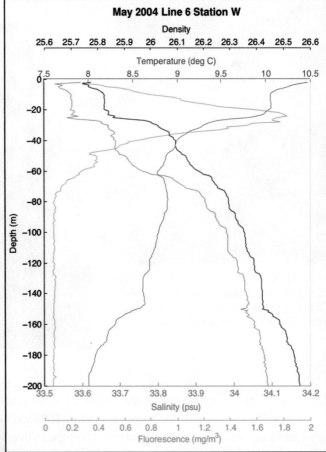

FIGURE 12.41.

7. Which plot or plots show water at any depth with the:
   a. warmest temperature?
   b. coolest temperature?
   c. greatest salinity?
   d. least salinity?
   e. greatest fluorescence?
   f. least fluorescence?

8. At what station might you expect to find the most bioluminescent organisms? Why?

9. Compare the Eastern and Western Stations. Keeping in mind what you have learned, what major differences and similarities do you notice in the data? Include at least one similarity and two differences.

10. How do the observed data readings compare to your predictions?

Pink-footed Shearwaters are seabirds that are known to travel from their breeding grounds along Coastal Chile to as far north as Southern Alaska. When foraging, these animals dive up to 25 meters (~82 feet) to catch small fish and squid. The map shows the locations of Pink-footed Shearwaters off the coast of California in the summer and fall of 2009.

FIGURE 12.42. Pink-footed Shearwater.

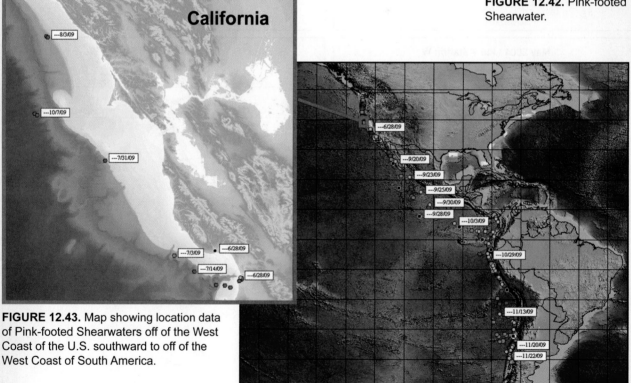

FIGURE 12.43. Map showing location data of Pink-footed Shearwaters off of the West Coast of the U.S. southward to off of the West Coast of South America.

11. According to the map above, the Pink-footed Shearwaters were tracked near stations 4W and 6W. Assuming the conditions in the summer of 2004 were similar to those in 2009, describe what the seabirds would experience (for each parameter) on their dives.

Evaluate

1. Explain the relationship between the depth of water and its temperature, density, salinity, and pressure, and available light.

2. What is bioluminescence? How does it help organisms living in the deep sea?

3. Identify two environmental conditions of the deep sea. For each, give one example of how marine organisms cope with the condition.

4. Explain how information from a CTD station in the polar seas might differ from one in the tropical seas.

FIGURE 12.44. CTD package being cast into icy waters.

13

Photosynthesis in the Ocean

INSIDE:

Objectives

You will be able to:

✓ Identify the reactants and products of photosynthesis and note the sources of the reactants in the ocean.

✓ Describe how carbon is cycled through Earth's spheres.

✓ Analyze chlorophyll imagery, looking for evidence of blooms of phytoplankton that contribute to the food sources of marine animals.

 Benchmarks

3e. The ocean dominates the Earth's carbon cycle. Half the primary productivity on Earth takes place in the sunlit layers of the ocean, and the ocean absorbs roughly half of all carbon dioxide added to the atmosphere.

4a. Most of the oxygen in the atmosphere originally came from the activities of photosynthetic organisms in the ocean.

5b. Most life in the ocean exists as microbes. Microbes are the most important primary producers in the ocean. Not only are they the most abundant life form in the ocean, they have extremely fast growth rates and life cycles.

5f. Ocean habitats are defined by environmental factors. Due to interactions of abiotic factors (e.g., salinity, temperature, oxygen, pH, light, nutrients, pressure, substrate, circulation), ocean life is not evenly distributed temporally or spatially (i.e., it is "patchy"). Some regions of the ocean support more diverse and abundant life than anywhere on Earth, while much of the ocean is considered a desert.

7d. New technologies, sensors, and tools are expanding our ability to explore the ocean. Ocean scientists are relying more and more on satellites, drifters, buoys, subsea observatories, and unmanned submersibles.

Engage

Some of the most important organisms in the ocean environments are those that you cannot see with the naked eye. If you were to put a drop of water from near the top of the ocean's surface under the microscope, you would see a remarkable number of organisms in it. Some of these organisms have the ability to use the Sun's energy to make food, through the process of photosynthesis. This extraordinary process supplies most living things in the ocean with the energy they need to live.

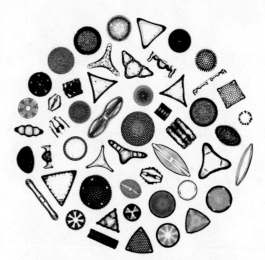

FIGURE 13.1. This image, taken with the help of a microscope, shows 50 different species of diatoms. Diatoms form the base of many marine and aquatic food chains. Upon their death, their glassy shells form sediments known as diatomaceous earth, which is sometimes used in pool filters.

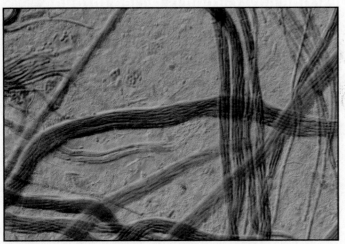

FIGURE 13.2. Cyanobacteria are some of the tiniest phytoplankton, but are also very important. They are believed to be Earth's first producers.

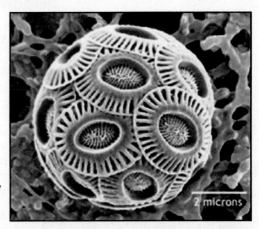

FIGURE 13.3. Like any other type of phytoplankton, coccolithophores are one-celled marine organisms that live in large numbers throughout the upper layers of the ocean. Coccolithophores surround themselves with a microscopic plating made of calcite, the mineral that makes up limestone. These scales, known as coccoliths, are shaped like hubcaps and are only three one-thousandths of a millimeter in diameter.

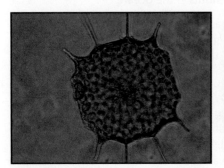

FIGURE 13.4. Through a microscope, the beautiful patterns that form the structure of diatoms are revealed.

FIGURE 13.5. Some diatoms form long chains.

FIGURE 13.6. Using a Scanning Electron Microscope (SEM), diatoms are magnified 270 times. Diatoms are found throughout the temperate and polar oceans.

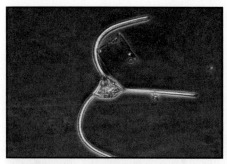

FIGURE 13.7. Dinoflagellates are another important type of marine phytoplankton. These organisms are easily identified by their long, whip-like projections called **flagella**, which they use to move. Many dinoflagellates produce their own food but others eat food from their environment.

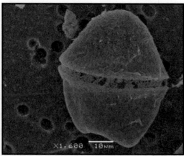

FIGURE 13.8. Some dinoflagellates, like this one called *Akashiwo sanguinea* (pronounced: ah-kah-SHEE-who sahn-gween-EE-ah), are toxic to both marine organisms and humans. This SEM photograph shows the structure of the organism's shell and flagellum.

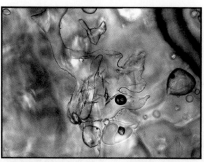

FIGURE 13.9. Some phytoplankton live within or just below sea ice, which floats atop the ocean. These algae are important producers in the polar seas.

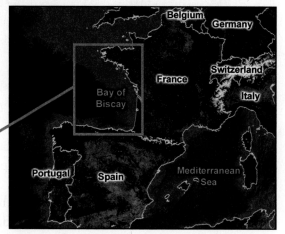

FIGURE 13.10. Although microscopic, when conditions are right, phytoplankton multiply and are even visible from Space. Phytoplankton in France's Bay of Biscay brought bright swirls of light blue and turquoise to the surface across much of the bay. Careful inspection of this true-color scene reveals there are likely a variety of species of phytoplankton blooming in the bay. Notice the dark green hues near the shore along France's Western Coastline. These hues are possibly due to the green pigment chlorophyll, which phytoplankton use for photosynthesis.

Think about what you know about photosynthesis. Work through the following Questions on your own, in small groups, or as a class.

1. Draw the chart below in your notebook. Then complete the chart by listing the substances necessary to complete photosynthesis and the products of the process. Substances required for a chemical reaction are called reactants.

Reactants	Products

2. Where do producers living in aquatic and marine ecosystems derive the reactants for photosynthesis?

3. Why are the end products of photosynthesis important?

Explore

Observing Photosynthesis

Demonstration

As a class, we will be making observations that will support our thinking about the reactants and products of photosynthesis. The following is a general equation for photosynthesis:

$$6CO_2 \text{ (carbon dioxide)} + 6H_2O \text{ (water)} \xrightarrow[\text{chlorophyll}]{\text{light}} C_6H_{12}O_6 \text{ (glucose)} + O_2 \text{ (oxygen)}$$

FIGURE 13.11. General equation for photosynthesis.

This equation tells us that carbon dioxide and water, in the presence of sunlight, nutrients, chlorophyll, and enzymes, complete a reaction that results in the production of glucose and the release of oxygen. Light energy is converted into chemical energy in the process of photosynthesis. Glucose, a sugar, is a form of chemical energy that can be used by living things. It is a chemical energy because the energy is actually stored in the chemical bonding between the carbon, hydrogen, and oxygen atoms.

Bromothymol blue is a chemical indicator that turns yellow in the presence of carbon dioxide. We will use this substance to make observations of photosynthesis. Is the process of photosynthesis occurring? The plant we will study is called Elodea (pronounced: el-Ō-dee-ah), a common plant found in freshwater ecosystems such as ponds, rivers, and streams.

Your teacher will set up the demonstration shown below.

FIGURE 13.12. Demonstration setup.

4. Draw what happens when CO_2 is added to the Bromothymol blue solution.

5. Observations: Day 1 – Draw and label each of the flasks containing Elodea.

6. Observations: Day 2 – Draw and label each of the flasks containing Elodea.

7. What happened in the flask when bubbles were blown into it? What color did the solution turn?

8. What happened in the flask with Elodea left under a light source? Why?

9. What happened in the flask with Elodea left in the dark cabinet? Why?

10. What happened to the control without Elodea? Why?

Explain

Part 1: Photosynthesis in Water

Organisms that make their own food are called **autotrophs** (pronounced: AW-tŏ-trōfs). Many producers are able to make their own food by first capturing sunlight energy—using chlorophyll from within their cells—to make sugar in a process called **photosynthesis**. Photosynthesis originates from the Greek word *photo*, "pertaining to light", and *synthesis* meaning "putting together". Therefore photosynthesis means "using light to put something together". Autotrophs combine light and substances to create sugar, or food, for themselves—and for other organisms.

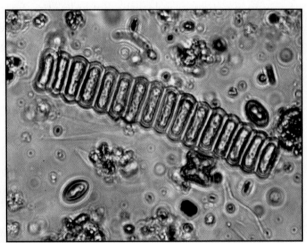

FIGURE 13.13. Tiny phytoplankton are some of the most important marine organisms. This photograph shows several different types of phytoplankton, including diatoms, dinoflagellates, and cyanobacteria.

The most important producers in the ocean are tiny, plant-like organisms called **phytoplankton**. These microscopic organisms, or **microbes,** are responsible for producing more than half of the oxygen on Earth. Most of the organisms in the ocean are microbes, the base of marine food webs. Microbes have extremely fast growth rates and life cycles. This means that more oxygen is produced in the ocean than is produced on the continents, including from all of the trees combined. An important group of phytoplankton are photosynthetic bacteria called **cyanobacteria** (pronounced: sī-ANN-ō-bak-teer-ē-uh). The oldest fossils found on Earth are from cyanobacteria that lived approximately 3.5 billion years ago. Thanks to these tiny plankton, there is plenty of oxygen in Earth's atmosphere. Before cyanobacteria existed on Earth, there was no oxygen at all. The changing atmosphere also led to changes in life on Earth. Oxygen in the upper atmosphere forms a compound called **ozone**, which protects living things from harmful solar radiation. Before there was oxygen in the upper atmosphere (due to cyanobacteria) there were no living organisms on land, as they could not tolerate the Sun's damaging ultraviolet (UV) light energy.

Other important phytoplankton include diatoms and dinoflagellates. The cell walls of diatoms are made of silica and are clear, allowing sunlight to penetrate to their internal structures. Many have spines or other features that help them to float and remain close to the sea surface. Dinoflagellates are named for their two whip-like cell structures called flagella. Dinoflagellates have both plant- and animal-like characteristics. Many are photosynthetic but can also ingest food.

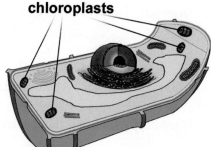

chloroplasts

FIGURE 13.14. A typical plant or phytoplankton cell contains many chloroplasts. You can often observe chloroplasts under normal compound microscopes, like those you probably use in your science lab.

Photosynthesis combines light, carbon dioxide (CO_2), and water (H_2O) and produces glucose ($C_6H_{12}O_6$), or sugar, a high-energy carbohydrate, and releases oxygen (O_2). This energy-capturing process occurs mostly in the cell organelle called the **chloroplast**. A chloroplast absorbs solar energy (sunlight) and converts it to chemical energy (in the chemical bonds of glucose) from the raw materials carbon dioxide and water.

Ingredients for Photosynthesis

Light: The Sun, an average-sized star in our galaxy, is the major source of energy for life on Earth. The sun emits a tremendous amount of energy in various wavelengths, but only a tiny fraction of that energy reaches our home planet. This includes visible light energy. Approximately 30% of the total amount of solar energy that makes it to Earth is reflected back into Space by all of Earth's materials combined (e.g., clouds, snow, ice, ocean surf, desert). Once within our Earth system, the Sun's radiation is absorbed by land, water, clouds, and living things. Nearly 50% of the energy that reaches Earth's atmosphere is ultimately absorbed by the land and oceans.

FIGURE 13.15. The tilt of the Earth on its axis and its revolution around the Sun result in seasonal differences in light availability. Therefore, there are seasonal differences in photosynthesis—both on land and in the ocean.

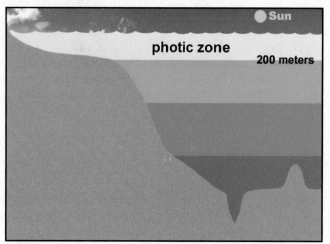

FIGURE 13.16. Sunlight penetrates only about 200 meters (~650 feet) into the ocean. Photosynthesis can only occur in this top layer, called the photic zone.

Sunlight does not reach very deep water. Its reach partially depends on how clear the water is. The photic zone, the layer of the ocean that allows light to penetrate, can extend from the surface to more than 200 meters (~656 feet) in clear, open areas. In coastal areas where there are more sediments and living things in the water, the light penetrates less. The amount of light also varies in strength with seasons during the Earth's revolution around the Sun. Below the upper part of the photic zone, there are no phytoplankton to photosynthesize, or make food, because there is not enough light available.

Carbon dioxide: Phytoplankton utilize CO_2 from the many living organisms that release it into the water as a result of respiration. This is not unlike the experiment in which we exhaled CO_2 into the flasks in the **Explore** section. In addition to living things, sources of CO_2 in the ocean include undersea vents and volcanoes; the breakdown of shells, rocks, and other materials; and diffusion from the atmosphere.

Nutrients: Nutrients necessary for photosynthesis include nitrogen, phosphorus, potassium, iron, and others. These substances are used in small amounts by autotrophs. There are both land- and water-based sources for nutrients. Phytoplankton can take in nutrients directly; the nutrients diffuse from the water across their cell membranes. In contrast, land plants must get nutrients through their roots. Nutrients are released when living matter and other organic materials break down, or **decompose**. Nutrients can reach the ocean from runoff from the land.

FIGURE 13.17. One major source of carbon dioxide (CO_2) in the ocean is from marine organisms. Living things release CO_2 as a byproduct of respiration. CO_2 is released from decomposers feeding on dead organisms.

FIGURE 13.18. Unlike phytoplankton in the sea, land plants derive nutrients from the soil. Most of the mass of the plant comes from carbon from the CO_2 in the air.

Chlorophyll and Enzymes: Chlorophyll and enzymes are present within organisms themselves. It is not necessary for organisms to get these ingredients from their surrounding environment. Within cells and other materials are colored substances called **pigments**. Chlorophyll, a type of pigment found inside chloroplasts, is responsible for most photosynthesis in phytoplankton. The green color typically associated with photosynthetic organisms results from chlorophyll's property of reflecting green wavelengths of light. It is actually the red and blue wavelengths of light that supply the energy absorbed and converted by phytoplankton during photosynthesis. Enzymes are proteins within all organisms that speed up chemical reactions, including photosynthesis.

11. Create a data table in which you list each of the ingredients for photosynthesis and sources for them.

Ingredients	Sources

The Carbon Cycle

Carbon plays a key role in photosynthesis. It enters the process as part of a carbon dioxide molecule, and, following a complex series of reactions, becomes an integral part of the chemical energy stored in the glucose molecule. When living plants and other producers grow, most of their mass is built from the carbon, right out of thin air. Other living things survive by tapping into that stored energy from producers—by eating them. Subsequent biotic and abiotic reactions involving carbon are found throughout the Earth system. The complex process in which the element carbon moves throughout the Earth system is collectively called the **carbon cycle**. Carbon is cycled from the non-living environment and is reused in living organisms for life to continue.

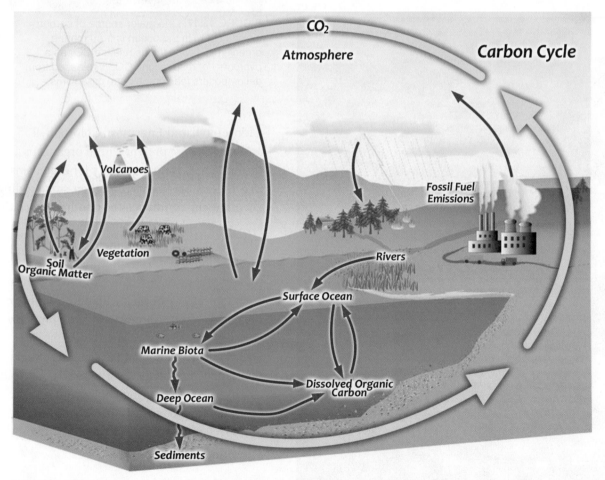

FIGURE 13.19. Not only is carbon found in all living things, but the element is present in the atmosphere, in the layers of limestone sediment on the ocean floor and in fossil fuels like oil. The complex process in which carbon moves throughout the Earth system is the carbon cycle.

The ocean plays an important part in the carbon cycle because it holds more than 90% of all of Earth's CO_2, while only trace amounts of CO_2 are found in the atmosphere. Besides photosynthesis, the CO_2 in the ocean is also used by some organisms (e.g., corals, clams, oysters) to build their shells of calcium carbonate ($CaCO_3$).

Plants take in CO_2 and use the carbon to build carbohydrates. The carbohydrates are passed along food webs to other organisms. Both producers and consumers die and release wastes, and the carbon returns to the water or the atmosphere. In the process of the decay of dead organic material, bacteria decompose the organic carbohydrates and release carbon dioxide and water back to the water, soil, or air. Both on land and in the ocean, buried remains of carbon-rich organisms become incorporated into rocks. Eventually, the remains can be converted into fossil fuels. Burning fossil fuels releases CO_2 into the atmosphere. The ocean absorbs about half of the CO_2 released into the atmosphere. Carbon dioxide gas is also released by volcanoes, found both underwater and on land. Carbon in the form of CO_2 and methane (CH_4) is released through activities such as mining and agriculture. Carbon is released through deforestation, as most trees that are taken down are burned.

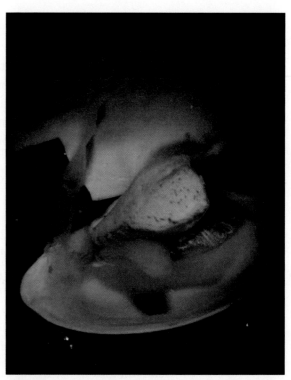

FIGURE 13.20. Clams and other animals make their shells from calcium and carbon dioxide found in seawater. You are probably familiar with calcium carbonate, also known as chalk.

FIGURE 13.21. Undersea volcanoes, such as the one shown here, contribute carbon dioxide and other compounds to seawater. The ocean holds more than 90% of the carbon dioxide in the Earth system.

12. Draw the data table in your notebook. Give one example of how cycling carbon enters and leaves each of Earth's spheres.

Sphere	Carbon Enters By:	Carbon Leaves By:
Atmosphere		
Biosphere		
Hydrosphere		
Lithosphere		

Elaborate

Scientists use extensive data and satellite imagery to learn about the ocean. Bathymetric data helps provide information about the ocean floor. Sea surface satellite imagery helps us to study environmental conditions on the sea surface. Similarly, satellites can gather information about phytoplankton. These "chlorophyll" satellite images provide details about the distribution and density of important food sources in marine environments.

Because they photosynthesize, the many different types of phytoplankton all contain chlorophyll. We have discussed that chlorophyll is the substance that makes trees, grass, and phytoplankton appear green. Scientists use satellite technology to visualize where chlorophyll is in the ocean. This is seen in satellite images. Instruments on satellites can detect exactly where chlorophyll is and assess its abundance.

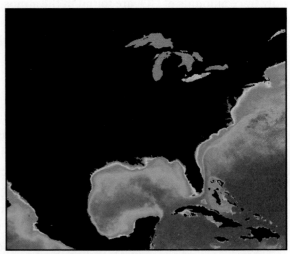

FIGURE 13.22. Phytoplankton image shows differing concentrations of chlorophyll. Chlorophyll levels are measured by remote sensing satellites.

Think about the concentration of chlorophyll as the amount of phytoplankton present in a certain volume in the top layer of the ocean. When chlorophyll concentrations are high, there are many phytoplankton; the organisms are meeting their needs and are reproducing. When chlorophyll concentrations are shown to increase in a short period of time, it is called a **phytoplankton** or **algal bloom**. Algal blooms occur when more light and nutrients are suddenly available and phytoplankton utilize these ingredients to grow and reproduce quickly. Conditions can become very favorable for growth, such that the algae will cover large surfaces. You will see evidence of algal blooms in some of the satellite imagery. Satellite-based instruments determine what the exact concentrations of phytoplankton are by calculating how much visible light is absorbed by chlorophyll.

Chlorophyll *a* concentration (mg / m³)

0.01   0.03   0.1   0.3   1   3   10   30   60

FIGURE 13.23. Average springtime image shows high concentrations of chlorophyll in North Atlantic waters. This image represents a typical average for monthly mean chlorophyll imagery for April, May, and June.

Just like the analyzed SST images, phytoplankton images also use false color. Use the image and color bar for FIGURE 13.23 to help you answer the following Questions:

13. According to the color bar, where are the areas with the highest chlorophyll concentration (that is, the most phytoplankton)?

14. Where are the places with the lowest phytoplankton concentration?

15. Look at the images below showing the same section of the North Atlantic Ocean. Describe the change between the circled areas of chlorophyll concentration from January to April.

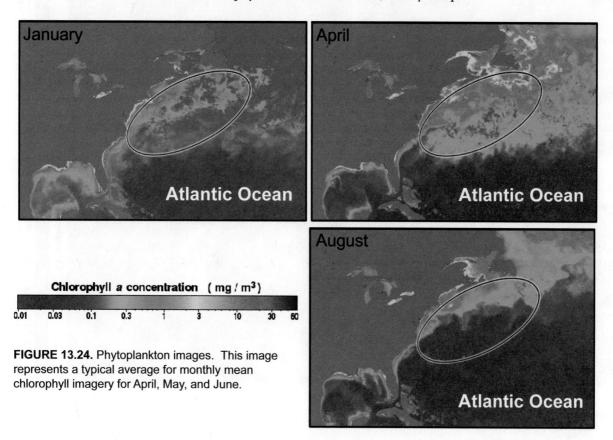

FIGURE 13.24. Phytoplankton images. This image represents a typical average for monthly mean chlorophyll imagery for April, May, and June.

16. What environmental factors would cause a major increase in phytoplankton over the time period?

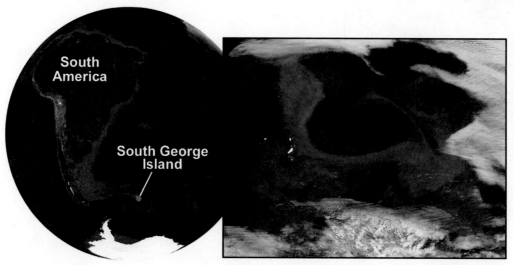

FIGURE 13.25. Real-color image of phytoplankton bloom off South Georgia Island in January 2004, photographed by a NASA satellite. Algal blooms like this occur naturally or as a result of human activities.

Living things in the ocean are not evenly distributed. Some areas have more organisms in them, supported by the processes of photosynthesis and chemosynthesis. Energy production through these processes is known as **primary productivity**. About half of the primary productivity that occurs on Earth takes place within the ocean's photic zone. In the chlorophyll images in the Lesson, you will observe areas of higher and lower productivity. Productivity in the ocean is affected by many factors, including bathymetric features, the movement of currents, light and nutrient availability, etc. You will further study these ideas in later Lessons.

The figures below illustrate chlorophyll concentrations for two consecutive years.

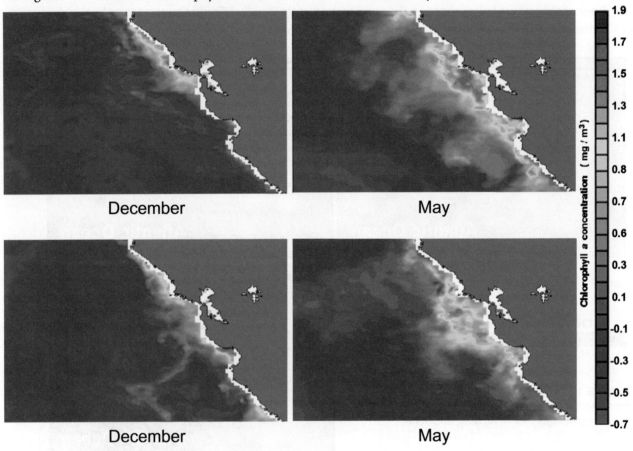

FIGURE 13.26. Chlorophyll images for two different years near the West Coast of the United States.

17. Identify the seasonal differences in chlorophyll concentrations seen in the West Coast satellite images above over two consecutive years.

The following image shows several Black-footed Albatross. These animals are often found along the coast of California during the spring and summer—times when the phytoplankton are quite abundant. In the next few Lessons, we will explore some of the connections between these seabirds and the plentiful plankton.

FIGURE 13.27. lack-footed Albatross chick waits on a beach in the Northwest Hawaiian Islands for its parents to return. Adult Albatross fly thousands of miles to more productive waters to gather food for their chicks.

FIGURE 13.28. Black-footed Albatross have a wingspan of up to 2 meters (~7 feet). This huge wingspan enables the seabirds to conserve energy as they fly for thousands of miles while soaring on wind currents.

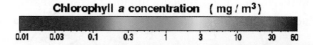

FIGURE 13.29. Select Albatross location data of a number of birds, each represented by a different color, on a phytoplankton image.

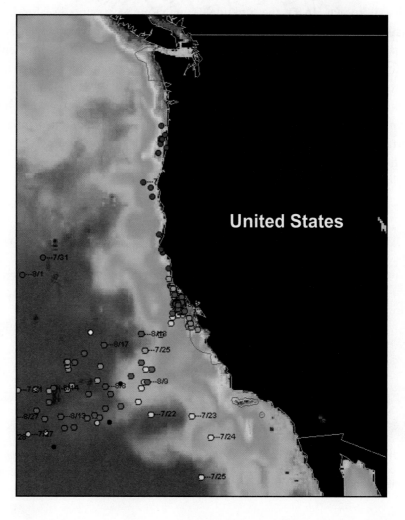

Harmful Algal Blooms

When a marine ecosystem receives a large input of excess nitrates and phosphates through agricultural runoff or sewage discharge, there is often an immediate increase in the amount of phytoplankton. This is an example of an algal bloom that is caused by human activities.

While most phytoplankton are not harmful, some species produce toxins that can have negative effects on animals and humans. These toxins are an example of disease-producing agents, or **pathogens**. When blooms of these phytoplankton occur, they are called **harmful algal blooms** or **HABs**. HABs have been responsible for mass die-offs of many species of fish, seabirds, and marine animals. Beaches in Florida can be closed due to HABs.

One well-known HAB is the "red tide" found along coastlines, particularly off the Gulf of Mexico. Harmful red tides are often created by a type of phytoplankton, *Karenia brevis*, which produces the neurotoxin **brevetoxin**. Red tide blooms cause a reddish discoloration in the ocean that can be seen for miles and can be responsible for extensive fish mortality and contaminated shellfish. The toxin in red tides can also become airborne, creating severe respiratory irritation in humans along the shore.

The diatom in the genus *Pseudo-nitzschia* creates a neurotoxin called **domoic acid** (pronounced: dō-MŌ-ic), which accumulates in the tissues of fish and filter-feeding organisms such as oysters, clams, and mussels, as well as large marine animals. In rare incidences, people who eat the tainted seafood can develop severe stomach pains, confusion, memory loss, and disorientation, or can even die. Marine mammals such as Sea Lions have also been known to travel long distances from the ocean and onto city streets and highways when sickened by domoic acid. Unfortunately, there is no cure for domoic acid poisoning.

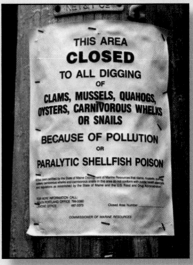

FIGURE 13.30. Shellfishing can be banned to prevent humans from getting sick due to contaminants such as brevetoxin or domoic acid.

FIGURE 13.31. The harmful algal bloom known as the "red tide" contains potent toxins. It can cause death of marine organisms and illness in humans.

FIGURE 13.32. Sea Lion pup is found wandering the streets of San Carlos, California. Scientists believe that the animal was disoriented because of effects of HABs.

HABs also played a role in a famous movie. Alfred Hitchcock's 1963 horror film, *The Birds*, was made at the same time an unusual incident occurred in Capitola (near Santa Cruz), California, in the fall of 1961. One morning, hundreds of Sooty Shearwaters were found dead, strewn throughout the streets of his sleepy coastal town, while others violently collided into the rooftops of residential homes. Scientists believe that the birds' bizarre behavior was caused by the accumulation of domoic acid in their bodies. This HAB was most likely caused by sewage discharge from a leaky septic tank.

Evaluate

1. Observe the chlorophyll image of North Carolina's waters.

   a. Identify areas of high chlorophyll.

   b. Identify areas of low chlorophyll.

   c. Give one example of a natural process that may result in increasing amounts of phytoplankton in North Carolina's waters.

2. How can phytoplankton result in a public health risk?

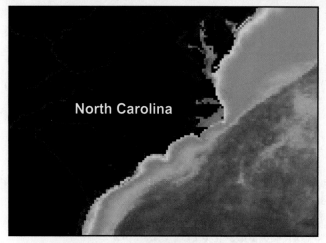

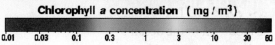

FIGURE 13.33. Phytoplankton image of coastal areas off of North Carolina.

3. The carbon cycle is a very important biogeochemical process within the Earth system. Using information in this Lesson, demonstrate that you understand the carbon cycle through one of the following "products":

   • a multimedia presentation
   • an essay
   • a poster

   Your product must include:

   • Each of Earth's spheres –Atmosphere, Biosphere, Hydrosphere, and Lithosphere
   • Processes in which carbon moves from one sphere to another
   • Carbon in at least three forms

14

Biodiversity in the Ocean

INSIDE:

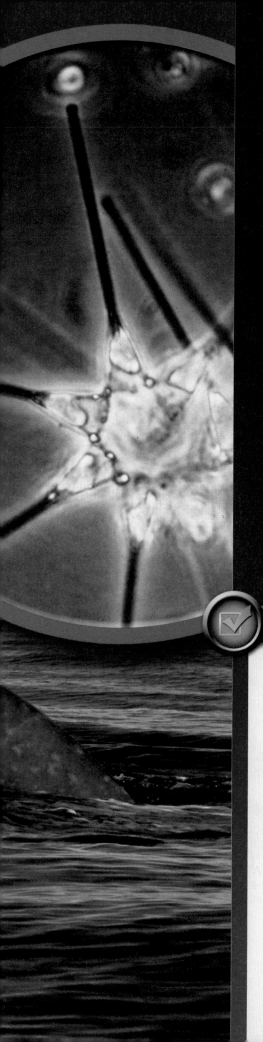

Objectives

You will be able to:

✔ Discuss the importance of biodiversity and provide examples of diverse organisms in the ocean.

✔ Describe the system of classification used by biologists.

✔ Classify organisms based on their characteristics.

✔ Analyze the similarities and differences between major groups of organisms.

✔ Explain how the structures of marine organisms support their functions.

✔ Identify the characteristics that all living things share.

Benchmarks

4b. The first life is thought to have started in the ocean. The earliest evidence of life is found in the ocean.

5a. Ocean life ranges in size from the smallest virus to the largest animal that has lived on Earth, the blue whale.

5b. Most life in the ocean exists as microbes. Microbes are the most important primary producers in the ocean. Not only are they the most abundant life form in the ocean, they have extremely fast growth rates and life cycles.

5g. There are deep ocean ecosystems that are independent of energy from sunlight and photosynthetic organisms. Hydrothermal vents, submarine hot springs, and methane cold seeps rely only on chemical energy and chemosynthetic organisms to support life.

Engage

1. Make a list of 5–10 of the most unusual marine organisms that you can recall.

From previous Lessons, you already know that the ocean is home to a wide variety of organisms. The number and variety of species within a habitat or area is known as **biodiversity**. For example, coral reef ecosystems have high biodiversity. These ecosystems are home to myriad algae, coral, fish, worms, slugs, sea turtles, sharks, plankton, and much more. Biodiversity is higher in the ocean than on land or in freshwater.

FIGURE 14.1. Coral reefs is one marine with very high biodiversity.

The term *biodiversity* does not only describe the many different types of organisms on Earth. Diversity within groups of organisms of the same species (within **populations**) also contributes to biodiversity. For example, when looking around your classroom, you may note the visible diversity within the population of humans—there are differences in height, hair color, eye color, skin color, and so on. Diversity extends to our metabolic processes as well. Some humans are more resistant to disease; some break down food or build muscle quite easily compared to others. Characteristics such as these came from our biological parents. Great internal and external diversity exists within populations of other organisms as well. Diversity within and among species based on inherited factors is **genetic diversity**. Genetic diversity results in biodiversity.

For example, within a species of albatross, no two birds are exactly the same. Some birds can fly faster or farther than others. Some look to attract stronger mates or choose the most protected place on the beach to raise their chicks. This quality of biodiversity is true for all species and can therefore help species to survive catastrophes. For example, imagine a mangrove forest is hit by a hurricane. It is likely that many of the mangrove trees would be destroyed by the high winds and big waves.

FIGURE 14.2. Within any species, no two individuals are exactly the same. These two individual Short-tailed Albatross have genetic differences.

Some of the trees in the mangrove forests, however, might have particularly strong root systems that help them to withstand the hurricane. That way, there are at least some mangrove trees living in the mangrove forest ecosystem even after a very bad hurricane. This is important because in ecosystems such as forests or coral reefs, every single species plays a very important role, and all of the species are dependent on one another. If there aren't very many mangrove trees in a forest, it's more likely that disease or a natural disaster could wipe all of them out, which would be bad for the forest ecosystem as a whole. For the same reason, ecosystems do not survive well with very few species because if all the members of

FIGURE 14.3. The mangrove trees with the strongest root systems are the ones most likely to survive a hurricane. Genetic diversity contributes to the survival of the tree species.

one of the species is wiped out, there are no other species to help take its place in the ecosystem. Simply put, biodiversity is important to the health of species, ecosystems, and the Earth system.

In this Lesson, you will explore and observe diverse members of the **plankton** community. The word *plankton* means "wanderers". The plankton community consists of organisms that wander at the mercy of the ocean's movements, including currents and tides. In contrast, marine organisms that can swim against these processes are called **nekton**. Examples of nekton include seabirds, fish, and marine mammals.

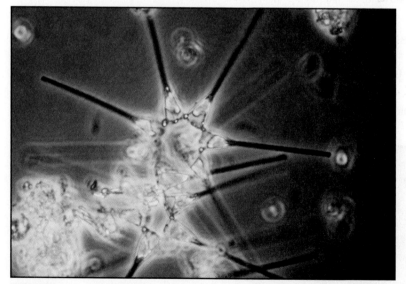

The phytoplankton that you studied in the last Lesson are plankton that are capable of photosynthesis. You will find that there are other types of plankton as well.

FIGURE 14.4. The plankton community is very diverse. Organisms that float along with current, tides, and other ocean processes comprise this community.

Explore

See Page 694 for how to access e-Tools.

Cyberlab

Virtual Plankton Exploration

The ocean is huge; it has vast space in which diverse organisms can live. Because living things on all of Earth are so many and diverse, scientists have developed ways to organize or classify them. The way in which organisms are classified has changed several times over the last few centuries, which you will read more about in the **Explain** section of this Lesson. A few of the major criteria used to classify organisms into broad groups are described below. You will work with these criteria during your Cyberlab investigation.

Cell type: Cells with a nucleus (**eukaryotic**) or lacking a nucleus (**prokaryotic**) (pronounced: you-kăr-ree-AWE-tic, pro-kăr-ree-AWE-tic)

Number of cells: One-celled (**unicellular**) or many celled (**multicellular**)

Mode of nutrition: Autotroph or heterotroph

Within the plankton population you will explore, you will note that the organisms have diverse characteristics. Some of these are suitable for classifying organisms; some of these are not.

With your team, you will conduct a virtual investigation of the plankton community, recording characteristics of the organisms that you find in a water sample.

Follow the instructions below with your group.

1. In the e-Tools, click on the *Plankton Cyberlab*.

2. Move the viewing tool over the sample, until you locate an organism.

e-Tools

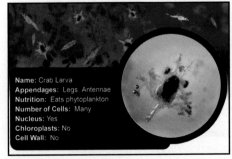

Name: Crab Larva
Appendages: Legs, Antennae
Nutrition: Eats phytoplankton
Number of Cells: Many
Nucleus: Yes
Chloroplasts: No
Cell Wall: No

FIGURE 14.5. Screenshot of the *Plankton Cyberlab*.

3. In your notebook, draw a table like the one below. Record data about your organism in the data table. The crab larva example is completed for you.

4. Repeat these steps until you have collected data for at least 5 organisms.

Organism Name	Sketch	Autotroph or Heterotroph?	Unicellular or Multicellular?	Prokaryotic or Eukaryotic?	Other Characteristics or Interesting Facts
Crab Larva		Heterotroph	Multicellular	Eukaryotic	Has appendages

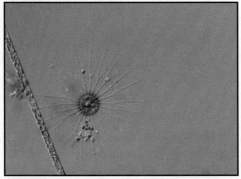

FIGURE 14.6. Diatoms are one of the most common types of phytoplankton. These organisms have a clear cell wall composed of silica that allows sunlight to easily penetrate.

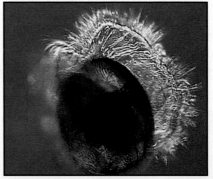

FIGURE 14.7. This mussel larva is a part of the plankton community. When the mussel becomes larger, it will attach to a rock, dock, or other hard surface.

Explain

In your explorations of plankton populations, you noted many similarities and differences among the organisms. The plankton population has high biodiversity and is very important to the functioning of the ocean. The three major types of plankton are:

- Phytoplankton – plant-like plankton
- Zooplankton – animal-like plankton
- Mycoplankton – fungi-like plankton

Zooplankton (pronounced: ZŌ-plank-ton) eat phytoplankton (pronounced: FĪ-toh-plank-ton) and are eaten by invertebrates and other organisms. Mycoplankton (pronounced: MY-kō-plank-ton) settle on a variety of organisms, including plants and animals, and derive nutrients through their cell walls.

Many organisms, including copepods (pronounced: CŌ-pah-podz), diatoms, and dinoflagellates (pronounced: dī-no-FLĂ-jel-lets), some of which you met in the Cyberlab, spend their entire lives as a part of the plankton community. Other organisms only spend their juvenile or larval stages among the plankton. Examples include crabs, lobsters, corals, and many fish. Because the plankton community, and life on Earth, is so diverse, it is important for scientists to use a general system to classify organisms. We will review our understanding of biological classification, and then classify planktonic organisms.

FIGURE 14.8. *Felis catus* is the scientific name given to the common housecat. By the rules of binomial nomenclature, *Felis* is the genus name, while *catus* is the species name. There are several wild cat species classified into the same genus as the domestic cat.

Biological Classification

The science of classifying organisms is called **taxonomy**. Taxonomy is always changing as scientists collect more and more data on organisms, allowing them to understand the relationships between groups. In the traditional system used by biologists, there are broad categories into which smaller ones fit. In other words, the system is hierarchical. FIGURE 14.13 (on the next page) shows the major taxonomic categories into which organisms are classified in using this traditional system. The narrowest classification is species, and the most broad is Kingdom. In a **hierarchy** such as this one, each group lower on the list is subordinate to the one above. Political distinctions are also hierarchical. For instance, you live in the United States, which is larger than the state of Florida, which is larger than your county, which is larger than your town, and so on.

FIGURE 14.9. California Sea Lion, *Zalophus californianus*, plays on the rocks in Monterey Bay, California. Sea lions are more agile on land than seals because sea lions can rotate their hind flippers forward and walk on them. In contrast, seals must hop along on their bellies.

FIGURE 14.10. This Cushion Sea Star, *Oreaster reticulatus*, is a common species throughout Florida and Caribbean Reefs. These animals live in shallow water, down to about 35 meters (~115 feet).

The names of organisms are their Genus and Species names; this is a system of naming organisms known as **binomial nomenclature**, which means "two-name naming". The scientific names of organisms are always italicized or underlined. In addition, the Genus name is capitalized, while the species name is not. Examples include: *Oreaster reticulates* (Cushion Sea Star), *Zalophus californianus* (California Sea Lion), and *Felis catus* (Domestic Cat).

Example classification of a Great White Shark:

- Kingdom Animalia
- Phylum Chordata SubPhylum Vertebrata
- Class Chrondrichthyes SubClass Elasmobranchii
- Order Lamniformes
- Family Lamnidae
- Genus *Carcharodon*
- Species *carcharias*

FIGURE 14.11. The Great White Shark, *Carcharodon carcharias* is the ocean's largest predatory fish. Its common name refers to its white underside, although its dorsal side (back) ranges from light to dark gray.

Scientists are always learning new things about organisms and groups of organisms. As they do so, classification systems have changed. For example, many scientists no longer think that using the term "Kingdom" is the best way to classify organisms. Recently, some taxonomists have begun to advocate another approach to classifying organisms. These scientists suggest dividing groups of organisms into **Domains** based on characteristics that include molecular evidence, such as DNA and cell structures. There are three Domains: Archaea (pronounced arr-KEE-uh), Bacteria, and Eukarya (pronounced: yoo-CAR-ree-uh).

Regardless of the system used, it is useful to consider similarities and differences among groups of organisms on Earth. Therefore, we will explore some of the major characteristics of organisms within the plankton population and beyond.

FIGURE 14.13. Organisms in the biosphere have traditionally been classified using a hierarchical system. Domain is the most general classification; species is the most specific.

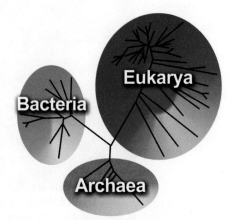

FIGURE 14.12. There are three Domains of life. The Domains are further classified into kingdoms, phyla, classes, and so on.

1. Copy the table below into your notebook. Use what you already know about land and freshwater organisms. On the next several pages, read the information about each of the categories. Record the characteristics in the data table.

Group/ Characteristics	Category					
	Plants	Animals	Fungi	Protists	Bacteria	Archaea
Cell structures?						
Autotrophs or Heterotrophs?						
Unicellular or Multicellular?						
Eukaryotic or Prokaryotic?						
Examples: Land and freshwater						
Examples: Marine						

Category: Plants

True plants are multicellular and perform photosynthesis. They take many different forms, and the floating seeds and fruit of some can travel along with the plankton population. For example, a coconut from a palm tree might float to another island where it takes root and a new tree grows.

In the ocean, true plants, such as cordgrass, are limited to coastal areas and more shallow water, because they require light to make food. They get nutrients through their roots, which grow into the soil.

The most important marine producers, phytoplankton, are not true plants. The majority of phytoplankton are considered to be Bacteria and Protists, even though they do photosynthesize.

FIGURE 14.14. Cordgrass, common in salt marsh ecosystems, is an example of a plant that can grow in brackish water.

Category: Animals

When we think of ocean animals, we often think of animals like those we will track: whales, dolphins, sea turtles, large fish, and so on. However, some of the most important animals in the ocean are tiny members of the plankton community. The large majority of animals on Earth are unlike humans and other mammals. These animals include jellyfish, sea stars, clams, squid, and many more. These animals are called **invertebrates** and none of these animals has a backbone. Most marine invertebrates spend at least a part of their lifetime within the plankton community. Many marine invertebrates do not move very fast, if at all. To ensure the survival of their species, invertebrates must find a way to reproduce, even if they never meet another of their kind.

FIGURE 14.15. Clams are simple animals but have muscles and organs, including gills and an intestine.

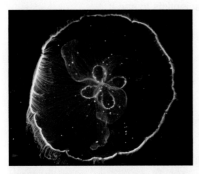

FIGURE 14.16. Jellyfish, such as the Moon Jellyfish shown here, are simple animals that are considered to be a part of the plankton community because they are at the mercy of ocean movements.

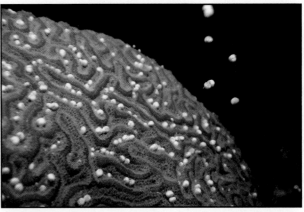

FIGURE 14.17. A Brain Coral releases eggs. Brain Corals are hard corals that can form large coral heads that are several meters across.

FIGURE 14.18. Copepod with eggs. Copepods are an important type of zooplankton, and remain in the plankton population through adulthood.

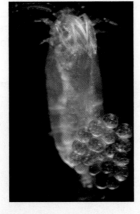

FIGURE 14.19. These zooplankton have been magnified hundreds of times so that you can see their characteristics. Normally, thousands of these plankton can fit into a single drop of water.

Corals are one type of invertebrate animal that does not move. Their reproduction strategy is to release eggs and sperm directly into the water. When these two cells meet, the egg is **fertilized**, and the cell begins to divide. The baby, or larval stage, floats within the plankton community until it gets too big and settles on the ocean bottom. This is a way for organisms that move slowly, or not at all, to colonize new habitats. Other organisms that you might not think of as animals, but are, follow the same strategy. These include sponges, clams, and anemones. Animals have true organelles, including a nucleus. They feed on other organisms.

Category: Fungi

You are probably familiar with mushrooms and mold. These are both examples of fungi. Fungi latch onto other organisms and eat them by absorbing the food through their cell wall. For example, you have probably seen a mushroom growing on a tree. This fungus is taking nutrition away from the tree through its cell wall and membrane. Fungi have true organelles, making them eukaryotic. Fungi on land and in estuaries are also important decomposers. They break down waste and dead organisms, releasing nutrients back into the ecosystem. In the ocean, fungi can be very harmful. Some types of marine fungi make fish very sick by invading their tissues. These fungi can remain in the plankton population until they latch onto a victim. Most marine fungi can only be seen with a microscope. Such organisms are called **microbes**.

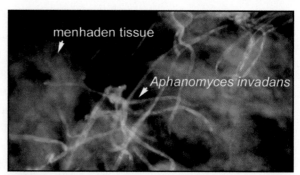

FIGURE 14.20. Taken under a microscope from within a fish's body tissue, this is a picture of a harmful marine fungus called *Aphanomyces invadans*. The fungus has been injected with a fluorescent stain to make it easier for scientists to see it.

Category: Protists

Protists are very strange organisms and a very diverse group. Some protists photosynthesize; others are heterotrophic. Some can cause diseases, such as malaria.

Most protists have cell walls, some have chloroplasts, and all have a nucleus and cell membrane. Diatoms and dinoflagellates are important marine producers. These protists are unicellular. Other protists are multicellular. Interestingly, most seaweeds, such as kelp and rockweed, are not plants at all: they are multicellular protists.

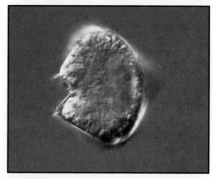

FIGURE 14.21. Some dinoflagellates can cause harmful algal blooms. You read about HABs in Lesson 13: Photosynthesis in the Ocean.

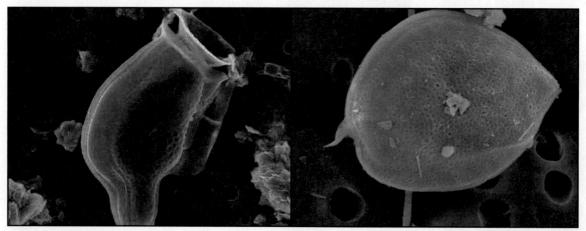

FIGURE 14.22. Many protists are so small that high-powered scanning electronic microscopes are necessary to fully study their structures.

Category: Bacteria

Bacteria are also known as true bacteria. These microbes are the most abundant organisms in the ocean. You were introduced to an important type of Bacteria, the cyanobacteria, in the last Lesson. Not all true bacteria are producers, however. True bacteria live in most Earth habitats, including inside our bodies. For example, there are bacteria that live inside our intestines that help us to produce vitamins. These bacteria are heterotrophs that get their nutrition from your body, but your cells use the vitamins created to help complete the body's processes. Many of the true bacteria are decomposers. They break down dead organisms and waste and return their nutrients to the Earth system.

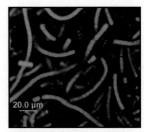

FIGURE 14.23. Cyanobacteria are smaller than other phytoplankton but are important marine producers.

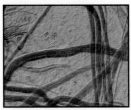

FIGURE 14.24. Cyanobacteria are thought to have been the first producers on Earth.

Some of the true bacteria are not as helpful. Some cause diseases that infect humans and other organisms. For example, some types of true bacteria cause strep throat, pneumonia, and ear infections. True bacteria are unicellular, but they reproduce quickly so there will be a lot of them, fast, if they are meeting their needs.

Category: Archaea

Archaea are similar to Bacteria in that they are single-celled microbes. Their cells do not have nuclei or true organelles. They differ from the true bacteria, or Bacteria, in biochemical ways. For example, they have different enzymes and mechanisms for building proteins within their cells.

When they were first identified, these organisms were also known as the "extreme bacteria" because of the extreme habitats in which they are found. Archaea live in some of the harshest environments on Earth, including hot springs, super salty lakes, and places with absolutely no oxygen. Prior to the discovery of these types of organisms, scientists assumed that nothing could live under such extreme conditions.

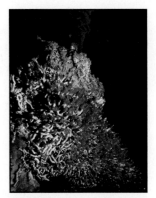

FIGURE 14.25. Archaeans live within Giant Tube Worms in hydrothermal vent communities.

Archaea can be autotrophs or heterotrophs. The autotrophic Archaea do not only photosynthesize, however. Instead of using sunlight to make sugar, some of these unique organisms use chemicals. The process of using chemicals to make sugar is called **chemosynthesis**.

Archaeans that live and thrive in very salty seas and lakes are called **halophiles** (pronounced: HAL-ō-fī-uls). Those that thrive on natural gas, or methane, are called **methanogens** (pronounced: meth-AN-ō-jenz). Methanogens are found in the deep ocean and also on land. Archaeans, found in very hot conditions, both in fresh water and salt water, are called **thermophiles** (pronounced: THER-mō-fī-uls).

More recently, however, scientists have learned that Archaea are found in almost every Earth environment, and are especially abundant in the ocean. There are Archaea in the plankton population, in estuaries, in the deep sea, and throughout marine ecosystems.

The Tree of Life

Scientists find it useful to group organisms based on the characteristics that they share and to create groupings like the ones in your chart. They show the relationships between organisms and the shared characteristics in a diagram known as the Tree of Life. The Tree of Life is a symbolic tree based on scientific evidence illustrating the relationships between all living things on Earth. It classifies all organisms on Earth alive today. Like a living tree with branches that are connected to and grow from a trunk, the branches of the Tree of Life have grown over millions and millions of years and are all connected to a **common ancestor** to which all other organisms that have ever existed on Earth are related. An ancestor is someone, or in this case, something, that came before. Your grandparents and great-grandparents, for example, are your ancestors. A common ancestor would have been a species that lived many years ago, and had similar characteristics to one of today's organisms, but is now extinct. When you look at the Tree of Life, you will see that all of the groups of living things that now live on Earth are related to one common ancestor.

As you explore the Tree of Life, you will meet the many different groups of living things that live on Earth today. During the process, think about what characteristics these groups share, and what differences each "branch" of the Tree of Life has from another. Groups of organisms shown at the bottom of the Tree of Life have been on Earth the longest. These groups are considered the oldest. Groups of organisms toward the top of the Tree of Life have appeared more recently on Earth and are considered "younger". All of the groups are related to a common, single-celled ancestor. The ancestor was a simple, one-celled organism with no nucleus that lived in the ocean. It is not shown on the Tree, because this organism no longer lives on Earth. Over several billion years, living things have changed as the Earth changed. New groups formed, and as such, they are shown as branches of the Tree. Groups and branches that are closest together on the Tree are most similar to each other; that it to say, they are most related. The groups at the top of the tree, including Plants and Animals, are connected to all others because they share the common single-celled ancestor.

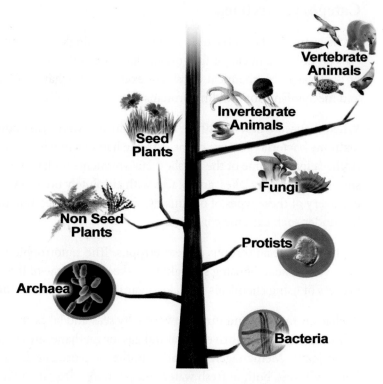

FIGURE 14.26. The Tree of Life is one way to picture our planet's biodiversity. All of the species currently living on Earth are a part of this Tree. The Tree also depicts the relationships between groups of organisms.

The Unity of Life

As you are now aware, there is great biodiversity on Earth, particularly in the ocean. There are, however, a number of characteristics that all living things share.

First, all organisms are made up of one or more cells. Cells are often referred to as the structural unit of life. This means that some organisms survive with only one cell; others, of course, are multicellular. As you have also read, there are cells that contain no nucleus and true organelles, prokaryotic cells; there are cells that have these components, eukaryotic cells. All cells attain and use energy.

FIGURE 14.27. Octopuses and other animals often spend parts of their lives within the plankton community. Eventually, many species become much larger, illustrating the life function of growth.

Cells and whole organisms carry out specific functions conducted by all living things, the **life activities**. The life activities are: growth, nutrition, transport, respiration, synthesis, excretion, regulation, and reproduction. Also called life processes, or life functions, each of these processes is described below, along with examples to illustrate them.

- **Growth.** All living things have increases in size, the life process of **growth**. Some living things grow by adding more cells. In some cases, the cells themselves get bigger. Picture an octopus larva, like one you might have encountered during the Cyberlab in the **Explore** section. Over time, this tiny organism, best observed under a microscope, becomes a much larger animal.

- **Nutrition.** The processes involved in obtaining and processing energy and nutrients are known collectively as the life function of **nutrition**. In heterotrophs such as fish, food, which contains nutrients and energy, is taken in from the external environment. Then, the animal's digestive system processes the food, breaking it down into small enough particles to be used by individual cells.

- **Transport.** Materials, including nutrients and waste materials, must be moved around within organisms. This life activity is known as **transport**. In unicellular organisms such as diatoms, transport is accomplished by the jelly-like substance that makes up much of the cell, called **cytoplasm**. Complex animals, including whales and humans, have complete systems dedicated to moving materials throughout the body. Our circulatory system, which includes the heart and blood vessels, carries oxygen, nutrients, and other necessities to cells. Waste products such as carbon dioxide are carried away from cells.

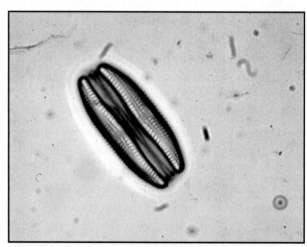

FIGURE 14.28. Freshwater diatoms, such as this one found in the Great Lakes, must accomplish all of their life functions within their single cell. This is true of all unicellular organisms.

- **Respiration.** Energy is stored in chemical substances inside of cells. The process of releasing energy from food is called **respiration**. In most instances, the chemical reaction of respiration requires oxygen. In many simple marine organisms, every cell remains in contact with the environment, allowing the exchange of gases such as oxygen. Oxygen can be brought into the cell and used in the respiration reaction.

FIGURE 14.29. Fish, such as this Speckled Parrotfish, accomplish the life function of respiration underwater. This fish takes in water through its mouth. The water then passes over the gills, which extract oxygen. The oxygen is used to release energy that is stored in its cells.

- **Synthesis.** Inside organisms, simple materials are made into more complex ones, a process known as **synthesis**. There are many examples of organisms building materials, including photosynthesis and chemosynthesis, both of which were discussed in the last Lesson. Another example of synthesis is the building of proteins. In fish, for instance, small molecules join to form complex chains of molecules, which eventually become important components of muscle tissues, allowing fish to swim.

- **Excretion.** Chemical reactions inside cells, whether building things up or breaking them down, result in the creation of waste products. The process of releasing waste products of reactions, as well as other non-useful materials, is known as **excretion**. For example, in most organisms, carbon dioxide is a waste product that is excreted in various ways, whether through cell membranes, skin, gills or lungs. Another example of excretion is observed in marine reptiles such as sea turtles, which excrete excess salt from their bodies.

- **Regulation.** All living things must maintain a stable internal environment, or **homeostasis**. The process of keeping homeostasis is known as **regulation**. You read about an example of regulation in Lesson 3: More About Water. Freshwater fish are constantly absorbing water through their skin, resulting in improper water balance in their cells. To maintain homeostasis, these fish release a high amount of diluted urine. The life process of regulation is the organisms way of responding to their environments. Something that causes a response in an organism is called a **stimulus**. In the ocean, many types of zooplankton migrate up and down in the water column, in response to the stimulus of changes in light. At dusk, when light levels decrease, many of these organisms push to the surface. At dawn, they reverse direction.

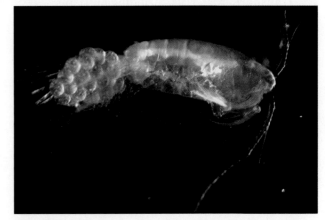

FIGURE 14.30. Copepods, such as the one shown, are a type of zooplankton known to undertake daily vertical migrations. Scientists believe that migrating plankton respond to changes in light levels. The eggs, shown in blue, also indicate that the organism is undertaking the life function of reproduction.

- **Reproduction.** In order for species to continue, living things must create other organisms of their own kind, the process of **reproduction**. Unlike the other life activities, reproduction is not necessary for continuing the life of individual organisms, but is required for the species.

The life activities are not distinct from one another—they work in tandem. For example, the freshwater fish regulating its water and salt balance does so by excreting excess water. The tiny molecules distributed during the life process of nutrition are combined during synthesis. In order for something to be deemed living, it must carry out *all* of the life functions. Consider that a salt crystal can seem to grow, but it does not respire, regulate, and so on. Collectively, within a living organism, all of the chemical reactions that occur to maintain its life are known as its **metabolism**. Because organisms perform their life functions in different ways, their is a great diversity of life forms. Seaweeds, for instance, respire, regulate, and reproduce in very different manners than do dolphins.

FIGURE 14.31. Water is required for all living things. About 95 percent of a jellyfish's body is water.

Living things share similar needs; as organisms' cells are growing they are reproducing and conducting their life activities. All living things require water to maintain their metabolism. Water is the universal solvent. Many substances dissolve in water and are then available for chemical reactions within cells. Nutrients, oxygen, and waste products are carried by water. Water comprises a significant percentage of the bodies of living organisms. Most jellyfish, for example, are 95 percent water, whereas an average human is approximately 60 percent water.

In addition to hydrogen and oxygen, which make up water, there are other elements that are important to living things. These elements include carbon, phosphorus, nitrogen, sulfur, and metals such as sodium, potassium, iron, and zinc. These are needed by living things to build their structures, and assist their cells in functioning. All living things have a limited life span; that is, no organism, including animals and plants (e.g., trees), can live forever.

2. Read the descriptions below and indicate which life function is being described.

    a. Corals often release eggs and sperm into the ocean at the same time. These sex cells meet in the water and develop into larvae.

    b. At low tide, a mussel living on a rock at the beach becomes exposed to sunlight. The animal closes its shell to prevent water loss.

    c. Some types of mangrove trees release excess salt through their leaves.

    d. In flatworms, every cell remains in contact with the environment. Oxygen and carbon dioxide are exchanged across its cell membranes. Oxygen is used to release energy from food.

    e. Sea stars deliver materials throughout their bodies through a system of water-filled canals.

    f. Whale Sharks strain plankton from water. They digest the food using a system that includes a stomach and intestine.

    g. *Spartina alternaflora* is a common grass that grows in salt marshes. From the glucose molecules built during photosynthesis, the plant creates large carbohydrates called starches.

    h. A certain species of kelp increases in size at an astonishing rate, up to ½ meter (~ 1.5 feet) per day.

Census of Marine Life

In 2010, a global network of scientists from more than 80 nations released the world's first comprehensive **Census of Marine Life**. The Census of Marine Life began in 2000 and was coordinated by the Consortium of Ocean Leadership in Washington, D.C., and supported by international government agencies as well as private organizations and companies interested in science, the environment, and fisheries. The purpose of this Census was to assess the diversity, distribution, and abundance of all marine life in the ocean. In addition to discovering new species throughout the world's ocean, the Census cataloged species that existed in museums and other collections around the world. This recent, enormous undertaking highlights the need to study the ocean—so much remains to be learned.

Scientists involved in the Census conducted assessments in fourteen major field projects around the world. Eleven projects addressed specific habitats (e.g., the Southern Ocean) and three projects focused on animal migrations, as well as those species that are distributed globally. The diverse technologies employed highlight the need for scientists, technologists, and engineers to work together, as well as the interdisciplinary nature of ocean sciences.

Researchers used bioacoustic surveys to examine the sounds produced by organisms, underwater cameras, and light sensors. They also performed genetic tests. Many animals were tagged with satellite transmitters, allowing scientists to examine their migratory behavior, as well as to collect data (e.g., temperature, salinity, fluorescence) below the surface in the areas where the animals dive. The genetic analysis of organisms helped researchers to match larvae with adult organisms and explore relationships between species. Using a variety of technological tools and scientific techniques allowed for the collection of complementary data sets.

The hope was that this ten-year study of the ocean's biodiversity would provide information needed to globally manage our marine resources, by providing baseline information to preserve species diversity, prevent habitat loss, and decrease pollution in our oceans. By understanding the distribution of marine organisms, humans can better manage fisheries and predict the effects of climate change. While this effort was an exciting and important undertaking, it still highlights how much there is left to learn—the ocean is an unexplored wilderness.

FIGURE 14.32. Coral reefs are known for their high biodiversity. The Census of Marine Life sought to examine biodiversity throughout the ocean's ecosystems.

FIGURE 14.33. In addition to fish, the Census examined the diversity and distribution of plankton and invertebrate species.

Elaborate

Lab

Local Plankton Exploration

Now that we have done a virtual exploration of plankton, it is time to do a real one. There are normally plankton in any natural body of fresh- or saltwater, including bays, sounds, streams, and ponds. Because most plankton are so tiny, it helps when studying them to use a tool that will bring more of them together, or concentrate them. You can build a plankton net that will do just that.

Part A: Building a Plankton Net

Materials:

- Scissors
- Embroidery hoop set
- Panty hose
- Nylon line, 6–8 meters (~20–26 feet) long
- 2 pieces of wire, about 2 meters (~2 yards) long each
- Small plastic bottle with cap
- Thick rubber bands
- Needle-nose pliers

FIGURE 14.34. Scientists in the field using plankton nets. The nets are towed using a research vessel where, at the end, a funnel helps deliver the plankton.

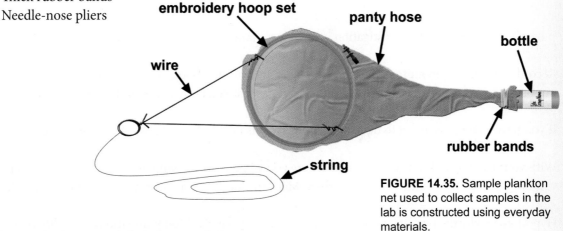

FIGURE 14.35. Sample plankton net used to collect samples in the lab is constructed using everyday materials.

To build your plankton net, follow the steps below:

1. Cut one leg of the panty hose off for use. Set aside the rest.

2. Attach the wide end of the leg to the inner embroidery hoop. Place the outer hoop over the inner hoop and snap closed.

3. Cut the toe off of the panty hose.

4. Uncap the bottle—do not lose the cap. Use the rubber band to attach the plastic bottle to the panty hose (see FIGURE 14.35). Wrap the rubber band around several times to be sure that the bottle is secure.

5. Gently fold the pieces of wire in half. Attach the ends of the wire, evenly spaced, to the net by threading the wire through the panty hose and around the hoop, and then wrapping it back on itself. Use the pliers to help manipulate the wire.

6. Twist the wires together at the top, leaving a loop to which the line can be attached.

7. Attach the string securely to the loop in the wire.

Part B: In the Field

Materials:

- Plankton net
- Masking tape
- Markers
- Clipboards
- Compass (to create an accurate map) (*optional*)

FIGURE 14.36. Scientists remove their sample from a plankton net. The plankton were collected by dragging the net slowly across the water near the surface.

Safety Note: Pay close attention to the safety rules noted by your teacher.

The purpose of this part of the investigation is to collect plankton.

8. Record information about the data collection site. In your notebook, draw a map of your site. Label any important features such as jetties, pipes, docks, marsh grasses, large rocks, and so on.

9. If you have a compass, use it to determine which way is north. Indicate this direction on your map.

10. With your team, decide on two locations where you will take your samples. Try to choose two sites that you think will be different from one another. Mark the locations on your map as Site 1 and Site 2.

11. Hypothesize why the two sites you have selected would have plankton populations with different characteristics. Note the Date and Time on your map. Indicate current weather observations and conditions (i.e., approximate temperature, wind observation, cloud cover, precipitation).

12. Site 1: Move to your first collection site. Make qualitative observations about the site, such as noting any shadows, rocks, plant life, and so on.

13. To use your net, hold onto the end of the line and toss your net as far as you can into the body of water. Slowly drag the net across the surface of the water by pulling the line in toward you. Remove the rubber band and cap the bottle.

FIGURE 14.37. The mouth of a plankton net being dragged slowly across the water's surface.

14. Use the masking tape and markers to label the sample with the site number and your group name.

15. Make qualitative observations about the sample in the bottle— describe what you see.

16. Use a rubber band to attach a new bottle to the plankton net.

17. Repeat steps 12–16 at Site 2.

18. Place all of your equipment and samples back into your bucket or bag. Be sure that you do not leave anything at the field site.

Part C: In the Laboratory

Now it is time to observe your samples and record your observations.

Materials:

FIGURE 14.38. A plankton net is properly towed alongside a NOAA research vessel. Note that the net is skimming the surface.

- Petri dishes
- Dissecting microscopes
- Compound microscopes
- Slides
- Coverslips
- Eyedroppers
- Quieting solution, which increases water velocity, slowing down zooplankton—available from many laboratory supply companies (*optional*)
- Books, pamphlets, online resources (to identify local plankton) (*optional*)
- Microscope camera and television (to show good examples of plankton to the class) (*optional*)

Follow the instructions with your group.

Safety Notes:

- Be sure to follow all laboratory safety rules.
- When using compound microscopes, remember, do **not** use the coarse adjustment knobs under high magnification.

19. Begin with your Site 1 sample. Place the tip of the eyedropper near the bottom of the bottle to extract some water and material from the sample. Transfer the sample to a Petri dish.

20. View the sample under the dissecting microscope. When your specimen is in focus, describe what you see in words.

21. Draw a sketch of the organism or organisms that you see.

22. If quieting solution is available, add it to the sample. Describe any changes you observe.

23. Use the eyedropper to extract a drop of water from the Petri dish and to prepare a wet mount slide.

24. View the slide you have prepared under the compound microscope. When you find an organism that is easy to view, focus on it.

25. Draw a sketch of the organism. Label any structures you can identify, such as a nucleus, cell wall or chloroplast.

26. Find a different organism to view, sketch, and label. You may need to prepare another slide.

27. Repeat steps 19–26 with your Site 2 sample.

28. Clean up your laboratory station as directed by your teacher.

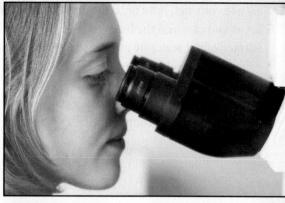

FIGURE 14.39. Microscopes allow biologists to extend their sense of sight in order to make observations of tiny organisms, cell structures, and so on.

FIGURE 14.40. Scientists onboard a research vessel near Antarctica prepare to examine zooplankton.

Part D: Analysis of Results

29. Compare the samples collected from your two Sites. Do you see any differences? If so, describe.

30. Did any of your specimens have chloroplasts? Were any of your specimens autotrophic?

Part E: Extending Ideas

31. If you had collected your sample in significantly deeper water, how might it have been different?

32. If you had collected your sample in a similar body of water, but in a different part of the world, how would your results compare?

33. How would you expect your observations to change seasonally? Describe how you would test this hypothesis.

34. Give an example of a human activity that might alter the biodiversity of your sample. What would the consequences of this activity be?

Evaluate

1. Scientists estimate that 90 percent of the wading birds that once inhabited Florida's salt- and freshwater bodies are gone due to various human activities. Why is this loss of biodiversity important? Give one specific example of how an ecosystem can be affected by the depletion or loss of a bird species.

2. Here is a scenario: You collect a sample of plankton in a local bay while you are on vacation. You take it to a local lab and observe it under a microscope. One organism that you find has chloroplasts, but also seems to be eating other organisms. In which kingdom would you classify this organism? Why?

3. While conducting fieldwork at a local body of water, you and your lab partner encounter something that looks like a rock. Your partner insists that the specimen is composed of many marine and aquatic organisms. They are stony, but are actually alive. Describe at least four criteria that would indicate that this thing is in fact alive.

FIGURE 14.41. Salt marshes, such as the one shown here, are very productive ecosystems with high biodiversity. With brackish water, there is a dominance of only salt-tolerant plants, but with the promotion of algae growth in certain times of years, they provide for an extensive food chain.

15

Marine Populations

INSIDE:

Objectives

You will be able to:

✔ Explain the concepts of carrying capacity and population density.

✔ Identify the factors that increase or decrease population sizes and analyze changes in animal populations.

✔ Describe the importance of the Endangered Species Act and give examples of species that are listed under the Act.

Benchmarks

1h. Although the ocean is large, it is finite and resources are limited.

5d. Ocean biology provides many unique examples of life cycles, adaptations, and important relationships among organisms (e.g., symbiosis, predator-prey dynamics, energy transfer) that do not occur on land.

6g. Everyone is responsible for caring for the ocean. The ocean sustains life on Earth, and humans must live in ways that sustain the ocean. Individual and collective actions are needed to effectively manage ocean resources for all.

Engage

Analyzing Human Population Changes

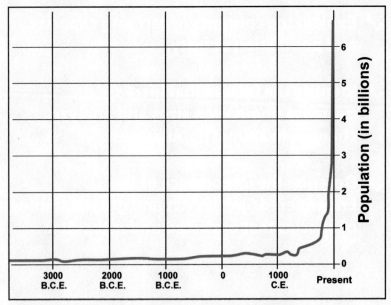

FIGURE 15.1. Human population for the past 6,000 years.

Changes in human population affect all of Earth's ecosystems. Examine the graphs and data table on this page, and answer the Questions that follow.

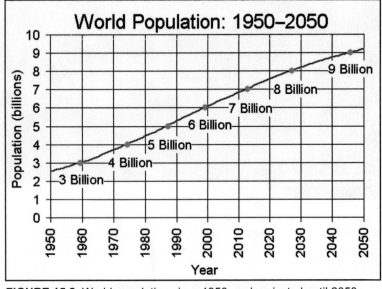

FIGURE 15.2. World population since 1950, and projected until 2050.

Population in Billions	Year
0.5	1500
1	1804
2	1927
3	1960
4	1974
5	1987
6	1999

1. Make three unique observations about the data.

2. How has the doubling time—the time it takes for a population to double—changed over time?

3. What are some factors that cause human populations to increase? To decrease?

Explore

Activity

Analyzing Marine Populations

Like the human population, the population of marine organisms also changes over time. Recall that all the members of a species in a specific area are a **population**. We will analyze three case studies of marine animal populations. For each case, your task will be to determine the factors that are causing a species to increase or decrease over time.

4. Record your findings in a chart similar to the one below.

Case Study	Population Trend (Increasing, Decreasing, or Stable)	Factors That Increase Population Growth	Factors That Decrease Population Growth
Florida Manatee			
Green Sea Turtle			
Common Dolphinfish			

Case Study 1: The Florida Manatee

The Florida Manatee is a beloved, gentle marine mammal. The manatee is one of two types of animals in Order *Sirenia* (pronounced sī-REE-nee-ah), the other being the dugong (pronounced: DOO-gong) of Australian waters. In general, manatees live in warm tropical waters. Populations of manatees are observed in the warm waters of West Africa, Caribbean Islands, and North and South America.

The Florida Manatee and Antillean Manatee, found throughout the Caribbean Sea, are considered to be separate subspecies, but members of the same order of species. Florida Manatees have a limited range. They are found year-round primarily throughout the shallow waters of Florida, but are frequently observed in other states lining the Gulf of Mexico, including Texas. During the summer months, when waters are warm, some individuals stray up the Atlantic seaboard as far north as New England. For example, in the summer of 2010, residents of Connecticut were surprised to observe a manatee visiting harbors along the Long Island Sound.

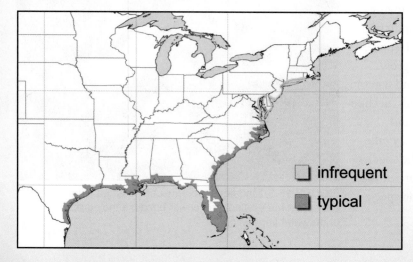

infrequent

typical

FIGURE 15.3. Typical and infrequent range of Florida Manatees.

These herbivores feed primarily on seagrasses, but they eat a variety of available plants. They can tolerate a wide range of salinity, mangrove forests, salt marshes, and canals, in addition to the coastal ocean. Their bodies are gray or brown, they are quite chubby and they have a paddle-shaped tail. Their faces are lined with whiskers, similar to seals. Adult Florida Manatees will average approximately 1,000 kilograms (~2,200 pounds) and 3.5 meters (~11.5 feet) in length. Like cetaceans, such as whales and dolphins, females tend to be larger than males.

Manatees are very sensitive to temperature changes. In the winter, they tend to congregate near warm water flows, including natural springs and outflows of power plants. Cold stress is a major issue for manatees. In the winter of 2010, for example, there was an increase in deaths of manatees, because of an unusual cold spell. Manatees are also very sensitive to human activity. Most manatee deaths result from collisions with motorboats. As a result, signs are commonly posted in Florida waters warning of speed restrictions to prevent high-speed boat and manatee collisions. The animals are also susceptible to entanglement in fishing gear. Human attempts at managing water flow, such as using locks and flood gates, can also entrap manatees. They have no real predators that threaten their survival, but in the past they were often hunted for food. In Florida, the hunting of manatees was outlawed in 1893.

FIGURE 15.4. Manatee Crossing signs to warn boaters of the slow-moving marine mammals are common throughout Florida's waters.

Manatees can live to about 60 years of age. Beginning at around the age of 5, and continuing through their mid-30s, female manatees can produce one calf about every 3 years. They are slow to reproduce; pregnancy, or gestation, lasts approximately 13 months. Calves tend to be born in the summer months. The young generally stay alongside their mothers for a couple of years.

While the overall population size of the Florida Manatee is stable, in some areas, such as in Northwestern Florida, the population is growing. Scientists believe that a larger manatee population could be supported. There is enough food, space, and other resources for the population to grow. Hunting, boat strikes, diseases, red tide, and habitat destruction have contributed to the animals' decline in the past. Of course, their slow growth and reproductive rates suggest that recovery may take a very long time. Scientists believe that the species will ultimately survive, but they are concerned that there are many factors that could cause the species to again decrease in population.

FIGURE 15.5. Manatees are unusual-looking animals. They are sometimes called "sea cows" because they graze on underwater vegetation.

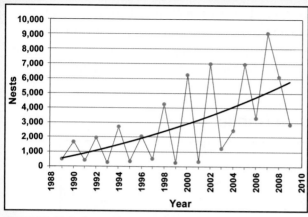

FIGURE 15.6. Green Sea Turtle nests in Florida from 1988–2010. Populations of the sea turtle are still considered to be too low.

FIGURE 15.7. The sub-population of Hawaiian Green Sea Turtles are unique in that they can often be observed sunning themselves on the beach. These turtles were photographed in the Northwest Hawaiian Islands.

Case Study 2: Green Sea Turtles

Green Sea Turtles are found throughout the ocean's tropical and temperate waters. The United States and its territories are home to many nesting spots for this species. For the Atlantic population, nesting spots include beaches in North and South Carolina, Georgia, Puerto Rico, the U.S. Virgin Islands, and in Florida, with the largest percentage in Florida. In the Pacific, many Green Sea Turtles nest in the Hawaiian Islands, as well as in American Samoa and the Mariana Islands.

It is believed that female Green Sea Turtles reach sexual maturity sometime between 20 and 50 years of age. Then, every 2–4 years, a female will return to her nesting beach and lay an average of 3–5 egg clutches approximately every two weeks throughout the nesting season. The average number of eggs in a clutch is around 135. When the hatchlings emerge from the nest, they are very susceptible to predation by birds, fish, and land animals such as raccoons. Adult Green Sea Turtles can grow to 1.2 meters (~4 feet) in length and 200 kilograms (~440 pounds) in weight. This sea turtle species gets its name from the green color of both its flesh and the fat under its shell. A notable characteristic is that the Green Sea Turtle's head looks too small for its body. It has only one distinguishable set of scales in front of its eyes, in contrast with the majority of other species of sea turtles, which have two sets of scales.

Adult female turtles migrate more than one thousand miles, yet remarkably they return to the same beach from where they hatched in order to lay their eggs. Green Sea Turtles prefer to live along coastlines where there are beds of seagrass and algae, the staple of their diet. When they are young hatchlings, they eat insects, worms, crustaceans, grasses, and algae. However, as adults they are strict herbivores, eating only plants and plant material.

The coastal areas where Green Sea Turtles live are also popular fishing areas. Turtles are sometimes caught in gillnets, trawls, traps, longlines, and other fishing gear. Also, Green Sea Turtles are a valuable delicacy in many countries. Over time, removing eggs and turtles from their nesting beaches to use as a human food has impacted the existing population.

FIGURE 15.8. Green Sea Turtles are named for their greenish flesh, which gets its color from the animal's vegetarian diet. They have a worldwide population and spend their time in shallow waters except while migrating.

Today, the endangered Green Sea Turtle is protected by national and international laws. In order to help protect this species, fishers and scientists are working both to improve actual fishing gear so they will not ensnare the animals and to reduce human interference with their eggs and nesting sites. Green Sea Turtles are also threatened in some areas of the world by a disease known as fibropapillomatosis (FP) (pronounced: fǐ-brō-pah-pǐl-lō-mah-TŌ-sǐs).

Green Sea Turtle Range

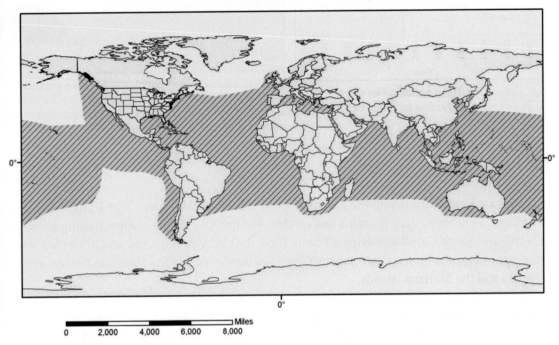

FIGURE 15.9. Green Sea Turtles have a wide range and habitats throughout the Atlantic, Pacific, and Indian Oceans. They appear to range in both tropical and mid-latitudes.

Case Study 3: The Common Dolphinfish

The Common Dolphinfish, sometimes called mahi-mahi, is an important predator in the open ocean. As an adult the dolphinfish is important to both recreational and commercial fishers. This large sport fish normally ranges between 1 to 2 meters (3 to 6 feet) in length and about 14 kilograms (~30 pounds) in weight. Because of its popularity, fishing regulations are now in place in both the Atlantic and Pacific Oceans to protect this species from becoming depleted. For recreational fishers, there are rules regarding the minimum size of a fish that can be taken. Commercial fishery regulations include restrictions on the types of gear used, minimum fish size requirements, and caps on total weight of fish caught. Fishery management in both the Atlantic and Pacific is strong. This means

FIGURE 15.10. Dolphinfish are easily distinguished by their turquoise and yellow colors. Father and son recreational fishers enjoy testing their strength against large pelagic fish. This pair of Mahi Mahi was caught near Oahu, Hawaii.

that fishing companies get together to create regulations that support the industry and ensure that the species population remains stable. The population of the Common Dolphinfish is believed to be stable, although it is hard to assess the numbers of these wide-ranging, open ocean (pelagic) fish.

Dolphinfish, which are brightly colored turquoise and yellow, are migratory and range throughout warm tropical and subtropical waters in the Atlantic, Pacific, and Indian Oceans. Adult Dolphinfish tend to migrate north and south seasonally. The animals live only about 4 years and are able to reproduce by about 5 months of age. They grow very rapidly and reproduce year round. Females produce an average of approximately 50,000 eggs per spawning episode, and the fish can spawn every 2–3 days if waters are warm enough. Spawning is believed to occur on the continental shelf. Eggs and juveniles hide in mats of *Sargassum*, a type of seaweed in which juvenile sea turtles are also reported to hide.

Dolphinfish feed on a wide variety of food sources. These include small fish (e.g., flying fish, triggerfish, and juveniles of larger fish such as tuna and jacks) and invertebrates (e.g., jellyfish, octopus, squid, krill, shrimp). Basically dolphinfish will eat anything they can find; they are **opportunists**. Their predators include larger fish (e.g., marlin, swordfish) and some marine mammals (e.g., Rough-toothed Dolphin).

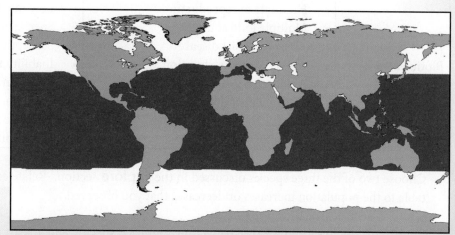

FIGURE 15.11. The range (marked red) of the Common Dolphinfish. The population of the species is thought to be stable throughout its range.

Explain

Population Dynamics

To protect species whose populations are at risk, it is important to first understand how populations are sustained in their environments overall. Wildlife biologists study changes in the numbers and composition of the population, or **population dynamics**. If resources (i.e., food, water, space) were unlimited, any population that stayed healthy would increase exponentially. Of course, resources are limited. The maximum number of organisms of a species that can be supported in an environment without damaging the habitat is known as the **carrying capacity**. In a typical population, growth will level off at the carrying capacity. A population can exceed carrying capacity, but a number of individuals will not survive, and the population will decrease to below the carrying capacity. Carrying capacity is not fixed. It varies based on factors that include food supply, space, and competition within and between species.

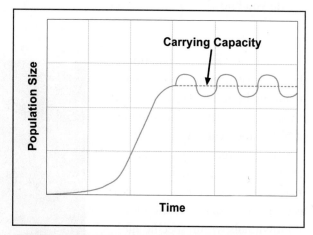

FIGURE 15.12. This graph shows the typical pattern of population growth for organisms. When the population reaches carrying capacity, it will fluctuate but will not usually increase or decrease dramatically.

A variety of factors affect populations of organisms. Basic factors include the number of births and deaths that occur over a fixed time. Fluctuations in populations are normal. These differences can be natural or due to human influences. The chart below illustrates factors that increase or decrease population sizes in the ocean.

	Factors Increasing Population Size	Factors Decreasing Population Size
Abiotic Factors	• Favorable amounts of nutrients • Favorable light availability • Favorable salinity • Favorable temperature	• Too few nutrients • Too little light • Salinity too high or too low • Temperature too high or too low
Biotic Factors	• Adequate food supply • High rate of reproduction • Multiple food sources • Ability to resist disease • Ability to change location • Ability to compete for resources • High genetic diversity • Human conservation efforts • Reduction of predators	• Lack of food • Low rate of reproduction • Specialized food sources • Susceptibility to disease • Inability to move to new locations • Poor competitive abilities • Low genetic diversity • Negative human impacts • Predation

5. Choose two of the three species discussed in the **Explore** section. Relate one or more of the factors in the table to the population increases or decreases that you observed.

6. Return to your chart in the **Explore** section. For each species, add at least one additional factor that increases or decreases population size.

7. Which, if any, of the species you studied in the **Explore** section are likely at their carrying capacity? How do you know?

Let's examine typical population dynamics of animal populations, including humans. The most basic things to consider are the number of births and deaths within a population over a period of time, let's say each year. Other factors include the ratio of males to females, as well as the relative abundance of individuals within specific age ranges. The easiest way to study these factors is by using age structure diagrams. Age structure diagrams, sometimes called population pyramids, are a type of frequency histogram. FIGURE 15.14 on the next page is based on United States census data.

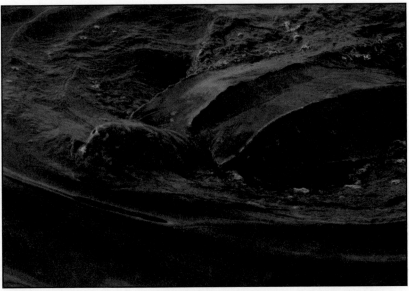

FIGURE 15.13. Scientists believe that the population of Leatherback Sea Turtles is increasing in the Atlantic Ocean, but decreasing in the Pacific Ocean. Many biotic and abiotic factors can increase or decrease population size.

United States Population (2000)

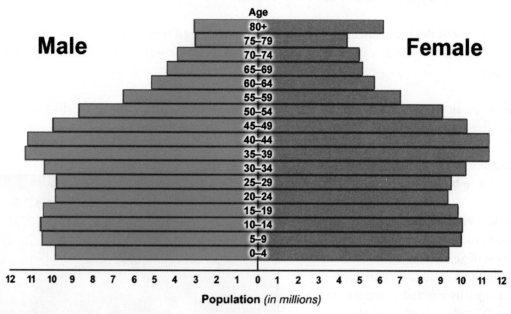

FIGURE 15.14. A population pyramid showing the United States population structure in 2000. The U.S. Census Bureau breaks up the data into 17 distinct age ranges.

Answer the following Questions about the age structure diagram of the United States population in 2000.

8. In which age categories are the populations the highest?

9. In which age category is the population of males and females vastly different? How can you explain this difference?

10. How many millions of males and females are shown in your (current) age category?

Examining age structure diagrams can tell us quite a bit about populations and assist us in predicting population changes. For example, if the bottom of the pyramid is very wide, it indicates that a population is expanding. There are many individuals who will be theoretically able to reproduce in the future, increasing population. In contrast, a narrow base indicates a population that will decline in the future.

Theoretical Population Comparison

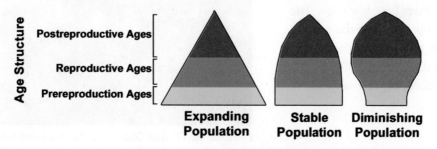

FIGURE 15.15. Theoretical age structure diagrams illustrate changes in populations.

11. Review the age structure diagram of the United States. Based on that diagram, is the population of the United States expected to increase or decrease? Explain.

12. One concern about the Hawaiian Monk Seal, a highly endangered species, is that there are few "teenage" females. With a life expectancy of 25–30 years if kept out of harm's way, the females mature by about 6 years of age.

    a. Sketch the age structure diagram for this scenario, showing just the shape of the diagram, not the specific age structures.

    b. Explain why this scenario is a serious concern to biologists.

13. In the mid-1990s, a disease caused high mortality in the female California population of Sea Otters, which have an average life span of 10 to 12 years. The disease primarily affected young adult females. Describe the effects of this pathogen on the Sea Otter population in subsequent years.

FIGURE 15.16. Following the passage of the Endangered Species Act of 1973, NOAA reviewed the population status of a number of marine animal species and determined that several, including the Hawaiian Monk Seal, are endangered. The Hawaiian Monk Seal is currently one of the rarest marine mammals in the world with populations declining annually. Scientists are concerned because of the species' low genetic diversity.

14. Studies show that the sex of sea turtle hatchlings is determined by environmental conditions, specifically temperature. When eggs are incubated at a temperature warmer than 30 °C, the sex is female. Those developing at a temperature cooler than 30 °C become male. In a typical nest, temperatures vary due to depth, proximity to cool sand, and so on.

    Earth is experiencing a warming trend. How might this affect sea turtle populations? Draw a potential population pyramid to support your ideas.

The number of individual organisms per unit of space is known as **population density**. Some marine ecosystems have high population densities, whereas others have low ones. The density of specific populations in the ocean varies depending on the species. There are three basic types of distribution patterns in habitats: uniform, clumped, and random.

FIGURE 15.17. Sea Otters in California have experienced high death rates, attributed to pathogenic agents including parasites. Sea Otters are the smallest marine mammals on the planet.

Oysters, whose larvae travel with the plankton population, often exhibit a random distribution. These mollusks settle on the seafloor in unpredictable patterns. Many pinniped species, including Northern Elephant Seals and California Sea Lions, show a clumped population pattern, as do fish that exhibit schooling behavior. Clumped distribution patterns improve access to mates, and are often formed near areas of abundant resources, such as coral reefs or estuaries. Clumped distribution patterns are the most common in the ocean because resources are not evenly distributed—they are "patchy".

Uniform distribution can be thought of as "evenly-spaced organisms". Within a coral colony, a smaller area of unit space, individual polyps can be uniformly distributed. Uniform distribution is also observed in some eel populations as well as certain sponges, which create chemicals that keep competitors at bay. On land, a human-manipulated example of uniform distribution is in a farm or orchard, where crops are planted equidistant from one another.

15. Would the Florida Manatees' population distribution be considered to be clumped, uniform, or random? Explain your answer.

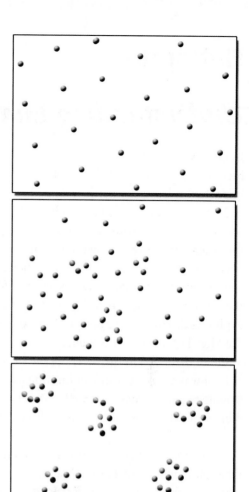

FIGURE 15.18. The distribution of populations throughout the ocean is varied. They may be uniform, random, or clumped.

FIGURE 15.19. Dolphins, which generally travel in pods, are an example of a population that has a clumped distribution.

Elaborate

Understanding Endangered Species

In Lesson 14: Biodiversity in the Ocean, we examined the many reasons for protecting biodiversity on Earth, including the fact that humans rely on organisms as a source of pharmaceuticals. Diverse species each have important roles in the Earth system. For example, losing just one plant species can result in the extinction of 30 other species. Plants provide food for a variety of species, and affect others through the food chain. In addition, plants provide habitat for many species, including birds and insects. They can also provide shade for other plants, preventing them from drying out due to intense sunlight. Extinction of species is expected over time as a result of natural phenomena and stresses on ecosystems, but human activities are significantly increasing the rate of species loss on our planet. For example, in 1741 explorers discovered the Steller's Sea Cow, a close relative of the Florida Manatee. The Steller's Sea Cow was a kelp-eating Sirenian that lived in the waters of the Bering Sea. By 1768, the animal was extinct because of hunting by European explorers. Scientists today believe the Steller's Sea Cow was already in danger of extinction at the time of discovery.

You probably have heard of species that are endangered. Examples include the Florida Manatee and the Green Sea Turtle, which you read about in the **Explore** section. Have you ever stopped to think about what the word *endangered* really means?

In 1973, the United States passed the Endangered Species Act (ESA). The ESA is one of the strictest environmental laws on Earth. The law authorizes the National Marine Fisheries Service (NMFS) and the U.S. Fish and Wildlife Service (FWS) to identify and list species that are in danger of extinction. All species of plants and animals, except pest insects, are eligible to be listed as endangered or threatened. Congress recognized when they wrote the law that although humans pose a danger to other living organisms, they are also responsible for protecting these organisms. Organisms that are protected under the ESA are *listed*. An *endangered* species is one that is in danger of extinction throughout all or a significant portion of its range. A *threatened* species is one that is likely to become endangered in the foreseeable future.

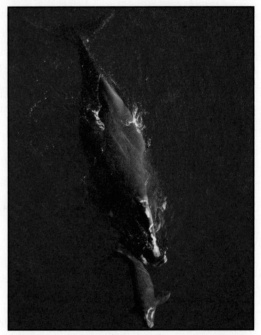

FIGURE 15.20 The North Atlantic Right Whale is one the most critically endangered species of marine mammal. These animals are plagued by a slow reproductive rate. Observing a mother and calf, such as those shown here, is an encouraging experience.

Under the Endangered Species Act, the U.S. Congress made it unlawful for a person to take or attempt to take a listed animal without a permit. Species permits are often given to scientists who are conducting research to help protect animals. The law defines *take* as "to harass, harm, pursue, hunt, shoot, wound, kill, trap, capture, or collect or to attempt to engage in any such conduct".

Listed plants are not protected in the same way as listed animals, but it is illegal to collect or maliciously harm them. This includes buying products made from listed plants and animals and trying to bring them into the United States. For example, it is possible to buy jewelry and other products made from sea turtle shells in other countries. It is illegal, however, to bring these products into the United States.

FIGURE 15.21. The Leedy's roseroot is an endangered wildflower found in Minnesota and upstate New York only. Scientists believe that the plant was more widespread during the last ice age but has lost habitat since the Earth has warmed.

People who break the law face large fines and potential jail time. Therefore, if you come across a sea turtle on a beach, or a manatee while snorkeling, you must increase your distance from the animal and leave it alone.

Species may be upgraded or downgraded from endangered or threatened status as their populations change. Once a species is listed, scientists and the government work together to develop a Recovery Plan, which includes ways to protect the species and to help increase its numbers. The goal of the Recovery Plan is for organisms to be *de-listed* and to be taken off the Endangered Species List completely. Organisms that are de-listed no longer need protection under the Endangered Species Act. Decisions about the listing and de-listing of species require much scientific data collection about the organisms, the characteristics of their populations, and their habitats.

The ESA is not accepted by all, however. Some believe that protections afforded to these species cause economic and social problems. For example, endangered plants in wetlands can stymie coastal development, meaning that jobs can be lost. Some people contend that since extinction is natural, humans should let nature take its course and allow endangered species to perish. Biologists, however, respect the inherent value of each species and of biodiversity as a whole. They realize that human activities are accelerating the extinction of many species, and may in fact be endangering species that would not otherwise face extermination. Once species are listed, their protection under the law becomes paramount; humans must accommodate the species and allow them to flourish.

FIGURE 15.22. Johnson's Seagrass is a threatened species throughout its range. It is found exclusively off of the Southeast Florida Coast.

A number of the animal species tracked in *Signals of Spring* are on the endangered species list. Wildlife biologists and marine biologists perform research to gain and provide information that will assist them in increasing animal populations. By learning about the species' behavior and critical habitats, the animals' chances for survival increase. There are strict rules about the permits required to work with these species, including tracking animals. Scientific study is carefully regulated.

Nations around the globe have banded together to protect endangered species. One of the most far-reaching international agreements is the Convention on International Trade in Endangered Species (CITES) signed in 1973. This treaty lists almost 900 species that cannot be commercially traded as live organisms or products. For example, shells and meat of sea turtles and the pelts of tigers cannot be transported from country to country. Unfortunately, not every country has signed this agreement and it can be difficult to enforce. When one of these products enters the United States, customs agents are authorized to confiscate items related to endangered species, and to advise prosecution for those who carry them.

16. Some critics of the ESA say that the law does not do enough to protect species. They say that whole ecosystems must be protected, rather than individual species. Do you agree or disagree? Use scientific ideas to support your claim.

Activity

Researching Endangered Species

While habitats in the United States support much biodiversity, many species of plants and animals are endangered. Your task is to prepare a presentation introducing others to a specific endangered species. The audience for your presentation is the general public.

Use resources on the *Marine Science: The Dynamic Ocean* website to choose a species and to learn more about it.

Be sure to include to the extent possible:

- Pictures of your species
- Habitat and range of the species
- Human-induced and natural factors that contribute to the species' vulnerability to extinction

1. During your classmates' presentations, take notes in your notebook about each species. Be sure to include at least the following:

- Name and description of the species
- Factors causing it to be endangered or threatened

FIGURE 15.23. The Elkhorn Coral is a threatened species native to the Caribbean Sea. Threats include disease, climate change, and hurricane damage.

FIGURE 15.24. The Polar Bear was listed as a threatened species in 2010. The species is susceptible to habitat loss due to climate change.

Evaluate

1. The following is an age structure diagram for Guatemala for 1998. Based on these data, what predictions would you make about the country's future population? Explain.

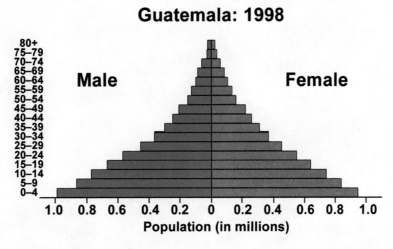

Guatemala: 1998

Male   Female

Population (in millions)

FIGURE 15.25.

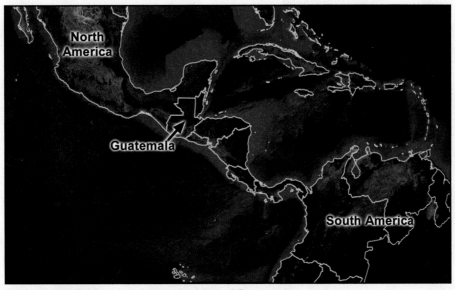

FIGURE 15.26. Map showing the location of Guatemala.

2. What is carrying capacity? Why can't populations exist above carrying capacity for long periods of time?

3. The Florida Manatee is an endangered species throughout its range. Describe at least two characteristics of this animal that make it vulnerable to extinction.

16

Population Changes

INSIDE:

Objectives

You will be able to:

✔ **Explain how the process of natural selection influences the evolution of species.**

✔ **Determine how invasive species can result in biodiversity loss.**

✔ **Give examples of adaptations in diverse marine ecosystems.**

Benchmarks

5e. The ocean is three-dimensional, offering vast living space and diverse habitats from the surface through the water column to the seafloor. Most of the living space on Earth is in the ocean.

5f. Ocean habitats are defined by environmental factors. Due to interactions of abiotic factors (e.g., salinity, temperature, oxygen, pH, light, nutrients, pressure, substrate, circulation), ocean life is not evenly distributed temporally or spatially (i.e., it is "patchy"). Some regions of the ocean support more diverse and abundant life than anywhere on Earth, while much of the ocean is considered a desert.

6e. Humans affect the ocean in a variety of ways. Laws, regulations, and resource management affect what is taken out and put into the ocean. Human development and activity leads to pollution (e.g., point source, nonpoint source, noise pollution) and physical modifications (e.g., changes to beaches, shores, and rivers). In addition, humans have removed most of the large vertebrates from the ocean.

Engage

Living organisms did not emerge from the sea to live on land until about 400 million years ago, and mammals did not emerge until 250 million years ago. Mammals are air-breathing, warm-blooded organisms that give birth to live young. The first land mammals were quite small compared to dinosaurs and other large reptiles that shared the land. It was not until after dinosaurs become extinct approximately 65 million years ago that mammals began to flourish.

FIGURE 16.1. A Humpback Whale performs a dive, revealing its tail fluke. Marine mammals are animals that, through evolutionary time, have returned to the sea.

Today, we are familiar with mammals living in the ocean. Have you ever wondered how a mammal such as a whale came to live its life in the sea?

The diagram in FIGURE 16.2 illustrates how scientists infer cetaceans have changed over time. Note that over millions of years, this group of animals began to show traits such as modified front limbs and tails. Today, the major groups of cetaceans are the baleen whales and toothed whales, which include dolphins and porpoises. In this Lesson, we will examine how species change over time.

1. Describe the changes in cetaceans over time.

2. How do scientists create a diagram like FIGURE 16.2? What data do they use?

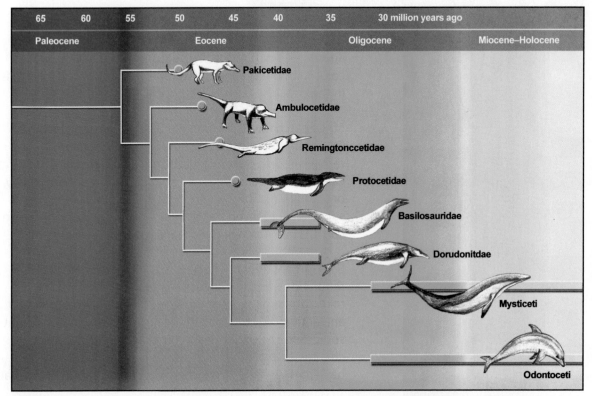

FIGURE 16.2. Evolution of cetaceans over time. The dots and bars in the illustration demonstrate the approximate time the species was or has been living on Earth.

Explore

This activity allows you to model changes over time in a species of sea stars. It is important to understand that genetic variations within species (color patterns, shape of lips, etc.) occur *randomly*. As a result, they may or may not be beneficial to individual organisms. In this activity, you and your classmates will act as predators—selecting prey—in a specific environment. Look for changes that occur in the population over time.

FIGURE 16.3. The Mottled Sea Star naturally occurs in many different colors. These sea stars are found along the Alaska Coast, often on rocky beaches, and can grow to 1/2 meter (~20 inches) in diameter.

Activity

Materials:

For each group:

- Sea star cutouts: 35 red, 35 orange, and 35 gray (to simulate a population)
- Die (to randomly select genetic variations)
- 2 Pieces of red paper taped together (to act as a habitat)
- Cup

Procedure:

Part I

1. You will work in groups of three or four. Divide your group into the following:

   - The **Predator** will use his or her first finger and thumb to pick up as many sea stars as possible with one hand. The other hand must be kept in a pocket.

   - The **Sea Star Counter** will count how many of each color sea star remain on the paper and how many have been "consumed" by the predator.

   - The **Data Recorder** will complement the **Sea Star Counter** (Predator) and record data on the *Sea Star Data Worksheet*.

   - The **Die Roller and Timekeeper** will determine how many and what type of offspring will be in successive generations, and they will place them on the "habitat". They will also provide timing for each "hunting period".

2. The two pieces of paper taped together act as the habitat of the sea stars and predator in this activity. Place the habitat on a desk. Place 35 gray sea stars on the habitat.

3. Direct the **Predator** to turn around, now facing the habitat. Time the **Predator** for 10 seconds as he or she tries to grab as many sea stars as possible. *Remember*: The **Predator** may use only his or her first finger and thumb. The other hand must be kept away in a pocket.

    Just like in nature, the **Predator** can "consume" only one sea star at a time. So the **Predator** may grab only one sea star on each try and place it in the cup. The **Predator** should choose the sea star first felt or noticed.

4. The **Sea Star Counter** then counts the number of each type of sea star remaining on the habitat. The **Data Recorder** records the information on the *Sea Star Data Worksheet*.

Sea Star Data Worksheet

Generation	Red	Orange	Grey	Total	# of pairs	% of red	% of orange	% of grey	
1	0	0	35			0%	0%	100%	Starting Population
									Survivors
									Offspring
2									New Population
									Survivors
									Offspring
3									New Population
									Survivors
									Offspring
4									New Population
									Survivors
									Offspring
5									New Population
									Survivors
									Offspring
6									New Population
									Survivors
									Offspring
7									New Population
									Survivors
									Offspring
8									New Population
									Survivors
									Offspring
9									New Population
									Survivors
									Offspring
10									New Population
									Survivors
									Offspring
									New Population

FIGURE 16.4. Screenshot of the *Sea Star Data Worksheet*.

Part II

For this part of the activity, to determine the type of color variation produced by the sea star pairs, the **Die Roller** will roll the die. For each pair of remaining sea stars, one offspring will be produced. Genetic variation, caused by mutation within a species, is also random, like the roll of the die.

> If the die roller rolls a: **1 or 2** = Red offspring are produced
> **3 or 4** = Orange offspring are produced
> **5 or 6** = Gray offspring are produced

Note: The color is the only thing determined by the roll of the die. For example, if your group has 15 sea stars left, that would indicate 7 pairs. The group would roll the die only once to determine the color of the 7 new sea stars. If the **Die Roller** rolls a 3 the group would add 7 orange sea stars to the environment.

5. Record the number of each color sea star that remains. For the 1st round, this would be the number of gray sea stars, as this is the only color with which you started.

6. The **Predator** turns away from the environment indicating that reproduction may successfully occur. The **Die Roller** rolls the die for the first time to determine the offspring. The "offspring" are added to the red paper. Mingle or mix the offspring with the sea stars.

FIGURE 16.5. Sunflower Sea Stars are large, voracious predators ranging in color from orange to purple. Notice the work boot to the left of the sea star, giving you perspective on the scale— a Sunflower Sea Star's arm span can reach up to 1 meter (~3 feet). They feed upon clams, snails, sea cucumbers, and other sea stars, but must escape from predators such as large fish, often by leaving one of their 16–24 arms behind.

Part III

7. Repeat steps 3 through 6, ten times. Make sure to keep careful track of your data.

8. Clean up before your group continues to the next portion of the activity.

Part IV

9. Calculate the percentages of offspring in each generation of sea stars. Show your work on a separate sheet of paper and record the percentages on the **Sea Star Data Worksheet**.

   To determine the percentage:

   % of surviving sea stars of a particular color = $\dfrac{\text{\# of surviving sea stars of a particular variation (red, orange or gray)}}{\text{Total number of sea stars (red + orange + gray)}}$ x 100

   Complete this calculation for each color of sea stars for each successive generation trial.

10. Using graph paper, create a bar graph using the percentage of red offspring.

11. What, if any, changes did you observe in the generations of offspring?

12. How can you explain your results? What did the experiment show about how prey are selected by predators?

13. Which color was the most difficult to hunt? Explain.

14. What caused differences among the offspring in this activity? How does this relate to real life?

15. What do you think would happen if the offspring colors were pink, red, and orange? Why?

16. How would changing the initial environment background color to orange have changed your results?

Explain

All species change over time, or **evolve**. Evolution in species occurs over many generations. In short-lived organisms, evolution is observable. For example, have you ever taken an antibiotic in response to an infection such as strep throat, bronchitis, pneumonia, or another illness? Antibiotics are chemicals that kill bacteria. When we take antibiotics, they kill the bacteria that are causing illnesses in our body. However, a lot of people tend to stop taking the antibiotics when they begin to feel better. This practice is problematic, because only the weakest bacteria in one's system are killed by the first few doses of antibiotics. The ones left behind have survived their interaction with antibiotics. These bacteria will reproduce, passing on their genes. Bacteria that are able to multiply even after exposure to antibiotics exhibit **antibiotic resistance**. Antibiotic resistance is one example of observable evolution. Because bacteria can multiply in as little as about 20 minutes, we are able to observe changes that occur over many generations within a relatively short time (i.e., days or weeks). The new bacteria are closely related to the bacteria that were killed by the antibiotics, but they have slight differences. In this case, the difference is the ability to resist antibiotics.

FIGURE 16.6. Antibiotics kill bacteria, but used improperly, can lead to antibiotic resistance. Bacteria are often a good example for studying observable evolution since they reproduce so quickly.

All living things share similar cellular functions and basic needs such as water, shelter, and nutrients. However, since these resources are limited, organisms must compete for them. Some groups of organisms compete more successfully than others, and thus are able to pass their traits on to their offspring. This process is called **natural selection**. Species that are not successful become extinct, and in fact, most species that have lived on Earth are now extinct. Nature "selects" those organisms that are better equipped to survive and pass on their genes. In the previous activity, the color of the habitat allowed some sea stars to survive better than others.

The **Theory of Evolution by Natural Selection** is also simply called the **Theory of Evolution**. Recall that in science a theory is a well-developed and supported explanation of events in the natural world. Scientists developed the Theory of Evolution based on evidence including fossils, body structures, and other observable similarities. Later, genetic observations including DNA comparisons between species provided stronger evidence. The Theory of Evolution is widely accepted by scientists around the world. It is a scientific explanation based on evidence obtained through scientific methods.

Fossils give us information about organisms that lived in the past. Fossils are a valuable source from which to learn the history of Earth's biosphere. The **fossil record**—the collective, fossilized history of different groups of living organisms—can indicate whether

FIGURE 16.7. Fossils, the mineralized remains of organisms, give scientists important clues to the past. Fossils and other data provide scientists with evidence that support the Theory of Evolution.

some fossils are older or younger than others. The fossil record suggests relative ages of the organisms. Fossilized remains of organisms introduce us to species that lived in the past and have become extinct. Fossilized remains may also illustrate changes in organisms that have occurred within species or groups of species over time. Scientists have discovered fossils of species that are similar to modern species but appear to no longer exist on Earth. Identified organisms that are "in between" ancient and modern forms are called **transitional species**. The transitional species is extinct but it may represent a link to modern groups. A classic example of this is *Archeopteryx* (ar-kē-ŎP-ter-ix), a species seen in fossil form only but frequently considered the evidence, or "missing link", between birds and reptiles, because it has characteristics of both birds and reptiles.

FIGURE 16.8. Scientists believe that the Tiktaalik (pronounced: TIK-tah-lĭk) was a transitional species between fish and four-legged land animals, such as modern crocodiles. This ancient organism had characteristics of a fish, yet had similar features to tetrapods, organisms that walk on four legs.

Extinct species, with the exception of their fossils, are gone from Earth forever. The Earth has gone through many changes in its history. For example, there have been ice ages, extreme warm periods, changes in the concentration of gases in the atmosphere, movements of the continents, and so on. As a result of the changes on our dynamic Earth, life on Earth has also changed. Sometimes changes in Earth's environments are significant enough that species or even groups of species are unable to survive, and species can then become extinct.

FIGURE 16.9. An illustration of what a Tiktaalik might have looked like 375 million years ago.

Recall that scientific theories must be widely supported with strong evidence. There are many pieces of evidence to support the Theory of Evolution. In addition to contrasting the fossil record with modern species, scientists compare the structures of organisms that live today. Similar structures, even when used for different purposes, can suggest that organisms had a common ancestor. For many years, scientists considered the way organisms appeared in order to understand the relationships between them. Looking at the body structures of organisms allowed scientists to establish relationships for many groups. However, later evidence showed that scientists sometimes drew the wrong conclusions. As new evidence was uncovered, scientists devised new explanations. The whale and the shark, for instance, look somewhat alike. These animals have similar body shape and color patterns, share a habitat, and are vertebrates. But, more importantly, these two groups of animals meet their life functions in very different ways. For example, whales are mammals and breathe through lungs, whereas sharks are fish and breathe through gills.

Scientists have learned that internal structures are more useful to compare than are external features for establishing evidence that species have changed over time. As it relates to the internal structure, scientists observe similar bone elements in the limbs of many closely related animals. Sharing similar characteristics can indicate that the species share a common ancestor. Such structures are called **homologous structures**. While whales share homologous limb structures with organisms such as humans, bats, and lizards, the pectoral fins of sharks are very different because sharks are not as closely related to the other organisms.

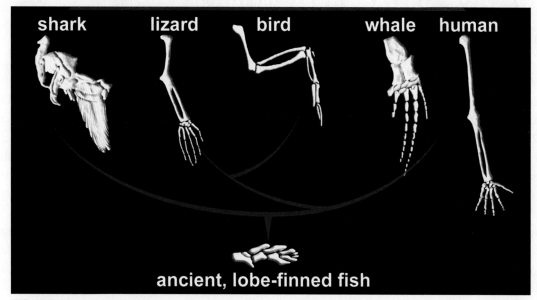

FIGURE 16.10. The similar bone structure of these vertebrates indicates that many share a common ancestor. Observations also reveal when species are less closely related. Humans, whales, and lizards are more closely related to one another than they are to sharks.

DNA evidence also illustrates change over time. DNA is the "blueprint of life". Contained in cells of every living thing, this blueprint is built by the sequences of only four "bases". They are represented by the letters A, T, C, and G, which stand for adenine, thymine, cytosine, and guanine. DNA is a double-stranded molecule. The bases are paired with their "complements"—A with T, C with G. Simply stated, it is the order of the base pairs that determines the characteristics of an organism. Of note, one molecule of human DNA contains about 3 billion chemical base pairs, whereas bacteria have as few as 600,000 base pairs.

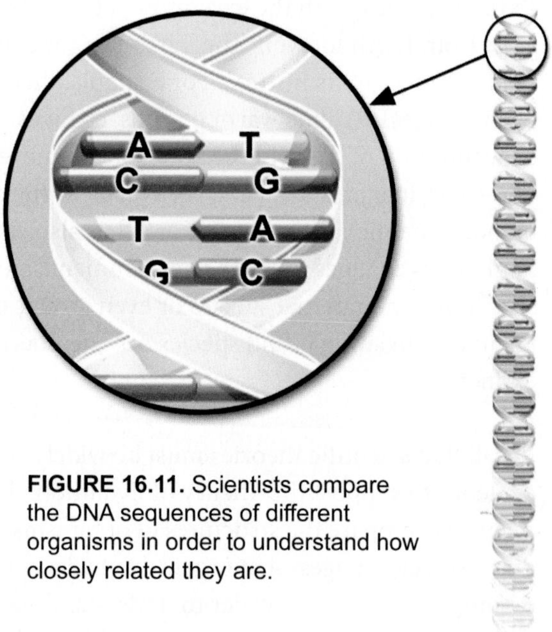

Genes are segments of DNA, usually thousands of base pairs long. Tiny differences in the sequence of the DNA change the genes. This may change the outward appearance, internal structure, or even the viability of an organism. When changes occur in genes, they are called **mutations**, and they are very common. Like the roll of the die in the sea star activity, mutations are random. Mutations are the sources of differences within populations. They are the reason why species can change over time. By examining differences in DNA sequences, scientists can determine whether the genetic code of individual organisms, or groups of organisms, are closely or distantly related. For example, DNA sequences can be used to establish relatedness between a parent and child (e.g., paternity tests), or between groups (e.g., between fish and mammals). The greater the percentage of similarity in DNA sequences between two organisms, the more closely related are the organisms.

FIGURE 16.11. Scientists compare the DNA sequences of different organisms in order to understand how closely related they are.

Study Spotlight

Charles Darwin and the Voyage of the *HMS Beagle*

In December of 1831, Charles Darwin set sail on a worldwide expedition aboard the *HMS Beagle*. At the age of 22, Darwin was invited by the ship's captain, Robert FitzRoy, to join the vessel as a naturalist and assistant to the captain. The journey itself was expected to take about two years, but lasted almost five. Darwin later explained that this trip was one of the most important experiences in his life as a scientist. Following the expedition, he published his Journal of Researches about his trip, which helped to establish his fame and respect as a scientist. In this publication, Darwin discussed geology, biology, paleontology, and anthropology, a great example of the interdisciplinary nature of the sciences. Despite his prominence as a scientist, Darwin was incredibly seasick throughout the journey, so most of his ideas and findings relate to observations he made during the ship's many stops on islands and continents around the world.

The trip began in Plymouth, England, and headed south, toward the Canary and Cape Verde Islands off of Northwestern Africa. A natural scientist, Darwin took copious notes and made many sketches throughout his journey. He observed geological features, such as volcanic islands, the rock formations

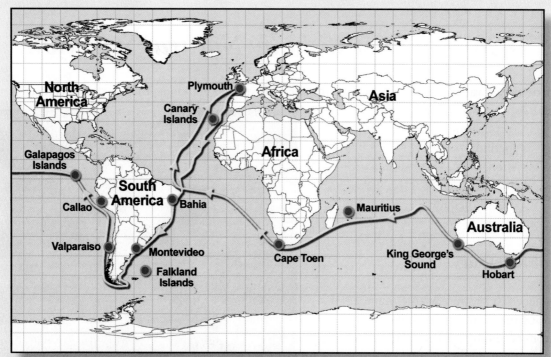

FIGURE 16.12. Darwin's 5-year voyage brought him to several continents and many isolated islands. The trip is famous for its influence on Darwinian Theory.

of river valleys and rugged coastlines, and began to hypothesize about their origins and changes. For example, in the Cape Verde Islands, he observed within the rocks of the cliffs a layer of shells that must have originated in the ocean. When visiting the Andes Mountains, he again noticed fossils of marine organisms high in the cliffs. He began to consider changes in the Earth's surface that result in the raising and sinking of continents. The evidence he found supported the theory of another scientist of the time, Charles Lyell, who had suggested that the continents were slowly rising over long time periods.

As the vessel's team collected biological specimens around the world, Darwin made special notes and many thorough sketches in his field journals. In South America, for instance, he collected hundreds of specimens of plants and animals from the rainforests. From the ocean, he collected birds, fish, and invertebrates, sending several shipments of specimens back to England during the journey. Darwin observed giant fossils in South America, and hypothesized that to support such large land animals, the area, now sparsely covered in vegetation, must once have been lush and different climatically. He noted the uniqueness of animals in Southern South America, as well as similarities between fossils found along African and South American coastlines. In the Galapagos Islands, he noted minute differences

in seemingly related species of finches. In Australia, he noted that the plants and animals were incredibly unique, unlike any others he had observed around the world. These and other observations were very curious and confusing to Darwin at the time, but led to his formulation of his Theory of Evolution by Natural Selection.

The *Beagle*'s worldwide voyage was a great example of science at work. Darwin made careful observations, and used these observations to support his new ideas. His field notebooks were incredibly detailed, inspiring all of us as scientists to record our findings carefully and completely.

FIGURE 16.13. This illustration is an example of variation in the size and shape of bird's beaks, as observed by Darwin.

The Theory of Evolution by Natural Selection

Darwin described various factors as components of his Theory of Evolution. These factors included:

- Overproduction
- Competition
- Variation
- Adaptation
- Survival of the Fittest
- Speciation

Overproduction

Species generally produce a larger number of offspring than is necessary to prevent them from becoming extinct. Earth does not have enough natural resources to support such large numbers of offspring. Yet, most species continue to overproduce. This overproduction leads naturally to competition between individuals within a species. Darwin noted that a very small number of offspring

FIGURE 16.14. In a school of fish, more animals are produced than can survive. This phenomenon is called overproduction. Individual fish will compete with one another, and some members of the school will not survive.

survive long enough to reproduce; those that do survive have the greater **fitness**. Many species of organisms overproduce at very high rates, particularly sessile species and organisms that have many predators.

Competition

Since such a large number of offspring are produced, they compete for the limited amount of space and food available. There is competition not only within a species but also with other species that live in the same habitat. Competition leads to some individuals and species surviving over others.

FIGURE 16.15. One can observe variations in a population of jellyfish, including size, length of tentacles, color, and strength of sting. Some of these individuals will outcompete others and pass on their genes.

Variation

Darwin further noted that individual organisms within the same species show differences in genetic traits. Genetic differences include swimming ability, size, shape, and so on. These differences within a species are called **variations**. These variations occur randomly due to mutation. Some variations will not affect an individual organism; other variations may harm or benefit an organism.

Adaptation

Earth's diverse environments have changed radically over geologic time. Not every organism is equipped to survive environmental changes. Some organisms are "lucky enough" to be born with genes that give them characteristics that improve their chances of survival. Of course, no organism lives forever; they must reproduce to pass on their genes and ensure the survival of their population and species. When organisms reproduce, they sometimes pass on the "lucky genes"—the ones that helped them survive—to their offspring.

Characteristics or genetic traits that enhance an organism's survival and reproductive success are **adaptations**. Characteristics are adaptations only if they are in an organism's DNA. Adaptations can take many forms, some of which are not visible. Archaea, for example, are specially adapted to create sugar in an unusual way. This helps them survive, but it occurs on the cellular level. Many Archaeans live in very harsh environments.

Behavioral Adaptations. Behaviors can be adaptations. They include how organisms move, respond to danger, find nutrients, and reproduce. For example, sponges are animals that do not move. Because they are stationary, or sessile, sponges have adapted and they reproduce by releasing their eggs and sperm into the water. These sex cells meet to form larvae and become a new sponge. In several sponge species, many of its members have adapted to release their eggs and sperm on the same night. Sponges that release their sex cells at other times have a slimmer chance of their sperm or egg meeting to form offspring. Therefore, releasing the cells directly into the water and releasing them at a specific time are behavioral adaptations that lead to the survival of sponges.

Another behavioral adaptation is migration. Some of the marine animals that *Signals of Spring* and scientists track by satellite, such as whales and albatross, migrate seasonally. For these animals, migration means that they find the best food sources available so that they can take the best care of their young—ensuring their young's survival. Remember that fitness means having offspring that reproduce their own offspring.

FIGURE 16.16. A behavioral adaptation in Christmas Tree Worms is coordination of the timing of the release of eggs and sperm. This adaptation is also observed in other sessile organisms including sponges and corals.

Structural Adaptations.
Organisms also have structural adaptations that lead to differences in survival. Let's consider diatoms, the type of phytoplankton we studied in Lesson 14: Biodiversity in the Ocean. Diatoms have many structural adaptations that help them to survive and perform photosynthesis in their water habitat. For example, they have clear cell walls made up of two spiny plates. The spiny plates help the diatoms to float, keeping them close to the surface and the available sunlight. The clear cell wall lets in as much sunlight as possible, which the organisms use to perform photosynthesis. Both of these structural adaptations of the cell wall help diatoms to survive in environments that might not necessarily support photosynthetic organisms.

FIGURE 16.17. These Atlantic Bluefin Tuna have torpedo-shaped bodies. This and other structural adaptations allow these fish to swim more quickly than most other species.

Fitness

Overproduction, competition, variation, and adaptations are essential components of the Theory of Evolution by Natural Selection. Natural selection posits that organisms that are best genetically adapted to an environment will be the most successful and survive to reproduce. Biologists explain that some organisms within a population are better adapted to pass on their genes to the next generation. They call this explanation **fitness**. Fitness does not necessarily mean the strongest individuals survive, but rather the organisms within the population that are best genetically suited will pass on their genes at a higher rate. Fitness takes into account the ability to survive in a specific environment, to find mates, and to produce offspring. All of these are important components of fitness.

Speciation (pronounced: spē-shē-Ā-shen)

Natural selection over a long period of time can cause significant changes in a species' characteristics. When combined with some form of isolation of the species, these changes can lead to the development of a new species. For example, the populations of finches that Darwin observed on the Galapagos Islands became so different from the finches on the mainland that they could no longer reproduce with one another. This process is called **speciation**.

1. How are overproduction, competition, and variation related? How do they ultimately lead to an adaptation?

Let's look at a specific example of a familiar marine organism in order to understand Darwin's theory.

See Page 694 for how to access e-Tools.

View the **Market Squid Behavior Video** (3:40) from the e-Tools.

FIGURE 16.18. Screenshot of the **Market Squid Behavior Video**.

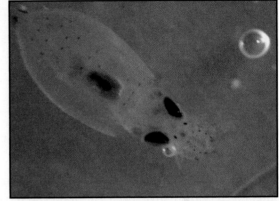

FIGURE 16.19. A newly hatched squid larva. Like many other invertebrate animals, squid produce many offspring, helping to ensure the survival of some individuals.

2. Copy the table into your notebook. After you watch the video, work with a partner to discuss how each of the following ideas are illustrated. Note that the ideas will not be discussed specifically—you will need to apply what you have learned to what is shown in the video. Describe at least one example of each.

Overproduction	
Competition	
Variation	
Fitness	
Adaptation	

Elaborate

Non-native Species

Human interference can influence the changes in species over time. One example of this influence is when animals and plants are introduced by humans into an area in which they have never lived before. These species, new to an area, are called **non-native species**, **introduced species**, or **invasive species**, while the species already inhabiting the environment are called **native species**. Some of these introductions have been done on purpose. For example, swans were introduced to the Northeastern United States as ornamental birds for wealthy property owners. In other cases, the introduction is accidental. Invasive species can be plants, animals, or microbes.

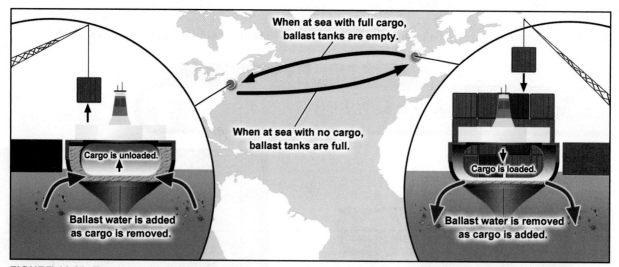

FIGURE 16.20. Transport of cargo around the world can also result in the introduction of non-native species. This problem is being addressed in the United States with regulations for ballast water.

Since the invasive species often do not have any natural predators in their new ecosystem, they tend to outcompete some native species for food and territory and they may reproduce quickly. As a result, they endanger the native species, making their extinction a possibility.

It is important to study invasive species to learn about the effects they may have on native organisms and the physical environment. Invasive species are prevalent in marine ecosystems. Many can be traced to the use of **ballast water**. Ballast water is simply water carried in special tanks on ships that is used to provide stability for the vessel. When a ship carries less than a full load of cargo, ballast water keeps the ship at the proper depth in the water. When the ship is loaded with cargo, the ballast water is released into surrounding waters; when the ship is empty, it takes on even more water to keep it upright. The problem is that the ballast water is simply water from the ocean. Ocean water contains organisms, including, in this case, larvae of many species from wherever the water came. When the ballast water is released in a new area, the larvae are also released and can colonize a new environment. To combat this problem, some vessels use sand as ballast rather than water. Many regulations have been enacted about the use of ballast water in United States waters.

The Red Lionfish – A Case Study

One example of an invasive species in the waters of the United States is the Red Lionfish. Lionfish are naturally found in the warm, tropical waters of the South Pacific and Indian Oceans and are coral reef fish. They are commonly collected from those reefs and displayed in aquariums across the globe. It is believed that in 1992, during Hurricane Andrew, a beachside aquarium broke and released 6 Red Lionfish into Biscayne Bay, near Miami, Florida. Over a period of time, the non-native species was spotted off the coast of Long Island, New York, in water as cold as 56 °F. Scientists believe that even more were purposely released when people

FIGURE 16.21. Red Lionfish are beautiful fish whose native distribution is generally in the Western Pacific Ocean. They have been outcompeting some native species in Florida and elsewhere along the East Coast in recent years.

no longer wanted them as aquarium pets because they grew too large for the tank—or they learned the hard way that lionfish will eat the other fish in the tank.

Along the continental shelf of the East Coast near the Gulf Stream, the temperatures are very similar to the Red Lionfish's native waters in the Indo-Pacific. The swift and warm current, which likely transported buoyant lionfish eggs and larvae from Florida northward, helped the lionfish's Atlantic journey.

FIGURE 16.22. The Indo-Pacific Lionfish (Red Lionfish) is an invasive species found along the coastline from North Carolina to Florida.

The Red Lionfish is now as abundant as many of the native fish in and around the Florida coastline. Lionfish are voracious feeders, and they quickly adapted to their new prey opportunities. They feed on just about anything, including fishes locally important to the Southeast, such as groupers, snappers, and sea bass. They outcompete other predators in these ecosystems, yet the lionfish has no confirmed predators in its new habitats. Its ability to succeed in its new environment, coupled with its lack of natural enemies due to being covered in venomous spines, has become a dangerous combination.

The Red Lionfish has distinctive maroon and white stripes, with fleshy tentacles above the eyes and below the mouth. A lionfish's sting is incredibly painful, but not usually life threatening. Relatives of the lionfish, including the Scorpionfish and Stonefish, produce a much more severe poison; in fact, the sting of the stonefish is sometimes fatal to humans. After the lionfish's spine punctures the victim's skin, the venom travels up a groove in its spine and into the new wound.

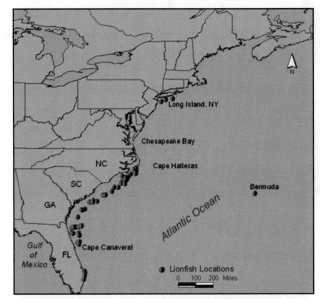

FIGURE 16.23. It was initially believed that the Red Lionfish was a species that could only survive in warm waters. Then the non-native species was spotted off the coast of Long Island, New York, in water as cold as 56 °F.

The sting causes intense pain, redness, and swelling around the wound site. Although the worst of the pain is gone after an hour or two, some people report pain and tingling sensations around the wound for several days or weeks. On rare occasions, when the poison spreads to other parts of the body, people may experience headaches, chills, cramps, nausea, and even paralysis and seizures.

Another negative impact of these nocturnal predators to the local coral reef communities is that they have drastically reduced the number of invertebrate and vertebrate larvae that are able to develop into adulthood. In time this will decrease many ecologically important species such as the Parrotfish and other herbivores that keep seaweeds and algae from overgrowing.

3. How are invasive species related to natural selection?

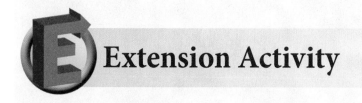 Extension Activity

Invasive Species Awareness

Each state has its fair share of invasive species.

Research one invasive species that is prevalent in your area. In your research you should address the following:

- Describe the invasive species.
- Where is its native range?
- What does it look like? How does it reproduce? What are its natural predators and diet?
- How was it introduced into the area where you live?
- What threats does it pose to other populations or the ecosystem?
- Why should people be concerned about the species?
- What can local residents do to help mitigate damage caused by this species?

Create an informational brochure with the information you have gathered. Remember that these brochures should bring attention to the seriousness of the problem and provide a way for people to help. Do not forget to include pictures of the invasive species and a map of where in your local area the invasive species is of great concern.

Evaluate

1. Go back to the ecosystems you "met" in Lesson 1: Diving Into Ocean Ecosystems. Copy the following chart into your notebook. Give an example of an adaptation exhibited by species in each ecosystem, and describe how the characteristic enhances survival in the specific environment.

Ecosystem	Adaptation
Open Ocean	
Coral Reef	
Kelp Forest	
Deep Sea	
Mangrove Forest	
Polar Seas	
Salt Marsh	
Rocky Shores	

2. Describe Darwin's Theory of Evolution. Use an example and expand on the following points: overproduction, competition, variation, adaptation, and survival of the fittest.

3. How can invasive species result in biodiversity loss?

4. In science, what is a theory? Describe three pieces of scientific evidence that support the Theory of Evolution by Natural Selection.

FIGURE 16.25. The Zebra Mussel, originally from Europe, has staked its claim throughout the Great Lakes and many rivers throughout much of the continental United States. These animals have no natural predators in North America and reproduce quickly.

FIGURE 16.24. Originally from South America, the fast-growing Water Hyacinth has clogged waterways throughout much of the United States.

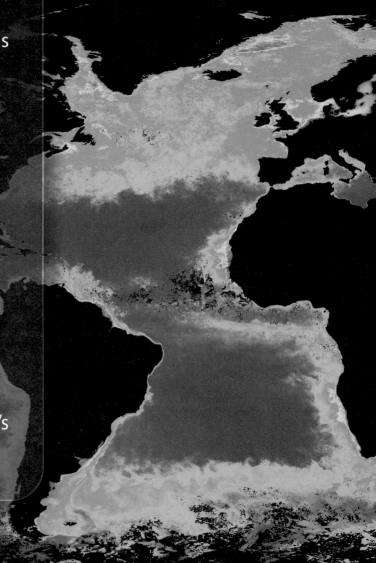

17

Food Webs in Action

INSIDE:

Objectives

You will be able to:

- ✔ Construct a sample marine food web.

- ✔ Describe the critical role of phytoplankton in marine food webs.

- ✔ Make predictions about changes in food webs that result from natural disruptions and human activities.

- ✔ Explain why nutrient cycling is critical within the Earth system.

Benchmarks

2a. Many Earth materials and geochemical cycles originate in the ocean. Many of the sedimentary rocks now exposed on land were formed in the ocean. Ocean life laid down the vast volume of siliceous and carbonate rocks.

2c. Erosion—the wearing away of rock, soil, and other biotic and abiotic earth materials—occurs in coastal areas as wind, waves, and currents in rivers and the ocean move sediments.

2d. Sand consists of tiny bits of animals, plants, rocks, and minerals. Most beach sand is eroded from land sources and carried to the coast by rivers, but sand is also eroded from coastal sources by surf. Sand is redistributed by waves and coastal currents seasonally.

5d. Ocean biology provides many unique examples of life cycles, adaptations, and important relationships among organisms (e.g., symbiosis, predator-prey dynamics, energy transfer) that do not occur on land.

7e. Use of mathematical models is now an essential part of ocean sciences. Models help us understand the complexity of the ocean and of its interaction with Earth's climate. They process observations and help describe the interactions among systems.

Phytoplankton and Marine Animals

In the previous Lesson, we discussed how marine animal populations change over time through natural selection. We investigated examples of structural and behavioral adaptations. In this Lesson, you will explore how each species plays an important role in the Earth system through complex interactions with other populations of organisms.

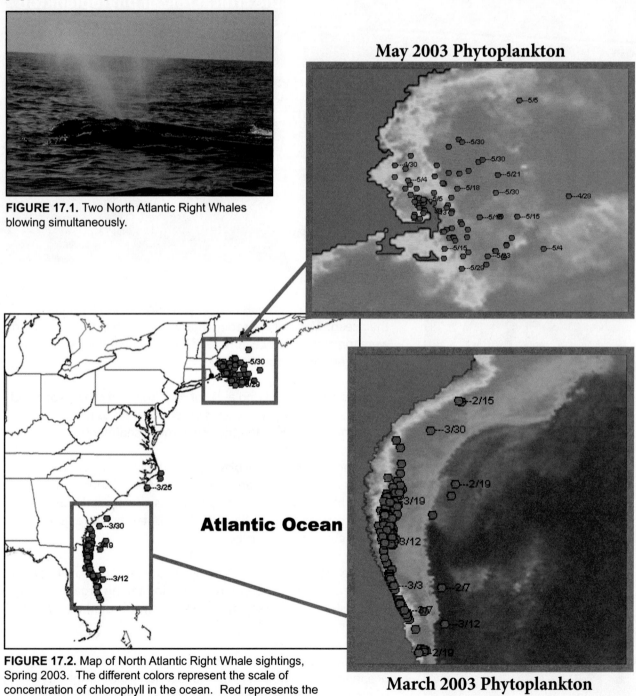

FIGURE 17.1. Two North Atlantic Right Whales blowing simultaneously.

May 2003 Phytoplankton

Atlantic Ocean

March 2003 Phytoplankton

FIGURE 17.2. Map of North Atlantic Right Whale sightings, Spring 2003. The different colors represent the scale of concentration of chlorophyll in the ocean. Red represents the highest concentrations. Orange then yellow are sequentially lower concentrations. Lowest concentrations are seen as blue.

The images in FIGURE 17.2 show sighting locations of North Atlantic Right Whales together with average chlorophyll concentrations for March and May 2003. Chlorophyll concentrations detected in satellite imagery indicate the presence of phytoplankton near or not far from the sea surface. As you observe the area off the coast of New England in May, notice that there are many whale sightings near the very high phytoplankton areas. North Atlantic Right Whales do not eat phytoplankton, however. These animals use broom-like plates in their mouth, called **baleen**, to filter and feed on zooplankton and small fish out of the water. The North Atlantic Right Whale is a type of baleen whale.

During the whaling era, particularly in the Northeastern United States, this species became known as the "right whale" because whalers thought they were the "right" ones to hunt. These animals often swam within sight of shore and also floated when killed, so they were both easy to catch and to transport. Intensive hunting has brought their numbers down to near extinction—it is believed that there are only about 300 individuals left in the North Atlantic. They are among the rarest of marine mammals on Earth. The short videos show footage of North Atlantic Right Whales.

FIGURE 17.3. Baleen whales—the one shown here is a Humpback Whale—use broom-like plates made of the protein keratin to sieve small organisms from large mouthfuls of seawater.

See Page 694 for how to access e-Tools.

View **North Atlantic Right Whale Video Clip 1** (0:10) and **North Atlantic Right Whale Video Clip 2** (0:21) from the e-Tools.

Video 1 (0:10)

e-Tools

Video 2 (0:21)

FIGURE 17.4. Screenshots of the **North Atlantic Right Whale Video Clips 1 and 2**.

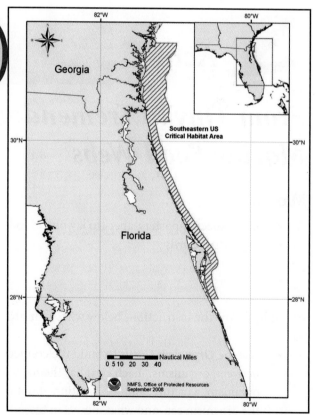

FIGURE 17.5. The red hatched area off the Central East Coast of Florida and northward to the Georgia Coast shows the critical habitat of the North Atlantic Right Whale. Federal law prohibits ships from coming closer than 500 yards to a Right Whale. They have been protected since 1970.

One of the three *critical habitats* for this imperiled species is Coastal Florida and Georgia. The other two areas are off the coast of New England, which is the summer habitat of these animals.

 # Extension Activity

International agreements and laws have been in place to protect North Atlantic Right Whales since the 1930s. This species, however, is still considered to be critically endangered. Some scientists predict that the species could face extinction within 200 years.

Conduct research online on the *Marine Science: The Dynamic Ocean* website and determine:

- The factors that contribute to the precarious existence of the North Atlantic Right Whale
- Current protections afforded to the species
- Additional scientific questions about the species that still must be answered

Present your findings through an essay, poster, or presentation.

Explore

 ## Activity

From Tiny to Tremendous: Marine Food Webs

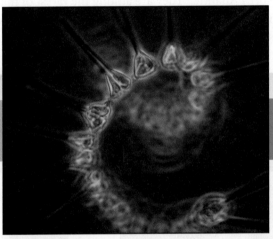

FIGURE 17.6. Phytoplankton are a primary producer in marine ecosystems. Some species are capable of moving up and down the water column as much as a few hundred meters in a day.

Materials:

- Large sheet of poster paper (to lay out a food web)
- *Organism Cards*
- Glue sticks
- Markers

Carefully follow the instructions below with your group.

- Use the *Organism Cards* to build the connections between organisms. Each card has the name of the organism, a picture, and information about what the organism eats and what it is eaten by.

  Begin with the different types of phytoplankton because they use the Sun's energy to make food. Place the phytoplankton Organism Card near the bottom of a blank piece of poster paper.

FIGURE 17.7. *Organism Cards*.

- Draw the Sun near the phytoplankton, and draw an arrow *from* the Sun *to* the phytoplankton to show how the *energy is transferred.*

- Read through the Organism Cards and determine which consumers eat the phytoplankton. This means that the organisms are deriving energy from the phytoplankton. Place these cards on the poster above the phytoplankton. Use arrows to indicate the flow of energy.

- Continue to add the different Organism Cards to the poster. Connect them using arrows. *Remember that the arrow shows the direction in which the energy flows.* There may be one or many arrows connected to a single organism.

- Once all of the organisms are connected, glue the Organism Cards to the poster.

The complete diagram your group created represents the transfer of food energy within a community of organisms. This diagram is a marine **food web**.

1. What is the initial source of energy for this food web?

2. Is this a complete food web? Why or why not?

3. What would happen if the Sun did not continue to shine?

4. Why are phytoplankton called the *base* of the marine food web?

5. If the amount of phytoplankton in an area decreased, what do you predict would happen?

6. How might some of the larger consumers cope with fewer phytoplankton in an area?

FIGURE 17.8. The Killer Whale, or Orca, is the top predator in many oceanic food webs. Depending on the region, this toothed whale species is known to feed on seals, seabirds, bony fish, and even sharks!

Explain

Producers, Consumers, and Decomposers

A marine ecosystem represents an intricate balance of life among all its organisms: plants, vertebrate, and invertebrate animals, fungi, protists, true bacteria, and Archaea, which rely on the ocean and each other for survival. As you have learned, phytoplankton play a major ecological role in the ocean. These organisms capture energy from sunlight and use that energy to make their own food through the process of photosynthesis. Phytoplankton are responsible for more than half of photosynthesis carried out on Earth. Organisms that produce sugars inside their cells are called **producers**. Also called **autotrophs**, these organisms also provide a direct source of nourishment for all living things.

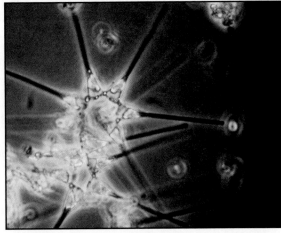
FIGURE 17.9. Phytoplankton capture energy from sunlight and use that energy to make their own food.

FIGURE 17.10. Kelp is a producer that belongs to Kingdom Protista. Though kelp grows from deep in the ocean, it grows toward the light and can get longer by as much as half a meter per day.

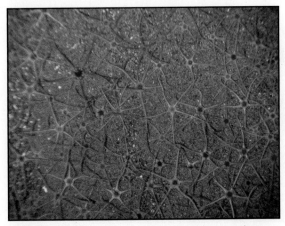
FIGURE 17.11. Brittle Stars are benthic organisms and detritus feeders.

Organisms that cannot make their own food and are dependent on the autotrophs for survival are called **heterotrophs**. Since these organisms rely on autotrophs for food, they are also called **consumers**. When consumers complete their life cycles, they die and are broken apart as they are eaten by scavengers such as crabs, lobsters, and sharks. Scavengers break down materials and release wastes with other organic particles, called **detritus** (pronounced: deh-TRI-tuss), which sinks and provides food for animals that live below the photic zone. Detritus is a major source of food for organisms living on the seafloor. These are called benthic organisms. Organisms that live attached to rocks or do not travel very far (e.g., snails, limpets, sand worms, Brittle Stars) feed on the detritus that drifts down from the surface. Bacteria and fungi that break down dead organisms and convert them back into nutrients available to the ecosystem are called **decomposers**. Decomposers are critical to the health of all ecosystems. Without them, nutrients would be used up and photosynthesis and other biological processes could not take place.

Energy Flow: Food Chains and Food Webs

A **food chain** is a simple way to picture how energy moves through a system—from producers to consumers to decomposers—in a pathway that has one direction. It is another example of how models are used in science to visualize complex processes. Energy flows through ecosystems. It starts with the Sun and moves through to producers (autotrophs) and then consumers (heterotrophs). In most ecosystems, many different food chains overlap to form an intricate food web of different types of organisms within the biological community. Of course, most organisms eat more than one type of food and can be eaten by more than one predator.

In the food chain shown below, the producers are microscopic phytoplankton. These are eaten by zooplankton, such as krill. The krill, in turn, are eaten by small fish. The krill and small fish are then eaten by a much larger baleen whale—the North Atlantic Right Whale.

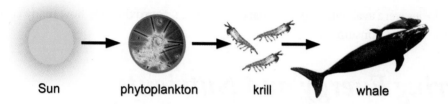

FIGURE 17.12. Simple food chain of a North Atlantic Right Whale.

A more complex portrayal of this community is illustrated as a food web shown below. Although this diagram appears complex, there are still more species, and even links between species, that are not shown. Note that the arrows indicate the direction of energy flow.

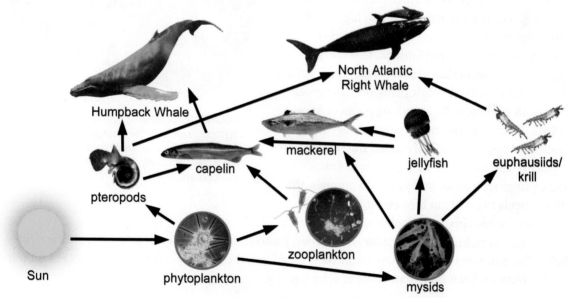

FIGURE 17.13. A food web.

Each step within a food chain is defined as a **trophic level**. The first level is made up of producers. Consumers that eat producers are called **primary consumers**. Those that eat the primary consumers are called **secondary consumers**; predators that eat secondary consumers are known as **tertiary consumers**. In summary, consumers comprise the second, third, and higher trophic levels. A consumer depends on the level below for its food, or energy.

Not all the energy within a trophic level is transferred to the next. Actually, depending on the ecosystem, only 5-20% of the available energy is passed on; the average is about 10%. This principle of ecology, which states that only 10% of energy is passed between trophic levels, is known as the **10% rule**. Food energy is normally measured in calories. Imagine that in the food chain above, the phytoplankton contained 10 million calories of energy. According to the 10% rule, only 1 million calories would be available to the krill.

1. From the North Atlantic Right Whale food web on the previous page, give examples of each of the following:

   a. Producers
   b. Primary Consumers
   c. Secondary Consumers
   d. Tertiary Consumers

2. If 500 million calories were available to the primary consumers, approximately how many calories would be available to the tertiary consumers?

Transferring Energy and Nutrients

Nearly all of the energy that fuels marine ecosystems comes from the Sun. A producer, such as a phytoplankton, captures the Sun's energy and converts it into organic compounds through photosynthesis. Recall from Lesson 13: Photosynthesis in the Ocean that photosynthesis is a complex biological process in which carbon dioxide (CO_2) and water (H_2O) are transformed into high-energy sugars called glucose ($C_6H_{12}O_6$). Oxygen (O_2) is also released as a byproduct. In phytoplankton, this energy-capturing process occurs in their chloroplasts. Chloroplasts are the green organelles inside phytoplankton. The green color comes from colored, light-absorbing pigment known as chlorophyll. Producers also need chemicals necessary for metabolism. These chemicals are called **nutrients**. From the glucose and nutrients, they are able to create more complex sugars, proteins, and so on. In animals, the prominent nutrients to carry out life's essential functions and build tissues are proteins, carbohydrates, lipids, nucleic acids, water, vitamins, and minerals. Producers use energy and abiotic compounds to conduct life activities within their cells. Since consumers cannot make their own food, they are dependent on producers for their survival—they must get both energy and nutrients by feeding.

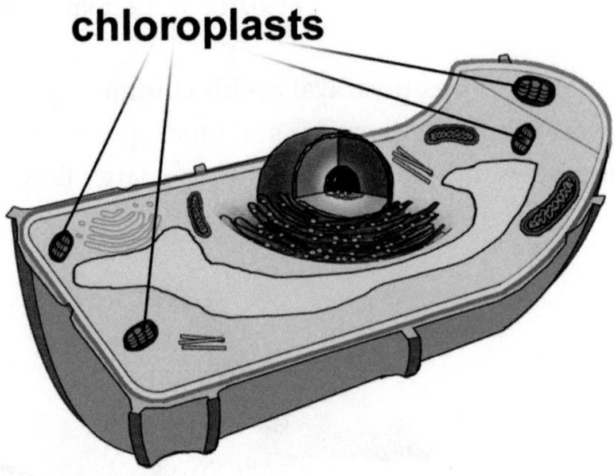

chloroplasts

FIGURE 17.14. During photosynthesis, phytoplankton use the energy in sunlight to make food (glucose) from carbon dioxide and water. Photosynthesis takes place in the chloroplasts.

Although consumers get the energy they need from food, their cells cannot process a squid or mackerel directly. The food must be broken down so that the energy it contains can be converted into a form usable by an organism's cells. In fact, *all* organisms must break down food molecules in order to release the energy stored within them, a process known as **cellular respiration**. When chlorophyll absorbs light, much of the energy is transferred directly to its electrons, raising the energy level of the organism. This energy is eventually stored within the chemical bonds of the glucose molecule.

This energy also helps to build nutrients that an organism's body needs for growth, maintenance, and activity. Nutrients include compounds that usually contain carbon and hydrogen and are held together by covalent bonds. These compounds are **organic compounds**. Proteins, carbohydrates, lipids, nucleic acids, and vitamins are all types of organic compounds. Minerals and water do not have the characteristics above, and are inorganic. The functions of each of the major types of nutrients are briefly described below:

- **Proteins** contain the element nitrogen and are responsible for building an organism's body structures (e.g., leaf tissues, organs, muscles) and controlling the rates of chemical reactions in cells.

- **Carbohydrates** are the main source of energy for organisms. They can be simple, such as the glucose created through photosynthesis, or complex, such as the starch that creates a plant's cell wall.

- **Lipids** (e.g., fats, oils) are incorporated into body structures, providing energy and controlling the use of vitamins and chemical signals within the body.

- **Nucleic acids**, DNA and RNA, store and transmit genetic information. The information contains the formula for the manufacturing of new proteins needed for cells to survive.

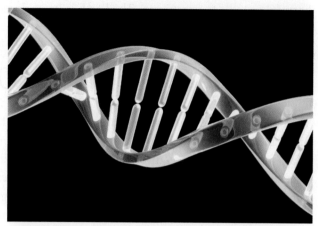

FIGURE 17.15. DNA is one of the organic molecules built by all living things. It stores genetic information, carrying it from generation to generation.

- **Vitamins** are organic compounds that are necessary in very small quantities for carrying out metabolic processes. Examples include Vitamin A, Vitamin C, and Vitamin D.

- **Minerals** such as iron, zinc, and sodium are inorganic substances required in small quantities for carrying out processes such as the transmission of nerve signals in animals.

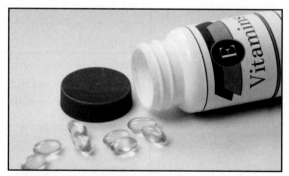

FIGURE 17.16. Animals usually derive vitamins and minerals in their food, but humans take vitamin supplements because they may not eat a quality balanced diet or the foods available do not have enough of specific vitamins and minerals needed.

Water is required by all living things. As the universal solvent, water is critical for transporting materials within organisms, including food molecules to be broken down and waste products to be removed.

Many of the nutrients above contain the elements carbon, hydrogen, oxygen, nitrogen, sulfur, and phosphorus. In ecosystems, decomposers are essential in breaking down waste and returning these elements back to the water and soil. The passing of these elements and the compounds they form within the Earth system is called **nutrient cycling**.

Decomposers break animal waste and dead organic matter into basic elements. For example, in the ocean, where carbon, calcium, and oxygen are found in abundance, many organisms have shells made of calcium carbonate ($CaCO_3$). When the animals die, decomposers break the compound into calcium ions and carbon dioxide molecules. The carbon dioxide is released into the water or atmosphere, and the calcium ions (Ca^{+2}) are then available within the ocean water for other organisms to use. Reusing nutrients through nutrient cycles is essential to sustain marine ecosystems as well as those on land. The Earth system is a closed system for matter—very little matter enters or leaves the ecosystem. Matter, therefore, must be cycled. Nutrient cycling also prevents the concentration of certain chemicals from becoming high enough that they could be harmful or toxic to organisms. The Earth is *not* a closed system for energy. There is a constant influx of energy from the Sun.

Nutrient Cycling in the Ocean

The ocean contains all of Earth's natural elements, but the concentration of these elements varies across the miles and with depth. Many elements, such as oxygen (O), nitrogen (N), carbon (C), phosphorus (P), sodium (Na), and iron (Fe) are required by almost all living things. Other elements are required by some living things. One common example is silicon (Si). The ocean is essentially a closed system made up of atoms of elements. These elements, which make up nutrients that all living things require, must be cycled. You are already familiar with the water and carbon cycles. Other important material cycles in the ocean are the nitrogen, phosphorus, and silica cycles. These elements cycle through all parts of the Earth—including living things. Therefore, these cycles are known as **biogeochemical cycles**.

3. The paragraphs to follow will discuss the major concepts of the nitrogen, phosophorus, and silica cycles. Copy the data table below into your notebook. As you read, complete your table to organize your understanding of each biogeochemical cycle.

	Nitrogen	**Phosphorus**	**Silica**
Biosphere (life) component			*Marine organisms use silica to build hard parts of their bodies (e.g., diatom tests). Dissolved silica is taken up by producers and passed through the food web.*
Lithosphere (land) component			*Abundant in the mineral quartz (SiO_2), found in beach sands, rock, and seafloor sediments.*
Hydrosphere (ocean) component			

Nitrogen Cycle

An element that needs to be cycled is nitrogen. It is incorporated into many nutrients, including proteins and nucleic acids. Nitrogen is important for living things, as it is essential for protein-building within cells. In humans, for example, proteins are particularly important for building muscle. Phytoplankton take up nitrogen compounds dissolved in seawater to create proteins and other compounds which are then consumed by zooplankton and other organisms within the food chain. The process of living things taking materials from their environment is known as **assimilation**. Living things will also release nitrogen compounds, such as urea, as waste products.

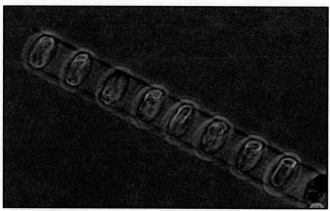

FIGURE 17.17. Phytoplankton, like the chain of organisms shown here, assimilate important compounds through their cell membranes. Nitrogen cannot be used in the form of N_2, but instead must be transformed by bacteria, fungi, or lightning.

Nitrogen that is in a form readily usable by organisms, however, is not always available. Although Earth's atmosphere is 78% nitrogen gas (N_2), producers will only take in nitrogen when it is in its ionic form, such as from a nitrate (NO_3). Some types of bacteria are able to convert atmospheric nitrogen to usable forms, a process known as **nitrogen fixation**. Within living organisms, nitrogen is combined during life functions into several different compounds, including amino acids and ammonia. Nitrogen fixation can also occur as a result of lightning, burning, and other non-biological processes.

When living things are decomposed in the ocean, their nitrogen compounds may settle to the ocean floor and become a part of the ocean's sediments. Over geologic time, these sediments may become rock. Through processes like uplift and accretion, they may become part of a continent. Eventually, weathering and erosion processes will return them to the ocean. Alternatively, nitrogen compounds within the ocean's water may be brought to the surface via upward movements of water, called **upwelling**. Near the surface, nitrogen compounds are once again available to phytoplankton for growth and reproduction.

See Page 694 for how to access e-Tools.

View the *Nitrogen Cycle Animation* from the e-Tools to learn about the different forms in which nitrogen is found within the Earth system.

e-Tools

FIGURE 17.18. Screenshot of the *Nitrogen Cycle Animation*.

Phosphorus Cycle

A distinction between the phosphorus cycle and the nitrogen and carbon cycles is that there is no atmospheric component of the phosphorus cycle. That is, there are no naturally occurring phosphorus compounds in Earth's atmosphere. The source of most oceanic phosphorus is the weathering and erosion of rocks from the land. Organic and inorganic phosphorus compounds are found in seawater to be assimilated by phytoplankton or other algae. If these compounds are not taken up by producers, they may sink and become incorporated into ocean sediments, becoming rock over long periods of time. Eventually, these rocks become parts of continents through uplift and accretion.

All organisms require phosphorus to build structures such as their cell membranes, DNA, and energy-rich compounds like ATP. Marine producers incorporate phosphorus into their structures, and the element is passed on to heterotrophs through the food web when consumed. When living things die, decomposers break them into much smaller components, including phosphorus compounds such as phosphates. Phosphorus compounds throughout the water column are either incorporated into seafloor sediments or upwelled toward the surface.

FIGURE 17.19. Phosphorus is very important to living things as it is used to construct nucleic acids, which store our instructions for life. Upwelling brings compounds, including those containing phosphorus, from the depths to the surface, making them available to phytoplankton, seaweed, and other producers.

FIGURE 17.20. Most phosphorus in the ocean comes from the land. Over geologic time, phosphorus in seafloor sediments is incorporated into continental rocks. The cycle continues as these rocks are then weathered and eroded, bringing phosphorus back to the ocean.

Silica Cycle

Compounds made of silicon and oxygen are known as **silica**. Quartz, one of the most abundant minerals in Earth's crust, is a silica, with a chemical formula SiO_2. Not surprisingly, many beach sands have high silica content. Recall that sand is made up of tiny particles weathered and eroded from living things (e.g., the shells of organisms) and rock. The majority of beach sand comes from land, but the ocean's processes, such as waves and currents, will also weather and erode sand along the coast.

Some marine organisms rely on silica to build hard parts of their bodies. Examples of parts are the spines of certain sponges and the shells of some plankton. The tiny clear shells, or tests, of diatoms are composed of silica, which allows sunlight to pass through them for photosynthesis. Just like the processes that involve nitrogen and phosphorus, phytoplankton and other producers take up silica that is dissolved in the water. The element is passed on through the food web to other organisms. When silica-containing organisms die, their compounds are also incorporated into seafloor sediments or upwelled back to the sea surface. Many rocks on Earth were created from the silica or carbonate-rich shells of living organisms.

FIGURE 17.21. Many beach sands are made primarily of silica. Volcanic eruptions and weathering and erosion of rock on land are the primary source of silicon in the ocean.

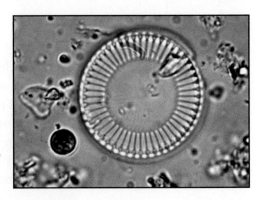

FIGURE 17.22. Silica makes up the tests, spines, and other hard parts of many marine and aquatic organisms. Diatoms, like the ones seen here under a microscope, have clear silica tests comprised by two halves.

Elaborate

Cyberlab

As nutrients cycle throughout various components of the Earth system, man-made compounds move throughout biotic and abiotic systems. Chemicals and heavy metals often deadly to organisms are known as **toxins**. Many toxins are created, purposefully, to serve human desires. For example, a group of chemicals called **pesticides** will kill unwanted insects and plants that harm farmer's crops. Some pesticides are used to kill mosquitoes that can transmit diseases like malaria and dengue fever (pronounced: DEN-gay). Some chemicals are created as a part of useful products like electronics, plastics, and paints, but they are unfortunately harmful, or **toxic**, to humans and other organisms.

PCBs, polychlorinated biphenyls (pronounced: bī-FĔN-ĭlls), are toxins created for use in manufacturing plants. Until the 1970s, they were used extensively in the United States in transformers, capacitors, and fluids used as coolants and insulators. After being proven toxic to organisms, they were banned from most uses. PCBs are very stable compounds; they do not easily break down chemically in the environment. Once they enter the water, air, or soil, PCBs persist. They are found in the environment and, when encountered, taken into the body tissues of living organisms.

One of the reasons that toxins like PCBs are not soluble in water is because their chemical structure repels water; they are hydrophobic. Instead of water these compounds are attracted to lipids, fats and oils, which are often stored in an organism's body to provide energy. PCBs are therefore referred to as "fat-loving" compounds.

Earlier in the Lesson, you constructed a marine food web using *Organism Cards* and demonstrated how food and energy both transfer throughout a community of organisms. When PCBs and other toxins exist in water, air, or soil in an organism's environment, they, too, can be taken into an organism's body. Plankton and other producers low on the food web accumulate toxins within their bodies in small amounts. As primary consumers feed on producers, they take in the toxins with their food. Secondary consumers eat primary consumers, taking in the toxins stored in the tissues of their prey, and the passage of toxin up the food web continues.

In the following Cyberlab, you will investigate a specific food chain in the Arctic Ocean ecosystem. The data presented come from scientific studies of the concentration of PCBs observed in Arctic organisms.

See Page 694 for how to access e-Tools.

View the **Arctic Food Web** from the e-Tools.

FIGURE 17.23. Screenshot of the *Arctic Food Web*.

e-Tools

Procedure:

1) Click on an organism to learn about what it eats and the toxins found through scientific investigation.
2) Beginning with a primary consumer, choose a line of organisms to follow from one trophic level to the next until you reach the tertiary consumer.
3) Click on each organism in your food chain and learn about the organism's diet and level of PCBs found in its body. Record the data.

(continued on next page)

4) Complete the Questions below utilizing your data.
5) Review your answers with classmates who followed other food chains within the *Arctic Food Web*.

1. Copy the chart into your notebook. Identify the trophic level of each organism in the chart.

Category of Organism/Description	Trophic Level	Organisms Represented
Tertiary Consumers	4	
Secondary Consumers	3	
Primary Consumers	2	
Producers	1	

2. Create a bar graph to help you analyze your data. (Hint: Place the PCB level on the *y*-axis.)

3. What happens to the levels of PCB as trophic level increases?

4. Interpret your graph from Question 2.

5. Large organisms tend to eat the most food and often have the greatest amount of fatty tissues, perfect for accumulating toxins. The building up of toxins in fatty tissues is known as **bioaccumulation**. The higher an organism is on a food chain, the greater the amount of toxin that is potentially accumulated and stored in organisms' bodies from the food they eat. This phenomenon of increasing concentration of toxins with increasing trophic level, from one (1) to four (4), is known as **biomagnification**.

Explain any evidence for bioaccumulation and biomagnification that you observe in your food chain.

Putting It Together

4. Why is it important to look at chlorophyll imagery when tracking marine animals?

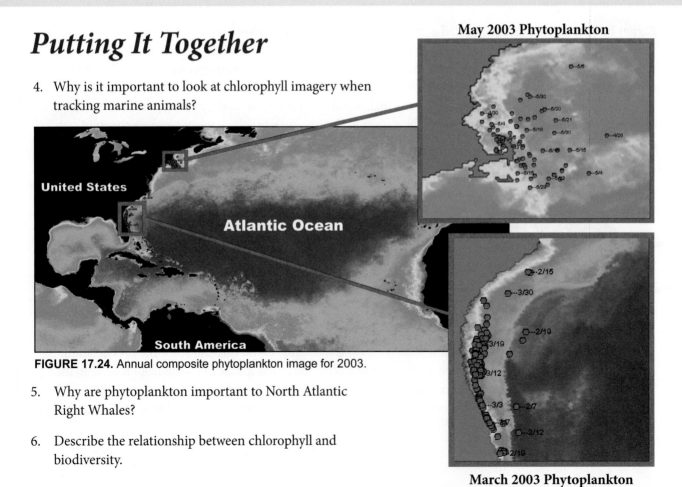

May 2003 Phytoplankton

FIGURE 17.24. Annual composite phytoplankton image for 2003.

5. Why are phytoplankton important to North Atlantic Right Whales?

6. Describe the relationship between chlorophyll and biodiversity.

March 2003 Phytoplankton

Who Is the Ocean's Greatest Predator?

by Carol A. Keiper, Marine Scientist

I've been leading natural history trips to the Farallon Islands located in the Gulf of the Farallones National Marine Sanctuary off the California Coast for more than 20 years. The big lesson I've learned over the years is to always expect the unexpected when you are on the Pacific Ocean.

On October 4, 1997, I was leading a natural history trip to look for whales and other marine life and experienced one of the most amazing predator-prey events I would ever see in my lifetime. I was standing by (and holding onto) the railing on the right side and near the back of the vessel, when all of a sudden I saw something swim out from under the boat right in front of where I was standing. I shouted out, "What was that?" The captain replied, "That's a Great White Shark!" This sighting occurred soon after we had also sighted two Killer Whales in the area just north of the Southeast Farallon Islands. In the next instant we saw the Killer Whale holding the Great White Shark in its mouth about 30 feet from our boat.

We couldn't believe what happened next: the Killer Whale brought the shark over to the side of the boat where we were standing and lifted the shark partially out of the water so we could see the entire shark's head, lower jaw, and teeth. Because of the strong grip the Killer Whale had on the shark in the area of its gill slits, it most likely suffocated and was killed quickly because there was no blood or evidence of any kind of struggle.

FIGURE 17.25. Scientist, Carol Keiper, conducting research off the California Coast.

We called the biologists on the island and told them of this incredible event. They launched their small, 18-foot-long Boston Whaler boat and zoomed over to where the Killer Whale was feeding on the shark. They put an underwater camera in the water near this feeding event and filmed the Killer Whale about to take a big bite from a table-sized chunk of shark's liver. Seeing the natural ocean world in action was truly awesome!

The shark was about 10–13 feet long, and the Killer Whale was at least 15 feet long. Based on the shape and size of the saddle patch behind the dorsal fin, the Killer Whale was identified as a known female, CA2, from the Los Angeles (LA) Killer Whale Pod.

Alisa Schulman-Janiger, a marine biologist who tracks the LA Pod for the American Cetacean Society, recognized CA2 from the footage. She described the LA Pod as an opportunistic group that preys on whatever they can find. Although they are usually seen near Los Angeles, she said they have been sighted from Northern Baja California to Monterey Bay. Killer Whales will prey on some species of sharks, but this was the first evidence of attacking a Great White Shark. Killer Whales are not commonly sighted around the Farallones, but Great White Sharks are, during the months of September to November. An important footnote to this story is that the Great White Sharks almost completely disappeared from the area immediately following the predatory event for several months.

FIGURE 17.26. The Gulf of the Farallones National Marine Sanctuary is located off the California Coast near San Francisco.

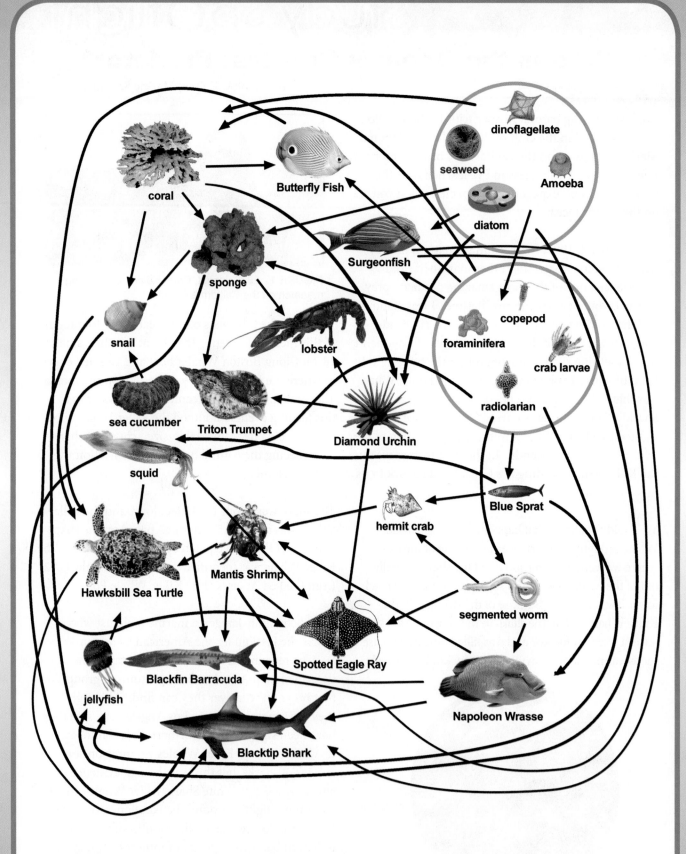

FIGURE 17.27. Complex food web of a coral reef ecosystem.

Evaluate

Base your answers to the Questions below on the complex food web of a coral reef ecosystem to the left.

1. Give at least 2 examples for each of the following:

   a. Producer
   b. Primary consumer
   c. Secondary consumer
   d. Tertiary or quaternary (4th level) consumer
   e. Scavenger

2. Explain why an arrow points from the Yellowtail Wrasse to the Blacktip Shark, and not the other way around.

3. If 1 billion calories of food are available to primary consumers in this ecosystem, approximately how many calories are available to the tertiary consumers?

4. Why must nutrients be cycled in this ecosystem? Is energy cycled in this ecosystem?

5. Name two organisms in this illustration that would be susceptible to biomagnification of toxins. Explain why.

FIGURE 17.28. Coral reef.

18

Introduction to Marine Invertebrates

INSIDE:

Biodiversity in Animals

Investigating the Animal Kingdom

The Animal Kingdom

Structure and Function of Feeding in Invertebrates

Investigating the Structure and Function of the Squid

Objectives

You will be able to:

✔ **Identify common organisms classified into the major invertebrate phyla.**

✔ **Give examples of how the structures of marine invertebrates support their functions.**

✔ **Describe diverse strategies for obtaining food in the ocean.**

✔ **Analyze the internal and external anatomy of a common marine invertebrate, the squid.**

Benchmarks

5c. Some major groups are found exclusively in the ocean. The diversity of major groups of organisms is much greater in the ocean than on land.

5d. Ocean biology provides many unique examples of life cycles, adaptations, and important relationships among organisms (e.g., symbiosis, predator-prey dynamics, energy transfer) that do not occur on land.

5e. The ocean is three-dimensional, offering vast living space and diverse habitats from the surface through the water column to the seafloor. Most of the living space on Earth is in the ocean.

Engage

While all living things must accomplish the same life functions— as you learned when you studied Lesson 14: Biodiversity in the Ocean—there is great diversity of life on Earth, especially in the ocean. Recall the life functions, which must be accomplished by all organisms: growth, nutrition, transport, respiration, synthesis, excretion, regulation, and reproduction. This Lesson is the first in a series focusing on the biodiversity of the animal kingdom. In this Lesson, you will study the invertebrates. In the next few Lessons, you will learn about the vertebrates, including fishes, reptiles, birds, and mammals.

When making observations in the ocean, it can sometimes be difficult to tell what is living and non-living, and whether something would be classified as an animal, plant, protist, Archaean, bacterium, or fungus. In this first exercise, you will try to pick out the animals from an array of photographs.

1. Observe the series of pictures on the next four pages.

    a. Which of the organisms pictured could you classify as an animal?

    b. How might you classify the other organisms? Why?

FIGURE 18.1.

FIGURE 18.2.

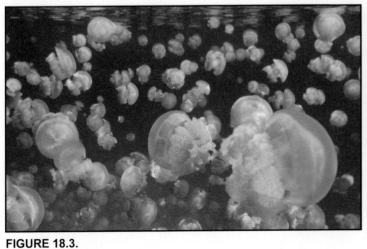

FIGURE 18.3.

FIGURE 18.4.

FIGURE 18.5.

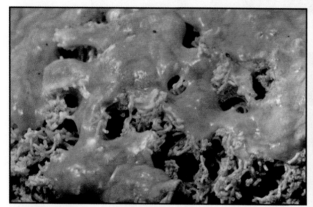

FIGURE 18.6.

FIGURE 18.7.

FIGURE 18.8.

FIGURE 18.9.

FIGURE 18.10.

FIGURE 18.11.

FIGURE 18.12.

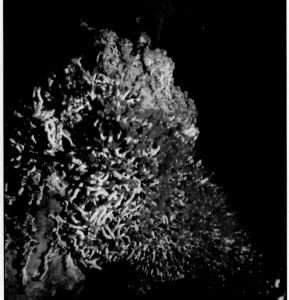

FIGURE 18.13.

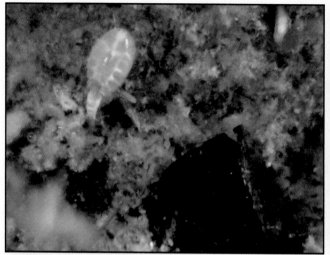

FIGURE 18.14.

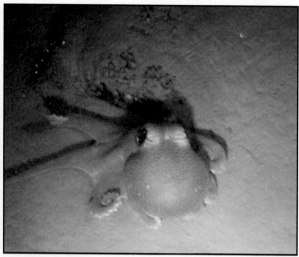

FIGURE 18.15.

FIGURE 18.16.

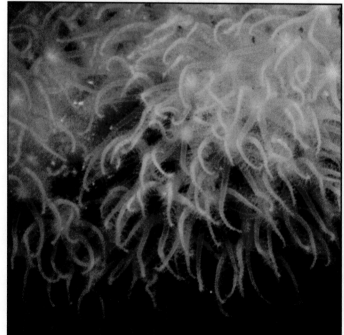

FIGURE 18.17.

FIGURE 18.18.

Explore
Biodiversity in Animals

In Lesson 14: Biodiversity in the Ocean, you were introduced to the Tree of Life. You discussed that each main branch of the Tree of Life continues to branch, or break, into more branches of groups of organisms with defining, similar characteristics. Since the huge ocean has so many different habitats, it can support a wide variety of organisms from different branches. The ocean contains tremendous biodiversity. We will be tracking and studying marine animals, so we will focus on Kingdom Animalia. Within this Kingdom, there are many different phyla.

Although there are even more, the major animal phyla are shown on the diagram below. Almost all of the animals in these phyla are **invertebrates**, animals without backbones. The exception is Phylum Chordata, which contains both invertebrates and vertebrates. All of the vertebrates are classified into Phylum Chordata, and subphylum Vertebrata. Ninety-seven percent (97%) of animals on Earth are invertebrates. The diagram below shows the evolutionary relationships between groups of organisms as they branch out on the Tree of Life.

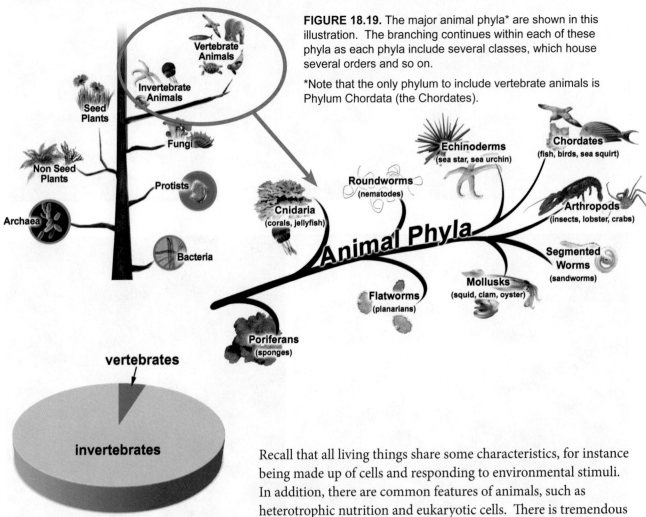

FIGURE 18.19. The major animal phyla* are shown in this illustration. The branching continues within each of these phyla as each phyla include several classes, which house several orders and so on.

*Note that the only phylum to include vertebrate animals is Phylum Chordata (the Chordates).

FIGURE 18.20. 97% of animal species on Earth are invertebrates. On Earth today, insects are the most numerous invertebrates. Many vertebrates are described as "fish", encompassing a large group of disparate classes or subphyla.

Recall that all living things share some characteristics, for instance being made up of cells and responding to environmental stimuli. In addition, there are common features of animals, such as heterotrophic nutrition and eukaryotic cells. There is tremendous biodiversity within the animal kingdom.

Activity

Investigating the Animal Kingdom

Materials:

- Poster paper or chart paper
- Markers
- ***Invertebrates Graphic Organizer***

See Page 694 for how to access e-Tools.

View the **Interactive Tree of Life** from the e-Tools.

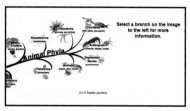

FIGURE 18.21. Screenshot of **The Tree of Life**.

e-Tools

www

Each student group will prepare a poster to introduce other students to one major invertebrate animal group, or phylum. Be sure to make your poster very easy to understand. Provide many pictures, including ones that you draw or print out. Be sure to cite your pictures. Your poster must be clearly labeled with the name of your branch, and include the information on the topics below:

- **Characteristics.** What do all of the organisms on this branch have in common (e.g., body structures, symmetry, organ systems)?
- **Subgroups.** What are the major subgroups (i.e., Classes, Orders) of this branch? What are some examples of organisms classified in these subgroups? Provide at least five photographs or sketches of organisms.
- **History.** How long have the species on this branch been known to exist on Earth?
- **Interesting facts.** What are some interesting facts about this branch?
- **Feeding Strategies.** What are some ways that organisms in this branch eat?

Explain

Use your classmates' posters to complete your ***Invertebrates Graphic Organizer***. Then, answer the following Questions.

1. Which groups share the characteristic of radial symmetry?

2. Compare and contrast the annelids (pronounced: AN-eh-lĭds) and platyhelminthes (pronounced: plăt-ĭ-HELL-mĭnths).

3. List three groups of mollusks, and at least two examples of each.

4. Which phylum is most interesting to you? Why?

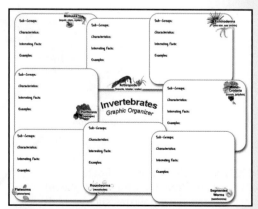

FIGURE 18.22. Screenshot of the ***Invertebrates Graphic Organizer***.

The Animal Kingdom

The diverse physical and chemical features of the ocean support a wide diversity of life. However, this life is not evenly distributed in the sea. As you discovered in Lesson 1: Diving Into Ocean Ecosystems, some ecosystems are much more productive than others, and support a more diverse and plentiful biological community. There are, however, living things in every part of the ocean, across distance and with depth; the diversity of phyla is greater in the ocean than on land or in fresh water. Within the six kingdoms, all of the major phyla have marine representation. In fact, the majority of phyla existing on Earth today are found exclusively in the ocean, with few existing solely on land.

FIGURE 18.23. Phylum Echinodermata, which includes sea stars such as the one shown here, is a phylum in Kingdom Animalia that exists exclusively in the ocean. The three seaweed phyla, which represent the green, brown, and red seaweeds, are also exclusively marine.

FIGURE 18.24. Note that the chordates are just one phylum of animals. There are many invertebrate phyla, several of which are shown in this diagram from earlier in this Lesson.

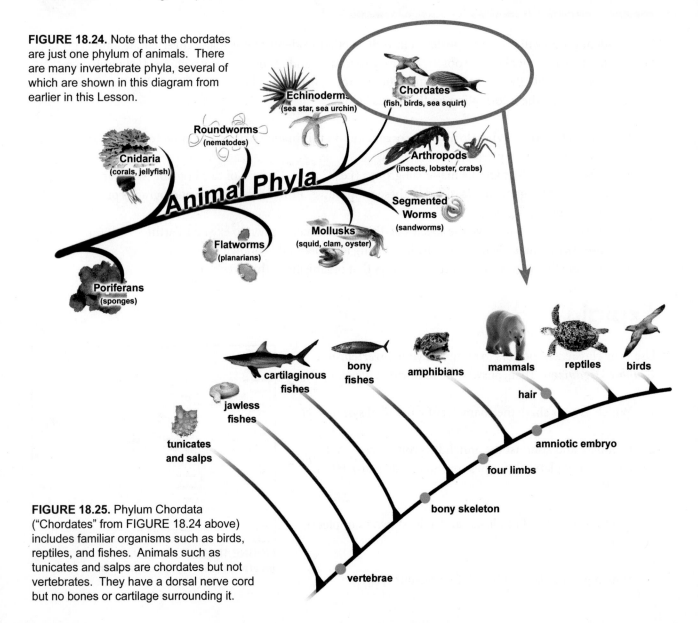

FIGURE 18.25. Phylum Chordata ("Chordates" from FIGURE 18.24 above) includes familiar organisms such as birds, reptiles, and fishes. Animals such as tunicates and salps are chordates but not vertebrates. They have a dorsal nerve cord but no bones or cartilage surrounding it.

Recall that in the animal kingdom, 97 percent of all animal species are invertebrates. Except for insects, most invertebrates are marine animals as compared to land or freshwater animals. Vertebrates, the 3 percent of animal species with a backbone, are one of the classes within Phylum Chordata. Vertebrates are animals with a nerve cord along their backs, or **dorsal** sides. These are classified in subphylum Vertebrata. Other members of Phylum Chordata include the tunicates, or sea squirts, and salps, both of which are described below. The defining characteristics of Phylum Chordata are described below:

- **Dorsal nerve cord**—a hollow nerve cord that runs along the dorsal side of an organism. In vertebrates, this becomes the brain and spinal cord.
- **Notochord**—a flexible rod that supports the dorsal nerve cord. In vertebrates, this becomes the bones that support and protect the spinal cord, or **vertebrae**.
- **Post-anal tail**—an extension of the notochord past the anal opening. This disappears in many adult vertebrate forms. In humans, it disappears during gestation.
- **Pharyngeal slits**—openings between the throat and the outside environment. In fishes, these become the gills. In mammals, these are present in embryos, but are not found in adults.

Tunicates and salps are chordates that are not vertebrates, and are examples of groups that exist exclusively in the ocean. Tunicates are known as "sea squirts", and as adults are slimy animals found attached to a substrate. Adult salps are jelly-like organisms that often form long chains, as shown in FIGURE 18.26. These organisms are classified as chordates because, in the larval form, they exhibit all of the characteristics described above. Tunicate and salp larvae resemble tadpoles and are free-swimming. As they become adults, most of their nervous system actually disintegrates. They become filter feeders, drawing in water through a siphon, and releasing it through another siphon. It is this behavior that gives the tunicates their nickname, "sea squirts". These simple-seeming animals are more closely related to humans than any of the other organisms you studied in the **Explore** section! In the next few Lessons, you will learn more about chordates that are members of Subphylum Vertebrata—fish, amphibians, mammals, reptiles, and birds.

FIGURE 18.26. This photograph shows a gelatinous salp, an example of chordate that is not a vertebrate. Like the echinoderms and tunicates, salps are only found in the ocean.

FIGURE 18.27. Several species of tunicate inhabit the Great Barrier Reef in Australia. Humans are more closely related to these organisms than to lobsters, squid, or other invertebrates.

FIGURE 18.28. Whales and other marine mammals are more familiar members of Phylum Chordata. These animals, like all chordates, will at some point all have pharyngeal slits, a dorsal nerve cord, as well as a notochord, and a post-anal tail.

Structure and Function of Feeding in Invertebrates

As you learned through your poster activity in the **Explore** section, invertebrates are found nearly everywhere in the ocean. The majority of marine invertebrates spend some portion of their lives, typically as juveniles, in the plankton community, typically as primary consumers, eating phytoplankton. As *adults*, invertebrates are found attached to substrates on the seafloor, inside their self-created shells or skeletons, floating among plankton, crawling on the sea bottom, or swimming within the water column. The variety of body forms allows invertebrates to take on different roles, or **niches**, within marine ecosystems. A niche is sometimes described as a species' "job" within its ecosystem. Each species occupies a different niche in an ecosystem; two species do not occupy exactly the same niche. For example, two species of fish might eat the same smaller fish species, but one may hunt at night, and another during the day. The niches of the two species are slightly different.

In the ocean, food is not equally distributed. It is abundant in many coastal areas and ecosystems such as kelp forests, salt marshes, and coral reefs. In ecosystems such as the deep sea and open ocean, food is scarcer. All animals must obtain energy and nutrients, accomplishing the life function of nutrition, by eating other organisms. There are many different ways in which invertebrates obtain food, and different niches for invertebrates to fill. An important part of an animal's niche is what and how the species eats, its mode of feeding, or feeding strategy. The structures and processes of all living things help to perform life functions, including nutrition. The study of the structures of organisms is known as **morphology**. In animals, this is termed **anatomy**. You have known the term *human anatomy*, which is the study of the structure of the human body. The study of the processes within organisms in known as **physiology**. Of course, there is a strong connection between anatomy and physiology—the structures of organisms support their processes, or functions. Invertebrates have some diverse strategies, some unique ways of accomplishing their life functions. Let's look at examples of feeding behaviors within the invertebrate phyla to better understand this concept.

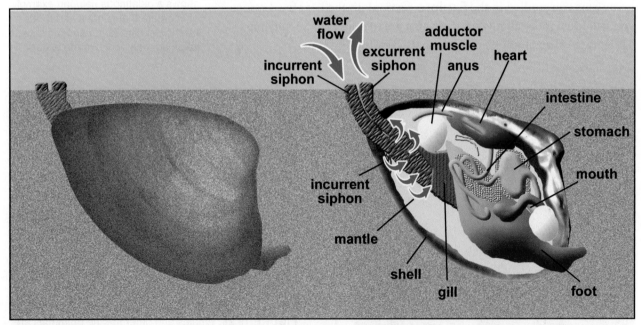

FIGURE 18.29. Clams, common bivalve mollusks, look like simple organisms, but have complex organ systems. The structures you see in the diagram have different functions. For example, gills extract oxygen from the water, while the heart pumps blood carrying oxygen and other materials to the animal's other organs.

Filter Feeding. A great deal of food is suspended in the water column; food can be planktonic organisms or the remains of larger organisms. Many bivalve species from the ocean floor or at the coast pump water through their bodies and are known as **active filter feeders**. FIGURE 18.29 shows a clam burrowed in the sand. The characteristic muscular foot of the bivalves appears at the bottom; the siphon is at the top. This clam will pump water in through an **incurrent siphon**, and across its gills. Feather-like gills of the clam are enlarged in order to gather both oxygen and food particles. The gills and siphon are covered in tiny hairs called cilia, which beat to maintain a constant water flow throughout the animal. Food particles are trapped by the cilia on the gills, which then push food to the digestive system, which includes a mouth, stomach, intestine, and anus. Wastes, including carbon dioxide and digested food, are released through the **excurrent siphon**, which also delivers water out of the animal, back into the ocean. The active pumping of water by a filter feeder allows the animal to counteract buoyancy of the plankton. Filter feeders such as clams filter large quantities of water to gather the food that they need to survive.

FIGURE 18.30. This large Geoduck Clam dug by divers near Discovery Bay of Washington State is often called a "gooyduck". It shows the large siphons that some bivalves have. Water is sucked in through the incurrent siphon, and then filtered by the gills before the water is expelled through the excurrent siphon.

Suspension Feeding. Suspension feeding is a type of filter feeding in which organisms do not create their own currents of water flows like filter feeders do. Instead, they rely on the movement of water to bring food to them. Crinoids, members of Phylum Echinodermata, are suspension feeders. The feathery arms of crinoids are lined with tube feet that are connected to the animals' **water vascular system**, a network of water-filled tubes characteristic of the echinoderms. The sticky tube feet capture food particles, and transfer them to the mouth and digestive system. Scientists have observed crinoids changing the positions of their arms and tube feets by manipulating their muscles and water vascular system in response to changes in the external environment, such as in local currents.

FIGURE 18.31. Crinoids are also known as sea lilies. They look like flowers but are actually echinoderms. They use their feathery arms to suspension feed.

Deposit Feeding. Some animals feed by eating detritus, the remains of decomposing plants and animals found along the seafloor. Like filter feeders sifting through water, deposit feeders sift through sediment, taking out food particles from among the grains of sand, mud, and soil. One common deposit feeder is the sea cucumber. Sea cucumber species range from nearshore to deep sea habitats, and can appear from fairly plain looking to brightly colored and diverse in texture. While they may look like worms to the eye, recall that sea cucumbers are echinoderms and therefore have five-part radial symmetry and also a water vascular system. Typical sea cucumbers feed

FIGURE 18.32. Some sea cucumbers, such as the California Sea Cucumber shown here, are brightly colored. Most species feed on detritus upon the bottom.

by using the modified tube feet around their mouth to scoop in sand and other sediments. They eat sand almost constantly, removing detritus and bacteria from this sediment. Food passes through their long, coiled digestive system and wastes are released through the anus.

Deposit feeders are important to the marine ecosystem because they help to recycle nutrients and make them available to the ecosystem. Nutrients within the detritus eaten by the sea cucumbers become available to the animals' predators. Predators include fish, sea turtles, crabs, snails, lobsters, and also humans. Sea cucumbers are a delicacy in Asian countries, including China, where many feel they benefit one's health, serving to reduce high blood pressure. Sea cucumbers have a slimy, rubbery texture when eaten and because they are tasteless, are often prepared with flavorful ingredients.

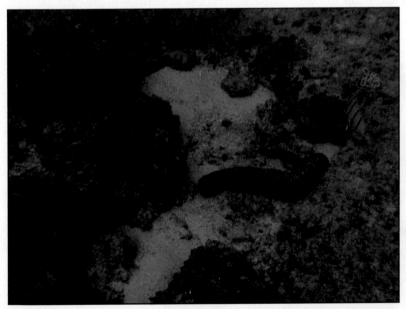

Some sea cucumbers have a unique strategy for evading their predators. When threatened, they permanently eject all of their internal organs out through their mouth or anus, a process known as **evisceration**. Scientists hypothesize that this behavior surprises and distracts predators, allowing the animal to escape. The internal organs eventually grow back and the sea cucumber is as good as new.

FIGURE 18.33. A Black Sea Cucumber sits among corals and fish in the Papahānaumokuākea Marine National Monument. This species is found in rocky or sandy bottom habitats and can grow to about 50 centimeters (~20 inches).

Herbivory (pronounced: er-BĬV-or-ee). Like deer, rabbits, and other vegetarian animals on land, there are **herbivores** in the ocean as well. These organisms eat plants and algae, including seaweed, some which are categorized as protists. An interesting herbivore is the sea urchin, another echinoderm.

Within the kelp forests of the Coastal Pacific, the Purple Sea Urchin serves an important role in the food web. A favorite food of sea otters, these sea urchins are kept in check by the furry mammals, which will often roll on their backs to take apart and enjoy their catch. The sea urchins graze on the kelp for which the kelp forest gets its name. These echinoderms coordinate the action of both their tube feet and spines in order to slowly move along the seafloor, rocks, and sediment along the beach, and on algae such as kelp. To bite or scrape pieces of kelp and other algae, the urchin uses a specialized organ known as an **Aristotle's Lantern**, which resembles an ancient Greek lantern. The Aristotle's Lantern is a structure composed of five teeth, which the animal pushes out through its mouth. It is a very effective structure for grazing. If there are not enough predators for the sea urchin in their ecosystem, they have been known to scrape habitats completely clean of kelp and other algae.

FIGURE 18.34. Sea urchins, shown here along with some Bat Stars, are particularly common along rocky shorelines. Watch where you step— these spines will easily puncture a foot, and some even contain toxins.

FIGURE 18.35. The broken sea urchin in this photograph allows us to get a view of Aristotle's Lantern, a sharp structure used to bite off pieces of algae. Notice the five teeth made up of calcium carbonate that make up the structure. Recall that one of the characteristics of echinoderms is their five-part radial symmetry.

FIGURE 18.36. The Southern Sea Otter is a common marine mammal in waters along the West Coast. In addition to clams and abalones, sea urchins are an important part of the otters' diet.

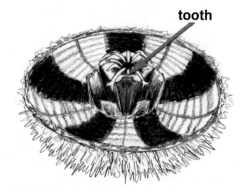

tooth

FIGURE 18.37. Side view of a broken sea urchin.

Predation. Many invertebrates feed on other animals; they are **predators**. Organisms, including predators that subsist almost solely on other animals are called **carnivores**. Predators typically have several adaptations that make them well equipped for capturing and eating prey. One example of an invertebrate predator is the sandworm, a member of Phylum Annelida. There are many species of sandworms in diverse marine environments. These sandworms look like the more-familiar earthworm in that they have the classic segmentation, the crosswise rings. However, being polychaete (pronounced: PAWL-ee-keet) worms, they have fleshy extensions to each segment called **parapodia**. The parapodia often have bristles on them and are used for swimming or crawling through sediment.

FIGURE 18.38. Polychaete worms, such as this bloodworm found off the South Carolina Coast, have visible parapodia that are used for locomotion. The sandworm is another common example of a polychaete worm.

You might not think of sandworms, sometimes called clamworms, as a predator. But, they have powerful and hook-like jaws, with which they can grab their prey. This includes other worms, small crustaceans such as amphipods and even bivalves. Some species are even able to inject poison into their victims. Once the worm grasps its prey, it pulls the food into its mouth. Sandworms can use their parapodia to "swim" through the sand to hunt other burrowing animals.

2. Choose two of the invertebrates described above. For each, describe how at least one of the animal's structures supports the function of feeding.

3. In the **Explore** section, you learned about the diversity of invertebrates. From your findings, describe another example of how an invertebrate employs feeding strategies.

FIGURE 18.39. The head of the sandworm includes a hook-like jaw for grasping prey. There are many species of sandworm throughout the temperate water surrounding the United States.

Elaborate

Lab

Investigating Structure and Function in the Squid

Squid are classified in Phylum Mollusca and Class Cephalopoda, along with octopuses and cuttlefish. Common invertebrates, species of squid are found in waters around the world—at the surface, in the deep sea, and everywhere in between. Squid can be smaller than your finger or as long as a tractor trailer truck. They are well suited for withstanding pressure, blending in with their environments, and capturing prey. Some are even bioluminescent. They are a very interesting invertebrate to dissect, and a tasty one to eat.

FIGURE 18.40. Some squid species lay their eggs in finger-shaped egg cases, such as the ones seen here. Each case contains hundreds of tiny squid eggs.

Materials:

- Whole squid
- Cardboard lunch trays or thick paper plates
- Sharp knife
- Surgical scissors
- Toothpicks
- Wooden coffee stirrer
- Plastic or latex gloves
- Paper towels
- Hand lens
- Clean plastic ruler
- Microscopes, slides, and coverslips (*optional*)
- Dissecting microscope (*optional*)

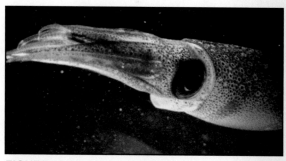

FIGURE 18.41. Market Squid has been an important commercial catch in California since the 1800s. Squid are baited using lights and they are then netted. They spawn at night and deposit their eggs at the sea bottom approximately 20–70 meters (~65–230 feet) below the sea surface.

Safety Note: Be very careful when using knives.

Part A: External Anatomy

Follow the procedures with your lab group. Have one group member read each step aloud. Remember that each individual squid is slightly different. Be sure to make observations based on what you see, feel, and smell. Use the hand lens to make more detailed observations.

1. Check to be sure your group has all of the necessary materials for the investigation.

2. Assign roles within the group. Some students may have more than one role. Roles include:
   • Reader/Lead Investigator
   • Dissectors
   • Recorder
   • Illustrator

3. Those students who will be touching the squid must put on gloves. Once wearing gloves, place the squid on the tray dorsal (back) side up, with the siphon face down.

4. Describe your squid in words. Make as many quantitative and qualitative observations as possible.

5. The Illustrator should draw an accurate diagram of the squid. As you read through the instructions, label each structure on the diagram.

6. At the top of the "torpedo" shape are two fins. They are attached to a structure that covers and protects many of the internal organs. This structure is the mantle. Describe the structure of the mantle.

7. Note the size and the location of the eyes.

8. The squid should have 8 arms and 2 tentacles that surround the mouth. Compare and contrast the arms and tentacles.

9. Carefully examine the mouth. Describe what you observe.

10. Lift your squid and examine the siphon, which sticks out from beneath the mantle. As it swims, a squid sucks in water to pass over its gills. The siphon also helps to determine the direction in which the animal swims.

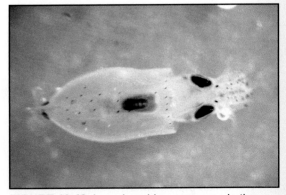

FIGURE 18.42. Larval squid are common in the plankton community.

Part B: Internal Anatomy

11. Place the squid back on the tray with the siphon down on the pan. Use a coffee stirrer to gently lift the mantle and hold it taut. A Dissector should use the scissors to carefully make a long slice, from the head to the fin, to open the mantle. **Do not cut too deep.** You do not want to damage the underlying organs.

12. Open the "flaps" of the mantle and lay them out on the tray. The internal organs will now be exposed.

13. Direct the Illustrator to draw a diagram of the internal anatomy of the squid. Also assign a student to take notes about things you find as you proceed through the dissection.

14. Use the Squid Anatomy Diagram to help you identify and label the internal structures as you proceed through the dissection.

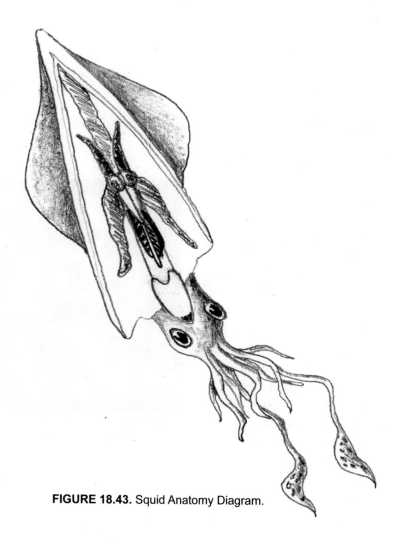

FIGURE 18.43. Squid Anatomy Diagram.

15. Near the fin, farthest from the head, you will notice the reproductive organ, or gonad. There are several other organs, a bundle of them, just below the gonad. Organs in this bundle can be hard to distinguish, but include the systemic heart and kidney.

16. To the sides of the bundle are the long, feathery gills. Use the hand lens to examine them more closely. Describe the gills.

17. Next to the gills you will find the flat, white, brachial (pronounced: BRAYK-ee-ill) hearts. A squid has three (3) hearts.

18. Now look for the ink sac. Try not to rupture it. Beneath the ink sac and the bundle of organs you observed earlier, you should find the stomach. Slice open the stomach. Describe its contents. Use the hand lens to examine the contents if necessary.

19. Below all of the organs, within the mantle, feel around until you note a hard, long, clear, stick-like structure. This is the shell, or pen, of the squid. This is the only shell that this mollusk has. Do some cutting to remove the pen. Describe its structure.

20. If time allows, investigate anything else you would like to about your squid. Use the hand lenses and observe structures under the dissecting microscope. Provide diagrams, descriptions, and other information below. Things worth investigating include:
   - The eyeballs
   - The beak
   - The liver
   - The ink sac

21. Clean up your station as directed by your teacher. Once you are done, begin working on Part C with your group.

Part C: Synthesis Questions

Let's focus on understanding the connection between the structure and function of the squid organism and its parts.

22. Answer the following Questions:

   a. Examine your diagram of the external anatomy of the squid. The longer appendages are called tentacles and are used primarily for catching food. The eight (8) arms push food particles into the mouth. Describe how the structures of these appendages support their functions.

FIGURE 18.44. A close-up of Boreo Atlantic Armhook Squid, *Gonatus fabricii*. This squid species is found in the North Atlantic.

   b. Describe how the external structures of the squid help it to move.

   c. Why would an individual squid with bigger eyes be more likely to survive than one with smaller eyes?

   d. As you noted, squid have three hearts. One of those hearts is located near the gills. Why is this placement of organs useful to these animals?

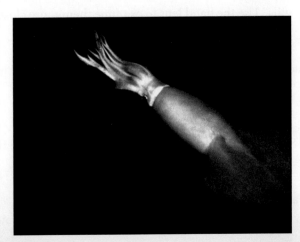

FIGURE 18.45. Humboldt Squid swimming. They move at speeds of greater than 20 kilometers per hour (~12 miles per hour) by ejecting water through a siphon and using fins. Their size can be more than 2 meters (~6 feet) in length.

Evaluate

FIGURE 18.46. Surfaces in the rocky inter tidal zone are all utilized by something. A typical tide pool like this one located in Olympic Coast National Marine Sanctuary is home to seaweed as well as invertebrates. Here, predatory ochre sea stars roam among communities of green sea anemones and rockweed searching for mussels. How many different phyla are there to identify in this picture?

FIGURE 18.47. The rocky shore ecosystem is rich with tidepools, which are puddles of water left between and within rocks on the beach when the tide goes out. Taken in Monterey, California, this photograph shows organisms growing in tidepools and along the rocks.

1. Imagine that your class takes a trip to a tidepool, looking for invertebrates in order to practice what you have learned about these "spineless animals", as well as your observation and description skills. Your teacher instructs you to choose four animals observed in the tidepool and to vividly describe them, without naming them.

   Back in the classroom, you are given the following descriptions written by another group of students. Based on the information the students have given, into which phylum would you classify each of the organisms? Support your answer.

   a. This flat animal has very rough, bumpy skin and is orange in color. It has five arms extending from a round part in the middle. On its bottom side, it has tiny, clear tube feet that allows it to walk slowly on our hands.

   b. This specimen is pink in color and is round with lots of tentacles extending out from around an opening in the middle. It is about 2 centimeters high, and is stuck to the rock. Juan touched the tentacles and it stung him!

   c. This organism has a mushy texture with a lot of holes in it, including a large hole in the top. It does not seem to be moving and is a light brown color. There are no obvious structures – no mouth, legs, or tentacles.

   d. The specimen is walking through the tidepool sideways on its jointed legs. Its entire body, including its legs, is covered in a shell, which feels smooth to the touch but is strong. The animal has eyes, as well as tiny structures that it is using to push water into its mouth.

2. Many species of squid fill the role of voracious predators in a variety of marine ecosystems. Describe two structures of the squid, and how these structures contribute to the animal's predatory abilities.

3. Choose two phyla of invertebrate animals. Compare and contrast the phyla.

19

Biology of Fishes

INSIDE:

Exploring the Structures and
Functions of Fishes

An Introduction to Fish

Fishes and Niches

Sharks: Great Ocean Predators

Objectives

You will be able to:

✔ **Identify and analyze the external structures of fish.**

✔ **Compare and contrast cartilaginous and bony fishes.**

✔ **Give examples of adaptations of fish species in various marine ecosystems.**

✔ **Give the reasons for sharks' evolutionary success over the last 450 million years.**

 Benchmarks

5d. Ocean biology provides many unique examples of life cycles, adaptations, and important relationships among organisms (e.g., symbiosis, predator-prey dynamics, energy transfer) that do not occur on land.

5e. The ocean is three-dimensional, offering vast living space and diverse habitats from the surface through the water column to the seafloor. Most of the living space on Earth is in the ocean.

6b. From the ocean we get foods, medicines, and mineral and energy resources. In addition, it provides jobs, supports our nation's economy, serves as a highway for transportation of goods and people, and plays a role in national security.

7a. The ocean is the last and largest unexplored place on Earth; less than 5% of it has been explored. This is the great frontier for the next generation's explorers and researchers, where they will find great opportunities for inquiry and investigation.

Engage

More than 480 million years ago, the first fish swim in the ocean. Today, more than half of the living vertebrates are fish. Fish are found in a wide variety of sizes, shapes, and color patterns, and are members of all marine ecosystems. Fish have played an important role in a variety of human cultures. For instance, in some Asian cultures, goldfish can symbolize wealth, and Koi fish, perseverance. Some fish are dangerous to humans; others provide us with food or medicine.

What knowledge do you have of fish? Perhaps you have been fishing, snorkeled, eaten fish, seen them in aquaria, or have observed these animals in a pet store.

FIGURE 19.1. Fish are a very diverse group. These eels are fish with elongated bodies.

FIGURE 19.2. Some types of fish swim in schools. What else do you know about fish?

FIGURE 19.3. In addition to being important members of marine ecosystems, fish have health and economic benefits for humans. Do you eat fish? What kinds?

1. You have certainly had experiences with fish. Based on these experiences, what observations can you make about fish?

2. What characteristics help you to realize that the animals are fish? What questions do you have about them?

Activity

Exploring the Structures and Functions of Fishes

Fish make up the largest group of vertebrates. According to NOAA there are more than 28,000 different species. Fish can be found in freshwater bodies, including lakes and streams, brackish areas such as estuaries and throughout the ocean's diverse ecosystems. With only about 5 percent of the ocean fully explored, scientists continually discover new species.

FIGURE 19.4. The Northern Pike is a freshwater fish found throughout much of North America, although it was introduced to some lakes in the West and is outcompeting native fish. This species is often a top predator in its ecosystem and is a fast swimmer, indicated by its fusiform body shape.

Observing the body shapes, fins, mouths, and other structures of a fish species can give you clues about its habitat, as well as its niche. For example, by observing the body structures of fishes it may help you determine the type of food a fish species eats, and hint at how the animal goes about getting its nutrients.

In this activity, you will analyze the different body structures of fish. Fish have a wide variety of adaptations for survival in diverse marine ecosystems. Some of the adaptations are structural; others are behavioral. By simply examining a fish's structures, you can predict a lot about the animal's niche within its ecosystem.

FIGURE 19.5. An angler fish lies in wait on young lava flows on the seafloor near New Zealand. Do you think this fish is a fast swimmer?

1. Complete the chart below, which introduces some structures of fish and their functions. You are asked to *describe the structure* (Column 2). In addition, you will speculate and *predict the function of the structure* (Column 3), in other words, how a fish might use it. Sometimes you are asked for both.

    For each body part, you will also *identify two marine ecosystems* (Column 4) in which you think this body part would be a successful structure, and give a brief explanation to support your prediction.

Body Part Description	Description of Structure	Predictions. Function of Structure	Predictions. Identification of Ecosystems.
Mouth			
Small mouth 		Can "nibble" on coral, algae, etc.	
Terminal 		Open water feeder; May chase and capture things	
Up-Pointing 		Feeds on prey above it in the water column	
Sub-Terminal 	Mouth located on the underside of the head		
Strong Jaws 			
Sucker-Shaped 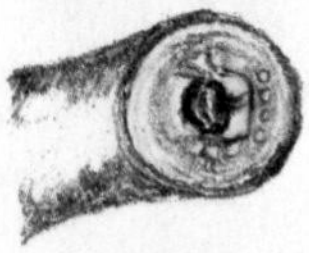		Sucking blood or rasping	
Large mouth 			

Body Part Description	Description of Structure	Predictions. Function of Structure	Predictions. Identification of Ecosystems.
Tail			
Crescent		Support fast speeds for long distances	
Forked		Fast, continuous swimmers.	
Truncated	Similar to fan; May be rounded or square-shaped		
Continuous		Allows fish to swim in cracks and crevices	
Color Pattern			
Red	Red in color	Found in dark or dimly lit areas, because without light, red looks gray; Most of the red light wavelength is absorbed in the first 10 meters so red objects appear dark/black because there is no red light to reflect.	
Counter shading	Dark top, light bottom		
Disruptive	Stripes or lines, either horizontal or vertical		

(continued on next page)

Body Part Description	Description of Structure	Predictions. Function of Structure	Predictions. Identification of Ecosystems.
Eyespots	Pattern that looks like an eye usually found near tail		
Warning Coloration		Signals fish is likely poisonous	
Mottled	Color pattern spotty		
Body Shape			
Flat Bottom		Feeds and lives on the bottom of the sea	
Elongated		Hides in crevices and within vegetation	
Fusiform (pronounced: FEW-sĭh-form)	Streamlined; torpedo shaped		
Laterally Compressed	Flattened from side to side		
Humpback		Helps to stabilize fish in fast-moving water	

2. Your teacher will assign you to an ecosystem. Describe the habitat.

   a. Describe the habitat (biotic and abiotic factors, etc.).

   b. What challenges would fish have to face in this environment?

See Page 694 for how to access e-Tools.

View the **Ecosystem Fish Pictures** from the e-Tools.

e-Tools

3. Copy the table below into your notebook. Using the e-Tools, view pictures of fish from your ecosystem. For at least <u>four</u> of the fishes, list the fish's name, and then determine the type of mouth, body shape, tail shape, and coloration pattern using the chart.

   In the final column, give a prediction about the animal's behaviors and niche in its ecosystem, based on the structures you have observed.

Ecosystem: _____

Fish	Mouth Shape	Body Shape, Mouth Shape, Fins, etc., Related to Its Niche	Coloration Pattern	Predictions. Description of Fish's Behavior and Niche

4. What patterns do you observe of the fishes in your ecosystem? Do they have similar structures? Why or why not?

5. Choose one of the fish from your chart. Imagine this fish was transported to another marine ecosystem.

   a. Choose and identify any new ecosystem.

   b. How would your fish species fare in this new ecosystem? Why? Point out specific characteristics of your fish and the new ecosystem to support your answer.

Explain

An Introduction to Fish

When thinking of marine organisms, many people first think of fish. A short note on terminology: while the plural form of the word *fish* is still *fish*, the term *fishes* normally refers to multiple species of fish. So, it is correct to say, "There are many fish in my tank", and "The various fishes in the ecosystem demonstrate the diversity of animals".

FIGURE 19.6. A flounder's mottled coloration allows it to camouflage with its surroundings. The eye spots serve as a defense against predators, and the flat shape allows this fish to remain near sandy and rocky bottoms. Can you find the fish in this photograph?

Fishes have a variety of different appearances (e.g., shapes, sizes, colors) and have diverse characteristics that have allowed them to survive in a variety of habitats. Fishes belong to Phylum Chordata and Subphylum Vertebrata. Vertebrate animals possess an internal skeleton, including a backbone and skull. There are three major groups, or classes, of fishes: **jawless fishes** (e.g., hagfishes, lampreys), **bony fishes** (e.g., tuna, salmon, carp), and **cartilaginous** (pronounced: kar-till-ADJ-in-us) **fishes** (e.g., sharks, skates, rays).

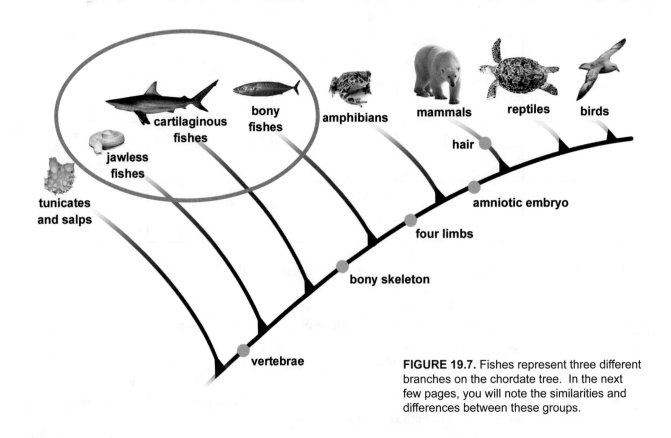

FIGURE 19.7. Fishes represent three different branches on the chordate tree. In the next few pages, you will note the similarities and differences between these groups.

Jawless Fishes

Jawless fishes are the most primitive fish species on Earth. They do not have scales, paired fins, or jaws—hence their name—and have elongated bodies. Jawless fishes have sucker-shaped mouths and feed by sucking on their prey. Hagfishes are typically parasitic and feed on dead or dying fish.

Some species of lampreys breed in rivers and move to the ocean as adults. As juveniles, lamprey feed on benthic invertebrates. Some adult lamprey are parasitic, feeding on the blood of other fish.

FIGURE 19.8. This photograph shows two lampreys, which are jawless fish with snake-like bodies, feeding on a lake trout. Notice the elongated bodies, typical of jawless fishes.

FIGURE 19.9. This close-up photograph of a Sea Lamprey's mouth illustrates its sucker shape and sharp teeth. The Sea Lamprey is an invasive species throughout the Great Lakes.

Bony Fishes

This group of animals is called bony fishes because bone comprises their skeleton, which you will learn is different from the cartilaginous fishes. The bony fishes are an incredibly numerous and diverse group. Approximately half of all vertebrate species are bony fishes, the majority of which are marine. Fish are economically very important as they are a vital protein source for many communities around the globe.

Have you ever watched a goldfish opening and closing its mouth? This is how many bony fish breathe. They take in water through their mouth and pass it over the gills, where oxygen is extracted. Some bony fish, especially those in the open ocean, must keep moving to allow the water to pass over their gills.

FIGURE 19.10. A tuna is ensnared near the mouth of a pelagic drift gillnet. This tuna weighed 270 kilograms (~600 pounds). A tuna is a bony fish.

The oxygen is then transferred to the fish's bloodstream to be brought to the body's cells. Oxygen-poor water is released from the body out through the flap of flesh that covers the gills, the **operculum** (pronounced: oh-PERK-ū-lum). Bony fishes have one gill opening on each side of the head, covered by the operculum.

FIGURE 19.11 illustrates some of the major structures of bony fish species. Examine the diagram as you read about many of the structures of bony fish. Note that the tail is also known as the **caudal fin**. As you studied in the **Explore** section, the caudal fin is critical to a fish's swimming ability, providing propulsion in water. Note that the caudal fins of fish move side-to-side, whereas marine mammals such as dolphins and whales swim by thrusting their tails up and down.

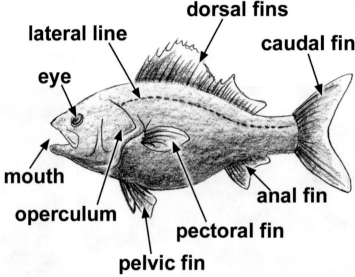

FIGURE 19.11. Note the major external structures of bony fish. Modifications of these structures occur over many generations as populations adapt to their environments.

On a fish's back, or **dorsal** side, are back fins that help to stabilize the animal and keep its body from rolling over. These are **dorsal fins**. The opposite of the dorsal side is the **ventral** side, or belly side, the bottom of the organism. On the ventral side, the **pelvic** and **anal fins** also provide stability. On the animal's sides are **pectoral fins**, which provide lift and propulsion and assist the fish in steering and moving up and down in the water column. The fins of bony fish tend to have fleshy, translucent membranes covering bony spines.

These fins are modified in many fish species; others do not have all of the fins described here. For example, in some eel species, the dorsal, pelvic, anal, and caudal fins are joined together to line the animal's elongated shape. In mudskippers, which are fish that have adapted to come *out* of the water for periods of time, the modified pectoral fins allow the animal to crawl.

FIGURE 19.12. Note the different fins on the Giant Trevally, shown swimming along the reef in the Northwest Hawaiian Islands. This large fish is a powerful predator and important game fish. It is also known by its Hawaiian name, Ulua Aukea.

FIGURE 19.13. A Witch Eel swims among rocks in the Monterey Bay National Marine Sanctuary. Notice the elongated shape and joined fins on the animal, which help it to sneak in and out of cracks, crevices, and caves.

Many bony fishes have a special structure that helps them to regulate their depth in the water. This organ is called a **swim bladder**. A swim bladder is a balloon-like structure that is filled with air, located inside a fish's body, usually near the stomach and intestine. The swim bladder prevents a fish from sinking if it stops swimming.

Notice on FIGURE 19.11 the line that runs along the middle of the fish, between the dorsal and ventral surfaces. This line is actually made up of a bunch of small cavities, which together form an organ to detect vibrations in the water. It is called the **lateral line organ**.

Other notable structures of bony fishes are their scales, which are covered in slimy mucus. These scales have a rounded shape, and, if you touch a bony fish, you are likely to find that scales rub off onto your hand. Some of the many examples of diverse bony fish include species of parrot fish, flounder, rockfish, trout, puffer fish, and salmon.

3. Describe the function of each of the following types of fins in fish.

    - Caudal fin
    - Pelvic fin
    - Anal fin
    - Dorsal fin
    - Pectoral fins

FIGURE 19.14. Mudskippers crawl on rocks and sand using their modified pectoral fins. In addition to having gills, recent studies show that these land-loving fish can breathe through their skin, like many amphibians.

FIGURE 19.15. Unless the animal is disturbed, the spines of a puffer fish remain close to their bodies. These fish have a short caudal fin, indicating that they are strong but relatively slow swimmers.

Cartilaginous Fishes

This group of fishes includes sharks, skates, and rays. These animals have been on Earth for almost 450 million years, and evidence suggests that many of their characteristics have not changed much for over 100 million years. Their skeletons are made of the bone-like substance that makes up your nose and ears, called **cartilage**. They have no true bones and do not have a swim bladder.

Their lack of bones allows cartilaginous fishes to be very flexible, but cartilage is not easily fossilized because it decomposes quickly and is not often replaced by minerals. As a result, the most commonly found pieces of evidence of past sharks are fossilized teeth. Sharks typically have hundreds of teeth, which are arranged in rows within an animal's mouth. The teeth are made of very hard substances called enameloid and dentine.

FIGURE 19.16. Fossilized shark teeth are fairly easy to find throughout much of the continental United States, much of which was once covered by ocean. Teeth are often the only part of a cartilaginous fish's body to become fossilized.

The bodies of cartilaginous fishes are covered in spiny tooth-like scales that are sharp to the touch. These scales are called **placoid scales** and are embedded in the animal's skin; they will not flake off in your hand as when you touch a bony fish. Placoid scales make the skin of cartilaginous fish feel a bit like sandpaper when rubbed from the tail toward the head. On the other hand, a ray, for example, feels like velvet when rubbed from the head toward the tail. Cartilaginous fishes have fleshy fins, different from the spiny fins of bony fish.

Unlike bony fishes, cartilaginous fishes have five or more gill slits on the sides or bottoms of their bodies as shown in FIGURE 19.18. Some cartilaginous fishes take in water through structures called **spiracles** located on their heads, and then pass the water over the gills, and out through the gill slits. Many species of shark, except for those that rest on the sea bottom, tend to breathe through their mouths, and must remain swimming to maintain the flow of water over their gills. The nostrils of cartilaginous fish are not for breathing but are related to their sense of smell. Sharks, in particular, have very acute smelling ability.

Skates are cartilaginous fishes with flattened bodies and long tails. They generally live on the sea bottom. There are many different species of skates that live in both shallow and deep waters that range from tropical to much colder temperatures. Rays have similar body shapes, but also have poisonous stingers.

FIGURE 19.17. A Southern Stingray shows off its spiracles, which look like holes near the fish's eyes. Stingrays have a body structure similar to skates and rays, but they also have a poisonous stinger.

FIGURE 19.18. A manta ray glides through the water with much grace. The pectoral fins are modified to appear like "wings", giving the appearance of the fish flying through the water. Notice the gill slits on this cartilaginous fish's underside.

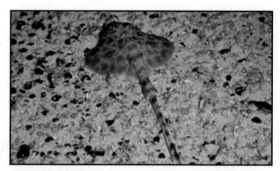

FIGURE 19.19. A skate is seen here hovering above the ocean floor. Notice the flattened body shape and mottled coloration pattern.

Sharks are probably the best-known cartilaginous fishes, but unfortunately they have a bad reputation. There are actually very few shark attacks on humans each year, and scientists believe that these incidents mostly occur when the fish mistakes humans for tastier prey like sea lions and seals. While certain species of shark, such as the Great White, Tiger Shark, and Bull Shark, are certainly fierce, others, such as the Whale Shark, the largest fish on Earth, are harmless to us. Whale Sharks eat only plankton. To that end, sharks and their cousins, the skates and rays, take on several different niches.

There are more than 300 shark species living on Earth today, many of which are talented predators. Many species have a fusiform body shape, which is streamlined, reducing friction as they speed through water. Their large caudal fins also propel the animals forward. Unfortunately, shark species are experiencing rapid declines due to human activities, including pollution, climate change, and overfishing. Humans have decimated shark populations, as well as those of many other large vertebrates, throughout the ocean. Several countries have enacted protections for sharks, many of which are important predators that keep the food chain in balance.

4. Give three ways in which cartilaginous fish are different from bony fish.

FIGURE 19.20. Whale Sharks are the largest fish on Earth today and are not harmful to humans at all—they eat plankton.

FIGURE 19.21. Leopard Sharks, such as the one shown here, are named for their spotted coloration pattern. This species has a sub-terminal mouth type, allowing it to feed on prey below it.

FIGURE 19.22. A Blacktip Reef Shark shows off its fusiform shape and its large, crescent-shaped, caudal fin. This species feeds primarily on fish and invertebrates throughout coral reefs of the Indian and Pacific Oceans.

Fishes and Niches

As you now know, fish are a very diverse group of organisms. Why did this diversity develop? The answer is competition. As you observed in the activities of the **Explore** section, observing the features of fish can give you a clue about both an organism's habitat and niche. For example, leafy sea dragons (FIGURE 19.23), bony fish that are relatives of seahorses, have interesting body structures that blend in with their vegetation-rich environment. The sucker-shaped mouth lets the fish suck in plankton.

FIGURE 19.23. Leafy Sea Dragons are unusual bony fish that are relatives of seahorses and pipefish. These fish are typically found in habitats such as salt marshes and seagrass beds.

Sea dragons and seahorses use their tails to hold onto vegetation and avoid being swept away by currents or waves.

Unlike relatively small, delicate seahorses and sea dragons, groupers are big fish with huge mouths. These slow swimmers wait patiently for their prey—typically fishes and invertebrates such as octopuses and lobsters—to come near, then use their large mouths to create suction, taking in the food. There are several species of grouper, all of which get fairly large; recorded weights of greater than 100 kilograms (~220 pounds) are not uncommon.

FIGURE 19.24. Groupers use their large mouths to suck in their prey. Their large, plump bodies do not allow for fast swimming.

There are many niches within an ocean ecosystem to be filled. This is a good thing, because no two species can occupy the exact same niche at the same time and place; the presence of many niches provides opportunities for many animals. If the same niche were being filled by more than one species, the result would be competition between the two species until one outcompeted the other. If you examine the organisms in an ecosystem, it might appear that two species are occupying the same niche. Upon closer inspection, however, you will see this is not the case.

Take, for example, doctorfish and surgeonfish. Both of these fish are herbivores that feed primarily on algae. Both live in and around a coral reef. Both have similar body and mouth shapes (See FIGURES 19.25 and 19.26). Yet, through close observation, one can note that doctorfish will feed high on the reef, toward the top of the water column. Surgeonfish feed low on the reef near the sandy bottom. The slight differences in their niches prevent the two species from competing for food.

FIGURE 19.25. A type of surgeonfish in the Northwest Hawaiian Islands hides under a shelf of coral. This fish will graze on algae along the lower portions of a coral reef, near the sandy bottom.

FIGURE 19.26. Doctorfish are herbivores that graze on algae in coral reefs. They tend to feed near the top of the reef or in nearby seagrass beds.

Elaborate

Sharks: Great Ocean Predators

Sharks are considered to be some of the ocean's most successful predators. Although few species ever attack humans, most sharks prey on other animals, including fish and marine mammals such as seals, sea lions, and dolphins. Sharks have many adaptations that allow them to occupy their predatory niche.

FIGURE 19.27. Horn Sharks are a small species of shark common to California coastal waters, typically measuring about 1 meter in length. These sharks prey on invertebrates and small bony fish.

See Page 694 for how to access e-Tools.

Before we explore some of these adaptations in more detail, view the *National Marine Sanctuaries— Channel Island: Swell Shark Video* from the e-Tools and consider the following Questions.

FIGURE 19.28. Screenshot of the *National Marine Sanctuaries— Channel Island: Swell Shark Video*.

e-Tools

5. What adaptations do these sharks exhibit?

6. What physical characteristics do all the sharks in the video have in common?

Sharks possess keen adaptations that enable them to be great hunters. Whether they are pelagic predators or bottom-dwelling consumers of mollusks and crustaceans, the most famous feature of a shark is its teeth. Unlike you, sharks have anywhere from 6 to 20 rows of teeth. The back rows serve as replacement teeth for when active rows of teeth in the front of the mouth are destroyed or lost. This ensures the shark is always using strong and sharp teeth when eating. It is believed that a shark can go through about 20,000 teeth in its lifetime. Shark teeth are clues to the niche of specific species. Predatory sharks have razor-sharp teeth used to tear their prey into small pieces. The bottom-dwelling sharks have large flat teeth used to crush the shells of invertebrates.

FIGURE 19.29. Sharks are well known for their sharp teeth, which frequently fall out. The shape of the teeth varies depending on what the species eats.

How do sharks locate their prey? A typical shark's eyesight is comparable to that of humans—not terrible, but not fantastic compared to some other animals. In contrast, a shark's sense of smell is impressive. Sharks have been known to detect blood nearly half of a kilometer away (~0.3 miles). A shark's ability to smell is so important to its survival that nearly two-thirds of the animal's brain is devoted to detecting and processing smells. Along with the shark's keen sense of smell, it is also able to detect the slightest sound vibrations in the water. This is made possible by a faint line along the entire body of the shark, called the lateral line organ, which is shown in FIGURE 19.30. This specialized structure, also present in many bony fishes, detects movements of other animals, and is similar to a human's sense of hearing.

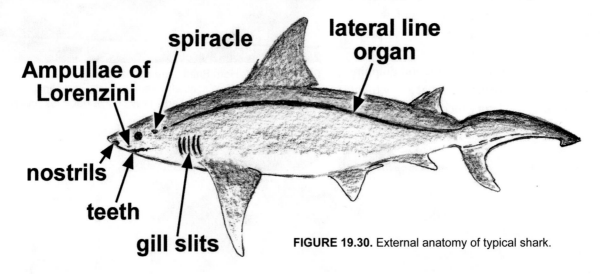

FIGURE 19.30. External anatomy of typical shark.

Sharks actually have a *sixth sense*. A sensing organ, consisting of tiny pores, located near the shark's snout is able to pick up the smallest electrical impulses produced by other organisms. An animal, for example, produces electrical impulses when its muscles contract as it swims or runs, or when its heart beats. These electricity-sensing pores are called the **Ampullae of Lorenzini**.

Once a shark detects its prey, it is on the move. The caudal fin propels the fish forward, while the pectoral fins provide lift. The streamlined, or fusiform, body shape is designed and set to slice through the water with minimal drag.

7. Shark teeth can provide clues about the fish's niche. From the following pictures, hypothesize each shark's niche. Support your answer.

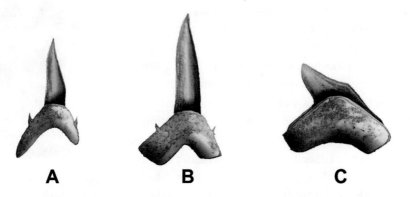

FIGURE 19.31. Shark's teeth vary by species and niche.

Evaluate

1. Create a graphic organizer to compare and contrast cartilaginous and bony fishes.

2. Describe three different structural adaptations of fish. Note the marine ecosystem(s) for which the organism possessing each structure is best adapted and why.

3. Sketch the diagram of the bony fish below in your notebook. Label the following structures:

   a. Dorsal fin
   b. Caudal fin
   c. Operculum
   d. Pectoral fin
   e. Pelvic fin
   f. Lateral line

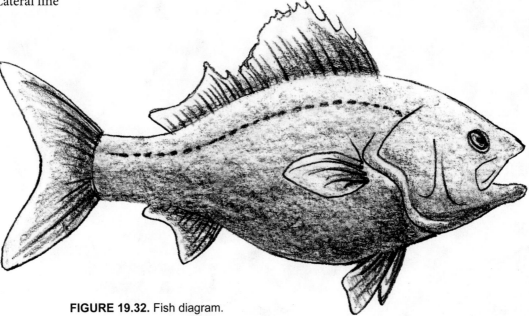

FIGURE 19.32. Fish diagram.

4. Write the script for a radio commercial in which you advertise a shark as an effective predator. Highlight at least three adaptations used for predatory behaviors.

20

Marine Reptiles and Birds

INSIDE:

Objectives

You will be able to:

✔ Compare and contrast the characteristics of marine reptiles and birds.

✔ Give examples of adaptations that allow some reptile and bird species to inhabit the ocean.

✔ Explain the adaptations that allow birds to be more far-ranging than reptiles.

Benchmarks

1a. The ocean is the dominant physical feature on our planet Earth—covering approximately 70% of the planet's surface. There is one ocean with many ocean basins, such as the North Pacific, South Pacific, North Atlantic, South Atlantic, Indian, and Arctic.

5d. Ocean biology provides many unique examples of life cycles, adaptations, and important relationships among organisms (e.g., symbiosis, predator-prey dynamics, energy transfer) that do not occur on land.

5e. The ocean is three-dimensional, offering vast living space and diverse habitats from the surface through the water column to the seafloor. Most of the living space on Earth is in the ocean.

7b. Understanding the ocean is more than a matter of curiosity. Exploration, inquiry, and study are required to better understand ocean systems and processes.

Engage

In the activity below, you will observe some examples of sea turtles and marine birds. There are seven species of sea turtles on Earth. These animals spend nearly all of their time in the ocean, except for when females come ashore to lay eggs. An exception to the rule is the Hawaiian population of Green Sea Turtles, which can often be observed enjoying Hawaii's beautiful beaches. You may already be familiar with turtles that inhabit fresh or brackish water.

Birds are found in nearly every environment on the planet, including the ocean. Those that spend a significant portion of their lives at sea are known as **seabirds**. Some seabirds with which you might be familiar are penguins, pelicans, and albatrosses. Many of the birds we observe along shorelines, including ducks, geese, egrets, and herons, are not true seabirds since they spend much of their lives on land. Many of the animals still rely on the ocean for food, and thus can be called **marine birds**. You will learn about both seabirds and other marine birds in this Lesson.

See Page 694 for how to access e-Tools.

View the *Marine Reptiles and Marine Birds Pictures and Videos* in e-Tools to make observations.

e-Tools

Observe videos as well as images of sea turtles and birds provided, and answer the Questions. Your observations will focus on the marine turtles and seabirds themselves. There are, of course, birds and turtles in other environments on Earth, including on land and in fresh water.

1. What do all the birds you observed have in common? What differences do you observe?

2. What do the turtles have in common? What differences do you notice between the turtles?

3. Compare the body structures and behaviors of turtles and birds.

FIGURE 20.1. This Loggerhead Sea Turtle with barnacles on its shell is swimming the vicinity of Carysfort Reef in the Upper Florida Keys.

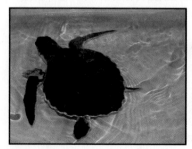

FIGURE 20.2. Many Kemp's Ridley and other sea turtles were rescued from the Gulf of Mexico following the 2010 gulf oil spill. This turtle is recovering in a small pool at a rehabilitation center.

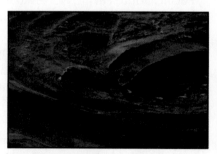

FIGURE 20.3. A Leatherback Sea Turtle surfaces to take a breath. This species is the largest of all sea turtles.

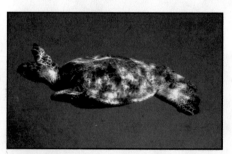

FIGURE 20.4. A Green Sea Turtle swims among schools of fish. This and other sea turtle species are available for students to track in Lesson 27: Student Expert Analysis. Green Sea Turtles are named for their green flesh.

FIGURE 20.5. A Hawksbill Sea Turtle rests on the seafloor off Texas' Gulf Coast as scuba divers observe it from afar. The bird-like beak of this species gives it its name and is useful for crushing the shells of mollusks and other invertebrates, as well as ripping apart marine algae.

FIGURE 20.6. Piping Plovers are small birds common to sandy shores of the Atlantic Ocean and Great Lakes.

FIGURE 20.7. White Terns are seabirds that nest in trees, like this pair on Midway Atoll.

FIGURE 20.8. Red-footed Boobies are seabirds that plunge into the ocean to catch fish, squid, and other prey.

FIGURE 20.9. Great Frigate Bird in the Northwest Hawaiian Islands. The wing design of some seabirds allows them to soar distances and conserve energy.

FIGURE 20.10. Egrets are long-legged wetland birds. There are several species that inhabit fresh- and saltwater marshes of North America.

FIGURE 20.11. Emperor Penguins are the largest penguins and are native to Antarctica. They breed on the ice but feed on fish, crustaceans, and mollusks out at sea.

Explore

Activity

Examining the Ranges of Marine Reptiles and Birds

In this activity, you will analyze Range Maps for different marine bird and sea turtle species. They illustrate the geographic areas and locations in which the species is most commonly found. Range Maps include areas where the species is found for all different times of year. Many of these specific species migrate, and will not be found in all areas during all seasons.

Tracking Maps represent general animal movement for one season (e.g., Spring 2012). They illustrate the actual locations of just a few individual animals of the species. The Tracking Maps display the animal locations for a relatively short time period.

1. Use the range and tracking maps on the next several pages to complete the following data table.

	Marine Birds		Sea Turtles	
	Latitude	Species	Latitude	Species
Northernmost latitude				
Southernmost latitude				

2. Compare the tracks of the marine bird species and the sea turtle species.

3. How do the ranges for the marine bird and sea turtle species compare?

4. List any adaptations that you know of or can identify from the information given that might account for the differences in ranges observed between the seabird and sea turtle groups.

5. Based on the maps on the next few pages, list at least three scientific questions that you could ask about these animals' movements.

Caspian Tern

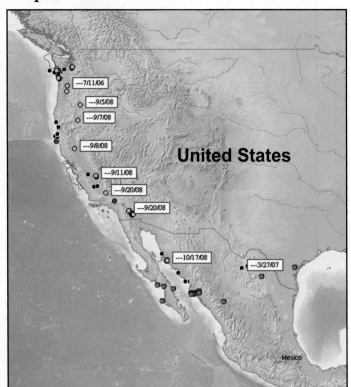

FIGURE 20.12. Caspian Tern Tracking Map shows bird locations over time along the west coast of North America and the coast of the Gulf of Mexico.

FIGURE 20.13. Caspian Terns are the largest terns on Earth. They are easily identified by their red bills.

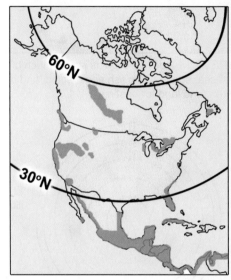

FIGURE 20.14. Caspian Tern Range Map illustrates general locations of the birds during the year from Canada to Central America and the north coast of South America.

Black-footed Albatross

FIGURE 20.15. Black-footed Albatross Range Map illustrates where birds are found across the Central and North Pacific Ocean.

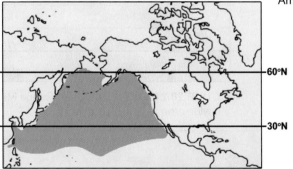

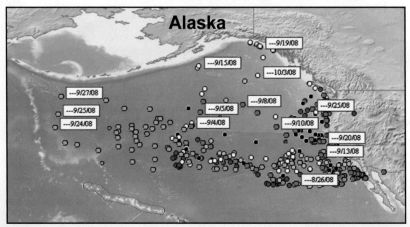

FIGURE 20.16. Black-footed Albatross spend much of their lives at sea, scooping up fish eggs, squid, and other prey. They return to land for nesting.

FIGURE 20.17. Black-footed Tracking Map shows dozens of specific birds' locations over a season.

Adelie Penguin

FIGURE 20.18. Adélie Penguins spend much of their lives at sea, scooping up fish eggs, squid, and other prey. They return to land for nesting.

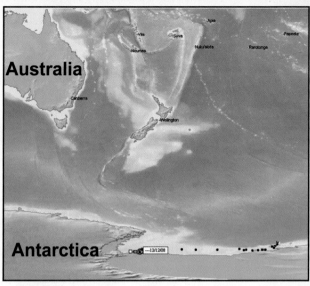

Australia

Antarctica

---12/12/08

FIGURE 20.19. Adélie Penguin Tracking Map shows the location of individual birds throughout the Antarctic region.

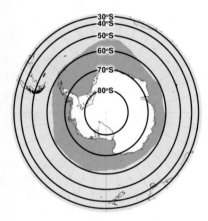

FIGURE 20.20. Adélie Penguin Range Map illustrates that the species remains south of 60° S latitude.

Sooty Shearwater

FIGURE 20.22. Sooty Shearwater are "endless summer" birds. When the seasons change, they migrate to the opposite hemisphere to enjoy another summer. These birds are opportunists, feeding mostly on fish such as anchovies.

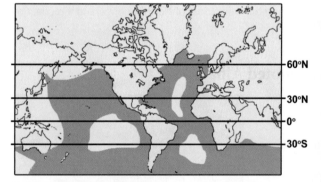

FIGURE 20.21. Sooty Shearwater Range Map shows the wide area used by this species.

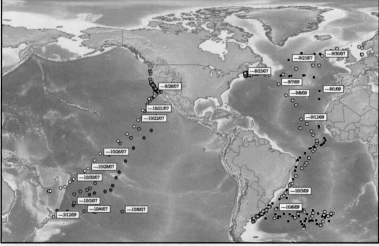

FIGURE 20.23. Sooty Shearwater Tracking Map illustrates several individual birds tracked by marine scientists as they migrate throughout their range.

Glaucous Gull

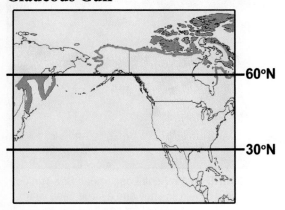

FIGURE 20.24. Glaucous Gull Range Map shows specific locations where populations of the birds live.

FIGURE 20.25. Glaucous Gulls can be observed searching for food along sandy beaches, rocky intertidal zones, and even in garbage cans and dumps.

FIGURE 20.26. Glaucous Gull Tracking Map highlights several individual birds that live in Alaska and across the North Pacific.

Surf Scoter

FIGURE 20.27. Surf Scoters make use of both marine and aquatic habitats, depending on the season. These ducks are able to dive for prey, mostly mollusks, in shallow water.

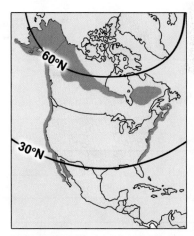

FIGURE 20.28. Surf Scooter Range Map illustrates the coastal areas and inland regions where Surf Scoters spend their time.

FIGURE 20.29. Surf Scooter Tracking Map depicts individual locations of birds tracked across the United States and Canada.

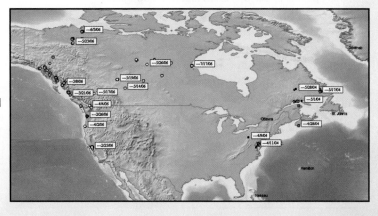

Loggerhead Sea Turtle

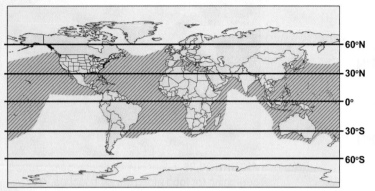

FIGURE 20.30. Loggerhead Sea Turtle Range Map shows the wide range of this turtle within specific latitudes.

FIGURE 20.31. Adult Loggerhead Sea Turtles have a brownish shell and a large head with powerful jaws perfect for crushing the shells of invertebrates. They are thought to reach maturity between 20 and 30 years of age.

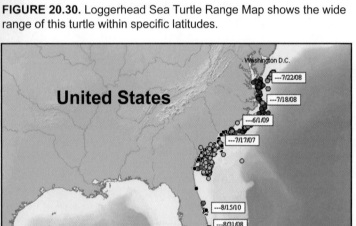

FIGURE 20.32. Loggerhead Sea Turtle Tracking Map focuses on several turtles tracked by marine scientists along the East Coast of the United States.

Green Sea Turtle

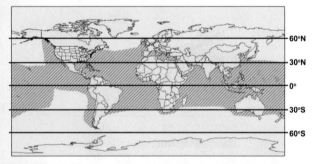

FIGURE 20.33. Green Sea Turtle Range Map illustrates that this specific species of turtle is found throughout the ocean.

FIGURE 20.34. As adults, Green Sea Turtles feed on seaweeds, seagrasses, and other plants and algae, making them herbivores. The species is generally found in tropical and subtropical waters throughout the world's ocean.

FIGURE 20.35. Green Sea Turtle Tracking Map identifies the locations of individual turtles tracked in the Atlantic Ocean.

Hawksbill Sea Turtle

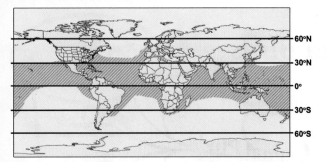

FIGURE 20.36. Hawksbill Sea Turtle Range Map illustrates the turtle's preference for areas of the tropics within the range of 30° N to 30° S.

FIGURE 20.37. Hawksbill Sea Turtles are known for their beautiful shells, which have been used to make jewelry, hair pieces, and other items. As a result of these and other activities, this species is critically endangered. It is illegal to sell or buy merchandise made from endangered species.

FIGURE 20.38. Hawksbill Sea Turtle Tracking Map shows individual turtles tracked in water surrounding the Caribbean Islands.

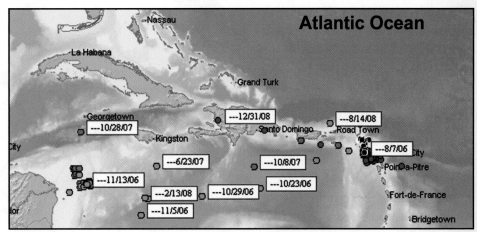

Kemp's Ridley Sea Turtle

FIGURE 20.40. Kemp's Ridley Sea Turtles are the smallest of the seven sea turtle species. Female Kemp's Ridleys are known to return to the beach at which they were hatched to lay their own eggs.

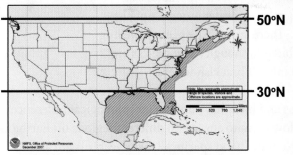

FIGURE 20.39. Kemp's Ridley Sea Turtle Range Map illustrates that the range of this turtle species extends into the Gulf of Mexico and northward from the Caribbean to the coast of Nova Scotia.

FIGURE 20.41. Kemp's Ridley Sea Turtle Tracking Map shows the path of one turtle on its journey along the U.S. East Coast.

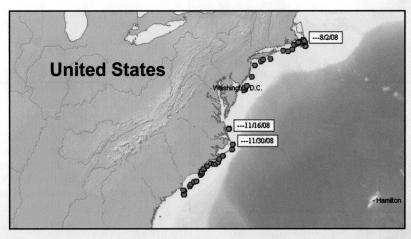

Explain

Amphibians, Reptiles, and Birds

So far, in our studies of Phylum Chordata, we have studied the urochordates, cartilaginous fishes, and bony fishes. This Lesson focuses mostly on reptiles and birds, but first let's examine amphibians.

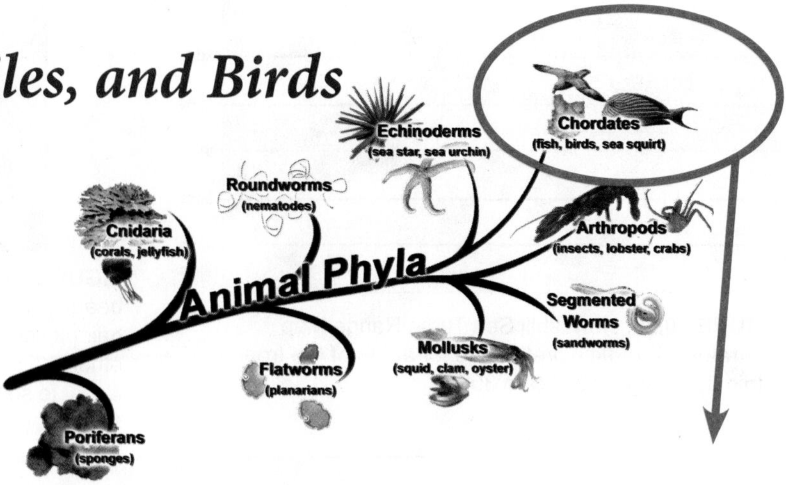

You are familiar with frogs and salamanders. As adults, these animals will spend considerable time on land. However, their juvenile forms, often called tadpoles, are very fish-like; they have gills and a tail for swimming. Once adults, amphibians breathe through small lungs, as well as through their skin, which must remain moist to facilitate gaseous exchange. Amphibians have never evolved to be considered true land animals, because they require a water environment at some portions of their life cycles. Almost all amphibians lay their eggs in the water around aquatic plants. There are no true ocean-dwelling amphibians, although a few species are able to inhabit brackish waters.

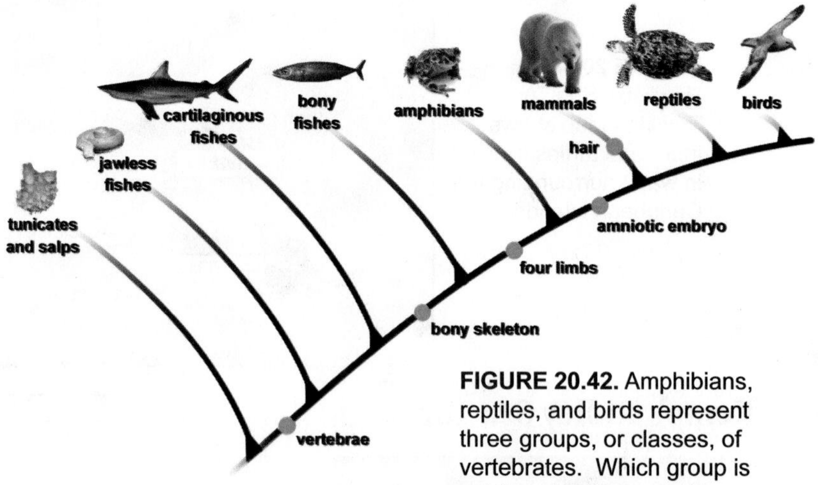

FIGURE 20.42. Amphibians, reptiles, and birds represent three groups, or classes, of vertebrates. Which group is not found in the ocean?

Reptiles and birds have unique morphological differences that allow them to survive in different regions on Earth. In order to understand specifically why seabirds are able to inhabit a wider range of latitudes than sea turtles, we will explore the specific characteristics of each group.

FIGURE 20.43. Called tadpoles, amphibian juveniles are common throughout the U.S. freshwater bodies.

FIGURE 20.44. Salamanders, such as the juvenile Barred Salamander seen here, newts, frogs, toads, and others are all amphibians. There are no true marine amphibians. Members of this group are found throughout a variety of North American habitats.

4. In your notebook, draw two graphic organizers like the ones below. These tools will guide your reading and note-taking about reptiles and birds. In the center, write general characteristics of marine reptiles or birds. Then use each of the outer circles as a place to take notes about each of the major groups of marine reptiles and seabirds. Include special adaptations and/or interesting facts.

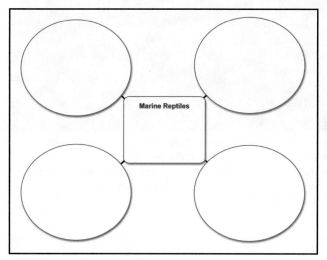

FIGURE 20.45. Sample Graphic Organizers.

Characteristics of Reptiles

Approximately 300 million years ago, reptiles evolved from amphibians, which were the first animals to successfully live out of water for part of their lives. Reptilian adaptations, including well-protected eggs, tough skin and scales to reduce water loss, stronger skeletal structures, and more complex organ systems, allowed for an entirely land-based existence. However, over time, some reptiles returned to water. There are approximately 7,000 species of reptiles. Sea turtles, sea snakes, saltwater crocodiles, and marine lizards (iguanas) all share common characteristics of reptiles, but due to evolutionary change are now able to survive in saltwater environments.

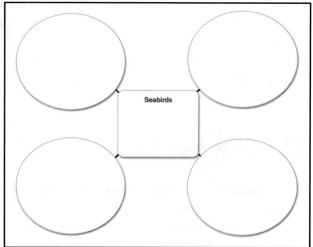

FIGURE 20.46. Lizards and other reptiles have thick, scaly skin that prevents water loss, making them well adapted to dry conditions. Interestingly, some reptile groups have returned to the ocean, including marine iguanas like the one seen here.

All reptiles breathe using lungs. Therefore, marine reptiles must visit the surface often to take in air. They have dry, scaly skin that helps the animal to maintain water and to reduce water loss to the external environment. Additionally, almost all reptiles lay their eggs on land. The reptilian **amniotic egg** was the first to contain a nourishing yolk sac, or **amnion** (pronounced: AM-nee-ŭn), to feed the developing embryo. It has a protective case to prevent water loss. Note in FIGURE 20.42 that reptiles are not the only group to possess an amniotic embryo.

Perhaps you have seen a turtle, snake, or lizard sunbathing on a rock or log. This behavior is common for animals that depend on the external environment to moderate their internal temperature. These organisms are called **ectotherms**. Ectotherms modify their behavior in order to change their body temperature. For example, if a snake lying on a rock in the Sun becomes too warm, it can retreat to the shade or cool off in the water. The metabolic rate or activity level of ectotherms is directly related to the amount of warmth they receive from the Sun; therefore, reptiles are most successful in warm climates. Cold temperatures cause ectotherms to become lethargic.

FIGURE 20.47. The ectothermic nature of reptiles' bodies makes them likely to bask in the Sun for warmth. Don't confuse turtles seen in ponds and estuaries with sea turtles; there are only seven species of truly marine, saltwater turtles. These are the only ones known as sea turtles.

Marine Reptiles

Marine reptiles have additional, special adaptations for survival in saltwater environments. Many are able to control the amount of salt in their bodies with specialized glands, located above the reptiles' eyes, that secrete excess salt. These structures are called **salt glands**. Reptiles also excrete urine with a high salt concentration, conserving fresh water within their body. These adaptations allow marine reptiles to live without access to fresh water. Recall that marine fishes also have to control the salt concentration in their bodies. They accomplish this through the process of osmoregulation.

Sea Snakes

Sea snakes very closely resemble their land relatives. However, they tend to have flatter, more streamlined bodies and a paddle-like tail for moving through the water. More than 50 species live in tropical waters of the Indian and Pacific Oceans. They typically measure 1 to 2 meters (~3 to 6 feet) in length and prefer shallow, coastal areas. Ocean-dwelling snakes tend to be venomous and carnivorous, hunting for fish and their eggs. Some sea snakes can dive for up to two hours because of their highly efficient lung capacity. Some lay their eggs on sandy beaches, but most give birth to live young in the water. Many species are hunted for their skin and as a food delicacy.

FIGURE 20.48. The Banded Sea Snake is a highly venomous species native to the Pacific and Indian Oceans. Despite its deadly poison, this snake is usually docile.

Marine Lizards

Marine Iguanas are famous for their uniquely unattractive faces and spiny scales that extend along their dorsal side. They are the only type of lizard adapted for life in the ocean. This unique lizard exists solely on the remote Galapagos Islands, off the coast of South America. Its clumsy movements on land are juxtaposed with graceful swimming in the ocean. They swing their bodies from side to side and use their streamlined tail to propel through the water.

Marine iguanas dive into the ocean in search of food. They scrape algae and plants off underwater rocks. After a chilly swim and a meal, they return to rocky islands to bask in the Sun for warmth. They congregate in large groups and lay their eggs on land in sandy burrows. They have salt glands on their heads to eliminate excess salt from their bodies.

Marine iguanas are vulnerable to changes in temperature that impact algae growth. They are also susceptible to oil spills, like all marine organisms. Past spills have significantly impacted their populations.

FIGURE 20.49. Map showing the location of the Galapagos Islands.

FIGURE 20.50. Marine iguanas sitting on the rocks in the Galapagos Islands. These herbivores dive into the ocean to scrape algae off of the rocks.

Saltwater Crocodiles

Saltwater crocodiles make their homes in estuaries and Mangrove Swamps, and sometimes pass into rivers and the open ocean. Crocodiles are predatory, often hunting by hiding beneath the surface of the water with only their eyes and nostrils visible. They wait quietly and catch their prey by snatching them up by surprise. One of the distinguishing features between alligators and crocodiles is the possession of salt glands—crocodiles use these features to excrete excess salt from their bodies, a consequence of living in marine environments. Alligators are freshwater species.

One species, the American Saltwater Crocodile, can be found in Puerto Rico and Florida as well as throughout the Caribbean Islands, Central America, and the northern coasts of South America. While some crocodiles are feared by humans, this non-aggressive species is uniquely shy. This species is endangered; its population has been reduced significantly by coastal development. The snout of many species of crocodiles tends to be more V-shaped, allowing them to eat a broader range of prey, including fish and other organisms. The U-shaped jaws of alligators provide the stronger force needed to crack the shells of organisms including freshwater turtles and invertebrates.

Sea Turtles

Most sea turtles have a hard shell that protects most of their bodies. The Leatherback Sea Turtle is the exception, named of course for its leathery shell. Each of the seven species of sea turtle has a unique pattern of scales on top of their shell, which varies in size and shape. Shells of sea turtles grow with them during their lifetime, unlike other animals such as lobsters or crabs whose shells are discarded, or molted. Sea turtles are not able to hide their head and limbs inside their shell like land turtles. Their streamlined bodies include powerful front flippers that move up and down to swim. The back flippers stabilize the animals in the water. Sea turtles are also well adapted for diving and do so often to forage for food. Sea turtles of course return to the surface to breathe using their lungs; they can remain underwater for tens of minutes, depending on the species.

FIGURE 20.51. A zoomed-in view of the head of a Kemp's Ridley Sea Turtle. This species is the smallest of the sea turtles. Adults weigh only 35–45 kilograms (~75–100 lbs) and are less than 1 meter long.

Although their specific diets vary by species, sea turtles feed on various foods including jellyfish, crabs, sponges, squids, and marine vegetation. They have strong jaws that are noticeably different depending on the species and type of food they eat. For example, Loggerhead Sea Turtles have jaws adapted for crushing the shells of crabs and other invertebrates, while Green Sea Turtles have serrated jaws for chewing plant material.

Sea turtles spend almost all of their lives at sea. In fact, after hatching, male sea turtles never return to land again. The females, usually returning to the same beach where they were born, come up on beaches to lay their eggs in the sand. A notable exception to these rules occurs in Hawaiian Green Sea Turtles. In the Hawaiian Islands, both male and female turtles are often observed resting on beaches, basking in the Sun.

All seven species of sea turtle are threatened or endangered. The one species not found in U.S. waters is the Flatback Sea Turtle, which has a limited range of waters near Australia, Papua New Guinea, and other islands in the South Pacific.

FIGURE 20.52. Hawaiian Green Sea Turtles on the beach on Kure Atoll, in the Northwestern Hawaiian Islands. After hatching, most sea turtles spend their entire lives at sea, except for when females come ashore to lay eggs.

5. What characteristics do the marine reptiles discussed here have in common?

The Leatherback Sea Turtle

Leatherback Sea Turtles are the largest of all sea turtles, growing to as much as 2 meters (~6 feet) and weighing nearly 900 kilograms (~2,000 pounds). As you may observe in FIGURE 20.54, Leatherbacks have a very wide range and, in fact, have the largest geographic range of all reptiles. To survive in chilly waters, such as those north of Scandinavia or south of New Zealand, these turtles must maintain a body temperature warmer than their surrounding environment—something ectotherms are normally unable to accomplish.

FIGURE 20.53. Leatherback Sea Turtle.

The Leatherback's large size plays a part in its ability to maintain internal heat. The turtle's shell is called a **carapace** (pronounced: KĀR-uh-pās). Leatherbacks release heat through their skin and shell. Leatherback Turtles are typically 1 to 2 meters (~3–6 feet) in length, although scientists have recorded individuals measuring over 3 meters (~10 feet). Given their large bodies, the surface area for heat exchange—the surface area of the carapace—is low compared to its mass. In addition, Leatherbacks have a layer of insulating blubber beneath their carapaces, a characteristic unique to this species. These characteristics assist them in maintaining body heat farther from the Equator than one might expect.

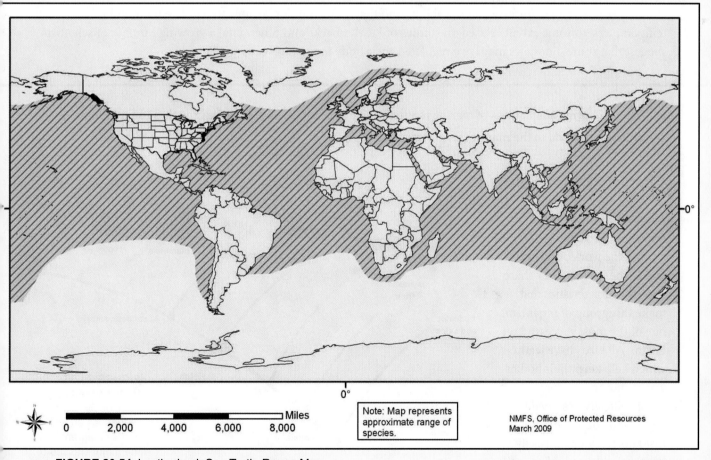

FIGURE 20.54. Leatherback Sea Turtle Range Map.

All sea turtles can control their internal blood circulation. Combined with their large size, Leatherbacks use this adaptation to their advantage when migrating into cold water. When they need to conserve heat, they reduce the amount of blood flow to areas of their body only covered by skin, specifically the flippers. This reduces the amount of heat flowing to the flippers, and therefore reduces the overall heat loss. Blood flow is concentrated in insulated regions of their body. In warm water, where the turtle may release internal heat, blood flow to the flippers is increased.

Their ability to regulate blood circulation and the Leatherbacks' large size allow them to migrate farther than any other sea turtle. Studying Leatherback Sea Turtles has caused biologists to challenge their ideas about what it means to be ectothermic. Some scientists now believe that there

FIGURE 20.55. A Leatherback Sea Turtle wearing a satellite transmitter swims out to sea. Notice the animal's dark, leathery shell, for which this species is named.

are "degrees" of temperature-regulating ability, and that many reptiles are able to regulate their bodies' temperatures to some extent. Based on studies of Leatherbacks and other data, a growing number of scientists suggest that some dinosaurs may have regulated their body temperatures as well.

6. What are some adaptations of marine reptiles? Give at least two and describe how these adaptations enhance survival in the marine environment.

Characteristics of Birds

There are around 10,000 species of birds living all around the world, on land and in the ocean. They share special characteristics that make this group of organisms one of the most successful on Earth. All birds have feathers, which help keep their bodies warm and dry. Some feathers are specifically designed for flight while others function as insulators. Not all birds fly, but they all have feathers and wings.

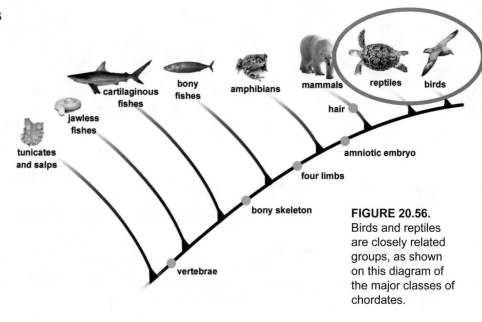

FIGURE 20.56. Birds and reptiles are closely related groups, as shown on this diagram of the major classes of chordates.

All birds have the ability to control their body temperature, an evolutionary advantage over their reptilian ancestors. As endothermic organisms, by definition, they are able tolerate diverse temperature conditions and inhabit all regions of Earth. In order to maintain a high internal temperature, birds have a high metabolism. Birds consume a huge amount of food each day.

Most birds have lightweight, hollow bones—an adaptation that makes flight possible. There are a few species of marine birds, such as penguins, that have heavier bones for diving and swimming beneath the water. The ability to fly has allowed birds to get to and inhabit nearly every Earth environment, from high on the planet's mountains to remote oceanic islands. Flight has also allowed some species of birds to undertake extremely long migrations. Taking advantage of favorable environmental conditions, birds can move quickly, moving when conditions such as weather become unfavorable.

A small percentage of all birds live in and rely on the ocean, and have unique adaptations for doing so. Marine and aquatic birds usually have webbed feet for swimming and, like terrestrial birds, their beaks are adapted for the type of food they eat. These include the many species of wetland and shorebirds that live along the coast.

Shorebirds

There are plenty of birds that use marine and aquatic environments but do not do much swimming or flying over the ocean. Therefore, they are not considered to be seabirds. Instead, these birds are referred to as shorebirds. The beaks of shorebirds tell a lot about what they eat as we observe them along the coast. Sandpipers and plovers search for food in the sand, poking their long slender beaks into the ground and retrieving small invertebrates. Oystercatchers, plovers, turnstones, and a variety of other shorebirds are able to reach the top few centimeters beneath the surface to find worms, bivalves, and crustaceans. A few shorebirds, such as curlews and godwits, all with relatively very long bills, can reach deep beneath the surface.

FIGURE 20.57. A sandpiper in Mississippi pokes in the sand along the Gulf of Mexico. Notice the thin shape of the beak, perfect for picking out small crustaceans and other prey.

Other shorebirds such as ducks and egrets inhabit coastal and inland aquatic environments. Ducks have adaptations such as webbed feet for swimming. Some have flat beaks for straining organisms out of mud. Egrets and wading birds are able to stand still on stick-like legs and quickly snatch fish from the water.

Seabirds

One subset of marine birds, birds that spend most of their lives at sea, are called **seabirds**. This term is not a taxonomic group. Seabirds include members of various groups, which are described below. Seabirds return to land to lay eggs, and they often breed in large groups called **colonies**. Many species travel great distances between their breeding grounds and regions where food is most available, their feeding grounds. Like reptiles, marine birds must remove excess salt from their bodies. Their salt glands are located in their nostrils.

FIGURE 20.58. Different species of birds sit on the rocks alongside sea lions and invertebrates in Monterey Bay, California. Observe the bill shape of different birds to hypothesize about their diets.

Penguins

Penguins are unique birds because they are extraordinary flyers—underwater. Penguins do not take flight in the sky as most birds do. Instead, their wings, akin to flippers, are adapted to propel them through water; penguins can reach 40 kilometers per hour (~25 miles). When they are ready to come ashore, most penguins jump out of the water. They are awkward on land, waddling around in large groups. Antarctic species often get around by gliding along on their bellies on the ice and snow.

FIGURE 20.59. Penguins, such as the Emperor Penguin shown here, use their wings to swim at top speeds, usually when looking for food. Like other seabirds, they lay their eggs on land.

Penguins live in a variety of habitats, but no species is found north of the Equator. Most penguins live in the Antarctic Region and are adapted for extremely cold temperatures. Other species live on Southern Hemisphere coastlines, such as in Africa and South America. A layer of fat beneath the skin and thick, waterproof feathers help insulate their bodies against the cold. Like all birds, penguins **preen** their feathers, cleaning them and spreading oil throughout their layers. A gland, located at the bottom of the penguin's tail, secretes oil that helps condition the bird's feathers and keeps them waterproof. The important chore of preening maintains the bird's ability to conserve body heat in extreme cold.

FIGURE 20.60. Gentoo Penguins grow to approximately 75 centimeters (~30 inches) in height. They are easily identified by their bright red bill and long, stiff tail feathers. These seabirds can dive to more than 100 meters (~328 feet) in search of crustaceans and fish.

Antarctic penguins lay their eggs during the cold winter so that their chicks hatch during the summer when food is most available. In one species, the large Emperor Penguin, adult birds mate for life and share the responsibilities of caring for the eggs and chicks. They breed in large groups and each pair cares for one or two eggs at a time.

The most northern population of penguins, the Galapagos Penguin, lives in the temperate waters of the Galapagos Islands. Ocean currents bring cold water and nutrients north to the Galapagos Islands, providing this small penguin the conditions it needs to survive so far north of its relatives.

Depending on the species, penguins feed on krill, fish, small crustaceans, and squid, and have strong thick beaks, like most seabirds. Their natural predators include whales, seals, and other seabirds that feed on eggs.

FIGURE 20.61. Emperor Penguins perform elaborate mating rituals before choosing a lifetime partner. Both parents contribute to caring for the young. Breeding takes place during the harsh Antarctic winter.

Tubenoses

This group of birds is named for its characteristically long, straw-like nostrils and thick beaks. They are amazing flyers and can spend months and even years soaring and diving into the open ocean to find food. Many species of tubenose seabirds, such as albatrosses, shearwaters, and petrels, migrate thousands of kilometers each year across the ocean, following their food sources, which they locate using their keen eyesight and sense of smell.

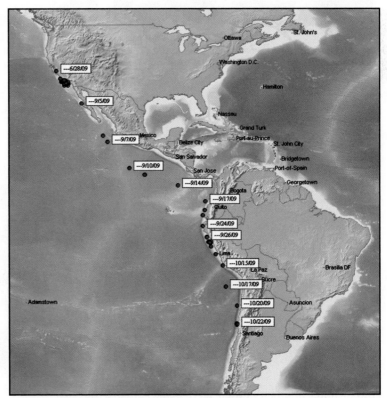

FIGURE 20.62. Map showing the movement of a Pink-footed Shearwater.

Some of these species have other unique adaptations for their long journeys. For example, albatrosses can lock out their wing joints, their "elbows", and take advantage of wind currents to avoid having to expend energy by flapping their wings. This technique is known as **dynamic soaring**.

Tubenoses are some of the most interesting animals to track because in their search for nutrition they are some of the farthest migrating birds. These seabirds often have hooked beaks to assist with catching fish and squid. They also commonly eat krill and plankton. Like penguins, tubenoses mate for life and have unique courting behaviors.

FIGURE 20.63. A Cape Petrel soars above the ocean surface near Drake's Passage in the Southern Ocean. During the winter, this species has been spotted as far north as the Galapagos Islands.

FIGURE 20.64. A Black-footed Albatross chick sits on the beach as two adult Laysan Albatross take flight over the water in the Northwestern Hawaiian Islands. Albatrosses often travel thousands of miles, for example from the Northwestern Hawaiian Islands to islands off Alaska, to gather food for their chicks, who remain at the nest.

Pelicans and Other Diving Birds

This group of birds lives along seacoasts, often in colonies, and hunts for their prey by diving into the ocean. Although beak shape varies, diving birds in pursuit of food generally have long, hooked beaks to catch and carry fish. Some eat their prey while flying.

Pelicans are large birds with deep bills. In the United States, Brown Pelicans are found along the East and California Coasts, throughout the Gulf of Mexico, and along Puerto Rico. They splash into the ocean, take a gulp of water and fish in their large beak, squeeze the water out of their beak pouch, and swallow the fish whole. The American White Pelican, which breeds only at inland locations, dips its head in both salt- and freshwater bodies to catch fish. This species is both marine and aquatic.

FIGURE 20.65. Pelicans, such as the Brown Pelican shown here, use their large bills to scoop up their prey and swallow it whole. Because they feed by diving into water, pelicans are very susceptible to oil pollution.

FIGURE 20.66. The American White Pelican is a very large bird that breeds in the Midwest and Western United States. In the winter, these birds are seen as far south as Central America. This species relies on both saltwater and freshwater environments.

Another type of bird in this group, frigate birds, is interesting because they do not typically enter the water—their feathers are not very waterproof. This fact is true although they spend the majority of their lives at sea. Instead, they snatch fish, turtle hatchlings, and other foods at the surface or bully other birds into regurgitating their meal in mid-flight. Their hooked beaks are well equipped for grabbing food on the go.

FIGURE 20.67. A frigate bird soars above the Northwestern Hawaiian Islands. These birds spend most of their time soaring above the sea, swooping down to snatch food. They return to land for nesting.

In contrast to frigate birds, the cormorant is a common, long-necked bird that dives and chases its prey underwater. Cormorants prey mostly on fish and nest on cliffs and rocks of coastlines. Some species are also found in freshwater habitats; they are a highly adaptable group.

FIGURE 20.68. There are about 40 species of cormorant found around the world. This Brandt's Cormorant is common on the Pacific Coast and is often seen diving into the water to catch a variety of fish species.

Gulls and Terns

Gulls are usually associated with the shore, perhaps because of their tendency to eat anything available—even the food out of your hand. There are many different species of gulls. The Greater Herring Gull and Black-backed Gull are particularly common in the United States. Gulls generally scavenge food from landfills and garbage cans and feed on dead, or sometimes living, marine animals, including crabs and invertebrates.

Terns are relatives of gulls. Many species undertake long migrations, including the Arctic Tern, which flies from the Arctic to the Antarctic. Terns tend to be lighter than gulls and have thinner, more pointed wings. Most plunge into the water to catch fish, although others skim for their prey at the surface.

FIGURE 20.69. Black-backed Gulls, like other gulls, often scavenge for food. The term *seagull*, although commonly used, is inaccurate and misleading. Many species of gulls are strictly inland, freshwater birds.

FIGURE 20.70. A Brown Noddy guards its egg in the Northwestern Hawaiian Islands. This species relies on large, predatory fish to scare prey up to the surface.

7. Of the adaptations discussed, which specific characteristic of seabirds allows them to inhabit a wider range of latitudes than marine reptiles?

Elaborate

Sea Turtle Nesting

While seabirds and sea turtles spend most of their lives at sea, they must return to land to nest. Seabirds tend to nest in colonies, which are large groups of nests, often on remote islands.

The reproductive and nesting behaviors of sea turtles are extremely interesting. In several species of sea turtles, females return to the actual nesting beach on which they themselves hatched, in order to dig their nests. In the United States, the sandy, coastal beaches, and barrier islands off the many coasts of North Carolina, South Carolina, Georgia, Florida, Alabama, Mississippi, Louisiana, Texas, Puerto Rico, the U.S. Virgin Islands, Hawaii, Guam, and American Samoa are critical nesting habitats for most species of sea turtles. Sea turtles nest in other areas around the world as well, including in Africa, Asia, the Middle East, and Australia.

FIGURE 20.71. Loggerhead Sea Turtle laying eggs. This sea turtle species is most common along the East Coast of the United States.

During the spring and summer months, sea turtles mate just off the coasts of these areas. Several weeks or months later, the female turtle climbs up the beach and builds a nest in the sand by digging a hole, and deposits her eggs. Adult female turtles return to the same beach for nest-building. Male turtles almost never leave the ocean. Female turtles lay eggs 3–5 times during the summer nesting season and will lay between 80 and 90 eggs in each nest, depending on the species. Once incubated, the hatchling sea turtles emerge from the nest and scramble toward the water, trying to avoid predators such as seabirds, raccoons, crabs, and other hungry beach dwellers.

FIGURE 20.72. Loggerhead Sea Turtle covering up her eggs. In the United States, the nesting season peaks in June and July.

FIGURE 20.73. Loggerhead Sea Turtle returning to the ocean. Only female Loggerheads return to shore after leaving land as hatchlings.

FIGURE 20.74. Hatchlings making their way to the ocean. Scientists believe that once they enter the surf, the hatchlings swim out to sea for several days.

Some beaches are closed to the public at night during nesting season. Inadvertently walking on nests can disturb or kill the eggs, and nesting females are known to get "spooked" by beach activity, preventing them from laying their eggs. Building lights are another source of disturbance. Scientists believe that nesting females prefer dark beaches for nest-building. When hatchlings break out of nests, their instinct tells them to head for the ocean. One way they seem to orient themselves is by seeing the natural starlight and moonlight reflecting off the ocean. Lights on land disorient turtles, causing them to head in the wrong direction, usually resulting in them getting picked off by a predator or dehydrating in the next day's sunlight, or even being run over by cars.

Observations of sea turtles heading in the wrong direction have, over the years, led to the inference that the lights were affecting these hatchlings. The result is that local citizens, organizations, communities, cities, states, and even the federal government have teamed up to enact regulations intended to protect these animals. Recall that all species of sea turtles are listed as threatened or endangered under the Endangered Species Act. Many communities have rules that prevent nighttime lights near the beach during nesting season. Outdoor lights on the beach also are often prohibited. People in homes and hotels along the beach are asked to use thick curtains to prevent their lights from being visible outside. Streetlights often have dim yellow bulbs that are not as disruptive to the turtles.

FIGURE 20.75. Hatchling emerging. Once they emerge from the nests, hatchlings are susceptible to predation by birds, raccoons, and even dogs.

See Page 694 for how to access e-Tools.

View the *Videos of Several Species of Sea Turtles as They Go Through the Nesting Process*.

e-Tools

Cyberlab

Lights at Night

1. View the *Earth at Night Map* from the e-Tools and zoom in to the state you were assigned.

e-Tools

www

FIGURE 20.76. Screenshot of the *Earth at Night Map*.

2. Using the map buttons at the top of the web page, or an atlas, determine which areas (counties, parishes, cities, parks, communities) in the specific area you were assigned have the most and least light pollution.

3. Based on your findings and the information you have read, how might sea turtles be affected by light pollution in the area you observed?

Evaluate

1. In a Venn Diagram, compare and contrast the characteristics of marine birds and marine reptiles.

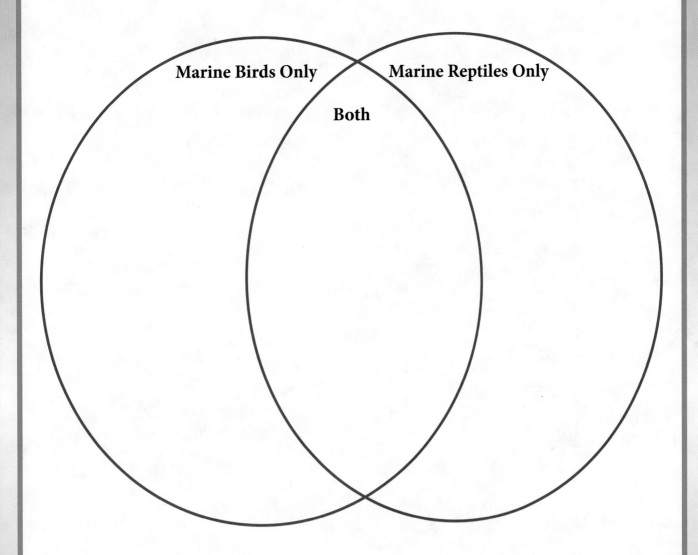

Marine Birds Only

Marine Reptiles Only

Both

2. Choose one type of marine bird and one type of marine reptile. For each, describe at least two characteristics that exhibit adaptions to the marine environment.

3. Explain why birds have adapted to a wider variety of latitudes on Earth than have reptiles.

21

Marine Mammals

INSIDE:

Objectives

You will be able to:

✔ **Observe and describe characteristics and behaviors of marine mammals.**

✔ **Classify marine mammals into their major groups.**

✔ **Give examples of behaviors observed in marine mammals.**

✔ **Describe ways in which marine biologists study marine mammals.**

 Benchmarks

1a. The ocean is the dominant physical feature on our planet Earth—covering approximately 70% of the planet's surface. There is one ocean with many ocean basins, such as the North Pacific, South Pacific, North Atlantic, South Atlantic, Indian, and Arctic.

5a. Ocean life ranges in size from the smallest virus to the largest animal that has lived on Earth, the blue whale.

5e. The ocean is three-dimensional, offering vast living space and diverse habitats from the surface through the water column to the seafloor. Most of the living space on Earth is in the ocean.

7a. The ocean is the last and largest unexplored place on Earth; less than 5% of it has been explored. This is the great frontier for the next generation's explorers and researchers, where they will find great opportunities for inquiry and investigation.

7b. Understanding the ocean is more than a matter of curiosity. Exploration, inquiry, and study are required to better understand ocean systems and processes.

7f. Ocean exploration is truly interdisciplinary. It requires close collaboration among biologists, chemists, climatologists, computer programmers, engineers, geologists, meteorologists, and physicists and new ways of thinking.

Engage

Scientific Studies of Marine Mammals

As you know, most of the living space on Earth is found in the ocean. The ocean is huge, and it contains huge animals—including the largest animal, the Blue Whale. Marine mammals are some of the most familiar ocean organisms. It is common to see images of whales breaching, Polar Bears stalking prey, or sea lions barking in commercials in today's media. Perhaps you have "met" some of these animals in real life at a local zoo or aquarium or on a visit to the ocean. This group of animals gets a lot of attention, perhaps because the animals are our most closely related ocean dwellers. Many of their characteristics and behaviors are familiar to humans, but there is still so much for scientists to study and learn.

FIGURE 21.1. The Blue Whale is the largest animal ever to have lived on Earth. Seen here is its tail fin, or fluke. The tails of marine mammals move up and down, in contrast to those of fish, which move from side to side.

FIGURE 21.2. California Sea Lions resting on the rocks in Monterey, California. Sea lions and seals can often be observed onshore relaxing, breeding, or nursing. These and other marine mammals are very familiar to us.

In Lesson 16: Population Changes, you learned that the groups of marine mammals on Earth today are descendants of animals that returned to the sea. Living in ocean habitats has allowed some of these groups to develop extremely interesting characteristics—and some incredible sizes. Use the chart on the next page to assist you in better visualizing the sizes of land and marine mammals, including the largest in each habitat, the African Elephant and Blue Whale, respectively.

FIGURE 21.3. The largest land animal is the African Elephant, yet this mammal's size seems small next to that of the Blue Whale.

Species	Length or Height in meters (feet)	Weight in kilograms (pounds)
Human (U.S. Male, 20+ years)	Typical is 1.8 meters (~5 feet 9.4 inches).	Typical is 88.3 kilograms (~195 pounds).
Human (U.S. Female, 20+ years)	Typical is 1.6 meters (~5 feet 3.8 inches).	Typical is 74.7 kilograms (~165 pounds).
Giraffe	up to 5.5 meters (~18 feet)	up to 1,900 kilograms (~4,200 pounds)
One-Horned Asian Rhinoceros	1.8 meters (~6 feet) tall, up to 3.7 meters (~12 feet) long	up to 2,300 kilograms (~5,000 pounds)
Nile Hippopotamus	1.4–1.7 meters (~4.5–5.5 feet) tall, up to 4.6 meters (~15 feet) long	up to 3,600 kilograms (~8,000 pounds)
Northern Elephant Seal	4 meters (~13 feet) long	up to 2,000 kilograms (~4,500 pounds)
African Elephant	up to 3.4 meters (~11 feet) tall, up to 7.6 meters (~25 feet) long	up to 6,400 kilograms (~14,000 pounds)
Sperm Whale	16 meters (~52 feet) long	up to 41,000 kilograms (~90,000 pounds)
North Atlantic Right Whale	14 meters (~45 feet) long	up to 64,000 kilograms (~140,000 pounds)
Fin Whale	23 meters (~75 feet) long	up to 73,000 kilograms (~160,000 pounds)
Blue Whale	While males are enormous, the somewhat larger females can approach 33 meters (~108 feet) long.	Females have been found to be over 150,000 kilograms (~330,000 pounds).

* The lengths, heights, and weights above represent males, with the exception of the Human, which includes females, and the Blue Whale, which represents females.

1. Create a visual representation to scale to compare *either* the lengths (or heights) or the weights of these animals. Include at least one marine mammal. You may draw the animal or use symbols to create comparative representations.

2. Based on the data and your visual representation, what pattern do you see?

FIGURE 21.4. A scuba diver encounters a much larger curious Humpback Whale in its breeding grounds near the Dominican Republic. During their seasonal migrations, Humpbacks travel incredible distances.

Explore

Marine biologists who study marine mammals study many aspects of the animals' lives. In previous Lessons, you learned about scientists using satellite tracking to study large- and small-scale movements of animals, including marine mammals. For example, scientists use satellite tags to study the migrations of Ringed Seals in the Atlantic and Arctic, movements of False Killer Whales around the Hawaiian Islands or **foraging** (feeding) trips of California Sea Lions in the Pacific.

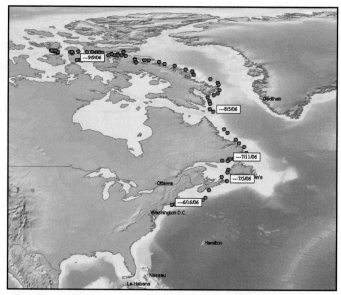

FIGURE 21.5. Map showing locations of a Ringed Seal.

FIGURE 21.6. False Killer Whale.

FIGURE 21.7. Ringed Seal.

FIGURE 21.8. California Sea Lion pup.

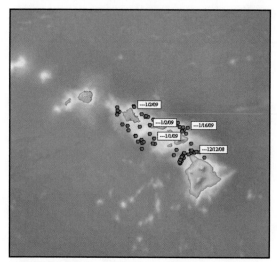

FIGURE 21.9. Map showing locations of a False Killer Whale.

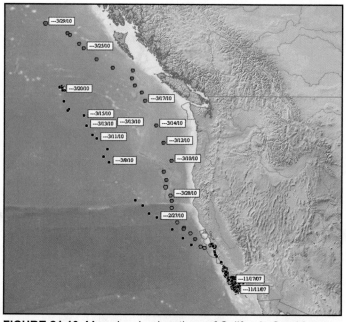

FIGURE 21.10. Map showing locations of California Sea Lions.

In addition to studying satellite tracks of marine mammals, biologists go out "into the field" on boats, walking along beaches, or by other means, to observe and study animals in their natural habitats. For instance, they conduct genetic analyses to learn about their ancestry, take blood samples to learn about susceptibility and resistance to disease, and use various types of tags to observe their migratory movements and underwater behaviors. An important aspect of studying and learning about marine mammals is conducting field research. One area of study is animal behavior.

FIGURE 21.11. Scientists in Antarctica prepare to take measurements of Southern Elephant Seals. This is the largest seal species.

FIGURE 21.12. Abandoned chairs on a beach in the Northwestern Hawaiian Islands due to the presence of an endangered marine mammal, the Hawaiian Monk Seal (near the middle of the photograph). If you encounter endangered marine mammals while on your boat, place the engine in neutral and wait for the animal to leave the area.

Studying animal behavior is no easy task. First, all marine mammals are protected by the Marine Mammal Protection Act, an act of the United States Congress in 1972. Many mammals are endangered or threatened species and are also afforded protection under the Endangered Species Act. As a result of these and other laws and regulations, scientists must obtain special permits to get close to these animals and perform research on them. For example, under the Endangered Species Act, which is generally updated every few years, humans must remain 50 meters (~150 feet) from Hawaiian Monk Seals. When one of these seals comes up on a Hawaii beach, all of the beachgoers are asked to move, affording the endangered mammal its space to relax.

To observe animal behaviors in the field scientists must follow strict protocols. Animal research groups use standard recording sheets in which they keep track of the date, time, latitude and longitude coordinates, and other general information. They also record behaviors observed and any measurements or other tests conducted on or with the animals. Scientists attempt to be as descriptively accurate as possible, which can be a challenge while working in the field, as they have to deal with rough seas, changing weather conditions, and many organisms to observe at once.

FIGURE 21.13. Scientist observes the behaviors of Killer Whales, or "Orcas", in the field in the Puget Sound off Washington State and the Canadian Province of British Columbia. Fieldwork can be an important part of marine biologists' research. Learning how animals spend their time can help scientists develop plans to protect them.

See Page 694 for how to access e-Tools.

Cyberlab

Observing Marine Mammal Behavior

In this Cyberlab, you will use videos collected by scientists in the field to simulate fieldwork in which you study behavior. For this activity, you will record the animal species as well as any behaviors you observe. Read the information below in the *Marine Mammal Behavior Guide*, which suggests some aspects of movement to look for when recording behavioral data.

e-Tools

Marine Mammal Behavior Guide		
Behavior	**Description**	**Things to Note**
Swimming	Marine mammals swim for many reasons—to forage for food, escape predation, migrate, etc.	• Is the animal underwater? Does it break the surface? • Which body structures are involved in swimming (e.g., tail, fins)? • Is the animal swimming from place to place, in circles, etc.?
Porpoising	This activity is common in dolphins, porpoises, and sea lions. Animals are observed jumping out of water for short distances as they swim forward.	• For how long is the animal out of the water?
Group behaviors	Many species of marine mammals may be observed in groups. For example, dolphins often travel in pods and exhibit social behaviors such as playing. Some seal species lounge on the beach and rocks.	• Approximately how many animals do you observe? • How do the animals interact with one another?
Feeding	All animals, of course, must feed to obtain energy and nutrients to perform life functions. Differences may be observed in the types of food eaten, body structures used, etc.	• What body structures are involved in feeding? • What type of food is the animal eating? • Is the animal feeding above or below water, or on land?
Nursing	A characteristic of mammals is that they nurse their young.	• Are the mother and baby on land or in the water? • For how long does the baby nurse?
Breathing	Marine mammals, like all mammals, breathe air. Animals spending a lot of time underwater, such as whales and seals, will often be observed surfacing to breathe.	• Are there any special behaviors associated with breathing? • What body structures are involved in breathing? (Hint: Not all marine mammals rely primarily on noses and mouths like humans do.)

1. Watch at least 6 of the videos available in the Cyberlab, choosing from at least 3 different marine mammal groups.

2. As you watch each video, carefully observe and record the behaviors exhibited by the animal(s). On the data sheet, check off behaviors you observe. Give a short description of each using the Marine Mammal Behavior Guide for assistance. You may need to watch the videos more than once, a luxury that scientists don't often have in the field.

Marine Mammal Observation Sheet							
Species name	Behaviors Observed						Description of Behaviors
	Swimming	Porpoising	Group Behaviors	Feeding	Nursing	Breathing	

3. Based on your observations, what are some scientific questions that you could ask about the animals' behaviors?

4. Answer the Questions below:

    a. Why is it important to conduct field studies in addition to satellite tracking?

    b. Why would studying fish in the field be different from marine mammals?

FIGURE 21.14. Bottlenose Dolphins are some of the most familiar marine animals to humans, thanks to television, aquarium visits, etc. In the wild, one can observe these marine mammals porpoising, swimming near boats, or even leaping high out of the water.

Explain

The Marine Mammals

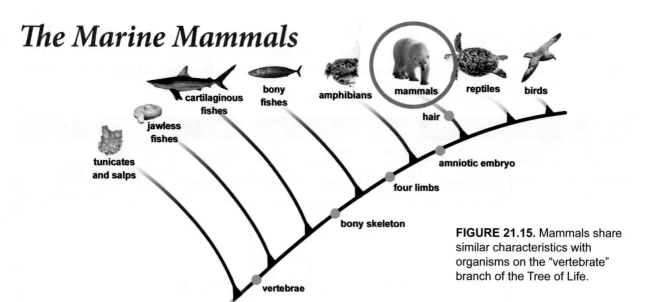

FIGURE 21.15. Mammals share similar characteristics with organisms on the "vertebrate" branch of the Tree of Life.

Marine mammals are found in different marine ecosystems, from polar seas to coral reefs, mangrove forests to sandy beaches. Whether they inhabit land, seawater, or fresh water, mammals share the following characteristics, with few exceptions:

- Mammals give birth to live young. Baby mammals develop inside the mother.
- Mammals nurse their young. Mother mammals produce milk.
- Mammals are endothermic, sometimes called "warm blooded". They can maintain their body temperature separately from their environment.
- Mammals have hair, which can either be full, such as a Polar Bear, or just a few hairs on the chin, such as a dolphin.

Marine mammals have been classified by scientists into a few major Groups:

- Cetaceans (pronounced: seh-TAY-shŭns) (whales, dolphins, and porpoises)
- Pinnipeds (seals, sea lions, and walruses)
- Sirenians (pronounced: sī-REEN-ee-ins) (manatees and dugongs)
- Polar Bears
- Sea Otters

Cetaceans

For swimming, these marine mammals have sleek, bullet-shaped bodies, and a strong tail that they use to propel themselves. Most have a long "mouth" area, or **rostrum**, and a dorsal fin on their back. Cetaceans move their tails, or **flukes**, up and down to push themselves through water. Fish, in contrast, move their tails from side to side.

FIGURE 21.16. A Humpback Whale surfaces, exposing its blowhole. The blowhole can be seen in action during the Cyberlab in the **Explore** section of the Lesson.

Cetaceans must breathe voluntarily — unlike humans who breathe without thinking about it. To breathe, cetaceans come up to the ocean's surface and breathe through a special hole on the top of their head called a **blowhole**. Deep-diving cetaceans often remain near the surface for several minutes to "catch their breath" before heading back down for a dive. While a whale is at the surface, observers will often see the cloud-like "blow", which is a mixture of air, including carbon dioxide and unused oxygen, liquid water spray, and mucus.

Unlike most mammals, cetaceans do not have much hair. Instead they have layers of fat under their skin called **blubber**. Blubber helps to keep the animals warm and to regulate their body temperatures.

FIGURE 21.17. A North Atlantic Right Whale and calf are seen swimming off of the U.S. East Coast. Notice the "double blow", which is characteristic of right whales.

There are two major groups of cetaceans. One group is the toothed whales. They include the dolphins and porpoises, and some species of whales including the Beluga Whale, Killer Whale, and Sperm Whale. Most toothed whales eat fish or squid and use their teeth to rip apart their prey. Recall that many toothed whales use sound to echolocate, navigate, and communicate.

While most cetaceans are marine mammals, there are several species of dolphin, including pink dolphins in the Amazon River, which live in freshwater habitats and are therefore considered to be aquatic mammals, like beavers and river otters.

The other major group of cetaceans includes species that all have large "broom-like" plates in their mouths called **baleen**; they are known as the "baleen whales". Their baleen allows these animals to strain their food out from the water. Their diet tends to include smaller prey such as krill, a shrimp-like animal, small schooling fish and squid. Examples of baleen whales include Blue Whales, Humpback Whales, Gray Whales, and Fin Whales. NOAA describes 11 species of baleen whales and 67 species of toothed whales.

The behaviors of cetaceans vary widely by species. For example, Spinner Dolphins swim in large pods, whereas Blue Whales are observed typically alone or in pairs. Some cetaceans, like Harbor Porpoises, prefer shallow waters, whereas species like Sperm Whales are known to make very deep dives chasing their favorite prey—squid. Cetaceans communicate with one another using clicks, whistles, and groans, some of which can be heard underwater over very long distances.

FIGURE 21.18. These Northern Right Whale Dolphins, photographed off of Washington State, are easily identified by their lack of a dorsal fin. Like other dolphins and porpoises, these animals are toothed whales.

Pinnipeds

Pinnipeds are unique marine mammals because they must come on land to give birth and to nurse their young. While they use both land and sea habitats, they are much more agile in the water. Pinnipeds have front and hind flippers. They use their long front flippers to propel themselves and steer through water. Pinnipeds are found in a range of marine environments. For example, one might observe Leopard Seals in icy Antarctic waters, Ribbon Seals in the Arctic, Harbor Seals resting along temperate shorelines, or Hawaiian Monk Seals diving near a coral reef.

There are three main groups of pinnipeds: eared seals, true seals, and walruses.

FIGURE 21.19. Sea lions and fur seals can rotate their hind flippers forward, allowing them to walk on land. California Sea Lions, like the one seen here, are often a nuisance to fishers and boaters as they like to rest on docks, buoys, and even boats!

FIGURE 21.20. Walruses rest on sea ice before diving to the seafloor to find tasty mollusks and crustaceans. These Arctic mammals were once hunted for their tusks. Some indigenous peoples still practice limited hunting of walruses, and traditionally use the animals' tusks, blubber, meat, and hide.

FIGURE 21.21. Harbor Seals hauled out on a Northern California Shoreline. Many pinniped species form colonies for breeding, nursing young, and relaxing between foraging trips.

Eared seals, a group which includes the seals with fur and the sea lions, have an earflap on the outside of their bodies. They use their longer flippers to walk on land by twisting their back limbs forward. Eared seal species include California Sea Lions, Steller Sea Lions, and Northern Fur Seals. True seals move on land by flopping around on their bellies. Species of true seals include Hawaiian Monk Seals, Harbor Seals, and Ringed Seals. Most true and eared seals eat fish.

Pinnepeds are excellent swimmers and can chase down fish underwater. Walruses are distinguished by their long tusks. They use these tusks to help dig up shellfish from the seafloor, as well as to break through ice and haul themselves up onto ice floes. Unlike other pinnipeds, walruses have very little hair on their bodies, which are covered in thick skin. The coarse, sensitive bristles around their mouths are shed and replaced yearly.

Many pinniped species relax, or "haul out", on land in large groups called colonies. This is true when mothers give birth to, or pup, their young, and also when the animals lose their fur, or molt. Some species, such as Northern Elephant Seals, undergo a period of time in which they lose their entire top layer of skin and hair.

Haul out areas are not always peaceful, however. Some pinniped species engage in violent fights, usually over mates. In Northern Elephant Seals, for example, the males establish dominance over one another through intense fighting, winning the right to mate with many females. Walruses follow similar procedures.

Sirenians

The sirenians include manatees and dugongs. Dugongs are found in the Indo-Pacific, in shallow waters of Eastern Africa, the South Pacific, and Australia. Manatees live on both sides of the Atlantic Ocean, in shallow waters near Western Africa, Eastern South America, the Caribbean, the Gulf of Mexico, and along the Southeastern Coast of the United States.

These animals are sometimes referred to as "sea cows", and are plump, vegetarian marine mammals with flattened tails. Like cetaceans, sirenians spend their entire lives in water. Like walruses, they have stiff bristles around their mouths.

FIGURE 21.22. A Florida Manatee, one of three manatee species, floats near the surface in a mangrove forest. Manatees and dugongs, the two types of sirenians, are found in warm waters.

Polar Bears

Most members of the bear family are land-dwellers, but Polar Bears spend most of their lives at sea on sea ice, hence they are considered to be marine mammals. The habitat of these carnivores includes far northern land, sea and, most importantly, sea ice. Polar Bears have coarse, hollow fur that traps heat close to their bodies, helping them to survive in their cold Arctic environment. Their white color camouflages them as they stalk their favorite prey, seals. Each individual hair on the bear's body is a tube that channels heat from the Sun directly to the layer of black skin that helps them stay warm.

Polar Bears live throughout Earth's entire circumpolar Arctic Region. They are found in Russia, Canada, Greenland, Norway, and the United States. There are several thousand Polar Bears in Alaska and less than 25,000 worldwide. Female Polar Bears can bear young when they are as young as 5 years old; they can live to over 30 years of age. They build a den for their young by digging into large snowdrifts. The den provides shelter for the mother and her cubs. Females will generally have twins. The mother bear stays with her cubs for at least two years, teaching them how to survive in the polar seas.

Polar Bears were listed as a threatened species in 2008. In 2010, the United States Fish and Wildlife Service designated areas along the Alaskan Coast as critical habitats for the marine mammal. These habitats included areas on the Alaskan Mainland and nearby islands that are used for denning, as well as areas of sea ice that are important for food gathering.

FIGURE 21.23. A Polar Bear cub curiously stands on its hind legs while its mother stays nearby. Polar Bears are the only bears that spend most of their lives at sea.

Sea Otters

Sea Otters are more closely related to land and freshwater animals such as weasels and river otters than other marine mammals. They do not have blubber. Their ability to survive the cold ocean water comes from extremely dense, water-resistant fur. Throughout history, Sea Otters have been hunted for their beautiful coats. In the United States waters, Sea Otters are found along the West Coast and northward along Alaska.

FIGURE 21.24. A Sea Otter floats among kelp, as they are commonly observed off the West Coast of the United States. Notice the animal's long whiskers, which are very sensitive and are useful for finding food in murky water.

Although they can only hold their breath for a few minutes, Sea Otters are very good divers. They gather benthic invertebrates including crabs, clams, snails, octopuses, sea urchins, and Abalone to eat, putting them in competition with fishers. They tend to float on their backs and use their teeth or rocks to break open shelled food items. Sea Otters are very flexible as their lack of a collarbone allows them to both perform twisting maneuvers in and out of kelp and to groom their entire body. Their hind limbs are very flipper-like, allowing them to propel through water. A Sea Otter pup typically weighs a couple of kilograms, up to 5 pounds, and adult females generally weigh in the 20–30 kilograms (~44–66 pounds) range, making these animals the smallest marine mammals.

3. Compare and contrast the cetaceans and pinnipeds.

Observing Marine Mammals in the Field

In the **Explore** section, you observed videos of marine mammals taken in the field. In real life, it is very important that all humans practice responsible viewing behaviors. Advice like this may sound obvious, but sometimes when humans encounter marine life, particularly marine mammals, they feel compelled to try to feed or touch the animals. Such behaviors can damage habitats, hurt the animals or, in rare cases, can result in injury or death to the person. Seals and dolphins, for example, have been known to bite humans to protect themselves. Breaching whales can land on a boat.

FIGURE 21.25. It may seem tempting to try to touch or feed wild animals like these Pacific White-sided Dolphins off the coast of California. For their protection and yours, remain safe distances from any animal you encounter in the wild.

The following holds true not just for mammals, but for all animals. Here are several rules of thumb to keep in mind when encountering wildlife:

FIGURE 21.26. Some marine mammals, such as the Hawaiian Monk Seal, have additional protections due to the Endangered Species Act. Sometimes humans must move away from these and other pinnipeds during chance encounters in order to comply with regulations. An account in Hawaii tells of a seal borrowing a tourist's beach towel—which the woman had to relinquish to the endangered mammal.

- Never touch, handle, or try to ride animals. If you are snorkeling, scuba diving, swimming, or in your boat, do not try to pet a dolphin, manatee, fish, sea turtle, or any other animal. It is easy to hurt animals, for example, by wiping scales off of a fish or introducing bacteria to a seal.

- Never feed wild animals. This includes trying to attract animals using food items or other decoys. Animals fed by humans may become sick or die from food not healthful for their species or containing contaminants. Animals that become used to humans become more vulnerable to being hit by boats or entangled in fishing gear.

- Do not approach wildlife. Never chase animals, whether you are in a boat, on foot, or using another form of transportation. These behaviors can cause animals distress and endanger them. Instead, use binoculars, zoom lenses, or other technologies that allow you to observe them from afar.

Remember, all marine mammals are protected by the Marine Mammal Protection Act. Many are also protected by the Endangered Species Act. These and other regulations make it illegal to approach or harass these animals. In some cases, the law dictates the distance from which you must observe animals. In general, a recommended distance for viewing is around 50 meters (~55 yards).

If you suspect that a marine animal you are observing is sick or injured, do not try to help the animal yourself. Each region of the United States has a network of scientists, veterinarians, and others trained in the rescue and rehabilitation of marine animals, known as a **stranding network**. Report any problems to the stranding network, and let the professionals take care of the animal.

FIGURE 21.27. A North Atlantic Right Whale entangled in fishing gear, which is visible near the animal's head and tail. Marine mammals can become ill or injured due to natural causes, but many injuries are the result of human activities. If you are a fisher, dispose of your fishing line responsibly—do not throw it into the water.

FIGURE 21.28. Marine mammals, like this Northern Fur Seal, may become entangled in fishing gear or other debris. If you observe any animal that appears hurt, let the experts help. Do not attempt to assist the animal yourself.

Activity

See Page 694 for how to access e-Tools.

View the **Whale Fluke Catalog** from e-Tools.

e-Tools

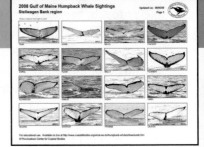

FIGURE 21.29. Screenshot of **Whale Fluke Catalog**.

Identifying Individual Whales

Scientists are constantly gaining insights into the behavior of marine animals. They learn about a variety of behaviors and family structures in order to better understand how the animals use their environments, communicate, care for young, and more. One way in which scientists study cetaceans is by observing characteristic markings on individual animals. In dolphins, biologists note scars, body markings, and the shape of the dorsal fin. For some whale species scientists use the patterns observed on the animals' flukes.

Some marine biologists liken a Humpback Whale's distinctive fluke patterns to a fingerprint. No two whales have the exact same patterns. You will examine the flukes of several whales that were photographed during Humpback Whale tagging cruises. Over time, a number of these whales were given satellite tags for tracking. Others were seen feeding in the research area, but not tagged. The catalog is a collaborative project of the Center for Coastal Studies in Provincetown, Massachusetts, along with the Stellwagen Bank National Marine Sanctuary. Similar studies are conducted in other areas of the world, as Humpback Whales are found throughout the ocean.

FIGURE 21.30. A Humpback Whale breaches in open water off the coast of Southern California. Marine biologists use many different techniques to find the answers to their research questions.

Humpback Whale tails are classified from all-white to all-black, with varying amounts of pigmentation and scarring in between. The range goes from 1 (all-white) to 5 (all-black).

FIGURE 21.31. Map of Cape Cod on Massachusetts features the town of Provincetown, a popular summer destination for whale watching, on its tip.

When you look at the undersides of the flukes, determine the white-to-black ratio and look for distinctive marks which are usually scars. The most distinctive marks are usually the basis for the animal's name. In the **Whale Fluke Catalog** within the e-Tools, look at the whale, Apex, on Page 10 with the inverted "V", or mountaintop, on the right fluke. See Dracula on Page 3 and the two "fangs" on its left fluke. See Liner on Page 7 with a line on its right fluke. Sometimes the whale's name is based on the shape of the trailing edge of its tail.

FIGURE 21.32.
Distribution map of Humpback Whales shows this species is found throughout the world's ocean. This cetacean species undertakes long migrations, and scientists use many techniques for studying these animals.

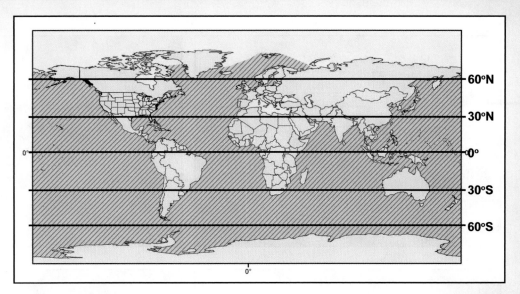

1. Copy a table similar to the one below into your notebook. Compare each photograph in this activity to the *Whale Fluke Catalog* and identify the individual animals.

Photo	Name
A	
B	
C	
D	
E	
F	
G	
H	
I	
J	
K	
L	

2. Answer the Questions below:

a. Is identifying individual whales easy or difficult? What would have made the task easier?

b. Why is it useful for marine biologists to identify individual animals? Give at least two possible reasons.

c. Give one advantage and one disadvantage of photograph identification as a research technique.

d. What can scientists learn from satellite tracking that they may not be able to learn from identifying individual animals?

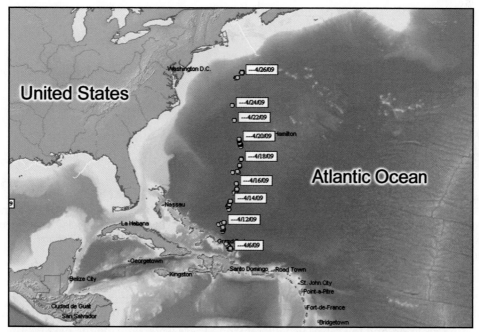

FIGURE 21.33. Satellite tagging of Humpback Whales and other whale species reveal their large-scale movements. Scientists also study these animals in the field to learn details about their behaviors, family structures, and more.

Humpback Whale Behaviors

Knowing the names of individual Humpback Whales greatly helps researchers in the field. Teams of scientists organized by NOAA's Stellwagen Bank National Marine Sanctuary went to study whales and place different types of tags on them, including SPOTs and SRDLs, about which you read in Lesson 5: Migrations in the Sea. Recall that SRDLs allow scientists to record oceanographic conditions and diving behaviors of marine animals.

FIGURE 21.34. A Humpback Whale with its pectoral fin out of the water, possibly engaging in pectoral fin slapping. This and other behaviors may be one way in which whales communicate with one another.

By identifying the individual animals, the scientists were able to know which animals were tagged and additional information about them, such as their age, sex, and areas in which they are frequently observed. For example, if scientists snap a photograph of a mother and calf, they now know the approximate age of the calf, as well as that the older whale is a female. Wildlife biologists can also determine if a whale is associating with any other individuals on a regular basis or engaging in group behaviors such as **cooperative feeding**, in which whales work together to herd and stun prey. This behavior, sometimes called **bubble netting**, occurs when a whale swims in a circular pattern below prey (e.g., a school of small fish) and exhales, letting out bubbles that rush to the surface, taking the prey with them. The bubbles are in the shape of a cylinder, and it is inferred that the fish are trapped in that cylinder; the whale will swim through the cylinder with its mouth open and feed on the fish. Scientists have observed whales perform bubble netting as individuals and in groups.

FIGURE 21.35. Orcas in the Antarctic. Notice the animal farther from the camera is spyhopping, allowing it to view the icy surface waters. This behavior is observed in many cetaceans.

FIGURE 21.36. Whale flukes are helpful in identifying individual animals, but they may also be used to warn other whales or in other communications.

Because Humpback Whales have been studied on Stellwagen Bank for more than 30 years, there is a large database of whale sightings and family histories. For instance, mother whales bring their calves back to specific local feeding grounds, and the calves usually return to these waters during the next feeding season. For some Stellwagen Bank whales, researchers know two, three, and even four generations in whale families. For example, Thalassa, a whale photographed during the tagging cruise, is the daughter of Salt and the mother of several calves. One calf, Etch-A-Sketch, was also tagged for closer study during the cruise.

Studies of Humpback Whales, using a variety of techniques, have taught us that these animals engage in fascinating behaviors. By observing these behaviors repeatedly, scientists can develop hypotheses about their purposes. Behaviors include:

- **Spyhopping.** The whale rises vertically above the water's surface, sticking its head out. This allows the animal to see what is happening above the water.

- **Pectoral fin slapping.** The whale slaps one or both of its pectoral fins, or flippers, on the water. Scientists believe this may be a form of communication with other individuals.

- **Tail slapping.** A humpback slaps its flukes repetitively on the surface, which is thought to be a form of communication, possibly a warning to other whales.

- **Breaching.** The whale launches itself out of the water and lands on its back, causing a huge splash. This behavior is often observed in breeding grounds, during migrations, and at feeding grounds. Some scientists believe that it is associated with mating, communications, play, or all of these reasons, including some we haven't considered.

Study SpOtlight

Studying to Save Whales

Scientists conduct research for many reasons. In NOAA's Stellwagen Bank National Marine Sanctuary, the most important reason is conservation. Dr. David Wiley, Research Coordinator for the Sanctuary, explains that what scientists working with the Sanctuary do is identify conservation problems such as **ship strikes**, which are collisions between boats and whales. In turn, they assist whales by performing research to help find solutions to the problems.

Dr. Wiley and other scientists have worked diligently with members of the shipping industry in New England to change the locations of shipping lanes to prevent ship strikes. This goal was complex as it required years of data collection and interpretation. Researchers considered data sets such as sighting and distribution information indicating where whales were most likely to be found.

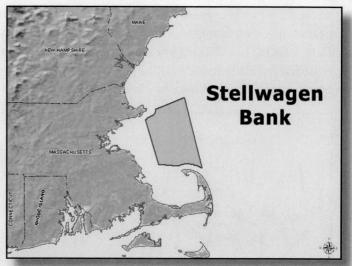

FIGURE 21.37. Map showing the location of Stellwagen Bank National Marine Sanctuary.

Another consideration was sediment type. On Stellwagen Bank, Humpback Whales feed primarily over sand; a favorite prey species in this area is the sand lance, or sand eel, which can burrow in the sediment. Several miles north, in areas over granite, the Humpbacks feed primarily on herring and squid. A model was developed to predict the locations of copepods, the favorite prey of North Atlantic Right Whales. When considering these data sets, scientists discovered that some of the locations of sandy bottoms, high copepod concentrations, and above-average whale sightings were smack in the middle of shipping lanes. With data in hand Dr. Wiley's team approached the shipping community to collaboratively decide locations to where the shipping lanes could be moved. They decided on lanes at locations with a mud and gravel bottom that was not copepod-heavy; the new course only took large ships several minutes out of their way.

In addition to being susceptible to ship strikes, whales are also affected by the noise produced by ships. Using underwater listening devices called **hydrophones**, Stellwagen scientists record underwater noise and discover places and times at which there is a lot of underwater noise. How can shipping interfere with whales' communication? Dr. Wiley explains: "We know that whales call for a reason, maybe to let other whales know where they are or the location of food. If they can no longer hear each other making these calls, that is a problem". Data collected in the Sanctuary suggest that ocean noise has reduced the communication space for North Atlantic Right Whales by close to 80%.

FIGURE 21.38. An acoustic tag is being placed on the back of a Humpback Whale. The tag is the small white object on the whale.

Wiley claims: "The evidence points to the acoustic space of whales being severely diminished by human-made noise in the ocean".

Another Stellwagen Bank project uses specialized tags to help indicate the types of behaviors in which whales are engaging. While satellite tagging is incredibly interesting and important, these specific tags give specialized data on a much finer scale. A special tag will indicate a whale's pitch, its front-to-back movement or roll, or side-to-side movement. It will provide the direction of movement as well as depth. It will also record every sound that the whale makes and hears. Using all of these data, scientists create careful models of animal movement for the express purpose of studying whale behavior. This example of scientists, technologists, and engineers working together to study a problem is one where a solution will follow.

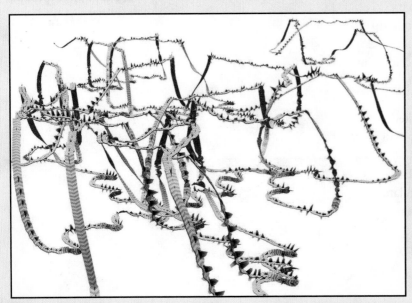

FIGURE 21.39. This is a 3-dimensional map of the movements of a Humpback Whale feeding along the ocean bottom over a period of several hours. The red lines on the ribbon indicate one-second intervals. The loops, turns, and rolls indicate the body position of the whale. Body rolls greater than 40 degrees are indicated in yellow. This behavior makes Humpback Whales vulnerable to gillnets and other fishing gear that is used along the seabed.

Evaluate

1. Describe at least 3 examples of behaviors exhibited by marine mammals. Be sure to indicate the types of mammals that engage in the behavior.

2. Observe each of the photographs below. Using what you know about the major groups of marine mammals and their characteristics, indicate the marine mammal group in which each animal would be classified.

FIGURE 21.40.

FIGURE 21.41.

FIGURE 21.42.

FIGURE 21.43.

FIGURE 21.44.

22

Relationships in the Sea

INSIDE:

Objectives

You will be able to:

✔ Describe examples of mutualism, parasitism, and commensalism in the ocean.

✔ Consider the costs and benefits of diverse reproductive strategies used by species.

✔ Record notes from secondary sources and attribute the sources of information recorded.

Benchmarks

5b. Most life in the ocean exists as microbes. Microbes are the most important primary producers in the ocean. Not only are they the most abundant life form in the ocean, they have extremely fast growth rates and life cycles.

5d. Ocean biology provides many unique examples of life cycles, adaptations, and important relationships among organisms (e.g., symbiosis, predator-prey dynamics, energy transfer) that do not occur on land.

5g. There are deep ocean ecosystems that are independent of energy from sunlight and photosynthetic organisms. Hydrothermal vents, submarine hot springs, and methane cold seeps rely only on chemical energy and chemosynthetic organisms to support life.

Engage

An Unlikely Pair

Have you ever seen two very different organisms together, and thought that they seemed like an odd pair? As you learned in Lesson 17: Food Webs in Action, the relationship between different species is often one of predator and prey—someone gets eaten. A sea star pries apart an oyster, or a seal snatches up an unsuspecting penguin. Sometimes, however, two species form an unusual relationship, similar to a tug-of-war game, in which the species each give and take from the other. Sometimes the relationship is beneficial for both organisms, other times one is harmed or unaffected.

Relationships between two or more different species are known as **symbiotic relationships**. Scientists estimate that up to 50% of species have some sort of symbiotic relationship with at least one other species.

FIGURE 22.1. In the biosphere, it is common for species to form relationships with one another. This photograph shows barnacles and other organisms growing on mussels.

Materials:

- Chart paper (to create a K-W-L chart)
- Markers

1. In groups, discuss all the possible relationships you can think of between different species—both in the ocean and on land.

   Create a K-W-L Chart. Divide the chart paper into 3 columns. Label the columns K, W, and L. K stands for What You Know, W for What You Want to Know, and L for What You Learned.

K	W	L

   a. In the first column, write down all the different relationships that your group _knows_ about.

   b. In the middle column, write down all the questions you have, what you _want_ to know about relationships between species. Include at least 3 questions for your group.

Explore

Part I: Conducting Background Research

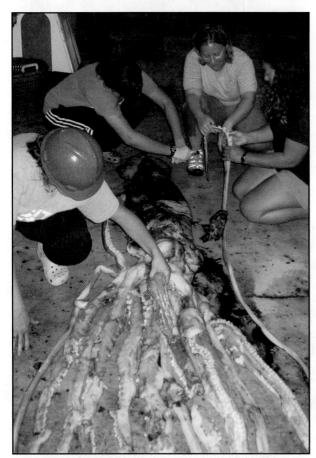

In this Lesson, you will be conducting background research on symbiotic relationships, using a variety of sources. Conducting background research is an important skill for scientists. Scientists must determine for themselves what is already known in their field before they proceed with new investigations. They use books, journal articles, and the Internet to do this. They may also talk with other researchers performing similar work directly, hear them speak at a conference, or contact them privately to ask about their work. This type of research, this establishment of a strong foundation in the subject matter, is called **secondary research**, as opposed to when you collect and analyze data yourself, which is **primary research**. In this Lesson, you will use secondary research to learn about one type of symbiotic relationship.

FIGURE 22.2. Scientists aboard a NOAA research vessel examine a giant squid. This work is an example of primary research, where scientists themselves are collecting and analyzing data.

FIGURE 22.3. When conducting research, it is important for scientists to learn what is already known about their topic. They use diverse sources to do so.

2. Draw this chart in your notebook. In your chart, list at least three types of resources that you could use to learn about symbiotic relationships. Note at least one pro and one con of each resource.

Resources	Pros	Cons

The Internet, invented only in the late 20th Century, has revolutionized the ways in which information is accessed and shared. Before you begin the activity, as a class you are going to review *how to find the most useful and accurate results* when using the Internet as a research tool. When conducting secondary research on the Internet, one thing to consider is the website from which you collect your information. Anyone can create a web page and write anything they want. To find accurate results, here are a few aspects of web pages to consider.

FIGURE 22.4. Online access to information allows for quick sharing of digital assets across the globe, but information may not always be reliable.

- *Who wrote the article? Where is the site housed?* Many web pages do not indicate who has authored them. If authors are noted, try to learn more information about them. Pay attention to where the website is housed; the URL (Uniform Resource Locator), or domain or "web address", will usually give you clues as to a website's origin. For example, good sources of scientific information include government and university sites. Scientists often work at these institutions. Their findings are reported through journal articles and then summarized on web pages aimed at educating the public.

   One can identify a government agency name by looking for a *.gov* indication at the end of many United States government website URLs (e.g., www.nasa.gov, www.noaa.gov). University sites normally include the school name or initials and have a *.edu* extension (e.g., you can visit the University of West Florida at www.uwf.edu or Cornell University at www.cornell.edu).

   Non-profit organizations, often denoted by a *.org* extension, may also be a good source of information. Such organizations include groups that conduct scientific studies as well as museums and science centers. Beware of political or special interest organizations, which do not usually share the most accurate, non-biased, and up-to-date scientific findings on their websites. Also beware of community encyclopedia sites, which allow almost anybody to contribute and update information. Most average citizens are not up to date on the latest scientific findings, so it may be best to forgo including sites that are open to public contributions when conducting secondary research for scientific purposes.

- *What are the sources of information?* Scientific articles on credible websites often include a bibliography or reference list that you may use to learn more about a topic. Additional links at the bottom or sides of a website should direct you to other reputable sources. Strong references will also introduce other specific scientific studies and reference them within the text. These additional sources can help you to verify details about what you are studying.

- *How current is the information?* Many web pages will indicate when they were last updated, often near the bottom of the page. Sources that are regularly updated are better supported and may indicate more reliable information. Another useful tip is to gather information from multiple websites and compare results. Accurate and accepted scientific ideas will be represented on several websites.

3. As an example of how to conduct research on the Internet, we are going to use a search engine to find out the life span of a Loggerhead Sea Turtle.

    a. Before you open your favorite search engine page:

        •   Guess how many hits you will get if you type "Loggerhead Sea Turtle".
        •   List 5 types of information you would expect to get in the first 5 hits.

    b. Try it. Type "Loggerhead Sea Turtle" in the search box and click Enter. How many website matches did you get?

    c. It might take hours to find the information you need with these results. Now type "Loggerhead Sea Turtle life span". Click Enter. How many website matches did you get?

    d. If you are specific in a search, you can decrease considerably the number of websites given in search results. To refine your search even more, you can use quotes around some words and group them. Try typing "loggerhead turtle" "life span". How many matches did you get?

FIGURE 22.5. Close-up of the head of a Loggerhead Sea Turtle. Being as specific as possible when using search engines will help you find the most relevant information.

    e. Fortunately, search engines order their responses, or hits, with the most relevant matches at the top. They provide a brief description of the information found on a particular, accessible web page. Click on one or two of the links. Did you get the answer to the original question? What is the typical life span of a Loggerhead Sea Turtle?

    f. What type of websites did you look at to get your answer? Is it a reliable source? How do you know?

FIGURE 22.6. It is important to credit the secondary sources used in your research. Using citations and a Works Cited list will help you to present your findings.

As you conduct research about symbiotic relationships, remember to keep in mind your ability to identify reliable sources. When conducting and reporting on secondary research, it is important to keep track of and attribute information to your sources—cite them. This practice helps to establish your credibility as a person who is knowledgeable about the work in your field as it relies on data collected by others. Citing your sources of information is very well respected and must be practiced whenever possible. It also allows readers to learn more about your topic, because they can easily access the sources that you used. Using someone else's words without citing them this way is called **plagiarism**, which is a serious crime.

Most high schools encourage their students to use the Modern Language Association (MLA) style to recognize their sources. In a research paper or report, citations would be used throughout the text, and a Works Cited page at the end of the work would include full resource information. For the purposes of our research on symbiotic relationships, we will only use the Works Cited page. The Works Cited page is a list of sources alphabetized according to authors' names.

The formats used for some typical resources are given below. You will practice with these formats when you conduct your research on symbiotic relationships. When using or referencing a physical book or magazine, the *medium of publication* will be noted as "print". When using Web-based resources, write "Web" in your Works Cited list.

FIGURE 22.7. Reputable print and electronic resources are useful sources of information worthy of being cited by the writer. By law, you must use your own words to avoid plagiarism.

Book:

Last name, First name. *Book Title*. Place of Publication: Publishing Company, Year of Publication. Medium of publication.

For example:
Cramer, Deborah. *Smithsonian Ocean: Our Water, Our World*. Washington, D.C.: Smithsonian Institution, 2008. Print.

Website:

Editor, or author name (if given). *Name of website*. Name of institution or organization, date listed on site. Medium of publication. Date you accessed the site.

For example:
NOAA Ocean Service: Estuaries. National Oceanic and Atmospheric Administration, 25 September 2008. Web. 16 March 2010.

Magazine Article:

Last name, First name. "Article Title". *Magazine Title*. Day Month Year: page numbers. Medium of publication.

For example:
Pavia, Robert. "Marine Protected Areas as a Management Tool". *Current: The Journal of Marine Education*. February 2008: 10–11. Print.

While conducting secondary research, it is important to take notes in your own words whenever possible. *Do not* copy information word for word, unless you are indicating a quotation from the text. Do not simply rephrase or restate text using the same, or nearly the same, words, without citing your source. If you do rephrase or restate text using nearly the same words, a technique call **paraphrasing**, be certain to give credit to the original author for their idea—however, in this case, you do not have to use quotes. As you read, think about what you are reading. Think about how you would explain it to someone else. Then write that explanation down and indicate the source of the information. This is your note on that piece of text. In the next activity, you will take some notes on index cards.

Part II: Symbiotic Relationships in the Ocean

Activity

Materials:

- Research resources—Internet access, reference books, etc. (to research examples of symbiosis)
- Index cards (to record information gathered from research resources)
- Large paper clips (to group index cards together)

As we noted earlier, symbiotic relationships between species are fairly common. There are three main types of symbiotic relationships:

- Parasitism
- Commensalism
- Mutualism

FIGURE 22.8. Symbiotic relationships between two different species are common in all of Earth's ecosystems, on land and in the ocean. This photograph shows one species of plant, a moss, benefiting from another species of plant, a tree.

Each Investigative Team will be assigned one type of symbiotic relationship. First, define and describe the characteristics of the symbiotic relationship you've been assigned. Use resources including the Internet, books, and magazines to look up this information. Then find examples of this type of relationship between marine species. Use the same resources to find these good examples. Take notes about everything you learn, and be sure to also record the source from which you collect each piece of information.

Use index cards to organize your note-taking with your team. Use two types of index cards: 1) Source Cards and 2) Note Cards. Use the following steps to take good notes and make attributing sources much easier later.

Source Cards:

- When identifying a source of useful information, write all of the information possible about that source (e.g., title, author, URL if using a website, publisher) as well as today's date on an index card.
- Number that index card at the top.
- Organize this information for your Works Cited list later.

Note Cards:

- Read the information that you gather and wish to use. Think about it. In your own words describe what you are reading.
- Label the Note Card with the number of the source that you used, as well as the page number(s) from which you recorded the notes on the card.

FIGURE 22.9. Sample Source Card shows information gathered from a National Park Service website. The information can be organized later and included in a Works Cited list.

1. Take notes about the characteristics of your assigned symbiotic relationship using resources including the Internet, books, and magazines. (Note: This does not mean simply copying the definition of the term using a glossary of a textbook or the dictionary.)

2. Once you have thoroughly defined your assigned symbiotic relationship, use your available resources to describe at least 5 marine examples of this relationship. Each symbiotic relationship should be described on a Note Card. To accomplish this task:

   - Write the names of the two chosen species (or types of organisms) at the top of an index card.
   - Describe the relationship between the two species you are highlighting (Parasitism, Commensalism, or Mutualism).
   - Note how each species is affected by the relationship.
   - Indicate the source number—this should correspond with your Source Cards.

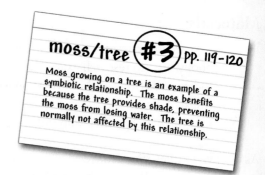

3. Write the names of your group members and the symbiotic relationship on a blank index card. Clip this card together with your Note Cards. The first card after your names should be the card in which you described your symbiotic relationship.

FIGURE 22.10. Sample Note Card on the moss/tree example.

4. Using the Source Cards, create a Works Cited list in your notebook for your Investigative Team's work. Access the MLA style resources on the *Marine Science: The Dynamic Ocean* website.

FIGURE 22.11. Bees and flies feed on nectar and visit many flowers for food, playing an important role in flower pollination. This is an example of symbiosis on land.

Activity

Part III: Symbiosis Game

You will now reconvene as a class to learn more about symbiotic relationships and identify examples of each—in a game format.

Game Rules:

- There are three teams: Parasitism, Commensalism, and Mutualism.
- Your teacher will randomly choose a card (created by students) and read aloud the description of the symbiotic relationship.
- A student on any team may "buzz in" to make a guess.
- If a student correctly *identifies* and *explains* the symbiotic relationship, points will be awarded as follows:
  - If the correct answer is *mutualism*, that student's group will receive 1 point and the other groups 1 point because in mutualism, all species benefit.
  - If the correct answer is *commensalism*, that student's group will receive 1 point and the other groups get 0 points because only one organism benefits.
  - If the correct answer is *parasitism*, that student's group will receive 1 point and the other groups will lose 1 point, because one organism is harmed.
  - If a student incorrectly identifies the symbiotic relationship, another team may attempt to answer correctly.

1. Draw a chart like the one below. In your chart, first write a description of each relationship. As the game is played, list examples of each type of relationship in your chart.

	Commensalism	Mutualism	Parasitism
Definition			
Examples			

2. How do these symbiotic relationships demonstrate the interdependence among different species? Illustrate your answer with at least 2 examples from the chart.

Explain

Symbiosis in Action

When different species live in close proximity, relationships that aid in the survival of a species can evolve. When such a relationship is beneficial to one or both species, it is referred to as a symbiotic relationship or **symbiosis**. Symbiosis is a relationship between different species, or an **interspecific** relationship. There are many unique examples of symbiotic relationships in the ocean. A relationship between two organisms of the same species is an **intraspecific** relationship.

FIGURE 22.12. A Nurse Shark with a Remora near its gill illustrates commensalism. The Remora benefits, but the shark is unaffected by the relationship.

Looking at FIGURE 22.12, notice that there is a Remora (a type of fish) near the gill of a Nurse Shark. This is a common scene—the Remora is "catching a ride" with the larger fish, and at the same time receiving protection from predators and eating the bits of food that get away when the shark eats. The shark is unaffected by having the Remora around. A relationship in which one organism benefits (+) while the other is not affected (0) is called **commensalism**.

Sponges, animals classified into Phylum Porifera, are commonly involved in commensal relationships. Crabs, worms, and other invertebrates can make their homes in sponges, using the organism as a place to hide. The sponge is generally unaffected by these organisms and goes about its business—straining phytoplankton and zooplankton from the water.

FIGURE 22.13. Sponges, such as this one found on a Caribbean coral reef, provide hiding places for a variety of other creatures. Sponges usually are not affected by their guests.

FIGURE 22.14. Clownfish and sea anemone species form mutualistic relationships in which both organisms benefit.

When both species benefit from each other (+,+), the relationship is called **mutualism**. In this case each organism is providing an advantage to the other, increasing both of their chances for survival. A well-known example of mutualism is shown in FIGURE 22.14, a picture of a clownfish and a sea anemone. The clownfish lives in the protective stinging tentacles of the sea anemone, and the sea anemone is able to eat the scraps of food floating in the water when the clownfish has a meal. For a long time, scientists classified this relationship as commensalism, until clownfish were observed actually feeding their anemone.

There are entire ecosystems that are dependent upon the mutualistic relationship between Giant Tube Worms and bacteria. These communities are unique because they thrive without the presence of sunlight. The bacteria that live inside the tubes of the worms turn the mineral-rich water that comes from hydrothermal vents into food. Instead of photosynthesis, they support the entire community through chemosynthesis. Surrounding these clusters of Giant Tube Worms you will find clams, crabs, shrimp, and fishes. The food web is completely dependent upon the mutualistic relationship between the worms and bacteria.

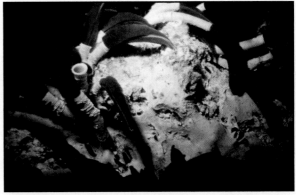

FIGURE 22.15. The relationship between Giant Tube Worms and chemosynthetic bacteria is another example of mutualism. The worms derive energy from the bacteria that live in their plumes.

Not all symbiotic relationships are positive ones. In some cases one organism benefits (+) while the other is harmed (-). The harmed organism is known as the **host**. This type of symbiosis is referred to as **parasitism**. Parasitism is the most common type of symbiotic relationship. An example of parasitism is seen in FIGURE 22.16, a photograph of an isopod parasite attached to the head of a squirrelfish. The isopod is able to get its meal, but unfortunately the squirrelfish can become paralyzed and die. Isopods are crustaceans, related to lobsters and crabs and classified into Phylum Arthropoda. In fact, isopods are the most diverse group of crustaceans. Isopods are found in nearly every ocean habitat, including in the deep sea, where they have been observed to be as large as 50 centimeters (~20 inches) long.

FIGURE 22.16. The isopod parasite sucks blood from the head of a squirrelfish.

Parasites are common in all marine and land environments. They can live in or on a host. A typical scenario for internal parasites is for them to live within the host's digestive tract or blood. There they can get the nutrients they need to survive. Many marine animals can survive for many years with parasites inside or on them. It is not until they become stressed or ill that the parasite causes the host to get sick or even die. Parasitic worms are incredibly prevalent in fish species. Some scientists estimate that for every species of fish in the ocean, there are 3–4 parasitic worm species. Be careful— undercooked fish may lead to these worms being transferred to humans. However, shellfish and fish species sold at fish markets and supermarkets are normally checked for worms and other parasites. This prevents members of the public from getting very sick.

Coevolution

How do these relationships begin? When two species compete or cooperate with each other, some members of one of the species influence the adaptations of the other species. Over time, the populations of one or both of the two species begin to gradually change. Each species serves as the agent of selection to the other species. The adaptations of one species affect the response of another, and the response of that species affects the traits of the first. When change occurs to two or more species over a long period of time in response to each other, the process is known as **coevolution**.

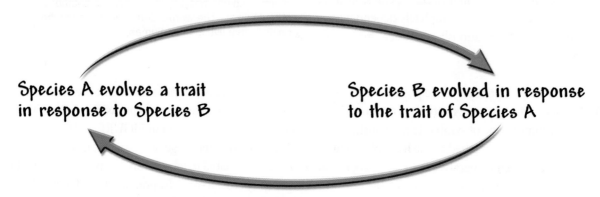

Species A evolves a trait in response to Species B

Species B evolved in response to the trait of Species A

FIGURE 22.17. Diagram of coevolution. Over time, each species has affected the other.

Let's look at the example of the clownfish and sea anemone again. In this case, the clownfish is receiving protection from its enemies while the sea anemone is receiving food particles when the clownfish eats. In mutualism, each species must provide a benefit to the other. How is the clownfish able to hide in the stinging tentacles of the sea anemone? Over many, many generations, the clownfish species developed a protective mucus covering. This adaptation prevents the clownfish from feeling the effects of the cnidarian's (pronounced: nī-DARE-ee-an) stinging tentacles.

FIGURE 22.18. The clownfish and anemone have coevolved. Clownfishes typically do not react to the anemones' stings, whereas the anemones benefit from food scraps left by the fish.

Predator-prey relationships can also lead to coevolution. Many small fish, for example, exhibit schooling behavior, which makes individuals less susceptible to predation. Larger fish are likely to snatch the slowest fish within a school, meaning that the ones with better swimming ability survive and pass on their genes. The species as a whole becomes faster. Then, only the predators who are fast enough to catch the food survive. This means the predator species evolves to become faster, too. These species cause selection pressure on one another.

FIGURE 22.19. The predator-prey relationship between small and large fish species is another example of coevolution. As prey species become faster and more agile, so do the predators.

4. Create a graphic organizer to summarize the information on coevolution.

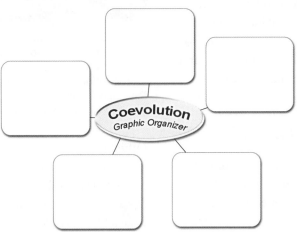

FIGURE 22.20. Example of a graphic organizer.

5. What have you *learned*? With your original groups, revisit your K-W-L charts. Now that you are close to the end of the Lesson on the different types of relationships in the sea, fill out the last column with all the things you have *learned*.

K	W	L

Chemosynthesis

Ecosystems on our planet are powered by the Sun via photosynthesis, right? As you have already learned, this is typically the case—but it isn't always the case. There are areas on our planet where the Sun doesn't reach. Deep areas. Dark areas.

Sunlight doesn't reach the dark vastness of the deep abysses of our ocean, the cold depths of our largest freshwater lakes, the Great Lakes or the hot, dark expanse of the deepest lithosphere. Is life found in these places? Yes!

There are areas on our planet far removed from the light of the Sun where life flourishes. It had long been thought that the depths of the ocean were sterile, devoid of life except for the isolated oasis around the corpse of a whale or large fish that had sunk to the bottom and provided a source of nutrients for a variety of scavengers. The first known exceptions to these isolated cases were the complex communities found around underwater "geysers" of mineral-rich heated water known as **thermal vents**.

The minerals found in the water coming from thermal vents support the growth of a type of bacteria that can use these minerals as an energy source— independent of the Sun. These organisms use the minerals in a form of energy production known as **chemosynthesis**. Chemosynthetic organisms serve as the base of a rich, diverse ecosystem. These vent communities have a much higher biomass than do the isolated temporary ones that develop around animal carcasses on the seafloor.

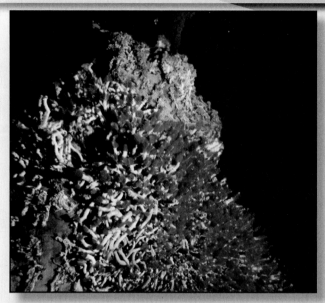

FIGURE 22.21. Chemosynthetic bacteria thrive within the Giant Tube Worms growing in the hydrothermal field on the Juan de Fuca Ridge in the Northeast Pacific Ocean. Vibrant colonies of tube worms with red gills are shown on this rocky structure, which is predominantly composed of iron and sulfur-bearing minerals.

Other areas where communities based on chemosynthesis have been found include Lake Huron, located between Michigan and Ontario, Canada, and deep within caverns, including a system found on the Coastal Plains of Israel. The Lake Huron ecosystem is associated with submerged depressions in the limestone bedrock of the region, known as **sinkholes**. Preliminary results of current research indicate the possibility of chemosynthesis occurring in the bacterial community associated with the sinkholes.

In addition to serving as food for organisms higher up on the food chain, some bacteria have entered into partnerships with other organisms in the community, creating a symbiotic relationship. An animal associated with vent communities, the Pompeii Worm, holds the record as the most heat-tolerant animal on Earth. This animal lives with its rear end bathed in water at a temperature as high as 80 °C (176 °F). On its back, the Pompeii Worm hosts a cloak of symbiotic bacteria that feed off a gluey secretion from the worm. Exactly how this animal is able to live in such hot water is an area of current research.

FIGURE 22.22. In Hydrothermal Vent Ecosystems, chemosynthesis provides the energy for other organisms to thrive, much like photosynthesis does in the photic zone. Notice the clams, crabs, and other organisms that could not live in this environment without the chemosynthetic processes of bacteria.

Elaborate

Reproduction and Life Cycles in the Ocean

In addition to interspecific relationships, there are also **intraspecific** relationships (between organisms of the same species). For example, for a species to avoid extinction, organisms must reproduce. There are many marine organisms that depend on unusual strategies for reproduction.

Some organisms are able to reproduce without a partner. In this case, the offspring are genetically identical to the parent. This type of reproduction is called **asexual reproduction**. The benefits of asexual reproduction include fast growth rates and the ability to reproduce with little energy expended. Many microbes, such as cyanobacteria, reproduce asexually. These organisms do not have to find a mate or risk their lives to do so. Asexual reproduction can also be disadvantageous. These organisms are not able to produce genetically diverse offspring. This leaves them vulnerable should their environment suddenly change, either by natural or human-induced means.

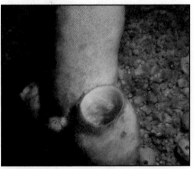

FIGURE 22.23. This White Vase Sponge has small buds that will become individual organisms eventually. Budding is a form of asexual reproduction requiring minimal amounts of energy to occur.

Organisms that reproduce by the union of gametes (sperm and egg). This form of reproduction is called **sexual reproduction**. The offspring from sexual reproduction are similar to both parent organisms, but not identical to them. Offspring receive half of their genetic information from each parent. Unlike those organisms that reproduce asexually, the offspring from sexual reproduction are genetically *different* from their parents. Sexual reproduction allows for the species to evolve more quickly in response to environmental changes.

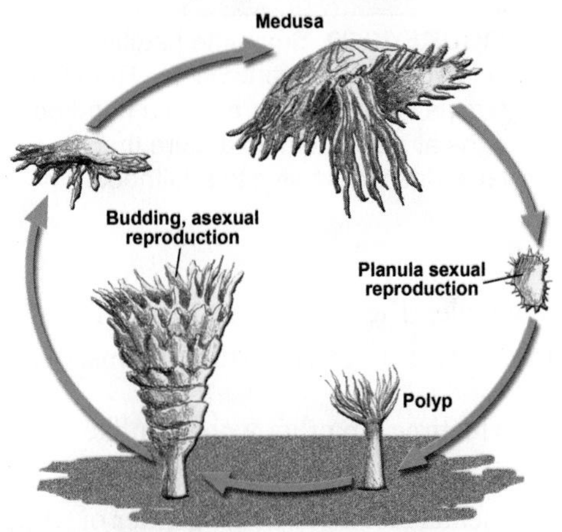

Life Cycle of a Jellyfish

Medusa

Budding, asexual reproduction

Planula sexual reproduction

Polyp

FIGURE 22.24. Jellyfish alternate between sexual and asexual reproductive strategies. The commonly seen medusa phase represents the sexual portion of the life cycle. While in the polyp stage, jellyfish reproduce asexually.

Some species in the ocean are able to shift between sexual and asexual reproduction in different phases of their life cycle. For example, jellyfish life cycles include both sexual and asexual components.

Many species are able to reproduce both sexually and asexually. Sponges are a good example. One method of asexual reproduction in which the parent divides itself in unequal parts is called **budding**. FIGURE 22.23 shows a White Vase Sponge with smaller buds to the left. The buds will break off from the parent and become individual sponges. The new sponges will be genetically identical to the original parent sponge.

When it comes to sexual reproduction, the sponges have a challenge to overcome. They are permanently attached to a hard surface, or substrate. Organisms such as sponges that do not move are considered **sessile** (pronounced: sess-sil). Since they are unable to move in order to find a mate, they rely on the water column (and a little luck) to get their eggs fertilized. The Star Coral on the next page, also sessile, releases millions of sperm and eggs into the water, a process called **spawning**. The gametes float around, fusing with one another. Sponges and corals are excellent examples of sessile organisms that rely upon spawning for external fertilization. They have evolved behavioral adaptations that time the release of sperm and egg cells to ensure a higher rate of fertilization.

Corals and other sessile organisms need to produce large numbers of **gametes**, the male and female reproductive cells, not only to ensure fertilization, but also to ensure survival of the species. These organisms do not provide any parental care or nurturing to their offspring. As a result, most of the eggs that are fertilized do not survive to adulthood. In fact, during this time of mass spawning, other invertebrates take advantage of the opportunity to feast on the released gametes, just as this Brittle Star is doing in FIGURE 22.27. In other cases, the larvae are eaten by fish and other organisms before they have a chance to settle and attach to a substrate.

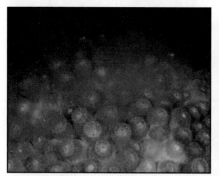

FIGURE 22.25. Star Coral releasing sperm during mass spawning.

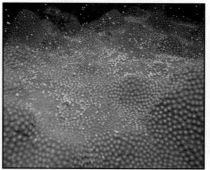

FIGURE 22.26. The eggs and sperm will meet in the water column, and the egg will be fertilized. A new coral polyp with genetic traits of both parents will be formed.

FIGURE 22.27. Brittle Star captures gamete bundles released by the Star Coral during spawning.

In addition, the mass production of fertilized eggs is a common form of reproduction for many different species in the ocean. Most larvae do not find a viable environment for development or to prevent becoming a meal for another organism. Fish, squid, clams, and even sea turtles are examples of different species that mass-produce offspring.

Some marine species have both male and female sex organs; they are **hermaphrodites**. This characteristic can lead to interesting behaviors. For example,

FIGURE 22.28. Many worm species, including flatworms like the one here, are hermaphrodites. Hermaphroditism is common in invertebrates and is also observed in some fish species.

FIGURE 22.29. Sea turtle hatchlings are very vulnerable to predation. Therefore, female turtles lay more than a hundred eggs at a time to help ensure that at least one will survive to adulthood.

hermaphroditic flatworms fight with other individuals for the right to act as a male. The loser of the battle is forced to carry eggs, investing a great deal of energy into species survival. Hermaphrodites very rarely fertilize themselves.

Another reproductive strategy is to actually change sexes during an organism's lifetime. In other words, unlike the case with mammals, gender is not determined at birth. Changing sexes can occur in response to population dynamics (e.g., if there are too many males a fish might turn female), environmental factors (e.g., the gender of some fish is based on temperature), and other reasons. This strategy is very common among reef fish, where competition for mates is intense.

In a group of mollusk species, typically called slipper shells, gender is dependent upon other organisms in the local populations. As adults, these animals live by stacking on top of one another. The slipper shell on the bottom attaches to a substrate such as a rock, pier, or another animal such as a Horseshoe Crab or oyster. These organisms begin their lives as males, and then switch to females for easy reproduction when another male lands above them. Thus, when you observe a stack of slipper shells, the individual on the bottom is typically a female, whereas the one on top is likely male.

6. Many species in the ocean are able to reproduce both sexually and
    asexually. Why is this an advantage for these species?

Some animal species produce very few offspring—in some cases, as few as
one or two at a time. These species invest a significant amount of energy
into raising and nourishing their young. Mammals, many seabirds, some
sharks, and seahorses exhibit varying degrees of parental care. The more time
invested by the parent, the fewer offspring that a species produces. However,
the parental care increases the chance that individual organisms will survive to
adulthood and pass on their genes by reproducing.

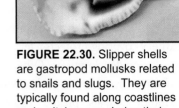

FIGURE 22.30. Slipper shells
are gastropod mollusks related
to snails and slugs. They are
typically found along coastlines
and switch sexes during their
lifetime.

The Adélie Penguin (pronounced: uh-DAY-lee) is a species that puts a
tremendous amount of energy into the parental care of its fertilized eggs. The
birds must overcome harsh weather conditions, including the extremely cold temperatures and blustery winds of the
Antarctic. To help improve the chances of offspring survival, unlike the sponges and coral that release thousands of
eggs, the Adélie Penguin lays only 1 or 2 eggs at a time. Adélie Penguins mate for life. Both parents incubate the egg
and subsequently nurture the chick. One of the adults will perform parental duties while the other goes to forage for
food. This will continue from the moment the egg is laid until the chick is old enough to forage for itself. This type
of pairing behavior is observed in many seabird species, including seaducks and albatrosses. To form pair bonds,
some seabird species perform elaborate mating rituals such as dances or feather displays. Some fish are also thought
to mate for life.

Male seahorses are the exception to the generally believed rule that males can't carry offspring, and in fact, the
male seahorse carries the fertilized eggs in his brood pouch until they hatch. Unlike placental mammals, the male
seahorse is not providing nutrients to the developing offspring. Instead he is providing a safe and protective place
for the eggs to develop. The young hatchlings later will emerge from the pouch fully developed, which increases
their chances of survival to adulthood.

FIGURE 22.31. Adélie Penguins typically
lay only one egg at a time. Both parents
will split duties and care for the egg, and
when it hatches, they both care for the
chick.

FIGURE 22.32. Many seabirds, such as
Laysan Albatross, commit to a lifetime pair
bond. Providing care to the young requires
a lot of time and dedication on the part of
the adults, but this priority improves the
chances of chicks surviving to adulthood.

FIGURE 22.33. Male seahorses
carry fertilized eggs, providing a safe
place for them to develop until they
hatch.

In most species of shark, the females lay eggs. Some species of sharks lay eggs that develop externally, with no parental care. Sharks and their relatives (e.g., skates, rays) that lay eggs often produce eggs contained in a pouch that has a tough covering, called a mermaid's purse. The leathery covering protects a fertilized egg during development. Other species, including invertebrates such as whelks, a kind of snail, also produce egg cases that protect developing eggs. These organisms lay many eggs to help increase chance of survival.

FIGURE 22.34. Some mollusks, such as whelks, lay their eggs in protective egg cases. This spiral-shaped whelk egg case was photographed on Assateague Island in Virginia.

FIGURE 22.35. Large skate case. Some species of sharks and their relatives deposit their eggs in pouches for protection.

In other species of sharks, the eggs develop inside the female. There are two major ways in which development occurs. The females of some shark species do not provide internal nourishment, but rather a protective environment in which eggs can develop. In other species, the mother provides direct nourishment to the developing sharks, much like in mammals. The species of sharks that develop young internally also have live births. Since the mother is protecting the young during development, this increases chances of survival. These sharks usually give birth to two pups (young sharks) at a time. In some species, such as the Sand Tiger, the pups begin to practice their predatory skills while developing inside the mother—the pups may actually hunt and attack their siblings.

FIGURE 22.36. Sharks use different strategies to provide care to their eggs, but pups are on their own once they hatch or are born.

In other species, including Mako and Thresher Sharks, fast-developing pups will sometimes eat the other eggs developing inside the female. In either case, following hatching or birth, sharks do not care for their young, and the newly born or hatched are on their own for survival.

FIGURE 22.37. Blue Whales, such as the two shown in this photograph, invest much time and energy into caring for their calves. A nursing Blue Whale mother produces about 200 liters (~50 gallons) of milk per day until the calf is weaned at about 6 months of age.

As you know, there are many mammals in the ocean, including pinnipeds, cetaceans, sirenians, and Polar Bears. These groups of organisms provide the most parental care to their young. For example, a Blue Whale creates a very strong bond with its calf after birth. The female Blue Whale's gestation period is approximately one year. She will then nurse the calf for just over six months after it is born. The milk contains 35% to 50% fat and has a high concentration of nutrients. The calf can gain up to 110 kilograms (~250 pounds) a day for the first 6 months of its life. Blue Whales take 7 to 10 years to reach sexual maturity, and will reproduce every 1 to 3 years after that. The reproductive cycle of whales occurs at a slow pace. They invest a lot of time and energy into raising their young. This increases the chance that the few that are born do survive to adulthood and reproduce themselves.

FIGURE 22.38. Polar Bears are marine mammals that invest a great deal of parental care in their cubs. Females nurse and remain with their young for up to 2½ years.

7. Explain how the role of the male in both the penguin and seahorse helps increase chances of survival of the offspring. What would be the result if the males did not take an active role in the parental care of the offspring?

8. How do live-birth shark pups have an advantage over those that hatch from a mermaid's purse?

9. What are the advantages and disadvantages for species that reproduce by mass production of fertilized eggs and species that provide increased parental care for their young?

Evaluate

1. How are mutualism, parasitism, and commensalism similar? How are they different?

2. Compare internal development to external development for the embryos of marine species. How does each increase the chances of survival for the species as a whole?

3. What is coevolution? Provide 2 examples to illustrate your answer.

4. Create a cartoon or diary entry from the point of view of the organism in a symbiotic relationship of your choice. Be creative as well as scientifically accurate.

FIGURE 22.39. Sea urchins, such as this common member of deep coral communities, typically reproduce by spawning. This reproductive strategy has both benefits and risks for the species.

23

The Ocean's Waves

INSIDE:

Objectives

You will be able to:

✓ Use mathematical calculations as you analyze the characteristics of waves.

✓ Determine the factors that influence wave height and wave speed.

✓ Evaluate a proposal for constructing a wave power plant.

Benchmarks

2c. Erosion—the wearing away of rock, soil, and other biotic and abiotic earth materials—occurs in coastal areas as wind, waves, and currents in rivers and the ocean move sediments.

2d. Sand consists of tiny bits of animals, plants, rocks, and minerals. Most beach sand is eroded from land sources and carried to the coast by rivers, but sand is also eroded from coastal sources by surf. Sand is redistributed by waves and coastal currents seasonally.

2e. Tectonic activity, sea level changes, and force of waves influence the physical structure and landforms of the coast.

5h. Tides, waves, and predation cause vertical zonation patterns along the shore, influencing the distribution and diversity of organisms.

6b. From the ocean we get foods, medicines, and mineral and energy resources. In addition, it provides jobs, supports our nation's economy, serves as a highway for transportation of goods and people, and plays a role in national security.

6e. Humans affect the ocean in a variety of ways. Laws, regulations, and resource management affect what is taken out and put into the ocean. Human development and activity leads to pollution (e.g., point source, nonpoint source, noise pollution) and physical modifications (e.g., changes to beaches, shores, and rivers). In addition, humans have removed most of the large vertebrates from the ocean.

6g. Everyone is responsible for caring for the ocean. The ocean sustains life on Earth, and humans must live in ways that sustain the ocean. Individual and collective actions are needed to effectively manage ocean resources for all.

7d. New technologies, sensors, and tools are expanding our ability to explore the ocean. Ocean scientists are relying more and more on satellites, drifters, buoys, subsea observatories, and unmanned submersibles.

7e. Use of mathematical models is now an essential part of ocean sciences. Models help us understand the complexity of the ocean and of its interaction with Earth's climate. They process observations and help describe the interactions among systems.

7f. Ocean exploration is truly interdisciplinary. It requires close collaboration among biologists, chemists, climatologists, computer programmers, engineers, geologists, meteorologists, and physicists and new ways of thinking.

Engage

Waves are what people picture first when they think about the ocean—slow, steady waves when out at sea, thundering waves crashing on the shoreline, or tsunami waves that can wipe out coastlines. In this Lesson, you will learn more about waves, what causes them, how they are measured, and why they can be important to humans.

See Page 694 for how to access e-Tools.

View the **Wave Video** (0:58) from the e-Tools and the **Wave Photographs** on Pages 444 and 445.

e-Tools

Carefully observe the wave photographs and view the short video. Think about what you know about waves and the ways in which you have experienced them.

FIGURE 23.1. Waves approaching the shoreline. What characteristics do you notice? Are these waves organized or erratic?

FIGURE 23.2. Waves out at sea take on a rolling quality.

FIGURE 23.3. Screenshot of **Wave Video**.

FIGURE 23.4. Surfer takes a ride on Oahu's North Shore.

FIGURE 23.5. Wave breaks on a California beach.

FIGURE 23.6. Storm waves as viewed from *MV Noble Star* in the North Pacific Ocean.

Demonstration

You and your classmates are going to create two different types of waves. After you experience the waves, you will sketch what occurred in your notebook. Be sure to label your diagrams.

Wave 1:

FIGURE 23.7. Students standing with their arms linked.

Wave 2:

FIGURE 23.8. Students standing shoulder to shoulder.

Explain

Wave Basics

Anything through which energy flows is called a **medium**. A medium can be metal, string, water, land, air—even people! A disturbance caused by the transfer of energy moving through a medium is called a **wave**. Waves are measured and described in different ways. Electromagnetic waves, which we will also discuss, travel through space and, hence, do not need a medium to propagate energy. In the ocean, the source of energy for most waves is wind. The energy is propagated through the ocean's water, which functions as the medium.

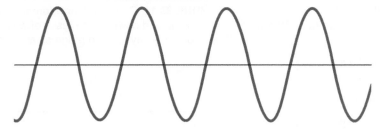

FIGURE 23.9. A wave.

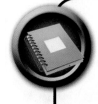

1. Copy the diagram above into your notebook and label the following:

    a. The highest part of a wave is called the **crest**; the lowest point is called the **trough** (pronounced: trawf).
    b. The vertical distance between a crest and its nearest trough is the wave height.
    c. The horizontal distance between two crests or troughs, or one complete "wave cycle", is known as the wavelength.

Think back to Wave 1, your human wave, as an example. The direction in which the energy flowed through the wave was from one end of the line of students to the other. The students themselves, the medium, were pulled in a direction *perpendicular* to that of the flow of energy. As the wave moved along in one direction, you noticed the students moving perpendicular to that direction. A wave in which the motion of the medium (students) is perpendicular to the motion, or direction of the wave, is called a **transverse wave**.

Light energy, or electromagnetic energy, travels in transverse waves. Here, there are actually two transverse waves traveling at the same time. Both the electric "E" and magnetic "M" wave elements run perpendicularly to the direction of the flow of energy. The two also run perpendicularly to each other. Ultraviolet waves, infrared waves, and all light waves are transverse waves.

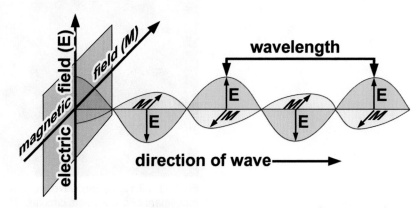

FIGURE 23.10. Electromagnetic energy waves consist of two components, each of which is a transverse wave.

One thing you should have noticed is that after the wave passed through them, the students returned to their original spot. Their *net movement* was no change in position. Something similar happens in the ocean, but ocean waves are slightly different from the student examples. These waves do transfer energy, but let's consider the *motion of the medium* (the medium being the water) with the wave.

A little boat on the surface goes up and down a lot, but doesn't move too far too fast. If you could look at the ocean in cross-section, the surface wave would look like a transverse wave. It appears to act like a transverse wave, bobbing up and down, but it is not because forward progressive movement of the water takes place. Below the surface, the movement of water molecules—the motion of the medium—is a circular motion. The ocean wave is an **orbital wave**.

We observe the relationship of the orbital diameter of a wave to water depth. FIGURE 23.12 provides a graphical explanation of why surface waves wouldn't interact with the ocean floor in deep oceans. Notice how the orbitals diminish to just about zero with depth.

FIGURE 23.11. Common Murre (pronounced: merr) on the water will bob up and down as the result of waves on the water. They will not make any forward progress as a direct result of the wave.

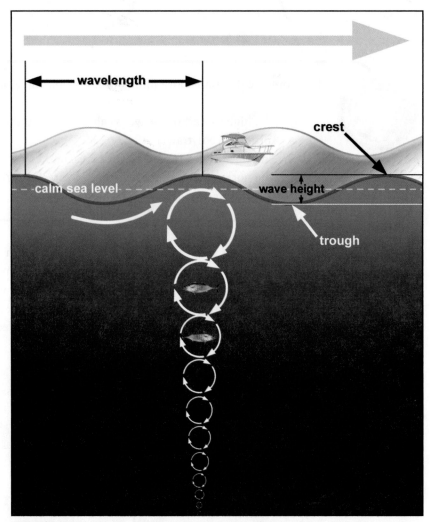

FIGURE 23.12. Ocean waves appear to be transverse waves, but the movement of the water is circular. This cross-section of the ocean's surface shows a boat on a wave's crest as well as the orbital wave, the flow of water, and its influence with depth.

See Page 694 for how to access e-Tools.

View the *Seabird Bobbing Animation* from the e-Tools.

e-Tools

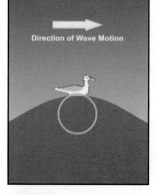

This seabird rides a wave, making no forward progression. This shows that while energy is transferred through the wave, the water is moving up and down.

FIGURE 23.13. Screenshot of the *Seabird Bobbing Animation*.

The bird moves up and down. Below the surface, energy transfer between particles of water causes the particles to move in a circular pattern. The bird rides up and over the crest of a wave, but remains in the same spot with respect to something stationary, such as the beach. It is the circular motion of the wave that causes things on the surface to bob up and down.

The demonstration of Wave 2 showed an example of a wave in which the motion of the medium traveled *parallel* to the flow of energy. This type of wave is sometimes called a compression wave, but is more properly called a **longitudinal wave**. P-waves, generated from earthquakes and sound waves, are examples of longitudinal waves. You studied sound waves when you read about using sonar to map the seafloor and echolocation by marine mammals. Another common example to show longitudinal waves is the wave produced with a Slinky® when you pull the coils apart to simulate wave motion.

Motion of Water Molecules Associated with Sound

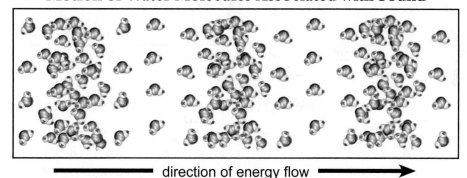

direction of energy flow

FIGURE 23.14. Sound waves moving through water. Energy is flowing from left to right in the figure as the transfer of energy moves through the water molecules.

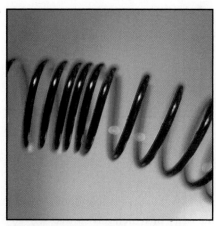

FIGURE 23.15. Longitudinal waves moving through a Slinky®-like coil.

Let's consider ocean waves again. From a dock or other fixed vantage point, one can make additional calculations about waves. Imagine you are standing on a dock, watching the waves pass by. The number of waves passing a fixed point per second is called the **frequency**. Related to frequency, the time it takes for the wave to move the distance of one complete wavelength is called the **wave period**. Frequency and wave period are inversely proportional to one another; as one increases, the other decreases. To find the period or the frequency, you can use the following formulas:

$$\text{period} = \frac{1}{\text{frequency}} \quad or \quad \text{frequency} = \frac{1}{\text{period}}$$

For example, if the period of a wave is 20 seconds, the frequency is 1/20 second, or 0.05. This number means that in one second, 1/20th of a wave will pass a fixed point. It would take the period, or 20 seconds, for the complete wave to pass this point. In the ocean, the wave period of wind-driven waves is normally 20 seconds or less.

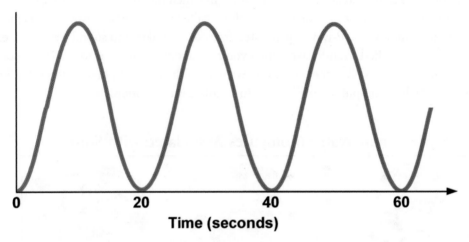

FIGURE 23.16. A wave with a period of 20 seconds and a frequency of 0.05 waves/second.

It is important to note that the measurable properties of waves change when waves enter different mediums. For example, the speed of sound will vary in different mediums. In air sound travels at approximately 340 meters (~1,115 feet) per second, as opposed to about 1,500 meters (~4,921 feet) per second in seawater. Imagine a loud sound (e.g., a ship's horn) traveling in waves through the air. When the sound waves enter the water, their wavelengths increase.

2. As wave period increases, what happens to frequency?

3. Using a ruler, measure and record the wavelength and wave height of the wave illustrated above.

4. If you were standing on a dock and it took 200 seconds for 20 waves to pass you, how long was the wave period?

5. What is the frequency of the waves at this spot on the dock?

Most waves at sea are generated from wind in Earth's atmosphere. Wind's mechanical energy is transferred into the ocean, producing waves, the majority of which have *wave heights* of less than 3 meters (~10 feet). The *wavelengths* of wind-driven waves are normally in the range of 60–150 meters (~200–500 feet).

Activity

Wind and Waves

Materials:

- Rulers
- Graph paper
- Atlases or Internet access (to look up locations on a map)
- String or rope, about 2–3 meters in length (*optional*, to model a transverse wave)
- Slinky® (*optional*, to model waves)

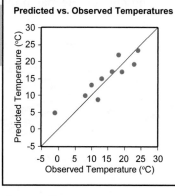

FIGURE 23.17. Example scatter plot shows average forecasted temperatures with actual temperatures for a select time period. The fact that the dots are close to the line suggests the forecasted temperatures were generally close to the actual ones.

Let's investigate the relationship between wind speed and wave height by plotting data about the two variables on a pair of axes. You will use a dot to represent each data point. The resulting graph will produce a plot used to compare variables, called a **scatter plot**. You will analyze your scatter plot to assess the relationship between the two variables, *wind speed* and *wave height*.

1. The following data were collected at various buoy stations on a date in February 2010. Follow the instructions below to create your scatter plot.

Data Point Number	Location	Wind Speed (knots)	Wave Height (feet)
1	48 miles NE Saint Augustine, FL	13	2.6
2	75 miles SE Boston, MA	15.5	3.9
3	456 miles E Halifax, Nova Scotia (Canada)	1.9	10.5
4	68 miles SE Virginia Beach, VA	15	4.3
5	23 miles SW Montauk, NY	7.8	3.9
6	28 miles SE Bridgeport, CT	15.5	2.6
7	756 miles E Bermuda	7.6	14.4
8	534 miles E West Palm Beach, FL	23.2	18.8
9	490 miles W Naples, FL	13.6	8.5
10	130 miles W/SW Tampa, FL	13.6	6.6
11	152 miles W Portland, OR	9.7	10.8
12	78 miles SW Los Angeles, CA	3.9	8.5
13	362 miles WSW Juneau, AK	11.7	15.4
14	290 miles S Honolulu, HI	11.7	13
15	778 miles SW Lima, Peru	13.6	16.2
16	687 miles NW London, England	18.2	19

a. Draw axes on graph paper. Choose which variable, *wind speed* or *wave height*, you will plot on the *x*-axis and which you will plot on the *y*-axis.

b. Give your graph a title and create an appropriate scale for each axis.

c. Plot each data point as a dot, labeling each dot with the *data point number* from the first column. Do not connect the dots.

2. Based on your scatter plot, describe the relationship between wind speed and wave height.

3. Use the scale to plot each data point number on the map provided. Use atlases or Internet resources to help you find the locations.

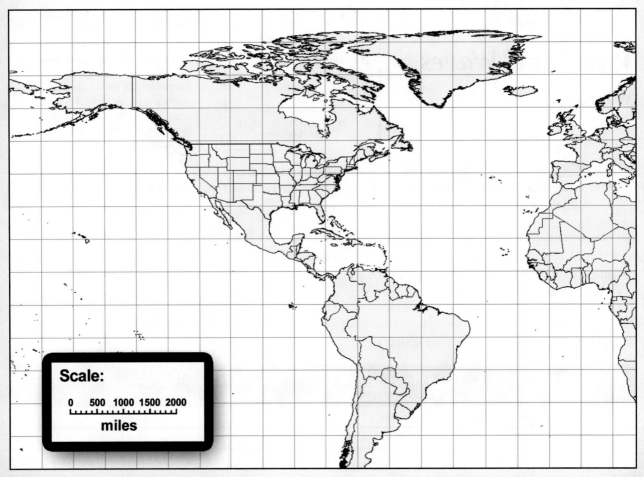

FIGURE 23.18. Wave Height Plotting Map.

4. Observe both your map and your scatter plot and compare the data. Other than wind speed, what factors do you think might influence wave height? List at least two possibilities.

As you probably realized by creating your scatter plot, predicting wave height is not simple. Both the strength of the wind and the period of time over which it blows are important factors in wave creation. When you plotted the data above, you noted wind speed, but not how long the speed had been sustained. In order for a wave to form, the wind must blow with sufficient strength and over a long enough period of time to overcome the force of friction that exists between the water and the air. As the wind blows for a while, the wave height increases, as do the wavelength and wave period. If you were observing wave development out at sea, first you would notice whitecaps forming and then waves would begin crashing down, or breaking.

FIGURE 23.19. When waves reach shallow water, they break or crash down. Out at sea, high winds and a long fetch can cause waves to break.

Another important factor is the distance of open water over which the wind can blow, called the **fetch**. A storm of the same magnitude can generate larger waves in the Pacific Ocean than in the Atlantic Ocean because of more fetch. When you look at an ocean wave, it may have been generated by a local wind, but, more likely, it was generated by a faraway storm.

FIGURE 23.20. Whitecaps form as wind speeds approach 10 knots (~11.5 miles per hour) and a wave is blown over. Higher wind speeds mean more whitecaps.

See Page 694 for how to access e-Tools.

View the **Hurricane Waves Video Clip** (1:12) from the e-Tools.

e-Tools

FIGURE 23.21. Screenshot of the Hurricane Waves Video Clip.

In the National Weather Service video, meteorologist John Metz describes the formation of waves due to a hurricane. He provides an overview of the factors that influence wave development, including wind speed, wind duration, and fetch.

Waves on the Move

The longer the wavelength, the faster the wave moves. Soon, waves with longer wavelengths outrun shorter ones, and the waves "organize" themselves by wavelength. They create a series of waves passing at regular intervals, called a **wave train**. Wave trains travel very long distances across oceans, with the waves with the longest wavelengths leading the way.

Out in the open ocean, wave trains encounter one another. When the crest of one wave encounters the trough of another, the wave heights tend to cancel one another out. When two or more wave crests run into each other, they create a wave much larger than other waves in the area, called a **rogue wave**. At sea, rogue waves are incredibly dangerous because they are usually completely unexpected. The result of many wave trains traveling in different directions over wide areas of ocean is that the ocean's surface is complex and seems quite random.

If you have ever been to the beach, you have observed waves "breaking" at the shore. In shallow water, waves crash, or break, when the wave height is large compared to the depth of the water. A gentle slope up to the beach or coastline causes the top of the wave to move ahead of the bottom water underneath. Out at sea, waves break when they become too steep or crash into one another.

FIGURE 23.22. Rogue waves often involve more than two wave crests combining. In some cases, rogue waves seem to be generated when waves interact with strong surface water currents. Researchers model rogue waves as a non-linear process, meaning they do not involve simple wave crest addition, but more complex interactions of wave energy.

To calculate wave speed, use a simple formula:

$$\text{speed} = \frac{\text{wavelength}}{\text{period}} \quad or \quad \text{speed} = \text{wavelength} \times \text{frequency}$$

Case Study #1: Wind-driven Wave

Let's work through an example: A buoy in the Atlantic Ocean is reporting a dominant wave period of 5 seconds and wavelength of 25 meters. What are the speed and frequency of the dominant wave?

$$\text{speed} = \frac{\text{wavelength}}{\text{period}} = \frac{25 \text{ meters}}{5 \text{ seconds}} = \frac{5 \text{ meters}}{\text{second}}$$

$$\text{frequency} = \frac{\text{speed}}{\text{wavelength}} = \frac{5 \text{ meters}}{\text{second}} \times \frac{1}{25 \text{ meters}} = \frac{1}{5 \text{ seconds}}$$

1/5 second or 0.2/second means that every second, 1/5th of a wave will pass through the fixed point where the measurement is taken at the buoy.

Case Study #2: Tsunami Wave

A very interesting case study of wavelength is to study tsunamis. What can you say first about tsunamis? They carry a lot of energy. A typical wave period is about 20 minutes, and the typical wavelength is about 200 kilometers. Waves with long wavelengths can have more energy. While the tsunami's wavelength is very long, its wave height is not. In fact, out at sea, it is barely noticeable when passing under a ship or buoy. Tsunami warnings may be automatically issued in many parts of the world when earthquakes occur and generate them. This may allow people a certain number of minutes to prepare and seek higher ground. Alternatively, tsunamis may be caused by underwater landslides or volcanic eruptions.

6. How could you find the speed, in meters per second, of the tsunami wave described above? Write down the procedure and calculate the answer.

7. Compare the wave speed of the wind-driven wave in Case Study #1 to the tsunami in Case Study #2.

8. Explain this result based on what you know about the energy of these types of waves.

FIGURE 23.23. Waves approach the beach with thick fog seen offshore. Although tsunamis can be deadly due to their sheer magnitude and energy, they can also be very small and measure less than a centimeter in height.

Surfing

The art of riding a wave on a board is the sport of surfing, a sport that originated more than 3,000 years ago in ancient Polynesia. While surfing styles and boards have changed over the years, finding the perfect-sized wave to ride is still determined by two factors: initial wave formation and local surf spot conditions.

Wind speed, wind duration, and the fetch are the three main components that affect the size of a wave. The stronger the wind speed and the longer the wind blows, the larger the wave. The area over which the wind affects the wave is known as the fetch. The greater the fetch is, the larger the wave. Surfers monitor the weather not only locally, but they also keep an eye on the weather in the open ocean. A storm in the middle of the Pacific Ocean has the ability to produce massive waves in Hawaii and in areas along the West Coast of the United States.

Factors at a particular surf location will also affect the size of a wave. The break of a wave is determined by the ocean floor. When the depth of the water is about one-half the height of the wave, it will break. A place such as Virginia Beach, Virginia, which has a gently sloping shelf, has small waves because they gently roll, form a tip at the top, and crumble down the face of the wave onto itself. A place such as the North Shore in Oahu, Hawaii, has a sudden change in ocean floor depth due to coral reefs. When the wave reaches the reef, it gets pitched up quickly and cannot maintain its shape. The wave will curl and crash violently. As a result, waves can grow higher than 12 meters (~40 feet), which draws the attention of surfers around the globe. Places such as Hawaii and Australia get big waves because the fetch is large around these locations; the wind has a long distance to push the water before the waves reach shore.

Surfers consider all these factors before heading out to the beach. By understanding how waves form and the conditions at a surf spot, surfers are able to predict how the waves will be on a given day. For many there would be no reason to head to the beach if the waves were not "perfect" for good surfing.

FIGURE 23.24. The science behind surfing is there for those that wish to study it. Surfing enthusiasts are always in search of the perfect wave.

How Do Waves Affect Organisms?

Out at sea, waves have little impact on marine organisms. Plankton are carried along by currents, and nekton swim among them freely. What about life below the sea surface? The orbital wave motion of water particles with depth will affect water to about the distance of half the wavelength. Even in stormy waters, high waves will only have an impact below to about 250 meters (~800 feet). Waves crashing on the shoreline, however, affect the patterns of biological communities along the coast. Many states have both high-energy coastline, where wave action is intense, and low-energy coastline, where one finds ecosystems such as salt marshes and mangrove forests, and wave action is more subdued.

FIGURE 23.25. Looking closely at sand dunes, one will notice a thriving biological community in which organisms are well adapted to the harsh conditions of a high-energy beach.

High-energy shorelines are greatly affected by wave action. Sand is constantly being added to and taken away from beaches. In some areas, these changes are seasonal. The movement of sediment by wind, water, or ice is called **erosion**. On a typical sandy beach, you would not observe many plants. Wave action, wind, and other processes are constantly moving sand. During peak periods of wave action, such as during a storm, the entire beach will be underwater. These factors make it very difficult for plants to grow.

FIGURE 23.26. A wooden path leads through the sand dunes, protecting them from erosion. When beachgoers walk on sand dunes, they may disturb plants and accelerate erosion.

Along sandy coastlines, one will find large hills of sand, or **sand dunes**, created primarily by blowing wind. Have you ever noticed signs on a beach advising you not to walk on the dunes, but to use established paths instead? Sand dunes are made up of loose sand and are therefore very susceptible to erosion. Walking on them leads to even more erosion, and disrupts native plants. Most beachfront parks and communities have established specific paths and boardwalks for crossing over the dunes.

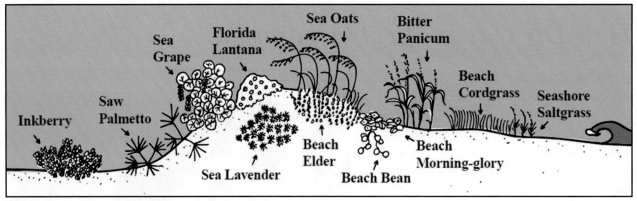

FIGURE 23.27. This image shows a typical zonation pattern of plants in a sandy beach ecosystem in the Southeastern United States.

FIGURE 23.28. Dune plants, including dune grasses and sea grapes, help to stabilize the dunes, preventing erosion.

Despite their fragility, dunes are important protectors of the coastline, preventing damage to buildings, roads, and other infrastructure behind them. Plants are critical to the stabilization of sand dunes and erosion prevention. They also provide a habitat for animals, forming a whole biological community. Nearest to the shore are plants that can withstand occasional wave action, salt, being buried in sand, and other harsh conditions. This area is known as the **pioneer zone**. Plants in the pioneer zone are well adapted to this environment. Some have waxy leaves to prevent water loss due to inundation with salt water; others have mechanisms for releasing excess salt. Most of these plants are fast-growing, which is an advantage when they become buried in sand. Sandy beach ecosystems are very common along United States coastlines. While the exact species vary by region, the zonation patterns and types of plants are similar. Common plants in this area include cordgrasses, dune grasses, salt grasses, beach beans, and sea oats. These plants have extensive root systems that trap sand and prevent it from being carried away.

FIGURE 23.29. Sea oats, beach grasses, and cordgrasses have extensive root systems that help the plants capture any available fresh water. The roots also stabilize the dunes, preventing erosion.

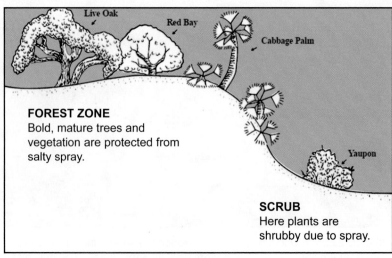

FIGURE 23.30. The scrub and forest zones are progressively farther from the water. These plants are different from those in the pioneer zone.

Just beyond the pioneer zone, one encounters shrubs and trees growing low to the ground, including types of berries, cactus, and elder plants. By remaining short and growing on the land side of the dune, plants in this **scrub zone** escape most winds and salt spray coming off the ocean. In this zone, the soil is still poor—sandy and salty—but inundations by waves are infrequent. The scrub zone only becomes submerged during intense flooding, such as during a storm.

FIGURE 23.31. Land animals like the deer shown here, are typical of the scrub and forest zones of sand dune communities. In the pioneer zone, one might encounter crabs, clams, shrimp, and other marine organisms.

The third zone of the sand dune community consists of larger trees and is protected from salt spray. This zone is known as the **forest zone**. In this zone, you would observe cabbage palm, pine, elm, or oak trees, depending on the region. These trees are not subjected to wave action very often as they are protected by the dunes and communities that are nearer to the shoreline.

In addition to plants, many animals are adapted to high-energy shorelines. In the pioneer zone, insects, crustaceans, and mollusks, including beach fleas, tiger beetles, mole shrimps, fiddler crabs, and clams, create burrows in the sand, waiting to be inundated at high tide in order to eat. Sandpipers, plovers, and other birds with long beaks can bore into the sand in search of a tasty treat. The scrub and forest zones provide habitat for animals, including reptiles such as snakes and lizards, mammals such as rabbits, mice, raccoons, and deer, and plenty of birds and insects. Following these animals are predators including foxes, bobcats, and birds of prey. All of these organisms and others are well adapted to the harsh environment of the sandy beach.

FIGURE 23.32. The scrub zone is composed of primarily short plants. Growing low to the ground allows these organisms to escape most winds and salt spray.

FIGURE 23.33. This image shows primarily the pioneer zone, which includes plants that can withstand occasional inundation with water, such as during a hurricane or another storm. Notice the stairs and walkways, which were erected to prevent people from walking on the dunes, which disturbs plants and can result in erosion.

FIGURE 23.34. The East and Gulf Coasts of the United States are dotted with barrier islands, which are dominated by sand dune communities. This photograph shows sand dunes in Cape Hatteras National Seashore in North Carolina.

FIGURE 23.35. Winds create wave patterns in sand dunes at Great Sand Dunes National Park. Although the Park is located in Colorado far from the coast, this photograph demonstrates how winds will affect an ecosystem of sand deposits inland as well as along coastlines.

9. Give two examples of adaptations of plants living in sand dune communities. Explain why each is an adaptation.

Elaborate

Harnessing the Power of Waves

As oil prices continue to rise and fossil fuels contribute more greenhouse gas to our atmosphere, everyone is looking to new sources of energy to create electricity for our homes and businesses. One way to meet our energy needs is to look to renewable resources, such as the ocean's waves. As you know, ocean waves have tremendous energy. Experts estimate that about 7% of energy needs in the United States could be met through wave power. In California, however, wave power could meet nearly 25% of the state's electricity needs.

Wave power is a clean technology, meaning when the electricity is generated, no pollutants are emitted into the atmosphere or into the ocean. Construction of clean energy power plants is very expensive. However, once they are operational, the maintenance costs are low because they use only seawater—a free, renewable resource. The image below shows *wave power densities* along worldwide coastlines. Not all coasts have natural areas of high waves; these areas may not be as suitable for wave energy plant construction.

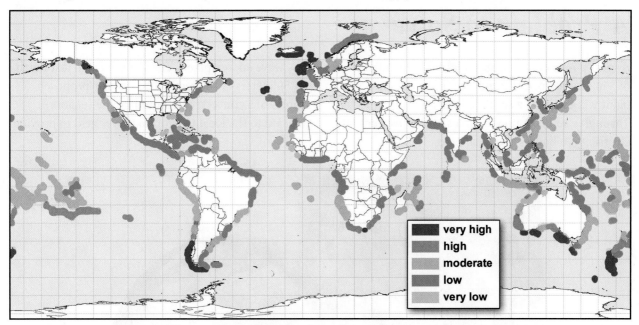

FIGURE 23.36. Wave power potential densities along worldwide coastlines.

There are several different modern designs for wave power plants, and they can be located either nearshore (in very shallow water), offshore (in greater than 40 meters [~131 feet] of water), or far offshore (in very deep water). Some designs use a series of small buoys to capture wave energy. Another design involves a series of 150-meter-long (~500-foot-long) *booms* that are placed at the water's sea surface and are perpendicular to the primary direction of wave action. The mechanical energy of the wave action is transformed, through a converter, into electricity.

FIGURE 23.37. Machines on the seafloor harness wave energy at the surface and convert it into electricity. A group of 30 of these are being deployed in the North Atlantic and will be able to provide electricity for up to 7,500 residences through an underwater cable.

FIGURE 23.38. Wave farm power booms in place off the Coast of Portugal. Wave power devices will derive energy from the surface waves' motion to effectively harness energy.

Activity

A Problem to Solve

A local power company has selected a potential site for a new wave energy plant. The site is located just north of San Francisco, California, on the continental shelf in over 50 meters (~160 feet) of water. The proposed plant will establish a series of long booms connected with cables to a converter anchored on the seafloor. Through a series of power cables, the converter will be connected to the local California power grid to provide electricity to homes and businesses.

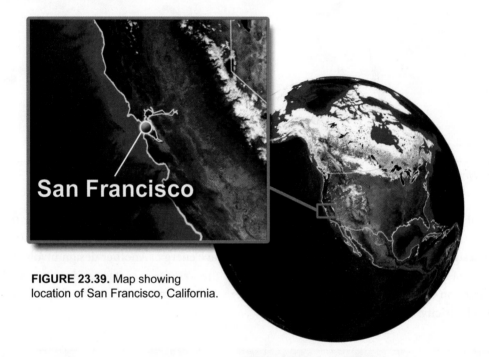

FIGURE 23.39. Map showing location of San Francisco, California.

Your team has been asked, as ocean experts, to consult with local governments on this project. Your task is to describe the potential impacts that these wave stations would have on the marine environment and make a recommendation either *for* or *against* creating this wave power site.

Answer the Questions below in order to make your recommendations:

1. Discuss the situation with your group. Write down at least three questions that you would ask the power company developers and the local marine scientists.

2. What are some of the possible positive effects of the wave energy plant? Be very specific as you list at least three.

3. What are some possible negative effects of the wave power plant? Be very specific as you list at least three.

4. What is your team's final recommendation? Are you for or against the construction of this wave power plant? Give at least two reasons that support your decision.

Evaluate

1. At a local stadium, fans often engage in "the wave". Explain why this wave does not fit the true definition of a wave.

2. Draw a typical transverse wave, including at least two crests and two troughs.

   a. Label and measure your wave height and wavelength.
   b. If 12 crests of your wave pass a given point in one minute, what is your wave period?
   c. What is the wave frequency?
   d. Calculate the speed of your wave.

3. A tsunami is generated from an undersea earthquake. Eventually the wave hits a coastline.

   a. A wave hits a particular beach, and the local residents warn that another wave will hit many minutes later. Are they correct in their assumption? Explain.

   b. In this case, the energy is transferred between three mediums. What are they? How does the wave change as it moves from one medium to another?

4. Describe one cost and one benefit of wave power plants.

FIGURE 23.40. Waves, found throughout Earth's ocean, are complex phenomena but are important to understand. They affect biological communities, can be harnessed for human electricity needs, and have tremendous impacts on ships at sea.

24

A Time for Tides

INSIDE:

Objectives

You will be able to:

✓ Relate tides to the alignment and natural gravitational forces of the Earth, Sun, and Moon.

✓ Distinguish between tides, currents, and waves.

✓ Give examples of how tides affect marine organisms.

Benchmarks

1c. Throughout the ocean there is one interconnected circulation system powered by wind, tides, the force of the Earth's rotation (i.e., Coriolis Effect), the Sun, and water density differences. The shape of ocean basins and adjacent land masses influence the path of circulation.

5f. Ocean habitats are defined by environmental factors. Due to interactions of abiotic factors (e.g., salinity, temperature, oxygen, pH, light, nutrients, pressure, substrate, circulation), ocean life is not evenly distributed temporally or spatially (i.e., it is "patchy"). Some regions of the ocean support more diverse and abundant life than anywhere on Earth, while much of the ocean is considered a desert.

5h. Tides, waves, and predation cause vertical zonation patterns along the shore, influencing the distribution and diversity of organisms.

6f. Coastal regions are susceptible to natural hazards (e.g., tsunamis, hurricanes, cyclones, sea level change, storm surges).

A Nighttime Mystery

It is a very strange night in the ocean—everything seems to be happening at once. Silver fishes called grunion (rhymes with *onion*) have left the ocean for the shore and are flopping along the beach. Lettuce-like seaweeds are releasing eggs at the water's surface. Fiddler Crabs are scampering sideways down the beach, waving their gigantic claws. Sand Shrimp are literally crawling out of their shells. The coral reef is covered by a thick, white, underwater cloud. Pairs of armored Horseshoe Crabs stuck together crawl away from the waves onto the sandy shore.

FIGURE 24.1. Grunion are common silver fish in the coastal waters of California and Mexico. They are known for their unusual mating rituals, which take place onshore.

FIGURE 24.2. Horseshoe Crabs are easily recognizable by their armored shell and spiky tail. This species has undergone few changes in the last 300 million years.

FIGURE 24.3. A coral in the Flower Garden Banks National Marine Sanctuary, located in the Gulf of Mexico, releases sperm into the waters above it.

FIGURE 24.4. Fiddler Crabs are common in mudflat and salt marsh ecosystems. Male Fiddler Crabs wave their enlarged claws to attract females.

Beach Trip

Samantha, Ahmed, Mei Ling, and Roberto are a group of friends enjoying their summer vacation. Samantha was watching her six-year-old brother Chris for the day. As a group they had decided to spend a day at the beach, soaking up some sun, playing volleyball, swimming, and having a good time.

The group arrives at the beach at around 10:15 in the morning. They place their beach blanket close to the water and near a lifeguard stand. After lathering up with sunscreen, they hang out for a while, take a swim, and decide to get some lunch. They walk up to a concession stand, eat at a picnic table, and start making their way back to their blanket. On the way back, some other kids ask them to join in a beach volleyball game. It is an intense game, and all four of them work up a sweat. They switched off watching Chris. By the time they finish the "best of five", it is nearly 3:00 in the afternoon and everyone is ready for another swim in the ocean.

As the friends walk back to their blanket, young Chris notices something strange. The blanket is no longer next to the water. The water is far away.

"What on Earth?" Chris exclaims, "Someone moved our blanket!"

"I'm not so sure about that," Samantha said, looking around. "Look, our blanket is still right next to the lifeguard stand."

The day is still bright and sunny; nothing else seems to have changed—the water just seems to be moving away.

1. What could have happened to the water? Explain.

FIGURE 24.5. In just a few hours, the beach seemed to change dramatically.

Explore

The level of the ocean's water along the shore changes in predictable patterns. These patterns repeat themselves twice each day. The patterns of rise and fall of the ocean's surface are called **tides**. The vertical distance between the high tide and low tide lines is known as the **tidal range**. The mean tidal range is the difference in height between the average high water and the average low water levels.

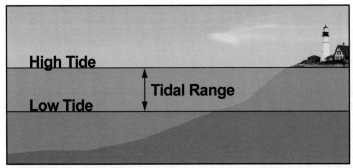

FIGURE 24.6. The tidal range represents the general difference in sea level height between high and low tides.

FIGURE 24.7. This photo is a double exposure (a photographic technique where a film is exposed twice, thus superimposing one image on top of another) of the NOAA Ship *Fairweather* docked at a pier in Anchorage, Alaska. The two photos were taken from the same location, capturing the ship at both high tide and low tide. The tidal range was between 9 and 11 meters (~30–36 feet).

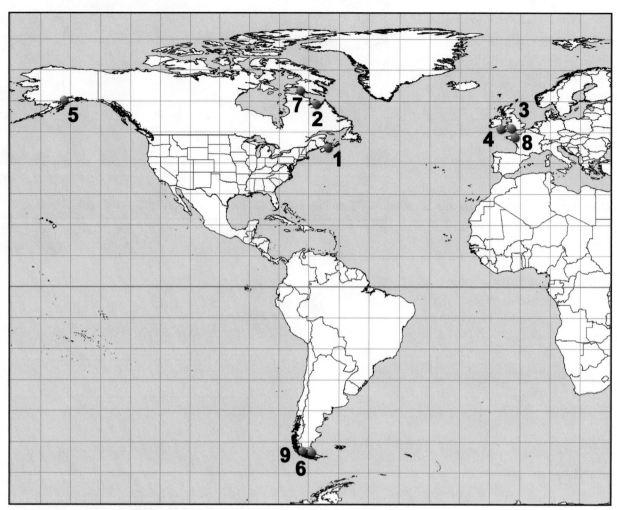

FIGURE 24.8. Map showing the locations of the stations listed in the table below.

	Locations of Some of the Largest Tidal Ranges	
Station		**Mean Tidal Range in Meters (~Feet)**
1	Burntcoat Head, Minas Basin, Bay of Fundy, Nova Scotia	11.70 (38.4)
2	Leaf Lake, Ungava Bay, Quebec	9.75 (32.0)
3	Port of Bristol (Avonmouth), England	9.60 (31.5)
4	Newport, Bristol Channel, England	9.24 (30.3)
5	Sunrise, Turnagain Arm, Cook Inlet, Alaska	9.24 (30.3)
6	Rio Gallegos (Reduccion Beacon), Argentina	8.84 (29.0)
7	Koksoak River Entrance, Hudson Bay, Canada	8.69 (28.5)
8	Granville, France	8.60 (28.2)
9	Banco Direccion, Magellan Strait, Chile	8.53 (28.0)

The Bay of Fundy

The Bay of Fundy with its great tidal range is famous. Tour groups actually travel to Nova Scotia to see the tides move in and out. The extreme tidal range is caused by the long, shallow, funnel-like shape of the bay, which squeezes the incoming tide into a narrow channel. When the tide rises, the water actually forms a wave that moves against the current. This wave is called a **tidal bore**.

When the tide goes out, wide expanses of mudflats are exposed. Wildlife living in coastal areas have adapted to this daily rhythm of the tides. Many animals burrow down into the sand or mud to avoid drying out as the water recedes. Barnacles and limpets close up at low tide, retaining water to get them through this dry spell.

Many people have a mental image of the changing tides that is gentle and serene. To them, tides are gradual changes in water levels of not more than a meter. This is not always the case. In some places on our planet, through a confluence of geography and physics, conditions lead to extreme tides. The Bay of Fundy, in Canada between Nova Scotia and New Brunswick, is such a place.

In the Bay of Fundy the range between high and low tide can be as much as 16 meters (~52 feet). To put this in perspective, 16 meters is approximately the height of five one-story homes stacked on top of each other. The average range between high and low tide is approximately 11.7 meters (~38.4 feet). This is an impressive flow of water into and out of the bay, occurring twice each day.

How is it possible to have such a dramatic difference between high and low tides at the Bay of Fundy? The bay is a shallow basin. Its length allows for it to fill and empty with tidal movements every 12 hours. This natural oscillation closely matches the period of the tidal forcing from the Moon and Sun. The resonance between these two periods greatly amplifies the height of the tides.

The vast amounts of water moving through the Bay of Fundy four times each day are a potential source of energy for Canada. According to FORCE (Fundy Ocean Research Centre for Energy), well over 100 billion tons of water is pushed through the bay along with every tide. This is more than all of the freshwater rivers and streams on our planet combined. The potential for generating clean electric power is tremendous. FORCE is pursuing the development of in-stream tidal power generation in the Bay of Fundy in order to provide up to 100,000 homes with emissions-free electric power.

Bay of Fundy

High Tide in the Bay of Fundy

Low Tide in the Bay of Fundy

FIGURE 24.9. The Bay of Fundy as seen from an orbiting satellite in Space during high tide and low tide.

Analyzing Tides in Three Locations

Activity

To explore tides, we will plot sample tidal data. Tide charts are widely available and are of interest to boaters, fishers, and scientists alike. Follow the instructions carefully to create your plot.

Materials:

- Graph paper
- Scissors
- Tape
- Pencil

Setting up the graph:

1. Cut graph paper in half lengthwise. Tape the two strips together making an even longer strip of graph paper. Take care to match up the lines.

2. Draw a horizontal axis, 3 lines up from the bottom, along the longest length of the graph paper.

3. Draw a vertical axis, 3 lines from the left.

4. Divide the horizontal axis into 6-hour intervals. Where the vertical axis crosses the horizontal axis, label this "12 am". Mark the next line "6 am"; then, "12 pm" or "noon"; "6 pm"; and "12 am" once again. Continue numbering in this way across the graph paper.

5. At each "12 am" mark, indicate a new date. Start the axis with March 1 and end with March 31.

6. To label the vertical axis start where the vertical axis crosses the horizontal axis. Label this intersection "-3 feet".

7. Mark every other line with a hash mark. Each hash mark represents 1 foot. You will need to mark lines for -3, -2, -1, 0, +1, +2, +3, +4, +5, and +6.

8. Draw a thin, dark horizontal line for the line you have marked as "0".

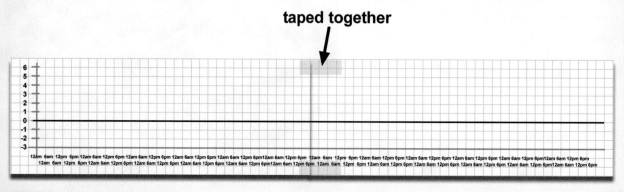

FIGURE 24.10. Example of setup.

Part 1: Plotting the Data

1. Plot each high and low tide level from the Tide Table onto your graph paper. Use a sharp pencil.

2. Remember, tides alternate from high tide to low tide, back to high tide, etc. You will never have two consecutive high tides or low tides. Connect the dots.

3. Once you have finished plotting the tides, place labels for the Moon Phases (New Moon, 1st Quarter, Full Moon, and 3rd Quarter) above the appropriate day.

4. Attach your graph to a page in your notebook.

Tide Table for Port Canaveral, Florida   March 2010

Date		Height (ft)		Height (ft)		Height (ft)		Height (ft)		Moon Phase
1	Mo	1:37am	-1.0	7:56am	+4.2	2:03pm	-0.9	8:23pm	+4.3	
2	Tu	2:30am	-0.9	8:45am	+4.0	2:49pm	-0.9	9:14pm	+4.3	
3	We	3:24am	-0.6	9:32am	+3.7	3:37pm	-0.7	10:04pm	+4.2	
4	Th	4:19am	-0.3	10:19am	+3.4	4:27pm	-0.5	10:55pm	+4.0	
5	Fr	5:17am	0.0	11:08am	+3.1	5:19pm	-0.3	11:49pm	+3.8	
6	Sa	6:16am	+0.2	12:01pm	+2.8	6:15pm	0.0	---	---	
7	Su	7:17am	+0.4	12:49am	+3.5	7:13pm	+0.2	1:01pm	+2.6	3rd Quarter
8	Mo	8:18am	+0.6	1:56am	+3.3	8:13pm	+0.3	2:10pm	+2.5	
9	Tu	9:20am	+0.6	3:04am	+3.2	9:14pm	+0.3	3:18pm	+2.5	
10	We	10:15am	+0.6	4:02am	+3.2	10:11pm	+0.3	4:15pm	+2.6	
11	Th	11:02am	+0.5	4:50am	+3.3	11:02pm	+0.2	5:02pm	+2.8	
12	Fr	11:41am	+0.3	5:31am	+3.3	11:40pm	+0.1	5:44pm	+3.0	
13	Sa	12:15pm	+0.2	6:09am	+3.4	---	---	6:24pm	+3.2	
14	Su	12:28am	0.0	7:45am	+3.4	148pm	0.0	8:02pm	+3.4	
15	Mo	2:07am	0.0	8:21am	+3.4	221pm	-0.1	8:39pm	+3.5	New
16	Tu	2:45am	0.0	8:56am	+3.3	254pm	-0.1	9:16pm	+3.6	
17	We	3:23am	0.0	9:32am	+3.2	327pm	-0.1	9:53pm	+3.7	
18	Th	4:03am	+0.1	10:08am	+3.1	403pm	-0.1	10:31pm	+3.8	
19	Fr	4:46am	+0.2	10:45am	+3.0	442pm	-0.1	11:12pm	+3.8	
20	Sa	5:32am	+0.3	11:26am	+2.9	527pm	0.0	11:57pm	+3.7	
21	Su	6:24am	+0.4	12:11pm	+2.8	618pm	0.0	---	---	
22	Mo	7:20am	+0.4	12:49am	+3.7	716pm	0.0	1:04pm	+2.7	
23	Tu	8:20am	+0.4	1:49am	+3.6	819pm	0.0	2:07pm	+2.7	1st Quarter
24	We	9:21am	+0.4	2:55am	+3.7	925pm	-0.1	3:17pm	+2.9	
25	Th	10:21am	+0.2	4:01am	+3.7	1031pm	-0.2	4:25pm	+3.2	
26	Fr	11:19am	-0.1	5:03am	+3.9	1135pm	-0.4	5:27pm	+3.5	
27	Sa	12:12pm	-0.3	5:59am	+3.9	---	---	6:25pm	+3.9	
28	Su	12:36am	-0.6	6:52am	+4.0	102pm	-0.6	7:20pm	+4.2	
29	Mo	1:32am	-0.6	7:43am	+3.9	149pm	-0.7	8:12pm	+4.5	
30	Tu	2:25am	-0.6	8:33am	+3.8	235pm	-0.8	9:03pm	+4.6	Full
31	We	3:16am	-0.5	9:21am	+3.7	320pm	-0.7	9:52pm	+4.6	

FIGURE 24.11. Port Canaveral, located on the Atlantic Coast of Florida, experiences a semidiurnal (twice daily) tidal pattern. This port is an important location for cruise ships and transport of goods.

Tide Table for Pearl Harbor, Hawaii   March 2010

Date		Height (ft)		Height (ft)		Height (ft)		Height (ft)		Moon Phase
1	Mo	4:44am	1.9	11:00am	-0.3	5:22pm	1.6	11:11pm	0	
2	Tu	5:20am	1.6	11:30am	-0.3	6:11pm	1.7	---	---	
3	We	12:10am	0.2	5:55am	1.3	12:01pm	-0.3	7:03pm	1.7	
4	Th	1:18am	0.3	6:31am	1	12:34pm	-0.2	8:00pm	1.7	
5	Fr	2:44am	0.4	7:09am	0.7	1:10pm	-0.1	9:07pm	1.7	
6	Sa	4:45am	0.4	8:00am	0.5	1:56pm	0	10:23pm	1.6	
7	Su	6:44am	0.3	9:51am	0.4	3:04pm	0.1	11:37pm	1.6	3rd Quarter
8	Mo	7:39am	0.2	11:57am	0.4	4:33pm	0.2	---	---	
9	Tu	12:39am	1.7	8:10am	0.2	1:05pm	0.5	5:51pm	0.1	
10	We	1:27am	1.7	8:34am	0.1	1:47pm	0.7	6:50pm	0.1	
11	Th	2:06am	1.7	8:54am	0.1	2:21pm	0.8	7:37pm	0	
12	Fr	2:38am	1.7	9:12am	0	2:53pm	1	8:19pm	0	
13	Sa	3:06am	1.7	9:30am	0	3:24pm	1.1	8:59pm	0	
14	Su	3:33am	1.6	9:48am	-0.1	3:56pm	1.3	9:39pm	0	
15	Mo	3:58am	1.5	10:08am	-0.1	4:29pm	1.4	10:19pm	0.1	New
16	Tu	4:24am	1.4	10:28am	-0.1	5:03pm	1.6	11:02pm	0.2	
17	We	4:51am	1.3	10:50am	-0.2	5:40pm	1.7	11:50pm	0.2	
18	Th	5:18am	1.1	11:15am	-0.2	6:22pm	1.7	---	---	
19	Fr	12:45am	0.3	5:48am	0.9	11:43am	-0.2	7:10pm	1.7	
20	Sa	1:56am	0.4	6:21am	0.7	12:16pm	-0.1	8:09pm	1.7	
21	Su	3:35am	0.4	7:06am	0.5	1:00pm	-0.1	9:20pm	1.7	
22	Mo	5:29am	0.3	8:36am	0.4	2:05pm	0	10:36pm	1.8	
23	Tu	6:36am	0.2	10:48am	0.4	3:36pm	0	11:45pm	1.8	1st Quarter
24	We	7:15am	0.1	12:19pm	0.5	5:09pm	0	---	---	
25	Th	12:43am	1.9	7:46am	-0.1	1:19pm	0.8	6:26pm	0	
26	Fr	1:32am	1.9	8:15am	-0.2	2:08pm	1	7:33pm	-0.1	
27	Sa	2:16am	1.9	8:43am	-0.2	2:53pm	1.3	8:32pm	-0.1	
28	Su	2:56am	1.7	9:11am	-0.3	3:36pm	1.6	9:29pm	-0.1	
29	Mo	3:35am	1.6	9:39am	-0.4	4:19pm	1.8	10:25pm	0	
30	Tu	4:12am	1.3	10:08am	-0.4	5:02pm	2	11:21pm	0	Full
31	We	4:50am	1.1	10:37am	-0.3	5:46pm	2	---	---	

Tide Table for Gulfport, Mississippi   March 2010

Date		Height (ft)		Height (ft)		Height (ft)		Height (ft)		Moon Phase
1	Mo	1:27am	+0.9	8:26am	+0.2	1:26pm	+0.3	6:37pm	0.0	
2	Tu	3:37am	+0.6	6:39am	+0.5	12:59pm	+0.8	8:55pm	-0.2	
3	We	---	---	---	---	1:24pm	+1.2	10:58pm	-0.5	
4	Th	---	---	---	---	2:05pm	+1.4	---	---	
5	Fr	---	---	12:44am	-0.6	2:53pm	+1.7	---	---	
6	Sa	---	---	2:07am	-0.8	3:46pm	+1.7	---	---	
7	Su	---	---	3:15am	-0.8	4:44pm	+1.7	---	---	3rd Quarter
8	Mo	---	---	4:13am	-0.8	5:51pm	+1.5	---	---	
9	Tu	---	---	5:02am	-0.6	7:05pm	+1.5	---	---	
10	We	---	---	5:45am	-0.5	8:20pm	+1.4	---	---	
11	Th	---	---	6:21am	-0.3	9:29pm	+1.4	---	---	
12	Fr	---	---	6:48am	-0.2	10:32pm	+1.2	---	---	
13	Sa	---	---	7:03am	0.0	11:32pm	+1.1	---	---	
14	Su	---	---	7:59am	+0.3	2:47pm	+0.5	5:10pm	+0.3	
15	Mo	1:37am	+0.9	7:27am	+0.5	1:38pm	+0.6	7:08pm	+0.3	New
16	Tu	3:00am	+0.8	6:20am	+0.6	1:26pm	+0.9	8:33pm	+0.2	
17	We	---	---	---	---	1:37pm	+1.2	9:51pm	0.0	
18	Th	---	---	---	---	2:00pm	+1.4	11:09pm	-0.2	
19	Fr	---	---	---	---	2:31pm	+1.7	---	---	
20	Sa	---	---	12:30am	-0.3	3:11pm	+1.8	---	---	
21	Su	---	---	1:49am	-0.5	3:59pm	+2.0	---	---	
22	Mo	---	---	3:00am	-0.6	4:57pm	+2.0	---	---	
23	Tu	---	---	4:05am	-0.6	6:05pm	+2.0	---	---	1st Quarter
24	We	---	---	5:03am	-0.6	7:26pm	+2.0	---	---	
25	Th	---	---	5:57am	-0.5	9:00pm	+1.8	---	---	
26	Fr	---	---	6:44am	-0.3	10:42pm	+1.5	---	---	
27	Sa	---	---	7:23am	+0.2	---	---	---	---	
28	Su	12:33am	+1.4	7:38am	+0.5	1:23pm	+0.8	6:05pm	+0.5	
29	Mo	2:54am	+1.1	6:45am	+0.9	12:23pm	+1.1	7:54pm	+0.2	
30	Tu	---	---	---	---	12:27pm	+1.5	9:20pm	-0.2	Full
31	We	---	---	---	---	12:58pm	+1.8	10:37pm	-0.3	

FIGURE 24.12. Tidal differences are noticeable along beaches and at docks. Boaters must be sure to leave enough slack in their lines to accommodate the changes in water level.

Part 2: Describing Tides

Use the information in the graph in FIGURE 24.14.

FIGURE 24.13. Screenshot of the *Ebb and Flood Tides Animation*.

e-Tools

See Page 694 for how to access e-Tools.

View the *Ebb and Flood Tides Animation* from the e-Tools.

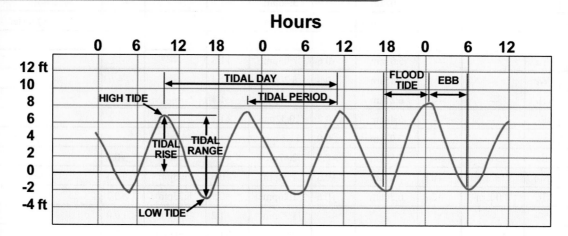

FIGURE 24.14. Tides graph illustrates terminology associated with tides over a 60-hour period.

1. Using the graph you created in the Project section on the previous pages, label a flood tide and ebb tide for March 9 (see FIGURE 24.14).

2. Label the tidal range for March 17 on your graph.

3. Describe the overall pattern of the plots of the tides as shown on the graphs.

4. What is the difference between the Flood Tide and the Ebb Tide?

5. Explain the relationship between the tides and the phases of the Moon you have drawn on your graph. What is happening to the tides because of the Moon during the month?

6. Copy the following chart into your notebook. Calculate the mean tidal range for Port Canaveral, Florida, Pearl Harbor, Hawaii, and Gulfport, Mississippi, for March 2010. Compare your findings to the mean tidal range of the Bay of Fundy, which is 11.7 meters (~38.4 feet). To find this value, determine the difference in height between the mean high tide and the mean low tide for the month.

	Mean Tidal Range for Three Locations in March 2010		
	Port Canaveral, Florida	**Pearl Harbor, Hawaii**	**Gulfport, Mississippi**
Mean High Tide			
Mean Low Tide			
Mean Tidal Range			

7. Which location(s) typically experience(s) one high and one low tide per day? Two high tides and two low tides?

8. Which location has the largest tidal range?

Explain

Top View (Looking Down at the North Pole)

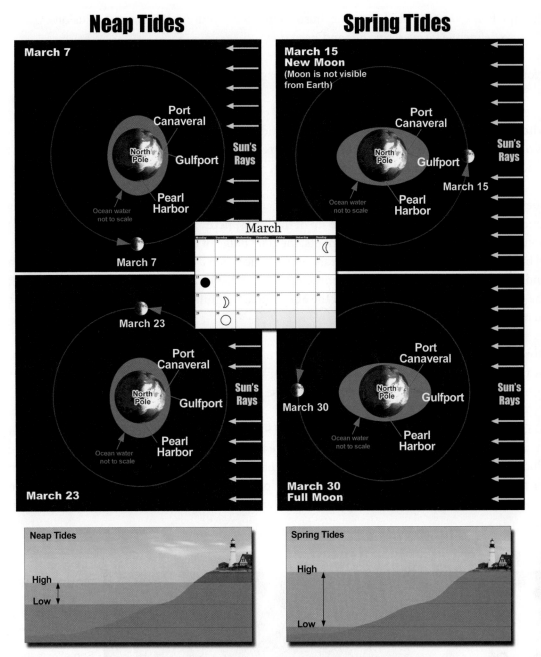

FIGURE 24.15. Diagrams illustrating neap tides and spring tides during March 2010. Water bulges in spring tides differ from that of neap tides. The difference in the magnitudes in the tides when the phenomena take place are shown.

9. Consider that the Earth is rotating on its axis once each day. Note the location of the Moon illustrated for each date. Look at the water levels for Port Canaveral, Pearl Harbor, and Gulfport in each of the four panels of FIGURE 24.15. On what days would you expect the biggest differences in the rise and fall of the tides?

10. Describe the alignment of the Sun, Earth, and Moon on the days you listed for Question 9.

11. When would you expect the smallest change between high and low tides?

12. Describe the alignment of the Sun, Earth, and Moon on the days you listed for Question 11.

13. Review the four Questions above and the illustrations. State your findings as a conclusion. Use the findings to define the terms *spring tide* and *neap tide*.

14. On your graph from the **Explore** section, note the spring tide and neap tide.

The gravitational pulls of the Moon and the Sun create tides on the Earth. The force of attraction exerted by the mass of an object is referred to as a **gravitational force**, or **gravity**. Gravity is the force that keeps the planets, including Earth, in orbit around the Sun.

While tides are most commonly associated with the ocean, gravitational forces also cause tides in the gases of the atmosphere and even in the solid make-up of the lithosphere. Most of us are not even aware of these gravitational effects. Without precise instruments, the tidal bulge of the lithosphere would not be detectable. The tidal bulge of the lithosphere, like the ocean, occurs twice each day at most locations on Earth. The bulge of the land is limited to approximately 30 centimeters (~12 inches). The nature of bodies of water, as fluids, allows the gravitational pull of the Moon and the Sun to create significant bulges or swells in water in the direction of the Sun and the Moon.

Two factors, mass and distance, determine the strength of the gravitational attraction between objects. Large objects with more mass have more pull, exerting a larger force than smaller objects. Objects exert more gravitational force on bodies close to them than on those that are far away.

The Moon, which is approximately 384,170 kilometers (~238,712 miles) from the Earth, has a greater influence on Earth's tides than the Sun. The Sun's average distance from Earth is approximately 150 million kilometers (~93 million miles) from Earth. Because the Sun is so massive, its gravitational pull on Earth is approximately 178 times that of the Moon's. The Moon, however, is responsible for more of Earth's tidal changes than the Sun because the Moon is much, much closer to Earth: the Sun is nearly 400 times farther from the Earth than the Moon is.

FIGURE 24.16. The force of gravity is a function of the mass of objects as well as their proximity. The Sun affects the Earth because it is so large, while the Moon's proximity to Earth is the main reason for its role in the tidal cycle.

2. Why does the Moon have a greater influence on the tides than the Sun?

Most of the time we think of tides from the frame of reference of the coast. Instead, let's think of the high tide as a constant bulge of water being pulled toward the Moon.

See Page 694 for how to access e-Tools.

View the **Earth Moon Animation** from the e-Tools, which shows the relative positions of the Earth and Moon over the course of a day. View it a number of times.

18 hrs
37.5 min

Low Tide

e-Tools

FIGURE 24.17. Screenshot of the **Earth Moon Animation**.

The Moon and this bulge in the ocean take nearly a month to revolve around Earth. However, the Moon is not the only body moving. The Earth spins eastward on its axis, making a complete rotation every 24 hours. Because the Moon and the Earth are both in motion, however, their positions relative to each other are constantly changing. These motions affect the timing and the magnitude of the tides. It takes an extra 50 minutes or so for the Moon to "catch up" with the Earth each day. The result is that the high and low tides occur about 50 minutes later each day, as you saw on your tide chart in the **Explore** section. Typically, tides occur approximately 12 hours and 25 minutes apart. This means that it takes about 6 hours and 12½ minutes for a tide to change from high to low, or from low to high.

As you noted in the **Explore** section, not every location experiences two high and two low tides per day. If Earth were entirely covered by ocean, without land, water would shift evenly during tidal changes. Nearly 30% of Earth's surface, however, is covered with continents, which block water movements. The continents, of course, are not evenly distributed. The result is differing tidal patterns.

There are three basic patterns of tides experienced along coastlines. Most areas on Earth experience two high tides and two low tides per day, a **semidiurnal tide** pattern, dependent on the orientations of coastlines. In some locations, there is one high and one low tide per day. This is called a **diurnal tide** cycle. Still others experience a combination of the two—two highs and two lows per day, but with one set of tides more dramatic than the other. This pattern is known as a **mixed tide** pattern.

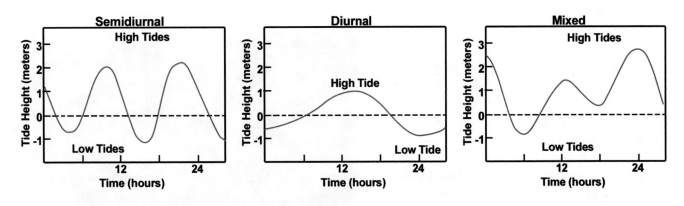

FIGURE 24.18. There are three major tidal patterns observed on coastlines. The most common pattern is semidiurnal, in which there are two high and two low tides per day.

3. List which of the locations you plotted in the **Explore** section experiences a:
   - semidiurnal tidal cycle
   - diurnal tidal cycle
   - mixed tidal cycle

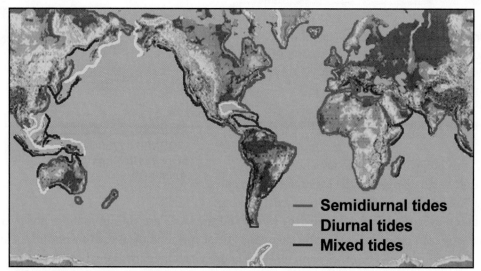

FIGURE 24.19. Due to the interactions between the ocean and landmasses, not every Earth location experiences two high and two low tides each day. Which type of tides are experienced near your region?

Tides are more than just the pattern of the rise and fall of the ocean's surface. Tides are the result of the gravitational forces of the Sun and the Moon. As seen in the diagrams, not all tides are created equal. The time of the most dramatic tides, those with the highest high tides and the lowest low tides, are called **spring tides**. Spring tides occur when the Earth, Sun, and Moon are in a straight line. The true spring tide happens about twice each month—not just in the springtime.

The tides with the least difference between high and low tides are called **neap tides**. Neap tides occur when the Earth, Sun, and Moon form a perpendicular angle to one another. True neap tides also happen about twice a month, approximately seven days after each spring tide. During the rest of the month, while the Moon is making its orbit around the Earth, the tidal changes on sea levels are somewhere in between a spring and neap tide.

FIGURE 24.20. Diagrams showing spring tides (above) and neap tides (below).

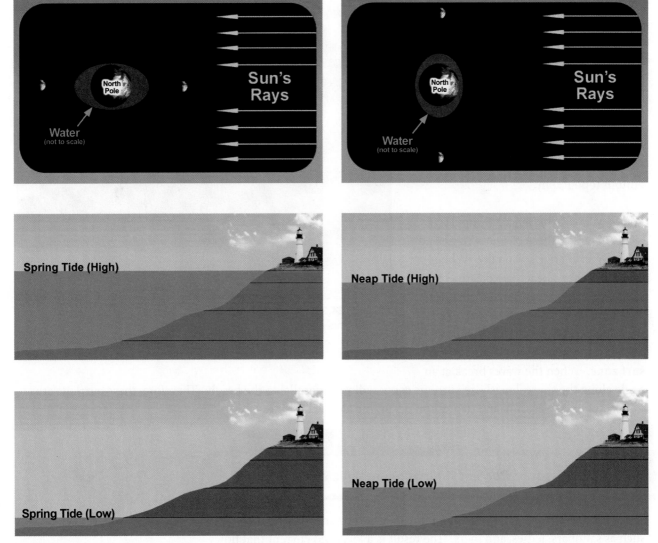

FIGURE 24.21. Diagrams showing spring tides and neap tides. During spring tides, coastlines experience the highest highs and lowest lows.

Ocean Motion: Waves, Tides, and Currents

The ocean waters are in constant motion, driven by waves, tides, and currents. All three contain energy of motion and can greatly affect many aspects of life on Earth.

Waves are a result of winds that are transferring energy from the atmosphere to the ocean. Winds affect the surface of water bodies. In fact, wave motion only involves the surface waters. The up-and-down movement of a wave is the actual wave energy—the wave energy moves forward through the water without moving the water forward along with it. The water molecules only actually travel in small circles as the wave energy passes through them, lifting them up as it approaches and then setting them down again as it passes.

Waves can be very gentle with lower energy, such as the waves we enjoy at the beach, or have higher energy, such as the waves in a storm surge pushed by a hurricane and its winds coming onshore. Tsunamis are also waves but are transferring energy from an earthquake rather than from atmospheric winds.

Currents in the ocean are in many ways similar to the currents in the atmosphere, driven by differences in pressure and modified by the Coriolis Effect. Surface currents, such as those you studied in Lesson 9, are driven by the constant global prevailing winds in certain latitudes. At a local level, other factors that affect currents are: salinity, tides, rain, wind, storms, runoff, and ocean bottom topography.

You may have experienced examples of local currents. These currents come and go, and can change seasonally. When a wave reaches a beach or coastline, it releases a burst of energy that generates a current called a **longshore current**. These currents form circular patterns in the region of breaking waves, or the **surf zone**. When the waves break at an

FIGURE 24.22. Rip currents are much more easily recognized from above. This rip current in Florida occurred after Hurricane Jeanne in 2004.

angle along the shore, longshore currents carry sediment parallel to the beach. Therefore, these currents are important for the erosion and deposition occurring along coastlines.

See Page 694 for how to access e-Tools.

View the *Longshore Current Animation* from the e-Tools.

e-Tools

As longshore currents move on and off the beach, they encounter barriers such as sandbars, jetties, and piers. The result is a localized current that flows away from the shoreline toward the ocean, called a **rip current**. Rip currents are more likely to occur when there are offshore storms causing intense wave action. Rip currents can be dangerous because swimmers may be pulled from shore. If you experience a rip current, swim parallel to the shoreline and then swim back to the beach when you have escaped the current's pull. Do not try to swim against a rip current—you will likely tire quickly, and it will be very difficult to swim to shore. Rip currents can be seen from the air, but are difficult to detect on the beach.

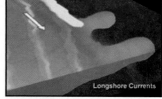

FIGURE 24.23. Screenshot of the *Longshore Current Animation*.

View the *Rip Current Animation* from the e-Tools.

Tides are observed along shorelines as a pattern of high and low water levels. They follow a regular pattern, cycling through the day. In most locations there are two high tides and two low tides in a cycle. Many shoreline animals and plants are dependent on the tides for various life functions. Tidal changes can cause local currents.

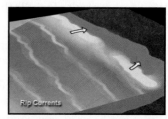

FIGURE 24.24. Screenshot of the *Rip Current Animation*.

4. How are waves, tides, and currents similar? How are they different?

Elaborate

Tides and Marine Organisms

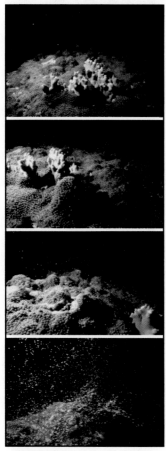

FIGURE 24.25. Coral spawning.

Fishers know that tidal movements affect marine organisms. During peak times of tidal water movement, fishers follow the many fish that move through narrow areas such as channels. In the **Engage** section, we read about a number of strange oceanic events happening at once. All of these activities, and many more, are timed to coincide with the spring tide. Many marine organisms, in fact, have adapted to reproduce at spring tide. Their stories are remarkable.

The grunion, a common fish along the West Coast, actually comes on to shore to lay its eggs in the sand. By coming onto the beach at spring tide, the fish get a "ride" as far up the beach as possible. The ocean tends to erode sand from the beach as the tide rises and to deposit sand as the tide falls. So if grunion spawned on a rising tide, the water would wash the eggs out to sea and they would not hatch. Instead, the grunion lay their eggs just after the highest tide. The next time there is a very high tide, the spring tide nearly two weeks later, is the next time that the sand above the eggs will get totally wet. This water is the signal for the eggs to hatch and the baby fish "catch a ride" out to sea with the eroding sands of the rising tide.

FIGURE 24.26. Grunion spawn on the beach 2–6 nights following the full and new moons. Female grunions bury their tails in the sand, at which time a male wraps around her, and eggs and sperm are deposited into the new nest.

FIGURE 24.27. Turtles tend to lay their eggs above the high spring tide line. This protects their eggs from being washed away by the water.

See Page 694 for how to access e-Tools.

View the **Brittle Stars Spawning Video** (1:19) and **Christmas Tree Worms Spawning Video** (0:59) from the e-Tools.

e-Tools

FIGURE 24.28. Screenshot of the **Christmas Tree Worms Spawning Video**.

The coral reef ecosystem is home to many invertebrates that move slowly or not at all, including hard corals, clams, mussels, and sea anemones. These types of animals cannot travel to find a mate. Instead, many different invertebrates in the coral reef spawn, or release eggs and sperm. During the spring tide, water becomes so thick with the gametes that it looks cloudy. By timing their spawning, these animals ensure that eggs will be fertilized and the species continued. Scientists also hypothesize that the wide tidal range at spring tide carries the fertilized eggs away from the reef and potential predators. This video shows Christmas Tree Worms spawning in the midst of the annual coral spawning event. The Christmas Tree Worms in this video are located in the middle of a Brain Coral colony that is also spawning.

Brittle Stars also get in on the mass spawning event after the Full Moon in August at the Flower Garden Banks National Marine Sanctuary in the Gulf of Mexico. View the video, which shows male Red Serpent Brittle Stars releasing their sperm into the water through small openings along the sides of their central disks. The animals tend to do this in groups. Notice that at the end of the video, a female Ruby Brittle Star is actually "standing up" on the tips of her arms and releasing tiny, bright red eggs.

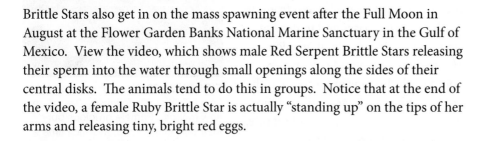

FIGURE 24.29. Screenshot of the **Brittle Stars Spawning Video**.

FIGURE 24.30. Sea stars are common in intertidal zones and many other habitats.

Tides also play an important role in coastal ecosystems. On rocky shorelines, for example, tides result in a specific pattern of organisms in a narrow area, similar to what we read about on sandy beaches in Lesson 23. The area along the coast between the high tide and low tide line is known as the **intertidal zone**. Organisms in the intertidal zone are submerged at high tide, but exposed to air and sunlight at low tide. These organisms are also subject to intense wave action. As a result, the adaptations we see in the rocky intertidal ecosystem allow organisms to cling to the rocks and to resist drying out. Sea stars, common in intertidal habitats, have thousands of tube feet that allow them to hold tightly to rocks and to other organisms. These star-shaped echinoderms (pronounced: eh-KĪ-neh-derms) feed by prying open mollusks such as mussels and clams, and then pushing their stomachs outside themselves and into the bivalves to digest their food externally!

There are four major zones within an intertidal community:

- The **splash zone** is almost always exposed to air, getting wet only during storms or other high water events. Therefore, there are relatively few species found in this area, which include some algae and snails that are well adapted for retaining moisture.

- The **high-intertidal zone** is submerged roughly twice a day, during high tides, and is otherwise exposed to air, wind, sunlight, and predators along the beach.

- The **mid-intertidal zone** is exposed to air only about twice a day, for short periods of time. Bivalves, particularly mussels, dominate this zone.

FIGURE 24.31. Close-up photograph of a Sunflower Star's tube feet. The tube feet allow sea stars to cling to hard substrates and to pry apart their prey.

- The **low-intertidal zone** is exposed only during the lowest tides. Anemones, seagrasses, sea stars, and other organisms are able to survive in this zone.

Tide pools are rocky areas along the coast filled with water. Tide pools are common in rocky intertidal ecosystems.

FIGURE 24.32. Rocky intertidal ecosystems show clear zonation patterns. The area farthest from the water is the splash zone, which has few inhabitants. The mid- and low-intertidal zones are most densely populated.

FIGURE 24.33. A close-up of a tide pool in Monterey, California, reveals anemones, snails, tunicates, and other organisms.

5. What are some of the conditions to which rocky intertidal organisms must adapt?

See Page 694 for how to access e-Tools.

View the *Elkhorn Slough Estuary Animation* (0:35) from the e-Tools. In this estuary in Monterey Bay, California, tidal cycles have a huge effect on the local environment. The animation is a time sequence.

e-Tools

FIGURE 24.34. Screenshot of the *Elkhorn Slough Estuary Animation*.

This animation illustrates one example of an estuary which is greatly affected by the tides. The black and white-striped stick you see is about 8 feet high. You can see at the tide's highest point, the man has to wear a mask and snorkel just to be able to stand in the same spot.

There are other examples of ecosystems affected by tides. Coastal ecosystems in which there are wide expanses of mud are called **mudflats**. Mudflats are common in estuaries, where rivers deposit sediment at their mouths. Mudflats are often associated with mangrove forests.

Organisms such as Fiddler Crabs, worms, and mollusks dominate mudflats. These Intertidal ecosystems are vastly different at high and low tide. At low tide, birds swoop in to dine in the exposed mud. Some birds bore into the mud, while others take advantage of the exposed crustaceans and mollusks and snatch them up.

6. Why would mudflats, estuaries, and rocky shores all be considered intertidal zones?

FIGURE 24.35. Low tide in Alaska's Cook Inlet reveals a broad mudflat. This mudflat is often dredged to allow ships to enter the port in the city of Anchorage.

FIGURE 24.36. A mudflat in Virginia is dotted by invertebrates. Exposure during low tide invites many bird species to enjoy the feast.

Evaluate

1. Describe three ways that tidal cycles affect organisms' adaptations or reproductive strategies.

2. Draw a picture that shows the causes of tides on Earth.

3. What causes tides and why do they vary from one day to the next?

4. Distinguish between ocean tides, waves, and currents.

FIGURE 24.37. The ocean's tides are due to gravitational interactions between the Earth and Moon, and to a lesser extent, the Sun. This picture of Earth was taken by astronauts on the Moon.

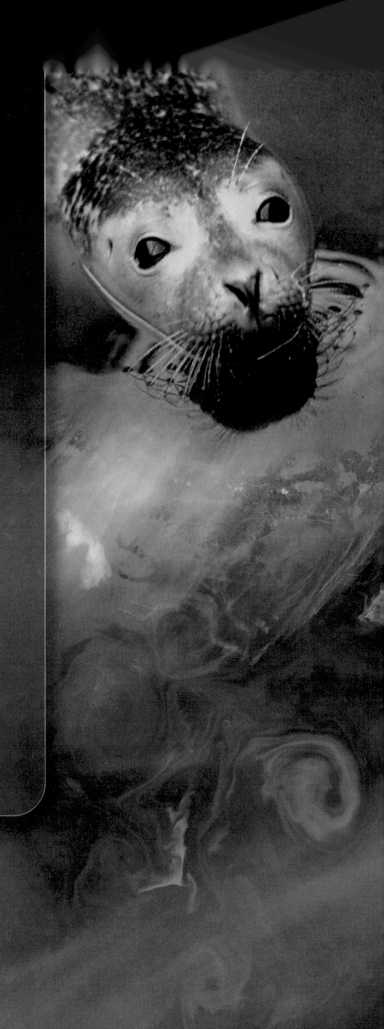

25

Animal Needs and Animal Tracking

INSIDE:

Objectives

You will be able to:

✔ Describe the relationship between water temperature, and dissolved oxygen.

✔ Explain the process of upwelling and relate the process to atmospheric winds, ocean currents, eddies, and bathymetry.

✔ Identify areas of upwelling and eddies in sea surface and phytoplankton satellite imagery.

✔ Relate the process of upwelling to the tracking of marine animals.

Benchmarks

1c. Throughout the ocean there is one interconnected circulation system powered by wind, tides, the force of the Earth's rotation (i.e., Coriolis Effect), the Sun, and water density differences. The shape of ocean basins and adjacent land masses influence the path of circulation.

1e. Most of Earth's water (97%) is in the ocean. Seawater has unique properties: it is saline; its freezing point is slightly lower than fresh water; its density is slightly higher; its electrical conductivity is much higher; and it is slightly basic. The salt in seawater comes from eroding land, volcanic emissions, reactions at the seafloor, and atmospheric deposition.

5f. Ocean habitats are defined by environmental factors. Due to interactions of abiotic factors (e.g., salinity, temperature, oxygen, pH, light, nutrients, pressure, substrate, circulation), ocean life is not evenly distributed temporally or spatially (i.e., it is "patchy"). Some regions of the ocean support more diverse and abundant life than anywhere on Earth, while much of the ocean is considered a desert.

Engage

Oxygen in the Ocean

In Lesson 17: Food Webs in Action, we focused on how phytoplankton support the marine food web by transforming carbon dioxide (CO_2) and water (H_2O) into sugar through the process of photosynthesis. Phytoplankton play another important role in the Earth system: they provide more than half of the oxygen in Earth's atmosphere. Before phytoplankton, the atmosphere was very different. The amount of oxygen was far less than it is today. Essentially, without phytoplankton, humans could not exist on Earth.

FIGURE 25.1. Phytoplankton produce more of the oxygen found in Earth's atmosphere than all the rest of the terrestrial vegetation combined. In one of the most important biological processes on the planet, they provide for the flow of energy between Earth's ecosystems.

Most organisms require oxygen in order to release energy from their food. This process is called cellular respiration. It is during this complex process that glucose, the energy-rich compound formed during photosynthesis, is broken down and energy is released. Oxygen allows for a more efficient retrieval of the energy stored in the glucose molecule. All aerobic organisms depend on oxygen, along with food, for survival.

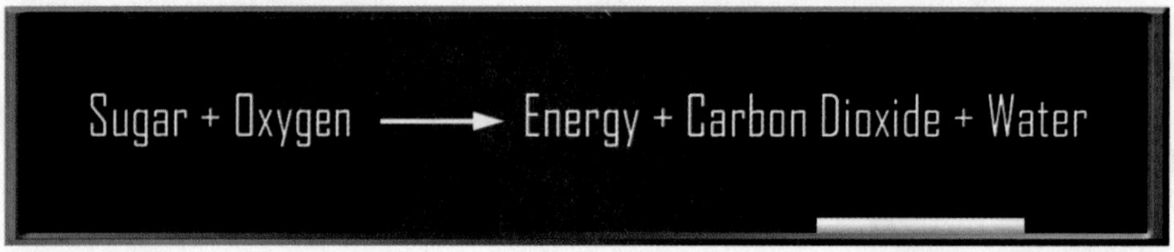

$$\text{Sugar + Oxygen} \longrightarrow \text{Energy + Carbon Dioxide + Water}$$

FIGURE 25.2. The chalkboard illustrates the simplified formula of releasing energy from food, cellular respiration.

Water is an excellent solvent. Seawater is well known for its salinity, or salt content, and common salt (NaCl) easily dissolves in water to form the ions Na^+ and Cl^-. Other salts, such as Mg^{+2}, $(SO_4)^{-2}$, and Ca^{+2}, are also components of seawater. In addition, seawater contains dissolved atmospheric gases, including oxygen, nitrogen, carbon dioxide, and argon. Because of its importance to cellular respiration, the amount of dissolved oxygen (DO) in seawater provides important data to marine biologists studying the distribution and movements of marine animals.

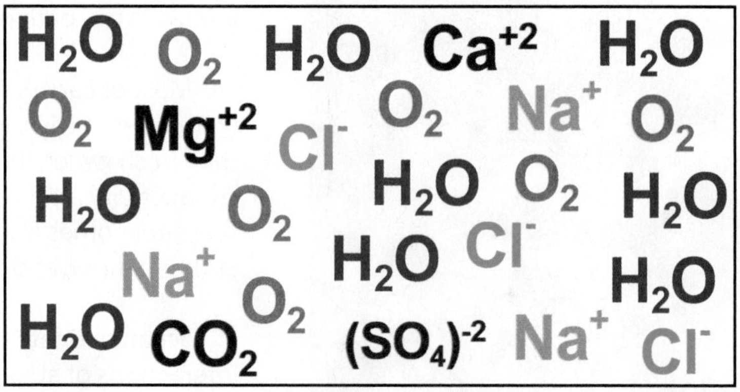

$$H_2O \quad O_2 \quad H_2O \quad Ca^{+2} \quad H_2O$$
$$O_2 \quad Mg^{+2} \quad Cl^- \quad O_2 \quad Na^+ \quad O_2$$
$$H_2O \quad O_2 \quad H_2O \quad O_2 \quad H_2O$$
$$Na^+ \quad H_2O \quad Cl^- \quad H_2O$$
$$H_2O \quad CO_2 \quad O_2 \quad (SO_4)^{-2} \quad Na^+ \quad Cl^-$$

FIGURE 25.3. Substances that dissolve in seawater include salts and gases from the atmosphere, such as oxygen.

There is much less oxygen freely available in seawater than there is in the atmosphere, which is approximately 21% oxygen. Oxygen gas dissolves in seawater; it is appropriately called **dissolved oxygen**, or **DO**. Many different substances are dissolved in seawater, including salts. This includes more than the ions Na$^+$ and Cl$^-$. The other prevalent salts are sulfates, magnesium, calcium, and potassium. FIGURE 25.4 illustrates the amounts of sea salts in seawater. The box on the left represents the percentage of water versus salts in a typical seawater sample. An enlargement of the small box labeled "Salt" is shown in the diagram on the right. The percentage of common seawater salts is illustrated in the different colored areas. Note that these percentages can vary by location and depth.

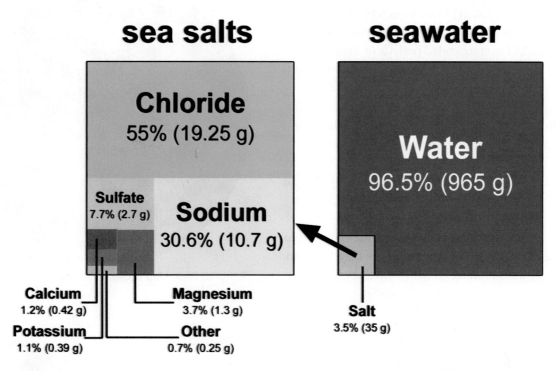

FIGURE 25.4. Dissolved salts compose the salinity, or salt portion, of Earth's seawater.

Some animals, such as fish and many invertebrates including crabs and squid, have gills with which to breathe and take DO directly from seawater. Other animals such as whales, sea turtles, and dolphins have lungs. These animals must come up to the surface of the water to breathe, where oxygen is much more plentiful.

FIGURE 25.5. The cuttlefish is a close relative of octopus and squid. These invertebrates have gills that help them extract DO from seawater.

Explore

See Page 694 for how to access e-Tools.

Cyberlab

Scientists measure physical properties of water (e.g., temperature, pH, clarity) to assess ecosystem health and to determine "normal" conditions and trends in data. Collecting data over extended periods of time allows scientists to determine the average measurements for different characteristics of the ocean. If they observe changes, it may be an indicator of a problem, something to continue monitoring. Scientists measure dissolved oxygen and temperature using instruments such as oxygen-sensitive probes and thermometers. Dissolved oxygen is measured as either milligrams per liter (mg/L) or parts per million (ppm).

In lieu of collecting your own data, use the Cyberlab to simulate data collection in the field. The data are from Rabbit Key Basin, located in the Florida Keys.

FIGURE 25.6. Map showing location of Rabbit Key Basin, Florida.

1. Go to the **DO Data Tool** in e-Tools.

   Virtually collect dissolved oxygen (DO) and temperature data using the data tool.

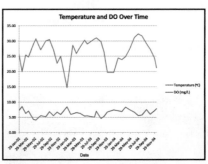

FIGURE 25.7. Screenshot of the **DO Data Tool**.

2. Record your data in a table in your notebook, similar to the one below.

Date	Temperature (°C)	Dissolved Oxygen (mg/L)

3. Use the *DO Data Tool* to create a line graph of the data you collected.

4. Compare your data with a classmate's.

5. Describe the results of the data. What is the relationship between dissolved oxygen and temperature?

6. How does seasonal variation influence temperature and dissolved oxygen data?

7. Are temperature and dissolved oxygen biotic or abiotic factors of ecosystems?

8. Over what period of time was the temperature and dissolved oxygen data collected?

9. What advantage is there for scientists to collect data over an extended period of time?

10. Explain why the procedure includes a step for comparing data with another classmate's.

Explain

Based on the data collection and analysis in the Cyberlab, one would expect that in areas of colder waters there is quantitatively more oxygen than in warmer waters. Take a look at the two images below. They each represent a season's average (three months) of temperature and chlorophyll concentrations. This means that three months of data (in this case, a period during the Northern Hemisphere Winter of 2007) was used to create each image. Pay careful attention to the area where the arrow is pointing.

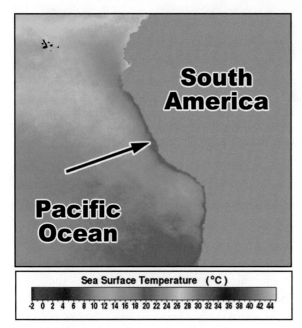

Sea Surface Temperature – Winter Mean 2007

FIGURE 25.8.

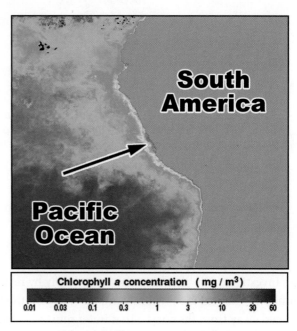

Chlorophyll – Winter Mean 2007

1. Explain the relationship between the SSTs and chlorophyll concentrations near where the arrow is pointing.

2. Become acquainted with the landscape of South America. FIGURE 25.9 shows the topography of most of the continent. What geographic land features do you observe in the vicinity of the high chlorophyll concentrations? Reconsider the chlorophyll (phytoplankton). Since there are high concentrations of chlorophyll (phytoplankton) near the coast, from where are all the nutrients coming?

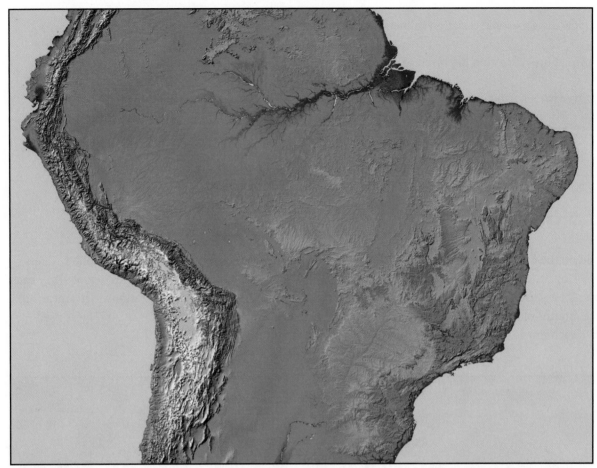

FIGURE 25.9. The image of South America was generated with data from NASA's Shuttle Radar Topography Mission (SRTM). The variety of landforms that make up the South American Continent is readily apparent. The topography is dominated by the Andes Mountains, which extend along the Pacific Coast.

3. Explain the connection between the cold water and the nutrients that phytoplankton need. How does the influx of cold water affect the nutrients available?

Let's investigate this phenomenon more deeply by revisiting a familiar graphic. In FIGURE 25.10, the Humboldt Current is shown moving westward off the South American Coastline. Surface water is swiftly dragged away from the coast. That water must be replaced. As warm surface water moves offshore, cold, nutrient-rich water from below rises upward to replace it. As you discovered, cold water holds more dissolved oxygen than warm water. The cold water that comes to the surface carries nutrients that accumulate from decomposed organic material that fell from shallower depths.

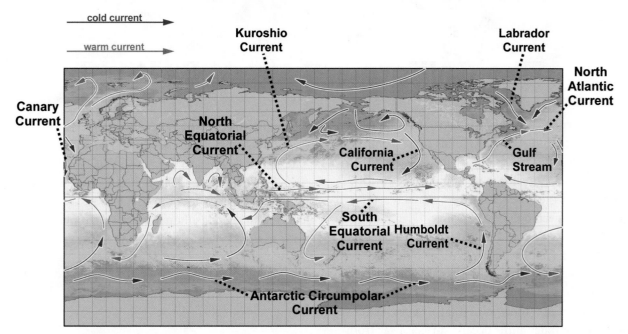

FIGURE 25.10. Select major surface currents are revisited. Note the movement of the Humboldt Current away from the South American Coast.

When cold water with a lot of nutrients rises from the ocean depths, the process is known as **upwelling**. Upwelling fuels phytoplankton growth. While nutrients are often scarce on the ocean's surface, upwelling brings ample nutrients up from the depths. An aspect of an environment that limits the growth, reproduction, or distribution of organisms is known as a **limiting factor**. In the ocean, nutrient and light availability are often limiting factors for phytoplankton growth.

Wind is a very important factor in upwelling. When wind blows from over land to over the ocean, it helps to move warm surface waters away from the land. This allows the cooler water that was underneath the warm water to rise to the surface. Since the water being brought to the surface by upwelling is cold, it is also able to hold more dissolved oxygen.

See Page 694 for how to access e-Tools.

View the *Upwelling Animation* from the e-Tools.

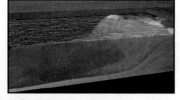

e-Tools

FIGURE 25.11. Screenshot of the *Upwelling Animation*.

Bathymetry also affects upwelling. Areas off of the coast with steep continental slopes tend to generate much upwelling when the wind conditions are right. There is a great supply of deep water available there that can flow to the surface fairly easily. The water is not impeded by a shallow seafloor.

4. Explain why one might expect to find an animal that is being tracked in areas of upwelling.

5. Look at the simplified currents map again. If the winds are consistent with the previous examples, where are some other areas where you might expect to find upwelling?

6. How could you use Earth imagery to verify whether the response to Question 5 is correct?

The California Current System

The California Coast is one of the most productive ocean areas in the world. Animals come from faraway places to feed in this special place. One of the main reasons for these animals' travels to California is the physical environmental response known as upwelling.

Upwelling Season

During the spring and early summer, winds blow from north to south along the California Coast. The steady winds and rotation of the Earth contribute to pushing the water at the ocean's surface away from the shoreline. Phytoplankton in the area use the resources available for photosynthesis, and suddenly there is a lot of phytoplankton. An eruption of phytoplankton is called a **bloom**. Nutrients contribute to the process by which the organisms grow and multiply. This is the base for a very diverse food web that includes invertebrates, marine mammals, seabirds, and sea turtles.

Relaxation Season

When the winds from the north slow down in the late summer and early fall, upwelling also slows. This is called **relaxation**. The water at the surface warms up; there are not a lot of nutrients. The sea surface is calm. During relaxation, offshore phytoplankton on the top ocean layer ease back toward the coast.

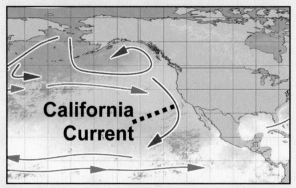

FIGURE 25.12. Map showing the California Current.

Winter Storm Season

In the winter, there are many storms and the seas are rough; there is high surf. The water at the surface mixes with water a bit below; the temperatures and amounts of nutrients are similar at the surface and at depth. There is less sunlight in winter, and phytoplankton do not bloom as readily.

FIGURE 25.13. During Upwelling Season in the California Current System, nutrients and dissolved oxygen are brought to the surface, fueling a robust food web.

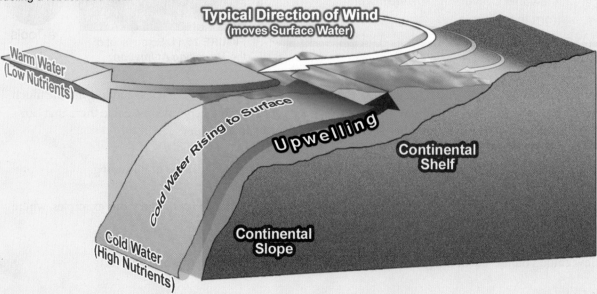

Nutrients, Oxygen, and Animals

Take a look at the two images below. The image on the left shows chlorophyll concentrations; the one on the right indicates SSTs. The animal tracks you see are for Sooty Shearwaters, which are a type of seabird. These birds nest in the South Pacific, on the beaches of New Zealand, and on other islands. Notice that all of the tagged animals are congregating in a very productive area off California, thousands of miles from their nesting grounds.

FIGURE 25.14. Sooty Shearwater.

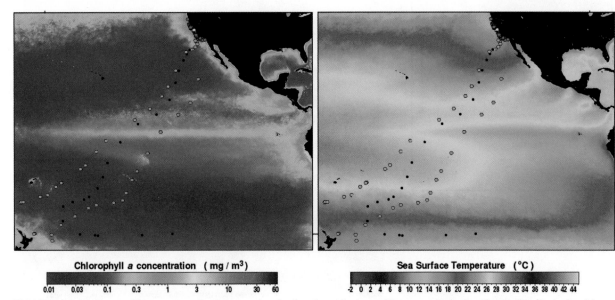

Chlorophyll *a* concentration (mg / m^3)

0.01 0.03 0.1 0.3 1 3 10 30 60

Sea Surface Temperature (°C)

-2 0 2 4 6 8 10 12 14 16 18 20 22 24 26 28 30 32 34 36 38 40 42 44

FIGURE 25.15. Sooty Shearwaters fly thousands of miles from their nesting grounds in the South Pacific to feed in the productive waters of the California Current. Each dot of the same color on the maps represents a location of an animal at a particular time.

A wide variety of organisms, including seabirds, whales, fish, and invertebrates use upwelling areas as feeding grounds—making them areas with high biodiversity.

7. Why does abundant phytoplankton in an area support high biodiversity?

While many of the animals we track must come to the surface to breathe with their lungs, there are many animals that breathe underwater. Many invertebrates and all cartilaginous (pronounced: kahr-tǐ-LAJ-ǐn-ǐss) and bony fishes use gills to breathe beneath the surface. Oxygen is much less abundant in water than in air. Therefore, gills must be highly specialized to extract every possible oxygen molecule.

Observe FIGURE 25.16, an image of an area along the coast of California during upwelling season. The high-resolution satellite image shows temperatures along the coast in late May 2000 just above 10 °C (50 °F).

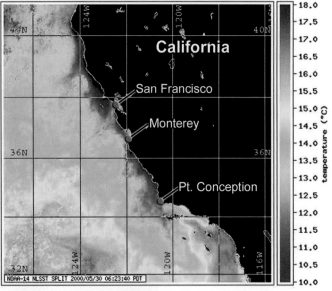

FIGURE 25.16. Water temperatures are typically colder near to shore than farther offshore for most of the California Coastline north of Point Conception—the bend in the coastline at 34.5° N. Notice the strength of the upwelling, as evidenced by how far the cold water extends offshore. Some areas show upwelled water pushed hundreds of miles offshore.

Elaborate

Eddies and Upwelling

The image below shows the location of a Leatherback Sea Turtle. There is something special about the location of this animal. Can you determine what it is?

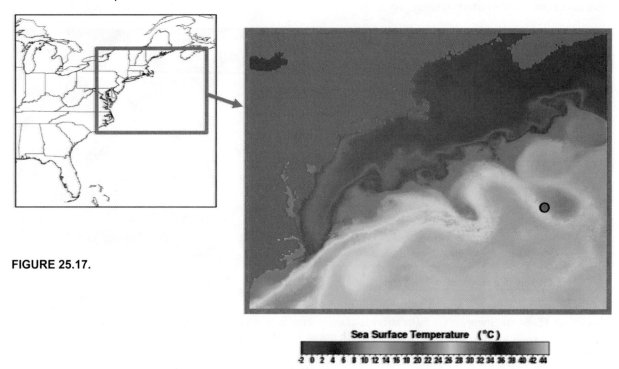

FIGURE 25.17.

8. Observe the image below (FIGURE 25.18) and FIGURE 25.19 on the next page. Describe the path of the Gulf Stream.

FIGURE 25.18. SST image of the Gulf Stream.

Eddy Formation

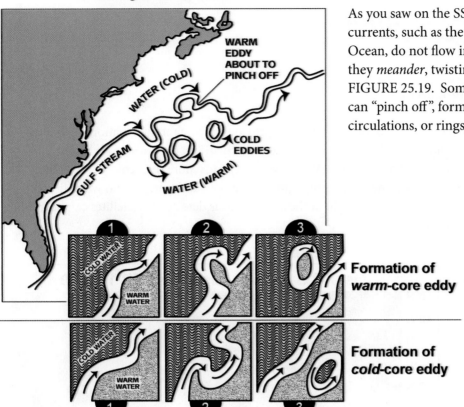

As you saw on the SST image, warm water currents, such as the Gulf Stream in the Atlantic Ocean, do not flow in a straight line. Rather, they *meander*, twisting and turning as seen in FIGURE 25.19. Sometimes, these **meanders** can "pinch off", forming huge swirling ocean circulations, or rings, called **eddies**.

FIGURE 25.19. Warm- and cold-core eddies "pinch off" and form meandering currents or rings.

As seen by studying FIGURE 25.19, the direction in which eddies pinch off and form from the Gulf Stream determines whether they carry warm surface waters or cold waters in their insides. Cold-core eddies circle counterclockwise. They carry nutrient-rich, colder waters through warmer regions of the ocean. The oxygen levels in cold-core eddies are also higher than warm-core eddies, encouraging the growth of phytoplankton and marine organisms. As a result, cold-core eddies are often the site of high productivity and feeding grounds for marine organisms, including marine mammals. Warm-core eddies pinch off and migrate north of the Gulf Stream. These waters (those seen in FIGURE 25.18) originated where warm water is generally found. The Gulf Stream flow waters are warm and as a result will often lack nutrients.

Eddies normally measure in the 50–200 kilometer (~30–120 mile) range in diameter, but they can have diameters as great as 300 kilometers (~190 miles). These rings may be stationary or they can travel about 1 kilometer per hour. They typically last for a few months before they dissipate and the water from within a ring mixes with the surrounding water. Large, warm-core eddies can move huge amounts of warm water northward to a particular region. There is significant heat transfer from the ocean to the atmosphere in these processes that potentially may affect weather.

9. Describe what you observe in the FIGURES 20.18 and 20.19.

10. In which type of eddy would you expect to find more marine organisms, cold-core or warm-core? Explain thoroughly by giving at least two reasons to support this hypothesis.

Sea Height Data—What Is Sea Surface Height? What Do Images Show?

Materials:

- *Identifying Eddies Worksheet*

Sea surface height is another characteristic of ocean water that provides important information to scientists. Although influenced by gravity, tides, and the Earth's active ocean circulations, the sea surface height represents a measure of the heat content of the water. Warm water expands more than cold water. Water molecules move around when they absorb heat, bumping into one another, and warm liquid water literally expands, taking up more space. Therefore, the height of the sea surface as detected by satellites can be used to calculate how much heat is stored in the ocean.

Sea surface height data from remote sensing satellites help oceanographers and other Earth scientists to identify the patterns of warm and cold water. The patterns provide important information for studying climate and weather. For example, short-term climate changes or events such as the El Niño and La Niña are dramatically visible in sea height data. In addition to tracking currents, this data can also be used to pinpoint eddies. Warm-core eddies have higher sea heights than the sea heights of the surrounding ocean water.

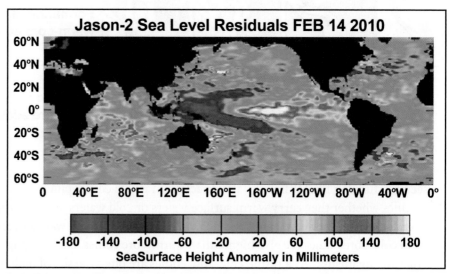

FIGURE 25.20. This image shows sea height difference from what is normal. The higher-than-normal sea heights off of the west coast of South America suggest an El Niño event. The higher waters are warmer waters and indicate low production activity and lower DO concentrations.

The images in FIGURE 25.20 and FIGURE 25.21 show sea surface height differences between what we see and what is normal for regions. Warmer water appears red. Each image is a 10-day average of data, centered on the date indicated.

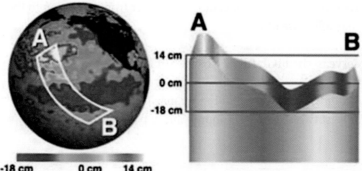

FIGURE 25.21. Sea height data from satellites measure differences in the height of the ocean from what is normal.

11. On your worksheet, place a circle around where you think there may be a warm-core eddy and a cold-core eddy.

12. Why might it be useful and important to be able to track eddies in the ocean?

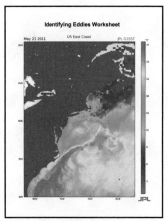

FIGURE 25.22. *Identifying Eddies Worksheet*.

Evaluate

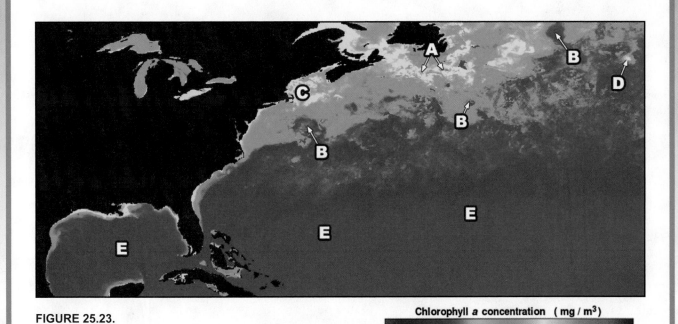

FIGURE 25.23.

Chlorophyll *a* concentration (mg / m^3)

0.01   0.03   0.1   0.3   1   3   10   30   60

1. Describe the phytoplankton concentrations at all points labeled A–E. If any of the regions include an eddy, indicate whether it is a warm-core or cold-core eddy. How do you know?

2. Where would the dissolved oxygen concentration be greater, at an A location or at a B location?

3. Explain why so much of the ocean has phytoplankton concentrations similar to area E.

4. Why is it important to study eddies and upwelling when tracking marine animals?

Phase II:

Research and Analysis –
Interpreting Satellite Imagery and
Analyzing Animal Movements

26

Student Expert Research

INSIDE:

Objectives

You will be able to:

✔ **Interpret real-time satellite data and imagery.**

✔ **Address student-developed questions about marine environments.**

✔ **Take notes from secondary sources and write a report, attributing ideas and facts to appropriate sources.**

Benchmarks

1c. Throughout the ocean there is one interconnected circulation system powered by wind, tides, the force of the Earth's rotation (i.e., Coriolis Effect), the Sun, and water density differences. The shape of ocean basins and adjacent land masses influence the path of circulation.

5b. Most life in the ocean exists as microbes. Microbes are the most important primary producers in the ocean. Not only are they the most abundant life form in the ocean, they have extremely fast growth rates and life cycles.

5f. Ocean habitats are defined by environmental factors. Due to interactions of abiotic factors (e.g., salinity, temperature, oxygen, pH, light, nutrients, pressure, substrate, circulation), ocean life is not evenly distributed temporally or spatially (i.e., it is "patchy"). Some regions of the ocean support more diverse and abundant life than anywhere on Earth, while much of the ocean is considered a desert.

(continued on next page)

7a. The ocean is the last and largest unexplored place on Earth; less than 5% of it has been explored. This is the great frontier for the next generation's explorers and researchers, where they will find great opportunities for inquiry and investigation.

7d. New technologies, sensors, and tools are expanding our ability to explore the ocean. Ocean scientists are relying more and more on satellites, drifters, buoys, subsea observatories, and unmanned submersibles.

7f. Ocean exploration is truly interdisciplinary. It requires close collaboration among biologists, chemists, climatologists, computer programmers, engineers, geologists, meteorologists, and physicists and new ways of thinking.

Engage

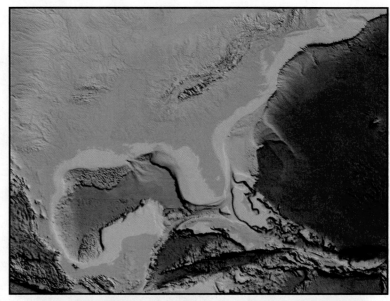

FIGURE 26.1. In this Lesson, Student Bathymetry Expert Teams will conduct in-depth research on seafloor features. Students will later discover these types of maps help to define the movement or migrations of marine animals.

Later in this Lesson you will be assigned to a "Student Expert Team". You will research answers to questions about <u>one of four</u> "expert" topics. Some groups will research Marine Animal "Species". Others will focus on data that can be observed in Earth imagery ("Bathymetry", "Phytoplankton", and "Sea Surface"). Throughout Lessons 1–25 you have learned to interpret different types of satellite imagery. Now, based on your research, you will become "Student Experts". In the next Lesson, you will take what you learn here to explain the movement of animals that are tracked by satellite.

1. Copy the table below in your notebook. Before breaking up into "Expert Teams", continue to review your work in the course by telling how different types of marine animals are affected by the environmental parameters listed in the table.

Environmental Parameters	Effects on Specific Marine Animals
Bathymetry (underwater landforms)	
Chlorophyll (phytoplankton)	
Sea Surface (includes temperature, sea ice, sea height, surface currents, and wind currents for seabirds)	

2. In Lesson 1: Diving Into Ocean Ecosystems, you developed your own questions about the ocean. At that point you had not studied about the ocean. In Lesson 5: Migrations in the Sea, you identified some of the environmental parameters that affect marine animal movement and asked additional questions for study. Review the questions generated. Together with the class, decide which questions would be appropriate for each of the four teams for further investigation. A chart similar to the one below will help you organize this step. Color code the questions on the chart paper, or reorganize them onto new pages.

Factors	How Are Marine Animals Influenced by the Factor?	Questions We Have
Landforms (above or below the ocean surface, shorelines)		
Food (types, location)		
Temperature (water, air)		

You will use this information in the **Elaborate** and **Evaluate** sections.

Explore

In this section you will practice how to interpret various forms of remote sensing satellite data. This will help you later in the **Explain** section when you are working to become "Experts". Each student will study and make observations based on data about each environmental parameter or about a marine species.

You will consider how the data in imagery changes over time and make inferences based on your observations. The processes of making observations and conclusions are essential steps in scientific inquiry. You may post your work on a *Scientific Community Research Wall* in the classroom or in the building hallways, for others to view and discuss.

FIGURE 26.2. Student Expert Research Teams make observations and write conclusions about SST and other types of data. In Lesson 27: Student Expert Analysis, you will relate these observations to animal movements.

Recall that observations are simply what your senses or tools, which are extensions of your senses, tell you. Scientists perform a lot of research and do a lot of reading to help them understand how their observations fit into a larger question. For example, how do Sea Surface Temperatures change over time? Scientists use background information and their observations to explain their findings, analyze data, and make conclusions.

In Lesson 27: Student Expert Analysis, you will use your observation and inference-making skills to explain how specific environmental factors affect the movement of marine animals. Let's practice by looking at sample environmental data for each parameter.

Bathymetry

Montserrat is one of the smaller volcanic islands, approximately 13 kilometers by 8 kilometers (~8 miles by ~5 miles), that make up the archipelago (pronounced: ar-kĭ-PELL-ĭ-gō) of the Lesser Antilles Islands (pronounced: an-TILL-lees). This chain of islands is located north of South America and over 2,000 kilometers (~1,243 miles) southeast of the Florida Keys. The islands sit along the tectonic plate boundary of the Caribbean Plate and the North and South American Plates. The North American Plate subducts under the Caribbean Plate, forming volcanoes. Montserrat's active volcano, Soufrière Hills (pronounced: soo-free-AIR) pictured in FIGURE 26.3, began its most recent activity in 1995.

The false color satellite image shows Soufrière Hills on the southern half of the island. The red areas indicate vegetation. The gray areas indicate volcanic material, including pumice rock, hot ash, and volcanic gas that flow down the side of the volcano toward the ocean like an avalanche.

FIGURE 26.3. The lava dome at the summit of Soufrière Hills collapsed in February 2010, causing an eruption and thick avalanche of debris that was 15 meters (~49 feet) thick in some areas.

See Page 694 for how to access e-Tools.

Interactive versions of all activities in this **Explore** section are available in the e-Tools. Use the slider to observe changes over time.

e-Tools

FIGURE 26.4. Screenshot of the slider.

1. List and describe at least three bathymetric features that you observe in the image below.

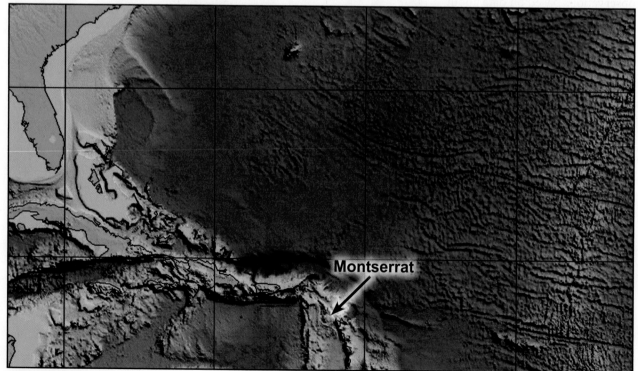

Montserrat

FIGURE 26.5.

2. Identify and provide the depths at Points A, B, and C in the image below.

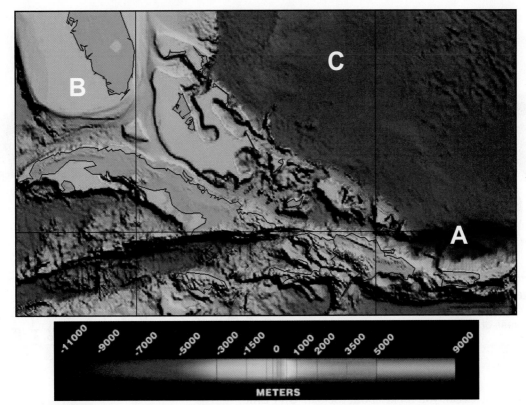

FIGURE 26.6.

3. What additional questions can you ask about the bathymetry data?

Sea Surface Temperature

e-Tools

1. What changes do you observe in sea surface temperatures over time?

FIGURE 26.7.

Sea Surface Temperature (°C)

-2 0 2 4 6 8 10 12 14 16 18 20 22 24 26 28 30 32 34 36 38 40 42 44

2. What changes do you observe in sea ice concentrations over time?

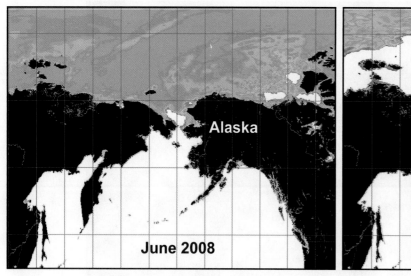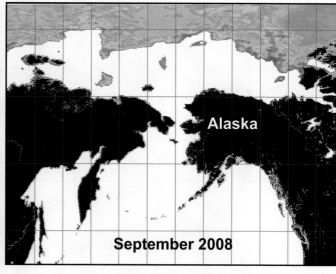

FIGURE 26.8. Sea Ice concentrations in June and September 2008. Land is black. White areas represent areas of open ocean.

3. What inferences can you make about the data over time?

4. What additional questions can you ask about the sea surface data?

Phytoplankton

e-Tools

1. What observations can you make about the change in chlorophyll concentration over time based on the data below?

FIGURE 26.9.

Chlorophyll *a* concentration (mg / m³)

2. What inferences can you make about chlorophyll concentration based on the data?

3. What additional questions can you ask about the data?

Explain

Now it is time to break into groups, your "Student Expert Teams", to perform research. In your Expert teams (Species, Bathymetry, Phytoplankton, Sea Surface), you will conduct secondary research and use the skills you practiced in earlier Lessons. Your team will be an important source of information and data for other Expert Teams. Using the *Marine Science: The Dynamic Ocean* website, books, and atlases, you will conduct research to answer the research questions so that you have very deep and informed answers. Here you will learn to organize your research using Note Cards and Source Cards, as you did in Lesson 22: Relationships in the Sea. Make sure to put answers in your own words. You should put together your responses to research questions from a variety of sources, and not rely on only one source. Write up your findings; print out pictures, and potentially post them on a *Scientific Community Research Wall*. You will also present your findings to the class.

Work through your Expert Team questions from the **Explain** section first. Then respond to those in the **Elaborate** section. Answer only the Questions for the Student Expert Team to which you are assigned. It will be helpful to use Note Cards to record your ideas as you conduct research. Then, compile your ideas and answer the Questions in a typed report to be submitted to your teacher and added to the *Scientific Community Research Wall* (described on next page). Use the following checklist to be sure you include everything.

- ✓ **All your research questions and answers from the Explain section**
- ✓ **All assigned class Questions and Answers as referred to in the Elaborate section**
- ✓ **Pictures/diagrams with captions**
- ✓ **Data tables if pertinent**
- ✓ **Graphs/plots if required**
- ✓ **Any charts your group has created**
- ✓ **Illustrations that help support your ideas**
- ✓ **A Works Cited page**

FIGURE 26.10. Examples of a Source Card and a Note Card.

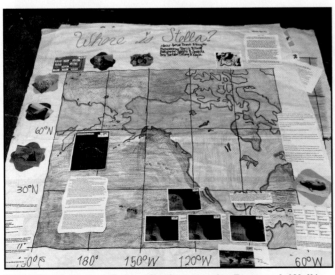

FIGURE 26.11. The *Scientific Community Research Wall* is an opportunity to teach students and faculty members about marine animals and dynamic ocean processes.

Optional Scientific Community Research Wall

During the current Research activity, the Wall Display is an opportunity for you to post your work and the responses to research questions. The work will demonstrate the successful completion of the Research Questions.

The *Scientific Community Research Wall* ultimately tells a story of an animal's movements. During Lesson 27: Student Expert Analysis, observers in other classes and throughout the school can observe the relationships between the animal's location and different types of Earth data.

Later, in Lesson 27: Student Expert Analysis, the *Scientific Community Research Wall* can illustrate special connections. Student Expert Teams will have the ability to regularly post updates about their animals. For example, one team's specific animal location may illustrate the connection between the animal's needs and cold sea surface temperatures. Another team could establish the relationship between a phytoplankton bloom north of the Gulf Stream in the Atlantic Ocean in spring and what an animal needs. The animal and the scientific remote sensing data can illustrate that the dynamic ocean functions as a system.

As you are working on your research, remember to create some highlights of your work in hard copy. Post your work to an area of the *Research Wall* that you are assigned. It is a way in which you can put together and share your research with the class.

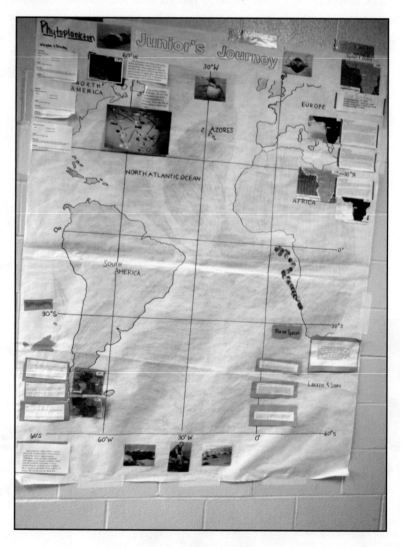

FIGURE 26.12. A *Scientific Community Research Wall* shows the movements of Junior, a sea turtle, off the coast of Africa. Notice that each Student Expert Team has contributed to the Wall.

Team 1: Species Expert Research

The job of a Species Expert Team member is to learn as much as possible about the assigned marine animal species. Go to the *Marine Science: The Dynamic Ocean* website. Go to Phase II. Click on Lesson 26: Student Expert Research. In *e-Tools*, access Research Links. This will take you to the *Signals of Spring* website. Utilize *Signals of Spring* Research Links to perform the following Research Activities:

1. Create a large chart that will describe the life stages of your animal species.

   a. Research the different life stages of your species. For example, the chart below includes the life stages of sea turtles. Create a chart similar to the one below. Fill in the left column with the titles of the specific life stages for your animal.

   b. In a chart similar to the one below, fill in details about your animal's preferred Habitat and Food. Identify its Challenges for Survival and Adaptations that help the animal at each life stage. The Life Stage column in the table below shows an example for a sea turtle.

FIGURE 26.13. Leatherback Sea Turtle hatchlings head for the waves. Species Expert Teams learn about animals in all of their life stages.

Life Stage	Habitat	Food	Challenges for Survival	Adaptations
	• In which environment(s) does this animal live during each life stage? • How does the habitat help the animal meet its needs? • Does the animal need specific environments for specific activities (e.g., reproduction, feeding)?	• What does the animal eat at each life stage? • How does the animal find food? • How much food does the animal require?	• What natural threats (including predators) does the animal face during each life stage? • What threats does the animal face as a result of human activities?	• What adaptations does the animal have that enhance its survival or reproduction at each life stage?
Egg				
Hatchling				
Juvenile				
Adult				

2. What does your animal look like throughout its life? Gather pictures of the species in various life stages to go with your data table.

Team 1: Species Expert Research (continued)

3. Where does the species you are researching generally move? Where do you predict their movements will be?

    a. Address whether you think your species travels through any National Marine Sanctuaries. If so, which ones? Discuss why that is important.

    b. Does your species normally migrate? If so, present the normal migration routes.

4. How are marine animals tracked by satellite and how do we know the animals' locations?

5. Is the population of the species you are researching stable or is it threatened or endangered?

Team 2: Bathymetry Expert Research

Bathymetry Experts will study the seafloor features of some of the National Marine Sanctuaries. Doing so will introduce you to the diverse features of these special places. Go to the *Marine Science: The Dynamic Ocean* website. Go to Phase II. Click on Lesson 26: Student Expert Research. In *e-Tools*, access Research Links. This will take you to the *Signals of Spring* website. Utilize Research Links to perform the following Research Activities:

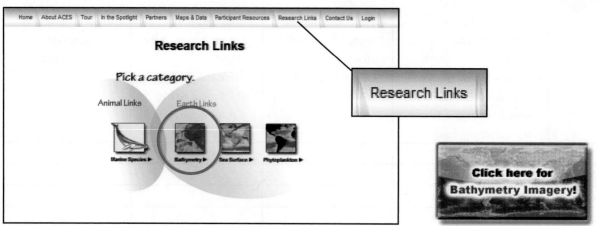

FIGURE 26.14. Screenshots from the *Signals of Spring* website illustrate the Research Links page. Bathymetry Expert Teams go to the website for practice Earth imagery and answers to research questions.

1. Copy the chart below. For each of the National Marine Sanctuaries (NMSs) listed in the table, use the Map Ruler Tool to measure the width of the continental shelf in the area of the sanctuary. Start at the coastline, and measure straight outward, through the sanctuary, to the edge of the continental shelf (i.e., the continental slope). Then, use the color bar to measure the greatest depth in the sanctuary.

Use the NMS map in Appendix D to help you locate these areas. For NMSs that are not close to the coast, measure the greatest width of the sanctuary.

Map Ruler Tool

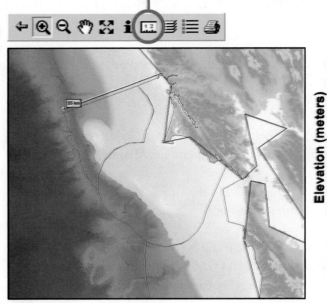

FIGURE 26.15. Screenshot showing a close-up of Cordell Bank National Marine Sanctuary.

Elevation (meters): 5000, 3000, 2000, 1000, 500, 250, 100, 1, 0, -25, -50, -100, -150, -200, -250, -500, -600, -750, -1000, -2000, -2500, -3000, -3500, -4000

	Width (km)	Depth (m)
Cordell Bank National Marine Sanctuary		
Stellwagen Bank National Marine Sanctuary		
Flower Garden Banks National Marine Sanctuary		
Gray's Reef National Marine Sanctuary		

2. Using bathymetry maps and world atlases, draw four cross-sectional plots (profiles) of the ocean floor. Begin at the closest part of the U.S. Coast and move outward into the ocean through each of the National Marine Sanctuaries listed below. For each sanctuary, create a data table in which you will record the seafloor depth every 50 kilometers.

Distance	50 km	100 km	150 km	200 km	250 km	300 km	Etc.
Depth							

Your plot should illustrate the depth of the water, starting at the sea surface on the *y*-axis. The *x*-axis illustrates the distance from the shoreline, through the sanctuary, straight out to sea. This is similar to the profile you created in Lesson 6: Explore the Seafloor.

Follow the directions to plot the data and create your graphs for each of the locations below:

> Hint: The ocean's surface will be represented at the top of the vertical scale on the graphs.

a. Through the Cordell Bank National Marine Sanctuary: from the California Coast to 500 kilometers into the Pacific Ocean

b. Through the Stellwagen Bank National Marine Sanctuary: from the Massachusetts Coast to 1,000 kilometers into the Atlantic Ocean

c. Monterey Bay National Marine Sanctuary: from the California Coast to 500 km into the Pacific Ocean

d. Gray's Reef National Marine Sanctuary: from the Georgia Coast to 500 km into the Atlantic Ocean

Prepare a short report and discuss your findings as you answer the following Questions:

• What bathymetric features (such as canyons, islands, continental shelves, continental slopes, etc.) can you detect in each of your plots? Label them on the graphs.

• Which of the four National Marine Sanctuaries has the most varied bathymetry? In which is the seafloor the deepest?

• How do these National Marine Sanctuaries compare with one another in terms of bathymetry?

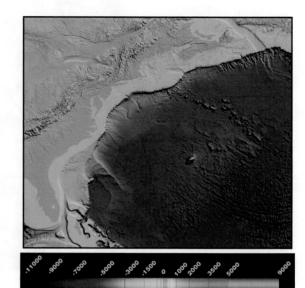

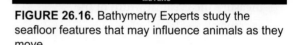

FIGURE 26.16. Bathymetry Experts study the seafloor features that may influence animals as they move.

Team 3: Phytoplankton Expert Research

Phytoplankton Experts become well versed in interpreting chlorophyll imagery. They help determine the concentration of phytoplankton and what it means for local food webs. Go to the *Marine Science: The Dynamic Ocean* website. Go to Phase II. Click on Lesson 26: Student Expert Research. In *e-Tools*, access Research Links. This will take you to the *Signals of Spring* website. Utilize *Signals of Spring* Research Links to perform the following Research Activities.

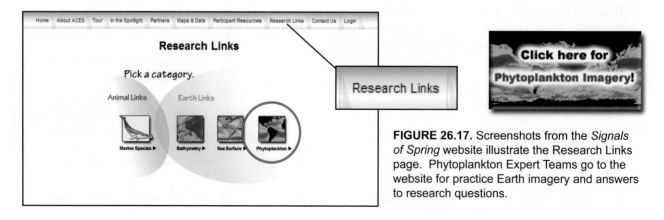

FIGURE 26.17. Screenshots from the *Signals of Spring* website illustrate the Research Links page. Phytoplankton Expert Teams go to the website for practice Earth imagery and answers to research questions.

Team 3: Phytoplankton Expert Research (continued)

1. Explain how satellites are used to determine the presence of phytoplankton. How is chlorophyll related to phytoplankton?

In the Phytoplankton Research Links, click the icons shown on the previous page, to find the information to respond to Research Question 2.

2. Compare and contrast the chlorophyll imagery for the East and West Coasts of the United States from January, April, and August for two different years. Print out the images.

3. Next, respond to a.–d.: (Hint: Use an atlas for assistance.)

    a. Study the satellite data imagery. Describe how the phytoplankton concentration changes in the Atlantic Ocean over the two years. Include the specific dates of the imagery in your descriptions. When and where do the biggest changes occur? Explain.

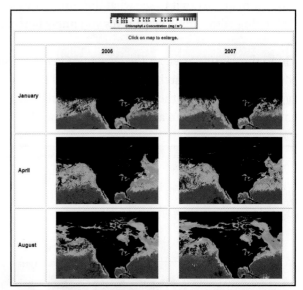

FIGURE 26.18. Phytoplankton Expert Teams explore chlorophyll satellite imagery to study food webs and sources for marine animals.

    b. Describe in words how the phytoplankton concentration changes along the California Coast over the two years. Include the specific dates of the imagery in your descriptions. When and where do the biggest changes occur? Explain.

    c. Where are the areas with the highest concentration of phytoplankton for the East Coast? For the West Coast? Explain.

    d. What are any major differences from year to year, if any?

4. Draw a sample food chain or web for your animal. Write a sentence, explaining why phytoplankton are so important.

5. In your notebook or on a piece of paper, explain why phytoplankton seem to be in greater abundance around the continental shelf, coastal river outlets, bays, shorelines, and islands. Identify some of these abundant areas you found in the chlorophyll imagery.

Team 4: Sea Surface Expert Research

Sea Surface Experts interpret several types of data. You will want to be able to first interpret a map, then begin to learn to see connections between data. For example, when you look at a SST map, you may put an ocean current map next to it to see what the similarities are. This helps to understand or tell a story about the data. Practicing with simple maps gives you important skills.

Go to the *Marine Science: The Dynamic Ocean* website. Go to Phase II. Click on Lesson 26: Student Expert Research. In *e-Tools*, access Research Links. This will take you to the *Signals of Spring* website. In the Sea Surface Research Links, click the icons shown below, to find the information needed to answer Research Questions 1 and 2.

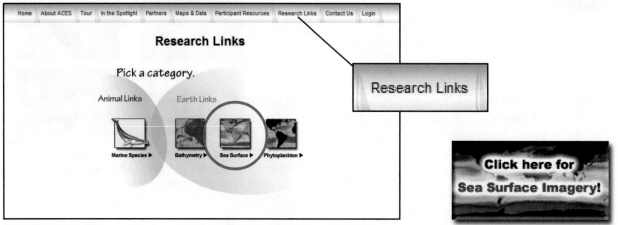

FIGURE 26.19. Screenshots from the *Signals of Spring* website illustrate the Research Links page. Sea Surface Expert Teams go to the website for practice Earth imagery and answers to research questions.

1. Print a set of the mean monthly SST images for January, April, and August 2007.

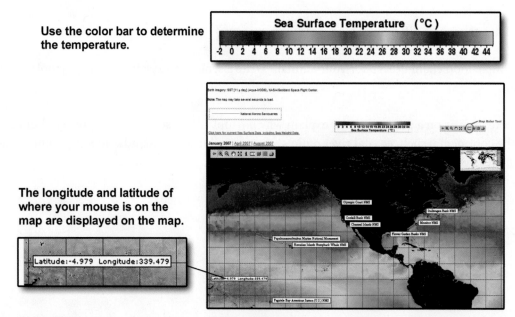

FIGURE 26.20. SST imagery can be correlated to other maps including surface current, sea heights, and sea ice data. A wealth of data is available from which Student Expert Teams can make connections and determine important relationships.

Team 4: Sea Surface Expert Research (continued)

2. Create a table similar to the one below and, for the general locations of each of the National Marine Sanctuaries listed, fill in the mean temperatures for each of the months listed:

National Marine Sanctuary (NMS)	Mean January 2007 SST	Mean April 2007 SST	Mean August 2007 SST
Fagatele Bay NMS			
Florida Keys NMS			
Cordell Bank NMS			
The Monitor NMS			
Olympic Coast NMS			
Stellwagen Bank NMS			
Channel Islands NMS			
Hawaiian Islands Humpback Whale NMS			

Write a short report in which you explain the answers to the following Questions:

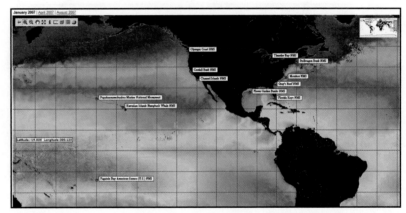

FIGURE 26.21. Screenshot of the interactive *Sea Surface Imagery* map.

- Which sanctuaries experience the warmest and coldest temperatures? Why?

- Which sanctuaries have similar latitudes? Compare the mean temperatures for the months between all the locations.

    - Are the mean temperatures at similar latitudes similar?
    - Do they follow the same patterns over the course of the seasons?
    - Why or why not?

- Using the tools available on the SST maps, find the temperatures 100 kilometers from the East and West Coasts of the United States at 35° N latitude.

    How can you explain the differences?

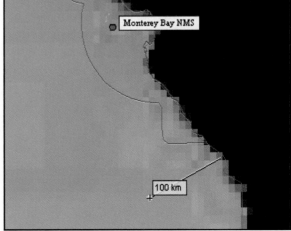

FIGURE 26.22. Use the *Map Ruler Tool* to determine distance.

Team 4: Sea Surface Expert Research (continued)

3. Scientists use many types of sea surface data to make observations including surface currents, sea heights, sea ice, and winds (affecting the ocean). Using the maps provided in the Research Links section of the *Marine Science: The Dynamic Ocean* website, print out imagery for a particular time and point out relationships between:

a. Wind and Currents
b. SSTs and Sea Height
c. SSTs and Currents
d. SSTs and Sea Ice

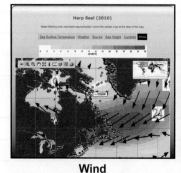

FIGURE 26.23. Screenshots of the various Sea Surface data available on the *Signals of Spring* website.

Wind   SST

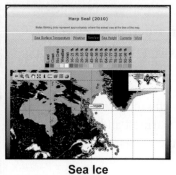

Sea Height   Currents   Sea Ice

Elaborate

In your Student Expert Teams, go back to the additional Questions that were assigned to your Team at the beginning of the Lesson. These are the Questions that you and your classmates had about the ocean and marine animal tracking.

Use a variety of resources to collect information to answer the Questions. It will be helpful to begin with the Research Links on the *Signals of Spring* website. Record your notes and sources on Note Cards and Source Cards. Answer the class Questions for your Expert Team, as directed by your teacher, in the form of a written report. Include pictures with captions and include a Works Cited page.

Evaluate

Part I: Expert Team Presentations

With your Expert Team, organize a 5–7-minute presentation to the class to share your Research findings. Be sure to include examples of how you observed and analyzed data. Include answers to at least one Question from the **Explain** section and one from the **Elaborate** section.

Decide which Questions your Expert Team will present and the order in which you will share your findings. Use the scoring sheet below to guide your presentation, as this is also how the public audience—your classmates—will be evaluating you.

1. Use a scoring sheet like the one below to evaluate the presentations. Look back to the **Explain** and **Elaborate** sections to become familiar with the tasks the Expert Teams were required to complete. Give a score (from 1–5, with 1 being the lowest score and 5 the highest) for each part, along with a constructive, useful comment.

Student Names/ Student Expert Research Team Type	Explain & Elaborate Score 1–5	Class Questions Score 1–5	Organization & Cooperation of Group Members Score 1–5	Most Interesting Aspects of Presentation/ Something I Learned
	How well does the team: • explain and elaborate answers to Questions? • interpret data (if applicable)? • use images to illustrate ideas?	How well does the team: • respond to class Questions?	How well does the team: • organize the presentation? • present clearly? • work cooperatively?	• What was the most interesting part of the presentation? • What is one thing you learned?

Part II: Data Analysis Quizzes

See Page 694 for how to access e-Tools.

Try the practice quizzes found in the e-Tools.

e-Tools

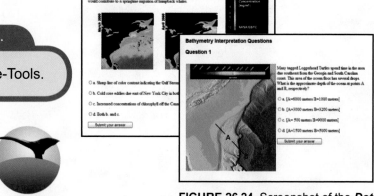

FIGURE 26.24. Screenshot of the *Data Interpretation Quizzes*.

27

Student Expert Analysis

INSIDE:

Objectives

You will be able to:

✔ **Use Earth imagery to explain the movements of animals that are tracked by satellite.**

✔ **Relate marine science content to animal movements.**

✔ **Differentiate between observations and explanations of animal movement.**

Benchmarks

1c. Throughout the ocean there is one interconnected circulation system powered by wind, tides, the force of the Earth's rotation (i.e., Coriolis Effect), the Sun, and water density differences. The shape of ocean basins and adjacent land masses influence the path of circulation.

5b. Most life in the ocean exists as microbes. Microbes are the most important primary producers in the ocean. Not only are they the most abundant life form in the ocean, they have extremely fast growth rates and life cycles.

5f. Ocean habitats are defined by environmental factors. Due to interactions of abiotic factors (e.g., salinity, temperature, oxygen, pH, light, nutrients, pressure, substrate, circulation), ocean life is not evenly distributed temporally or spatially (i.e., it is "patchy"). Some regions of the ocean support more diverse and abundant life than anywhere on Earth, while much of the ocean is considered a desert.

7a. The ocean is the last and largest unexplored place on Earth; less than 5% of it has been explored. This is the great frontier for the next generation's explorers and researchers, where they will find great opportunities for inquiry and investigation.

7d. New technologies, sensors, and tools are expanding our ability to explore the ocean. Ocean scientists are relying more and more on satellites, drifters, buoys, subsea observatories, and unmanned submersibles.

7f. Ocean exploration is truly interdisciplinary. It requires close collaboration among biologists, chemists, climatologists, computer programmers, engineers, geologists, meteorologists, and physicists and new ways of thinking.

Engage

In this Lesson the class finally gets the opportunity to track animals. There is plenty to learn about marine animal behavior. Your teacher will assign your Student Expert Team and animal.

1. Let's make a few hypotheses. Write a paragraph in which you answer the following Questions:

   - Where do you expect your individual animal to move? Why?

   - In what ways do you believe your animal will be influenced by bathymetry, chlorophyll concentrations, and sea surface data? Why?

FIGURE 27.1. Loggerhead Sea Turtle wearing a satellite tag heads for the waves. Loggerheads tend to remain in shallow waters of the continental shelf.

FIGURE 27.2. A Spotted Seal dives into the icy Arctic waters. Notice the tiny satellite tag on its rear flipper.

FIGURE 27.3. A NOAA scientist carefully attaches a satellite tag to a huge Humpback Whale. A suction cup is used to attach the device to the whale's rubbery skin.

FIGURE 27.4. Black-footed Albatross soars with the winds. With seabirds, satellite transmitters are glued to the animal's feathers.

Explore

Case Studies of Marine Animal Movements

In this section, the entire class will use case studies to make connections between Earth data and the movements of specific animals. We will model an individual animal's movement and relate it to environmental data parameters (bathymetry, chlorophyll, SST). In Lesson 26: Student Expert Research, we interpreted Earth data in satellite imagery—now we will add the animal tracks.

In the e-Tools, access the case studies for Bathymetry, Chlorophyll, and Sea Surface. Answer the Questions that follow.

Bathymetry

See Page 694 for how to access e-Tools.

Access the tracking and bathymetry data for Ginger, a Hawksbill Sea Turtle, in the e-Tools.

e-Tools

FIGURE 27.5. A Hawksbill Sea Turtle in Central America becomes equipped with a satellite transmitter. These marine reptiles feed primarily on sponges, although they are known to eat jellyfish and other invertebrates as well.

1. Near which seafloor features is Ginger found? At what depths?

2. Why might Ginger stay in these tropical regions?

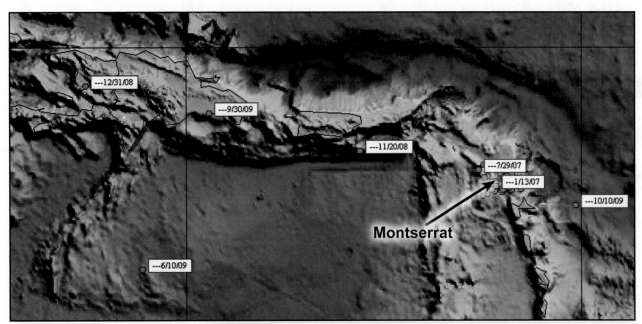

Montserrat

FIGURE 27.6. Screenshot of the tracking and bathymetry data for Ginger, the Hawksbill Sea Turtle.

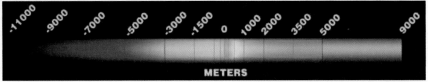

METERS

Recall the volcanic island of Montserrat and the changes to its landscape.

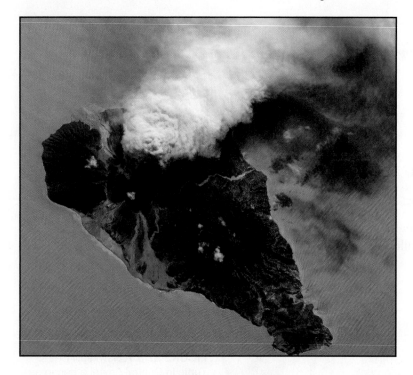

FIGURE 27.7. Montserrat in October 2009 shows off its active volcano, visible from the International Space Station (ISS). Much of the island is green; however, evidence of pyroclastic lava flows is also present.

3. How do you think the volcano could influence Ginger if she were nearby when the volcano was actively spewing debris?

4. Assuming there was no intrusion from volcanic activity, what questions might you ask about Ginger's movement, habitat requirements, life cycle, and so on, based on the bathymetry data?

5. How would you proceed in answering the questions you pose in Question 4?

Phytoplankton

See Page 694 for how to access e-Tools.

Access the tracking and phytoplankton data for Juno, the Hooded Seal, in the e-Tools.

e-Tools

Use the slider to adjust the date of the phytoplankton (chlorophyll concentration) image so that it coincides with the data point you are observing.

1. How do Juno's movements compare to the changes in chlorophyll concentration over time?

2. Why might Juno's movements be related to chlorophyll concentration?

3. How could other Student Expert Teams help you to explain why the seal moved as it did?

FIGURE 27.8. This Hooded Seal pup was nursed back to health at a marine mammal center and then released back into the wild. There are many organizations dedicated to rescuing sick marine animals. These pinnipeds primarily eat fish such as herring, capelin, halibut, and others.

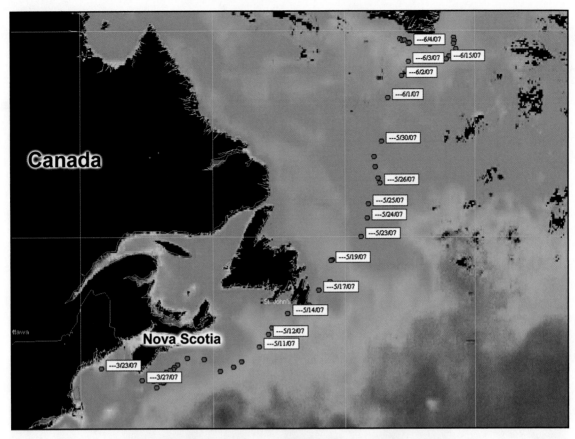

Chlorophyll *a* concentration   (mg / m³)

| 0.01 | 0.03 | 0.1 | 0.3 | 1 | 3 | 10 | 30 | 60 |

FIGURE 27.9. Screenshot of the tracking and phytoplankton data for Juno, the Hooded Seal.

FIGURE 27.10. Screenshot of the slider.

Sea Surface

See Page 694 for how to access e-Tools.

Access the tracking and Sea Surface data for Jaime, the Walrus, in the e-Tools.

You will focus on SST in this exercise.

e-Tools

FIGURE 27.11. Walruses hauled out on ice in the Bering Sea. Males often gather together on rocks offshore and it is not unusual to find 10,000 or more piled up in one place. Females, however, prefer lounging on the pack ice. These pinnipeds eat benthic invertebrates including clams, shrimp, and worms.

1. Create a data table similar to the one below and note the observed SST at Jaime's location for each point given on the map. Use the slider to adjust the date of the SST image, so that it coincides with the data point you are observing.

Date	Observed SST
6/13	
6/27	
7/10	
7/24	
8/10	

2. How can you explain Jaime's movements with respect to SST over the length of time illustrated on the map?

3. How does sea ice relate to SST?

4. What questions do you have related to Jaime's movements?

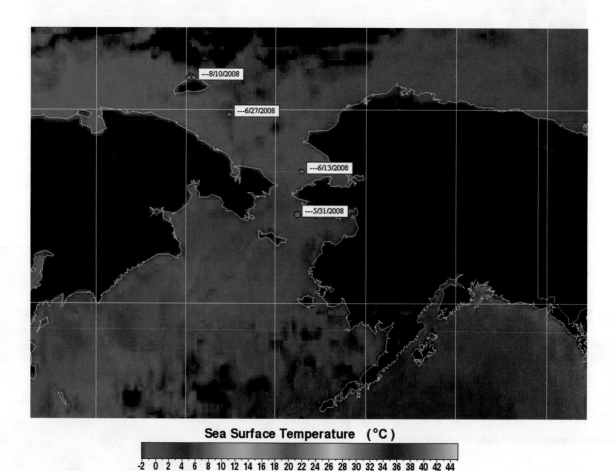

FIGURE 27.12. Screenshot of the tracking and SST data for Jaime, the Walrus, from May to August 2008.

Explain

Learning to Write Observations and Explanations

You are almost ready to begin explaining the movements of "your" marine animal. When you follow your animal, you write Analysis Journal entries regularly. Many students write one Analysis Journal Entry every two weeks for a period of time. The frequency differs from classroom to classroom. This case study takes you through some of the interesting aspects of an investigation of a California Sea Lion's movements.

Access the abundant tracking and Earth data for Tracey, the California Sea Lion, in the e-Tools. Use the data provided to carefully observe her movements with respect to sea surface data. Analyze each point independently. **Important:** A point on a map does **not** necessarily mean the animal stopped there. Remember the satellite picked up the location information from the transmitter on the animal when the satellite moved over it. The animal may have been actively moving at that moment.

e-Tools

FIGURE 27.13. California Sea Lions are highly social pinnipeds and can often be found sleeping in piles on the shoreline, particularly during the summer breeding season. While California Sea Lions eat a variety of seafood, they predominantly enjoy feeding on fish such as salmon, hake, pacific whiting, and anchovies and invertebrates such as octopus and squid.

Practice Analysis Journal Entry

Here is the scenario:

The Sea Surface Expert Team is ready to write an Analysis Journals Entry. Their assigned animal is Tracey, the California Sea Lion. The team studies the maps and also the location data. They analyze the latitude–longitude points in the Data Table.

The student team decides to write about the time period from February 21st to 25th, 2010. This is the time the animal leaves the coast of California and ventures out to sea.

This first time, for some practice, the maps have been captured. You can find them in e-Tools. When you do a real Analysis Journal Entry, you will need to log in to the website. This is after your teacher has given you your Username and Password. At that time you will utilize the complete mapping system to track animals.

1. Write a sample Analysis Journal entry for February 21st to 25th, 2010, in your notebook and include the following:

   a. **Observations:** Describe your observations of Tracey's movements and location with respect to SST and ocean surface currents during this time period. Be as specific as possible, including actual SSTs you observe.

   b. **Explanations:** Explain why, based on the SSTs you observed, Tracey might be found in this area at this time. (Hint: Include what you know about diving behavior, dissolved oxygen, seasons, etc.)

   c. **Questions:** Write at least one question that you could ask Bathymetery Experts about Tracey's location during this time period.

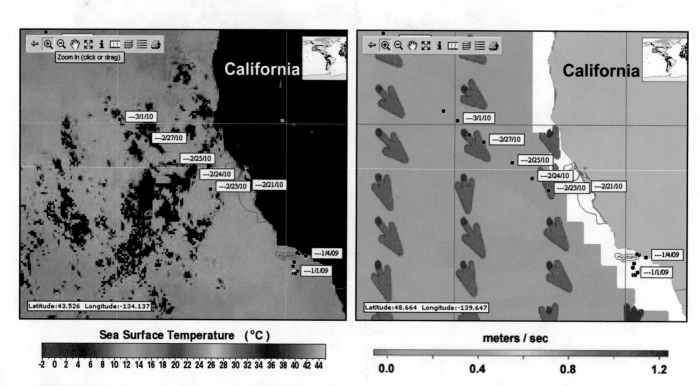

FIGURE 27.14. Screenshots of the geographic location of the animal at a particular time (dots on the map), SST, and ocean currents data for Tracey, the California Sea Lion. Data here is for the week ending February 25, 2010.

2. Perhaps it's weeks later and the SST Student Expert Team writes another Analysis Journal Entry. Again they study the data. This time they decide to write about Tracey's movement from February 26th to March 11th, 2010.

a. **Observations:** Describe your observations of Tracey's movements and location with respect to SST and currents during this time period. Be as specific as possible, including actual temperatures you observe. Create a data table to record the temperatures at Tracey's locations during this time period.

b. **Explanations:** Explain why, based on the SST you observed, Tracey might be found in this area at this time. (Hint: Include what you know about currents, adaptations, etc.)

c. **Questions:** Write at least one question that you could ask Phytoplankton Experts about Tracey's location during this time period.

Sea Surface Temperature (°C)

-2 0 2 4 6 8 10 12 14 16 18 20 22 24 26 28 30 32 34 36 38 40 42 44

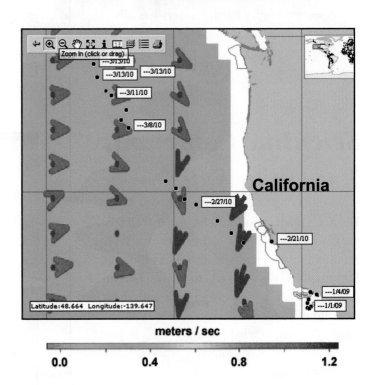

meters / sec

0.0   0.4   0.8   1.2

FIGURE 27.15. Screenshots of the geographic location of the animal at a particular time (dots on the map), SST, and ocean currents data for Tracey, the California Sea Lion. Data here is for the week ending March 13, 2010.

Elaborate

We will use Earth data imagery to explain the movements of specific animals and write about them in online Analysis Journals. You are encouraged to add and update to the *Scientific Community Research Wall* so that others in the school can learn about marine animal movements.

You will write in your Analysis Journal approximately every other week. At least twice over the coming months, you should confer with other Expert Teams and regularly update and check the *Scientific Community Research Wall* for new information from other Expert Teams and how they might be affecting the movements of your animal.

Note: Occasionally we may notice a "bad" data point in the animal track, one that does not make scientific sense. For example, you might notice a sea turtle in the middle of a continent, or even just a few miles inland. You might observe a location that is hundreds of kilometers away from recent animal tracks. These points occur as a result of problems with data entry or computer error and are fairly common. The *Signals of Spring* team will take notice to adjust or remove these data from the web pages, but in the meantime you should use your scientific reasoning skills and note that these points are probably not an accurate representation of your animal's location at the time. Therefore, you should not consider such points as you study your animal's movements.

Also, sometimes Earth imagery has missing data. Areas in black demonstrate that the satellite could not gather data for a particular area. This may be due to cloud cover or another technology issue. Scientists work with the data available in order to draw conclusions.

Scientific Community Research Wall

The *Scientific Community Research Wall* tells the stories of the animal movements and will serve as a visual organizer for Observations and Explanations. Students add to the display and share the observations and analysis with the school community. A good classroom display will include similar content to what you are writing in your team's online Analysis Journals. This includes maps and summaries.

Your teacher will assign each team a section of the wall display to post observations and analysis. 3-D artifacts and creations go a long way to making a nice display!

FIGURE 27.16. Former *Marine Science* students tracked Whitey, the Polar Bear, in her journeys north of Alaska. The Expert Teams collaborated to learn more about this animal and her movements.

Student Analysis Journals

The Analysis Journal is an online analysis tool. It is completely interactive and unique for each Student Expert Team. Each Team writes Analysis Journal entries. Each Journal entry contains an Observation and Explanation section.

Each Student Expert Team is provided a Username and Password by a registered teacher. Login information provides access to Student Expert Teams' Analysis Journals. Once logged in, you can create, edit, and read you team's Analysis Journal entries. You can embed specific maps that you are observing from the system into your Journal entries.

What data do I use to write Analysis Journal entries?

After logging in to the website, use *Signals of Spring* to obtain the following:

- Migration and animal movement data (latitude/longitude point data and maps)
- Earth data imagery corresponding to important days
- Other resources and links for background information

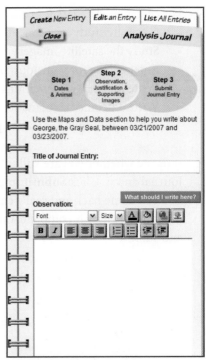

FIGURE 27.17. Screenshot of an Analysis Journal. Log in and follow these simple steps to begin writing Analysis Journal entries. Create a title for your team's Journal entry, select dates, and use familiar technology tools.

Creating Analysis Journal Entries

How do I create an Analysis Journal entry?

1. Go to the *Signals of Spring* website (accessed through the *Marine Science: The Dynamic Ocean* website) and log in with the Student Expert Team Username and Password provided by your teacher.

2. Click on **Open Analysis Journal**.

3. Click on the **Create New Entry** tab.

4. Select your animal and explore the maps. Select the specific dates you wish to write about, and then click **Continue to Step 2**. In general, write about a few days at a time so that each Journal entry will be somewhat different.

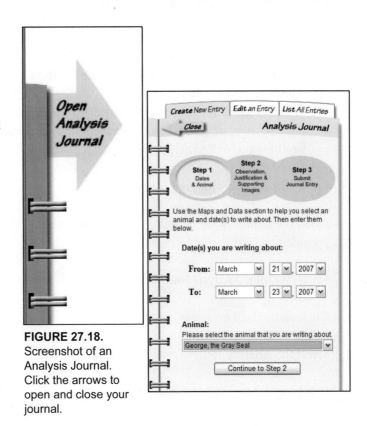

FIGURE 27.18. Screenshot of an Analysis Journal. Click the arrows to open and close your journal.

5. For each new Analysis Journal entry:
   - Carefully study location and map data.
   - Study the satellite imagery.
   - Enter a Title for your Journal entry.
   - Write detailed Observations (can be several paragraphs).
   - Write a detailed Explanation. Explain observations and behavior (should be several paragraphs).

6. Indicate whether you are still working on a Journal entry. Click **Submit Journal Entry**. You can come back and make changes. When the Journal entry is complete, uncheck the box and submit it.

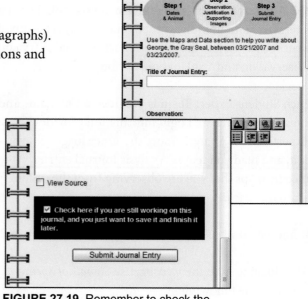

FIGURE 27.19. Remember to check the black box if you are still working on your Journal entry.

Editing Analysis Journal Entries

Student Teams can edit Analysis Journal entries in order to respond to some of the questions and comments from teachers (and possibly scientists).

Why would I edit an Analysis Journal entry?

- A teacher (or possibly a scientist) may have asked questions about a Journal entry. Students may improve the entry by responding.
- Teachers may make suggestions to students about changes to a Journal entry or to include some additional information.
- Errors (such as spelling or incorrect data) were discovered.
- Students may wish to take a break and simply add more information to a Journal entry after initially beginning to write one.

How do I edit Analysis Journal entries?

1. Go to the *Signals of Spring* website and log in with the Student Expert Team Username and Password, provided by your teacher.

2. Click on **Open Analysis Journal**.

3. Click on the **Edit an Entry** tab.

4. Select the Analysis Journal entry you wish to edit.

5. Resubmit the changed text and imagery.

You and your Expert Team will follow the directions for <u>one</u> of the "Teams" below (e.g., Team 1, Team 2)

Team 1: Species Expert Team Analysis

Analysis Journal Entries: Things to Think About When Writing

Now that you are assigned the animal species you will track, spend some time researching the animal. Your Expert Team may wish to refer back to the Questions you responded to in Lesson 26: Student Expert Research in order to become an "Expert" on your new species. Remember the Analysis Journal tells a story, so you should make entries every other week or so, particularly during your animal's movement. Journal entries may include or focus on some of the issues that are discussed with other student teams. The two sections to fill out in each Journal entry are the Observation and Explanation sections.

What do I write in the Observation section for each Analysis Journal entry?

What is an Observation? An observation is something you see or measure. You are not drawing conclusions when you observe.

You should describe how the animal's location has changed. Use the available maps and Data Table to help you give specific locations of the animal. Note references to locations on land, latitude and longitude points, and the direction the animal is moving. Use atlases and the map tools to reference specific locations and distances an animal travels. Excellent Analysis Journal entries will cite specific geographic locations or distances from them. Do this for each Journal entry.

What do I write in the Explanation section for each Analysis Journal entry?

Write about whether the animal movement is changing during the time period. Give possible reasons why. Think back to what you learned about the factors that affect the animal. Write about the inferences of how far it moved over a particular period of time, perhaps since the tracking of the animal started. If there are no changes in your animal's location, why might that be? Do the needs of the animal appear to be met? How? Consult with other Expert Teams and determine if they think the animal's needs are being met. Make predictions: Where do you think the animal will go next? Why?

Explanation Hints:

- Calculate distances of travel between two or more dates.
- Determine how fast the animal is traveling each day or week.
- Describe how the animal's location changes over time.
- Make predictions about future movements of the animal.
- Did the animal travel through any National Marine Sanctuaries? If so, why is that important?

FIGURE 27.20. A False Killer Whale makes its way through the waves. Species Expert Teams explain the movements of marine animals such as this cetacean over time.

Scientific Community Research Wall

Attach a large "X" or put up marine animal "icons" or arrows to show the locations where the animal has been. Be as precise as possible. Use other maps and atlases. Update your maps as necessary.

Prepare a reference area for the class about the species on the Research Wall display. Research and share the following characteristics of the species and the habitats:

- General size, shape, and color of the adults and the young. What are the different life stages?
- Food normally eaten
- The nature of the general habitat (coast, near coral reefs, bays, deep water, etc.)
- Preferred location for breeding, raising, and protecting young
- Information about natural predators
- Competition with other animals
- How humans positively and negatively affect the animals

Team 2: Bathymetry Expert Team Analysis

Analysis Journal Entries: Things to Think About When Writing

Analysis Journal entries may focus on some of the issues that are discussed with other student teams. Remember that the Analysis Journal tells a story, so you should make entries about every other week during your investigation of the animal's movements. At times, you may find it helpful to confer with other Expert Teams. The two sections to complete in each Journal entry are Observation and Explanation.

What do I write in the Observation section for each Analysis Journal entry?

What is an Observation? In the case of interpreting imagery, an observation is something you see or measure. You are not drawing conclusions when you observe.

Use maps and images from the *Signals of Spring* website as well as other resources to discuss the bathymetry of the area of the animal's location for different times. Include specific depths and names of basins, canyons, islands, and other locations, including coastal areas. List changes in location from one period of time to another.

In addition to the Internet and map tools, atlases allow you to reference specific locations and distances that the animal travels. Excellent Analysis Journal entries will cite specific geographic locations or distances from them. Do this for each Journal entry.

What do I write in the Explanation section for each Analysis Journal entry?

Write about evidence you think tells how the bathymetry and habitat are affecting the animal's movement. Suggest influences from the seafloor. If no changes in location are apparent, discuss why the area is seemingly meeting the needs of the animal. Discuss your conclusions.

Explanation Hints:

- Is the animal staying on the continental shelf? Is it moving? How does a particular location help the animal to meet its needs?
- Is the animal along the continental slope? How might the continental slope affect upwelling?
- Is the animal in deep water? How deep? Is it expected to be found in waters of this depth? Why or why not?
- Did the animal come into very shallow coastal areas such as harbors or bays? If so, why? How might these areas positively or negatively affect the animal?
- Did the animal travel through any National Marine Sanctuaries? If so, why is that important?

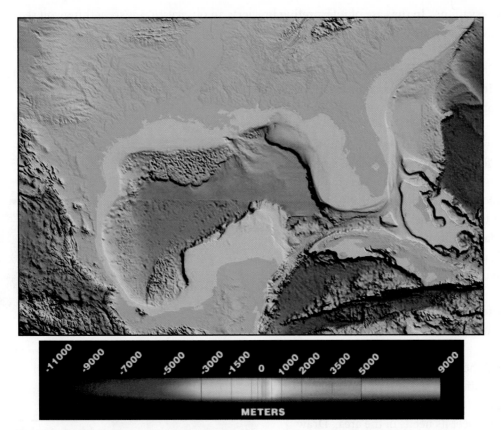

FIGURE 27.21. This image shows the bathymetry of the Gulf of Mexico. Bathymetry Expert Teams consider animal movements with respect to bathymetric features such as the continental shelf, seamounts, and abyssal plain.

Scientific Community Research Wall

Use your Research Wall display to visually explain your Observations and Explanations. It should contain much of the same information as the online Analysis Journal entries, including your writing summaries and maps.

Neatly add appropriate information to the display, including color sections of bathymetric data and their relation to and potential influence on the animal's location. Share your findings.

Team 3: Phytoplankton Expert Team Analysis

Analysis Journal Entries: Things to Think About When Writing

Remember that the Analysis Journal tells a story, so you should make entries about every other week during your investigation of the animal's movements. At times, you may find it helpful to confer with other Expert Teams. The two sections to complete in each Journal entry are Observation and Explanation.

What do I write in the Observation section for each Analysis Journal entry?

What is an Observation? In the case of interpreting imagery, an observation is something you see or measure. You are not drawing conclusions when you observe.

Use maps and images from the *Signals of Spring* website as well as other resources to discuss the phytoplankton concentration in the area of the animal's location. Include specific concentrations and locations. Discuss changes from one period of time to another.

Note: It is very important that you use a chlorophyll satellite image for a date that is very close to the animal location point that you are observing. Remember, chlorophyll changes relatively quickly over time. On the maps, the "animal location dot" closest to the date of the map imagery will blink. You will find it useful to use weekly, monthly, and seasonal mean data.

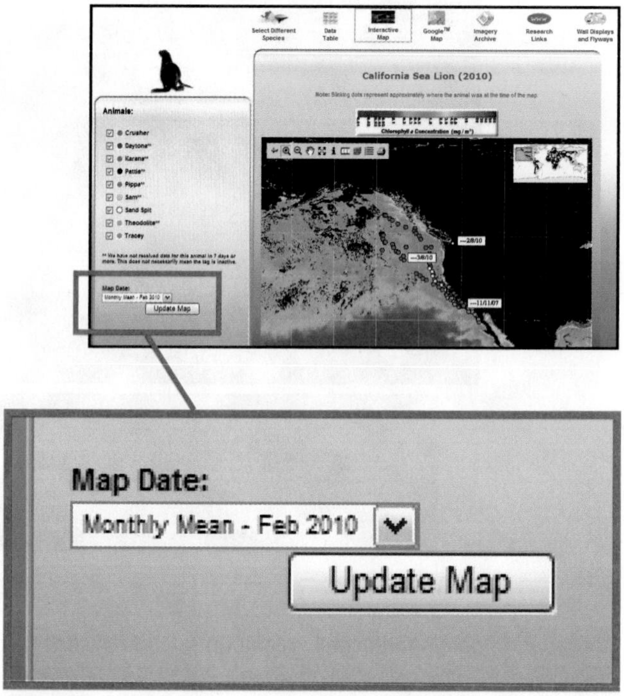

What do I write in the Explanation section for each Analysis Journal entry?

Write about whether you think the phytoplankton concentration is affecting the animal movement. If no changes in location are apparent, discuss why the animal is able to meet its needs in the area. Draw conclusions.

Explanation Hints:

- What does phytoplankton mean to this particular animal? Does it eat phytoplankton? If not, how many trophic levels is the animal above phytoplankton? How is the animal's prey affected by phytoplankton?
- How do seasonal changes affect the phytoplankton? Is this related to the animal movement?
- Is there evidence for upwelling in the animal's location? Why is that important for the animal meeting its needs?
- Does the animal pass through warm- or cold-core eddies? If so, how are the eddies related to phytoplankton and to your animal?

FIGURE 27.22. Screenshot from the *Marine Science: The Dynamic Ocean* website. Change the date of the map by selecting from the dropdown menu and clicking Update Map.

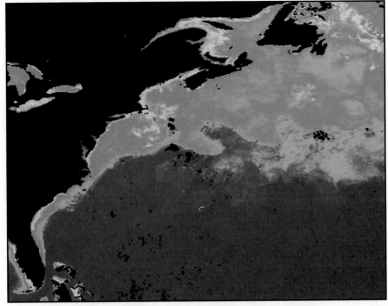

FIGURE 27.23. Phytoplankton Student Expert Teams make connections between animal movements and changes in chlorophyll concentration indicating phytoplankton. These students look for evidence of upwelling, eddies, and seasonal changes.

Scientific Community Research Wall

Use your Research Wall display to visually explain your Observations and Explanations. It should contain much of the same information as your online Analysis Journal entries.

Neatly add appropriate information to the display, including color phytoplankton images and their relationship to the animal's location. Share your findings.

Team 4: Sea Surface Expert Team Analysis

Analysis Journal Entries: Things to Think About When Writing

Remember that the Analysis Journal tells a story, so you should make entries about every other week during your investigation of the animal's movements. At times, you may find it helpful to confer with other Expert Teams. The two sections to complete in each Journal entry are Observation and Explanation.

What do I write in the Observation section for each Analysis Journal entry?

What is an Observation? In the case of interpreting imagery, an observation is something you see or measure. You are not drawing conclusions when you observe.

Utilize imagery from the *Signals of Spring* website. Report observations about SSTs, surface current velocities and directions, ice concentration (if relevant), sea heights, and so on of the area near and around your animal. Refer to specific locations. Provide actual temperatures for specific dates. Give the speed and direction of currents if they are important. You can reference sea heights and point out heights and temperatures at particular locations. If sea ice is relevant, examine those data. Discuss changes from one period of time to another.

Note: It is very important that you use a SST image for a date that is very close to the animal location point that you are observing. Remember, sea surface parameters change relatively quickly over time. On the maps, the "animal location dot" closest to the date of the map imagery will blink.

What do I write in the Explanation section for each Analysis Journal entry?

Write about how the SSTs or current velocities are affecting the animal's movement. Compare and contrast imagery and how this information changes over time. Determine if there are relationships between the animal location and SSTs or sea ice in particular, or if a surface current is affecting the animal's movement. Look for relationships between SSTs and sea heights. Discuss your conclusions.

Explanation Hints:

- Does the animal need a certain temperature range (talk with Species Expert Teams)? If so, why? Does the animal move when the water gets too warm or cold?
- Is the animal using surface currents in an area to help it move faster, or might currents be impeding an animal's progress? If the animal is a seabird, is it using winds?
- Is there evidence of upwelling in an area that the animal passes through? If so, why might that be important?
- Does the animal move into or around warm- or cold-core eddies? Is there evidence of this in sea height and SST imagery? If so, why is that important?

Scientific Community Research Wall

Use your Research Wall display to visually explain your Observations and Explanations. It should contain much of the same information as your online Analysis Journal entries.

Neatly add appropriate information to the display, including color phytoplankton images and their relation to the animal location. Share your findings.

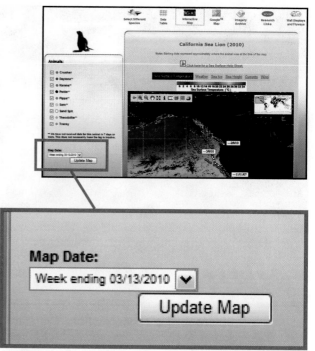

FIGURE 27.24. Screenshot from the *Marine Science: The Dynamic Ocean* website. Change the date of the map by selecting from the dropdown menu and clicking Update Map.

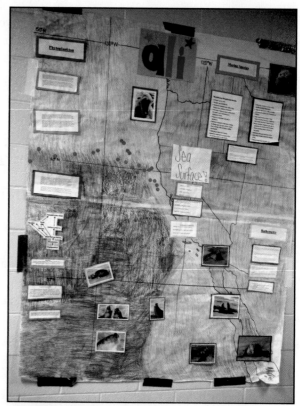

FIGURE 27.25. Each Student Expert Team has a designated place on the *Scientific Community Research Wall* in which they report their findings. These students were tracking the movements of Ali, a Northern Elephant Seal, as he moved west off the Coast of California.

Evaluate

e-Tools

Your teacher will grade your Analysis Journal entries using a rubric. Now it is time for you to assess your own work. Rubrics for each Student Expert Team are available in the e-Tools. Grade your Analysis Journal entry using the rubrics.

You may use *Individual and Group Rubrics* for consideration of each Student Expert Team's work.

Using the rubrics is one way to see how you might earn a higher grade by adding to your Analysis Journal entries. To make changes to your journal, use the "Edit an Entry" feature.

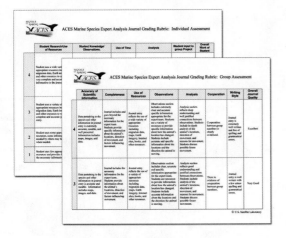

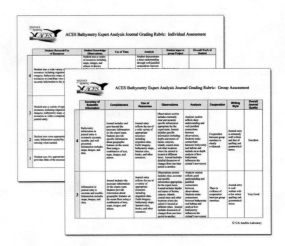

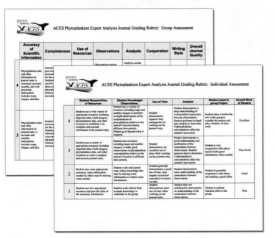

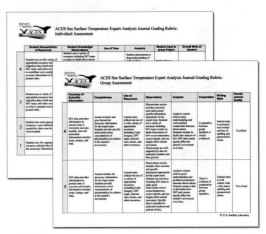

FIGURE 27.26. Screenshots of the *Individual and Group Rubrics*.
There is a set for each type of Student Expert.

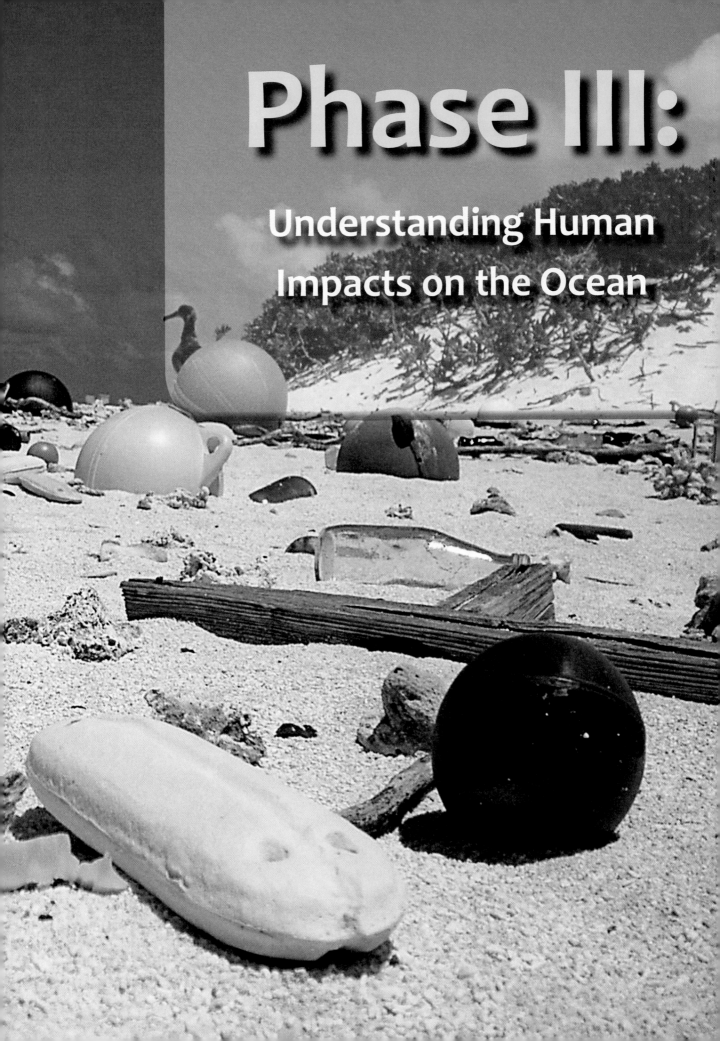

Phase III:

Understanding Human Impacts on the Ocean

28

Which Way to the Sea?

INSIDE:

Objectives

You will be able to:

✔ **Identify a watershed and its boundaries using a topographic map.**

✔ **Explain that most watersheds flow into the ocean.**

✔ **Give examples of water quality parameters.**

✔ **Use scientific techniques and field data to assess water quality.**

✔ **Compare local water quality data with data from other regions of the state or country.**

Benchmarks

1e. Most of Earth's water (97%) is in the ocean. Seawater has unique properties: it is saline; its freezing point is slightly lower than fresh water; its density is slightly higher; its electrical conductivity is much higher; and it is slightly basic. The salt in seawater comes from eroding land, volcanic emissions, reactions at the seafloor, and atmospheric deposition.

1f. The ocean is an integral part of the water cycle and is connected to all of the Earth's water reservoirs via evaporation and precipitation processes.

1g. The ocean is connected to major lakes, watersheds, and waterways because all major watersheds on Earth drain to the ocean. Rivers and streams transport nutrients, salts, sediments, and pollutants from watersheds to estuaries and to the ocean.

1h. Although the ocean is large, it is finite and resources are limited.

2c. Erosion—the wearing away of rock, soil, and other biotic and abiotic earth materials—occurs in coastal areas as wind, waves, and currents in rivers and the ocean move sediments.

(continued on next page)

2d. Sand consists of tiny bits of animals, plants, rocks, and minerals. Most beach sand is eroded from land sources and carried to the coast by rivers, but sand is also eroded from coastal sources by surf. Sand is redistributed by waves and coastal currents seasonally.

6e. Humans affect the ocean in a variety of ways. Laws, regulations, and resource management affect what is taken out and put into the ocean. Human development and activity leads to pollution (e.g., point source, nonpoint source, noise pollution) and physical modifications (e.g., changes to beaches, shores, and rivers). In addition, humans have removed most of the large vertebrates from the ocean.

6g. Everyone is responsible for caring for the ocean. The ocean sustains life on Earth, and humans must live in ways that sustain the ocean. Individual and collective actions are needed to effectively manage ocean resources for all.

Engage

Where Does the Water Go?

FIGURE 28.1. Where does rainwater travel?

e-Tools

FIGURE 28.2. Screenshot of the *Water Cycle Animation*.

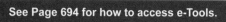

See Page 694 for how to access e-Tools.

View the *Water Cycle Animation* from the e-Tools.

1. What role does the ocean play in the water cycle?

2. How are freshwater systems connected to the ocean?

Explore

What Is a Watershed?

Whether you live 3 miles or 3,000 miles from the ocean, you are connected to its waters through your local environment. That means your everyday activities impact the ocean even if you live far from its shores.

The geographic land area on which runoff water from precipitation gathers and flows into a single body of water is called a **watershed**. Smaller watersheds, such as the area draining into a local stream or pond, are a part of larger watersheds. Eventually, the runoff water in many large rivers, from many larger watersheds, combines to drain into an ocean.

Each of us lives in a watershed. Everything we do—the decisions we make—affects the water quality and health of the watershed we live in. Because nearly all watersheds eventually drain into the ocean, our actions also affect the health of marine ecosystems. Since Earth is covered by one big ocean, this means that all of us are connected to marine organisms through our own local watersheds.

From some streets rain flows into storm drains, many of which empty directly into local bodies of water. In other places, runoff flows into a stream and may end up at a lake. The water will continue to move toward the ocean, but this is where it begins. On a much larger scale and for the biggest watersheds, the way that water flows is the same. Look at the big picture as it relates to the Mississippi River watershed.

FIGURE 28.3. In some areas runoff from the street collected by storm drains empties directly into local streams, rivers, bays, or sounds. Where does runoff in your area go?

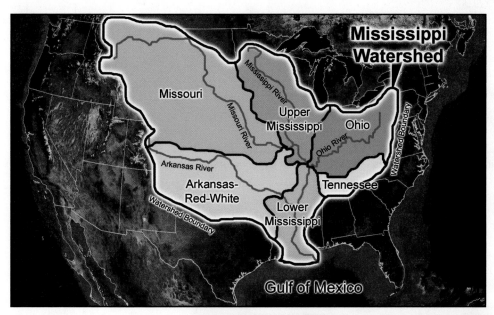

FIGURE 28.4. There are several major watersheds in the United States. The Mississippi River watershed is the largest. Each major watershed consists of smaller watersheds. Every body of water has its own watershed.

FIGURE 28.5. Topographic image of the continental U.S. shows vast differences in regional areas' elevation above sea level.

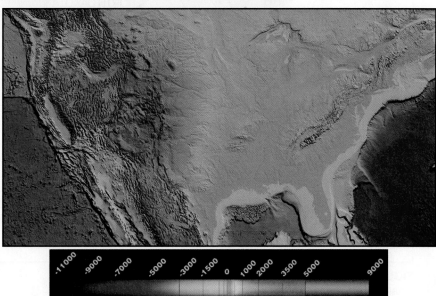

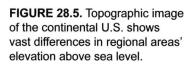

3. In your notebook, draw a sketch that illustrates the basic idea of a watershed and how watersheds are connected to the ocean.

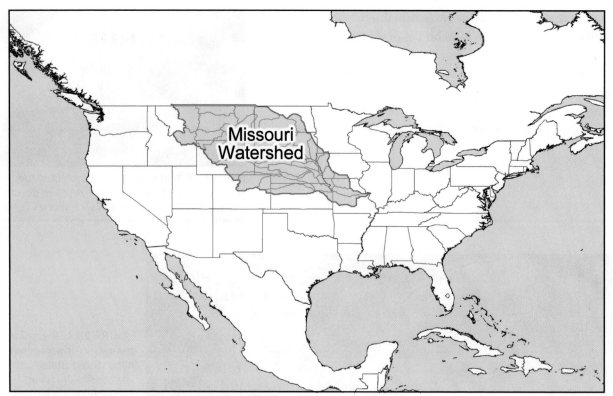

FIGURE 28.6. Map showing the Missouri Watershed. Water in this large watershed flows into the even larger Mississippi Watershed.

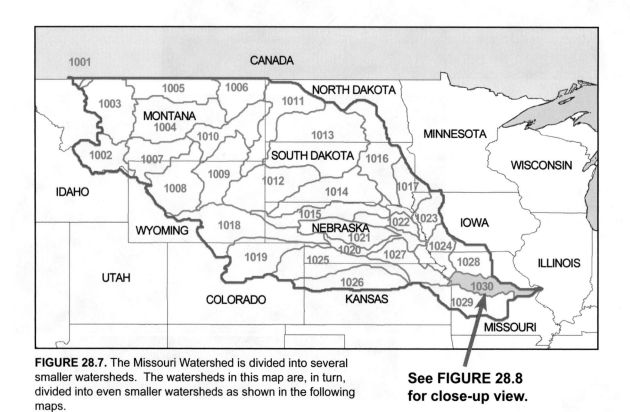

FIGURE 28.7. The Missouri Watershed is divided into several smaller watersheds. The watersheds in this map are, in turn, divided into even smaller watersheds as shown in the following maps.

See FIGURE 28.8 for close-up view.

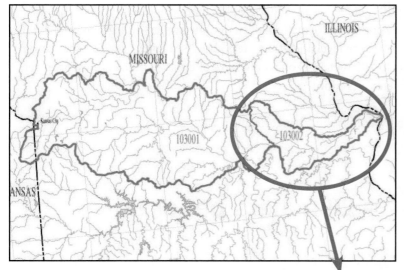

FIGURE 28.8. This map shows a close-up of one area of the lower Missouri River. Notice the number of streams and rivers that contribute just to this part of the watershed.

FIGURE 28.9. Each stream or river has a specific land area from which water drains to "feed" that body of water. As you can see from the series of maps, several small watersheds make up a larger watershed.

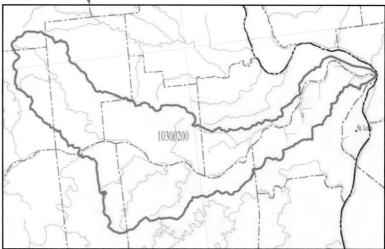

Reading Topographic Maps and Modeling Water Flow

Topographic maps show all types of landforms including mountains, hills, valleys, rivers, streams, lakes, ponds, and oceans. Lines drawn on maps to connect points of equal elevation (or height above sea level) are called **contour lines**. The distance between contour lines indicates the slope of the land, the change in elevation over a given distance. When contour lines are far apart, the change in elevation occurs over a greater distance, meaning the slope is gradual. Contour lines that are close together indicate a change in elevation over a shorter distance, meaning a steeper slope.

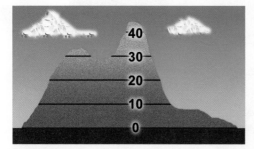
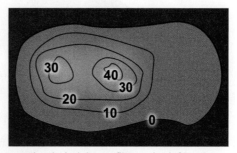

FIGURE 28.10. Representations of an island show a simple height profile on the left and a "bird's eye view" on the right. Each illustration represents the same island.

Not all maps provide contour lines at every 10 meters. Using a topographic map, you can figure out the difference in elevation between the lines by using the information given. For example, the segment of the map below illustrates elevations for 800 meters above sea level and 700 meters above sea level. Imagine that you must climb from an elevation of 700 meters to 800 meters. You would have to cross 4 contour lines, or travel over 5 areas, to do that and reach the 800 meter elevation.

You may divide the difference by the number of areas separating the given values.

$$\frac{100 \text{ meters}}{5 \text{ areas}} = 20 \text{ meters per area}$$

In the example below, each contour line represents 20 meters in elevation.

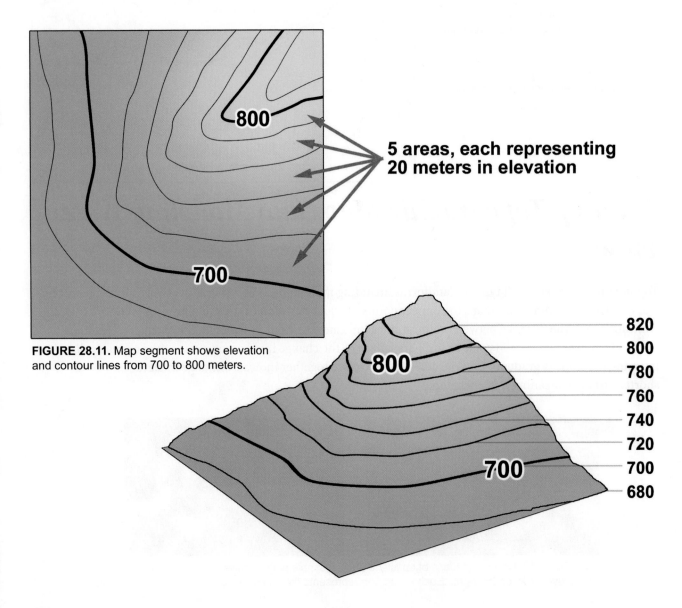

5 areas, each representing 20 meters in elevation

FIGURE 28.11. Map segment shows elevation and contour lines from 700 to 800 meters.

Activity

Your teacher will provide you with the *May Lake Topographic Map*.

1. This activity models water flow to help us to understand the concept of a local watershed. The contour lines represent elevation in feet above sea level. Identify two labeled contour lines.

   What is the change in elevation represented by each contour line?

2. Now that the change from one contour line to the next is known, identify the elevation above sea level of points A, B, and C.

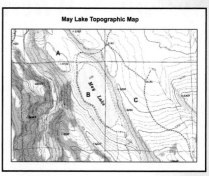

FIGURE 28.12. Screenshot of the *May Lake Topographic Map*.

Now let's identify a watershed.

3. Using a colored pencil or marker, outline the body of the May Lake.

4. Start on one side of the lake. Find the highest elevations on the map that surrounds the body of water. Place an "X" at each high point.

5. When the lake is completely surrounded with "Xs" try to connect them with a solid line. This line represents the highest elevations surrounding the lake. The land area between the line and the body of water is the lake's watershed.

   a. What will happen to rainwater that falls between the line and May Lake?

   b. What will happen to rainwater that falls outside this area?

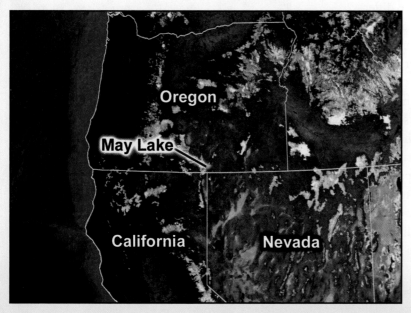

FIGURE 28.13. Map showing location of May Lake.

Explain

Part 1: Freshwater Systems—Where Does Water Flow?

Fresh water accounts for only 3% of Earth's total water. It is stored in ice, underground and in surface water bodies such as lakes, ponds, rivers, streams, and wetlands. All bodies of water, fresh or salt, have a watershed.

FIGURE 28.14. View of Lake Superior from Northern Minnesota. The Great Lakes are the largest freshwater system in the world. Parts or all of eight states (Illinois, Indiana, Michigan, Minnesota, New York, Ohio, Pennsylvania, and Wisconsin) and the Canadian province of Ontario form their watershed.

Lakes and ponds are surface water systems that store fresh water in depressions on the Earth. There is no real difference between a lake and a pond; however, generally lakes tend to be larger and deeper than ponds, and there are many exceptions to this rule. Lakes may be huge, covering thousands of square kilometers, or considerably smaller, some less than 20 acres. If they are large enough, such as the Great Lakes, they can affect local climates like an ocean can. In lakes, the water temperature is cooler with depth because sunlight will generally not reach the bottom. In ponds, there is often little temperature difference throughout the water; sunlight will often reach the bottom, and as a result, ponds support a wide variety of plant life. Some ponds are so small that they do not hold onto the same water throughout the year. Pond water may be completely recycled with the seasons.

Lakes, ponds, and rivers are sometimes surrounded by wetlands, which also store fresh water. Wetlands are transitional areas between land and water where the soil is inundated with water either permanently or periodically. The abundance of water determines the nature of the soil and the range of living organisms.

In Lesson 1: Diving Into Ocean Ecosystems you investigated salt marshes and mangrove forests, two types of wetlands. Swamps, bogs, mudflats, and other transitional areas are also characterized as wetlands.

Wetlands exist in a multitude of places and differ tremendously in size and location. They are prevalent in coastal areas where they hold salt water or a mixture of salt and fresh water, called brackish water. Freshwater wetlands are found throughout inland areas often alongside rivers and streams in floodplains. In **floodplain** areas water regularly flows over the banks of the river or stream. Wetlands exist in depressions where the contour of the land is low, and precipitation and runoff supply the water. They are found where land dips below the level of the water table, sometimes forming spring-fed lakes or ponds. The amount of water in a wetland varies depending on the season, weather, and climate. We will discuss wetlands and their importance in more detail in Lesson 31: Humans and Coastlines.

FIGURE 28.15. Coastal wetlands are home to a wide variety of organisms. In this image, a Great Blue Heron in a salt marsh eats a freshly-caught fish. This bird species is common throughout much of the United States.

Rivers and streams are flowing bodies of water. Rivers are the larger of the two and flow into large lakes, bays, or the ocean. Rivers may receive flowing water from smaller streams, which may be small enough to walk or wade across. Some streams exist only during rainy times, others flow year round. In addition to receiving water from the surrounding land, all rivers and streams have a source, a beginning from which water flows from high to low elevation until it reaches another freshwater body or the ocean. A river's source is often referred to as **headwaters**, which may include a lake, a pond, or melting glacier.

In addition to fresh surface water, some of Earth's fresh water is stored beneath its surface. Underground fresh water is known as **groundwater**. Groundwater forms when precipitation falls on the Earth's surface, and instead of running off the land into streams and rivers, it seeps down through layers of soil until it reaches a layer of rock. The water is unable to permeate the layer of rock, and it collects. In many areas, public drinking water comes from areas of groundwater known as **aquifers**. This water is also used for irrigation of farmland.

The Ogallala Aquifer, seen in light blue in FIGURE 28.16, extending beneath eight states throughout the middle part of the United States, is believed to be the largest in the world. Under parts of Texas, New Mexico, Oklahoma, Colorado, Kansas, Nebraska, South Dakota, and Wyoming, it is heavily relied upon as the irrigation source for this primary agricultural region, often referred to as "America's breadbasket". Of all the water used in the United States in the year 2000—approximately 408 billion gallons per day of fresh and saline water—about 21% came from groundwater sources. Water from surface water sources accounted for the remaining 79%.

Any area at which groundwater flows to the surface is known as a **spring**. Springs are an important connection between groundwater and surface water. There are many spring-fed streams, rivers, lakes, and ponds in the United States and around the world. The aquifers that provide water to these springs are important renewable freshwater resources.

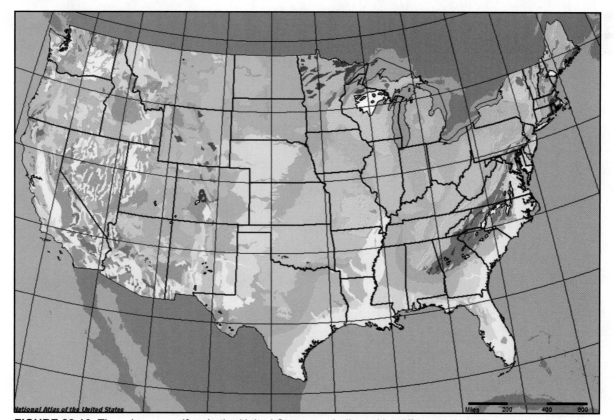

FIGURE 28.16. The primary aquifers in the United States are indicated by different colors. These represent specific geologic signatures. Are aquifers in your area or region shown on the map?

See Page 694 for how to access e-Tools.

View the **Spring Formation Animation** from the e-Tools.

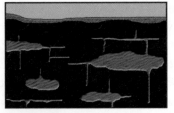

e-Tools

FIGURE 28.17. Screenshot of the **Spring Formation Animation**.

4. Describe the formation of a spring.

Rivers and streams are dynamic systems and they change as they flow from their sources and progress downhill to eventually meet the ocean. When you look at maps of rivers and streams, you notice that none of them flows in a straight line. The geology and the topography of the land through which water flows determine the path of a river.

Rivers and streams will take the path of least resistance—that is to say, liquid water will flow in the most direct route possible to reach its destination. In general, rivers and streams at high, mid and low elevations share common characteristics. At higher elevations water tends to flow quickly and most directly down a steep slope. The river channel is narrow at this point. When a river flows over an area where the slope of the land is less severe, as in a mid-elevation river, the river channel widens and the velocity slows. The path of the river bends, or meanders. At lower elevations, rivers typically have wide channels and form wide meanders.

5. Using your topographic map reading skills, identify this section of the Colorado River as high, mid, or low elevation. What is the elevation range in this area?

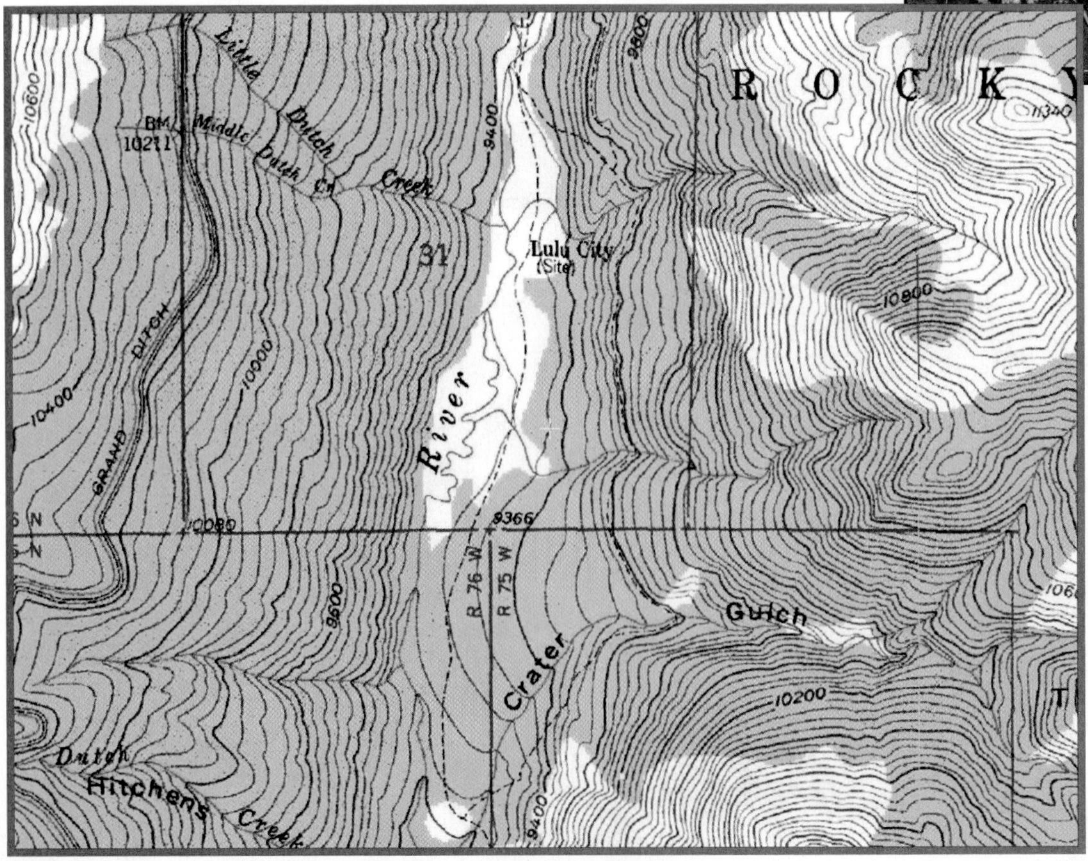

FIGURE 28.18. Topographic Map of part of the Colorado River.

As water flows, it weathers and erodes minerals and sediments. Water has a unique ability to dissolve minerals, hence its nickname, the "universal solvent". Some materials are more easily weathered and eroded than others. For example, limestone that exists throughout much of the state of Florida is readily dissolved by water. The erosion of underground limestone can form caves and even channels through which underground rivers will flow. In Florida, some underground rivers flow to the ocean and others return to the surface and spill into above-ground bodies of water. Other rock types, including igneous rocks (rocks of volcanic origin), resist weathering. When water can break apart rock, minerals, and salts from the rocks get washed downstream. Water is able to dissolve minerals and salts because its polarity allows it to pull upon and separate the ions of salts. Water then can carry these dissolved salt ions away downstream, eventually to the ocean.

In addition to salts, water picks up, transports, and deposits sediment. Sediment is made of tiny pieces of organic and inorganic material including bits of rock, silt, sand, clay, decayed organisms, tiny pieces of vegetation, and so on. Whenever faster-moving water in a river or stream meets a lake, pond, a wetland area, or the sea, the water slows down and deposits sediments. A significant amount of sediment is deposited at the mouth of a river. As fresh water meets the ocean it slows down, depositing sediment in a fan shape pattern called a **delta**. On a beach, sediment is sand. As the amount and velocity of water in a river increases and decreases, sediment is moved and deposited. Water carries sediment great distances, especially when the volume and velocity of the water is high. This happens to a great extent during storms. When the velocity of water slows, sediment falls to the bottom of the river and is deposited. The land surrounding either side of a river is the floodplain, ideal habitat for wildlife and good for farming because of the consistent influx of nutrients from deposited sediments. A significant amount of sediment is deposited at the mouth of a river.

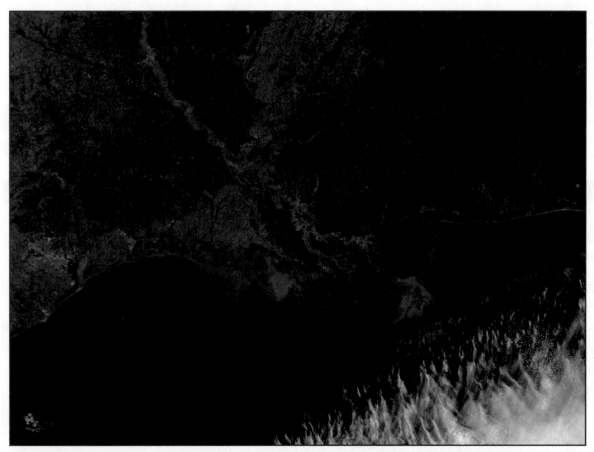

FIGURE 28.19. Satellite image from the MODIS instrument shows sediment from the Mississippi River filling the delta as it spills into the Gulf of Mexico. Sediments flowing off of the land are the result of erosion.

Part 2: Why Sample the Water?

Scientists sample water bodies to study the health of the environment. Scientists use biological, physical, and chemical tests to obtain a broad survey of **parameters**, or the measurable characteristics, of a body of water. The observations and data collected tell scientists if the environment will support living organisms or if there is something unhealthy about it. The quality of ocean water is directly linked to the quality of freshwater bodies that drain into it.

While scientists often use sophisticated tools to collect data, students can conduct similar tests using simpler instrumentation. In the upcoming activity we will conduct water chemistry tests and make an assessment of the local watershed. By studying the data and making observations, we can draw conclusions about water quality parameters that directly affect aquatic organisms. First, we will read about the tests that we will conduct.

Chemical Parameters

Chemical testing helps scientists to identify the presence of minerals, nutrients, and gases in water. If measurements of these compounds reach a certain threshold and become too high or too low, some organisms may be unable to survive.

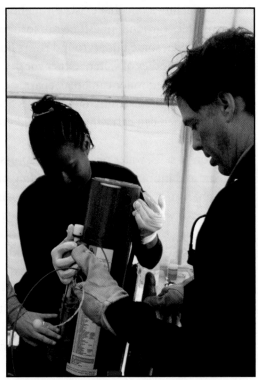

FIGURE 28.20. Scientists use specialized sampling equipment to collect lake water. Students can conduct many of the same tests as the researchers to assess a local body of water.

6. Copy the following chart into your notebook. Use the second column of your chart to write down "what you already know" about water quality. Then, read the paragraphs beginning on the next page and add to your notes in the next column, "What else did you learn?"

Water Quality Parameter	Why is the parameter important to living things in the water?		
	What do you already know?	What else did you learn?	What else do you want to know?
Nitrogen and Phosphorus			
pH			
Dissolved Oxygen			
Temperature			
Turbidity			

Read the following information about the different tests. Then, add to the final column of your chart: "What else do you want to know?"

Nitrogen and Phosphorus. Nitrogen and phosphorus are found in several different forms on land and in bodies of water. All organisms need nitrogen and phosphorus to build proteins, DNA, and other important compounds. Too much nitrogen or phosphorus, however, can cause serious problems, especially in water. Excess nutrients can cause **eutrophication**, out-of-control algae growth. When there is eutrophication, there is an algal bloom, and then all of the algae die at once. When the algae die, decomposers

FIGURE 28.21. A healthy stream near Smoky Mountains National Park in Tennessee. A healthy body of water typically has low levels of nitrogen and phosphorus.

begin breaking the organic matter down into basic compounds. The decomposers use up the oxygen supply very quickly. Other organisms, including fish, cannot live in the water without oxygen. Therefore, too much nitrogen and eutrophication cause organisms in the water to die from lack of oxygen.

High concentrations of nitrogen and phosphorus have also been linked to algal blooms that have produced harmful toxins, such as red and brown tides. According to the Environmental Protection Agency (EPA), the natural levels of nitrogen and phosphorus compounds in surface water tend to be less than 1 milligram per liter (mg/L) and 0.1 mg/L respectively. Levels above these measurements are more likely to cause eutrophication. Possible sources of these nutrients include wastewater treatment plants, runoff water from fertilized lawns and croplands, leaking septic and waste systems, runoff from animal manure storage areas, and runoff from industrial areas. Chemical tests and probes are used to measure nitrogen and phosphorus content. In Lesson 29: Nonpoint Source Pollution eutrophication is covered in much greater detail.

pH. A measure of how acidic or basic a substance is, is the pH. A substance with a pH measurement of less than 7.0 is acidic. A substance with a pH greater than 7.0 is alkaline, or basic. The ocean is slightly basic. The chart below shows the pH of common substances. pH affects many chemical and biological processes in water. For example, different organisms survive best within different ranges of pH. Most organisms in water require a range of 6.5–8.0 pH. pH values outside this range reduce the number of different types of organisms in the water. This affects the food web and health of the environment. Changes in acidity can be caused by atmospheric deposition (acid rain), surrounding rock, and wastewater entering the environment. The results of a single water sample are not as useful as pH measurements taken over time. It is possible that a seemingly "acidic" measurement of, say, 5.5 taken from a nearby creek could be the creek's "normal" value. If, however, a student or scientist noticed changes in the typical pH over time, these data might indicate a problem in water quality.

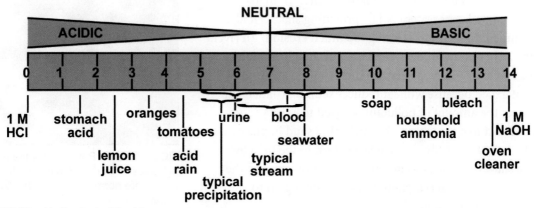

FIGURE 28.22. pH of selected liquids.

Dissolved Oxygen. Oxygen (O_2) is measured in water as dissolved oxygen (DO). This means that oxygen molecules are mixed with water molecules. Running water, because of its churning, dissolves more oxygen than still water, as in a reservoir behind a dam. In the ocean, wave action adds oxygen to water because of the interaction between the ocean and atmosphere. Oxygen enters the water from the atmosphere and from marine plants as a result of photosynthesis. Aquatic organisms go through respiration, decomposition, and other chemical reactions that use oxygen. Organisms such as fish and many invertebrates require dissolved oxygen from respiration to release energy from food. Most fish require at least 5 mg/L to survive, although the range of tolerance of different species varies. The units of measurement for dissolved oxygen are milligrams per

FIGURE 28.23. This sea slug, or nudibranch, found in the deep coral reefs, has feathery gills protruding outside its body. Underwater invertebrates such as the nudibranch require adequate levels of dissolved oxygen for survival.

liter (mg/L). Recall that cold water holds more dissolved oxygen than warm water. The normal range of DO can range from 5.0–15.0 mg/L. Dissolved oxygen levels of less than 3.0 mg/L are often stressful to fish and invertebrates. Waters with 2.0 mg/L or less dissolved oxygen are considered to lack oxygen, or be **hypoxic**.

Dissolved oxygen levels in the ocean can decrease as a result of human activity. Wastewater from sewage treatment plants entering the ocean contains materials that are decomposed by microorganisms in the water. The increase in the decomposition uses up dissolved oxygen. Other sources of oxygen-consuming waste include stormwater runoff from farmland or urban streets and failing septic systems.

Physical and Biological Parameters

Scientists study the physical nature of water and measure the size and depth of a water body and the velocity of water moving in it or through it. They assess the physical condition of the banks, the amount and type of vegetation, the size and location of sediments, and other factors. Scientists conduct field tests with measuring instruments, look at satellite imagery, and conduct various studies of habitats within the watershed. The amount and type of vegetation along the banks of a freshwater body, the **riparian vegetation**, has a significant impact on the health of the water body. Debris, including leaves, twigs, and branches, falls into the water; this provides some food for aquatic species. In many cases, riparian vegetation keeps water cool by providing shade. It also anchors sediment in place, preventing too much erosion. In rivers and streams, where water moves quickly, bank stabilization by plant roots is important. Vegetation is important in any location within a watershed because while it reduces sediment-laden runoff, it also reduces the amount of pollutants carried to a water body. Beach grasses act in a similar way by anchoring sand in place on a beach. Scientists study riparian vegetation in the field by conducting surveys of the amounts and types of plants, and they use satellite images and aerial photographs of the region to gain a larger perspective of the watershed.

FIGURE 28.24. Plants affect the health of bodies of water. Healthy freshwater bodies are normally surrounded by riparian vegetation.

The activities that take place within the watershed boundary affect the water quality. Disturbances to land as a result of agriculture, building, recreational facilities, and so on reduce the amount of vegetation, which in turn can change the water chemistry and overall quality.

FIGURE 28.25. Erosion is often easily noted in a physical survey of shorelines or banks. This photograph shows erosion along the Nemadji River in Wisconsin. Riparian vegetation helps to prevent erosion.

Temperature. Temperature is a measure of the average kinetic energy of molecules in the water; it is a very important parameter for organisms. Temperature is measured in degree Celsius. All organisms require a certain temperature range to survive. Some are able to survive in freezing temperatures while others require warm water in Earth's Equatorial Regions. If the temperature is too high or too low, an organism will become stressed and either die or leave the environment to find better conditions. Recall that there is a relationship between temperature and dissolved oxygen; warm water carries less dissolved oxygen molecules in it than colder water. Causes of temperature change in local bodies of water of course include seasonal differences and weather. Several other natural and human-induced factors can affect the temperature of water bodies. These include removing plants along the edge of a stream or lake; building dams and other structures that slow the flow of water; adding heated wastewater that was initially for purposes of cooling in industry; and the inflow of water from aquifers, springs, or urban storm drains.

Turbidity. The turbidity of water is a measurement of how cloudy or clear it is, or how easily light can be transmitted through it. As sediments and other suspended solids increase in the water, the amount of light that can pass through the water decreases. Thus, the cloudier the water, the greater is the turbidity. As algae, sediments, or suspended solids increase in the water, so does turbidity. Turbidity affects organisms that are directly dependent on light, such as aquatic plants, because it limits their ability to carry out photosynthesis. This, in turn, affects other organisms that depend on the plants for food and oxygen. Scientists often consider the causes and consequences of turbidity to better assess water quality. For example, high levels of turbidity can be caused by shoreline erosion or by malfunctioning sewage processing facilities, two things with very different impacts on water quality.

High turbidity means that less light can enter the water and as a result there is not as much photosynthesis taking place. Many organisms cannot live in turbid water. The suspended materials in the water can clog fish gills, and when the materials fall to the bottom they can smother eggs and bottom-dwelling creatures. In the ocean high turbidity means that phytoplankton and other organisms are not very abundant. Turbidity alone is not a good indication of overall ecosystem health, however. Some bodies of water are naturally more turbid than others. For instance, the productive waters off the California Coast will be more turbid than the clear, warm waters of the Caribbean Sea off of Puerto Rico. That is because there are more phytoplankton, zooplankton, and nutrients in the California waters, whereas the warm crystal-clear Caribbean waters do not support an abundance of plankton.

Turbidity is measured using an instrument called a **Secchi disk**. A Secchi disk allows researchers to determine the amount of light that reaches beneath the water's surface. The depth of water where a Secchi disk disappears and reappears is called the Secchi disk reading. The range for turbidity varies widely. Using a turbidity tube, students measure turbidity in centimeters. High readings indicate very clear water, because the Secchi disk at the bottom of the tube can be observed through a meter or more of water. A reading of less than 100 centimeters indicates turbid water. Secchi depth readings will vary. A very clear body of water may have a secchi depth reading of 40 meters while water with a high concentration of suspended solids may be only 4 centimeters.

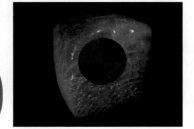

See Page 694 for how to access e-Tools.

View the **Secchi Disk Animation** (0:10) of a Secchi disk being lowered into turbid water from the e-Tools.

e-Tools

FIGURE 28.26. Screenshot of the **Secchi Disk Animation**.

A Secchi disk has black and white elements that will fade as it is lowered into the water. A calculation is performed based on the depth of water at which the Secchi disk vanishes to determine the disk reading. Secchi disks are most accurately used when lowered from a boat or dock. An adaptation of the Secchi disk is a clear tube with a Secchi disk inside of it. This is called a **turbidity tube**. Water is poured into the tube until the Secchi disk disappears.

FIGURE 28.27. A student and scientist work together to use a turbidity tube, measuring the turbidity of water from a stream. The second photo shows the view into the tube, when the Secchi disk has disappeared from view.

FIGURE 28.28. Students lower a Secchi disk into a lake. As the disk disappears from sight, the students record the depth to indicate the water's turbidity.

Elaborate

 **Lab**

Data Collection in the Field

Be sure your group has access to the following materials, which you may need to share with other groups.

Materials:

- Data recording sheet
- Clipboard
- Pencils
- Test kits or probes appropriate for the following water quality parameters:
    - o Nitrogen
    - o Phosphorus
    - o Turbidity
    - o Temperature
    - o pH
    - o Dissolved oxygen

FIGURE 28.29. A clipboard is useful for holding papers to record quantitative and qualitative data in the field—even underwater!

Physical Assessment: Watershed Survey

 Safety Note: Pay careful attention to the safety rules put forth by your teacher.

Field Notes

1. In your notebooks, sketch the sampling area and record other notes about the location. Record as much detail as possible, including the following:

    - The shape of the body of water
    - Details about the width of the riparian vegetation, including where it may have been changed by human activity
    - Areas where the bank is steep, undercut from erosion, or unstable
    - Large debris, rocks, fallen or overhanging trees, etc.
    - Any other notable aspects of the sampling area, including human disturbances such as pavement, boat ramps, docks, etc.

FIGURE 28.30. Field notes are an important part of a scientist's data. This scientist records field notes while conducting research in Nicaragua. A local farmer and his family watch the process from nearby.

2. What was the most significant human disturbance you observed in the watershed?

3. Hypothesize the connections between the human disturbance and the water chemistry.

4. Copy or make notes based on the following chart. Based on the physical survey, predict the results of the chemistry tests by indicating your choice of: average, above average, or below average.

a.	Nitrogen	average	above average	below average
b.	Phosphorus	average	above average	below average
c.	Turbidity	average	above average	below average
d.	Temperature	average	above average	below average
e.	pH	average	above average	below average
f.	Dissolved oxygen	average	above average	below average

Chemical Testing: Water Quality

Chemical tests help scientists identify the presence of minerals, nutrients, and oxygen in the water.

1. Follow the specific instructions for each water quality test and record your data on the **Water Quality Worksheet**.

2. Review the data. Do you see a relationship between any of the parameters?

3. Based on the pH data you collected, would you expect a mayfly larva, a juvenile insect that lives in cold water streams with a pH tolerance of 5.5 to 7.5, to survive?

4. Note the turbidity measurement. What factors within the watershed (e.g., recent rainstorms, construction activity) could have impacted this measurement?

5. When sampling your local body of water, you discover that the temperature and turbidity levels are high. What range would you expect DO to measure?

6. Describe ways you would perform a more in-depth study of the water quality in your local body of water.

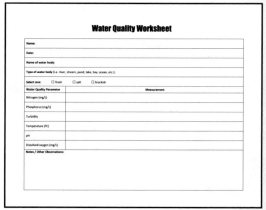

FIGURE 28.31. Screenshot of the **Water Quality Worksheet**.

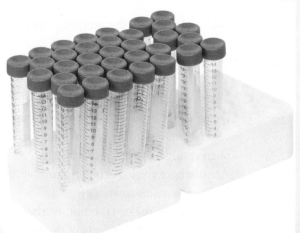

FIGURE 28.32. Chemical tests are an important component of assessing water quality.

As a class, calculate the average measurement for each parameter. Create a data table like the one below in which you will record the class observations.

Water Quality Parameter	Average Measurement
Nitrogen (mg/L)	
Phosphorus (mg/L)	
Turbidity	
Temperature (°C)	
pH	
Dissolved oxygen (mg/L)	

7. Based on these findings, what is your assessment of the water quality of this body of water? Is it average, above average, or below average? Support your assessment with data.

8. Compare your water quality measurements to those published by the Environmental Protection Agency (EPA) for your region or body of water. Does the use of additional data change your assessment? If so, how?

9. Why is it important for scientists to share data and record data for several years?

Website Data Entry Instructions

- As a class, go to the *Marine Science: The Dynamic Ocean* website.

- Select "My Class Water Study" under "Participant Resources".

- If your teacher is registered, enter your teacher's email address. Otherwise, if your class is participating in the water study only, select "Enter as Guest".

- Select the "Enter Data" icon.

- Assign a class representative to enter the class averages. Note: Remember the password you enter. This will enable you to log in to edit your data.

- Click "Submit".

- After the data are entered, you will be able to see them plotted on the **Water Study Map** along with that of other participating classes.

IMPORTANT: Make sure you use the correct units for each measurement when entering the data online.

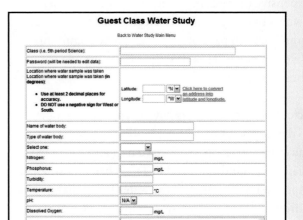

FIGURE 28.33. Screenshot of the *My Class Water Study* data entry form.

Salty Drinking Water?

Many aquifers throughout the United States and in other countries are in danger of contamination from pollutants. In some areas, including Long Island in New York, parts of Louisiana, and portions of Florida, it is salt water that is contaminating the groundwater. When the water level within an aquifer decreases, ocean water is able to flow in. The movement of salt water into fresh water is known as **saltwater intrusion**.

Most coastal aquifers are susceptible to saltwater intrusion, which can naturally occur in times of drought or due to storm surge during a tropical storm. Population growth, however, has increased the consumption of water from aquifers. When more water is pumped from the aquifer than is naturally returned to it (e.g., through rainfall), salt water flows into the fresh groundwater. In addition, the construction of canals, very common in Florida, allows for fresh- and saltwater mixing. When salt water pervades aquifers, some communities are forced to import water from other places.

Another option is the process of making salt water fresh, or to **desalinate** water. Desalination is a very expensive process, however, and home and business owners to really adopt this strategy for fresh water would have to pay a high price. Many communities have campaigns to encourage residents and visitors to conserve water.

Scientists and engineers have been working together to develop solutions for preventing and mitigating saltwater intrusion. They have developed extensive maps of groundwater and installed barriers and other systems to prevent the water from mixing. Through decades of study, scientists have recognized the importance of the wetlands in recharging groundwater.

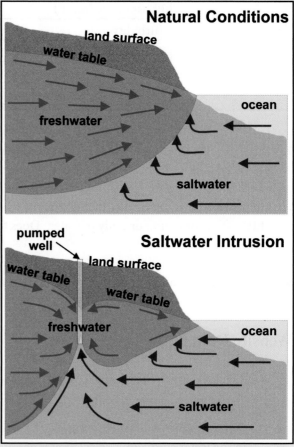

FIGURE 28.34. Aquifers in many coastal communities in Florida are being affected by saltwater intrusion. When fresh water is withdrawn faster than it is replenished, seawater can enter the aquifer.

FIGURE 28.35. The Florida Everglades are an important habitat for a myriad of species, including the Cypress Trees and Great Egret seen here. Fresh water in these wetlands also recharges the underlying aquifers.

Comparing Different Places

Now that you have taken your own measurements, it is time to look at the observations that other *Marine Science: The Dynamic Ocean* students have entered.

Water Study Map Instructions

- As a class, go to the *Marine Science: The Dynamic Ocean* website.

- Select "My Class Water Study" under Lesson 28: Which Way to the Sea? in Phase III.

- If your teacher is registered for the *Marine Science: The Dynamic Ocean* program, enter your teacher's email address. If your class is participating in the water study only, select "Enter as Guest".

- Select the "View Map" icon.

1. Choose two sites from the map to compare. (One may be the site that your class studied.)

2. Use the tools available to you on the map. Describe the surrounding areas of each site.

   (Hint: Click the "Satellite" button on the top right and zoom in so that you can get a good look at the surrounding area. For example, is the area a beach, forested, or urban area? Do you see a lot of concrete or a big, open field? Be very descriptive.)

3. Create a table like the one on Page 561 in your notebook for each of the sites you selected. Fill it out with the information provided. It will help you compare data easily for the two sites.

4. Why do you think the two sites' data differ in terms of the measurements? Explain how you have come to this conclusion.

5. Which parameters are similar?

6. Which parameters are different?

7. How do water quality data for freshwater environments throughout the country relate to the quality of the ocean water?

29

Nonpoint Source Pollution

INSIDE:

Objectives

You will be able to:

✔ **Discuss human impacts on the ocean and how they are detected by satellite imagery.**

✔ **Illustrate the process of eutrophication and its effects on aquatic ecosystems, while relating it to human activities.**

✔ **Identify the sources of marine debris and its impacts on marine organisms.**

✔ **Establish a connection between local debris and marine debris.**

Benchmarks

1a. The ocean is the dominant physical feature on our planet Earth—covering approximately 70% of the planet's surface. There is one ocean with many ocean basins, such as the North Pacific, South Pacific, North Atlantic, South Atlantic, Indian, and Arctic.

1c. Throughout the ocean there is one interconnected circulation system powered by wind, tides, the force of the Earth's rotation (i.e., Coriolis Effect), the Sun, and water density differences. The shape of ocean basins and adjacent land masses influence the path of circulation.

1g. The ocean is connected to major lakes, watersheds, and waterways because all major watersheds on Earth drain to the ocean. Rivers and streams transport nutrients, salts, sediments, and pollutants from watersheds to estuaries and to the ocean.

5b. Most life in the ocean exists as microbes. Microbes are the most important primary producers in the ocean. Not only are they the most abundant life form in the ocean, they have extremely fast growth rates and life cycles.

5f. Ocean habitats are defined by environmental factors. Due to interactions of abiotic factors (e.g., salinity, temperature, oxygen, pH, light, nutrients, pressure, substrate, circulation), ocean life is not evenly distributed temporally or spatially (i.e., it is "patchy"). Some regions of the ocean support more diverse and abundant life than anywhere on Earth, while much of the ocean is considered a desert.

6e. Humans affect the ocean in a variety of ways. Laws, regulations, and resource management affect what is taken out and put into the ocean. Human development and activity leads to pollution (e.g., point source, nonpoint source, noise pollution) and physical modifications (e.g., changes to beaches, shores, and rivers). In addition, humans have removed most of the large vertebrates from the ocean.

6g. Everyone is responsible for caring for the ocean. The ocean sustains life on Earth, and humans must live in ways that sustain the ocean. Individual and collective actions are needed to effectively manage ocean resources for all.

Engage

Many human activities on land impact ocean ecosystems. Over the next few Lessons, we will investigate this land-and-sea connection and examine how human actions affect the ocean. First, let's review our understanding of phytoplankton and chlorophyll imagery.

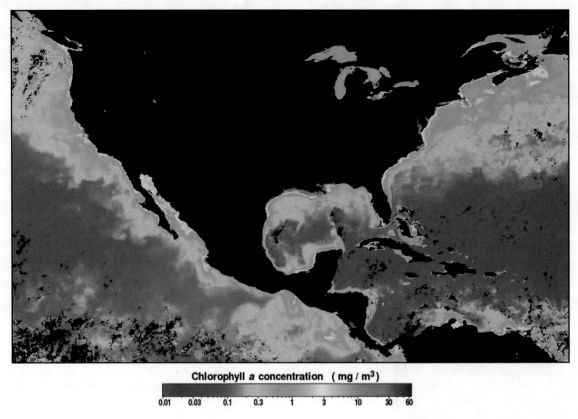

Chlorophyll *a* concentration (mg / m³)

0.01   0.03   0.1   0.3   1   3   10   30   60

FIGURE 29.1. Phytoplankton image composite of satellite data shows varying concentrations of chlorophyll.

1. Describe the patterns you notice of high and low chlorophyll. What do all of the high-chlorophyll areas shown on the map have in common?

In an earlier Lesson, we discussed how phytoplankton meet their needs.

2. What raw materials do phytoplankton require for survival? Why?

We have discussed how the amount of light available to phytoplankton varies—depending on the length of day and seasons, and with ocean depth. Without the light, photosynthesis cannot happen. Light availability limits photosynthesis; therefore, light is a limiting factor of photosynthesis.

Nutrients are also needed for photosynthesis, because phytoplankton use them to build the compounds necessary to carry out the process and make food. But, as you saw in Lesson 25: Animal Needs and Animal Tracking, nutrients are not always available. So, nutrients are a limiting factor for photosynthesis in the ocean.

 **Lab**

FIGURE 29.2. Sample setup.

Light or Nutrients

Let's investigate the effects of the limiting factors on phytoplankton growth first-hand. We are going to perform a 2-week experiment that explores the needs of phytoplankton, our most important marine producers. Follow the lab procedures listed on your worksheet. Each group of students will test the effect of light or nutrients, but not both.

Materials:

Per group:

- Three 1-liter transparent soda bottles (to conduct eutrophication experiment)
- Water from any local aquatic environment, enough for each student group to have ~1 liter
- Tap water, enough for each student group to have ~½ liter
- Liquid fertilizer containing nitrogen and/or phosphorus (to simulate the effects of excess nutrients)
- An area exposed to light
- An area in darkness
- Chart paper
- Masking tape
- Markers

Procedure:

1. Obtain two 1-liter soda bottles. Be certain that the bottles have been completely washed out. Using the water provided by the teacher, fill each bottle approximately halfway, making sure the water levels are equal.

2. Obtain a third 1-liter soda bottle. Fill it with tap water from the sink approximately halfway. Be sure the water level is equal with that of the other bottles.

3. Label the bottles with the limiting factor that your group is assigned and will test. On the bottle with the tap water, label that it as tap + the limiting factor.

An experimental factor of either light or nutrients will be your variable, the factor that you are testing in your experiment. It is important to make sure that your experiment has only one variable. All other conditions must be controlled.

4. Describe how your group will control the experiment to test for only one variable.

5. Describe the methods your group will use for collecting and recording data.

6. Create a data collection table like the one below. The data entered in the sample table are an example. Record data based on your observations.

Date and Time	Experimental (Bottle A)	Control (Bottle B)	Control (Bottle C)	Other Notes
Feb 2 11am	Clear water	Clear water	Clear water	*We added 2 teaspoons of fertilizer to bottle A. Both bottles were left in the classroom window.*
Feb 3 11:05 am	*Water is more cloudy*	*Clear water, no change*	*Clear water, no change*	

Our Results after 2 Weeks

7. What organisms are living in the water in the soda bottles? How do you know?

8. Describe what the groups who tested the effect of light found.

9. Describe what students who tested the effect of nutrients found.

10. Describe the effect of light and fertilizers on phytoplankton.

11. How does the excess fertilizer affect organisms living in the water?

Explain

As you learned in Lesson 17: Food Webs in Action, nitrogen and phosphorus are two important nutrients. Land and estuary plants take in these inorganic elements from the soil. In the ocean, phytoplankton and marine algae absorb the nutrients from the water. Nitrogen is used to build proteins and chlorophyll. Phosphorus is commonly found in organisms in the form of phosphate (a phosphorus atom bonded to 4 oxygen atoms). Phosphate is essential to the structure of DNA, RNA, and ATP. These molecules allow an organism to pass genetic traits to the next generation, build proteins, and store energy.

These nutrients and others—including iron and magnesium—are naturally found in small amounts in marine ecosystems. Unfortunately, human activities can result in too many of these nutrients in some areas. Human sources of these nutrients include fertilizers, sewage, and household cleaning supplies.

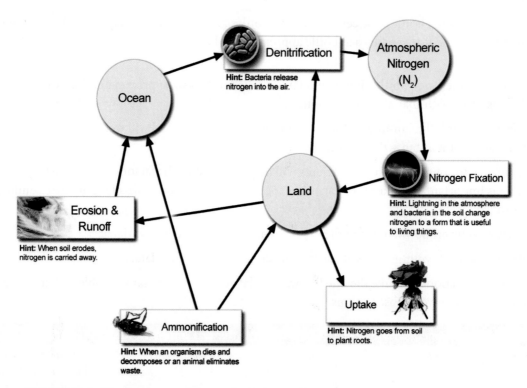

FIGURE 29.3. Nitrogen is one of the nutrients required to build compounds, such as chlorophyll, and proteins that include the enzymes needed for photosynthesis. Nitrogen is cycled through all of Earth's spheres in the nitrogen cycle.

FIGURE 29.4 shows the mouth of the Mississippi River, where it enters the Gulf of Mexico. The Mississippi Watershed drains fresh water from thirty-one (31) states, making it the largest watershed in the United States. The fresh water entering the Gulf contains many nutrients, from natural and human sources, which allow phytoplankton to reproduce at a much faster rate. This leads to an explosive growth of phytoplankton, including algae, along the Gulf Coast, called a **bloom**.

Major phytoplankton blooms can be seen in satellite imagery. The reddest areas in the image in FIGURE 29.4 of the Gulf of Mexico, indicate high phytoplankton growth seen in spring and early summer when nutrients are carried from land into the ocean. While phytoplankton blooms in other areas of the ocean occur naturally and often serve extensive marine food webs, the type of bloom shown here indicates that the water is in poor health.

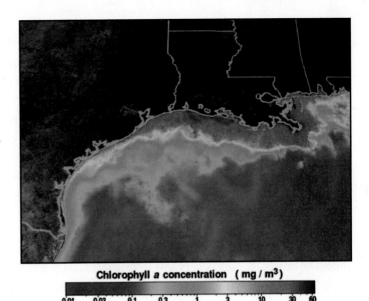

Chlorophyll *a* concentration (mg / m³)

0.01   0.03   0.1   0.3   1   3   10   30   60

FIGURE 29.4. The area around the Mississippi River Delta in Louisiana as shown from a satellite. Algal blooms are visible along the coast.

FIGURE 29.5. In some areas, storm drains feed directly into the ocean, contributing to pollution. In the Hawaiian Islands Humpback Whale National Marine Sanctuaries Watershed, sanctuary volunteers stencil storm drains like this one to increase awareness about such environmental threats.

FIGURE 29.6. True-color image from the Terra satellite shows the murky brown water of the Mississippi River flowing into the Gulf of Mexico.

Because phytoplankton provide food for many organisms in a marine ecosystem, it might seem that a large bloom of them would be beneficial. However, phytoplankton blooms can cause problems by upsetting the balance in a marine ecosystem. First, marine plants and small animals can die. The presence of too many algae, whether phytoplankton or seaweeds, in the water creates a "blanket" on the surface. Light cannot penetrate through this thick cover. As a result, other producers, such as algae living attached to rocks on the shallow seafloor, will likely die, as will the animals that feed on these organisms.

Second, bacteria can take over an aquatic ecosystem. With the abundance of nutrients available initially, phytoplankton will continue reproducing until they can no longer meet their own needs, eventually using up much of their resources. However, water, carbon dioxide, and sunlight may still be available. Phytoplankton do not live very long. Suddenly, the tiny organisms that were a part of the bloom begin to die. The dead phytoplankton begin sinking to the bottom and are broken down by decomposers. Decomposers, usually bacteria, use oxygen in the water to break down the tissues of dead organisms. Because so many phytoplankton die at the same time, the bacteria, which also reproduce quickly, are able to multiply rapidly because they have plenty to eat.

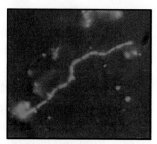

FIGURE 29.7. Deep sea sediment bacteria.

Each year, by late July, a large area within the Gulf of Mexico—15,000 square kilometers (~5,800 square miles) or more—becomes very low in dissolved oxygen (DO) concentrations. Millions of organisms die, including shrimp, oysters, clams, and numerous species of fish. Sometimes DO levels become so low that the area becomes known as a **dead zone**. Dead zones can persist for months. Scientists first became aware of dead zones in the 1970s. Studies now indicate that there are over 400 dead zones worldwide. Dead zones are **hypoxic**, defined as water containing less than 2 ppm (parts per million) of dissolved oxygen. DO levels at 6 ppm or above are considered normal; 5 ppm is the minimum to sustain life. Anything below 5 ppm is hypoxic to most marine organisms. When a marine ecosystem sustains hypoxic oxygen levels, the condition is known as **hypoxia**.

This entire process, from the addition of excess nutrients, to the phytoplankton bloom and die-off, to the resulting hypoxia, is called **eutrophication** (yoo-trō-fĭ-KAY-shŭn).

FIGURE 29.8. Tube anemones (pronounced: ah-NEH-men-eez), in the Flower Garden Banks National Marine Sanctuary in the Gulf of Mexico, are benthic invertebrates. When the water near the seafloor becomes hypoxic, these and other animals are affected.

See Page 694 for how to access e-Tools.

View the **Dead Zone Video** (3:50) from the e-Tools, which explains how the Gulf of Mexico Dead Zone develops each year.

e-Tools

FIGURE 29.9. Screenshot of the **Dead Zone Video**.

3. How can you explain the high levels of chlorophyll seen at the mouth of the Mississippi River?

4. Explain why the fertilizers used in many states can affect marine life in the Gulf of Mexico.

5. What harm can a phytoplankton bloom do to the marine ecosystem?

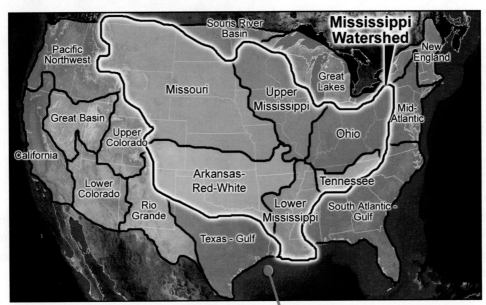

FIGURE 29.10. Map showing major watersheds. The red dot indicates the location of Flower Garden Banks National Marine Sanctuary, which protects important reef areas.

Flower Garden Banks National Marine Sanctuary

Fertilizers can be beneficial because they supply necessary compounds to help crops and plants to grow. When they reach bodies of water, however, they are pollutants. It is difficult to trace the origins of these pollutants. One wouldn't be able to determine, for example, from whose lawn excess fertilizer came.

Learning About Pollutants

Any substance that does not belong in an environment can be deemed a **pollutant** or **contaminant**. Pollutants can be solids (e.g., garbage thrown onto the street), liquids (e.g., chemicals that leak into the soil), or gases (e.g., bad smells that come from a garbage dump). Pollution can also be in the form of unwanted energy such as light coming from a neon sign disturbing sleep, loud noises emanating from a construction site, or excess heat being released into the environment from a power plant. Living things themselves can also be pollution. For example, bacteria that accidentally get into drinking water can pollute the water and make people sick.

FIGURE 29.11. Volcanoes are one natural source of pollutants. Volcanic activity releases noxious gases and particulate matter into the air, which can cause respiratory problems for many organisms.

Pollutants can be **anthropogenic**, meaning they result from human activities, but they can also be from natural sources. For example, volcanoes naturally release gases, ash, and rock into the air, making the air dirty and causing animals to have difficulty in breathing. Humans run factories and drive cars that release chemicals into the air, examples of anthropogenic pollution. All of Earth's environments—water, land, and air—can become polluted, and pollution can harm living things, including humans and marine animals.

FIGURE 29.12. Point source pollution is defined by the U.S. Environmental Protection Agency (EPA) as "any single identifiable source of pollution from which pollutants are discharged, such as a pipe". This image shows a point source of industrial pollution along the Calumet River in Illinois.

Some pollution comes from an obvious source. The source, for example, could be an oil tanker that crashes into rocks and spills oil into the ocean, or a smokestack that continuously spews thick black smoke into the air. Recall that pollution that comes from a specific, identifiable source is called **point source pollution**. It is very hard, however, to identify the sources of most pollution. For example, fertilizers or pesticides sprayed on a farm thousands of miles away from the sea may enter the ocean when it rains because these chemicals are carried long distances downhill and downstream. Pollution that comes from sources that are hard to identify is called **nonpoint source pollution**. Most pollution comes from nonpoint sources.

About 80% of the pollution in the ocean originates from land. There are two classifications of anthropogenic pollutants: organic and inorganic. Both of these types of pollutants were included in the nutrient runoff pollution that you investigated in the **Explore** section. **Organic pollutants** contain the element carbon. Sources of organic pollutants include sewage waste, some pesticides, gas leaks, and oil spills that can happen on land or at sea. These pollutants can affect marine organisms. Nonpoint sources of organic pollutants include poorly maintained waste systems aboard boats, which can release sewage, and oil and gas, which run off the land. If your family has a boat, be sure that the boat's waste system and the marina's pump-out station are checked each year.

Sewage waste can carry diseases that affect sea turtles and marine mammals. Pesticides have been linked to reproductive problems and difficulty fighting off diseases in seabirds and marine mammals such as seals and whales. Another organic pollutant is pet waste. Pet wastes, like any kind of fecal matter, can potentially carry bacteria and parasites that cause disease. The Environmental Protection Agency (EPA) estimates that in some areas, over 20% of bacteria found in water samples could be linked back to infected dogs. Pinnipeds (e.g., seals, sea lions) are particularly susceptible to the same diseases that affect dogs, meaning that dog waste that is carried into the ocean can make these animals sick. To dispose of pet waste, throw it into the garbage, flush it down the toilet, or bury it at least a meter into the ground.

FIGURE 29.13. Pet waste on land can easily lead to disease in the ocean. Cleaning up after your pet is one way to prevent additional organic pollutants from entering marine habitats.

Inorganic pollutants include metals, such as mercury and lead, as well as substances used as fertilizers and detergents. These contaminants may become highly concentrated as a result of many human activities including car washing, lawn and garden care, and mining for metals and minerals. Inorganic pollutants also affect marine animals. Studies have shown links between inorganic pollutants and hormonal and reproductive problems in seabirds, fish, and marine mammals. The organisms' livers and kidneys can also be affected. Animals exposed to these pollutants may have difficulty fighting disease. Consider the amounts of fertilizers and pesticides really needed for a lawn, and consider using a car wash, which must usually meet environmental safety requirements.

Marine pollution affects humans as well as other organisms. Inorganic contaminants such as heavy metals are incorporated into the food chain, of which humans are a part.

FIGURE 29.14. This image shows an adit (pronounced: Ă-dĭt) or mine opening, at Blackbird Mine in Lemhi County, Idaho. The water that can seep out of mine openings is often very acidic and can be contaminated with zinc, copper, or arsenic.

Human activities on land are leading to the build-up and transport of organic and inorganic pollutants in the ocean. Of course, some pollutants come from ocean-based sources. Examples include ships that empty their waste tanks into the ocean or cargo that falls off decks during rough seas. Another major ocean-based pollutant is fishing gear that is lost, either intentionally or unintentionally, from fishing boats. This type of gear is known as *ghost gear*. Lines, nets, and traps floating in the ocean can become ensnared on reefs or entangle marine animals, either in the water or once they wash up on shore. Using their understanding of healthy fish habitats, fishers can make responsible choices to dispose of fishing lines safely instead of leaving them in the water.

FIGURE 29.15. Florida and other states have begun recycling programs for fishing lines. By recycling used and broken lines, fishers prevent them from becoming ghost gear.

FIGURE 29.16. Laysan Albatross chick sits on a beach surrounded by ghost gear—including fishing lines and eel traps.

Marine Debris

One type of pollution that has both land and ocean-based sources is *marine debris*. Marine debris includes any solid material that persists in the ocean. Marine debris can range from a plastic bottle cap to an abandoned ship. Types of marine debris include plastics, glass, metal, Styrofoam, rubber, and ghost gear. This debris can be intentionally or unintentionally released into the ocean. For example, fishers might cut and release tangled lines, or irresponsible boaters may throw cigarette butts or plastic wrappers off the vessel's deck. Unintentional debris could occur when a storm causes a boat

FIGURE 29.17. The marine debris littering the remote shoreline of Kure Atoll in the Northwestern Hawaiian Islands demonstrates the diversity of items that are carried by ocean currents, including bottles, floats, shoes, and toys.

to crash into a coral reef; the shipwreck could remain on the reef indefinitely. A plastic bag could fly out of a litter bin and blow into the water, where it could float with or be ingested by an animal.

Regardless of the cause, marine debris is a serious problem. It is very difficult to estimate how much marine debris there really is, and how many organisms are injured or killed by it each year. However, a NOAA Pacific Islands Fisheries Science Center study from 1985 estimates the following: "Up to one hundred thousand marine mammals and possibly more die each year. Half or more of the individuals of certain marine reptile species are affected by the plastic litter, and beachcombing land mammals become snarled in nets and die". Marine mammals and sea turtles are not the only organisms affected—seabirds, fish, invertebrates, and algae can all be at risk. Because marine debris is such an important concern, NOAA has established a marine debris program to educate the public about marine debris, how it is being studied and what is being done about it.

FIGURE 29.18. This computer monitor washed up on the shore of Midway Atoll in the Pacific Ocean is believed to have been unintentionally lost from a cargo ship.

Plastics make up a large portion of all marine debris. A major problem with plastics is that they do not decompose naturally; they are not **biodegradable**. Plastics of all sizes can be ingested by marine animals, causing digestive and other problems. For example, clear plastic lunch bags are a threat to sea turtles, because when floating in the ocean, these bags closely resemble a favorite food—jellyfish. Plastic does break down into tiny particles called **plastic nodules**. Plastic nodules float along with the plankton population and have even been noted in analyses of beach sand. They can also absorb other chemicals, causing them to float on the surface of the ocean. While this is a new area of study, plastics and chemicals within them can have a toxic effect on organisms. Some of these chemicals, for example, will interfere with growth and reproduction in marine animals that are consuming the toxins through the food chain.

Plastic, whether small or large pieces, and other types of floating marine debris are pushed along by wind and ocean currents. In this way, marine debris, most of which originates on land and enters the ocean from the outflow of watersheds, can end up on the most remote beaches in the world. In some areas, where currents and winds cause a gyre, marine debris is more highly concentrated. One such area is in the North Pacific, where there are two huge areas of highly concentrated marine debris, referred to as the Eastern and Western Pacific Garbage Patches. Do not picture an area of ocean completely covered with garbage—rather, this area is simply one where debris is found in higher concentrations because of winds and currents. Much of this debris consists of tiny plastic nodules and other small items. Although there are thousands of pieces of debris per square kilometer over large areas, these "patches" cannot be easily seen with aerial photography or in satellite imagery. Similar areas of highly concentrated marine debris have been identified and investigated in the Atlantic, South Pacific, and Indian Ocean basins.

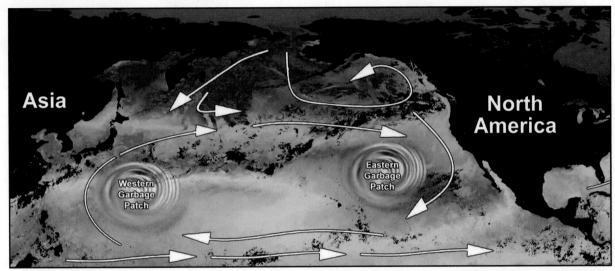

FIGURE 29.19. The Pacific Garbage Patches are areas where winds and currents create highly concentrated areas of marine debris. Mats of garbage do not cover these areas—most of the debris is tiny and floats along with the plankton community.

Preventing additional marine debris is possible, but we all must be committed to the concept of **Reduce, Reuse, Recycle**. According to studies of education programs, making impressions on students and others can cause people to change their practices. Many students have decided that if a simple bottle cap can flow from within a watershed out to sea and harm an animal, they will be sure to dispose of such items properly. We can reduce the amount of trash we generate in the first place by choosing products with less packaging or avoiding disposables (e.g., by using cloth lunch bags and metal water bottles instead of plastic) and simply by not being wasteful. When at all possible, we should reuse items, as by packing lunch in the same containers daily or storing household items in containers that we've collected. Depending on your area, glass, paper, metal, and some plastics can be recycled. Recycled items are turned into new products.

FIGURE 29.20. Hawaiian Monk Seal pup sunning on the beach surrounded by marine debris including plastic bottles, fishing floats, and even laundry baskets. Marine mammals such as Monk Seals easily can become ensnarled in nets, baskets, and lines.

6. Describe three ways in which nonpoint source pollution in the ocean can be prevented. Articulate how each strategy can specifically help.

7. How does pollution contribute to biodiversity loss? What are the consequences of these losses?

FIGURE 29.22. This photo shows plastic debris on a coral reef. Note that underwater, plastic bags resemble jellyfish; they are often ingested by sea turtles that prey on the jelly-like invertebrates.

FIGURE 29.21. A decomposing albatross carcass reveals a digestive system filled with plastics.

One type of marine animal that is particularly affected by marine debris is the albatross. There are several species of albatross that inhabit the world's ocean. In the North Pacific, these species include the Laysan Albatross, Black-footed Albatross, and Short-tailed Albatross. Albatross parents take special care of their chicks. They fly hundreds or thousands of miles from their nesting sites, such as in the remote Northwestern Hawaiian Islands, to productive waters just to scoop up fish eggs, squid, and other delicacies. From these food sources, they create nutrient-rich oil, which they regurgitate directly into the chicks' mouths.

Unfortunately, however, these caring parents will most often feed something else to their chicks—marine debris. Rotting carcasses of chicks, which died for any reason, reveal all kinds of plastics, including bottle caps, toys, and toothbrushes. One thing to consider is how long the adult birds spend in known areas with high concentrations of marine debris—such as the Pacific Garbage Patches.

FIGURE 29.23. Adult albatross, such as the Laysan Albatross shown here, trek thousands of miles to areas of high productivity to gather food for their young. This photograph shows the adult regurgitating its nutrient-rich liquid into the mouth of the chick.

FIGURE 29.24. Black-footed Albatross chick looks to the sea as an adult Laysan Albatross flies away.

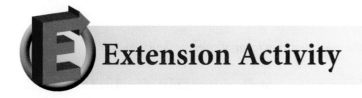

Extension Activity

1. Follow the instructions below:

   a. On the *Marine Science: The Dynamic Ocean* website, go to Animal Movement Maps and Data. Find the Pacific Plastics Map in Issues Data.

   b. Choose Black-footed Albatross or Laysan Albatross from real-time or archived data, from any year available.

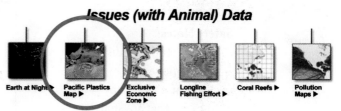

Issues (with Animal) Data

Earth at Night ▶ Pacific Plastics Map ▶ Exclusive Economic Zone ▶ Longline Fishing Effort ▶ Coral Reefs ▶ Pollution Maps ▶

FIGURE 29.25. Map icons.

   c. What does this map show?

   d. How do you think plastics get into the ocean?

   e. Based on the map, how much time did the albatross spend in the areas of the two garbage patches? Choose three of the birds and give specific amounts of time.

   f. Why does the amount of time spent in the areas of the garbage patches matter?

Elaborate

 **Lab**

Campus Debris Survey

Materials:

- Pair of work gloves for each student
- One kitchen-sized garbage bag for each pair of students
- *Campus Debris Data Sheet* for each group
- *Campus Debris Data Summary Excel® Workbook* or *Campus Debris Data Summary Sheet* for each group

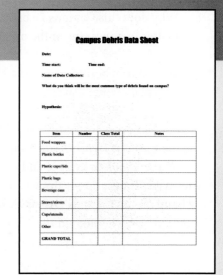

FIGURE 29.26. *Campus Debris Data Sheet*.

We are going to examine potential future marine debris on our school campus.

1. Make a hypothesis: *What do you think will be the most common form of campus debris found?*

2. Once at the assigned location, your group will be given 15 minutes to survey a plot of land and to place all human-made objects that do not occur in nature into your garbage bags. As you work, record the number of items found in each category on the data sheets.

Safety Notes:
- Every student must wear work gloves.
- Do not pick up any objects that are sharp or unidentifiable.

FIGURE 29.27. Debris found on a school campus could one day become marine debris. All schools, campuses, business buildings, and other developments sit in a watershed capable of distributing debris into the ocean.

3. a. What was your debris collection rate per minute?

   b. Which items can be recycled?

   c. What campus location had the most debris?

   d. Which items could entangle marine life?

   e. Which items could conceivably be eaten by marine life?

   f. Why does this Campus Debris Survey on land matter to organisms in the ocean far away?

   g. Was your hypothesis supported? Use evidence to explain your answer.

FIGURE 29.28. NOAA Scientists take time to clean up marine debris in a Virginia estuary.

4. If computer access is readily available, use the *Campus Debris Data Summary Excel® Workbook* to analyze and graph your data. If not, simply draw graphs by hand on the *Campus Debris Data Summary Sheet*, found in the e-Tools.

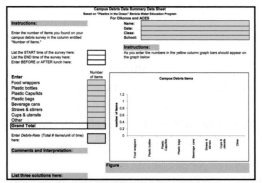

e-Tools

FIGURE 29.29. *Campus Debris Data Summary Excel® Workbook.*

Evaluate

1. Draw a comic strip that illustrates the steps of eutrophication in a pond, lake, or bay. Use 6 boxes similar to what is shown below. Draw and label as necessary to communicate what is happening at each step.

2. Now, draw a healthy body of water. What lives in there? Are there nutrients? Is there light? Be sure to show how the healthy body of water differs from a eutrophic one.

3. Share the responsibility of caring for the ocean and join the effort to promote ocean conservation. Now that you are aware of some of the consequences of land-based activities, it is your responsibility to teach others about the topic, and persuade them that they can make a difference. Think in terms of prevention—how can you convince others to do their part in taking care of ocean habitats?

Create a product in which you convince others that changing behaviors on land can have a positive effect on the marine environment. Your product may be a brochure, an advertising campaign consisting of a series of posters, or another idea approved by your teacher.

The product must:

- Be convincing. Catch the reader's attention and compel them to act.
- Use scientific evidence. Data (e.g., statistics, explanations of how specific organisms or ecosystems are affected) should support the ideas presented and establish the importance and credibility of your product.
- Be aesthetically pleasing. The product should be attractive, well organized, and "catchy".
- Use correct grammar and spelling. Products are not persuasive when there are obvious errors.

30

Point Source Pollution

INSIDE:

Objectives

You will be able to:

✔ **Describe examples of point source pollution.**

✔ **Compare and contrast methods of cleaning up oil spills.**

✔ **Discuss the effects of oil spills on marine organisms and ecosystems.**

Benchmarks

1g. The ocean is connected to major lakes, watersheds, and waterways because all major watersheds on Earth drain to the ocean. Rivers and streams transport nutrients, salts, sediments, and pollutants from watersheds to estuaries and to the ocean.

2a. Many Earth materials and geochemical cycles originate in the ocean. Many of the sedimentary rocks now exposed on land were formed in the ocean. Ocean life laid down the vast volume of siliceous and carbonate rocks.

5i. Estuaries provide important and productive nursery areas for many marine and aquatic species.

6b. From the ocean we get foods, medicines, and mineral and energy resources. In addition, it provides jobs, supports our nation's economy, serves as a highway for transportation of goods and people, and plays a role in national security.

6e. Humans affect the ocean in a variety of ways. Laws, regulations, and resource management affect what is taken out and put into the ocean. Human development and activity leads to pollution (e.g., point source, nonpoint source, noise pollution) and physical modifications (e.g., changes to beaches, shores, and rivers). In addition, humans have removed most of the large vertebrates from the ocean.

6g. Everyone is responsible for caring for the ocean. The ocean sustains life on Earth, and humans must live in ways that sustain the ocean. Individual and collective actions are needed to effectively manage ocean resources for all.

7c. Over the last 40 years, use of ocean resources has increased significantly, therefore the future sustainability of ocean resources depends on our understanding of those resources and their potential and limitations.

7f. Ocean exploration is truly interdisciplinary. It requires close collaboration among biologists, chemists, climatologists, computer programmers, engineers, geologists, meteorologists, and physicists and new ways of thinking.

Engage

Gusher in the Gulf

One of the largest oils spills in history began on April 20, 2010 as the result of an explosion on the Deepwater Horizon Oil Rig located in the Gulf of Mexico, about 80 kilometers (~50 miles) from the coast. As the name of the rig implies, owner British Petroleum (BP) was conducting exploratory drilling into the ocean floor approximately 1,500 meters (~5,000 feet) below the surface, in "deep water". As the drilling was taking place, a large bubble of methane gas traveled up from the well, through the pipe. It caused an explosion killing 11 of the 126 rig workers onboard.

FIGURE 30.1. Fire on the Deepwater Horizon Oil Rig in the Gulf of Mexico. Eleven workers were killed in the explosion on April 20, 2010.

Two days after the explosion, Deepwater Horizon sank to the seafloor. It is unclear how much of the estimated 16,700 barrels of fuel onboard burned before it sank. When the rig sank, a pipe connecting the well and the rig broke, releasing a quantity of oil estimated at 1,000 barrels each day into the water (~42,000 gallons/~160,000 liters). Within one week, another leak was discovered, and the U.S. Coast Guard reported that there was five times the amount of oil pouring into the ocean than was originally estimated.

Over several weeks, BP attempted to stop the leak using various methods. On September 17, 2010, a devastatingly long 86 days after the incident, BP announced they had successfully sealed the well. In addition to the human lives lost, thousands of marine animals including seabirds, dolphins, and endangered sea turtles, and hundreds of other species were killed. The livelihoods of fishers and business owners in Louisiana and throughout the Gulf of Mexico were severely impacted. Final estimates for the oil spill are equivalent to over 4.9 million barrels. The Deepwater Horizon oil spill and its effects on the environment will be studied for many years to come.

FIGURE 30.2. Oil quickly washed up on beaches in Southern Louisiana. This picture shows oil among sand, twigs and seaweed on Grand Isle.

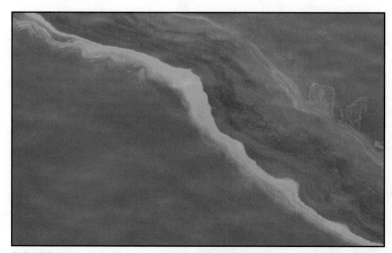

FIGURE 30.3. Scientists began assessing the oil soon after the spill. This photograph, taken from an airplane, shows a heavy band of oil in the Gulf.

1. Create a K-W-L (What do you Know—What do you Want to Know—What have you Learned) Chart like the one below in your notebook. Write what you know about oil spills and their effects on marine ecosystems in the first column. Then, write your questions, or what you want to know, in the second column. You will complete the chart at the end of the Lesson.

K	W	L

FIGURE 30.4. Precious wetlands were inundated with oil during the spring and summer of 2010. This photograph was taken at Pass a Loutre, Louisiana, on May 22, 2010, following a storm in the area.

FIGURE 30.5. A NOAA "overflight" on May 20, 2010, revealed plenty of oil on the Gulf's surface. NOAA and other agencies used many techniques to study the oil spill, including aerial and boat surveys, to assess the extent of the contamination subsequent to the spill event.

FIGURE 30.6. Dr. Brian Stacy, NOAA veterinarian, prepares to clean an oiled Kemp's Ridley Turtle. Veterinarians and scientists from NOAA, the Florida Fish and Wildlife Commission, and other partners worked tirelessly to capture heavily-oiled young turtles 20 to 40 miles offshore. The turtles were treated and released whenever possible.

Explore

Following an oil spill such as the Deepwater Horizon explosion, many groups of people mobilize for damage control as well as for action so that another catastrophic event can be averted in the future. There are often contrasting views on how to handle a large-scale cleanup; it is difficult to determine a right answer for how to best handle such an extensive mess.

One type of point source pollution, as a single location contributes to pollution or an event, is an oil spill. Recall that fossil fuels, such as oil, develop from the remains of living things and contain high amounts of carbon, making them organic materials. Oil spills may come from different point sources, including drilling, pipelines, or oil tankers.

Most oil found in the ocean is actually from nonpoint sources. It runs off the land, likely from sources such as leaky cars, spilling drops during oil changes, dripping fuel pumps at the gas station, and people improperly disposing of changed oil. After a rainstorm, have you ever noticed a rainbow pattern in a puddle on the pavement? If so, you have observed nonpoint source oil pollution.

The *Exxon Valdez* oil spill occurred when the ship leaked in Alaska's Prince William Sound in 1989. Almost 11 million gallons (~41.6 million liters) of crude oil were released into the Sound. NOAA estimates that this amount of oil could fill more than 9 average high school gymnasia. The Deepwater Horizon spill estimates as stated are at 4.9 million barrels, in which there are 42 gallons to a barrel; over 200 million gallons of oil were released into the Gulf of Mexico.

FIGURE 30.7. Motor oil and other oil-based chemicals can be recognized by a characteristic rainbow-colored sheen. As a liquid, oil will flow and contribute to marine pollution.

FIGURE 30.8. An oiled marsh in Southern Louisiana, May 2010. A variety of techniques were employed in the Gulf of Mexico to address the spill.

 # Lab

Cleaning Up Oil Spills

In this activity, you will design, test and refine mechanisms for cleaning up oil spills. You will create a model spill. You will follow an **Engineering Design Process**, a cyclical process for creating a way to solve a problem at hand. The oil spill on which you will work will consist of oil, water, and sand to model an oil spill near a coastline. A set of materials will be presented to each group in order to work through the Engineering Design Process.

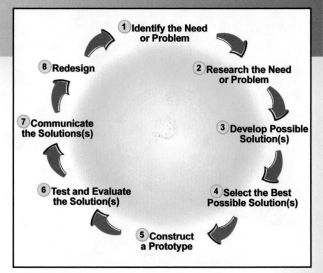

FIGURE 30.9. The Engineering Design Process.

Materials:

For the class:
* Buckets in which to pour contaminated water

For each student:
* Safety goggles
* Working gloves

For each group of 4–5 students:
* Water
* Motor oil
* Sand
* Disposable paint trays or aluminum casserole pans
* Small graduated cylinder
* Garbage bags
* Various tools for creating oil spill cleanup devices (examples shown to the right)

Various tools for creating oil spill cleanup devices	
String	Plastic spoons
Straws	Toothpicks
Styrofoam pellets	Wooden coffee stirrers
Dish detergent	Scraps of cloth
Spray bottles	Needles and thread
Cotton balls	Wire
Pieces of sponge	Tape
Paper towels	

Safety Note: Gloves and safety goggles must be worn when working with motor oil.

Follow the steps with your group.

1. **Identify the Need or Problem** – What question are you trying to answer as a group?

2. **Research the Need or Problem** – Conduct online, book, and journal research to determine ways in which real oil spills are cleaned up. Some starting points are available in the e-Tools. Take notes on the different strategies and put them into your notebook.

e-Tools

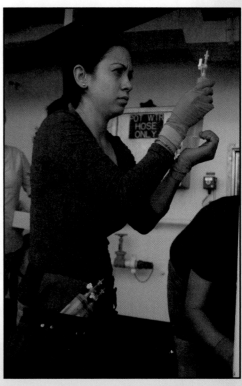

FIGURE 30.10. Following an oil spill scientists in all disciplines must work together and with engineers, technologists, and others to respond to the problem. In this image, Stephanie Mendes, a researcher from the University of California at Santa Barbara, is checking a water sample for air bubbles onboard the NOAA Ship *Pisces* during a September 2010 mission. Scientists collected water samples to analyze them for chemicals that could show the presence of natural gas and oil, as well as the dilution and decomposition of these products.

3. **Develop Possible Solutions** – With your group, discuss your research findings. Discuss which strategies you believe you can model in the classroom with the materials you have been given. Alternatively, develop new strategies that can work in the ocean and that you can model. Sketch at least three possible designs of spill cleanup devices in your notebooks.

4. **Select the Best Possible Solution** – Decide which solution you think will be most effective for cleaning up a spill in the model ocean as well as in real life.

5. **Construct a Prototype** – Build your device, the means with which you will address the problem, noting the steps you follow in your notebook.

6. **Test and Evaluate the Solution** –

> **Safety Note:** Gloves and safety goggles must be worn for this step.

FIGURE 30.11. Remediation team members, such as this worker helping to clean up the *Exxon Valdez* spill, must wear protective suits, gloves, and goggles when cleaning up oil spills.

a. To model your ocean, use the sand to create "land" on one side of your pan.
b. Fill your pan with water until it is about halfway full.
c. Add 20 mL of oil to one area of your pan. The oil will begin to spread out, eventually covering areas of your "ocean" and "coast".
d. Draw your setup.
e. Test your device. Make observations and drawings about how it works.
f. Now add a little more oil. In real sea conditions, the oil is constantly being pushed by winds and currents. Therefore, areas tend to become re-covered in oil even after cleanup efforts have occurred.
g. Test your device again. Make observations and drawings about how it works.
h. How can your device be improved? What else would you try? Why?
i. Clean up your station as directed by your teacher. Do not pour oil down the sink as it can clog sewage treatment plants.

7. **Communicate the Solutions** – If you were to *scale up* this device for use in the ocean, what would be the costs and benefits of using it? Use evidence from your tests to support your answer. Questions to consider include:

   - What real materials would you suggest using?
   - Would it be expensive to produce?
   - Is your system practical for large or small areas?
   - Is your system best used in the open ocean or near the coast?
   - How would it be deployed? How many people would be needed to do so?

8. **Redesign** – Refine your design based on your testing and discussion of scaling up your product. Build your new prototype.

Engineering Design Conference

Next we will compare the different solutions designed by our class groups, simulating a conference of environmental engineers. Each group will demonstrate the effectiveness of their prototype in a model ocean at the front of the room, address the three topics below, and answer questions posed by other groups. You will have an opportunity to rate each design in three topic areas:

FIGURE 30.12. Formulating a design to solve a problem helps to promote career-building skills. The process of design is a common activity carried out by engineers in the workplace.

1. Effectiveness at Sea – How well does this method work for cleaning up oil floating on the sea surface?

2. Effectiveness on Land – How well does the system work for cleaning up oil that has affected areas of coastline?

3. Value for Cost – How expensive would a real-life version of this tool be? Is it worth it for the effectiveness?

4. Copy the rubric below into your notebook. Then, for each team of students, use it to rate the aspects of each design, by indicating *high*, *medium*, or *low* in each column.

Design Rubric

Team Name	Quick Sketch of Design	Effectiveness at Sea	Effectiveness on Land	Value for Cost

5. After the conference, answer the Questions below individually.

a. If you were a town council member in a coastal community, which design would you purchase for your town to have on hand in case of an oil spill? Why?

b. What other materials would you have liked to use when building a prototype? Why?

c. Explain why the Engineering Design Process is considered to be cyclical.

d. Why are models important in the Engineering Design Process?

e. How can oil spills be prevented in the first place?

FIGURE 30.13. NOAA scientists and partners at work in the BP Training Center, Houma, Louisiana. NOAA provides response services to state and federal organizations.

Explain

Point Source Pollution and the Ocean

While oil spills probably come to mind first, there are many other point sources of marine pollutants, including factories and sewage treatment plants. According to the Environmental Protection Agency, point sources of pollution can originate from pipes, ditches, channels, tunnels, containers, and vessels, including ships and other watercraft, as well as places where animals are kept and fed. The Clean Water Act, enacted in 1972 and amended in 1977, made it illegal to discharge pollutants into U.S. waters without proper permits. Before this legislation, it was common practice for factories, power plants, and other sites to simply release chemicals into rivers, streams, lakes, bays, and the ocean.

FIGURE 30.14. Point sources of pollution take on many forms. This photograph shows a pipe leaking substances into a waterway.

For example, from approximately 1947 to 1977, in the Hudson River, which runs through Eastern New York State and separates New York City from New Jersey, General Electric released over a million pounds of polychlorinated biphenyls (PCBs) from its factories. PCBs are organic chemicals used in the manufacturing of electrical parts to release energy, such as transformers and capacitors. They are known to cause hormone and reproductive problems in humans and in some wildlife. The Lower Hudson River is an important estuary, protecting the juveniles of many Atlantic Ocean marine species. This point source pollution necessitated, at times, closing portions of the river to recreational activities, such as fishing and swimming. Many organisms were affected, including fish, birds, and invertebrates. Today, most of the PCBs are trapped on the river's bottom within the sediments, and the government has ruled that General Electric must pay to clean up this more than 30-year-old problem.

While intentional dumping of pollutants should theoretically be prevented by legislation, there are still occasional accidents worldwide. For example, in 2010, an accident occurred at an aluminum oxide plant in western Hungary. Aluminum oxide is used to produce aluminum metal, which is used to make a wide variety of familiar products such as cans and foil. The manufacturing plant had large concrete reservoirs, similar to swimming pools, which held toxic wastes leftover from processing. A wall in one of these containment tanks failed after heavy rains, releasing nearly one million cubic meters of thick, rust-colored "sludge" gushing into local waterways. The sludge was not only unsightly, but dangerous because of its high pH, measured at near 13 closest to the spill site. Substances with high pH, as well as those with low pH, can result in chemical burns. This is exactly what happened as over 100 people were injured and at least eight were killed as the sludge traveled downstream.

FIGURE 30.15. Sand dunes along Lake Michigan, with power plant in the background. Prior to the Clean Water Act, in some areas it was legal to discharge pollutants into bodies of water.

FIGURE 30.16. Map showing the location of the Hudson River.

FIGURE 30.17. This natural-color image was taken by NASA's Earth Observing-1 satellite on October 9, 2010. Notice the rust-colored sludge and nearby homes and farms.

The quick release also caused flooding—of water and sludge—damaging homes, bridges, and even sweeping cars off of the road. Hundreds of people were forced to relocate because villages became contaminated. The sludge flowed down tributaries into the Danube River, one of the largest rivers in Europe.

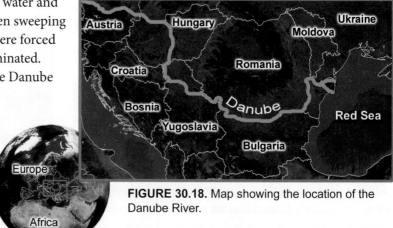

FIGURE 30.18. Map showing the location of the Danube River.

2. Neither of the spills described on these pages occurred directly in the ocean. Describe the process by which the ocean may be affected by point source pollution occurring in rivers.

Point source pollution can also originate from facilities that treat wastewater from homes and businesses, called **wastewater treatment plants**. In most urban and suburban areas, wastewater from toilets, tubs, and sinks is collected in a system of waste pipes called **sewers**. The sewers carry human and other waste to a sewage treatment plant where this wastewater is treated. Particles are removed, the water is disinfected, and so on. Bacteria and other organisms are used to consume organic materials such as fecal matter. Finally, cleaned water can be released into local water bodies.

FIGURE 30.19. The inner workings of a wastewater treatment plant. Wastewater is sent through several treatment processes by means of a series of pipes and tanks.

In some areas, urban runoff is combined with wastewater and is also treated. This means that storm drains seen in the streets also connect to the sewer system. This practice is excellent because oil, fertilizers, litter, and other materials seen in the street will not be dumped into bodies of water. At times, however, particularly after heavy rains, some wastewater treatment plants cannot handle the amount of material entering them. The system overflows, and water that is not completely treated is released into surface water.

3. What would happen if our wastewater were not treated?

Point Source Pollution from Oil Spills

Oil spills can occur for many reasons. Vessels can run aground, damaging their hull, allowing oil to gush out. This happened during the 1989 *Exxon Valdez* spill. Broken gas lines or other pipes can also be a point source. As you know, the 2010 main Deepwater Horizon spill occurred below the site of an oil rig. Let's learn more about offshore drilling for oil and natural gas, specifically in the Gulf of Mexico, so we can consider the events that led to this tragic spill.

With changing climate and varying evaporation rates over millions of years, at times of high evaporation rates, water evaporated and minerals remained, and large amounts of salt were left in thick layers on a shallow seafloor. Over time, rivers carried sediment—mud, sand, silt, and clay—to the Gulf of Mexico, depositing these materials in layers over the existing salt. Pressure from dense overlying sediment layers forced salt layers upward. In some places salt layers broke through completely, while in others the salt layers simply forced the seafloor to bulge upward in distinct domes, creating the characteristic peaks and valley of the seafloor in this region.

Over millions of years, the many plant and protist remains in the region become fossilized, until, under pressure, they became coal, natural gas, or oil. As you know this is why these energy sources are called **fossil fuels**. To understand how fossil fuels develop, consider diatoms, a type of phytoplankton. Diatoms take in carbon dioxide from the atmosphere to make sugars. Diatoms that died millions of years ago sank to the bottom of the ocean and were covered by layers of minerals, sediment, and rock. Over the millennia, heat and pressure from the geologic events in the area helped to convert carbon in these diatoms and other organisms to oil and natural gas. The Gulf of Mexico has a significant reserve of oil because of its geologic past. In fact, some of that oil naturally seeps from the seafloor into the water, meaning that there are natural oil spills deep within the Gulf. Microbes that live in these areas are adapted to consuming the oil and changing it into different forms.

FIGURE 30.20. Coal, shown here being transported by freight train, is one example of a fossil fuel. Others examples include oil and natural gas.

When the sequestered oil and gas is burned, the carbon dioxide is quickly returned to the atmosphere. Oil, in its various states, can be burned to provide energy for human activities including making electricity, heating homes, and fueling cars, trucks, and airplanes.

FIGURE 30.21. Layers of sand and deposits of dead organisms accumulated over time. Tremendous pressure transformed this matter into oil and gas. Deep drilling into the layers of rock now allows humans to tap natural fuel sources.

The removal of many deposits of oil and natural gas from beneath the seafloor (in the ocean) is referred to as **offshore drilling**. In U.S. waters, offshore drilling of fossil fuels is particularly prevalent in the Gulf of Mexico. According to a 2010 NOAA estimate, there are over 4,000 shallow-water drilling rigs in the Gulf. Oil platforms or rigs are huge structures anchored in an area to drill for oil below the seafloor. The oil is refined and made into energy-rich fuels such as diesel fuel and gasoline. These products are transported via pipelines, huge ships, barges, and, finally, trucks to local distributors and consumers. Oil transport requires that pipelines, canals, and other infrastructures be built. Oil and natural gas production is an extremely important industry for the U.S. economy, providing many jobs and resulting in huge sums of money paid to federal, state, and local governments. Oil companies, for example, pay governments for the right to lease the seafloor or land on which they will be working. The United States consumes about 25% of the world's oil supply, but produces only about 10% of it. Therefore, a majority of the oil we use is imported from other countries. To rely on such a crucial resource being provided by foreign countries is problematic. Gas and

FIGURE 30.22. Offshore oil platform on the continental shelf is a production facility for drilling and producing oil and natural gas.

home heating oil prices are high, in part, because quantities of these nonrenewable resources are limited. Therefore, many citizens and politicians have called for more offshore drilling to be conducted in U.S. waters. Current discussions about expanding offshore drilling focus on the extraction of oil from the continental shelf. Because the water is shallow, drilling is easier and less expensive in comparison than drilling in the deeper waters of the abyssal plain.

During the 20th Century, the practices of oil and gas extraction on offshore rigs resulted in waste products that were dumped directly into the ocean. Decomposition of wastes by microbes resulted in low-oxygen, or **anoxic**, conditions and hence the inability of marine species to breathe ample oxygen.

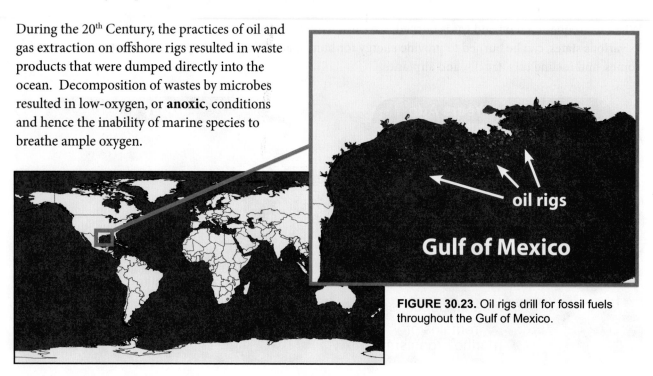

FIGURE 30.23. Oil rigs drill for fossil fuels throughout the Gulf of Mexico.

Oil seeping out from the drill site was common. There were frequent accounts of "blowouts", where oil spewed from drilling sites, and even fires, such as what happened with the Deepwater Horizon explosion. Regulation of offshore drilling by the United States Environmental Protection Agency began in the late 1970s. Today, there are processes in place to treat wastes, prevent blowouts and fires, and to reduce harm to marine environments resulting from drilling and other extraction and treatment activities. Of course, there are still accidents. Although regulations have reduced negative effects of offshore drilling, there are still serious potential environmental impacts associated with the process.

FIGURE 30.24. Oil truck transports liquid fuel from production sites to customers or fuel providers.

Before drilling begins, scientists use seismic processes to identify drilling sites. A common technique is to shoot an air gun and record how sound waves reverberate. This technique yields data about the densities of the substances beneath the seafloor. The initial waves propagate through solid rock and sediment in a somewhat different manner from how they characteristically pass through oil and gas.

Unfortunately, marine mammals can be disturbed by these loud noises, and their ability to use echolocation to find prey may be compromised. When oil is extracted from the seafloor, potential toxins such as mercury and lead can be released into the seawater. Pollutants no longer trapped in the seafloor can enter the food chain. A concern about creating new offshore drilling sites is related to the transport of the oil. Building canals and ports to move the oil requires dredging, which can be extremely disruptive to benthic habitats. The risk of accidental oil spills is always a concern—most spills at sea are the result of ships transporting oil. One last consequence of expanding offshore drilling is that if more fossil fuels are available, people may not have the incentive to seek renewable sources of energy production.

FIGURE 30.25. This 1992 oil rig fire occurred near the coast of Louisiana. Fires are one concern associated with offshore drilling.

4. Describe one cost, or negative result, and one benefit, or positive result, associated with offshore drilling.

See Page 694 for how to access e-Tools.

View the *Artificial Reef Video* (0:53) from the e-Tools of an artificial reef in the Gulf of Mexico. The video demonstrates how an offshore oil rig became a habitat for a wide variety of organisms in the Gulf of Mexico.

FIGURE 30.26. Screenshot of the *Artificial Reef Video*. Underwater, rigs have become artificial reefs for millions of marine organisms.

e-Tools

The Department of the Interior's (DOI) Bureau of Ocean Energy Management, Regulation and Enforcement (BOEMRE), formerly the Minerals Management Service (MMS), is the government agency responsible for energy development offshore. They lease the space to energy producers, who pay fees on the minerals they extract from the ocean floor. The MMS previously performed these same services and identified deepwater offshore sites in the Gulf of Mexico and permitted exploratory drilling to determine the extent of the reservoirs. In the past, drilling activities have been concentrated along the coast and in shallow waters. **Deepwater drilling sites**, located more than 1,500 meters below the surface, are considered the "final frontier" for oil and gas exploration.

FIGURE 30.27. A helicopter near the Deepwater Horizon rig site, where fire is visible. When the explosion occurred, the rig was in about 1,525 meters (~5,000 feet) of water.

Before oil companies drill in a certain location they are required to have an approved permit from BOEMRE. The MMS had allowed BP to continue their exploratory drilling at the Deepwater Horizon site without a careful assessment of the environmental impacts. This allowance is referred to as a "categorical exclusion" from the requirements of the National Environmental Policy Act (NEPA). NEPA requires an Environmental Impact Assessment (EIA) to be performed and reviewed to identify the potential environmental effects of specific actions, in this case drilling in deep water.

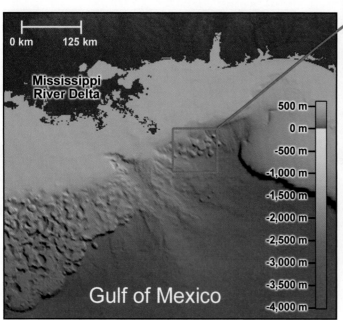

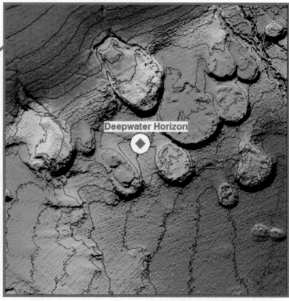

FIGURE 30.28. Examine the multibeam sonar image of the region near the Deepwater Horizon rig. Deepwater drilling takes place beyond the continental shelf.

Tracking the Deepwater Horizon Spill

Following the Deepwater Horizon spill, scientists worked hard to track the oil and to make predictions about where the oil would next head. FIGURE 30.29 shows a plume of smoke arising from the burning rig on April 20, 2010. Satellite imagery was able to detect some of the aftermath, but this was difficult because of weather conditions, the glare of sunlight off the water, and other complications.

While the oil quickly reached shore, including beaches and wetlands, in Louisiana and Mississippi, residents of the East Coast and Florida were concerned about if and when the oil might reach them. Scientists and citizens alike were concerned that the main oil slick would reach the Loop Current, which carries water from the Gulf into the Caribbean Sea. The Loop Current connects with the Gulf Stream, which carries water northward along the East Coast. FIGURE 30.31 shows the location of the oil slick on May 17, 2010, nearly reaching the Loop Current. Scientific reports indicated that the main slick never reached the Loop Current, but that a thin sheen of oil did so by May 19.

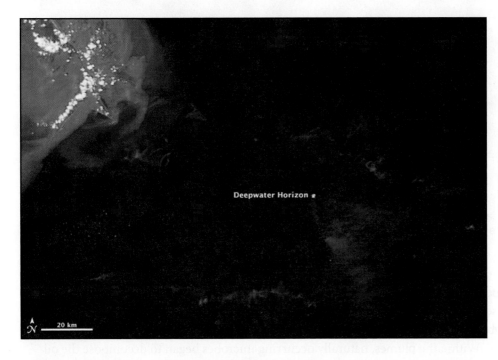

FIGURE 30.29. Smoke from the burning Deepwater Horizon oil rig was visible from NASA satellites. The oil itself was difficult to track.

FIGURE 30.30. This natural color satellite image shows the locations of the oil slick 18 days after the initial blowout and fire. Note how hard it is to distinguish oil from clouds and normal sea surface conditions.

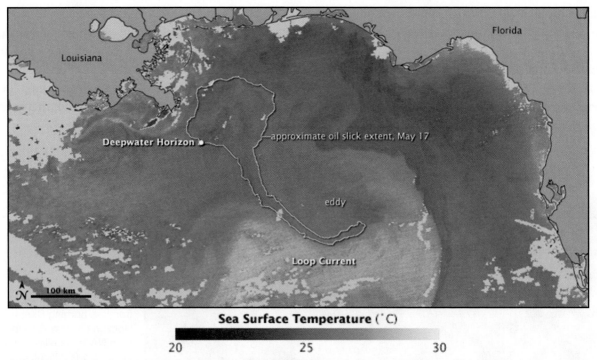

Sea Surface Temperature (˚C)

20   25   30

FIGURE 30.31. By mid-May of 2010, the oil slick had extended close to the Loop Current, which had the potential to carry oil to the Gulf Stream and ultimately up the East Coast.

On June 8, 2010, NOAA confirmed that not only was there abundant oil on the surface of the Gulf, but that within the water column there were massive layers of suspended oil droplets, called underwater **plumes**. These plumes were composed of oil droplets too small and dense to float to the surface. Scientists used ships, ROVs, and submersibles to collect data to detect these plumes. One plume, for instance, was over 35 kilometers (~22 miles) long. Within the plumes, naturally occurring microbes began to decompose the oil and quickly reproduced. Unfortunately, while this decomposition effectively removes the oil, it also removes oxygen from the water.

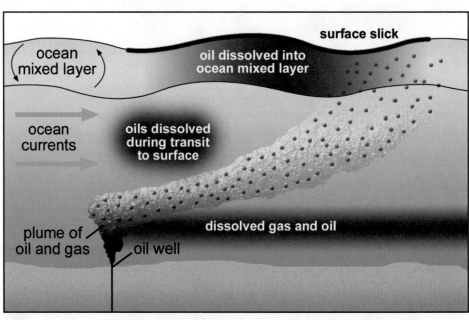

FIGURE 30.32. While most people worry about oil at the surface, oil from the Deepwater Horizon spill was distributed throughout the water column. Underwater plumes dozens of kilometers long were observed by scientists.

After 86 days and several unsuccessful attempts at capping the leaking pipe, BP announced that the leak had been capped on July 15, 2010. This cap significantly slowed the flow of oil into the Gulf. In September, the pipe was sealed and oil was no longer spilling into the Gulf at the Deepwater Horizon drill site.

Thanks to the cleanup efforts, the visible surface oil began to dissipate, and many people seemed to believe that the danger to wildlife was over. Of course, some of the oil was broken down by naturally-occurring microbes. The fate of the underwater plumes is unknown—scientists were unsure as to how long they would last and what the consequences would be. On the Gulf Coast beaches and in the wetlands, different forms of oil were being identified for many months. For example, weathered and degraded clumps of oil became **tar balls**, which washed up on beaches for a very long time following

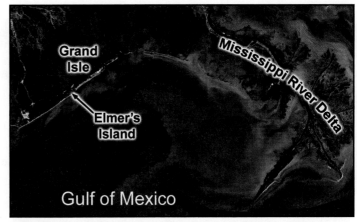

FIGURE 30.33. Map showing the location of Grand Isle and Elmer's Island in Louisiana.

the spill. The beaches on Elmer's Island, Louisiana, for instance, was re-closed in January 2011 after additional contaminants were identified within the sediment. In early 2010, a higher-than-normal number of dolphins began washing up dead on the Gulf Coast, some visibly oiled and some not.

FIGURE 30.34. Cleanup crews removing contaminated sediment on Elmer's Island in February 2011. The effects of the Gulf oil spill will be felt for many years to come.

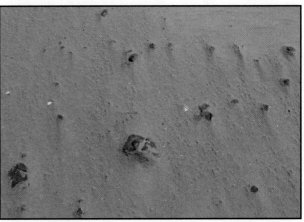

FIGURE 30.35. Tar balls were plentiful on the beach on Grand Isle, Louisiana, in February 2011, close to a year after the spill began. These by-products of oil breakdown and weathering are not considered to be hazardous to human health.

See Page 694 for how to access e-Tools.

View the *Timeline Tool* from the e-Tools.

e-Tools

5. Use the *Timeline Tool* and the information in the passage above to track the progression of the oil spill.

   a. Identify the date that oil reached land.

   b. What factors contribute to the oil appearing to move in a haphazard way, rather than flowing predictably in a certain direction?

   c. Identify other dates that stand out to you and explain why they caught your attention.

6. How might underwater plumes affect marine life in the Gulf?

See Page 694 for how to access e-Tools.

Cyberlab

Oil and Marine Life

Scientists at NOAA and other marine science agencies have been working diligently to protect wildlife in the Gulf of Mexico. Part of this effort includes locating, documenting, and treating or rehabilitating affected animals.

View the **Deepwater Horizon Response Consolidated Fish and Wildlife Collection Report** from the e-Tools.

The data table shows the documentation of birds, sea turtles, and mammals collected in the six months immediately following the oil spill. Scientists recorded whether an animal was covered with oil, or "visibly oiled", and whether it was alive or dead. If an animal is found dead, it is preserved for evaluation at a later time. Scientists are able to better identify the cause of death for an animal once the animal can be more closely examined.

1. Using the data provided, create the following graphs:

   a. A bar graph plotting the data for visibly oiled, alive animals

   b. A second graph for the visibly oiled, dead animals

2. Return to the bathymetry maps for the Gulf of Mexico and select Sea Turtle Observations. Where are sea turtles most often found by scientists?

3. Now select Avian Observations.

   a. Where are birds most often found?

   b. What is the connection between the location that birds are most likely found and the overall number of birds found to be affected by oil.

FIGURE 30.36. In addition to the mammals, sea turtles, and birds, fish, invertebrates, plankton, and other organisms are affected by oil spills. Air-breathing organisms are much easier to count.

FIGURE 30.37. Dead fish, invertebrates, and other organisms sometimes wash up onshore following oil spills. Many do not, making it difficult to estimate the number of animals lost.

How Does Oil Affect Marine Organisms?

The degree to which a species is harmed by oil in the water depends on the specific behaviors, characteristics, and life cycle of the organisms. Let's investigate the specific effects on several key groups of marine organisms: whales, fish, birds, seals, and sea turtles.

Whales and Dolphins

As mammals, whales must surface to breathe oxygen. They can be exposed to floating oil slicks and volatile fumes, which can cause organ damage, pneumonia, and death. When whales come in direct contact with oil, they may suffer from burns and infections to their skin and eyes. Many whales dive deep beneath the surface in search of food. Their habitats include several layers of the water column. Therefore, they are also exposed to dispersed oil and plumes beneath the surface.

Whales consume a large amount of food each day. Accumulation of toxins in the food chain is magnified for those whales that are tertiary predators. Sperm Whales that live in the Gulf of Mexico year-round feed primarily on squid. The impact of biomagnification in their food web will unfold over many years after the Deepwater Horizon oil spill.

Seals

Seals are surface swimmers, inhabiting coastal areas where they often haul themselves onto land. They need to surface to breathe, and as a result are susceptible to inhaling volatile fumes from the oil, as well as from swimming through oil floating on the surface. Seals have fur to which oil adheres, causing a seal to lose the ability to insulate itself. As with other organisms, seals experience burns and infections to skin and mucous membranes when exposed to oil. The internal organs of the nervous, reproductive, respiratory, and digestive systems can be damaged fatally as well.

FIGURE 30.38. Oil on the sea surface affects some animals more than others. Here, people use skimmers in an attempt to clean up a slick.

FIGURE 30.39. Striped dolphins are observed in emulsified oil on April 29, 2010. Pictures like these are commonplace with an oil spill.

FIGURE 30.40. Seals, sea lions, and other pinnipeds are very susceptible to health problems resulting from oil spills. Many pinnipeds were injured or killed due to oil following the *Exxon Valdez* spill in the 1980s.

Sea Turtles

Sea turtles are vulnerable to oil exposure by many different routes. Their habitat includes places where oil tends to aggregate. Turtles use fine-grain sand beaches for nesting and seek out sargassum mats as developing juveniles. They search for food in seagrass beds and coral reefs. These habitats hold oil more than the open ocean or other habitats; therefore turtles have a high likelihood of encountering oil.

Sea turtles do not have the ability to avoid oil through their behavior. For example, they continue their foraging activities despite the presence of oil. Scientists have learned that oil increases the incidence of egg mortality and developmental defects in young turtles. When covered in oil, turtles experience burns and infections, and the functioning of salt glands is compromised. When turtles take oil into their bodies through inhalation or ingestion, the blood, digestive system, respiratory system, reproductive system, and immune system are negatively affected.

See Page 694 for how to access e-Tools.

View the **NOAA Video of Turtles Being Released Back to Gulf** (1:39) from the e-Tools.

FIGURE 30.41. Mark Dodd, wildlife biologist from Georgia's Department of Natural Resources, surveying oiled Sargassum in the Gulf of Mexico. The offshore seaweed is important for young sea turtles.

FIGURE 30.42. A heavily oiled turtle rescued from the Gulf of Mexico following the spill. Many turtles were rescued and released back into the Gulf.

e-Tools

FIGURE 30.43. Screenshot of the **NOAA Video of Turtles Being Released Back to Gulf**.

Fish

Fish include a diverse group of organisms that inhabit the entire water column. They are exposed to oil on the surface as well as oil mixed at various depths. Fish eggs and larvae are immobile and cannot move away from oil in the water. As a result, the reproductive success of fish is significantly affected when oil coats eggs and keeps them from hatching. Scientific studies have shown that when exposed to oil, fish larvae may hatch with deformations and do not survive.

Fish breathe primarily through gills that can become clogged in the presence of oil, causing fish to suffocate. The presence of oil in the marine environment also decreases oxygen levels, affecting the amount available for fish. Oil, both external and ingested, prohibits the fishes' organ systems from functioning properly. Fish are an important link in the marine food web and can ingest oil through their food. They are also the prey of many larger marine mammals. Depending on the type and location of oil in the water, it may look like food, attracting fish and their predators.

Birds

Birds' feathers are intricately layered to protect the bird from the external environment, specifically extreme air and water temperatures. When feathers become oiled, they become matted and lose their overlapping pattern; a bird's ability to stay dry and control its temperature can be compromised. Often oiled birds experience hypothermia. When birds try to preen themselves and clean oil from their feathers, they will likely end up ingesting it. The oil causes damage to internal organs. Scientific research indicates that birds will focus primarily on preening themselves when oiled and may not spend time feeding, which leads to weight loss and dehydration.

FIGURE 30.44. Scientists wearing protective clothing attempt to clean a Brown Pelican. Birds are very susceptible to injury and death by oil at the sea's surface and in wetlands.

Birds also ingest oil by eating vegetation, plankton, fish, crustaceans, and other creatures that live in habitats susceptible to oil spills. Coastal areas are important breeding and foraging areas for many birds.

See Page 694 for how to access e-Tools.

View the **Bird Rescue Videos** (4:15 and 2:05) from the e-Tools to learn how oiled birds are cleaned and released.

e-Tools

FIGURE 30.45. Screenshot of a **Bird Rescue Video.**

7. Consider what you know about the characteristics of fishes. How do you think fish might initially be affected by oil in the water? How would you investigate further?

8. Which other groups of organisms should be closely monitored to best understand the total impact of the oil spill on the marine ecosystem?

9. Following the Deepwater Horizon spill, much oil was found along the wetlands of the Gulf Coast. What would you predict are the short-term and long-term consequences of oil pollution in wetland ecosystems?

FIGURE 30.46. Scientists assess salt marsh ecosystems in Southern Louisiana during summer 2010. How do you think wetlands were affected?

Coral Reefs of Kaneohe Bay, Oahu

Kaneohe Bay, Oahu

FIGURE 30.47. Map showing the location of Kaneohe Bay, Oahu.

Kaneohe Bay (pronounced: kah-nee-Ō-ay) is a unique estuary and coral reef ecosystem located on the east coast of Oahu just northeast of the capital, Honolulu. Set against the majestic Koolau (pronounced: kō-ō-LAH-oo) Mountain range, tourists and islanders alike flock here for the stunning views of islets and to enjoy all the bay has to offer in water recreation. Kaneohe Bay is about 13 kilometers long by 4 kilometers wide (~8 miles by 2.5 miles), and its average depth is 8 meters (~25 feet).

In the early 1900s, only about 5,000 people lived in the Kaneohe Bay area. When two tunnels were built to connect Kaneohe and

Honolulu, the population swelled to over 60,000 people. It was during this period of growth between 1950 and 1977 that two local sewage treatment plants and the U.S. Marine Corps Air Station began to increase the volume of sewage discharged directly into the shallow bay from three separate locations.

While some parts of the bay were rich in diversity with phytoplankton, coral, fish, and sharks, the areas closest to the sewage outfalls showed signs of ecological distress. Coral closest to the outfalls began to die, and dense mats of blue-green algae and diatoms grew in its place. Runoff and pollution from urban development further deteriorated Kaneohe Bay. Studies showed that almost all of the point source discharge came from two larger sewage treatment plants and was responsible for 80% of the nitrogen and 90% of the phosphorus compounds released into the bay.

FIGURE 30.48. Kaneohe Bay is a scenic bay, drawing snorkelers, sailors, recreational fishers, and tourists. For many years the area's ecosystem was not healthy.

In the late 1970s, two of these sewage treatment plants permanently diverted sewage away from the bay and into deep ocean outfalls. A study conducted shortly after the sewage diversion showed that the bay was responding positively to the decrease of nutrients and was no longer eutrophic. Furthermore, there were signs of coral recovery.

It was expected that with a decrease of sewage outfalls and algal blooms, the recovery of coral would continue. However, a 1990 reef study found the opposite. It showed that the algal cover had doubled and the coral recovery had reversed. Additional research found that the bay's phytoplankton had become phosphorus-limiting, meaning it needed phosphorus when it had once relied on nitrogen. Finally, high levels of the pesticides that had been banned five years earlier were found in the bay's oysters.

Kaneohe Bay has been the subject of many ecological studies since sewage outfalls ended in 1978. Scientists still have many questions about why this bay's ecosystem continues to change and how the coral reefs can be preserved.

FIGURE 30.49. As a result of eutrophication, dead corals become covered in algae, like those shown in this photo.

Elaborate

Activity

Cleaning Up Oil Spills: A Town Hall Meeting

Materials:

- *Dispersants Graphic Organizer*
- *Dispersants Note Sheet*

I. Preparing for the Meeting

Following the Deepwater Horizon spill, scientists and BP officials searched for the best possible options to clean the oil in the months immediately following the explosion. In this activity, you will debate controversial approaches to oil spill cleanup.

FIGURE 30.50. Plastic pom-poms were used to soak up oil that reached along the Louisiana shore. This was one of many methods used for cleaning up oil.

First, work with your group to learn about the major cleanup options that were used following the Gulf spill by reading the "Overview of Options", written by NOAA, either on the *Marine Science: The Dynamic Ocean* website or from handouts provided by your teacher.

See Page 694 for how to access e-Tools.

View the **NOAA "Overview of Options" Article** from the e-Tools.

1. What are the four major strategies for cleaning up oil spills?

The cleanup options described in the NOAA article were all used extensively in the Gulf of Mexico. Dispersants are petroleum-based chemicals used to break up oil into tiny droplets, which become spread out or dispersed in the water column. Use the *Marine Science: The Dynamic Ocean* website to learn more about the use of dispersants. You will use white papers, fact sheets, newspaper articles, videos, and diagrams to learn about this cleanup strategy.

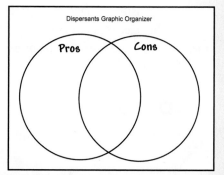

FIGURE 30.51. Screenshot of the *Dispersants Graphic Organizer*.

2. Use the **Dispersants Graphic Organizer** to record notes about the pros and cons of using dispersants as a strategy for oil spill cleanup.

3. As you go through the links provided, take notes in a format similar to the **Dispersants Note Sheet** that will help you to answer the following questions:

   a. What effect does the dispersant have on the oil?

   b. What effect does the dispersant have on the physical environment? the biological system? Present any past data from other oil spills to support your statement.

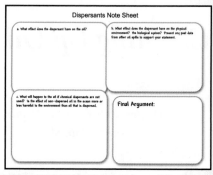

FIGURE 30.52. Screenshot of the *Dispersants Note Sheet*.

   c. What will happen to the oil if chemical dispersants are not used? Is the effect of non-dispersed oil in the ocean more or less harmful to the environment than oil that is dispersed?

4. Finally, with your team members, present an argument *for* or *against* the use of chemical dispersants. Be prepared to present your statement, supported by evidence, to the class at the Town Hall Meeting.

   To support your statement, you may wish to use visual aids and include graphs, tables, or images.

II. Town Hall Meeting

When controversial issues arise, people often come together in the form of Town Hall Meetings to discuss their perspectives. At this meeting, each group will tell about the cleanup strategy that they researched and present its findings. Then, all teams will debate the idea of using dispersants as a strategy for cleaning up spills.

In an ideal world, decisions like this are made based on sound scientific data. All data about the effects of dispersants on the health of marine life and human life should have been considered before BP applied the chemical treatment to the oil spill.

5. Based on all of the arguments presented, what is your personal stance on the use of dispersants? Give three pieces of evidence to support your position.

FIGURE 30.53. A NOAA veterinarian cleans a young Kemp's Ridley Turtle. Many dozens of sea turtles rescued survived; many others did not.

Evaluate

1. Give two examples of point source pollution.

2. Describe two strategies used for cleaning up oil spills. Give at least one positive and one negative about each strategy.

3. How do oil spills affect marine organisms? Give examples of the effects on two different types of organisms.

4. Return to your K-W-L Chart from the **Engage** section of this Lesson. Complete the "L" column with what you have learned about oil spills.

31

Humans and Coastlines

INSIDE:

Objectives

You will be able to:

✔ **Identify the properties of wetland ecosystems.**

✔ **Explain the many functions provided by wetlands, including the filtering of pollutants, providing habitats for diverse organisms, and reducing flooding.**

✔ **Define storm surge and make predictions about it using contour maps.**

✔ **Analyze the costs and benefits associated with coastal development.**

Benchmarks

2c. Erosion—the wearing away of rock, soil, and other biotic and abiotic earth materials—occurs in coastal areas as wind, waves, and currents in rivers and the ocean move sediments.

2d. Sand consists of tiny bits of animals, plants, rocks, and minerals. Most beach sand is eroded from land sources and carried to the coast by rivers, but sand is also eroded from coastal sources by surf. Sand is redistributed by waves and coastal currents seasonally.

5i. Estuaries provide important and productive nursery areas for many marine and aquatic species.

6d. Much of the world's population lives in coastal areas.

6e. Humans affect the ocean in a variety of ways. Laws, regulations, and resource management affect what is taken out and put into the ocean. Human development and activity leads to pollution (e.g., point source, nonpoint source, noise pollution) and physical modifications (e.g., changes to beaches, shores, and rivers). In addition, humans have removed most of the large vertebrates from the ocean.

6f. Coastal regions are susceptible to natural hazards (e.g., tsunamis, hurricanes, cyclones, sea level change, storm surges).

6g. Everyone is responsible for caring for the ocean. The ocean sustains life on Earth, and humans must live in ways that sustain the ocean. Individual and collective actions are needed to effectively manage ocean resources for all.

7b. Understanding the ocean is more than a matter of curiosity. Exploration, inquiry, and study are required to better understand ocean systems and processes.

7f. Ocean exploration is truly interdisciplinary. It requires close collaboration among biologists, chemists, climatologists, computer programmers, engineers, geologists, meteorologists, and physicists and new ways of thinking.

Engage

View the image below.

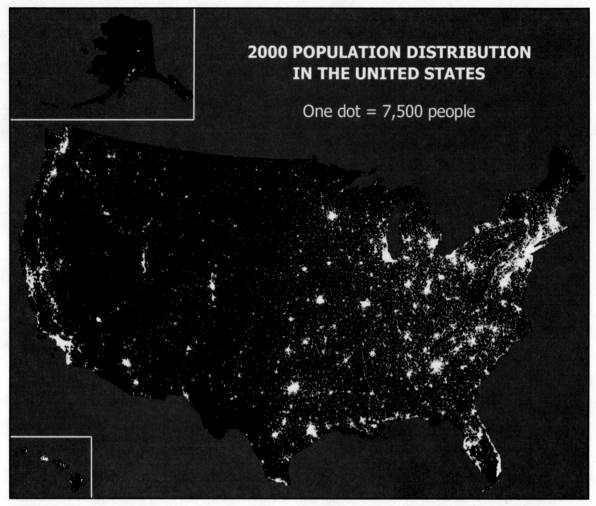

FIGURE 31.1. United States Census 2000 population distribution in the United States. Each dot represents 7,500 people. In densely populated areas, the white dots meld together.

Humans have lived along the coastlines for thousands of years. Access to the sea has afforded people the opportunity for food gathering, trade and travel, medicine, recreation, and much more. It is impossible to separate human history from the ocean. As human population increases, however, so does the demand on our coastlines.

Areas between water and land where soil contains tremendous amounts of water are often wetlands. Recall from earlier lessons that wetlands include areas called marshes, swamps, bogs, mudflats, and other regional names. There are freshwater and saltwater wetlands; they are found in all 50 states. Wetlands are especially prominent in the far north and along coastlines. They are found in a variety of climates—from tropical and subtropical mangrove forests to the bogs of the Tundra.

Before the first settlers arrived in North America in the early 1600s, what was to later be referred to as the continental United States had approximately 221 million acres of wetlands. By the mid-1980s, only about 103 million acres remained. Human activities have compromised and destroyed wetlands as we have built along the coastlines, rivers, and lakefronts. Here we will examine the importance of wetlands as a critical habitat and buffer between the land and water.

FIGURE 31.2. Wetlands support a wide variety of living organisms and are protected throughout the United States. In many areas, wetland loss has slowed as a result of federal and local regulations.

FIGURE 31.3. Freshwater and saltwater wetlands are found in diverse climates across the globe. They are defined by the fact that soil is temporarily or permanently covered in water.

The two images below are typical of United States coastlines. Some coastlines are relatively undisturbed and include extensive wetland habitats. Others include beachfront hotels, amusement parks, and houses.

FIGURE 31.4. Three Mute Swans swim through wetlands with Virginia's Assateague Lighthouse in the background.

FIGURE 31.5. Hotels and commerce are built up along the coastline in Ocean City, Maryland.

Explore
Investigating a Model of Wetlands

 **Lab**

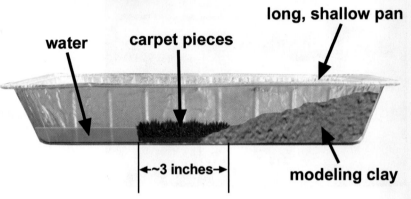

In this section, you will make a model to simulate a wetland. The model components represent land, wetlands and ocean.

Materials:

(for each group of about 4 students)
- Long, shallow pan
- Modeling clay
- Strips of carpet pieces, florist foam, or sponges cut to fit the width of the pan
- Spray bottle
- Food coloring
- Small cup of soil
- Dishpan or bucket
- Paper towels

FIGURE 31.6. Sample setup.

To build the model, follow the instructions below with your group:

- To represent the land, spread modeling clay all the way to the sides at one end of the pan. Form the clay into a gradual slope leading to the center of the pan. Make sure the edges are sealed along the sides of the pan, so that no water can flow underneath the clay.
- Place the carpet or foam next to the clay to serve as a buffer between your land (clay) and water (ocean). This will represent your wetland.
- Leave the remaining area of the pan empty. This will represent the ocean.

Follow the procedures with your lab group. You may wish to have one group member read each step aloud.

Procedures:

1. Use the spray bottle to sprinkle some "rain" on the land portion of your model.

   a. Describe what happens to the water.

   Pour out the excess water—the water that made it "to the ocean"—from the pan.

2. Place one or two small drops of food coloring on the land portion of your model. Again, slowly sprinkle some "rain" on the land.

   a. Describe what happens to the food coloring.

   b. What might the food coloring represent?

   Pour out excess water from the pan.

3. Sprinkle some soil on the clay. Again slowly sprinkle some "rain" on the land portion of your model.

   Describe what happened to the soil.

   Pour out excess water from the pan.

4. Remove the "wetlands" from the pan. Repeat steps 2 and 3.

   a. Describe what happened to the food coloring this time.

   b. Describe what happened to the soil this time.

   c. How might muddy water affect fish and other animals?

   d. How might muddy water affect plants?

5. Explain why rivers and streams often look cloudy and muddy after heavy rains.

6. Wetlands, such as marshes and mangroves, are often removed and filled in with sediment, to bring the land area above the water level to facilitate commercial development. Think about your model; what might happen to the houses right along the coast if there were a severe rainstorm?

7. How did this model help you to understand the functions of wetlands?

FIGURE 31.7. Wetland ecosystems, like the salt marsh shown here, are home to many invertebrates, fish, mammal, and bird species. Wetlands are especially important habitats for juveniles as they grow. Notice the young swans, or cygnets, in the photograph, along with adult swans and a sandpiper.

Explain

Globally, over 2 billion people live within 100 kilometers (~62 miles) of a coast. Over half of all people living in the United States lives within 80 kilometers (~50 miles) of the coast—and the numbers are increasing. Long, sandy islands that run parallel to the shore, **barrier islands**, often become prime vacation spots; homes, shops, and hotels sprout up along the waterfront. The building of homes and businesses along the coast, **coastal development**, has a tremendous impact on wetlands.

Wetlands can sustain a definable amount of stress from coastal development before the ecosystem begins to fail. At some point restoration efforts may assist problem areas and help them to become more healthy. Over the past 200 years, approximately half of wetland areas have been lost. The impacts of coastal development in conjunction with natural processes and other human activities affecting wetland ecosystems (e.g., dredging to make canals, making agricultural lands productive) are better understood after the initiation of research. These studies and constructions are another example of how interdisciplinary teams of scientists and engineers work together to explore the ocean and respond to natural and human-induced processes.

FIGURE 31.8. Humans have settled near coastlines for millennia. Coastal development, such as the building of cities like San Francisco shown here, can lead to pollution and changes to coastlines. In addition, coastal regions are susceptible to natural disasters such as storm surge and tsunamis.

Introduction to Barrier Islands

Barrier islands are found up and down the East and Gulf Coasts of the United States. In these areas, there is plenty of sand available and adjoining continental shelves are shallow and wide. In contrast, on the West Coast, the continental shelf is much more narrow and the coastlines are rocky. Barrier islands are separated from the mainland by bays and lagoons, which are subject to tidal flow. This type of activity causes mixing and interactions between the ocean and smaller bodies of water. These islands are normally dominated by sand dunes and have wetlands, including mangrove forests and salt marshes, on the side facing the bay.

FIGURE 31.9. Santa Rosa Island of Florida along the Northern Gulf Coast is a barrier island 64 kilometers (~40 miles) long, host of the communities Pensacola Beach, Okaloosa Island, and Navarre Beach.

Barrier islands form when coastal currents and wave action build ridges of sediment in shallow areas. Over time, ocean processes and wind deposit additional sand, building the islands higher. Eventually, winds, birds, and insects bring seeds, and dune plants take root. Wetland plants begin to settle on the inland side of the island, protected from energetic wave action. Eventually, animals begin to make their homes among both the land and water plants, and the barrier island community flourishes. The community behind the dune shifts from one dominated by grasses to one of shrubs, and eventually forests. The high dunes and sandy beaches of barrier islands prevent the mainland coasts from receiving the brunt of wind and waves.

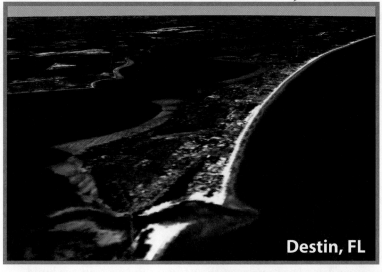

Destin, FL

FIGURE 31.10. The East and Gulf Coasts of the United States are dotted with barrier islands. Wide continental shelves and ample sand provide optimal conditions for these islands to form.

Cape Lookout, NC

Natural processes, including wind and water erosion, make barrier islands dynamic—they are always changing. Sand is constantly moving and being transported along the beaches, out to sea, and back again. Over geologic time, it is common for whole barrier islands to be moved by wind and wave erosion. During a strong storm, such as a hurricane, high winds cause water to pile up higher than the usual sea level, which is then pushed onshore. This phenomenon is called **storm surge**, and it is an important consideration for those living along the coast. Storm surge is one reason why people are asked to evacuate barrier islands and other coastal communities when a hurricane is forecasted. Storm surge can sometimes cause a break, or breach, in a barrier island. The photograph and satellite images below show one such example of a breach that resulted from a storm surge associated with Hurricane Isabel in 2003.

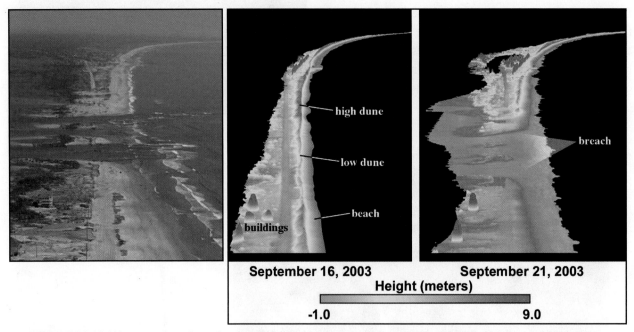

FIGURE 31.11. Water washes through a newly formed breach on Hatteras Island, North Carolina, a few days after Hurricane Isabel swept through the area. Imagery on the right was created from instrumentation onboard a research plane, NASA's Experimental Advanced Airborne Research Lidar.

Barrier islands are beautiful places—picturesque sandy beaches, pristine views of the ocean, abundant wildlife—so here we build homes, businesses, and roads. To prevent the natural sand erosion, we build jetties and breakwaters, rock structures that absorb wave energy before it reaches the beach. To allow our boats to dock, we dig the seafloor deeper, or **dredge**. Sometimes dunes are flattened to allow buildings to be constructed. Because barrier islands are such important properties, people try to prevent erosion by adding jetties, seawalls, and other constructions that prevent sand migration. These constructions prevent the normal migration of sand that would naturally be distributed by longshore currents along the coastline. When the sand is trapped by the jetty, the currents move along it, without sand. The currents can move even faster without the sand load, so they cause even greater erosion to shorelines, leading to the need for adding even more sand. One method is to dredge sand from offshore and deposit it along beaches, replacing the sand that is naturally carried away by wind and water.

1. Describe how barrier islands protect mainland coastlines.

2. Explain how barrier island vegetation provides an example of biological succession.

Moving the Cape Hatteras Lighthouse

The Cape Hatteras Lighthouse has been protecting one of the most dangerous sections of the Atlantic Coast for 140 years. At the end of construction of the tallest lighthouse in the United States in 1870, the Cape Hatteras Lighthouse boldly stood 64 meters (~210 feet) tall from the bottom of the foundation to the top of the tower and rested 457 meters (~1,500 feet) away from the sea.

After years of pounding waves and driving winds, the beach eroded to within 36 meters (~120 feet) of the lighthouse. Several attempts were made to control the erosion by pumping in extra sand, placing concrete breakwaters offshore, and using artificial seaweed to stabilize the sand. In 1997, a study done by the University of North Carolina decided the best option for saving the lighthouse was to move it.

FIGURE 31.12. The Cape Hatteras Lighthouse stands in its original location with the encroaching ocean creeping toward the foundation.

In June 1999, over a 23-day period, the National Park Service lifted the 4,400-ton lighthouse off its foundation with hydraulic jacks and rolled it 883 meters (~2,900 feet) across steel mats and track beams to its new location. The lighthouse was aligned using three zones of hydraulic jacks to keep it from leaning or falling over. Sixty automated sensors placed on the lighthouse constantly measured the transfer of load, tilt, vibration, and shaft diameter. At the top of the lighthouse, a weather station monitored wind speed and temperature.

The Cape Hatteras Lighthouse resumed its responsibilities on November 13, 1999. The lighthouse now stands a safe 487 meters (~1,600 feet) away from the ocean that once threatened its existence. The ocean should not be a menace to the lighthouse for at least another 100 years.

FIGURE 31.13. An aerial photograph shows its old location and the track to its new location as the Cape Hatteras Lighthouse began its move.

(continued on next page)

FIGURE 31.14. Steel mats and beams were used to roll the Cape Hatteras Lighthouse 883 meters (~2,900 feet) to the southwest of its original location.

Discovering Wetlands

Wetlands are areas that have saturated soils and are sometimes covered by shallow surface water. They have high biodiversity and provide many important ecological functions as they serve as a buffer between the land and water. Saltwater wetlands include mudflats, mangrove forests, salt marshes, and more. These wetlands actually include brackish water, water that is a mixture of salty and fresh. Saltwater wetlands are common habitats in estuaries, where rivers meet the sea.

The abundant plant life and muddy conditions of wetlands make an ideal habitat for juvenile fish and invertebrates, providing plenty of places to hide from larger predators. Plant roots are efficient at trapping soil and sediments, which then absorb excess water during storms, including both storm surge from the ocean and runoff from the land. Wetland organisms can process organic wastes through their own metabolic processes. Bivalve mollusks (e.g., clams, oysters) that filter water for food will also filter sediments and pollutants from coastal waters. As you experienced in the laboratory activity, land-based pollutants can be absorbed by plants and their roots, preventing them from washing out to sea. In some cases, contaminants may be buried within wetlands for hundreds of years—unless the plants are removed.

FIGURE 31.16. A salt marsh ecosystem in Coastal North Carolina.

FIGURE 31.15. Plants, including the poisonous Common Milkweed, of the John's Pond Bog in Massachusetts. Bogs are examples of freshwater wetlands.

FIGURE 31.17. Extensive root systems of mangrove trees in Southeast Florida. The root systems of mangrove trees are incredibly important as they trap sediment, preventing erosion, and provide habitat for juvenile fish and invertebrates.

Wetlands play a critical role in biogeochemical cycling. The abundant plants in these ecosystems remove nitrogen and phosphorus from water before they reach the ocean. Therefore, wetlands can help to prevent dead zones by reducing the amount of nutrients that lead to eutrophication. As a part of the carbon cycle, wetlands are important sinks for carbon. Dead organisms, including plants and animals, become trapped in wetland soils as they decompose. Scientists estimate that about 20% of all trapped land-based carbon is in wetlands. Trapped carbon is an important part of the carbon cycle, because it is prevented from entering our atmosphere in the form of CO_2 and CH_4, both of which are greenhouse gases that contribute to warming in our atmosphere.

Vegetation along the coast is often removed to make way for construction of structures, such as homes, businesses, roads, and bridges. Wetlands are often drained of their water and filled with sediment to facilitate the construction. Levee systems are created to prevent flooding from rivers and the ocean by redirecting water. When a storm surge breaks over the levees, water is then trapped by the levees. Water pools, or collects, in the areas that sit below sea level and is further prevented from returning to the ocean.

Without the buffering provided by the wetlands, homes and businesses are subject to flooding because there is nowhere for the water to flow. Wetland vegetation impedes the movement of flood waters and distributes them more slowly over floodplains. The combined water storage and slowing action lowers flood heights and reduces erosion. Docks and piers constructed for recreation affect underwater habitats (e.g., coral reefs, benthic communities) and seawalls are built to prevent erosion. These constructions affect sea turtles and other animals that use beaches and other coastal areas for breeding and nesting. Pinnipeds, such as seals and Sea Lions, use beaches for resting and caring for their pups.

Our wetlands are under great pressure and their destruction is a real concern. Research, education, and new laws promoting conservation have provided diverse ways to protect marine habitats successfully. Scientists studying marine organisms use their data to inform lawmakers about specific habitats that require protection. The more we research marine ecosystems, the more we learn about how best to protect them. We all have a responsibility to be good stewards of our coasts. The good news is that we can do something to prevent additional wetland loss and even restore wetlands that have been affected by human activities.

FIGURE 31.18. A pier under construction. Piers, jetties, docks, and other structures can disturb underwater habitats.

FIGURE 31.19. Jetties built along the beach are constructed to prevent erosion of sand. These and other constructions along coastlines can disturb benthic habitats.

FIGURE 31.20. Elephant Seal nursing her pup. Beaches are an important habitat for pinnipeds, such as seals and Sea Lions.

FIGURE 31.21. Tidal mudflats in estuaries are important foraging areas for shorebirds, including these dowitchers, which use their long bills to probe the mud for worms and other invertebrates.

FIGURE 31.22. Plants of all kinds, including these Pitcher Plants, help to stabilize a wetland by trapping soil with their roots. Wetland plants are very important in protecting coastlines.

FIGURE 31.23. Common animals found in mudflats are mollusks such as snails, clams, and mussels; crustaceans such as fiddler crabs; a variety of worms; and birds preying upon these organisms.

One way to replenish a wetland is to replant plants that have been removed. At the Palmetto Estuary Reserve, in Manatee County, Florida, the Tampa Bay Watch staff coordinated two salt marsh transplanting events. Approximately 300 students from Bloomingdale High School in Valrico, Florida, transplanted 10,000 *Spartina alterniflora* plants at the reserve. In a second planting, approximately 6–7 acres of coastal wetland habitat was restored with 22,000 plants, including salt marsh grasses and other coastal species. Volunteers used a wedge-shaped shovel called a dibble bar to create a hole in the marsh sediments and then inserted the plant plug. These plantings were intended to stabilize the wetlands by preventing further erosion. All of us are responsible for caring for our environment. One way to do so is to participate in local stewardship projects like the one in which the students shown here engaged.

FIGURE 31.24. Flooding in New Orleans due to storm surge from Hurricane Katrina.

FIGURE 31.25. A group of volunteers using dibble bars to plant **Spartina alterniflora**, a common salt marsh grass, in Manatee County, Florida.

FIGURE 31.26. Palmetto Estuary Reserve before the planting. Erosion is a problem due to the absence of grasses in the marsh.

FIGURE 31.27. Palmetto Estuary Reserve after the planting. The planting will help to stabilize the marsh. Restoration was conducted in part by students through the Tampa Bay High School Wetland Nursery Program.

Elaborate

Activity

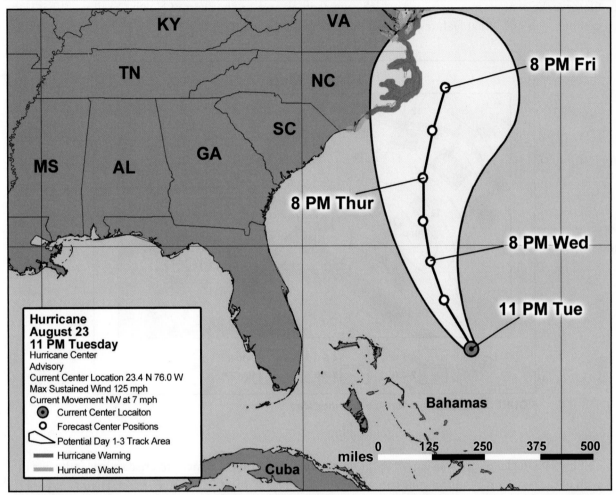

KY

VA

TN

NC

SC

GA

MS

AL

8 PM Fri

8 PM Thur

8 PM Wed

11 PM Tue

Hurricane
August 23
11 PM Tuesday
Hurricane Center
Advisory
Current Center Location 23.4 N 76.0 W
Max Sustained Wind 125 mph
Current Movement NW at 7 mph

⊙ Current Center Locaiton

◯ Forecast Center Positions

⬠ Potential Day 1-3 Track Area

━━ Hurricane Warning

━━ Hurricane Watch

Bahamas

| 0 | 125 | 250 | 375 | 500 |

miles

Cuba

FIGURE 31.28. Advisory Map issued by NOAA's National Hurricane Center during late August, an active time during the Northern Hemisphere's hurricane season. The graphic illustrates a threat to the Mid-Atlantic Coast of Virginia and North Carolina.

A hurricane with a diameter of 760 kilometers (~472 miles) is headed for the coast shown by the map above. As the storm moves closer to the coast of the United States, scientists make predictions about the strength of the storm as well as the associated storm surge. At this time, meteorologists are predicting a 10-foot storm surge. What does this mean? Who and what is safe? How are we protected from storm surge?

See Page 694 for how to access e-Tools.

For comparison, view the *Storm Surge Model from Hurricane Georges* (0:06) from the e-Tools, which shows the rising storm surge and the area hardest hit along the Mississippi and Alabama border. Note that storm surge was measured at up to 10 feet, and that water is pushed up into bays and rivers, making these areas particularly susceptible to flooding.

FIGURE 31.29. Screenshot of the *Storm Surge Model from Hurricane Georges*.

e-Tools

Materials:

- *Contour Maps*
- Colored pencils or crayons

1. Observe the contour map provided, which represents an area on the coast of North Carolina. What is the contour interval? What features are most prominent on the map?

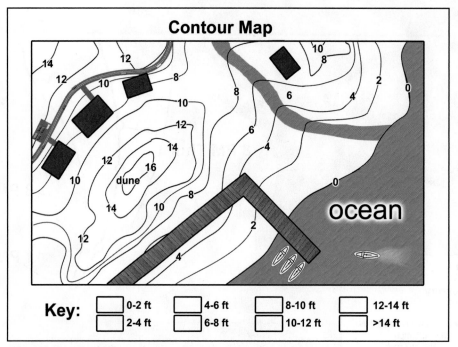

FIGURE 31.30. Screenshot of the *Contour Map*.

2. To illustrate the landward movement of the storm surge, use colored pencils to create a key and color in each of the elevation bands on your contour map: 0–2 feet, 2–4 feet, 4–6 feet, 6–8 feet, 8–10 feet, 10–12 feet, 12–14 feet, and >14 feet.

Recall that low pressure systems rotate counterclockwise in the Northern Hemisphere. Therefore, storm surge will be much higher north of the center of impact than south of the center because of the onshore waters.

3. Based on your map, what damage would a 5-foot storm surge inflict on this area? 10-foot?

4. Sometimes beach houses are constructed on stilts. Why? Is a beach house on 10-foot stilts safe from a 5-foot storm surge? Why or why not?

5. How would a storm surge affect a wetland-studded coastline, such as a marsh, compared to an area that has been developed with homes?

6. What recommendations would you make to a developer who is interested in constructing a new building in the area represented by the Contour Map?

Evaluate

1. A development company is proposing to develop a new beachfront community. The construction would require that local wetlands be drained and filled with sediment. Describe at least two costs and two benefits associated with this proposal.

2. The photo below depicts a typical healthy wetland ecosystem. In an essay of at least one page, address the following:

    - What are wetlands?
    - What sorts of organisms make their homes in wetlands?
    - Why are wetlands important to humans on the coast?

FIGURE 31.31. Salt marsh in Grand Bay National Estuarine Research Reserve, MS.

32

The Ocean's Resources

INSIDE:

Objectives

You will be able to:

✔ **Discuss what is meant by The Tragedy of the Commons.**

✔ **Give examples of ways in which fisheries can be more sustainable.**

✔ **Consider the perspectives of multiple stakeholders on issues that address the use of ocean resources.**

✔ **Use evidence to teach others about ocean resource protection.**

Benchmarks

6b. From the ocean we get foods, medicines, and mineral and energy resources. In addition, it provides jobs, supports our nation's economy, serves as a highway for transportation of goods and people, and plays a role in national security.

6c. The ocean is a source of inspiration, recreation, rejuvenation, and discovery. It is also an important element in the heritage of many cultures.

6e. Humans affect the ocean in a variety of ways. Laws, regulations, and resource management affect what is taken out and put into the ocean. Human development and activity leads to pollution (e.g., point source, nonpoint source, noise pollution) and physical modifications (e.g., changes to beaches, shores, and rivers). In addition, humans have removed most of the large vertebrates from the ocean.

6g. Everyone is responsible for caring for the ocean. The ocean sustains life on Earth, and humans must live in ways that sustain the ocean. Individual and collective actions are needed to effectively manage ocean resources for all.

7c. Over the last 40 years, use of ocean resources has increased significantly, therefore the future sustainability of ocean resources depends on our understanding of those resources and their potential and limitations.

Engage

Humans have lived along the coastlines and relied on the ocean as a food source for thousands of years. Seafood, including fish and invertebrates (e.g., shrimp, crabs, lobsters, clams), is an important source of protein and healthful fats for people around the world. For countless generations, the taking of food resources did not deplete the seafood available; it was able to be continued. Fishing practices were **sustainable**.

As the human population has increased and technologies for catching fish have improved, the amount of fish taken from the ocean on a yearly basis has skyrocketed. Sport, commercial, and personal fishing have all contributed to a reduction in the number of fish from each species, the **fish stocks**. Some fish stocks are severely depleted. The availability of fish and shellfish in the ocean is not what it once was.

Analyze the pictures (FIGURES 32.1–32.8) on pages 646 and 647, and then answer the Questions below.

1. Make several observations about fishing, based on these photographs and your personal experience or knowledge.

2. How do you think each of the fishing methods pictured impacts the environment?

FIGURE 32.1.

FIGURE 32.2.

FIGURE 32.3.

FIGURE 32.4.

FIGURE 32.7.

FIGURE 32.5.

FIGURE 32.6.

FIGURE 32.8.

The Ocean's Resources **627**

Explore

Fishing for Resources

Activity

Materials:

- Piece of blue construction paper for each group of 3–4 students (to simulate ocean)
- Large box of goldfish-shaped crackers (to simulate fish)
- Chopsticks, 2 for each student (to simulate fishing equipment such as nets and lines)
- Small, bathroom-sized paper cup for each student
- Prizes for students

Safety Notes: Observe the following safety procedures, as well as any other rules that are in place at your school.

- Students should not share chopsticks.
- Once a fish is "caught" it should not be put back into the "ocean".

1. We will be stimulating how humans extract or harvest resources from the ocean. Follow the instructions carefully with your group.

   - The piece of blue construction paper represents the ocean.
   - Crackers represent real fish.
   - Each student in the group represents a different country.
   - Chopsticks represent fishing equipment including boats, nets, and fishing poles.
   - Small paper cups represent boats and will hold each country's food supply.

2. Place the 16 fish on the "ocean".

3. Assign one student to be the timekeeper. The others get chopsticks. The timekeeper will give the other students in the group 10 seconds to fish. To do this, *you may not use your hands at any time*! Instead, follow the instructions below:

   a. Hold a pair the chopsticks over the "ocean".
   b. With the chopsticks, lift the fish gently. Lift up one fish at a time.
   c. Place the fish into your cup.

4. Describe what happened in this simulation.

FIGURE 32.9. Simulation setup.

Investigating Shared Fish Resources

In this section, you will record data by copying the table below into your notebook, as you use a procedure similar to the one used before.

5. Read all of the directions before beginning.

6. Place 16 more fish into your ocean.

7. Use the data table to record your results at the end of each "season".

Fish Caught During Each "Fishing Season"

	Country 1	Country 2	Country 3	Country 4	Remaining in Ocean
Season 1					
Season 2					
Season 3					
Season 4					

8. The timekeeper gives all fishers 10 seconds to use fishing poles (chopsticks) to "catch" fish. As you catch fish, place them into your "boat" (small paper cup). The fish in your boat will represent your country's food supply for the Fishing Season (round of 16 fish).

   You must catch at least one fish per season or your country will experience a terrible, widespread famine. There will be a prize for the best fisher at the end of the simulation. The only limit to the amount of fish you can catch is the time and your skill. Be sure to keep your fish in your cups until they are counted at the end of four seasons.

9. At the end of each season, count how many fish are left in your ocean and record that number in the data table.

10. Each fish remaining in the ocean after a season has a chance to reproduce before the next season, so add an additional fish for each fish that is left. Note, however, that there is a carrying capacity to the ocean. For this simulation, the "ocean" can hold a <u>maximum</u> of 30 fish.

11. Repeat Steps 8–10 for Seasons 2, 3, and 4.

12. Answer the Questions below.

   a. Was the fishing within your group sustainable? If not, what could have been done to make it sustainable?

   b. What happened when people thought it was the last season?

Explain

The ocean itself is a critical renewable resource. It is also the source of nonrenewable resources. Fish, invertebrates, and algae are renewable resources, meaning that they can be replenished in a reasonable amount of time. These renewable resources are critical for the food supply, medications, and other commercial products. Oil and gas derived from the ocean seafloor are nonrenewable resources—these resources take many thousands or even millions of years to be replenished. These nonrenewable resources are used to provide power to our communities, fuel our cars, and more. The ocean is so vast that its resources seem limitless. However, we know this is not the case. As the human population has increased, so has our dependence on the ocean for its natural resources. At the same time, the technologies used to obtain these resources have improved and become more efficient, putting an even greater strain on ocean assets. Through the activity in the **Explore** section of this Lesson, you observed how humans use resources that are open to all, and how these commodities are frequently used without concern for others. Resources become depleted because no one takes responsibility for preserving them to benefit future generations.

Garrett Hardin, an author and environmentalist, wrote an essay in 1968 called "The Tragedy of the Commons". In the essay, he describes a situation in which many shepherds and cattlemen allow their animals to graze on a public field. He explains:

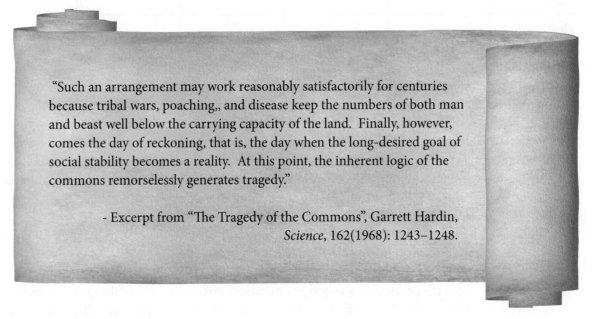

"Such an arrangement may work reasonably satisfactorily for centuries because tribal wars, poaching,, and disease keep the numbers of both man and beast well below the carrying capacity of the land. Finally, however, comes the day of reckoning, that is, the day when the long-desired goal of social stability becomes a reality. At this point, the inherent logic of the commons remorselessly generates tragedy."

- Excerpt from "The Tragedy of the Commons", Garrett Hardin, *Science*, 162(1968): 1243–1248.

Hardin's quote also applies to the degradation of resources.

3. How does the Fishing Season activity relate to The Tragedy of the Commons?

4. Write down examples of behaviors resembling The Tragedy of the Commons as observed:

   a. in your neighborhood
   b. in your state
   c. in the nation
   d. globally

Traditional Fishing and Whaling Practices

Humans have relied on the ocean as a protein source throughout our history. People who fish regularly to feed their families or their local communities are called **subsistence fishers**. Many cultures across the globe have practiced subsistence fishing for thousands of years. Most subsistence and recreational fishers (i.e., those who go out fishing on their personal boats) use either simple nets or fishing poles with baited hooks; this is normally referred to as **rod and reel** or **pole fishing**. The practice of drawing the fishing lines through the water, typically behind a boat, is called **troll fishing**.

Sometimes, fishers spot fish from either above or below the water's surface. They use a long pole with an arrow-shaped metal point attached, a technique known as **spearfishing**. Spearfishing is the oldest method of fishing, dating back thousands of years to when ancient humans used sharpened sticks and leaned into rivers, streams and bays to grab a meal. This technique is still practiced in traditional cultures, particularly in Pacific Islands and South America.

FIGURE 32.10. Fishers on a North Carolina beach practice pole fishing. Attached to the pole is a long line that ends in a baited hook. The fisher casts the line into the surf, hoping to catch local species like Bluefish, Red Drum, Striped Bass, or Croaker.

FIGURE 32.11. This photograph, dated in the 1890s, shows a Native American hunter using a spear to capture seals. Spears can also be used underwater to hunt fish.

In addition to fishing, whaling has also been practiced for thousands of years. Some anthropological evidence suggests that ancient peoples in the areas of Japan and Norway were hunting whales 4,000 years ago. Larger tools with larger heads designed to hunt marine mammals (e.g., seals, whales) are called **harpoons**. As with spearfishing, one must first spot the animal to be targeted and then thrust the harpoon directly at it. Modern harpoons are more powerful, as they can be powered by gunpowder or other means of ensuring thrust.

FIGURE 32.12. Traditional Inuit fishers in Nuuk, Greenland, preparing a boat for the day's activities. The harpoon, seen in both the small and enlarged insets above, is used to capture prey.

Today, indigenous peoples in the Circumpolar North, including the Inuit and Aleut in Alaska, still practice whaling. In the traditional culture, only resources needed by a local community are taken. In Northern Alaska, for example, a small number of Bowhead Whales are still caught each fall. Hunters in skin boats venture into the ocean to catch a whale. When they are successful, the community shares the resource, using the meat and blubber for food, and skin and baleen for other purposes including food, clothing, building structures, and more. Any parts of the whale not used (e.g., bones) are returned to the land or sea where they are subsequently eaten by scavengers and then decompose.

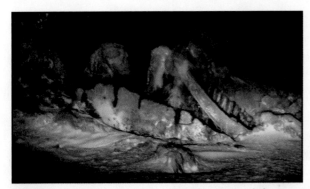

FIGURE 32.13. Seen at night, a whale carcass left by the sea's edge by local indigenous people at Point Barrow, Alaska.

FIGURE 32.14. Map showing the location of Point Barrow, Alaska.

Modern Fishing and Whaling Practices

The traditional strategies described in the previous paragraphs are sufficient for catching reasonable numbers of fish and other organisms, as is done by recreational and subsistence fishers. In the twentieth century, however, improvements in the technologies used to catch fish greatly increased the amount of fish that could be caught. Companies that use these technologies to catch large amounts of fish at sea and then transport them to be sold are called **commercial fisheries**. Commercial fisheries provide food for a larger population of people, which often means that local communities do not have to do their own fishing. Also, many fish are transported to inland areas, where seafood may not have been available in the past. Some of the tools and strategies used by commercial fisheries are described below.

- Fishing lines that are let out up to 130 kilometers (~80 miles) are appropriately called **longlines**. Along the main line, smaller lines are strung at even intervals, with baited hooks attached. Longlining is used primarily to catch large pelagic fish such as swordfish.

- A method in which a large net is dragged behind a boat at various depths—depending on the type of fish desired—is called **trawling**. Trawling conducted in the middle of the water column catches tuna, anchovies, and squid. Haddock and flounder are caught if the net is dragged along the bottom.

- A net stretched across the water intended to interrupt swimming fish is called a **gill net**. The fish do not see the net and try to swim through it. When they do so, their gills are caught in the net.

- A boat may loop a large net in a circle around a school of fish and then pull the net in toward the boat, in a method called **purse seine** (pronounced: sayn) fishing. This method is used to trap schooling fish such as mackerel and sardines.

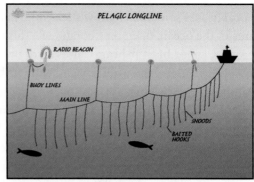

FIGURE 32.15. Used in the open ocean, longlines are typically used to catch large fishes, including swordfish and tuna.

FIGURE 32.16. Trawl nets are dragged behind boats. Shrimp are often caught in trawl nets.

FIGURE 32.17. Gill nets are set out to trap fishes as they swim forward.

FIGURE 32.18. Purse seine nets scoop up entire schools of fish at a time.

Local fishers sometimes throw sticks of dynamite into an area of the ocean, often on a coral reef. This often-illegal process, called **blast fishing**, causes all of the organisms in an area to die and to be quickly and easily collected and sold. Although spearfishing, as traditionally practiced, is considered sustainable because few fish are taken at a time, newer techniques have allowed some fish species to become locally depleted. Modern spears can include compressed gas or elastic bands to launch the spears long distances. In some local areas, spearfishers who sell their catch have depleted species. Examples include the Giant Black Sea Bass in California and certain species of grouper in the Caribbean.

FIGURE 32.19. Atlantic Bluefin Tuna have been commercially depleted.

FIGURE 32.20. Orange Roughy is a slow-growing species that reproduces late in its lifetime. These characteristics have caused the fish to become vulnerable to overfishing.

Commercial fishing and the methods described above are used around the world—in the open ocean, along coastlines, and in deep and shallow water. The present worldwide take of fish by commercial fisheries may not be sustainable. The advancements in fishing methods and tools have greatly increased the amount of fish humans take from the ocean. Sometimes, so many individuals of a fish species are taken that the species cannot reproduce fast enough to sustain its population. This problem is called **overfishing**. The Atlantic Bluefin Tuna, Chilean Seabass, Atlantic Salmon, and Orange Roughy are examples of fish species that have been overfished, and there are many more.

FIGURE 32.21. Atlantic Salmon are not considered to be a sustainable resource. At this point, most Atlantic Salmon are farmed.

The fishing methods described above also accidentally catch nontargeted marine animals such as seabirds, mammals, and sea turtles in the nets or lines. These mistakenly caught creatures are called **bycatch**. For air breathers, getting caught in a fishing line or net is almost certain death because they will drown. Other kinds of bycatch include young fish that are too small to be sold at market, and other species of fish and invertebrates outside the intended catch. Bycatch results in a lot of unnecessary waste. If fishers are trying to catch and sell shrimp, they may also net sea turtles, small fish, and invertebrates, all of which will be discarded. A recent study found that for every five pounds of seafood caught in United States waters at least one pound will be discarded. This statistic is even more dramatic in the shrimp industry. For every one pound of shrimp caught—normally by trawling—three to ten pounds of other animals are discarded.

5. Based on what you have read, which practices do you think would result in the most bycatch? Why?

6. Which practices do you think would result in the most overfishing? Why?

FIGURE 32.22. A commercial shrimper separating shrimp from bycatch.

Maintaining fish populations to ensure that they are not depleted is critical to protecting biodiversity, as well as to the sustainability of the ocean as a resource. To sustain our resources, individuals and governments must work together to take ownership of the ocean's assets and manage them responsibly. Fishing practices that do minimal harm to fish populations and result in little bycatch are known as **sustainable fishing** practices. Sustainable fishing practices also involve protecting the physical environments in which the animals live.

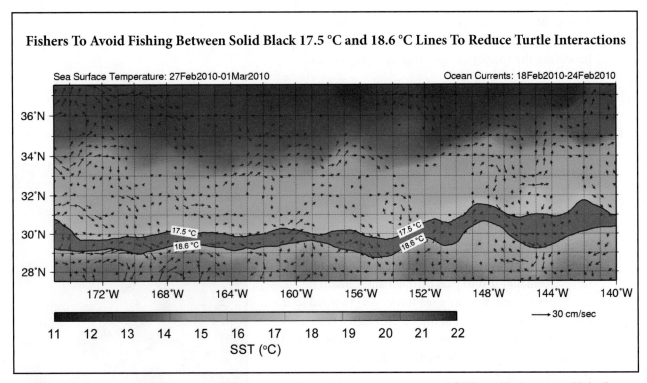

FIGURE 32.23. Newly derived visualizations from NOAA combine ocean current and SST satellite imagery with isolines of 17.5–18.6 °C (~63.5–65.5 °F). By tracking Loggerhead Sea Turtles in the Pacific Ocean, scientists have determined that these animals are more likely to be found in areas having these SSTs. This map, which changes often depending on SSTs, can be used by fishers in these areas whenever possible.

While it might seem simple to fix the problem of overfishing by not catching too many fish, it is difficult to control because there are many independent fishers as well as companies trying to make their living from fresh-caught fish. In addition, the demand for fish is high. The best way to maintain fish or shellfish populations is to allow time for the animals to reproduce in order to replace those that have been caught. To ensure that reproduction can occur safely, governmental regulations that specify fishing quotas, seasons, and size limits have been put into place. Based on the latest data and on trends observed in the data available to scientists and fisheries managers, these regulations change yearly, or even more often.

- **Quotas:** Until laws were enacted, fishers were allowed to catch as much as their boats could carry. Realizing that overfishing was causing damage to populations of fish and shellfish, quotas or daily limits for fish-per-species caught were determined. These quotas are determined by using many different types of scientific data and by making inferences about how much harvesting a particular fish species can withstand. Quotas usually regulate the number of pounds of fish for commercial fishing. For private fishing, the actual number of fish is counted.

- **Fishing seasons:** Fish and shellfish tend to reproduce at specific times every year. In order to ensure that mating is not interrupted, it has become common practice to regulate the time of year that certain fish and shellfish may be caught. Based on what scientists have observed in terms of reproductive patterns, harvesting is not allowed when the animals are actively reproducing.

- **Size limits:** It is also common practice to have a minimum size limit on fish and shellfish. These limits are based on scientists' observations about the life histories of a particular species. Regulators know, for example, the average length or weight for mature adults of a fish species. Animals that are caught and are below the minimum size limit must be thrown back. These limits ensure that fishers are catching only adults. Many species of animals do not reproduce until they are a certain size or age. Not catching fish and shellfish that are smaller allows time for the species to reach sexual maturity, providing the species an opportunity to reproduce.

While some fishing practices discussed are difficult to make environmentally friendly, advances in technology have made it possible for fishers to use methods that both help them decrease bycatch and earn more money. Laws on occasion require fishers to use these technologies or face severe fines. Some of these technologies are:

- **Turtle Excluder Devices (TEDs):** All species of sea turtles have been hard hit because they tend to migrate through the paths of the fishers and get caught in their nets and lines. The turtles then drown because they are unable to return to the surface to take a breath. TEDs are a series of bars located inside the net that allow for the targeted smaller fish to pass through and remain inside. If a larger animal, such as a sea turtle, gets trapped in the net, it is then guided out of the net through a flap. This device has prevented the drowning of countless sea turtles. It also allows larger fish to escape, reducing bycatch of these species as well.

FIGURE 32.25. A Turtle Excluder Device (TED). The oval metal ring and bars deflect the turtles. The cut in the netting is where the trap door will be placed. The bars force a turtle to the open trap door, allowing the turtle to go free.

See Page 694 for how to access e-Tools.

View the **TED Video** (0:35) from the e-Tools of a turtle escaping from a net thanks to a TED.

FIGURE 32.24. Screenshot of the **TED Video**.

e-Tools

- **Tori Lines:** Sea turtles are not the only species harmed through fishing practices. Seabirds are in danger of becoming entangled in longlines. Albatross that fly overhead dive down to scoop up bait on hooks and in the process get tangled. Even the fishers may not be aware that this is happening because the lines stretch far from the boat. Tori lines are longlines that have colored, flapping streamers attached to them in order to scare the birds away and prevent them from diving down toward the lines.

FIGURE 32.26. Tori lines' colored flapping streamers scare seabirds, preventing them from entanglement when diving down to pick up bait.

FIGURE 32.27. The hook on the left is the traditional J-hook. The circle hook on the right is more effective in catching fish and not snagging nontargeted sea animals.

- **Circle hooks on longlines:** Sea turtles can get caught on hooks that are attached to longlines. The original hook used—the J-hook—could easily snag a passing animal. Newly designed circle hooks cannot easily catch an animal that is swimming by. It is reported that using circle hooks has decreased hooking of the Loggerhead Sea Turtle by 65% and the Leatherback Sea Turtle by nearly 90%. Circle hooks yield more fish caught by their mouth because the fish remain on the hook. Previously used hooks often resulted in fish being snagged in the gills and not remaining on the line.

In addition to these technologies helping to ensure efficiency in the industry, purchasers of seafood have a tremendous amount of influence. An example of this is the Dolphin Safe Tuna campaign of the 1990s. From the 1950s to the 1990s, dolphins were routinely caught in purse seine nets along with tuna as these two species prey on similar fish and share habitats. While some 1970s regulations to prevent bycatch of the marine mammals were enacted, many dolphins were still being killed. In the 1980s, the idea of "dolphin safe tuna", or tuna "certified" to have been caught without ensnaring dolphins, was established; this became popular with consumers. Companies began labeling tuna cans as dolphin safe. By 1994, only dolphin safe tuna could be sold in the United States. According to NOAA, in order for tuna

FIGURE 32.28. NOAA has worked to ensure that tuna purchased in the United States is dolphin safe. Its work included a survey in which random cans and pouches of tuna were purchased and then traced back to the vessel and location at which the tuna was caught.

to be dolphin safe, it must be ensured that "no tuna were caught on the trip in which such tuna were harvested using a purse seine net intentionally deployed on or to encircle dolphins, and that no dolphins were killed or seriously injured in the nets in which the tuna were caught". These actions were critical to the survival of the canned tuna industry in the United States.

Unfortunately, most purchased seafood is not easily identified as sustainable. It is best to buy from fishers that use environmentally friendly fishing practices, and everyone should make an effort to do this. Several websites offer a free *wallet card* that promotes good practices. Access this information from the *Marine Science: The Dynamic Ocean* website. Consumers may keep these cards in their wallets to use as a reference when they are shopping or dining out. It helps to determine which species of fish to buy or order in a restaurant. This can then support the harvesting of fish that are being caught sustainably.

Blue Ocean Institute, a non-profit organization, distributes a "Guide to Ocean-friendly Seafood" for consumers to choose sustainable seafood while at restaurants, grocery stores, or fish markets. In the guide, fish species listed on a spectrum ranging from "green" ocean-friendly choices to "red" choices, species that have a combination of serious problems such as overfishing and high bycatch. For wild-caught fish, the criteria include life history of the species (i.e., its reproductive capabilities and how fast it grows) and the abundance of fish (how many individuals are thought to be available). Another important consideration is how the species is caught and managed. Questions to be answered include: Is there a lot of bycatch? Does the fishing gear damage habitats? Is the species well managed thanks to local, federal, or international regulations and enforcement? The information on this and other sites is updated often. Consumers should download the guides each year and educate others about choosing fish and shellfish species in order to promote a healthy and sustainable ocean.

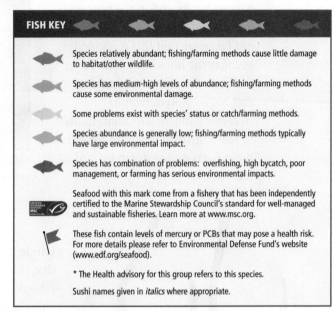

FIGURE 32.29. Fish Key developed by Blue Ocean Institute as part of their Guide to Ocean Friendly Seafood. Several criteria are used to determine the ratings. Fish and shellfish that receive a red ranking have a combination of serious problems; they are generally overfished, or catching them may result in habitat destruction or excessive bycatch. Seafood selections that receive a green ranking represent more ocean-friendly choices.

Visit the *Marine Science: The Dynamic Ocean* website to learn more about sustainable seafood and see which species are currently considered sustainable in your area.

7. Describe ways to maintain fish species as renewable resources.

8. Explain how scientific data are used to manage fish stocks.

A Brief History of Whaling in the United States

At the time of the American colonies, during the late 17th and 18th centuries, whaling was an important economic activity. Spotters onshore would look for the spouts of whales, such as the North Atlantic Right Whale. Then, whalers would row out to sea to harpoon the whale and tow it back to shore behind the boat. In fact, the North Atlantic Right Whale got its name because the species was very easy to target and tow after death—its big, fatty body was a relatively slow mover and readily floated.

FIGURE 32.30. North Atlantic Right Whales got their name because they were the "right" whale to hunt. Today, this species is one of the most endangered whales. These slow-moving animals are susceptible to ship strikes.

Whale oil became a very important fuel for lighting during that time; this continued well into the 1800s. By the mid-1700s, however, it became a bit more feasible to hunt whales from the sea. Particularly following the Revolutionary War, sailing ships began to set farther and farther out to sea, even heading to whale-rich waters of the Arctic and Antarctic.

The industry expanded in the 19th Century, particularly in New England and off of the California Coastline. For much of this time, large ships launched smaller boats from their decks when a whale was spotted. Men rowed to the whale and harpooned the huge animal—a similar procedure to what had been done from shore. This meant that slow-moving whales, like North Atlantic Right Whales, were the ones typically caught. Harpooning them was just a first step. Once harpooned, the injured whale would attempt to swim off; the whalers would follow the animal until it tired.

By the late 1800s, fast-moving steam ships allowed whalers to catch up with speedier species, including the tremendous Blue Whale. Another invention during this time period was a harpoon cannon, a device that would shoot a harpoon with a head like a grenade. It would explode within the animal, causing massive bleeding and slowing it down. These technologies and others allowed whalers to catch many more whales, and the depletion of whale stocks began. Whale oil was being used for lubricating machinery and creating margarine; other whale parts were made into fertilizers and livestock feed. Scientists estimate that the number of whales caught in the early 20th Century exceed the total number hunted in the 1600s through the 1800s combined. By the 1920s, whaling became even more efficient as "floating factories" allowed whales to be processed while ships were out at sea.

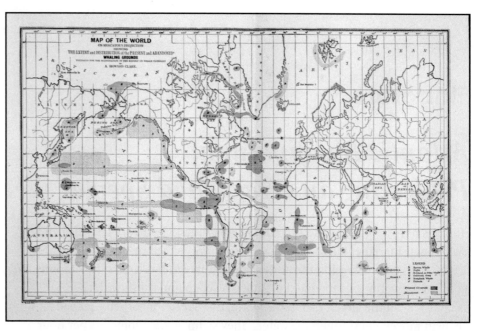

FIGURE 32.31. A map prepared in 1880 illustrated whaling grounds and areas in which whales were already depleted. The map also indicates the specific species of whale caught in specific locations.

In 1946, the International Convention for the Regulation of Whaling was held in Washington, D.C. The session was geared to regulating the whaling industry to ensure its continued success, because whaling nations realized that the world's whale stocks were becoming depleted. It was at this meeting that the International Whaling Commission (IWC) was established. The IWC still exists today. The 1946 meeting was largely unsuccessful at curtailing whaling activities, and the number of animals continued to fall. By 1971, the United States had outlawed whaling, and by the middle of the decade had listed eight whale species as endangered. The Marine Mammal Protection Act, enacted in 1972, prevented Americans, either in U.S. or international waters, from taking marine mammals, including whales and seals. The Act also outlawed bringing marine mammal products into the country. In 1982, IWC member nations voted to end whaling altogether. Japan and Norway voted against this policy.

In the United States today, indigenous peoples including Alaska Natives are allowed to take a limited number of whales for subsistence purposes. The populations of some whale species, including Gray Whales along the West Coast, have responded to protections in place since the 1970s. Other species, such as North Atlantic Right Whales, are susceptible to modern hazards including ship strikes and entanglement in fishing gear and remain at risk of becoming extinct. Practices including whaling and overfishing in the United States

FIGURE 32.32. This painting depicts the use of a "bomb lance", a type of harpoon with an exploding head. This technological advancement made whaling less dangerous for whalers and increased the number of whales caught.

have been very detrimental to marine ecosystems, as many of the large vertebrate populations have been removed. The strain on the ocean's resources, including fish and shellfish, increased tremendously in the late 20th Century, and continues today. By managing our ocean's renewable resources, we can protect marine ecosystems and their resources for the future.

9. Contrast traditional whaling practices of indigenous peoples with those of commercial whalers in the 19th and 20th Centuries.

Elaborate

Atlantic Bluefin Tuna: Protecting an Overfished Species

Humans have long found the Atlantic Bluefin Tuna to be a very tasty fish and it is a popular ingredient in sashimi—a dish of thinly sliced raw fish, of Japanese origin. This tuna is low in salt and is a good source of healthful oils, vitamins, and minerals. The Atlantic Bluefin Tuna is also a popular fish with sport fishers. One of the largest fish in the world, this species is torpedo shaped for swift movement through the water. They swim at 7.5 kilometers per hour (~4.7 miles per hour), but when they are chasing food, they can reach speeds of about 100 kilometers per hour (~62 miles per hour).

FIGURE 32.33. Bluefin Tuna sashimi is a healthful and delicious dish, but tuna populations are declining.

Atlantic Bluefin Tuna fishing tournaments became common in the middle of the 20th Century, because the fish were a challenge to catch. After the 1960s, however, sport and commercial overfishing caused the tuna population to decline, and it still has not recovered. Huge commercial fishing fleets that carry onboard freezing facilities catch the tuna. Unfortunately, the large purse seine nets used to catch entire schools of tuna can also result in the bycatch of sea turtles and dolphins.

The International Commission for the Conservation of Atlantic Tunas (ICCAT) helps to bring awareness of overfishing and the resultant decline in tuna populations to the public. They help set fishing limits and monitor the tuna populations. Recent studies indicate that this tuna species' populations have decreased by 90% since the 1970s and it is close to commercial extinction, meaning that fishers may no longer find it in the ocean in quantities worth harvesting. There are many different species of tuna, however, and this type of fish remains popular around the world. When purchasing tuna in a store or restaurant, you may hear of other types of tuna including Skipjack, Yellowfin, Bigeye, and Albacore.

FIGURE 32.34. Atlantic Bluefin Tuna has been one of the world's most sought-after game fish. This large migratory fish is at risk because of overfishing practices.

Scenario:

Data show that Atlantic Bluefin Tuna population numbers continue to decline, yet this species is still of interest to consumers, sport fishers, and others. Your task is to consider how different groups might view this issue. Each column in the table below represents a different stakeholder group in this discussion.

See Page 694 for how to access e-Tools.

Use the passage above and resources in the e-Tools and website to help you answer the Questions below.

e-Tools

10. Draw a table like the one below in your notebook. In each column, write at least two questions, concerns, suggestions, or ideas that each stakeholder group would have about this problem.

Marine Scientist	Recreational or Commercial Fisher	Consumer	Conservationist

11. Is it possible to make all groups happy at the same time? How?

12. What are the compromises that each group might be willing to make?

13. What are your suggestions on what should be done to stabilize the Atlantic Bluefin Tuna population?

Harvesting Salt from the Ocean

Our ocean has been providing mankind with important resources for millennia. Fish, mollusks, and sea mammals, such as seals and whales, provided food, oil for lighting, and fur for clothing. Camps and eventually settlements were established on the coastlines because the oceans had an abundance of food and a means of preserving it—salt. Salting meat dries the meat. Bacteria need water to grow, so the drying action of the salt prevents meat from spoiling or growing bacteria.

Seawater has a high concentration of the ions that make up table salt: sodium and chloride. The concentration of all dissolved ions in seawater, including sodium and chloride ions, averages 35 parts per thousand. When it rains over a continent's surface, runoff dissolves salts from soil and rock and carries them to the ocean. Over time, the concentration of these dissolved ions has stabilized. If a kilogram of seawater was evaporated it would provide approximately 35 grams of salt, mostly in the form of sodium chloride.

People have been harvesting salt from the ocean for thousands of years. Human-made drying ponds, such as those seen in the images below of the Dead Sea taken by the crew of two different Space shuttle missions, are a planned source for the extraction of salt from seawater even today. As global demand for salt rises, the extent of these drying ponds grows. The crew of Space Shuttle Mission STS-28 took the picture on the lower left in August 1989. NASA's Space Shuttle Mission STS-102 astronauts took the picture on the lower right, showing the increased production of salt, in March 2001.

Food preservation and dietary needs were some of the main uses of salt in the past. Salt was highly valued. Roman soldiers were even paid their wages in salt. If someone didn't perform well at their job, they were even said to be "not worth their salt".

A major use of salt today is for de-icing, helping to make our roads and highways safer in the winter months. Salt is also a source of chlorine. Chlorine is widely used in the chemical industry in processes for the making of rubber, polyvinyl chloride (PVC), and even aluminum. Being abundant and inexpensive, salt will remain a highly valued commodity for years to come.

FIGURE 32.35. Evaporation pools are used to get salt from seawater. The water evaporates, leaving salt behind.

August 1989

March 2001

Evaluate

Our ocean is under great pressure, and resource management is a real concern. The good news is that something can be done about it. As in The Tragedy of the Commons, recognizing how our actions can reduce and deplete resources is the first step. Putting into place laws and regulations will help to maintain our resources. We all have a responsibility to be good stewards of our ocean.

Choose one of the marine resources topics described in this Lesson (e.g., ovefishing, bycatch, regulation of fisheries). Alternatively, research a related issue such as aquaculture, oil and gas exploration, or mineral mining. Once you have chosen your issue, choose to complete Option A or Option B below.

Option A: Decide what your position is on a particular issue. For example, do you believe that fishing should be regulated? To what extent should commercial fishers have the right to make a living regardless of the effect on fish stocks? What should the government role be in preventing bycatch? Should offshore drilling be expanded? Should recreational fishers be exempt from quotas and size limits?

1. Research individuals or groups in your local area who are in a position to establish or rescind regulations related to the issue you chose. Write a letter to this person or group. Your letter should address a single topic and be typed.

2. Use a three paragraph format in which you:

    *   Include who you are and why you are writing.
    *   Provide detail about your issue.
    *   Close by requesting the action you want taken.

Option B: Decide what your position is on a particular issue. For example, could you or other citizens be more aware about choosing sustainable seafood or what the potential is for oil and gas exploration? Should recreational fishers better understand why there are quotas and size regulations in place?

1. Create a poster or PowerPoint presentation to educate others about your issue.

2. In the poster or presentation:

    *   Provide detail about your issue.
    *   Include graphics and other visual aids.
    *   Close with one action a person could take related to this issue.

33

Changing Climate

INSIDE:

Objectives

You will be able to:

✔ Cite evidence that Earth's climate is undergoing a warming period by analyzing diverse data sets.

✔ Analyze the impacts of climate changes on marine organisms, including corals and California Sea Lions.

✔ Describe changes in the Tropical Pacific associated with the El Niño Southern Oscillation.

Benchmarks

1a. The ocean is the dominant physical feature on our planet Earth—covering approximately 70% of the planet's surface. There is one ocean with many ocean basins, such as the North Pacific, South Pacific, North Atlantic, South Atlantic, Indian, and Arctic.

1c. Throughout the ocean there is one interconnected circulation system powered by wind, tides, the force of the Earth's rotation (i.e., Coriolis Effect), the Sun, and water density differences. The shape of ocean basins and adjacent land masses influence the path of circulation.

1d. Sea level is the average height of the ocean relative to the land, taking into account the differences caused by tides. Sea level changes as plate tectonics cause the volume of ocean basins and the height of the land to change. It changes as ice caps on land melt or grow. It also changes as seawater expands and contracts when ocean water warms and cools.

2b. Sea level changes over time have expanded and contracted continental shelves, created and destroyed inland seas, and shaped the surface of land.

3a. The ocean controls weather and climate by dominating the Earth's energy, water, and carbon systems.

(continued on next page)

3c. The El Niño Southern Oscillation causes important changes in global weather patterns because it changes the way heat is released to the atmosphere in the Pacific.

3e. The ocean dominates the Earth's carbon cycle. Half the primary productivity on Earth takes place in the sunlit layers of the ocean, and the ocean absorbs roughly half of all carbon dioxide added to the atmosphere.

3f. The ocean has had, and will continue to have, a significant influence on climate change by absorbing, storing, and moving heat, carbon, and water.

3g. Changes in the ocean's circulation have produced large, abrupt changes in climate during the last 50,000 years.

6b. From the ocean we get foods, medicines, and mineral and energy resources. In addition, it provides jobs, supports our nation's economy, serves as a highway for transportation of goods and people and plays a role in national security.

6c. The ocean is a source of inspiration, recreation, rejuvenation, and discovery. It is also an important element in the heritage of many cultures.

7b. Understanding the ocean is more than a matter of curiosity. Exploration, inquiry, and study are required to better understand ocean systems and processes.

7d. New technologies, sensors, and tools are expanding our ability to explore the ocean. Ocean scientists are relying more and more on satellites, drifters, buoys, subsea observatories, and unmanned submersibles.

7e. Use of mathematical models is now an essential part of ocean sciences. Models help us understand the complexity of the ocean and of its interaction with Earth's climate. They process observations and help describe the interactions among systems.

7f. Ocean exploration is truly interdisciplinary. It requires close collaboration among biologists, chemists, climatologists, computer programmers, engineers, geologists, meteorologists, and physicists and new ways of thinking.

Engage

Climate is a complex system because there are many factors that influence it, including insolation, surface and deepwater ocean currents, cloud cover, heat held by the atmosphere, soil moisture, and forested vegetation. Throughout the planet's history, Earth has undergone many periods of warming and cooling.

FIGURE 33.1. Fluctuations in climate affect all of Earth's systems, including biomes such as the tropical rainforest.

You've most likely heard about climate change all over the media, at home, and in school. In this Lesson you are given the opportunity to explore climate data for yourself so you can draw your own conclusions. You will observe some data sets and make inferences about whether, over the last century or more, Earth is experiencing a warming or cooling period.

Natural fluctuations in climate on Earth are generally cyclical; cycles range from every few years to many thousands of years. The impact of Earth's seasonal fluctuations on climate differs over thousands of years because of changes on Earth as it revolves around the Sun. Gravitational forces in Space cause Earth to wobble slightly, increasing and decreasing its angle of tilt on its axis. These changes are studied by Earth and Space scientists and are inferred to be reflected in ice ages. Professional scientists study climate change using multiple sources of evidence to determine past atmospheric temperatures, including **ice cores**, which are extracted cylindrical samples of ice from glaciers; **sediment cores**, which are extracted cylindrical samples of land; and chemical tracing. The graph in FIGURE 33.4 below shows the inferred average temperature changes at the Earth's surface for the past 150,000 years leading almost up to today. This shows the historical period of time when temperatures were warm and Earth was not in an ice age, and the colder times when Earth was experiencing an ice age. The plot is based on ice core data for a site located in Antarctica.

Satellite and other technologies have enabled scientists to see a complete picture about climate on a global scale. Studying these data reveals signals of a changing climate throughout history. FIGURE 33.5 shows at least four ice age cycles, with the last one ending about 7,000 years ago. The main reason for changing climate during these times has been small changes in Earth's orbit, which cause Earth to receive differing amounts of solar energy.

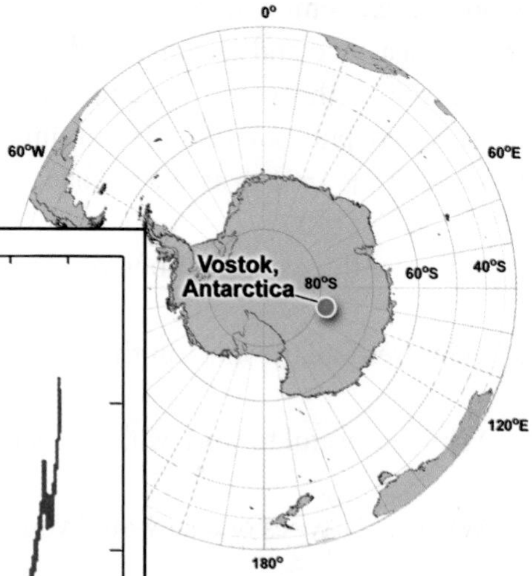

FIGURE 33.2. Ice core showing algae band.

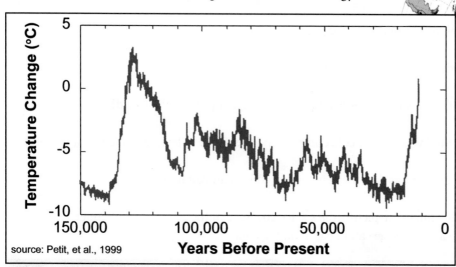

source: Petit, et al., 1999

FIGURE 33.3. Map showing the location of Vostok, Antarctica.

FIGURE 33.4. Data for the past 150,000 years show fluctuations and temperature differences from a modern baseline of data. Results were derived using measurements of a variation of common oxygen from ice core samples at Vostok Station in Antarctica.

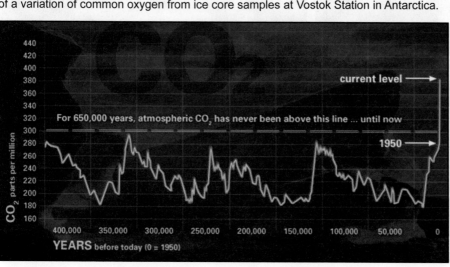

FIGURE 33.5. This graph, based on the comparison of atmospheric samples contained in ice cores and more recent direct measurements, provides evidence that atmospheric CO_2 has increased since the Industrial Revolution.

The next graph shows three scientific studies of temperatures at Earth's surface. It demonstrates how the Earth's temperatures have changed over the many past decades. Basically, the average global temperatures each year are being compared to the average global temperature from 1961–1990. So, if a point on the graph shows -0.4 °C, that means that at the time represented by the plot point, the temperature was 0.4 °C cooler on Earth than the average temperature for the time from 1961 to 1990. The plot on the right allows us to compare the average temperature from 1961 to1990 to more recent temperatures. The data were directly measured and recorded at different regions around the world. Note that the data sets were published at different times, from as early as 1881 to as late as 2006.

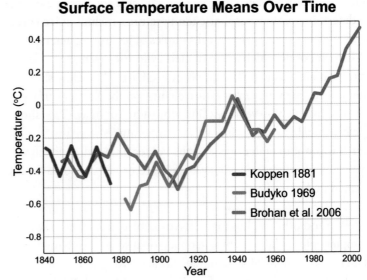

FIGURE 33.6. Average temperatures derived from land-based, ship, and SST data from around the globe.

1. What are three observations you can make based on the graph?

2. Why aren't all the lines on the graph exactly the same?

3. Why is it useful to work with temperature measurements in different parts of the world?

4. What other types of data would you suggest collecting around the world to learn about current climate?

5. Look at the most recent study that has data for many years. What can you infer about the study?

6. The images below are satellite images depicting the sea ice coverage in the Arctic in September 1979 and September 2007. Write at least one observation based on the data.

FIGURE 33.7. Arctic sea ice coverage in September 1979.

FIGURE 33.8. Arctic sea ice coverage in September 2007.

7. Write one inference based on these satellite images.

8. The graphs below show other measures of global changes. Write one observation based on each of the graphs.

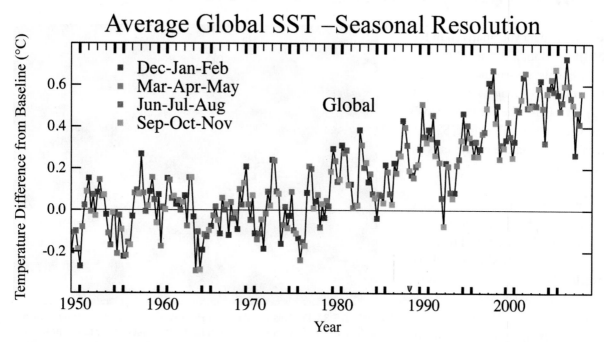

FIGURE 33.9. Each season's average global SST from 1950 is compared to the average SST for the 1951–1980 base time period.

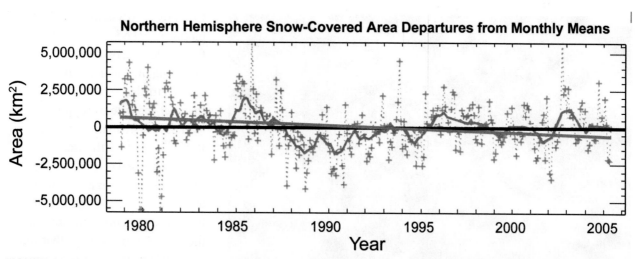

FIGURE 33.10. Annual Northern Hemisphere snow cover averages' *best fit line* (solid red) is created from data from NOAA snow charts and satellite data. Each point on the line of best fit, providing an approximation to what is happening, is compared to the average for 1978–2005.

9. Is Earth currently experiencing a warming or cooling period? Give two pieces of evidence, using the data sets above to support your inference.

Explore

Climate Changes and Coral Reefs

Based on the data you analyzed in the **Engage** section, it is evident that Earth is experiencing a warming period. Recall that the ocean is a major sink for heat energy on Earth. The ocean absorbs the Sun's radiation. Therefore, SSTs are increasing, and marine ecosystems will certainly be affected.

Scientists are concerned that coral reef ecosystems will be significantly impacted by a warming climate. Coral reefs are found in warm, tropical waters all over the world, including places such as the Florida Keys, Hawaii, American Samoa, and the Red Sea. Reefs are found in shallow waters, up to about 70 meters (~230 feet) deep. There are also deep

FIGURE 33.11. This coral reef in Puerto Rico provides a habitat for a wide variety of organisms. Coral reefs are susceptible to changes in temperature, sediment runoff, and other environmental impacts.

water coral ecosystems found in temperate (cooler) waters. In this Lesson we will focus on and consider the shallow, tropical corals that build reefs. These are sometimes called stony corals.

FIGURE 33.12. Florida's coastal reefs are visible in the Florida Keys in this image photographed from the International Space Station. One of the Station's solar panels is shown in the top left of the photograph.

Coral reef ecosystems have high biodiversity and provide habitat for a wide variety of organisms including invertebrates, fishes, and sea turtles. Scientists estimate that reef ecosystems support at least 25% of all marine species. Reefs are made of thousands of individual coral animals whose limestone skeletons are cemented together. Coral reefs are the largest biological structures on Earth, and they can become so large that some are visible from Space. Reefs grow very slowly, an average of 0.5–2 centimeters (~0.2–0.8 inches) per year. Most coral reefs on Earth today are between 5,000 and 10,000 years old.

Scientists have observed that in the past 100 years, the sea surface temperatures have increased on average across the globe by about 1 °C. This may not sound significant, but it can be. Let's consider some of the different SSTs being observed at coral reefs. Sometimes SSTs can be a bit above or below normal for a region. If measurements are way above or below normal, or they are not normal for a fairly long period of time, it can be of note. An observation that is different from what is considered normal or is uncommon in science can be described as an **anomaly** (pronounced: uh-NŎM-uh-lee). Therefore, an ocean sea surface temperature (SST) anomaly refers to an uncommon or unusual ocean temperature reading for a particular area.

You are going to observe SST difference imagery below. These data were derived from instruments onboard satellites orbiting the Earth. The SSTs are averaged over days, weeks, months, or years. The SST difference imagery for a particular month can tell you whether the temperatures in an area were higher or lower than the mean. Warmer-than-normal temperatures are indicated in yellows, oranges, and reds. Cooler-than-normal temperatures are indicated in greens, blues, and purples. The farther away from 0 on the color bar, the greater the difference from the mean SST and the greater the likelihood of an anomaly.

See Page 694 for how to access e-Tools.

View the *Coral Reef Interactive Map* from the e-Tools.

e-Tools

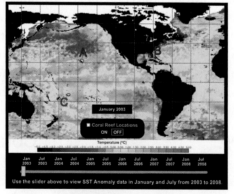

SST Difference (°C)

-5.0 -4.5 -4.0 -3.5 -3.0 -2.5 -2.0 -1.5 -1.0 -0.5 0.0 0.5 1.0 1.5 2.0 2.5 3.0 3.5 4.0 4.5 5.0

FIGURE 33.13. Screenshot of the *Coral Reef Interactive Map*.

1. Use the *Coral Reef Interactive Map* by moving the slider to view the SST anomaly data for various time periods.

    a. Describe two regions and time periods in which there is anomalously warm water (more than 2 °C greater than the mean), or the warmer pattern persists for more than 1 year.

    b. Describe two regions and time periods in which there is anomalously cool water (more than 2 °C less than the mean), or the cooler pattern persists for more than 1 year.

2. On the interactive map, Letters A, B, and C correspond to areas with coral reefs. Letter A shows Hawaiian Humpback Whale National Marine Sanctuary, Letter B is the location of the Florida Keys National Marine Sanctuary, and Letter C represents Fagatele Bay National Marine Sanctuary.

Copy this table into your notebook. Use the maps to record the observed SST differences for locations A, B, and C. For each time period, note whether the data indicate that the SSTs are *warmer* or *cooler* than average.

	Temperature (°C)					
	January			July		
	A	B	C	A	B	C
2003						
2004						
2005						
2006						
2007						
2008						

3. Which area, A, B, or C, experienced consistently warmer-than-average temperatures in the years studied?

In order to consider how a warming climate might affect coral reef ecosystems, let's look more closely at corals themselves. The coral polyps that make up stony reefs are invertebrate animals in the same phylum (Phylum Cnidaria) as jellyfish. At night, they use their tentacles to catch prey, which includes zooplankton. The polyps also hold and provide protection for photosynthetic algae called **zooxanthellae** (pronounced: zō-ah-zan-THELL-ee). Zooxanthellae are autotrophs and are classified as part of the Kingdom Protista. During the day, these algae perform photosynthesis, and the sugars they produce are available for the coral animals to eat. The coral polyps satisfy about 90% of their energy needs from activities of the zooxanthellae. Each polyp is tiny, usually only a few millimeters in length, but together they form large colonies. The polyps build the calcium carbonate skeletons that make up the reef.

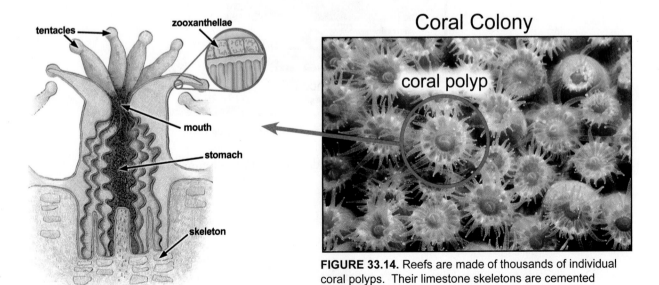

FIGURE 33.14. Reefs are made of thousands of individual coral polyps. Their limestone skeletons are cemented together.

Corals can only perform their life activities under certain physical conditions, within specific ranges of temperature, salinity, depth, and so on. In fact, all living things survive within a range of physical conditions, known as a **range of tolerance**. Prolonged exposure to conditions beyond their range of tolerance stresses the coral and can result in sickness and death. This is true for all organisms, including humans. For example, picture an earthworm in a puddle after a rainstorm. When the puddle dries up, the earthworm must return to the soil to retain moisture and avoid becoming overheated.

When reef-building corals become stressed over time, they expel their zooxanthellae. Their brilliant colors, seen in familiar coral reef pictures, fade and the corals appear white. This phenomenon is known as coral **bleaching**.

There are several other causes of coral stress including pollution, destructive fishing practices, and disease. Most of these dangers occur regionally. Prolonged warming in the ocean can cause widespread bleaching. High temperatures also increase the risk for coral diseases.

FIGURE 33.15. Healthy coral polyps display vibrant colors.

Most reefs are composed of several different stony coral species. The optimal temperature range for most of these species is 23–29 °C (~73–84 °F). The corals tend to grow much more slowly in temperatures above or below this range. Also, most coral species cannot withstand temperatures significantly above or below this range for more than a very short period of time. When water temperatures become too hot or too cold, corals will bleach, eventually causing death. In January 2010, for example, the Florida Keys experienced a record cold spell lasting several weeks, in which water temperatures at the coast dipped to almost 13 °C (~56 °F). Reefs in this area were devastated because the cooler temperatures caused a bleaching event to occur.

FIGURE 33.16. Bleaching causes the brilliant colors of the coral reef to fade to white.

Primarily because of their temperature constraints, Coral reefs are normally located between 30° N and 30° S latitude. Corals require relatively salty water, between 32 and 40 practical salinity units (PSU), and they become stressed when the salinity of the water becomes too low. They also require that water be very clear, as murky water prevents the zooxanthellae from performing photosynthesis.

FIGURE 33.17. When water temperatures become too hot or too cold, corals will bleach. Most will eventually die.

In addition to their inherent value as an ocean ecosystem, coral reefs are a renewable resource important to humans. While it is hard to put a price on such a valuable commodity, coral reefs provide many billions of dollars to the global economy yearly through industries such as tourism, scientific exploration, and commercial fishing. Many compounds found in reef organisms, such as corals, sponges, anemones, and fish, have proven to be useful in the pharmaceutical industry. Coral reefs have been the source of treatments for cancer, arthritis, bacterial infections, and other ailments. Approximately ⅓ of commercially harvested fish depend on coral reefs. Reefs also prevent coastal erosion and absorb land-based pollutants. Corals are significant in some human cultural traditions, particularly in the Indo-Pacific. Native Hawaiians, for example, revere coral polyps in their creation story.

FIGURE 33.18. Scientist studying an area affected by coral reef bleaching. Data collected in the water are analyzed along with those collected from satellites, buoys, and other sources.

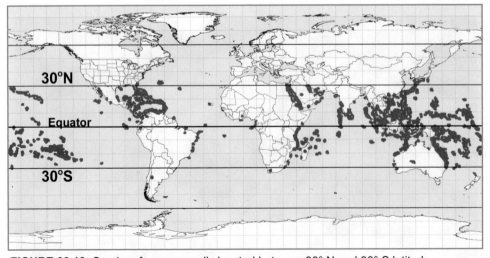

FIGURE 33.19. Coral reefs are normally located between 30° N and 30° S latitude.

10. Explain what happens to corals when they become stressed.

11. Describe the effects of the loss of coral reefs on the ocean as a whole.

12. Indicate the benefits and costs of protecting coral reefs. Give at least one benefit and one cost.

FIGURE 33.20. Tourism contributes to the economic importance of coral reefs. Have you or anyone you know ever visited a coral reef to go snorkeling, scuba diving, or to enjoy other activities?

As you just read, one problem with increasing SSTs is that corals release their zooxanthellae and become bleached. Scientists are interested and concerned about coral bleaching because of its effects on ocean ecosystems. Using several data sets, including temperature and salinity observations, researchers have created a computer program that makes ecosystem predictions, called a **computer model**. This model predicts the risk of bleaching and can be used by scientists and other decision-makers who manage coral reefs and how they are used (e.g., for fishing, for recreation, and scuba diving). Models can lead to strategies to limit coral bleaching, such as the restricting of activities, which can protect corals from additional stressors besides temperature anomalies.

Cyberlab

To gain an understanding of the model, you will use the data it has generated by following the steps below.

See Page 694 for how to access e-Tools.

View the *Coral Bleaching Interactive Map* from the e-Tools.

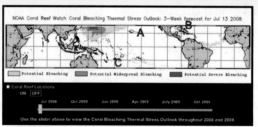

FIGURE 33.21. Screenshot of the *Coral Bleaching Interactive Map*.

e-Tools

1. Copy the table below into your notebook. Use the interactive map to record the coral bleaching thermal stress outlook for locations A, B, and C in your table.

	Coral Bleaching Thermal Stress Outlook		
	A	B	C
July 2008			
October 2008			
January 2009			
April 2009			
July 2009			
October 2009			

13. According to NASA, the decade of January 2000 through December 2009 was the warmest decade on record. If this warming trend continues, how will coral reefs and other ocean ecosystems be affected?

14. The graphs to the right show the inferred temperature and atmospheric CO_2 concentration for the past 400,000 years.

   a. Describe the correlation between temperature and atmospheric CO_2 concentration illustrated in the graph.

   b. Predict what would happen to coral reefs if both atmospheric CO_2 and temperature were to increase over the next 100 years.

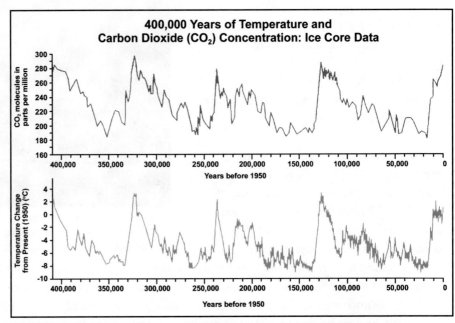

FIGURE 33.22. There have been many changes of climate in Earth's history. Major changes can happen gradually or over several decades.

Explain

Earth is a complex system, particularly when it comes to climate and understanding interactions between the ocean, atmosphere, land, and biosphere. The current warming being observed on our planet is termed **global climate change**. Sometimes, you might hear it referred to as "global warming". Understanding ocean processes is critical to the study of global climate change because the ocean absorbs and transports so much heat, carbon, and water. Studying global climate change and its effects has brought together oceanographers, geologists, biologists, meteorologists, engineers, computer programmers, and many other experts. Scientists from around the world have been collecting many pieces of data, such as those with which you worked in the **Engage** and **Explore** sections, to learn about past and present climate. From these data, researchers draw inferences and ask further questions. They build computer models to predict additional changes that will occur and the possible impacts on physical and biological systems.

Scientists, of course, do not always agree with one another about their inferences or most important questions. Ocean scientists come from different backgrounds, cultures, and areas of academic training. When looking at the same data, they may view them differently, and come up with a different explanation of what they see and believe the data are saying. Different perspectives also help scientists to better understand the way the natural world functions as a system. They can see relationships between factors that they might not notice if they worked solely within their own discipline.

FIGURE 33.23. A scientist studies a coral sample in a shipboard laboratory. Research can lead to reducing adverse impacts of human activities.

Scientists share their explanations through posters and presentations at scientific conferences and through publishing their work in scientific journals. Articles in scientific journals are peer-reviewed, meaning that other scientists examine the data and arguments made by the writers. When looking for scientific information, one should first consult these peer-reviewed scientific journals, rather than the Internet or other sources in which anyone can post their ideas and present them as facts, even if there is not strong supporting evidence.

Sharing work and ideas allows other scientists to consider and criticize new scientific views and test new ideas. Scientists sometimes engage in debates, arguing for their positions and supporting their claims with evidence. While this may seem confusing for outsiders, the fact that scientists do not always have the same perspectives actually makes scientific knowledge stronger. You have probably simulated many of these activities in your class by sharing posters and presentations and by engaging in debates.

Global climate change is a topic that is widely discussed among scientists around the world currently and in recent years. Most scientists agree that the data show that Earth's climate is warming. Their debates often center on the *causes* and *effects* of climate change. Let's now explore some of the issues that they are debating.

FIGURE 33.24. Scientists make observations of fish. All species are susceptible to changes in climate.

FIGURE 33.25. Dr. Ku'ulei Rodgers discusses coral bleaching and acidification with educators at the Hawaii Institute of Marine Biology.

FIGURE 33.26. Scientists in a submersible prepare to venture underwater. Deep sea corals' growth can indicate climate change over many years.

FIGURE 33.27. Scientists collect seafloor sediments. The ocean floor holds evidence of change over time.

FIGURE 33.28. *Marine Science: The Dynamic Ocean* scientist Michelle Hester studies penguins in Antarctica.

Causes of Changes in Climate

As you noted in the **Engage** section, Earth has gone through many variations and fluctuations in climate in the past. The changes in climate can be attributed to volcanic activity, the "wobble" of Earth on its axis, and even changes in ocean currents. Scientists have gathered evidence from many sources (tree rings, ice cores, sediment cores, and other sources) to learn about past climate. From these data, scientists explain that the Earth has undergone both slow and rapid climatic changes.

Scientists generally agree that there is strong evidence that human activities are contributing to global climate change. In an earlier Lesson, you studied greenhouse gases, including carbon dioxide (CO_2), methane (CH_4), nitrous oxide (N_2O), ozone (O_3), and water vapor (H_2O). Greenhouse gases trap infrared radiation that could go into Space. They are keeping the planet warmer by preventing the heat from escaping the atmosphere. An increase in greenhouse gases will correlate to an increase in heat on the planet, where much of that heat is stored in the ocean. This is due to the high heat capacity of water. The warmer ocean then also contributes to the warming of the atmosphere above it.

The figures on the right show the atmospheric changes in three greenhouse gases—carbon dioxide, methane, and nitrous oxide—over the past several decades. Each graph shows the global averages of the concentrations of the gaseous molecules in the air. The numbers on the y-axis represent the amount of the molecules in the air in parts per million (ppm) for carbon dioxide. This means, for instance, in 2006, the amount of CO_2 molecules out of 1,000,000 molecules in the air across the globe averaged 380. The graph shows an increase of approximately 40 ppm since 1982, when the global average was 340 ppm. The average had been approximately 275 ppm for the 2,000 years prior to the Industrial Revolution.

Methane and nitrous oxide are measured in parts per billion (ppb) and show increases over the recent past as well.

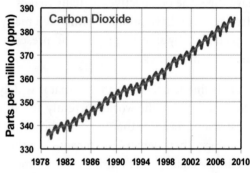

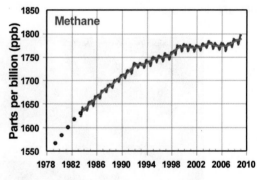

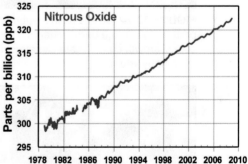

FIGURE 33.30. Average global concentrations of carbon dioxide (CO_2), methane (CH_4), and nitrous oxide (N_2O) molecules in the air as measured since the late 1970s from the NOAA global flask sampling network of 38 stations around the globe.

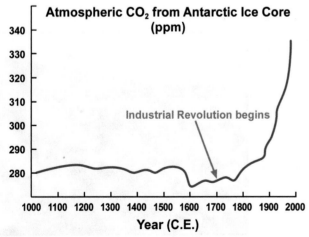

FIGURE 33.29. The amount of greenhouse gas CO_2 appears stable since before 1000 C.E. until the Industrial Revolution.

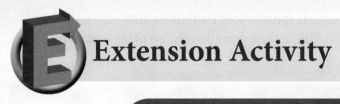 **Extension Activity**

e-Tools

See Page 694 for how to access e-Tools.

View the *Greenhouse Gas Interactive Tool* from the e-Tools.

The *Greenhouse Gases Interactive Tool* includes data recorded at stations in locations around the world. The stations report the atmospheric CO_2 concentration in parts per million (ppm) at various times of year. Scientists at the reporting stations work to ensure the accuracy of their tools in order to record and share the highest possible data quality.

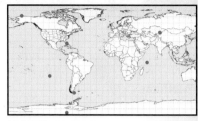

FIGURE 33.31. Screenshot of the *Greenhouse Gas Interactive Tool*.

Use the *Greenhouse Gases Interactive Tool* and follow the steps below.

1. Copy the chart below into your notebook. Choose three locations from the tool and record them in your chart. For each gas, record the highest and lowest observed concentrations of CO_2 for the years 2000 and 2005.*

Location	2000 High	2000 Low	2005 High	2005 Low
Barrow, AK				
Key Biscayne, FL				
Tierra Del Fuego, Argentina				
Mahe Island, Seychelles				
Plateau Assy, Kazakhstan				
Easter Island, Chile				
South Pole, Antarctica				

a. What trends do you observe in the data that you recorded?

b. Does every location on Earth emit the same amount of CO_2? Why or why not?

c. Does the concentration of CO_2 at different stations vary widely? Why or why not?

d. Predict: How would readings of N_2O and CH_4 vary across the globe?

* measured in parts per million (ppm)

There are both natural and human-made, or **anthropogenic** (pronounced an-thrō-pō-JEN-ick), sources of these greenhouse gases, as illustrated in the table below. The anthropogenic emissions of these gases have increased.

Greenhouse Gas	Sources of Gases	
	Anthropogenic	Natural
Carbon Dioxide	Fossil fuel burning (e.g., cars, industry, power plants)	Respiration, volcanoes, decomposition
Methane	Agricultural practices (e.g., cattle production, rice paddies), landfills	Decomposition in wet areas, thawing permafrost, animals, termites
Nitrous Oxide	Burning waste, agricultural soils	Tropical soils, ocean

Other human activities contribute to climatic changes in the atmosphere and ocean. For example, changing how humans use land areas affects the amount of heat that is absorbed or reflected by the land. Pollutants in the air that settle on ice, known as *black carbon*, change the albedo of the ice, causing energy to be absorbed rather than reflected. This effect alone contributes to the melting of glaciers. The factors that change Earth's heat balance—the amount of energy entering and leaving the Earth system— are called **radiative forcings**. An increase in radiative forcing of +1 W/m² (watts per square meter) is equivalent to shining a small, holiday light bulb over every single square meter on Earth's surface.

FIGURE 33.32. Holiday light bulbs are the example used to equate CO_2 concentrations with an amount of energy per square meter on Earth. Increasing CO_2 in the atmosphere suggests more heat energy per Earth's surface area.

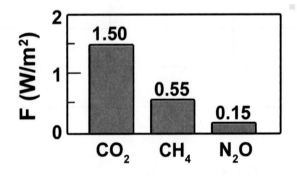

FIGURE 33.33. The bar graph illustrates the relative radiative forcings of the greenhouse gases since 1750.

15. Based on this graph, which radiative forcing agent has had the largest influence on climate change during the time period since the Industrial Revolution?

Effects of Climate Change

You worked with coral reef and SST anomaly data in the **Explore** section and saw that the effects of global climate change are already quite apparent in many areas. The public's perception of what is real, however, can be confused. Some of these effects are misunderstood or unclear. One of the major areas of confusion is with rising sea levels. Scientists have observed that sea levels are rising. The figure below shows the trends in sea level from 1992 to 2010. Note that in some areas of the ocean, sea level rose during that time period. In other places, it decreased. But, should we be concerned with slight increases? What would it take for there to be significantly higher waters across the globe?

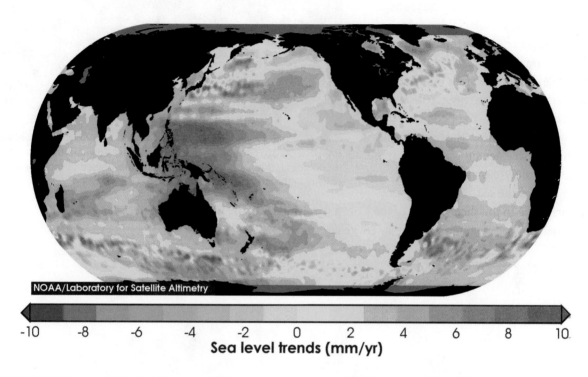

FIGURE 33.34. The image shows the average increase in sea level across the globe since 1992. The TOPEX, Jason-1, and Jason-2 satellites have provided this data since 1992.

Completing the following investigation will help to solidify your understanding of what really causes the sea level to rise or what could cause it in the future.

Investigating Sea Level Rise

As the Earth's atmosphere and ocean are warming, ice in many places on Earth is melting. There are different types of ice. **Sea ice** near Earth's Polar Regions rests on top of the ocean. **Glacial ice**, which is frozen fresh water, sits on top of land areas. Look at the image below, which shows Earth's Poles. The blue areas indicate frozen ocean water, the sea ice. Sea ice is salty because of salt crystals trapped between frozen water molecules. The light purple areas show freshwater snow and ice. These areas include slow-moving rivers of ice heading toward the sea. This movement

FIGURE 33.35. Greenland glaciers melt and flow into the ocean, to an extent, during summer. Scientists are poised to monitor this activity in the coming years.

is primarily due to the sheer weight of the frozen freshwater ice, the **glaciers**. Glaciers can be as small as a football field or large enough to cover an entire continent.

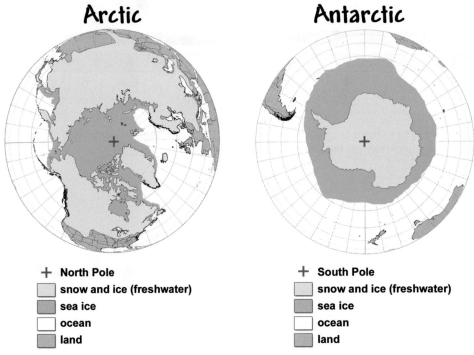

Arctic   Antarctic

+ **North Pole**
☐ **snow and ice (freshwater)**
☐ **sea ice**
☐ **ocean**
☐ **land**

+ **South Pole**
☐ **snow and ice (freshwater)**
☐ **sea ice**
☐ **ocean**
☐ **land**

FIGURE 33.36. Maps showing freshwater snow and ice and sea ice in the Arctic and Antarctic.

1. Compare the ice found in the Arctic and Antarctic.

2. Make a prediction: How will melting glaciers and sea ice affect sea levels?

FIGURE 33.37. Freshwater icebergs break off from glacial ice and eventually melt in the ocean.

Materials:

- 2 beakers half full of water (simulates ocean)
- Masking tape or grease pencil to mark water level on beaker (simulates sea level along a coast)
- Rock, brick, or other object (used as a landmass to support a "glacier")
- 4–6 ice cubes (simulates glacier and sea ice)
- Hair dryers, heat lamps, or another source to melt ice quickly
- Paper towels for cleanup
- Rulers

Your team is going to use the materials to design and conduct an investigation. The investigation focuses on the effect on sea levels of 1) sea ice melting and 2) ice sheets and glaciers melting. The masking tape is provided as a way to mark the starting level of the water.

3. How will you model sea ice? Draw your setup in your notebook.

4. How will you model glaciers on land? Draw your setup in your notebook.

5. What data will you collect?

6. Write a procedure for your investigation.

Now try your investigation.

7. What are your findings?

8. What conclusion can you draw based on your findings?

The Ocean and Heat

Sea level has changed many times in Earth's history. The data you observed earlier indicated that sea level is currently rising, and the laboratory model indicated that some of this increase is a result of glacial ice that melts and runs off the land. Another cause of sea level rise is the warming of water: as liquid water warms, it takes up a larger volume. This phenomenon is known as **thermal expansion**. Recall that as substances heat, their kinetic energy increases, and, in a liquid, molecules move farther apart. People living along coastlines and in low-lying areas or on islands are particularly concerned about rising sea levels.

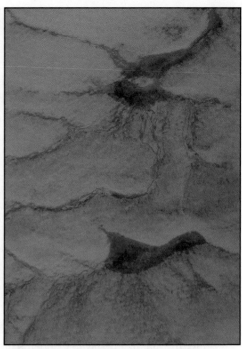

FIGURE 33.38. Close look at meltwater pools. Greenland glaciers in summer pool water that runs along the frozen surface over great distances.

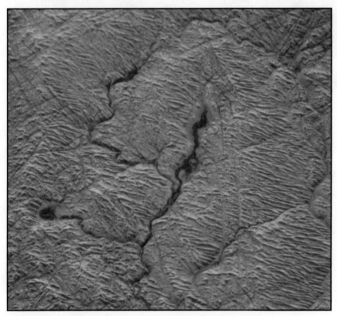

FIGURE 33.39. Wider view of meltwater pools accumulating during summer in Greenland, and the system of water flow they create.

FIGURE 33.40. The Global Conveyor Belt carries heat to Earth's Polar Regions. Scientists are concerned that as ocean temperatures increase, the water may not become cool enough to sink in the North Atlantic, altering the entire worldwide circulation of water and heat.

Besides rising sea levels, there is another effect of melting glaciers. As the freshwater ice melts and runs off into the more salty sea, this **meltwater** floats atop the saltier, denser water below. In the North Atlantic, the Greenland Ice Sheet is melting, and meltwater is being added to the ocean. Recall that this area is important in terms of the Global Conveyor Belt. Cold, salty water sinks to begin its journey through the deep ocean. The meltwater being added, however, is not salty enough to sink, and this may change the Global Conveyor Belt. Scientists are also concerned that as ocean temperatures increase globally, more heat will be carried to the Polar Regions. This heat transport may mean that in the North Atlantic, for example, the water does not cool enough to sink, which would also alter the Global Conveyor Belt. This change in ocean circulation could have important implications for ocean currents and the weather in Europe. Storm patterns may be altered.

The Ocean and Carbon

In addition to holding heat, the ocean is also a *sink* for carbon, which means it absorbs energy from the system. As humans have increased the amount of CO_2 in the atmosphere, the ocean has absorbed much of the compound into its waters. Scientists estimate that between ¼ and ⅓ of the anthropogenic CO_2 released during the 20th Century was absorbed by the ocean. They believe that the carbon absorption by the ocean has reduced the warming of the atmosphere. Without this ocean warming, predicted increase in temperature would be greater.

The absorption of CO_2, however, has altered the chemistry of the seawater. Recall that seawater is slightly basic on the pH scale. Absorption of CO_2 has resulted in reactions that are causing the ocean to acidify. This acidification poses a major threat to marine organisms. One reason for concern is related to the compound calcium carbonate ($CaCO_3$). Many shellfish, including crustaceans (e.g., lobsters, crabs), as well as mollusks (e.g., clams, oysters), combine calcium with available carbonate (CO_3^{-2}) to build calcium carbonate ($CaCO_3$) shells.

FIGURE 33.41. Spiny Lobster peeks out of its hiding place in the coral. Many marine invertebrates rely on carbonate ions (CO_3^-) in the ocean to build their shells.

By definition, a lower pH means that the water contains more hydrogen ions (H^+). These ions react with the carbonate ions (CO_3^{-2}) dissolved in the water. In more acidic water, more carbonate ions are able to form bonds. This means that fewer carbonate ions (CO_3^{-2}) are dissolved within water. This reduces the availability of (CO_3^{-2}) for marine invertebrates such as corals to build their shells. Slow-growing reefs may grow even more slowly if reef-building is impeded by ocean acidification and the lack of available (CO_3^{-2}). Slow growth makes it harder for reefs to recover from damage from storms or human influences. Data indicate that for stony reefs in Florida and the Caribbean, various factors are contributing to slower growth.

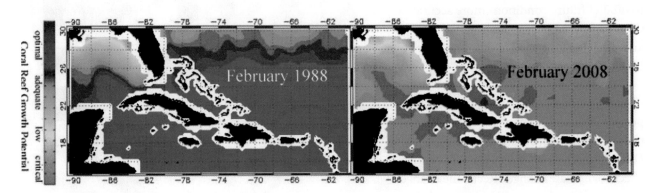

FIGURE 33.42. The growth potential in recent years for coral reefs near Florida and in the Caribbean has been dramatically reduced.

See Page 694 for how to access e-Tools.

...iew the *Sea Change Excerpt Video* (2:00) ...om the e-Tools, in which scientists discuss ...ome of the changes associated with ocean acidification.

FIGURE 33.43. Screenshot of the *Sea Change Excerpt Video*.

e-Tools

16. Describe two reasons why humans should be concerned about anthropogenic carbon dioxide entering the atmosphere.

Predicting Future Effects of Climate Change

Many of the changes you have read about so far, including ocean acidification and rising sea levels, are already occurring. Other worldwide changes being attributed to global climate change include changes in animal migration and hibernation patterns, thawing of frozen land in the Arctic, increased drought, and shrinking lakes in subtropical areas.

To make predictions about *future* effects of global climate change, scientists use computer models. You used data generated by a computer model when you analyzed the coral bleaching outlook in the **Explore** section. Part of the debate between scientists over global climate change is related to new climate change models. To build climate models, scientists input observed data and then the model predicts the future for many climatic variables, or parameters, including SSTs, air temperature, cloud cover, and precipitation. To test and improve a model, scientists run them for time periods that have already occurred. For example, they might input observed data from 1950 to 1970, and let the model make predictions for 1980–2000. Scientists can then compare a model's predictions with observed data for the same time period. They make adjustments to predict future conditions more accurately. Over time, computer models will be refined, and the science of climate change will be better understood in the future.

In the meantime, models are still far from perfect in their predictions, and the long-term effects of global change are unknown. Different models have predicted different effects of climate change. Recall the changes in the Global Conveyor Belt described above. The slowing of the system in a certain period of time represents one possible scenario.

FIGURE 33.44. Climate scientists actively assimilate Earth data from satellites and ground-based measurements in order to derive climate models, in an effort to better understand our changing climate.

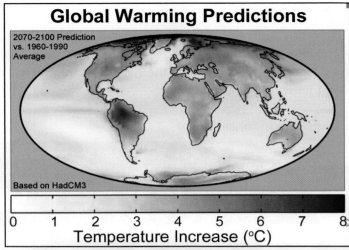

Global Warming Predictions

2070-2100 Prediction
vs. 1960-1990
Average

Based on HadCM3

Temperature Increase (°C)
0 1 2 3 4 5 6 7 8

FIGURE 33.45. Climate models compute complicated algorithms and generate forecasts. Potential increases in temperature could be extreme in the coming fifty years or more.

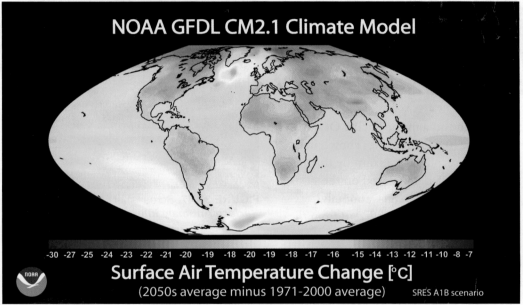

NOAA GFDL CM2.1 Climate Model

-30 -27 -25 -24 -23 -22 -21 -20 -19 -18 -20 -19 -18 -17 -16 -15 -14 -13 -12 -11 -10 -8 -7

Surface Air Temperature Change [°C]
(2050s average minus 1971-2000 average)   SRES A1B scenario

FIGURE 33.46. Computer models, using information from today, show examples of forecasted temperature increases in the future.

Above are two images created by two different climate models. Although they are showing predictions for slightly different time periods, it is useful to compare them.

Other climatic changes predicted by global climate change models include:

- Warming is most significant in the Polar Regions
- Increased frequency and intensity of storms
- Increase in ocean acidification
- Decrease in snow cover
- Increase in precipitation in the Polar Regions, decrease in precipitation in subtropical land regions such as Florida
- Decreases in soil moisture

17. Compare and contrast the temperature increases predicted by the NASA and NOAA climate models. Give at least two similarities and two differences.

Elaborate

In previous sections, we focused on long-term changes in climate. Changes in climate occur on shorter-term bases as well. We are going to examine SST images for specific times in the Pacific Ocean. You will discover a time period when the SST observations were unusual, an *SST anomaly*.

Both short- and long-term climate changes affect marine organisms.

See Page 694 for how to access e-Tools.

Cyberlab

With your group, follow the instructions below.

View the **Sea Surface Anomaly Interactive Map** from the e-Tools.

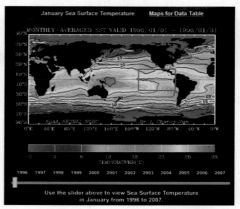

e-Tools

FIGURE 33.47. Screenshot of the **Sea Surface Anomaly Interactive Map**.

1. Look closely at the area in the Pacific Ocean near the Equator (0° latitude line) shown in the box. Use the scroll bar to examine the different years of SST data. Based on the maps, which year shows an SST anomaly? (*Hint: Which year looks very different from the others?*)

2. Describe the differences that you see in the map of the anomalous year.

3. Now click on the Maps for Data Table link at the top. Draw the table below in your notebook. Use the maps to complete the table. This table will help you to compare the different years quantitatively.

    Slide the bar across the screen to view the average January SSTs from 1996 through 2007.

    Record the temperature for locations A and B along the Equator, for each year.

	Temperature (°C)							
	January		April		June		October	
	A	B	A	B	A	B	A	B
1996								
1998								
2000								
2002								
2004								
2006								

Anomalies in Winds and Ocean Currents

The atmosphere and ocean are very closely connected. In the area just south of the Equator are **trade winds**. They blow from east to west. Recall, it is the *wind* that drives the direction of ocean currents. The major ocean current in this area is the Peru Current, also called the Humboldt Current.

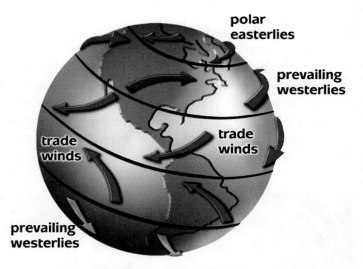

FIGURE 33.48. Earth's prevailing winds. Illustration shows common surface winds just above Earth's surface.

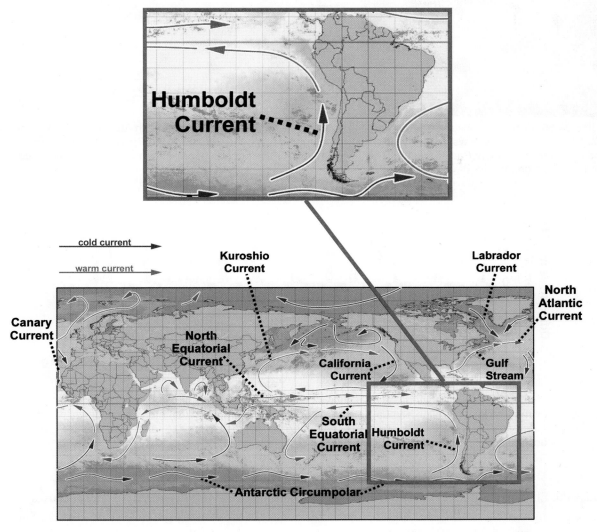

FIGURE 33.49. Maps showing the Humboldt Current as well as select warm and cold currents. Notice the relationships with Earth's prevailing surface winds from FIGURE 33.48.

The conditions that you observed in the data from 1998 are part of a climatic phenomenon that occurs in the ocean and atmosphere in the area of the Tropical Pacific Ocean. The phenomenon is known as the **El Niño Southern Oscillation**, often referred to as either El Niño or ENSO. *El Niño* refers to both the anomaly in the ocean temperatures and the height of sea level of the ocean's waters in the Tropical Pacific Ocean, the area you were just observing. In Spanish, *El Niño* means "The Christ Child". People in South America often notice the cyclical anomalies occurring around Christmas time, when many celebrate the birth of Christ. A phenomenon that is opposite to El Niño and results in cooler temperatures and drier air in the Tropical Pacific is called La Niña. Scientists are unclear of the reasons for these oceanic and atmospheric anomalies.

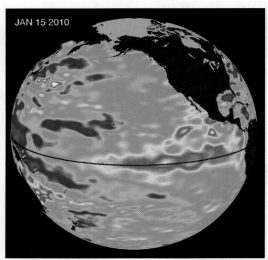

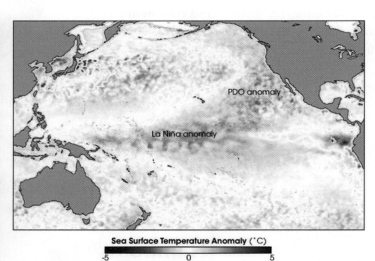

FIGURE 33.50. El Niño as observed in January 2010. Warmest surface sea waters are visible over the Eastern Equatorial Pacific Ocean. This anomaly is the signature for the phenomenon.

FIGURE 33.51. La Niña as observed in April 2008. Waters are colder than normal along the Equator in the Pacific. This occurrence is the signature for this phenomenon, influencing short term climate.

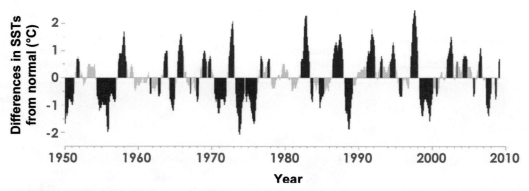

FIGURE 33.52. SST difference map shows cooler temperatures during a 2008 La Niña event. Cycles of El Niño and La Niña are apparent in the graph. When the *y*-axis index is > 0.5, an El Niño event was observed. When the *y*-axis index was < 0.5, a La Niña event occurred.

Because the El Niño anomaly is a result of changes in the atmosphere and the ocean, the event causes climatic changes throughout the world that can last anywhere from eight months to up to two years. An El Niño event will cycle in every 2–5 years. After the El Niño event is over, normal weather patterns resume across the globe.

Recall that the height of the ocean's surface is known as *sea level*. Sea level varies with changes in lithospheric plate movements, thermal expansion, tides, ice melting, and other factors. Winds will also affect sea height. Under normal conditions, the trade winds push the Peru Current from east to west, off the South American coast. Nutrient-rich, cold, deep water moves up to the surface, a process called upwelling.

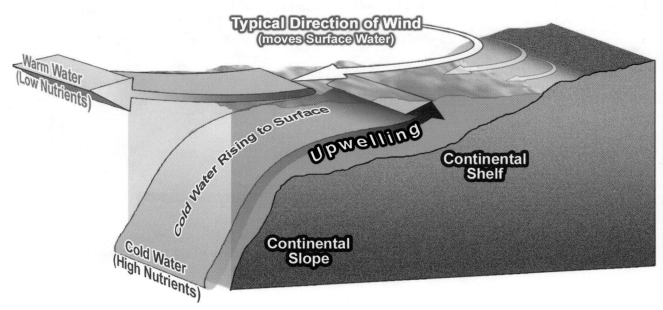

FIGURE 33.53. Upwelling diagram illustrates a scenario when cooler surface waters are exposed. Winds moving water offshore set the stage for this typical environmental condition. In the process, high-nutrient waters rise to the top of the water column.

FIGURE 33.54. Penguins, such as these Macaroni Penguins, and other seabirds are common along the Chilean coasts, where there is tremendous upwelling.

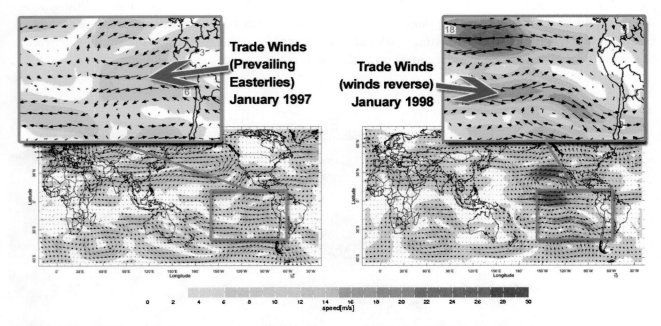

FIGURE 33.55. Surface wind data for January 1997 and January 1998 show varied conditions in the trade winds. When winds blow from west to east, they affect surface sea heights, and drive a potential El Niño event.

During an El Niño event, the trade winds (from east to west) slow down and even reverse. This causes warm water to shift eastward. The warm water piles up and upwelling is reduced or even stopped. The image below shows the sea surface heights for the same area during both a normal year and during an El Niño event. The colors indicate the differences in sea height above and below normal sea levels.

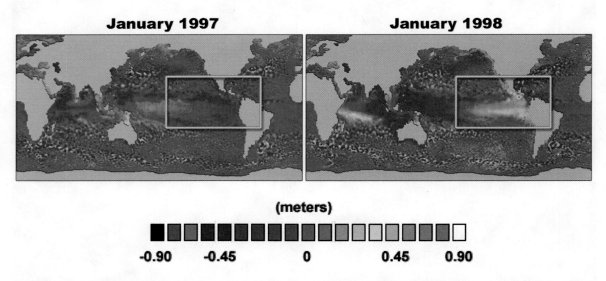

FIGURE 33.56. Sea height anomaly data show higher-than-normal sea heights off of the West Coast of South America in January 1998. This anomaly is characteristic of an El Niño event, which triggers changes in weather patterns around the globe.

In addition to changes at the ocean's surface, water below the surface is affected. Under normal conditions, strong upwelling processes bring cold water near the surface. During an El Niño event, warm water sits atop lower layers; cooler waters do not come to the surface.

While changes due to El Niño events are easiest to discern in the Tropical Pacific, the phenomenon's effects reach around the world. Among the observed short-term climatic change attributed to El Niño, look for the following:

- Cool and wet winters in Florida and other Southern states
- More intense winter storms on the East Coast of North America
- Warmer-than-usual winters in Canada and Alaska
- Extreme rainfall on the West Coast of North America
- A less intense monsoon season in India
- Severe droughts in Australia, parts of Africa, Indonesia, and Brazil

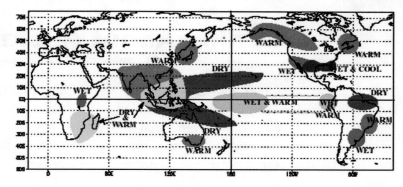

WARM EPISODE RELATIONSHIPS   DECEMBER - FEBRUARY

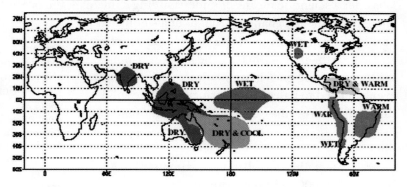

WARM EPISODE RELATIONSHIPS   JUNE - AUGUST

FIGURE 33.57. The effects of an El Niño event are felt around the world, for up to 18 months.

18. Copy the table below into your notebook. Compare and contrast the following oceanic and atmospheric conditions in the Tropical Pacific during normal and El Niño conditions.

	Normal	El Niño
Wind		
SST		
Upwelling		
Sea Heights		

19. How do you think El Niño events affect productivity in the Eastern Pacific?

20. The Humboldt Current supports a thriving fishing community. How might this industry be affected during an El Niño event?

Learning About Ancient Climates

The 143-meter (~469-foot) *JOIDES Resolution*, better known as the *JR* by those who have sailed aboard her, is a seagoing research vessel that drills cylindrical core samples and collects measurements from beneath the ocean floor. The ship provides scientists with evidence of Earth's development over the last 180 million years. Data generated in the *JR's* labs offer a scientific means of understanding climate and environmental change throughout a significant part of our planet's history—a research subject often termed Earth's **paleoclimate**. The *JR's* core samples are the "smoking gun" in evaluating many historical events related to paleoclimate, changes in the solid earth, and more—the extinction of the dinosaurs, for example.

Over 20 years, the *JR* drilled approximately 2,000 holes and 40,000 sediment cores in the ocean. Between 2007 and 2009, the ship was completely rebuilt with exciting new laboratories and equipment, new structural improvements, and living spaces that are more comfortable during the average two-month expedition for its approximately 60 scientists and 65 crew members. That's a long time to be away from home!

Credit: Integrated Ocean Drilling Program's Deep Earth Academy

Why "*JOIDES Resolution*"? The research vessel is named for the *HMS Resolution*, commanded by Captain James Cook over 200 years ago, which explored the Pacific Ocean, its islands, and the Antarctic Region. Like her namesake, the purpose of our current *Resolution* is to sail for scientific exploration. This time, those discoveries lie beneath the ocean floor.

FIGURE 33.58. This core sample from the bottom of the ocean provides remarkable evidence of an asteroid impact on the Yucatán Peninsula 65 million years ago, when dinosaurs went extinct. In geologic time, this was the Cretaceous-Tertiary Boundary. The *JOIDES Resolution* obtained the core 480 kilometers (~298 miles) east of Florida, over 1,920 kilometers (~1,193 miles) from the now-buried impact crater. The core was drilled 2,658 meters (~8,720 feet) below the ocean surface, and 128 meters (~420 feet) below the ocean floor. The layers include fossils, and are punctuated by dust and ash fallout, as well as material blasted from the crater.

Animals and Anomalies

As climate affects people and coral, it affects other animals, too. Climate change can be monitored by looking at SST data and chlorophyll data and watching for El Niño events. Learning to use imagery to see how their environments affect animals is an activity you can perform, just as scientist researchers will do.

2005 was not an El Niño year, but it was unusually warm in the North Pacific. Scientists were very interested in examining how animals such as pinnipeds (e.g., seals, sea lions) behaved during that time, and whether their travel patterns were any different than in years of average SSTs.

FIGURE 33.59. California Sea Lions swimming on the surface in the Cordell Bank National Marine Sanctuary.

See Page 694 for how to access e-Tools.

Cyberlab

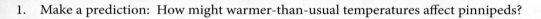

View the *California Sea Lion Interactive Map* from the e-Tools.

e-Tools

1. Make a prediction: How might warmer-than-usual temperatures affect pinnipeds?

2. Based on the maps, how do the Sea Lions' tracks differ in 2005 from their normal paths? (*Hint: Be sure to zoom in to the area of Sea Lions' locations.*)

3. How is the SST in this area in 2005 different from other years?

4. Why might the animals respond in this way to the anomalous conditions?

5. Use your answer to make a prediction about the following Question: How might California Sea Lions respond to an El Niño event? Use evidence from your investigation of the animals' tracks to support your prediction.

Evaluate

1. How would you describe what El Niño is to a middle school student?

2. Prepare a poster, PowerPoint presentation, or speech about the observed and predicted effects of global climate change. Include:

    *   3 pieces of evidence that Earth is warming
    *   3 natural or anthropogenic causes of global climate change
    *   2 predicted effects of global climate change
    *   1 way in which marine organisms could be affected by global climate change

34

Protecting Marine Habitats

INSIDE:

MPAs in the Hawaiian Islands

National and International Waters

International Cooperation for
Resource Management

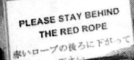

PLEASE STAY BEHIND
THE RED ROPE
赤いロープの後ろに下がって
下さい

Objectives

You will be able to:

✓ **Explain the importance of ocean literacy.**

✓ **Describe the functions of Marine Protected Areas (MPAs).**

✓ **Use scientific data to design new MPAs.**

Benchmarks

1h. Although the ocean is large, it is finite and resources are limited.

6e. Humans affect the ocean in a variety of ways. Laws, regulations, and resource management affect what is taken out and put into the ocean. Human development and activity leads to pollution (e.g., point source, nonpoint source, noise pollution) and physical modifications (e.g., changes to beaches, shores, and rivers). In addition, humans have removed most of the large vertebrates from the ocean.

6g. Everyone is responsible for caring for the ocean. The ocean sustains life on Earth, and humans must live in ways that sustain the ocean. Individual and collective actions are needed to effectively manage ocean resources for all.

7a. The ocean is the last and largest unexplored place on Earth; less than 5% of it has been explored. This is the great frontier for the next generation's explorers and researchers, where they will find great opportunities for inquiry and investigation.

7c. Over the last 40 years, use of ocean resources has increased significantly, therefore the future sustainability of ocean resources depends on our understanding of those resources and their potential and limitations.

7d. New technologies, sensors, and tools are expanding our ability to explore the ocean. Ocean scientists are relying more and more on satellites, drifters, buoys, subsea observatories, and unmanned submersibles.

Engage

In Lesson 1: Diving Into Ocean Ecosystems, you drew a picture of the ocean. Now it is time to complete this exercise again.

1. What do you picture when you consider the ocean's waters? Draw a sketch of what you think about when you picture the ocean.

2. In 4–5 sentences, list reasons you think the ocean is important.

3. Compare today's drawing with the drawing you completed in Lesson 1. Describe how the sketches differ.

4. In Lesson 1, you were also asked to note reasons the ocean is important. How has your understanding of the ocean evolved over this course of study?

FIGURE 34.1. We are constantly learning more about our ocean, and there is still so much to be discovered. Use these Questions to consider what you have learned about the ocean.

There is a growing movement in the United States and the world for students and citizens to know and understand more about the ocean. An understanding of the ocean's influence on you and your influence on the ocean is called **ocean literacy**. The goal of ocean literacy is for a person to be able to make important personal and societal decisions related to the ocean.

5. What personal decisions do you make that relate to the ocean?

6. What societal decisions related to the ocean are currently being made, either in the United States or worldwide?

When it comes to using our natural resources—whether renewable or nonrenewable—it is important to consider the scientific bases on which the decisions are made. We are all responsbile for caring for the ocean. Decision-makers (i.e., politicians, community members) often call upon science advisors for help in understanding key scientific principles. These advisors try to present unbiased data, models, and predictions with the hope of helping people make the best possible decisions that seem reasonable to all parties involved.

Ongoing decisions are being made with regard to marine protected areas (MPAs). On land, there are many protected areas. These include small local sites, such as gardens or bird sanctuaries, as well as huge National Parks. Since the ocean is so immense and borders so many nations, it is difficult to protect. The ocean is also largely unexplored. Scientists estimate that only 5% of the ocean has been explored thus far. The total area of international MPAs is minuscule compared with the expanse of the Earth covered by ocean. In this Lesson, you will read about some MPAs, and then use data to design a new one, simulating the decision making that can occur at a level such as county or state, or, at the federal level, by Congress.

The official federal definition of an MPA is: "any area of the marine environment that has been reserved by federal, state, tribal, territorial, or local laws or regulations to provide lasting protection for part or all of the natural and cultural resources therein."

– Executive Order 13158 (May 2000)

Explore

MPAs in the Hawaiian Islands

In your team, you will be discussing the issues that affect marine animals and their homes in the waters of the Hawaiian Islands. Hawaii is an interesting case study because it is the site of two very different MPAs: 1) the Hawaiian Islands Humpback Whale National Marine Sanctuary and 2) the Papahānaumokuākea Marine National Monument (pronounced: pa-pa-ha-now-mō-coo-ah-KAY-ah).

FIGURE 34.2. Bathymetric map showing the Hawaiian Islands Humpback Whale National Marine Sanctuary and the Papahānaumokuākea Marine National Monument. Each is outlined in red.

Hawaii is a remarkable place. The islands are always changing because of volcanic processes (e.g., eruptions), weathering, and erosion (e.g., landslides). Not all of the islands are experiencing volcanic activity at the present time. Currently the locus of that activity is ongoing on the southeastern side of the Big Island of Hawaii and on Loihi, which is currently a seamount. The remainder of the Hawaiian Islands are experiencing weathering and erosion, including landslides. The mountainous islands have fertile soil, gushing waterfalls, lush rainforests, and beautiful beaches. Surrounding the islands are coral reefs teeming with life and supporting a strong food web that includes Tiger Sharks, Humpback Whales, Hawaiian Monk Seals, and Black-footed Albatross. Your first task is to examine how different animals are using both of the MPAs.

FIGURE 34.3. The Hawaiian Islands are dynamic because of interactions between all of Earth's spheres. The volcanic islands reaching above the ocean waters that teem with life above and below sea level have high biodiversity.

See Page 694 for how to access e-Tools.

Cyberlab

Materials:

- *Hawaiian Animal Areas Maps I and II*
- Colored pencils
- Atlases (*optional*)

With your team, follow the instructions below.

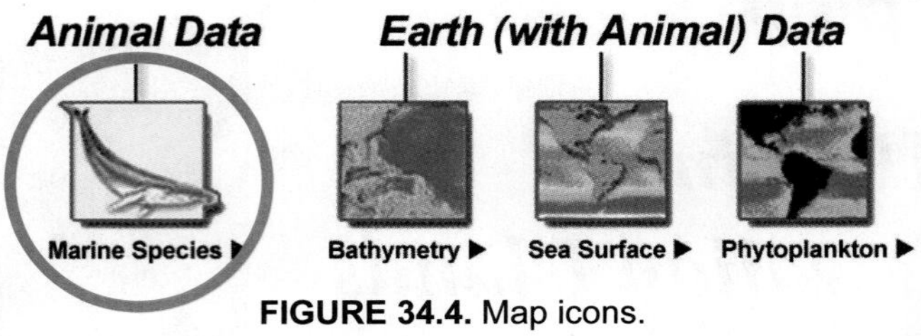

1. On the *Marine Science: The Dynamic Ocean* website, go to "Animal Movement Maps and Data" and choose Marine Species.

Animal Data   **Earth (with Animal) Data**

Marine Species ▶   Bathymetry ▶   Sea Surface ▶   Phytoplankton ▶

FIGURE 34.4. Map icons.

2. Click on any of the Hawaiian animals, current or archived. These may include Tiger Sharks, Black-footed Albatross, False Killer Whales, Short-finned Pilot Whales, Hawaiian Monk Seals, and others.

   Note: You must be logged in to view some of these maps and data.

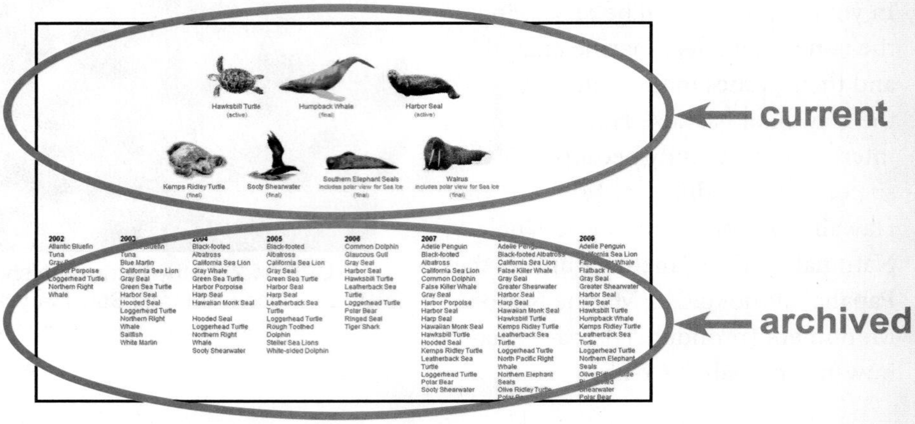

FIGURE 34.5. Screenshot showing where to find current and archived species.

3. First observe all of the individual animals' tracks for a particular species if available for a particular year. Do not simply consider a single animal.

4. On both *Hawaiian Animal Areas Maps I and II*, shade and label areas that show where each of the individual tracked animals for this first species traveled during the year you chose to observe.

5. Use a different color or symbol and perform this activity for 1–2 additional species for any year, noting it on the key provided.

   Alternatively, observe the tracks of some of these species from a different year, if available. To change species or year, click on the "Select Different Species" icon.

6. Describe the locations of these animal tracks in relation to each of the two MPAs in the Hawaiian Islands. Are the animals mostly traveling within the MPAs, or not? Does this vary by species? Explain.

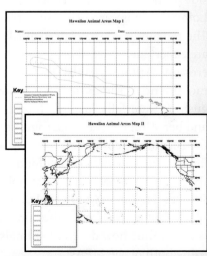

FIGURE 34.6. Screenshots of *Hawaiian Animal Areas Map I and II.*

Explain

Voyagers on sailing canoes arrived in the Hawaiian Islands from Polynesia as early as 300 C.E. and continued to arrive in groups for centuries to follow. These people settled throughout the Hawaiian island chain, or **archipelago** (pronounced: ahr-keh-PĔL-uh-go), and are now known as Native Hawaiians.

As you have learned, there are many marine protected areas (MPAs), including our National Marine Sanctuaries and Marine National Monuments. All of these special areas are contained within the United States' waters. Other countries have similar Marine Protected Areas. According to NOAA:

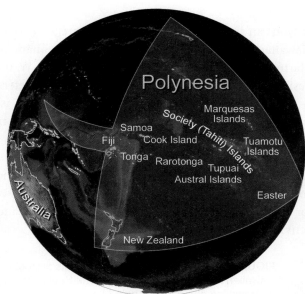

FIGURE 34.7. Today's Native Hawaiians are descendants of peoples from throughout Polynesia.

> *"The primary objective of a sanctuary is to protect its natural and cultural features while allowing people to use and enjoy the ocean in a sustainable way."*

There are a few ways to establish a new National Marine Sanctuary. Congress or the nation's Department of Commerce may designate new sanctuaries. The President may also create Marine National Monuments.

National Marine Sanctuaries offer special protection for animals within them. When a sanctuary is designated, site-specific rules are created to limit activities that could hurt the sanctuary ecosystem. Examples of rules include: 1) not allowing wastes to be released (e.g., from boats) and 2) not allowing the seafloor to be disturbed by dredging or anchoring. Sanctuary managers can issue permits for some types of activities that are otherwise prohibited. For example, a permit may be issued to place an oceanographic buoy in the ocean at a place that is attached to the seafloor, in order to collect scientific information. A permitted activity such as this is done with minimal impact to the habitat. It must also show a benefit to the public.

Sanctuaries also provide places for people to enjoy the ocean via boating, swimming, scuba diving, exploring, and fishing and to educate people about the importance of conserving marine resources.

The Hawaiian Islands Humpback Whale National Marine Sanctuary is an MPA located in the main Hawaiian Islands (see FIGURE 34.9 on the next page). The 3,600 square kilometers (1,400 square miles) was established to protect important breeding grounds for Humpback Whales.

FIGURE 34.8. Islanders throughout Polynesia used traditional double-hulled sailing canoes. Today, Native Hawaiian sailors are retracing their routes on ships such as the *Hokulea*, shown here.

As you can see from the online maps, there are two MPAs in Hawaiian waters. The second MPA is the Papahānaumokuākea Marine National Monument. President George W. Bush designated this area of over 362,074 square kilometers (~139,797 square miles) in 2006. This type of MPA is different from a National Marine Sanctuary. Fishing is much more closely regulated within the Monument area. In fact, as of June 2011, commercial fishing in Monument waters will be completely phased out, meaning that no fishing or shellfish collecting will be allowed. In addition, shipping lanes, drilling for resources such as oil and gas, dumping wastes, and other activities are limited within the Monument.

FIGURE 34.9. Map showing the the Hawaiian Islands Humpback Whale National Marine Sanctuary and the Papahānaumokuākea Marine National Monument. Each is outlined in red.

FIGURE 34.10. Among the many animals protected in the Northwestern Hawaiian Islands, the Hawaiian Monk Seal is one of the most endangered. Its Hawaiian name is "Ilio-holo-i-ka-uaua" (pronounced: ee-lee-ō-hō-lahw-ee-kay-oo-ă-oo-ă), which loosely translates to "dog that runs in the waves".

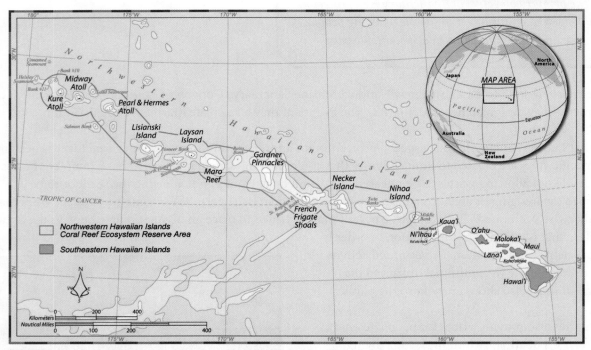

FIGURE 34.11. Map of the Northwestern Hawaiian Islands. The island chain is broken up on the map into the Northwestern Hawaiian Islands and the Southeastern Hawaiian Islands.

The Papahānaumokuākea Marine National Monument is culturally important to Native Hawaiians. The Northwestern Hawaiian Islands (NWHI), including Nihoa Island, Laysan Island, and Midway Atoll, are considered to be *kupuna* (pronounced: koo-POON-uh) islands, or ancestors.

Hoʻokuleana (pronounced: hō-ō-koo-lee-AH-nah) is a Hawaiian word that means "to take responsibility". Native Hawaiians believe that it is their responsibility to care for their natural and cultural resources, including the land and sea, as well as the plants and animals that inhabit these areas.

7. Compare and contrast the Marine National Monument and National Marine Sanctuary designations.

National and International Waters

Notice on the map below (from the *Marine Science: The Dynamic Ocean* website) that there are areas in blue off the coast of different countries. There are also lines that separate the waters near each country. Every country has special rights to use its own coastal waters and offshore resources. A country is allowed to make its own rules for its own respective geographic areas. For instance, countries make decisions about who is able to use or not use the waters for fishing and selling their catch, as well as decisions about other activities. The area "owned" by a specific country is a country's Exclusive Economic Zone, or EEZ. Most of these areas extend 200 miles (~322 kilometers) from each country's coastline. Areas outside of any country's EEZ are referred to as *international waters* (white areas on the map).

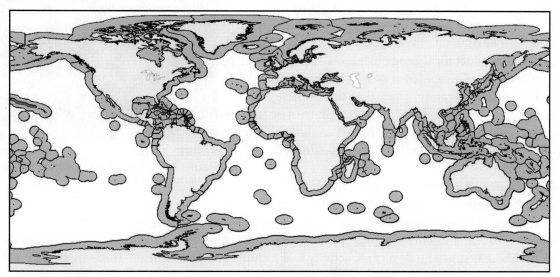

FIGURE 34.12. Map of global Exclusive Economic Zones (EEZs). Countries create their own regulations for these marine areas off of their coasts.

Within the United States EEZ, the country has put many rules in place to try to reduce the problems of bycatch and overfishing. For example, fishers must fish for certain fish during specific seasons. This regulation may give some species of fish time to reproduce, thus preventing the species from becoming overfished. At other times, the regulation is in place to prevent bycatch, the accidental killing of other species.

One important regulation within the United States EEZ is that no foreign longline vessels can legally operate within this zone. This regulation is in effect because the U.S. cannot easily enforce how fishers from other countries catch fish or whether they use methods that prevent bycatch. So the United States protects the environment by banning foreign fisheries from entering these areas. Many other countries do not have stringent requirements about safer fishing methods, or their use is voluntary.

As you have learned, NOAA has established many MPAs, including National Marine Sanctuaries and a Marine National Monument. All of these special areas are contained within the United States' EEZ.

FIGURE 34.13. Regulations in United States EEZs restrict the type of fishing gear permitted. New technology is helping reduce bycatch. This Loggerhead Turtle is escaping a net fitted with a turtle excluder device (TED). The TED consists of a series of bars that act like a door, allowing a turtle, shark, or other large animal to swim and leave the net.

International Cooperation for Resource Management

International agreements for responsible fishing have been established in the Pacific Ocean. Nations have formed Regional Fisheries Management Organizations (RFMOs). RFMOs encourage nations to agree that fishing should be sustainable, even in international waters. One problem in international waters is that many countries can fish in them without anyone overseeing fishing activities. Keeping fishing in the area sustainable so that the ecosystems in the area are not destroyed can be difficult. Even though the RFMOs have created a code of conduct for fishing businesses, this code is voluntary. It is enforced simply by trust and the hope that fishers will be honest and careful when they fish in these areas. The issue is whether to continue to rely on trust or to make stronger laws making fishers and others accountable for their actions, to ensure that ecosystems are not damaged.

FIGURE 34.14. The crab fishery in the North Pacific is managed through Regional Fisheries Management Organizations.

While strong cooperative efforts have protected marine resources in the Atlantic and Pacific Oceans, protecting resources in the polar oceans has been difficult. The Continent of Antarctica, however, has a long history of international resource management efforts. Earth's southernmost continent has tall mountain ranges and huge glaciers. There is substantial volcanic activity and tectonic plate movement. There are deserts and ice—lots of ice. Sea ice and freshwater ice make up 98% of the landscape. Much of Antarctica is perennially covered by very thick ice, and therefore its lands have been difficult to study. Many nations have established research bases on Antarctica in order to conduct scientific studies of the continent. In fact, countries have agreed to maintain Antarctica as an internationally important place for learning more about our planet and its

history. In 1959, twelve nations signed the Antarctic Treaty, in which all agreed that the continent would be shared between nations for research purposes and that no military action would be allowed there, nor can any country claim exclusive rights to the land. The treaty also prohibits dumping waste on or near Antarctica. Today, nearly 50 countries have signed the Antarctic Treaty, which is summarized in the following statements:

FIGURE 34.15. The Antarctic landscape as seen here across McMurdo Sound is dominated by snow and ice, but the bottom of the world also boasts mountains, valleys, and other features.

Antarctic Treaty – A Summary

[The Treaty covers Earth's Polar Region south of 60° S latitude.]

1. No military use shall be made of Antarctica, though military personnel and equipment may be used for peaceful purposes.

2. There will be complete freedom of scientific investigation.

3. Antarctic Treaty Nations will exchange plans for their scientific programmes, scientific data will be freely available, and scientists will be exchanged between expeditions where practical.

4. No activities under the Treaty will affect claims to sovereignty of any part of Antarctica made by any nation. All territorial claims are put aside for the duration of the Treaty.

5. Nuclear explosions and nuclear waste disposal are banned from Antarctica.

6. The Treaty applies to all land and ice shelves south of 60° South, but not to the seas.

7. All Antarctic stations and all ships and aircraft supplying Antarctica shall be open to inspectors from any Treaty nation.

8. Observers and exchange scientists shall be under the jurisdiction of their own country regardless of which national station they may visit. National laws do not apply to stations or areas, but only to the citizens of those countries.

9. Treaty nations will meet to consider ways of furthering the principles and objectives of the Treaty. Attendance at these meetings shall be limited to those countries that are engaged in substantial scientific research activity in Antarctica. Unanimous approval will be necessary for any new measures to become effective (i.e., everyone has to agree).

10. All Treaty Nations will try to ensure that no one carries out any activity in Antarctica that is against the Treaty.

11. Any dispute by Treaty Nations, if not settled by agreement, shall be determined by the International Court of Justice.

12. The Treaty may be modified at any time by unanimous agreement. After 30 years any consultative Party may call for a conference to review the operation of the Treaty. The Treaty may be modified at this conference by a majority decision.

13. The Treaty must be legally ratified (agreed to) by any nation wishing to join. Any member of the United Nations may join as well as any other country invited to do so by the Treaty Nations. All notices and records are deposited with the Archives of the United States of America.

14. The Treaty translated into English, French, Russian, and Spanish was signed on 1st December 1959 by 12 states and entered into force on 23rd of June 1961.

Credit: coolantarctica.com

Scientists are concerned that animals in the Antarctic are under increased pressures. Climate change is changing the patterns of sea ice, and therefore the habitats and food webs. Commercial fishing boats from a variety of nations have come to Antarctic waters to catch krill and cold water fish species. Ships from some nations also practice whaling in the area. In some cases, species have been overfished, which of course affects the entire ecosystem. In 1982, the Convention on the Conservation of Antarctic Marine Living Resources (CCAMLR) was created as a part of the Antarctic Treaty. The purpose of the CCAMLR was to agree upon fishing practices in the sea around Antarctica, to prevent overfishing and bycatch. Unfortunately, this agreement is hard to enforce, and there are many reports of illegal fishing practices. Some scientists say that the CCAMLR agreements are not strong enough and that the regulations are too loose. They believe that stricter rules must be created and enforced, and that rules regarding accountability must be established.

FIGURE 34.16. A mother Giant Petrel watches while U.S. Antarctic Program scientists weigh her chick. Bird surveys are conducted to track population numbers, sizes, and other characteristics.

8. Why is it so difficult to enact and enforce laws in international waters?

Elaborate

See Page 694 for how to access e-Tools.

Cyberlab

Your group will be assigned one of the two case studies: 1) Arctic Mammals or 2) Animals of the Antarctic. The ultimate goal is to design a new MPA based on data and your understandings of MPAs, EEZs, and so on. The Cyberlab will lead you through this process.

Materials:

- *Arctic Region Sea Ice Worksheet*
- *Antarctic Region Sea Ice Worksheet*

Case Study 1: Mammals of the Arctic

There are many different issues facing marine animals and their habitats. In the Arctic, scientists are concerned about the polar ecosystems involving animals such as Polar Bears, walruses, and Arctic seal species (e.g., Harp Seals, Bearded Seals, Ringed Seals). At this time, there are no MPAs in areas where Arctic marine mammals make their homes. However, there are protected areas on Arctic land (e.g., state forests, National Wildlife Refuges, National Parks).

Your team will be asked to design an MPA appropriate to protecting Arctic mammals and their habitats. You will be required to support your design with what you have learned about animals and physical processes in the ocean.

With your team, discuss and answer the following Questions:

1. Animals that live in the icy world of the Arctic are very special. They are well adapted to living in the harsh polar seas, using ice, ocean, and land as their habitat. What are some current threats to Arctic habitats? If necessary, do some research online about this issue.

2. Diagram a typical Arctic Ocean food web.

One of the most significant features of the physical Arctic ecosystems or habitats is the **sea ice**—ice on the surface of the ocean. You can use maps and data to examine the ice.

3. Go to the *Marine Science: The Dynamic Ocean* website.

   a. Click on "Animal Movement Maps and Data" and choose "Sea Surface".

   b. Click on any of the Arctic (not Antarctic) species from any year—these may include Polar Bear, walrus, Ringed Seal, Harp Seal,, and so on.

      Note: You must be logged in to view some of these maps and data.

   c. At the top of the map, choose "Sea Ice".

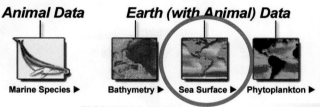

FIGURE 34.17. Map icons.

Walrus
includes polar view for Sea Ice
(active)

FIGURE 34.18. Example of Arctic mammal species icon.

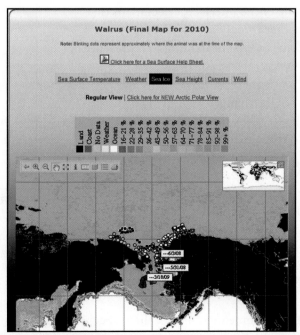

FIGURE 34.19. The "Sea Ice" link is located at the top of the map.

The colors on the Sea Ice Concentration map in FIGURE 34.20 indicate the percentage of a square area (4 kilometers × 4 kilometers) that is covered by sea ice. So if an area is essentially covered by sea ice, it is considered to be 99+%. This means that the ocean in this area is completely frozen over. Remember that even though the ocean's surface may be frozen, there is still plenty of liquid water underneath.

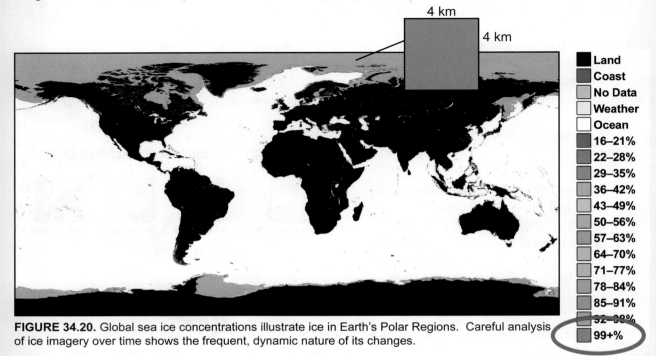

FIGURE 34.20. Global sea ice concentrations illustrate ice in Earth's Polar Regions. Careful analysis of ice imagery over time shows the frequent, dynamic nature of its changes.

4. Use the ***Arctic Region Ice Worksheet*** and the latest available maps and views. On the Sea Ice Concentration map, shade in the area of the ocean that is currently covered completely by ice (99+%).

5. Using the dates on the left side of the interface, select maps that represent ice in each of the other three seasons. On the same worksheet, use a different color or type of shading to represent each season.

6. Describe in words how the sea ice changes with the seasons.

7. Why is sea ice important to Arctic mammals?

8. From "Animal Movement Maps and Data", now choose a species of Arctic mammal. On the Arctic Mammal Areas map, shade areas where the tracked animals have traveled during the year you are observing.

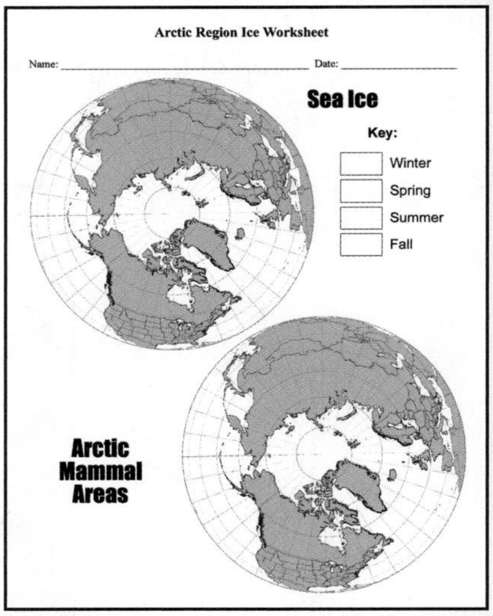

9. Click on "Select Different Species" at the top of the screen. Now choose a different Arctic mammal species and repeat Step 8.

10. In addition, observe the tracks of some members of these species from previous years and add to your shading as necessary.

FIGURE 34.21. Screenshot of the ***Arctic Region Ice Worksheet***.

Select Different Species

FIGURE 34.22. "Select Different Species" icon.

11. Go to the Exclusive Economic Zone Map.

    a. Within which country's EEZs did the Arctic mammals travel?

    b. Why do you think it is important to consider the amount of time that Arctic mammals spend within different EEZs?

    c. What do the EEZs have to do with creating an MPA?

    d. How might an MPA in the Arctic protect mammals there?

12. What might be some of the costs and benefits of designating an MPA in the Arctic?

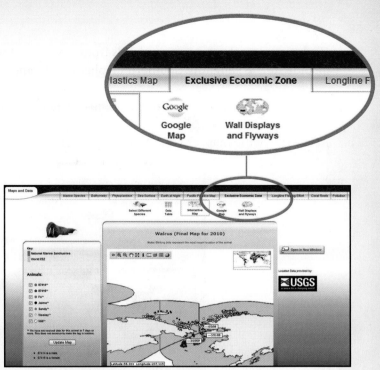

FIGURE 34.23. There is a link to the EEZ Map at the top of the screen.

Case Study 2: Animals of the Antarctic

There are many different issues involving marine animals and their habitats. In Antarctic waters, scientists are concerned about the polar ecosystems of animals including penguins, seals, whales, and so on. At this time, there are no MPAs in Antarctic waters, and the Antarctic Treaty applies only to land. Your team will be asked to design an MPA appropriate to protecting Antarctic mammals and their habitats. You will be required to support your design with what you have learned about animals and physical processes in the ocean.

With your team, discuss and answer the following Questions.

1. Animals that live in the icy world of the Antarctic are very special. They are well adapted to living in the harsh polar seas, using ice, ocean, and land as their habitat. What are some current threats to Antarctic habitats? If necessary, do some research online about this issue.

2. Diagram a typical Antarctic food web.

One of the most significant physical features of the Antarctic ecosystems or habitats along the coast of Antarctica is the sea ice—ice on the surface of the ocean at the edge of the continent. You can utilize maps and data to examine the ice.

3. Go to the *Marine Science: The Dynamic Ocean* website.

    a. Click on "Animal Movement Maps and Data" and choose "Sea Surface".

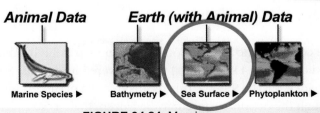

FIGURE 34.24. Map icons.

b. Click on any of the Antarctic animals from any year—these may include Adélie Penguins, Southern Elephant Seals, and so on.

Note: You must be logged in to view some of these maps.

c. At the top of the map, choose "Sea Ice".

Southern Elephant Seals
includes polar view for Sea Ice
(active)

FIGURE 34.25. Example of Antarctic mammal species icon.

FIGURE 34.26. The "Sea Ice" link is located at the top of the map.

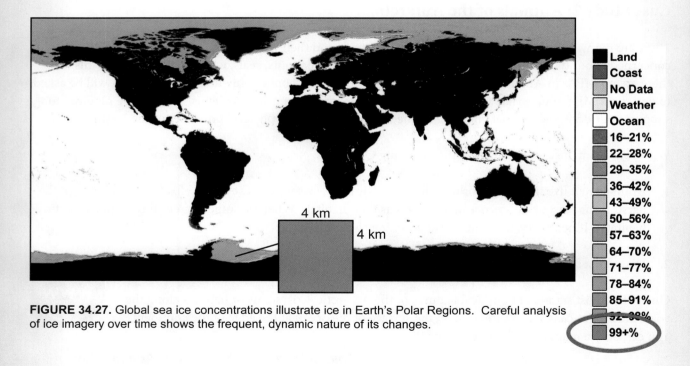

FIGURE 34.27. Global sea ice concentrations illustrate ice in Earth's Polar Regions. Careful analysis of ice imagery over time shows the frequent, dynamic nature of its changes.

The colors on the Sea Ice Concentration map in FIGURE 34.27 indicate the percentage of a square area (4 kilometers × 4 kilometers) that is covered by sea ice. So if an area is essentially covered by sea ice, it is considered to be 99+%. This means that the ocean in this area is completely frozen over. Remember that even though the ocean's surface may be frozen, there is still plenty of liquid water underneath.

4. Use the *Antarctic Region Ice Worksheet* and the latest available maps and views. On the Sea Ice Concentration map, shade in the area of the ocean that is currently covered completely by ice (99+%).

5. Using the dates on the left side of the interface, select maps to represent ice in each of the other three seasons. On the same worksheet, use a different color or type of shading to represent each season.

6. Describe in words how the sea ice changes with the season.

7. Why is sea ice important to animals in the Antarctic?

8. From "Animal Movement Maps and Data", now choose a species of Antarctic mammal. On the Antarctic Mammal Areas map, shade areas where the tracked animals have traveled during the year you are observing.

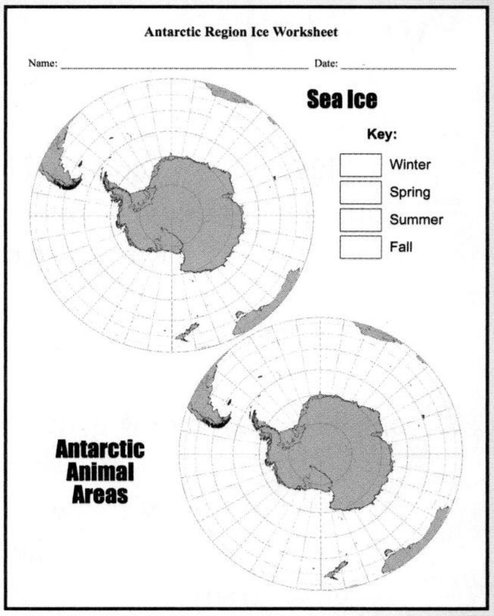

9. Click on "Select Different Species" at the top of the screen. Now choose a different Antarctic animal species and repeat Step 8.

10. In addition, observe the tracks of some members of these species from previous years and add to your shading as necessary.

11. How might an MPA in the Antarctic protect animals there?

12. What might be some costs and benefits of designating an MPA in the Antarctic?

FIGURE 34.28. Screenshot of the *Antarctic Region Ice Worksheet*.

FIGURE 34.29. "Select Different Species" icon.

FIGURE 34.30. A Southern Elephant Seal roars for the camera. Most of these pinnipeds' lives are spent at sea. They climb onto land mostly for breeding and molting.

Evaluate

1. Design an MPA based on the scientific data (e.g., sea ice, tracking data) you analyzed in the **Elaborate** section and from other online resources. Create a poster that describes your proposal. Your poster must include the following:

   a. A map of the proposed MPA

   b. Justification of why the team has chosen the proposed area

   c. A list of species that would be protected and reasons why an MPA is needed in the area (e.g., the MPA will protect biodiversity)

   d. If applicable, a list of nations that would be invited to share in decision making with respect to the proposed area

   e. A list of proposed rules for the MPA and reasons for enacting the rules, drawing upon what you have learned in other Lessons (e.g., fisheries regulation, pollution prevention, oil and gas exploration)

   In addition, your poster should be well organized and aesthetically pleasing.

2. Present your poster to the class. Be persuasive and use scientific data to support your ideas.

FIGURE 34.31. Polar Bears in the Arctic are very dependent on sea ice. Sea ice has markedly declined in recent years.

FIGURE 34.32. The scientific research vessel *Nathaniel B. Palmer* in Barilari Bay, Antarctic Peninsula. The ship was on a two-month expedition to the Larsen B. Embayment once occupied by a major ice shelf. In 2002, a portion of the ice shelf, approximately the size of Rhode Island, collapsed and left only a shard of the ice from it and a rapidly changed ecosystem in its wake. The ice shelf had been in place for at least 10,000 years.

3. Using the rubric below, evaluate each group's poster.

MPA Designation Rubric   Group Members' Names_____

Criteria/Score	4	3	2	1
Map of MPA	Area designated as MPA is clearly defined and well supported by scientific data, including animal tracking, sea ice data, and other sources.	Area designated as MPA is clearly defined and supported by scientific data, including animal tracking and sea ice data.	Area designated as MPA is clearly defined and supported by some scientific data.	Area designated as MPA is not well defined or not supported with scientific data.
Reasons for Protection	Poster cites clear and scientifically sound reasons why the MPA is needed. Specific species are noted, and poster/presentation thoroughly describes how species will benefit from MPA designation.	Poster cites scientifically sound reasons why the MPA is needed. Specific species are noted, and poster/presentation describes how species will benefit from MPA designation.	Poster cites reasons why the MPA is needed or specific species are noted. Description of how species will benefit from MPA designation is not thorough.	Reasons for the MPA are inadequate and/or it is unclear how specific species will benefit from MPA designation.
List of Proposed Rules	Rules are reasonable, scientifically sound and likely to be agreed upon by national and international decision makers.	Rules are reasonable and scientifically sound, but may be controversial with decision makers.	Rules lack scientific soundness and/or are unreasonable.	Rules are not indicated and/or are not based in scientific understanding.
Organization and Aesthetics	Poster is extremely well organized and aesthetically pleasing.	Poster is well organized and aesthetically pleasing.	Poster has some organizational problems.	Poster is poorly organized.

Appendix A

How to Access e-Tools and Website

e-Tools

The *e-Tools* are organized by Lesson on the DVD and are also on the *Marine Science: The Dynamic Ocean* website. The DVD includes files that can be loaded onto the school network for easy access during class time. This prevents the burden on school bandwidth as dozens of students may be downloading animations and videos simultaneously. You can also log in to the *Marine Science: The Dynamic Ocean* website to access *e-Tools* from home or school.

To access *e-Tools* from the DVD:

1. Launch the *Marine Science: The Dynamic Ocean e-Tools* from the DVD or, if it is installed on a computer or network, double-click on the Desktop icon.
2. Select the Phase (*see Figure A*). Lessons 1–25 are in Phase I; Lessons 26 and 27 are in Phase II; and Lesson 28–34 are in Phase III.
3. Select the Lesson (*see Figure B*).
4. The default tab is **Media** (*see Figure C*), which includes videos, animations, and interactive data tools. Click on a resource in the list to open. You may also access the figures from each Lesson under the **Figures** tab. Worksheets, such as graphic organizers, are located under the **Activity & Lab Worksheets** tab. The **Links** tab will direct you to the website for accessing online resources.

FIGURE A.

Note: Some *e-Tools*, particularly those required for Cyberlabs, require Internet access, even when accessed via the DVD. These are marked with a "www" icon as seen to the right. They are accessed as any other *e-Tool*, but you will need to be connected to the Internet.

www

FIGURE B.

To access *e-Tools* from the website:

1. Go to www.us-satellite.net/marinescience.
2. Select **National Edition**.
3. Select **Student/Demo** Login and log in with the Passcode provided by your teacher.
4. Select the Phase (*see Figure A*). Lessons 1–25 are in Phase I; Lessons 26 and 27 are in Phase II; and Lesson 28–34 are in Phase III.
5. Select the Lesson (*see Figure B*).
6. The default tab is **Media** (*see Figure C*). Click on a resource in the list to open. You may also access images, worksheets, and links by clicking on the tabs labeled **Figures**, **Activity & Lab Worksheets**, and **Links**.

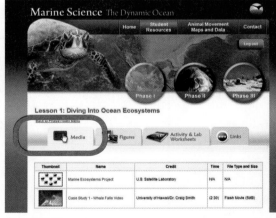

FIGURE C.

How to Access the Signals of Spring Website

In Phase II, you will be doing more extensive research and animal tracking, interpretation of Earth imagery, and writing Analysis Journals.

To access the *Signals of Spring* website:

1. Go to www.us-satellite.net/marinescience.
2. Select **National Edition**.
3. Select **Student/Demo** Login and log in with the Passcode provided by your teacher.
4. Select the Phase II.
5. Click on **Click here to go Signals of Spring** (*see Figure D*).
6. Log in with the Username and Password provided by your teacher.

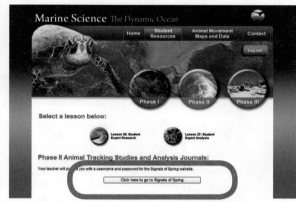

FIGURE D.

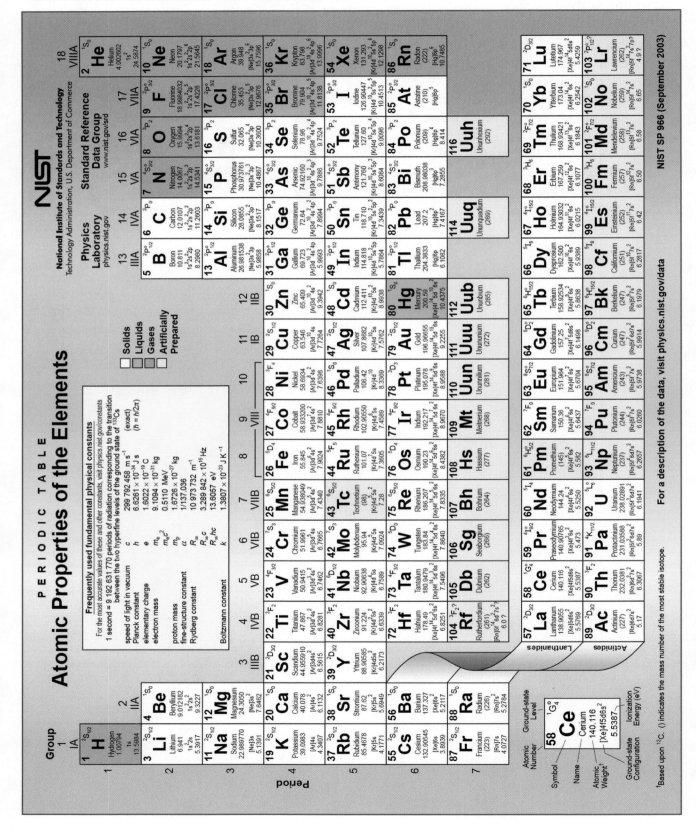

Appendix B

Atomic Properties of the Elements

PERIODIC TABLE

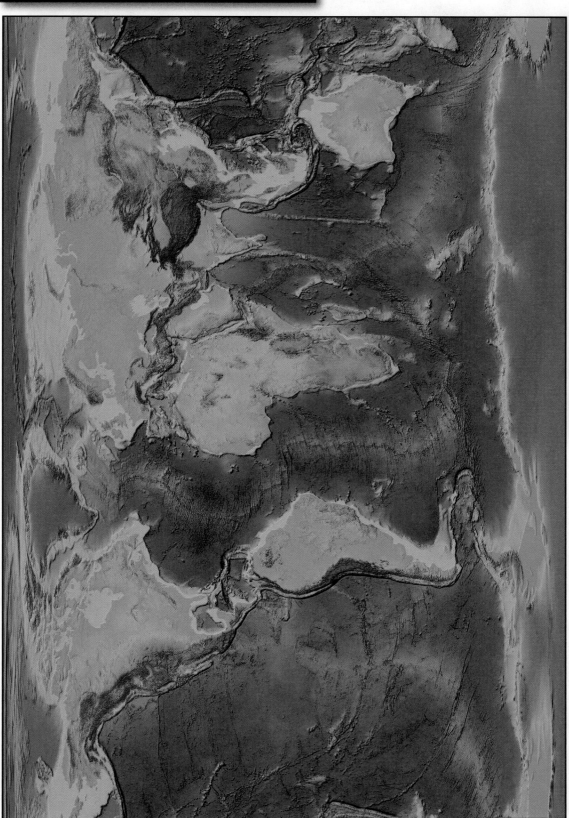

Global Bathymetry Map

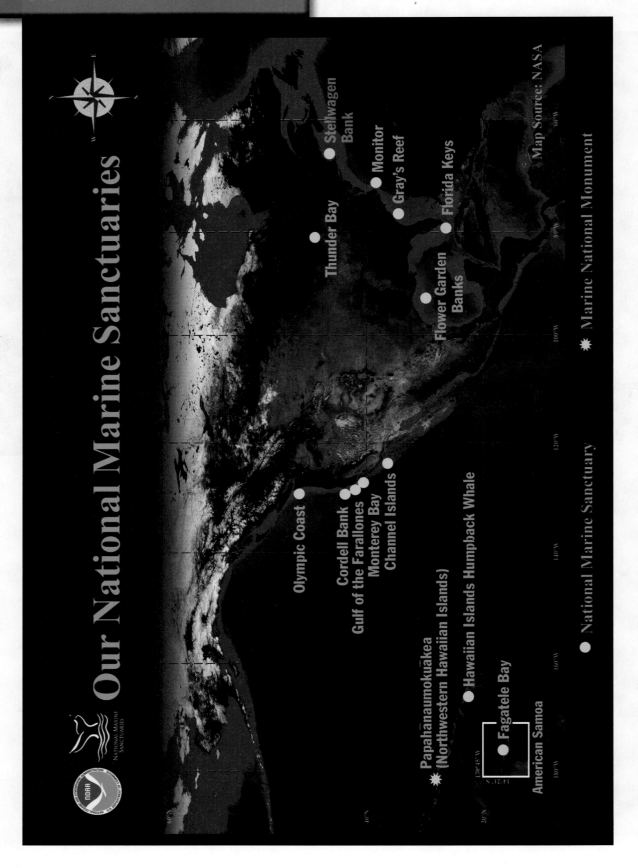

Our National Marine Sanctuaries

- Stellwagen Bank
- Monitor
- Gray's Reef
- Florida Keys
- Thunder Bay
- Flower Garden Banks
- Olympic Coast
- Cordell Bank
- Gulf of the Farallones
- Monterey Bay
- Channel Islands
- Papahānaumokuākea (Northwestern Hawaiian Islands)
- Hawaiian Islands Humpback Whale
- Fagatele Bay
- American Samoa

★ Marine National Monument

● National Marine Sanctuary

Map Source: NASA

Glossary

Symbols

10% rule: an ecological principle that states that only 10% of energy is passed from a lower trophic level to the next

A

abiotic: related to non-living things

adaptation: a characteristic or genetic trait that enhances organisms' reproductive success and survival

air mass: a large volume of air with uniform temperature and humidity

albedo: measure of the reflectivity of Earth's surface

angle of insolation: the angle at which the Sun's rays hit the Earth

anomaly: an observation that is different from what is considered normal; uncommon event

anthropogenic: anything resulting from human activity; human-made or human-caused

antibiotic resistance: the ability of populations of bacteria to evolve in response to antibiotics

aquifer: a natural area in which groundwater collects, usually as water seeps through layers of soil and rock from the Earth's surface

archipelago: an island chain

artificial satellite: object created by humans to orbit the Earth

asexual reproduction: the creation of offspring that are genetically identical to the parent

astrology: the study of celestial bodies and their influence on human activities

atmosphere: layers of gases surrounding a planet, the molecules of which hold thermal energy

atom: the most basic particle of an element that has the properties of that element

autotroph: an organism that makes its own food

Autumnal Equinox: a point in Earth's orbit that causes the greatest amount of solar radiation to be over the Equator and every location on Earth to experience 12 hours of day and 12 hours of night, after summer and before winter; for the Northern Hemisphere, occurs each year on September 22nd or 23rd; sometimes called Fall Equinox

B

baleen: broom-like plates that certain whale species use to filter zooplankton and small fish out of the water

ballast water: water carried in special tanks on ships that is used to provide stability for the vessel

barrier island: long, sandy island that runs parallel to the shore

basin: in the ocean, large water-covered areas between continents

bathymetry: the highs and lows of the seafloor; underwater topography

benthic: having to do with the seafloor

binomial nomenclature: two-name system of classifying species

biodegradable: able to decompose naturally

biodiversity: the number and variety of species within a habitat or area

biogenous: describing sediments that come primarily from living organisms

biogeochemical cycle: the movement of chemical elements or molecules through the Earth's spheres

biological community: all of the living things within an environment

biotic: related to living things

blast fishing: a method of fishing that uses sticks of dynamite to kill fish

bloom: a large increase in the number of phytoplankton over a short period of time

boiling point: the temperature at which a liquid changes to a gas

brackish: water with salt concentrations that are somewhere between those of fresh water and salt water

brevetoxin: a neurotoxin produced by a type of phytoplankton, *Karemia brevis*

budding: a method of asexual reproduction in which the parent divides itself into unequal parts

buoy: a floating device

bycatch: marine organisms that are unintentionally caught by fishers

C

carbohydrate: an organic compound that an organism uses as a main source of energy

carbon cycle: the complex movement of carbon through the Earth's spheres

carrying capacity: the maximum number of individuals of a species that can be supported in a habitat

cellular respiration: the process in which all organisms break down food molecules to release stored energy

chemosynthesis: the process in which an organism uses minerals or chemicals to make sugar (a process of energy production)

chlorophyll: a pigment contained in chloroplasts that is responsible for most photosynthesis in phytoplankton

chloroplast: an organelle that absorbs solar energy (sunlight) and converts it to chemical energy (sugar) using the raw materials carbon dioxide and water

circle hook: a longline hook design that prevents marine animals from becoming ensnared as they pass by

climate: global patterns of weather over time

closed system: a system in which only energy (no matter) is exchanged beyond the system

coastal development: the building of homes and businesses along the coast

coevolution: the occurrence of changes in two or more species over a long period of time in response to each other

cohesion: the property of water molecules that makes them attracted to each other

cold front: a boundary between air masses in which more dense, cold air wedges beneath less dense, warm air

commensalism: a relationship between two species in which one species benefits and one is not helped or harmed

commercial fishery: a company that uses technologies to catch large amounts of fish at sea and then transport them to be sold

common ancestor: the most recent organism or species that two or more different species have evolved from

competition: the struggle between species or within a population for natural resources; a component of the Theory of Evolution by Natural Selection

computer model: a program developed by scientists that makes predictions based on data sets

conclusion: a statement following the analysis of data that supports, fails to support, or contradicts a hypothesis

condensation: the process in which a substance changes from gas to liquid form

conduction: the movement of heat from one material to another through direct contact

conductivity: the ability to carry an electrical charge

consumer: an organism that cannot make its own food and so takes its energy from an external living source

contaminant: any substance that causes harm in an environment; also called pollutant

continental accretion: the process by which new land is added to the edge of existing land; for example, as Florida was added to North America

contour line: a line on a map that connects all points representing the same elevation, or height above sea level

convection: the transfer of heat by the movement of large groups of particles from one place to another; warmer areas lose heat and become cooler, and cooler areas gain heat and become warmer

convergent plate boundary: place where two tectonic plates are moving toward each other and colliding

cooling: the process in which a substance loses heat energy

coral bleaching: a phenomenon that occurs when reef-building corals become stressed, expel their zooxanthellae and, as a result, appear white

Coriolis Effect: the deflection of a mass moving over Earth's surface due to Earth's rotation

cosmogenous: describing sediments originating from particles from Space

covalent bond: a bond between atoms in which two or more electrons are shared among the atoms

crest: the highest point of a wave

crustal plate: a layer and piece of Earth's crust including the top layer of the underlying mantle

CTD device: a device that collects conductivity, temperature, and density data with respect to depth

current: a large mass of continuously moving ocean water

cytoplasm: a jelly-like substance that makes up much of a cell

D

data: facts and information based on observations collected and recorded by scientists

dead zone: a region in coastal waters with little or no oxygen available for living organisms, and so unable to sustain marine life

decompose: to break down; in living matter and some materials, this releases nutrients back into the ecosystem

decomposer: an organism, such as some true bacteria and fungi, that breaks down dead organisms and converts organic materials back into nutrients available to ecosystems

Deep-ocean Assessment and Reporting of Tsunamis (DART): real-time monitoring program using buoys to record violent seawater activity and warn people of potential tsunamis

delta: the fan-shaped land area formed when a freshwater system deposits sediment in the ocean

density: mass per unit volume

dependent variable: something that changes in a way that depends on other factors being measured in an experiment

detritus: wastes and other organic particles that sink in water

diatomic molecule: molecule composed of two atoms of the same element

differential heating: a process by which all places on Earth do not receive the same amount of energy from the Sun at all times of the year

dissolved oxygen (DO): a measure of the oxygen gas (O_2) dissolved in water

diurnal cycle: cycle of sunlight and darkness over a 24-hour period

domoic acid: a neurotoxin, produced by a diatom, that accumulates in the tissues of fish and filter-feeding organisms

downlink: signal sent down from a satellite to a ground station

dredge: to dig through an area of the seafloor, usually to create a channel to allow boat traffic to pass

dry ice: solid carbon dioxide (CO_2)

dynamic soaring: the method in which seabirds use wind currents to travel long distances without flapping their wings, in order to conserve energy

E

echolocation: the process by which organisms, including many marine mammals, emit sounds that bounce off objects and return to the animals' highly sensitive ears

ecosystem: a biological community in which the living things (biotic factors) interact with the non-living things (abiotic factors) and which includes an energy source

eddy: a circular current of water moving against or differently from the main current; formed when meanders separate from a major current

efficiency: a measure of the amount of energy conserved when energy is converted to a new form

Glossary (continued)

El Niño, or El Niño-Southern Oscillation: an anomaly of ocean temperature, sea height, and atmospheric pressure in the Tropical Pacific Ocean that results in worldwide changes in climate for a period of up to 18 months

electromagnetic radiation: full range of energy emitted from the Sun; also known as solar radiation

electron: the type of tiny particle that orbits the nucleus of an atom and has a negative electrical charge

energy: the ability of an object or system to do work on another object or system

energy transfer: the movement or transfer of energy from one part of the universe or Earth system to another

energy transformation: a change in energy from one form to another

engineering: the process of applying scientific concepts to a new problem in order to design solutions and systems

Engineering Design Process: a cyclical process for creating a way to solve a problem

enzyme: a substance made by an organism that speeds up biochemical reactions, such as photosynthesis

erosion: a natural process in which sediment is removed from an area

eukaryotic: related to cells with a nucleus

eutrophication: the result of excess nutrients being added to an ecosystem, which causes an undesirable and short-lived increase in phytoplankton populations

evolution: the process by which populations change over time

excretion: the process of releasing waste products that result from reactions and other non-useful materials from the cell

experiment: a scientific investigation to test a hypothesis

F

fertilization: the process in which sex cells merge, resulting in offspring

fetch: the length of open water over which wind can blow

fish stock: the number of fish available within a population

fishing season: a designated period of time during the year that certain fish and shellfish may be caught

fitness: the ability of a population to survive and reproduce in a certain environment

flagella: a whip-like projection that some single-celled organisms use to move

floodplain: an area where water regularly flows over the banks of a river or stream

fluorescence: measure of light availability in ocean water

food chain: a model of how energy moves in one direction through a system of producers, consumers, and decomposers

food web: a diagram that represents the transfer of food energy through a community of organisms

foraging: the practice of searching for food

forest zone: the most landward zone of a sand dune community, consisting of large trees and vegetation protected from salt spray and frequent wave action

fossil fuel: an energy source such as coal, natural gas, or oil that is made up of the fossilized remains of once living things

fossil record: all fossils preserved in rock and sediments, whether discovered or undiscovered; the collective history of living organisms

freezing: the process in which a substance changes from liquid to solid form

freezing point: the temperature at which a substance changes from liquid to solid form

frequency: the number of waves passing a fixed point per second

front: a boundary that separates different air masses

G

gamete: male or female reproductive cell

genetic diversity: the range of inherited traits within and among species

geostationary satellite: a satellite that remains fixed above one specific location on Earth by orbiting the Earth with the planet's rotation

gill net: a net that is stretched across the water, intended to interrupt schools of swimming fish by hooking them by the gills

glacial ice: frozen fresh water on top of land areas

global climate change: the alteration of Earth's climate currently being observed and studied by scientists

global conveyor belt: a system of deep water currents that connects all of the world's ocean basins

gravitational force/gravity: the force of attraction exerted by the mass of one object on that of another

Great Global Rift: a deep rift valley formed by the divergent boundary extending the length of the Mid-Ocean Ridge, and the site of frequent volcanic activity

greenhouse gas: a gas that holds or traps heat in Earth's atmosphere, heat that would otherwise escape into Space

growth: the life process of increasing in size

gyre: a circular flow of water formed by the wind's push and the shape of the continents

H

habitable: able to support life forms

halophile: an organism that lives and thrives in extremely salty seas and lakes

harmful algal bloom (HAB): a large increase in pathogen-producing phytoplankton over a short period of time

harpoon: an arrow-shaped metal point attached to a wooden or aluminum shaft and used for fishing or hunting

headwaters: the source area or the beginning of a river, where it begins to flow from high elevation to low elevation

heat capacity: the amount of energy it takes to increase or decrease a unit of temperature of a substance

heterotroph: an organism that cannot make its own food and must obtain its energy from an external source

hierarchy: a system in which groups are ranked one above the other according to importance or inclusiveness

high-intertidal zone: a coastal area submerged only about twice a day, during high tides, that is otherwise exposed to air, wind, sunlight, and predators

homeostasis: a stable internal environment

homologous structure: a characteristic observed in different species that indicates that the species have a common ancestor

host: the harmed organism in a parasitic relationship

hydrogenous: describing sediments that come primarily from water

hydrogen bonding: the attraction between water molecules due to the opposite charges of their hydrogen and oxygen "ends"

hydrothermal vent: a chimney-like tube that spews out seawater heated by the Earth's mantle beneath the seafloor

hypothesis: a testable explanation based on observations and used as a starting point for further investigation

hypoxia/anoxia: a fatal condition caused by a lack of oxygen available for organisms, occurring as the result of eutrophication

I

ice core: a cylindrical sample of ice extracted from a glacier or ice cap and used to study past environmental conditions

independent variable: something that changes in a way that does not depend on the other factors being measured in an experiment

Indigenous: related to groups of people that have lived in a certain place for thousands of years

inference: an explanation that is based on logic, knowledge, and experience

inorganic pollutant: a pollutant that does not contain the element carbon, including metals such as mercury and lead, as well as substances used as fertilizers and detergents

insolation: the Sun's energy entering Earth's atmosphere; incoming solar radiation

interspecific: occurring between species

intertidal zone: the area along a coast between the high tide and low tide levels

intraspecific: occurring within a species

invertebrate: an animal without a backbone

ionic bond: the strong bond formed when the positive and negative charges of atoms are highly attracted to each other

ionic compound: a compound that consists of atoms that each have an electrical charge

isobar: a line that connects all points of equal air pressure on a map

isocline: a line that connects points of equal gradient or change on a map

isolated system: a completely efficient system with no exchange of energy or matter beyond the system

isotherm: a line that connects all points of equal temperature on a map

L

latent heat: the heat absorbed during a phase change

Law of Conservation of Energy: a universal law stating that energy cannot be created or destroyed, only transferred or transformed

leeward: opposite of windward; side of a mountain that receives little precipitation

life activities: specific functions carried out by cells and whole organisms

limiting factor: a feature of the environment that limits the growth, reproduction, or distribution of organisms

lipid: an organic compound consisting of fats and oils

longitudinal wave: a wave in which the motion of the medium travels parallel to the flow of energy; a compression wave

longline: a type of fishing line that is up to 130 kilometers (~80 miles) long, used to catch large pelagic fish

longshore current: a current moving parallel to the shoreline; forms circular patterns in the surf zone

low-intertidal zone: a coastal area that is under water most of the time, exposed to air only during lowest tides

M

mangrove: a type of tree that lives in Tropical estuaries

mean tidal range: the difference in height between the average high water and average low water levels

meander: a bend or curve that forms in a current of moving water

medium: anything through which energy flows

melting point: the temperature at which a substance changes from solid to liquid form

meltwater: water that originates from freshwater ice

metabolism: all of the chemical reactions that occur to maintain an organism's life

methanogen: a bacterium that produces natural gas, or methane

microbes: organisms that can only be seen with a microscope

Mid-Atlantic Ridge: a continuous, mountain-like ridge that runs the length of the Atlantic Ocean to the southwest coast of Africa

mid-intertidal zone: the coastal area usually submerged in water that is exposed to air only about twice a day for short periods of time

migration: the seasonal movement of an organism

mineral: an inorganic substance that an organism requires in small quantities in order to carry out bodily processes, such as the transmission of nerve signals and transport of food and waste

model: a representation of something else, often on a larger or smaller scale so it can be more easily observed

mudflat: a coastal ecosystem made up of wide expanses of mud exposed by tides

multicellular: being made up of many cells

mutation: a random change that occurs in genes

mutualism: a relationship between species in which both species benefit from each other

N

native species: a species that naturally inhabits an environment

natural satellite: a planet or moon that orbits around another celestial body

natural selection: the scientific theory that describes how species best suited to survive in an environment will be the most successful at reproducing

neap tide: the tide with the least difference between high and low tide, or least tidal range

nekton: marine organisms that can swim against the ocean's movements

neutral buoyancy: able to maintain position in the water column; not floating or sinking

neutron: the type of tiny particle in the nucleus of an atom, with no electrical charge

nitrogen: an element found in many forms in nature; required by organisms to build proteins and DNA

noble gas: an element with atoms that have a filled outer electron shell, so it tends not to bond with other elements

non-native species: a species that humans have brought into an area in which it has never occurred before; also known as introduced or invasive species

nonpoint source pollution: any substances that cause harm in an environment that come from a source that is unknown, difficult to trace, or spread out over a very large area

nonrenewable resource: a resource that is used up faster than it is naturally replaced

nucleic acid (RNA and DNA): an organic compound that stores and passes on genetic information and uses that information to direct protein synthesis

nutrient: a chemical necessary for metabolism in a living thing

nutrient cycling: the movement of essential elements and compounds through the Earth's spheres

nutrition: the life function of obtaining and processing energy and nutrients

O

observation: the collection of information about the natural world using one's senses and tools to enhance human senses

ocean literacy: an understanding of the ocean's influence on humans and humans' influence on the ocean

offshore drilling: the removal of fossil fuels from beneath the seafloor

open system: a system that exchanges matter and energy with another system

opportunist: a species that has a varied diet based on what is available

orbital wave: the transfer of energy through a medium in a circular motion; an ocean wave

organic compound: a chemical compound made up mainly of carbon, hydrogen, nitrogen, and/or oxygen, held together by covalent bonds; part of the make-up of all living things

organic pollutant: a substance containing the element carbon that causes damage to an environment

organism: a living thing

overfishing: the practice of extracting fish at rates faster than stocks can be replaced

overproduction: a component of the Theory of Evolution by Natural Selection, describing the strategy of organisms to produce more offspring than will survive competition for natural resources

P

parameter: a measurable characteristic

Glossary (continued)

paraphrasing: rephrasing or restating text using nearly the same words and giving credit to the original author for their idea

parasitism: a relationship between species in which one organism benefits while the other is harmed

pathogen: a disease-producing agent

pH: a measure of the acidity or alkalinity of a substance

phase: a distinct and fixed form of matter separated by its surface from other forms

phase change diagram: a graph that shows the change in form of a substance as heat is added to or removed from a system

phosphorus: a chemical element found in many forms in nature; required by organisms to build proteins and DNA

photic zone: the layer of ocean surface water into which light is able to penetrate

photosynthesis: the process in which certain organisms are able to make their own food by using solar energy to make sugar

phytoplankton: tiny, plant-like producers that live near the water's surface

phytoplankton bloom: a large increase in a phytoplankton population over a short period of time, represented by increased chlorophyll concentrations observed through satellites

pigment: colored substances in cells, e.g., chlorophyll

pioneer zone: the area nearest to the shore in which plants are adapted to withstand occasional wave action, salt, being buried in sand, and other harsh conditions

pixel: a single data point captured by satellite sensors and represented as high-resolution imagery

plagiarism: the act of using someone else's words without giving them proper credit

plankton: marine organisms that are at the mercy of the ocean's movements

plastic nodules: tiny particles that result when plastic breaks down

plumb line: a weighted length of cable or other line with evenly spaced knots, used to measure the ocean's depth and map the seafloor

point source pollution: any substances that cause harm in an environment for which the source of the pollutants is known and traceable

polar covalent bond: a bond in which two or more different atoms combine, the electrons are not shared equally, and the shared electron pair tends to be negatively charged

polar covalent molecule: molecule formed by bonding in which electrons are not evenly distributed

polar satellite: a satellite that orbits Earth from Pole to Pole

pollutant: any substance that causes harm in an environment; also called contaminant

population: a group of organisms of the same species that inhabit a specific area

population density: the number of individual organisms of a species per unit of space

population dynamics: changes in the numbers of organisms of a population

Pop-up Archival Tag: a type of satellite tag that stores location data; used to track animals that do not surface often, and when released from the animal after a period of time floats to the surface and transmits its location and data to a satellite

pressure: force per unit area

prevailing easterly: a trade wind, which is a wind that blows from east to west, from the Tropics toward the Equator

prevailing wind: a wind current that moves heat in the atmosphere and affects ocean currents

primary consumer: an organism that does not make its own food and gets energy from producers

primary research: collection of data using one's senses and tools of observation

producer: an organism that captures energy from sunlight or chemicals and uses it to create food energy

prokaryotic: related to cells lacking a nucleus and true organelles

protein: an organic compound that contains the element nitrogen; used by an organism's cells to build body structures and control the rates of chemical reactions in cells

proton: the type of tiny particle in the nucleus of an atom, with a positive electrical charge

purse seine: a method of fishing that uses a boat to loop a large net in a circle around a school of fish and pull the net toward the boat

Q

qualitative data: information (data) recorded as descriptions

quantitative data: information (data) recorded as measurements

quota: a set limit on the number of fish or shellfish per-species that fishers may catch in a given time period

R

radiation: the movement of energy through space, for which no particles or mass are needed for transfer

radiometer: a tool used to collect data using microwave energy sensors

range of tolerance: the span of physical conditions in which a species can survive

Reduce, Reuse, Recycle: the steps promoted through education programs to encourage people to reduce human impact on the environment

regulation: the process of maintaining homeostasis

relaxation: a slowing of upwelling

remote sensing: the science of gathering and interpreting data from human-made satellites

remote sensing satellite: a satellite outfitted with tools that measure, survey, and map Earth's global environment and provide the data required to track and study marine animals

renewable resource: a resource that is naturally replenished over relatively short periods of time

reproduction: the process of creating other organisms of the same kind

respiration: the process of releasing energy from food

rip current: localized, swift currents that move water away from the shore

riparian vegetation: vegetation along the banks of a freshwater body or stream

rogue wave: the result of two or more wave crests running together and creating a wave much larger than other waves in the area

ROV: remotely operated vehicle

S

salinity: the measure of dissolved salts in water

sand dune: a large hill made up of sand, created primarily by wind moving sediment

Satellite Relay Data Logger (SRDL): a satellite transmitter tag that collects several types of data, used on large diving animals to measure salinity, temperature, and depth

scatter plot: a graph in which each data point is represented by a dot; used to compare variables

scientific inquiry: a cyclical process that includes asking questions, making inferences, developing hypotheses, forming data, and drawing conclusions that lead to additional questions

scrub zone: the area landward of the pioneer zone where plants grow close to the ground and on the landside of dunes, where wave action is infrequent

sea ice: a layer of frozen seawater on the ocean's surface

sea level: the ocean's average height relative to the land

sea surface temperature (SST): the measurement of the temperature of the very top layer of the ocean

Secchi disk: a round instrument with black and white markings that helps scientists to assess water turbidity

Second Law of Thermodynamics: a natural law describing the natural and spontaneous flow of heat from an object or mass of higher temperature to one of lower temperature

secondary consumer: an organism that obtains its energy from primary consumers

Glossary (continued)

secondary research: the use of books, journal articles, Internet, interviews, and other sources to develop background information on a subject matter

sediment core: a cylindrical sample of soil, dirt, and rock extracted from a seafloor or land surface by scientists and used to study past environmental conditions

sessile: (of an organism) fixed in one place

sexual reproduction: the creation of offspring through the union of gametes (sperm and egg) from two individual parents

sink: a body or process that removes heat, energy, or a substance from another part of the Earth system

sinkhole: a submerged depression in the bedrock of a region

size limit: the minimum size of a fish or shellfish that can be caught and kept

solubility: the ability to be dissolved in a solvent

solute: a substance that dissolves another substance

solution: a homogeneous mixture of two or more substances

solvent: a substance in which other substances can dissolve

sonar: a technique used to measure ocean depth by bouncing sound waves off the seafloor, which are then received by recording instruments at the surface

spawning: a form of sexual reproduction in which organisms release millions of gametes (sperm and eggs) into the water

speciation: the process by which a new kind of organism, or species, evolves

spiracle: a specialized organ located at the front of the head of a shark or cartilaginous fish that pumps water over the gills

splash zone: along the coast, the area that is almost always exposed to air, getting wet only during storms or other high-water events

spring: an area that forms in a place at Earth's surface where groundwater or an aquifer becomes saturated and cannot hold more water

spring tide: the tide with the greatest difference between high tide and low tide, or tidal range

stimulus: something that causes a response in an organism

storm surge: an unusual and temporary rise in sea level and movement of water onshore during a storm event, due to high winds

sublimation: the process in which a substance changes directly from solid to gas form, bypassing the liquid state of matter

submersible: a pressure-controlled chamber used when investigating beyond the safe depths for people with diving equipment

subsistence fisher: a person who fishes regularly to feed his or her family or local communities

substrate: a hard surface to which organisms attach themselves

succession: the process in which species progressively replace one another until they reach a stable community, after a change occurs in an ecosystem

Summer Solstice: the point in Earth's orbit that produces the longest day of a year, on which the greatest amount of solar radiation is received over a given hemisphere

surf zone: the area where waves break near a beach

surface current: a current within the top 400 meters of the ocean

surface tension: the attraction between molecules at a liquid's surface

survival of the fittest: a component of the Theory of Evolution by Natural Selection stating that when changes occur in the environment, organisms with the most useful characteristics for survival and reproduction are the most fit and pass on their genes

sustainable: able to be continued for a long period of time without damaging the environment

sustainable fishing: the use of fishing practices that do minimal harm to fish populations and result in the least bycatch

symbiosis: a relationship between species

synthesis: the process of making complex materials from simple materials

T

taxomony: the science of classifying organisms

temperature: a measure of the average heat energy of all the atoms, molecules, or ions in a substance or object

terrigenous: describing sediments that come primarily from land

tertiary consumer: a predator that obtains energy from a secondary consumer

theory: the most powerful explanation scientists have to offer about a topic; an explanation of all current evidence

Theory of Evolution by Natural Selection (or Theory of Evolution): the scientific theory that explains how species on Earth change over time by natural selection

thermal energy: the vibration and movement of particles

thermal equilibrium: the point at which heat going into an object equals the amount of heat flowing out of the object (i.e., two objects have the same temperature)

thermal expansion: the phenomenon that as liquid water warms, it takes up a larger volume

thermocline: the layer of water in which temperatures change rapidly, creating a boundary that separates the warmer, surface area from the colder water below

thermohaline circulation: deep water circulation driven by salt concentration and density of the water

thermophile: an organism that thrives in extremely hot conditions, whether in fresh water or salt water

tidal bore: a wave that moves against the current, formed when the tide rises

tidal range: the vertical distance between the high tide and low tide levels

tide: a pattern of rise and fall of the ocean's surface

tide pool: a depression in a rocky coastal area that retains water at low tide

topography: the study of the landscape of Earth's surfaces and features, particularly relating to land and water features, as well as elevation

tori line: a colored, flapping streamer attached to a longline to prevent birds from diving down toward the lines and becoming injured

transect: an imaginary line drawn through an area, along which scientists collect data

transform fault: a zone in Earth's crust along which rocks fracture and slide past each other with a side-to-side movement

transitional species: an identified type of organism that has characteristics "in between" those of more ancient and modern forms

transport: the life activity which involves moving materials around within organisms

transverse wave: a wave in which the motion of the medium is perpendicular to the motion, or direction, of the wave

trawling: a method of fishing in which a large net is dragged behind a boat

trend: the general direction or pattern of a data set

troll, or pole, fishing: a fishing technique using simple nets or fishing poles with baited hooks

trophic level: a step in a food chain that represents energy storage or feeding relationships

trough: the lowest point of a wave

tsunami: a high-energy wave caused by an earthquake, volcano, landslide, or other natural event that displaces and distributes energy through the ocean waters

turbidity: a measurement of how cloudy or clear the water is, or how easily light can penetrate water

turbidity tube: a clear tube with a Secchi disk inside it, used to assess the amount of light that penetrates the water surface

Turtle Excluder Device (TED): a grid of bars located inside a fishing net that allows large animals to escape through a flap while the targeted smaller fish remain inside

U

underground river: a cave or channel that forms from the erosion of underground rock, such as limestone

Glossary (continued)

unicellular: being made up of one cell

uplink: a communications signal sent from a transmitter to a satellite

upwelling: the process in which nutrient-rich, cold water moves up to the surface from ocean depths

V

valence electron: an electron in the outer shell around the nucleus of an atom that may be displaced by or shared with another atom

vaporization: the process in which a substance changes from liquid to gas form

variable: any factor, trait, or condition that changes

variation: genetic differences between individual organisms of the same species

Vernal Equinox: a point in Earth's orbit that causes the greatest amount of solar radiation to be over the Equator and every place on Earth to experience 12 hours of day and 12 hours of night, after winter and before summer; for Northern Hemisphere, occurs each year on March 20th or 21st; sometimes called Spring Equinox

vitamin: an organic compound that an organism needs in very small quantities in order to carry out metabolic processes

volume: the amount of space taken up by a given mass

W

warm front: a boundary where a mass of warmer air pushes into an area occupied by colder air

watershed: the specific land area from which precipitation gathers and flows into a body of water

wave: a disturbance caused by the transfer of energy through a medium

wave height: the vertical distance between the crest (highest point) and the trough (lowest point) of a wave

wavelength: the horizontal distance between two crests (highest points) or two troughs (lowest points) of a wave

wave period: the time it takes for a wave to move the distance of one complete wavelength

wave speed: a measurement calculated as wavelength times frequency

wave train: a series of waves passing a given point at regular intervals, lead by waves with greater wavelengths

wetland: a transitional area between land and water, where the soil is inundated with water either permanently or periodically

wind: the movement of air molecules from areas of high pressure to areas of low pressure

Winter Solstice: the point in Earth's orbit that produces the longest night of the year, on which the least amount of solar radiation is received over a given hemisphere

X

***x*-axis:** the horizontal axis of a graph on which the independent variable goes

Y

***y*-axis:** the vertical axis of a graph on which the dependent variable goes

Z

zooxanthellae: photosynthetic algae that live within corals

Index

Symbols

10-50 rule 165
10% rule 326

A

Abiotic factors 6, 7, 9, 12, 292
Abyssal plain 101, 122
Adaptation 320
  Behavioral **311**
  Structural **311**
Age structure diagram **293**
Air masses 209–215. *See*
    also Hurricanes
  Classification of 209, 210
  Climate and 210
Air pressure 211
Albatross. *See* Seabirds
Albatross, Black-footed. *See* Sea-
    birds
Algae **64,** 65. *See also* Phyto-
    plankton; *See also* Seaweed
  Brown 58, 64, 65
  Commercial uses 64
  Green 58, 64, 65
  Red 58, 64, 65
Algal bloom 256–261, **272,** 555,
    568–569, 603
  Cause of 570–571
  Harmful 260–261, 272
Alvin **72.** *See also* Submersibles
American Crocodile **296**
Amphibians **384–396**
  Salamander **384**
  Tadpole **384**
Analysis Journals 530–539
Anemone **434**
Anomalies 655, 668–674
Antarctic Treaty **684–686,** 689
Antibiotic resistance 305
Aquarius Underwater Habitat
    72–74

Aquifers. *See* Freshwater systems
Archaea 273
Archipelago 681
Arctic Ocean 20
Argos Instrument 83, 84
Asexual reproduction 437
Astrology 129
Atlantic Basin **102**
Atlantic Bluefin Tuna 312,
    640–642, **641**
Atlantic Ocean 20, 205, 236, **257,**
    684
  Marine debris 575
Atmosphere (air) 20, 48, **155,**
    156–157, 201, 656, 658,
    670. *See also* Earth Sys-
    tem; *See also* Earth System,
    Spheres
  Warming reduced 665
Atom 26, 27, 45, **187**
  bond 27
  Mass 26
Autonomous Underwater Vehicles
    (AUVs). *See also* Marine
    technologies
Autotroph 324

B

Baleen 78, **302**
Baleen whale. *See* Whales
Ballast water 314
Barrier Islands 612–623
  Formation of **613**
Basins 20, 134, 469
Bathymetry 110–119, 256, 504,
    506–514, 523
Bay of Fundy 468
Bearded Seal. *See* Seals
Beluga Whale. *See* Whales
Benthic 12, 324
Binomial nomenclature 269

Biodiversity 264–274, 317,
    342–345, 495, 616
Biogeochemical cycling 328, 617
Biological community 9, 325, **457**
  Sand dune communities **460**
Bioluminescence **237,** 351
Biomes **210**
Biosphere 20, 328, 424, 656. *See*
    also Earth System, Spheres
Biosphere (life). *See also* Earth
    System
Biotic factors 6, 7, 9, 12, 58, 292
Bird banding 70
Birds **384–396.** *See also* Seabirds
  Sandpiper **391**
  Shorebirds **391**
Black-footed Albatross. *See* Sea-
    birds
Black Smokers. *See* Hydrothermal
    vent
Blue Marble Animation 20
Blue Planet 6
Blue Whale. *See* Whales
Boiling point 24, 25
Bone-eaters 10–11
Bottlenose Dolphins. *See* Mam-
    mals
British Petroleum (BP) **596**
Budding 437
Buoyancy 34–37
Buoys **167,** 167–168, 451, 455,
    461
Bush, President George W. 15
Bycatch 634, 636, 640, 683, 686

C

California Sea Lion **260, 269,**
    410, 675
Calorie, heat 31
Cape Hatteras Lighthouse **615–**
    616
Carbohydrates 64, 252, 327
Carbon cycle **254–255**
Carbon dioxide 22–39, 132, 156,
    238, 252–255, 275, 326,
    328, 488, 656, 658–659, 665
  Atmospheric **647,** 656
Carrying capacity 291–292, 629

9.30. NOAA. 9.31. NOAA, OSCAR Project Office, Earth and Space Research. Page 180 *Scroll*: photos.com. Figures: 9.32. photos.com. 9.33. USSL, NASA/GSFC, NOAA/NMML. 9.34. NOAA. 9.35. MOTE Marine Laboratory. 9.36. photos.com. 9.37. NASA, GSFC. Pages 184–185: photos.com. Figures: 10.1. NPS/P. Valentine. 10.2. Glen Schuster. 10.3. photos.com. 10.4. photos.com. 10.5. photos.com. Page 188 *Earth and Moon*: NASA. Figures: 10.6. photos.com. Page 189 (TE) *Lab Setups*: photos.com. Page 190 *Stop Sign*: photos.com. Figures: 10.7. NASA, JPL. 10.8. Adapted from NASA, JPL. 10.9. photos.com. Page 192 *Energy Transformations Table*: U.S. Department of Energy, photos.com. Figures: 10.10. USSL. 10.11. photos.com. 10.12. USSL. 10.13. photos.com. 10.14. photos.com. 10.15. NSF. 10.16. photos.com. 10.17. USSL. 10.18. NOAA. 10.19. NOAA. 10.20. photos.com, NOAA/Andy Bruckner. 10.21. photos.com. Page 199 (TE) *Plant in Bottle*: photos.com. Figures: 10.22. NSF, U.S. Antarctic Program/Mike Casey. 10.23. NASA Jet Propulsion Laboratory. 10.24. NASA Goddard Visualization Analysis Lab. Pages 202–203 *Hurricane Frances*: NASA Johnson Space Center, Earth Sciences and Image Analysis Laboratory. Figures: 11.1. NASA. 11.2. NOAA/National Weather Service. 11.3. photos.com. 11.4. NOAA Environmental Visualization Laboratory. 11.5. NOAA, National Weather Service. 11.6. USSL. 11.7. NOAA. 11.8. NOAA Environmental Visualization Laboratory. 11.9. NASA, GSFC. 11.10. NASA. 11.11. NOAA. 11.12. USSL. 11.13. Adapted from USDA. 11.14. USSL. 11.15. USSL. 11.16. USSL. 11.17. USSL. 11.18. NOAA. 11.19. photos.com. 11.20. NOAA, NWS. 11.21. USSL. 11.22. Seth Schuster. 11.23. USSL. 11.24. NOAA. 11.25. USSL. 11.26. USSL. 11.27. USSL. 11.28. NOAA, NWS. 11.29. NOAA/Captain Budd Christman. 11.30. Oikonos, Hawaii Pacific University, NOAA, State of Hawaii, Papahānaumokuākea Monument, USGS, U.S. Satellite, NOAA. 11.31. USSL. Pages 221–222 (Climate Data): NOAA National Climatic Data Center. Figures: 11.32. NOAA National Climatic Data Center/USSL. 11.33. NOAA National Climatic Data Center/USSL. 11.34. NOAA National Climatic Data Center/USSL. 11.35. NASA. 11.36. USSL. Pages 224–225: photos.com. Figures: 12.1. USSL. 12.2. NOAA, Office of Exploration and Research, Bioluminescence 2009. 12.3. NOAA, Office of Exploration and Research. 12.4. NOAA, Channel Islands National Marine Sanctuary. 12.5. NOAA, Office of Exploration and Research. 12.6. NOAA, Office of Exploration and Research. 12.7. Ocean Explorer/L. Murphy. 12.8. NOAA Ocean Explorer. 12.9. photos.com. 12.10. photos.com. 12.11. photos.com. Page 229 (TE) *Lab Setup*: photos.com. Figures: 12.12. NOAA. 12.13. NOAA Ocean Explorer. 12.14. USSL. 12.15. USSL. 12.16. NOAA, Atlantic Oceanographic and Meteorological Laboratory. 12.17. NOAA, SFSC. 12.18. NOAA, NOAA Okeanos Explorer Program, INDEX-SATAL 2010, Gulf of Mexico 2002, NOAA/OER. 12.19. photos.com. 12.20. USSL. 12.21. USSL. 12.22. USSL. 12.23. Adapted from NASA, Goddard Earth Science Data and Information Services Center. 12.24. NOAA, Ocean Explorer, Bahamas Deep-Sea Coral Expedition Science Party. 12.25. NOAA Ocean Explorer. 12.26. NOAA, Office of Exploration and Research, Islands in the Stream 2002. 12.27. NOAA, Office of Exploration and Research, Islands in the Stream 2002. 12.28. NOAA, Office of Exploration and Research, Bioluminescence Team 2009. 12.29. NOAA, Office of Exploration and Research, Bioluminescence Team 2009. 12.30. NOAA, Office of Ocean Exploration and Research/E. Widder. 12.31. Bioluminescence 2009 Expedition, NOAA,

Office of Ocean Exploration and Research (OER). 12.32. NOAA. 12.33. NOAA/F. Nicklin. 12.34. NOAA. 12.35. NOAA, Southwest Fisheries Science Center. 12.36. Bahamas Deep-Sea Coral Expedition Science Party, NOAA-OE. 12.37. NOAA. 12.38. NOAA Ocean Explorer. 12.39. NASA, NOAA, National Marine Sanctuaries. 12.40. NOAA Ocean Explorer. 12.41. PRBO Conservation Science and NOAA Cordell Bank NMS. 12.42. USGS/Greg Lasley. 12.43. Josh Adams, USGS/David Hyrenbach, Duke University and Hawai'i Pacific University/Commission for Environmental Cooperation (CEC)/NOAA Office of International Affairs/Oikonos. 12.44. NOAA Ocean Explorer, The Hidden Ocean, Arctic 2005 Expedition. Pages 246–247: photos.com. Figures: 13.1. National Biological Information Infrastructure (NBII)/ Randolph Femmer. 13.2. NASA Microbes Image Gallery. 13.3. NASA. 13.4. NOAA Marine Biotoxins Program/Steve Morton. 13.5. NOAA Marine Biotoxins Program/Steve Morton. 13.6. NOAA Marine Biotoxins Program/ Steve Morton. 13.7. NOAA Marine Biotoxins Program/Steve Morton. 13.8. NOAA Marine Biotoxins Program/Steve Morton. 13.9. NOAA Arctic Program. 13.10. NASA Earth Observatory. 13.11. USSL. 13.12. photos.com. 13.13. EPA. 13.14. USSL. 13.15. USSL. 13.16. USSL. 13.17. photos.com. 13.18. photos.com. 13.19. NOAA. 13.20. NOAA, OER. 13.21. NOAA, NSF. 13.22. NASA, GSFC. 13.23. NOAA CoastWatch, NASA, GSFC/OceanColor Web. 13.24. NOAA CoastWatch, NASA, GSFC/OceanColor Web. 13.25. NASA. 13.26. NOAA CoastWatch, NASA, GSFC/OceanColor Web. 13.27. Meghan Marrero. 13.28. NOAA, Cordell Bank National Marine Sanctuary. 13.29. Exploring Albatross Movements. 13.30. NOAA. 13.31. EPA. 13.32. San Carlos Police Department. 13.33. NASA, GSFC. Pages 262–263: NOAA MESA Project - Blue Whale; NOAA/NMFS; NOAA. Figures: 14.1. NOAA, Florida Keys National Marine Sanctuary. 14.2. NOAA/Mike Levine. 14.3. Meghan Marrero. 14.4. NOAA, NMFS, Auke Bay Laboratories, Marine Ecology and Stock Assessment (MESA) Program. 14.5. USSL, NOAA/D.Forcucci. 14.6. NOAA Marine Biotoxins Program/Steve Morton. 14.7. NOAA/OER Gulf of Mexico. 14.8. photos.com. 14.9. Meghan Marrero. 14.10. USGS/Caroline Rogers. 14.11. Massachusetts Division of Marine Fisheries. 14.12. USSL. 14.13. USSL. 14.14. NPS. 14.15. NOAA Ocean Explorer/J. Dreyer. 14.16. NOAA, Florida Keys National Marine Sanctuary. 14.17. NOAA, Flower Garden Banks National Marine Sanctuary/Emma Hickerson. 14.18. NOAA, NMFS, AFSC/Matt Wilson, Jay Clark. 14.19. NOAA's Sanctuaries Collection/Jamie Hall. 14.20. NOAA. 14.21. NOAA, Marine Biotoxins Program/Steve Morton. 14.22. NOAA, Marine Biotoxins Program/Steve Morton. 14.23. USGS/Barry H. Rosen. 14.24. NASA Microbes Image Gallery. 14.25. NOAA Ocean Explorer, University of Washington. 14.26. photos.com, Florida Keys National Marine Sanctuary, USGS, NOAA/PMEL/E. D. Cokelet, NOAA, NOAA/Dr. James P. McVey, NOAA Sea Grant Program, NOAA Ocean Explorer/Art Howard/NAPRO, NASA Microbes Image Gallery, NOAA, Marine Biotoxins Program, NASA, NOAA Ocean Explorer/Deep Water Macroalgal Meadows 2004 Exploration, NOAA-OE. 14.27. Meghan Marrero. 14.28. EPA/ Great Lakes program. 14.29. NOAA/Claire Fackler. 14.30. NOAA NMFS Alaska Fisheries Science Center/Matt Wilson, Jay Clark. 14.31. NOAA MBNMS/Josh Pederson. 14.32. NOAA/ Dave Burdick. 14.33. NOAA. 14.34. NOAA/ Katrin Iken, NOAA Corps/Robert Pawlowski. 14.35. USSL. 14.36. USGS. 14.37. NOAA Pacific Islands Fisheries Science Center. 14.38. NOAA

Marine Operations. 14.39. photos.com. 14.40. NSF/Peter Rejcek. 14.41. Canadian Department of Water Resources. Pages 284–285: photos.com. Figures: 15.1. USSL. 15.2. United States Census Bureau. 15.3. USSL. 15.4. NOAA/William Folsom. 15.5. NASA. 15.6. Adapted from Florida Fish and Wildlife Conservation Commission. 15.7. NOAA/ Paolo Maurin. 15.8. NOAA/National Marine Fisheries Service, Office of Protected Resources/ Dwayne Meadows. 15.9. NOAA National Marine Fisheries Service. 15.10. NOAA. 15.11. USSL. 15.12. USSL. 15.13. NOAA, NOAA Ship David Starr Jordan Collection/Commander John Herring, NOAA Corps. 15.14. U.S. Census Bureau, International Data Base. 15.15. USSL. 15.16. NOAA. 15.17. NPS. 15.18. USSL. 15.19. NOAA Ocean Explorer and University of Louisiana at Lafayette/Scott France. 15.20. NOAA. 15.21. U.S. Fish and Wildlife Service/Phil Delphey. 15.22. NOAA, NMFS. 15.23. NOAA's Florida Keys National Marine Sanctuary. 15.24. USGS. 15.25. Adapted from U.S. Census Bureau, International Data Base. 15.26. NASA. Pages 300–301: photos.com. Figures: 16.1. OAR, National Undersea Research Program, National Marine Mammal Lab. 16.2. USSL. 16.3. NOAA, AFSC/Jan Haaga. 16.4. USSL. 16.5. U.S. Fish and Wildlife Service. 16.6. photos.com. 16.7. National Park Service. 16.8. USSL. 16.9. NSF/Zina Deretsky. 16.10. USSL. 16.11. photos.com. 16.12. USSL. 16.13. Tara Alvarez. 16.14. NOAA, NMFS, Office of Protected Resources/Dwayne Meadows. 16.15. Meghan Marrero. 16.16. NOAA/Dwayne Meadows. 16.17. NOAA. 16.18. NOAA National Marine Sanctuary Program, Encyclopedia of the Sanctuaries. 16.19. NOAA Office of Ocean Exploration and Research/ George Sedberry. 16.20. USSL. 16.21. NOAA/ David Burdick. 16.22. NOAA. 16.23. NOAA Ocean Service. 16.24. U.S. Department of Agriculture. 16.25. NOAA. Pages 318–319: NASA, GSFC. Figures: 17.1 NOAA. 17.2. NOAA CoastWatch, NASA GSFC/OceanColor Web. 17.3. NOAA/NMFS/OPR/Dr. Brandon Southall. 17.4. NOAA, NMFS. 17.5. NOAA. 17.6. NOAA MESA Project. 17.7. NOAA, NOAA Corps/Lieutenant Elizabeth Crapo. 17.8. NOAA, Protected Resources Division, SFSC/Michael Richlen. 17.9. NOAA MESA Project. 17.10. photos.com. 17.11. NOAA/Olympic Coast National Marine Sanctuary/ Bowlby. 17.12. *North Atlantic Right Whale*: NOAA; *Euphausiids/Krill*: NOAA National Marine Sanctuaries; *Phytoplankton*: NOAA MESA Project. 17.13. *Humpback Whale*: NOAA; *North Atlantic Right Whale*: NOAA; *Euphausiids/Krill*: NOAA National Marine Sanctuaries; *Mysids*: NOAA/Steve Pothoven; *Jellyfish*: NOAA Sea Grant Program/Dr. James P. McVey; *Mackerel*: NOAA/NMFS/SEFSC Pascagoula Laboratory/Brandi Noble; *Zooplankton*: South Carolina Department of Natural Resources/ NOAA Office of Ocean Exploration: Charleston Bump Expedition 2003/George Sedberry; *Copepods*: NOAA/D. Forcucci; *Phytoplankton*: NOAA MESA Project; *Pteropods*: UAF/NOAA/ Russ Hopcroft; *Capelin*: USGS/Alaska Science Center. 17.14. USSL. 17.15. USSL. 17.16. photos. com. 17.17. NASA. 17.1. NOAA. 17.18. USSL. 17.19. photos.com. 17.20. Meghan Marrero. 17.21. photos.com. 17.22. EPA, Great Lakes program. 17.23. USSL. 17.24. NASA, GSFC. 17.25. NOAA Cordell Bank NMS/Shannon Lyday. 17.26. NASA. 17.27. *Snail*: NOAA/NMFS/OPR/Dr. Dwayne Meadows; *Spotted Eagle Ray*: US Dept of the Interior, Fish and Wildlife Service; *Blue Sprat*: photos.com; *Radiolarian*: USGS; *Napoleon Wrasse*: NOAA Pacific Islands Fisheries Science Center Coral Reef Ecosystem Division; *Amoeba*: NOAA/ National Climatic Data Center; *Coral*: Florida Keys National Marine Sanctuary; *Sponge*: NOAA Ocean Explorer; *Blacktip Shark*: NOAA/NMFS/

SEFSC Pascagoula Laboratory/Brandi Noble; *Surgeonfish*: photos.com; *Butterfly Fish*: Florida Keys National Marine Sanctuary/Chris Huss; *Lobster*: photos.com; *Diamond Urchin*: NOAA; *Triton Trumpet*: NOAA/David Burdick; *Squid*: NOAA/NMFS/SEFSC/Andrew David; NOAA's Undersea Research Center: Phantom II ROV/ Lance Horn; *Hermit Crab*: NOAA/NMFS/SEFSC/ Andrew David; NOAA's Undersea Research Center: Phantom II ROV/Lance Horn; *Hawksbill Sea Turtle*: Florida Keys National Marine Sanctuary; *Jellyfish*: NOAA Sea Grant Program/Dr. James P. McVey; *Mantis Shrimp*: photos.com; *Blackfin Barracuda*: NOAA/NODC/Dr. Anthony R. Picciolo; *Sea Cucumber*: NOAA/Becky A. Dayhuff; *Segmented Worm*: NOAA; *Seaweed*: NOAA/Captain Albert E. Theberge; *Diatom*: USSL; *Dinoflagellate*: NOAA; *Copepod*: NOAA/D. Forcucci; *Crab Larvae*: NOAA/OER: Exploring Alaska's Seamounts 2002; *Foraminifera*: NOAA Historic Collections. 17.28. photos.com. Pages 336–337: NOAA/Kip Evans. Figures: 18.1. NOAA Ocean Explorer. 18.2. NOAA Ocean Explorer. 18.3. NSF. 18.4. Lawrence Livermore National Laboratory. 18.5. California Department of Fish & Game. 18.6. USGS. 18.7. NOAA Ocean Explorer. 18.8. NOAA. 18.9. NOAA/NMFS/PIFSC/CRED/ Kerry Grimshaw. 18.10. NOAA Ocean Explorer. 18.11. NOAA Ocean Explorer. 18.12. NOAA Ocean Explorer. 18.13. NOAA Ocean Explorer. 18.14. NOAA Ocean Explorer. 18.15. NOAA Ocean Explorer. 18.16. Meghan Marrero. 18.17. NOAA Florida Keys National Marine Sanctuary. 18.18. NOAA Ocean Explorer. 18.19. *Archaea*: NASA; *Non Seed Plants*: photos.com; NOAA Ocean Explorer/NOAA-OE: Deep Water Macroalgal Meadows 2004 Exploration; *Seed Plants*: photos.com; *Bacteria*: NASA Microbes Image Gallery; *Protists*: NOAA/Marine Biotoxins Program/Steve Morton; *Fungi*: photos.com; *Seal*: NOAA; *Polar Bear*: USGS; *Sea Turtle*: Florida Keys National Marine Sanctuary; *Fish*: photos. com; *Roundworms*: USSL; *Jellyfish*: NOAA Sea Grant Program/Dr. James P. McVey; *Coral*: Florida Keys National Marine Sanctuary; *Poriferan*: NOAA Ocean Explorer; *Flatworms*: NOAA; *Urchin*: NOAA; *Sea Star*: NOAA Ocean Explorer/ NAPRO/Art Howard; *Squid*: NOAA/NMFS/ SEFSC/Andrew David; NOAA's Undersea Research Center: Phantom II ROV/Lance Horn; *Clam*: NOAA Ocean Explorer/J. Dreyer; *Segmented Worms*: NOAA; *Lobster*: photos.com; *Crab*: NOAA/OER: Exploring Alaska's Seamounts 2002; *Sea Squirt*: NOAA; *Fish*: photos.com; *Bird*: NOAA/PMEL/E. D. Cokelet. 18.20. USSL. 18.21. *Roundworms*: USSL; *Jellyfish*: NOAA Sea Grant Program/Dr. James P. McVey; *Coral*: Florida Keys National Marine Sanctuary; *Poriferan*: NOAA Ocean Explorer; *Flatworms*: NOAA; *Urchin*: NOAA; *Sea Star*: NOAA Ocean Explorer/NAPRO/ Art Howard; *Squid*: NOAA/NMFS/SEFSC/ Andrew David; NOAA's Undersea Research Center: Phantom II ROV/Lance Horn; *Clam*: NOAA Ocean Explorer/J. Dreyer; *Segmented Worms*: NOAA; *Lobster*: photos.com; *Crab*: NOAA/OER: Exploring Alaska's Seamounts 2002; *Sea Squirt*: NOAA; *Fish*: photos.com; *Bird*: NOAA/PMEL/E. D. Cokelet. 18.22. *Roundworms*: USSL; *Jellyfish*: NOAA Sea Grant Program/Dr. James P. McVey; *Coral*: Florida Keys National Marine Sanctuary; *Poriferan*: NOAA Ocean Explorer; *Flatworms*: NOAA; *Urchin*: NOAA; *Sea Star*: NOAA Ocean Explorer/NAPRO/Art Howard; *Squid*: NOAA/NMFS/SEFSC/Andrew David; NOAA's Undersea Research Center: Phantom II ROV/Lance Horn; *Clam*: NOAA Ocean Explorer/J. Dreyer; *Segmented Worms*: NOAA; *Lobster*: photos.com; *Crab*: NOAA/OER: Exploring Alaska's Seamounts 2002; *Sea Squirt*:

NOAA; *Fish*: photos.com; *Bird*: NOAA/PMEL/E. D. Cokelet. Page 343 (TE) *Sample Poster*: *Urchin*: NOAA; *Sea Urchin Shell*: NOAA's National Marine Sanctuary Program/Paulo Maurin; *Sea Star (upper right)*: NOAA Ocean Explorer/NAPRO/Art Howard; *Sea Stars (orange)*: Hidden Ocean 2005 Expedition: NOAA Office of Ocean Exploration. Figures: 18.23. NOAA/Gray's Reef National Marine Sanctuary. 18.24. *Roundworms*: USSL; *Jellyfish*: NOAA Sea Grant Program/Dr. James P. McVey; *Coral*: Florida Keys National Marine Sanctuary; *Poriferan*: NOAA Ocean Explorer; *Flatworms*: NOAA; *Urchin*: NOAA; *Sea Star*: NOAA Ocean Explorer/NAPRO/Art Howard; *Squid*: NOAA/NMFS/SEFSC/Andrew David; NOAA's Undersea Research Center: Phantom II ROV/Lance Horn; *Clam*: NOAA Ocean Explorer/J. Dreyer; *Segmented Worms*: NOAA; *Lobster*: photos.com; *Crab*: NOAA/OER: Exploring Alaska's Seamounts 2002; *Sea Squirt*: NOAA; *Fish*: photos.com; *Bird*: NOAA/PMEL/E. D. Cokelet. 18.25. *Tunicate*: NOAA; *Jawless Fish*: NOAA/OER/Lewis and Clark 2001; *Cartilaginous Fish*: NOAA/NMFS/SEFSC Pascagoula Laboratory/Brandi Noble; *Bony Fish*: photos.com; *Amphibian*: photos.com; *Polar Bear*: USGS; *Reptile*: Florida Keys National Marine Sanctuary; *Bird*: NOAA/PMEL/E. D. Cokelet. 18.26. Gulf of the Farralones National Marine Sanctuary. 18.27. NOAA National Marine Fisheries Service/Office of Protected Resources/Dwayne Meadows. 18.28. NOAA. 18.29. USSL. 18.30. Washington Department of Fish and Wildlife/Kristina Wilkening. 18.31. NOAA Flower Garden Banks National Marine Sanctuary. 18.32. Monterey Bay National Marine Sanctuary/Steve Lonhart. 18.33. Meghan Marrero. 18.34. NOAA National Marine Sanctuaries/Claire Fackler. 18.35. NOAA Ocean Explorer/Art Howard. 18.36. NOAA Monterey Bay National Marine Sanctuary/Becky Stamski. 18.37. USSL. 18.38. NOAA/National Estuarine Research Reserve System. 18.39. Environmental Protection Agency (EPA). 18.40. Meghan Marrero. 18.41. NOAA, Southwest Fisheries Science Center. 18.42. NOAA Ocean Exploration Digital Video and Image Data. 18.43. USSL. 18.44. NOAA, Office of Exploration and Research. 18.45. NOAA, Sanctuaries Collection/Rick Starr. 18.46. Olympic Coast National Marine Sanctuary/Nancy Sefton. 18.47. Meghan Marrero. Pages 356–357: photos. com. Figures: 19.1. NOAA Ocean Explorer. 19.2. NOAA/Julie Bedford. 19.3. photos.com. 19.4. California Department of Fish and Game. 19.5. NOAA Ocean Explorer. 19.6. Meghan Marrero. 19.7. *Tunicate*: NOAA; *Jawless Fish*: NOAA/OER/ Lewis and Clark 2001; *Cartilaginous Fish*: NOAA/ NMFS/SEFSC Pascagoula Laboratory/Brandi Noble; *Bony Fish*: photos.com; *Amphibian*: photos. com; *Polar Bear*: USGS; *Reptile*: Florida Keys National Marine Sanctuary; *Bird*: NOAA/PMEL/E. D. Cokelet. 19.8. U.S. Fish and Wildlife Service. 19.9. Great Lakes Sea Grant Network Exotic Species Graphics Library. 19.10. NOAA/Courtesy of United Nations Food and Agriculture Organization/Danilo Cedrone. 19.11. USSL. 19.12. NOAA National Marine Sanctuaries / Claire Fackler. 19.13. NOAA/Monterey Bay Aquarium Research Institute. 19.14. Meghan Marrero. 19.15. NOAA/NMFS/SFSC/Andrew David, Lance Horn. 19.16. photos.com. 19.17. NOAA Flower Garden Banks National Marine Sanctuary/E. Hickerson. 19.18. NOAA/NMFS/Office of Protected Services/ Dwayne Meadows. 19.19. NOAA Ocean Explorer. 19.20. NOAA/NMFS. 19.21. NOAA Monterey Bay National Marine Sanctuary/Chad King. 19.22. NOAA/David Burdick. 19.23. Fotosearch. 19.24. Meghan Marrero. 19.25. NOAA/NMFS/OPR/Dr. Dwayne Meadows. 19.26. NOAA/NMFS/SEFSC/ Andrew David; NOAA's Undersea Research

Center: Phantom II ROV/Lance Horn. 19.27. NOAA Monterey Bay National Marine Sanctuary/ Chad King. 19.28. Channel Islands National Marine Sanctuary. 19.29. photos.com. 19.30. USSL. 19.31. USSL. 19.32. USSL. Pages 374–375: NOAA Corps/Captain Budd Christman. Figures: 20.1. NOAA/Florida Keys National Marine Sanctuary/Bill Precht. 20.2. NOAA. 20.3. NOAA/ Commander John Herring, NOAA Corps. 20.4. NOAA. 20.5. NOAA Flower Garden Banks National Marine Sanctuary/E. Hickerson. 20.6. NPS/Indiana Dunes National Lakeshore. 20.7. Meghan Marrero. 20.8. Meghan Marrero. 20.9. NOAA Corps/ Lieutenant Elizabeth Crapo. 20.10. Meghan Marrero. 20.11. ORA/Michael Van Woert. 20.12. Willamette University, College of Liberal Arts. 20.13. EPA. 20.14. USSL. 20.15. USSL. 20.16. NOAA National Marine Sanctuaries/Claire Fackler. 20.17. Oikonos, Hawaii Pacific University, NOAA, State of Hawai'i, Papahānaumokuākea Monument, USGS, USSL. 20.18. NSF/Robyn Waserman. 20.19. Penguin Science. 20.20. USSL. 20.21. USSL. 20.22. NOAA. 20.23. USGS/Western Research Center/Josh Adams. 20.24. USSL. 20.25. NPS/Indiana Dunes National Lakeshore. 20.26. Troy Ecological Research Associates. 20.27. USGS/ Patuxent Wildlife Research Center/Matthew Perry. 20.28. USSL. 20.29.USGS San Francisco Bay Estuary Field Station/Susan Wainwright-De La Cruz. 20.30. NOAA/NMFS/Office of Protected Resources. 20.31. NOAA Florida Keys National Marine Sanctuary/Bill Precht. 20.32. MOTE Marine Laboratory, Marine Turtle Research Group. 20.33. NOAA/NMFS/Office of Protected Resources. 20.34. NOAA/Andy Bruckner. 20.35. Marine Turtle Specialist Group. 20.36. NOAA/ NMFS/Office of Protected Resources. 20.37. USGS/Caroline Rogers. 20.38. Caribbean Conservation Corporation & Sea Turtle Survival League. 20.39. NOAA/NMFS/Office of Protected Resources. 20.40. NOAA. 20.41. WhaleNet. 20.42. *Roundworms*: USSL; *Jellyfish*: NOAA Sea Grant Program/Dr. James P. McVey; *Coral*: Florida Keys National Marine Sanctuary; *Poriferan*: NOAA Ocean Explorer; *Flatworms*: NOAA; *Urchin*: NOAA; *Sea Star*: NOAA Ocean Explorer/NAPRO/ Art Howard; *Squid*: NOAA/NMFS/SEFSC/ Andrew David; NOAA's Undersea Research Center: Phantom II ROV/Lance Horn; *Clam*: NOAA Ocean Explorer/J. Dreyer; *Segmented Worms*: NOAA; *Lobster*: photos.com; *Crab*: NOAA/OER: Exploring Alaska's Seamounts 2002; *Sea Squirt*: NOAA; *Fish*: photos.com; *Bird*: NOAA/PMEL/E. D. Cokelet; *Tunicate*: NOAA; *Jawless Fish*: NOAA/OER/Lewis and Clark 2001; *Cartilaginous Fish*: NOAA/NMFS/SEFSC Pascagoula Laboratory/Brandi Noble; *Bony Fish*: photos.com; *Amphibian*: photos.com; *Polar Bear*: USGS; *Reptile*: Florida Keys National Marine Sanctuary; *Bird*: NOAA/PMEL/E. D. Cokelet. 20.43. photos.com. 20.44. photos.com. 20.45. USSL. 20.46. photos.com. 20.47. photos.com. 20.48. NOAA/Julie Bedford. 20.49. NASA. 20.50. NOAA/Rosilin Cohen. 20.51. NOAA. 20.52. NOAA National Marine Sanctuaries/Paulo Morin. 20.53. NOAA/NMFS/SFSC. 20.54. NOAA/NMFS/ Office of Protected Resources. 20.55. NOAA/ NMFS/SFSC. 20.56. *Tunicate*: NOAA; *Jawless Fish*: NOAA/OER/Lewis and Clark 2001; *Cartilaginous Fish*: NOAA/NMFS/SEFSC Pascagoula Laboratory/Brandi Noble; *Bony Fish*: photos.com; *Amphibian*: photos.com; *Polar Bear*: USGS; *Reptile*: Florida Keys National Marine Sanctuary; *Bird*: NOAA/PMEL/E. D. Cokelet. 20.57. NOAA NESDIS, NODC/Mary Hollinger. 20.58. Meghan Marrero. 20.59. NSF/Emily Stone. 20.60. NSF/ Melissa Rider. 20.61. NSF/Glenn Grant. 20.62. Josh Adams, USGS, David Hyrenback, Duke University and Hawai'i Pacific University,

Commission for Environmental Cooperation (CEC), NOAA Office of International Affairs, Oikonos. 20.63. NOAA Corps/Elizabeth Crapo. 20.64. Meghan Marrero. 20.65. Department of the Interior/U.S. Fish and Wildlife Service. 20.66. U.S. Fish and Wildlife Service/John Foster. 20.67. NOAA Corps/Elizabeth Crapo. 20.68. Meghan Marrero. 20.69. NPS, Indiana Dunes National Lakeshore. 20.70. Meghan Marrero. 20.71. U.S. Fish & Wildlife Service. 20.72. U.S. Fish & Wildlife Service. 20.73. U.S. Fish & Wildlife Service. 20.74. U.S. Fish & Wildlife Service. 20.75. U.S. Fish & Wildlife Service. 20.76. USSL. Pages 400–401: photos.com. Figures: 21.1. Channel Islands Naturalist Corps/April Rabuck. 21.2. Meghan Marrero. 21.3. photos.com. Page 403 *Species Size Table*: National Marine Fisheries Service, NOAA, Smithsonian National Zoological Park, National Center for Health Statistics. Figures: 21.4. NOAA/Lieutenant Tony Perry III. 21.5. WhaleNet. 21.6. NOAA/NMFS/Pacific Islands Regional Office. 21.7. USGS/Steve Amstrup. 21.8. NMFS National Marine Mammal Laboratory. 21.9. Cascadia Research Collective. 21.10. University of California Santa Cruz and TOPP. 21.11. NOAA/Scott Seganti. 21.12. Meghan Marrero. 21.13. NOAA. 21.14. photos.com. 21.15. Tunicate: *Jawless Fish*: NOAA/OER/Lewis and Clark 2001; *Cartilaginous Fish*: NOAA/NMFS/SEFSC Pascagoula Laboratory/Brandi Noble; *Bony Fish*: photos.com; *Amphibian*: photos.com; *Polar Bear*: USGS; *Reptile*: Florida Keys National Marine Sanctuary; *Bird*: NOAA/PMEL/E. D. Cokelet. 21.16. Channel Islands Naturalist Corps/Josh Kaye-Carr. 21.17. NOAA/Northeast Fisheries Science Center/Peter Duley. 21.18. NOAA. 21.19. Monterey Bay National Marine Sanctuary/Becky Stamski. 21.20. NOAA/Captain Budd Christman. 21.21. Meghan Marrero. 21.22. Andy Collins, Papahānaumokuākea Marine National Monument. 21.23. NOAA Office of Exploration/Kelley Elliot. 21.24. photos.com. 21.25. NOAA/Southwest Fisheries Science Center Protected Resources Division/Michael Richlen. 21.26. NOAA. 21.27. NOAA. 21.28. NOAA/Alaska Fisheries Science Center. 21.29. Provincetown Center for Coastal Studies. 21.30. Barbara LaCorte, Channel Islands Naturalist Corps. 21.31. NASA. 21.32. NOAA/NMFS. Pages 415–417 (whale tail images): Photos courtesy of NOAA's Stellwagen Bank National Marine Sanctuary. Photos were taken under NOAA Fisheries Research Permits #605-1904 (2009) and #775-1875 (2008). Photographers: Cara Pecarcic, Jenn Tackaberry, Whale Center of New England, Ari Fiedlaender, Danielle Cholewiak, Elliott Hezen, Jeremy Winn, Michael Thompson. Figures: 21.33. NOAA/NMML. 21.34. Eileen Avery, Channel Islands Naturalist Corps. 21.35. NSF/Joe Stanford. 21.36. NOAA. 21.37. NOAA. 21.38. Photo taken under research permit # 605-1904 issued by the National Marine Fisheries Service. 21.39. Stellwagen Bank National Marine Sanctuary. 21.40. photos.com. 21.41. NOAA/Chris Cutler. 21.42. NOAA. 21.43. photos.com. 21.44. NOAA/NFSC/Northeast Fisheries Science Center. Pages 422–423: NOAA, Stellwagen Bank National Marine Sanctuary. Figures: 22.1. Meghan Marrero. 22.2. NOAA. 22.3. photos.com. 22.4. photos.com. 22.5. NOAA/NMFS/Southeast Fisheries Science Center. 22.6. photos.com. 22.7. photos.com. 22.8. photos.com. 22.9. USSL. 22.10. USSL. 22.11. NSF, University of California Santa Barbara (UCSB)/Bree Belyea. 22.12. NOAA/David Burdick. 22.13. NOAA/NMFS/OPR/Dwayne Meadows. 22.14. NOAA/David Burdick. 22.15. NOAA, OAR, National Undersea Research Program (NURP); College of William & Mary/C. Van Dover. 22.16. NOAA/Becky A. Dayhuff. 22.17. USSL. 22.18. NOAA/David Burdick. 22.19. NOAA, Florida

Keys NMS/Paige Gill. 22.20. USSL. 22.21. NOAA OER, University of Washington. 22.22. NOAA OER. 22.23. NOAA's Cordell Bank National Marine Sanctuary/Jodi Pirtle. 22.24. USSL. 22.25. NOAA's Flower Garden Banks National Marine Sanctuary/Emma Hickerson. 22.26. NOAA's Flower Garden Banks National Marine Sanctuary/Emma Hickerson. 22.27. NOAA's Flower Garden Banks National Marine Sanctuary/Emma Hickerson. 22.28. NOAA/David Burdick. 22.29. NPS. 22.30. NPS. 22.31. NOAA/NOS/OPR/Robert Ricker. 22.32. Meghan Marrero. 22.33. photos.com. 22.34. NOAA/NOAA Corps/Captain Albert E. Theberge. 22.35. NOAA Ocean Explorer/L. Rear. 22.36. NOAA. 22.37. NOAA Channel Islands National Marine Sanctuary/A. Lombardi. 22.38. U.S. Fish and Wildlife Service/Scott Schlieb. 22.39. NOAA Office of Ocean Exploration/Steve Ross. Pages 442–443: photos.com. Figures: 23.1. photos.com. 23.2. photos.com. 23.3. NOAA National Marine Sanctuary Program/John Brooks. 23.4. NOAA/Ian Masterson. 23.5. NOAA, Monterey Bay National Marine Sanctuary/Josh Pederson. 23.6. NOAA. 23.7. photos.com. 23.8. photos.com. 23.9. USSL. 23.10. USSL. 23.11. U.S. Fish and Wildlife Service. 23.12. photos.com. 23.13. NOAA, National Weather Service. 23.14. USSL. 23.15. photos.com. 23.16. USSL. 23.17. USSL. 23.18. USSL. 23.19. photos.com. 23.20. NASA GSFC/Jeff Johnson. 23.21. NOAA, National Weather Service. 23.22. photos.com. 23.23. photos.com. 23.24. photos.com. 23.25. photos.com. 23.26. Meghan Marrero. 23.27. Florida Department of Environmental Protection. 23.28. USGS/Tracy Enright. 23.29. NOAA/NMFS/William B. Folsom. 23.30. Florida Department of Environmental Protection. 23.31. Meghan Marrero. 23.32. NPS. 23.33. Meghan Marrero. 23.34. Meghan Marrero. 23.35. Glen Schuster. 23.36. USSL. 23.37. Southwest Regional Development Agency, United Kingdom. 23.38. U.S. Department of Energy, Energy Efficiency and Renewable Energy. 23.39. NASA, USSL. 23.40. photos.com. Pages 464–465: NASA/JPL-Caltech/University of Arizona, photos.com. Figures: 24.1. NOAA, Grunion Greeters/Bill Hootkins. 24.2. NOAA, NODC/Mary Hollinger. 24.3. NOAA Ocean Service Education/Brendan Holland. 24.4. NOAA, South Carolina Department of Natural Resources, Marine Resources Research Institute (MRRI). 24.5. photos.com. 24.6. USSL. 24.7. NOAA/George Leigh. 24.8. USSL. 24.9. NASA. 24.10. USSL. Pages 471–473 *Tide Tables*: NOAA. Figures: 24.11. NASA. 24.12. NOAA. 24.13. NOAA Ocean Service Education. 24.14. USSL. 24.15. NASA, photos.com. 24.16. USSL. 24.17. NOAA Ocean Service Education. 24.18. Adapted from NOAA/NOS. 24.19. NOAA/NOS. 24.20. USSL. 24.21. NASA, photos.com. 24.22. NOAA, National Weather Service/Dennis Decker. 24.23. NOAA Ocean Service Education. 24.24. NOAA Ocean Service Education. 24.25. NOAA/Emma Hickerson. 24.26. Julianne E. Steers/grunion.org. 24.27. NOAA, SWFSC/Scott R. Benson, photos.com. 24.28. NOAA, Flower Garden Banks National Marine Sanctuary. 24.29. NOAA, Flower Garden Banks National Marine Sanctuary. 24.30. NOAA, Olympic Coast National Marine Sanctuary/Nancy Sefton. 24.31. NOAA Monterey Bay National Marine Sanctuary/Steve Lonhart. 24.32. Meghan Marrero. 24.33. Meghan Marrero. 24.34. NOAA Ocean Service Education. 24.35. Meghan Marrero. 24.36. U.S. Fish and Wildlife Service. 24.37. NASA, Apollo8. Pages 486–487: NOAA; NASA, GSFC. Figures: 25.1. NASA. 25.2. USSL. 25.3. USSL. 25.4. Adapted from Argonne National Laboratory. 25.5. Meghan Marrero. 25.6. NASA. 25.7. Data credit: SERC-FIU Water Quality Monitoring Network (supported by SFWMD/

SERC Cooperative Agreements #4600000352 and EPA Agreement #X994621-94-0). 25.8. NOAA CoastWatch, NASA GSFC/OceanColor Web. 25.9. NASA, SRTM, Earth Observatory. 25.10. USSL. 25.11. NASA. 25.12. USSL. 25.13. USSL. 25.14. NOAA, Cordell Bank NMS. 25.15. U.S. Geological Survey/Western Ecological Research Center/Josh Adams, NOAA CoastWatch, NASA GSFC/OceanColor Web. 25.16. NOAA Ocean Explorer, OER Sanctuary Quest 2002. 25.17. NOAA CoastWatch, NASA GSFC/OceanColor Web. 25.18. NASA, GSFC. 25.19. USSL. 25.20. Jet Propulsion Laboratory, Jason. 25.21. NASA/JPL. 25.22. NASA/JPL. 25.23. NOAA CoastWatch, NASA GSFC/OceanColor Web. Pages 500–501: photos.com. Pages 502–503: photos.com. Figures: 26.1. NOAA, NGDC. 26.2. NASA, GSFC. 26.3. NASA, Earth Observatory. 26.4. USSL. 26.5. NOAA, NGDC. 26.6. NOAA, NGDC. 26.7. NASA, GSFC. 26.8. NOAA. 26.9. NASA, GSFC. 26.10. USSL. 26.11. USSL. 26.12. USSL. 26.13. NOAA/NMFS/Southwest Fisheries Science Center/Scott R. Benson. 26.14. USSL. 26.15. NOAA, USSL. 26.16. NOAA, NGDC. 26.17. USSL. 26.18. NASA, GSFC. 26.19. USSL. 26.20. NASA GSFC, USSL. 26.21. NASA GSFC. 26.22. USSL. 26.23. USSL. 26.24. USSL. Pages 520–521: NOAA, NGDC; NASA GSFC. Figures: 27.1. NOAA. 27.2. NOAA. 27.3. NOAA. 27.4. Oikonos Ecosystem Knowledge/Sophie Webb. 27.5. NOAA. 27.6. NOAA, NGDC. 27.7. NASA, ISS Expedition 21 Crew. 27.8. NOAA. 27.9. NASA, GSFC. 27.10. USSL. 27.11. NOAA/Captain Budd Christman. 27.12. USGS, NASA, GSFC. 27.13. NOAA, SFSC. 27.14. UC Santa Cruz and TOPP, NASA, GSFC, NOAA, NESDIS. 27.15. UC Santa Cruz and TOPP, NASA, GSFC, NOAA, NESDIS. 27.16. USSL. 27.17. USSL. 27.18. USSL. 27.19. USSL. 27.20. NOAA/Southwest Fisheries Science Center. 27.21. NOAA, NGDC. 27.22. USSL. 27.23. NASA, GSFC. 27.24. USSL. 27.25. USSL. 27.26. USSL. Pages 540–541: NOAA National Marine Sanctuaries Media Library/Claire Fackler. Pages 542–543: NASA, USGS. Figures: 28.1. photos.com. 28.2. USSL. 28.3. photos.com. 28.4. NASA. 28.5. NOAA, NGDC. 28.6. Adapted from USGS. 28.7. Adapted from USGS. 28.8. USGS. 28.9. USGS. 28.10. USSL. 28.11. USSL. 28.12. USGS. 28.13. NASA. 28.14. USDA Forest Service. 28.14. USDA Forest Service. 28.15. NOAA. 28.16. National Atlas, USGS. 28.16. USGS. 28.17. USSL. 28.18. NASA, USGS. 28.19. NASA, GSFC/MODIS Land Rapid Response Team/Jacques Descloitres. 28.20. NSF/Steven Profaizer. 28.21. Meghan Marrero. 28.22. USSL. 28.23. NOAA, OER/Valerie Paul. 28.24. United States Department of Agriculture, Natural Resources Conservation Service. 28.25. USDA Natural Resources Conservation Service. 28.26. NOAA Ocean Education Service. 28.27. NASA. 28.28. Oklahoma Conservation Commission. 28.29. NOAA/NMFS/OPR/Dr. Dwayne Meadows. 28.30. NSF/Essa Gross, Michigan Technological University. 28.31. USSL. 28.32. photos.com. 28.33. USSL. 28.34. USSL. 28.35. NPS. Pages 564–565: photos.com. Figures: 29.1. NASA, GSFC. 29.2. photos.com. 29.3. *Bacteria*: NASA; *Lightning*: NOAA/OAR/ERL/National Severe Storms Laboratory (NSSL); *Dead Bug, Waterfall, and Plant*: photos.com. 29.4. NASA, GSFC/Science Visualization Studio. 29.5. NOAA, Hawaiian Islands Humpback Whale National Marine Sanctuary/Wendy Wiltse. 29.6. NASA MODIS Team/Liam Gumley. 29.7. NOAA, OER, Arctic Exploration 2002/Shelly Carpenter. 29.8. NOAA, Flower Garden Banks National Marine Sanctuary. 29.9. NOAA. 29.10. NOAA. 29.11. USGS/Austin Post. 29.12. U.S. Environmental Protection Agency. 29.13. Meghan Marrero. 29.14. Meghan Marrero. 29.15. Meghan

Marrero. 29.16. Meghan Marrero. 29.17. NOAA National Marine Sanctuaries Media Library/Claire Fackler. 29.18. Meghan Marrero. 29.19. NASA, GSFC. 29.20. Meghan Marrero. 29.21. Sunny Seal-LaPlante. 29.22. NOAA/David Burdick. 29.23. Meghan Marrero. 29.24. Meghan Marrero. 29.25. USSL. 29.26. Adapted from "Plastics in the Ocean" Benicia Water Education Program developed by Oikonos Ecosystem Knowledge for the City of Benicia, CA. 29.27. photos.com. 29.28. NOAA. 29.29. USSL. Pages 580–581: NOAA, ENS Sandor Silagi, NOAA, U.S. Coast Guard/Timothy Tamargo. Figures: 30.1. NOAA. 30.2. NOAA. 30.3. NOAA. 30.4. NOAA. 30.5. NOAA. 30.6. NOAA and Georgia Department of Natural Resources. 30.7. NOAA Ocean Service. 30.8. NOAA. 30.9. Adapted from Massachusetts Department of Education. 30.10. NOAA. 30.11. NOAA, EXXON Valdez Oil Spill Trustee Council. 30.12. photos.com. 30.13. NOAA. 30.14. National Park Service, Indiana Dunes National Lakeshore. 30.15. NPS, Indiana Dunes National Lakeshore. 30.16. NASA. 30.17. NASA. 30.18. NASA. 30.19. NSF/Brien Barnett. 30.20. photos.com. 30.21. NOAA Ocean Explorer, USSL. 30.22. photos.com. 30.23. USSL. 30.24. photos.com. 30.25. NOAA Restoration Center. 30.26. NOAA, Flower Garden Banks NMS/Hickerson. 30.27. NOAA. 30.28. NOAA. 30.29. NASA GSFC/MODIS Rapid Response Team. 30.30. NASA GSFC/MODIS Rapid Response Team/Jeff Schmaltz. 30.31. NASA Earth Observatory. 30.32. NOAA, Geophysical Fluid Dynamics Laboratory. 30.33. NASA. 30.34. Meghan Marrero. 30.35. Meghan Marrero. 30.36. NOAA. 30.37. photos.com. 30.38. NOAA. 30.39. NOAA. 30.40. photos.com. 30.41. Georgia Department of Natural Resources. 30.42. NOAA. 30.43. Unified Commands Joint Information Center. 30.44. U.S. Fish and Wildlife Service/Kim Betton. 30.45. U.S. Fish and Wildlife Service. 30.46. NOAA. 30.47. NASA. 30.48. Meghan Marrero. 30.49. NASA Goddard Earth Sciences Data and Information Services Center. 30.50. NOAA. 30.51. USSL. 30.52. USSL. 30.53. NOAA, Georgia Department of Natural Resources. Pages 606–607: photos.com. Figures: 31.1. U.S. Census Bureau. 31.2. NOAA. 31.3. NOAA. 31.4. NOAA, NMFS, OPR/Dr. Dwayne Meadows. 31.5. NASA. 31.6. USSL. 31.7. Meghan Marrero. 31.8. NOAA/Captain Albert E. Theberge. 31.9. USGS. 31.10. NASA, USGS. 31.11. USGS Center for Coastal and Watershed Studies/A. Salleger and A. Nayengandhi; NASA/W. Wright. 31.12. North Carolina Department of Transportation. 31.13. North Carolina Department of Transportation. 31.14. North Carolina Department of Transportation. 31.15. NOAA, National Estuarine Research Reserve System/Alison Robb. 31.16. NOAA, National Estuarine Research Reserve System. 31.17. NOAA. 31.18. photos.com. 31.19. Meghan Marrero. 31.20. NMFS, OPR/Dr. Brandon Southall. 31.21. NOAA, National Estuarine Research Reserve System. 31.22. NOAA, National Estuarine Research Reserve System. 31.23. NOAA, National Estuarine Research Reserve System. 31.24. NOAA, National Weather Service, NOAA Corps, Marine and Aviation Office, Aircraft Operations Center/Lieut. Commander Mark Moran. 31.25. NOAA Restoration Center/Mark Sramek. 31.26. NOAA Restoration Center/Mark Sramek. 31.27. Adapted from NOAA, NWS. 31.28. USSL. 31.29. NOAA. 31.30. USSL. 31.31. NOAA, NESDIS, National Coastal Data Development Center/P. R. Hoar. Pages 624–625: photos.com. Figures: 32.1. NOAA. 32.2. NOAA/Bob Williams. 32.3. photos.com. 32.4. NOAA/Edward J. Pastula. 32.5. NOAA/Bob Williams. 32.6. NOAA/J.M. Olson. 32.7. photos.com. 32.8. photos.com. 32.9. photos.com. Page 630 *Scroll*: photos.com. Figures: 32.10.

Meghan Marrero. 32.11. Gulf of Maine Cod Project, NOAA National Marine Sanctuaries; Courtesy of National Archives. 32.12. Glen Schuster. 32.13. Glen Schuster. 32.14. NASA. 32.15. Australian Fisheries Management Authority. 32.16. U.S. Fish and Wildlife Service. 32.17. U.S. Fish and Wildlife Service. 32.18. NOAA/Robert K. Brigham. 32.19. NOAA. 32.20. NOAA/R. Waller. 32.21. NOAA. 32.22. NOAA Estuarine Research Reserve Collection. 32.23. NOAA/NMFS/Pacific Islands Fisheries Science Center. 32.24. NOAA, NMFS. 32.25. NOAA, NMFS/ William B. Folsom. 32.26. NOAA. 32.27. Massachusetts Division of Marine Fisheries. 32.28. NOAA Fisheries Service/Ed Gorecki. 32.29. Blue Ocean Institute. 32.30. NOAA/Northeast Fisheries Science Center. 32.31. NOAA/NMFS/A. Howard Clark. 32.32. NOAA/NMFS /painting by J.S. Ryder. 32.33. NOAA. 32.34. NOAA Fisheries Service. 32.35. NASA, Earth Observatory. Pages 644–645: photos.com. Figures: 33.1. photos.com. 33.2. NOAA. 33.3. USSL. 33.4. NOAA, National Climate Data Center (NCDC). 33.5. NASA, NOAA. 33.6. Koppen (1881), Budyko (1969) and Brohan et al. (2006). 33.7. NASA. 33.8. NASA. 33.9. NASA, Goddard Institute for Space Studies (GISS). 33.10. Adapted from National Snow and Ice Data Center. 33.11. NOAA CCMA Biogeography Team. 33.12. NASA. 33.13. NOAA, National Environmental Satellite, Data, and Information Service (NEDIS). 33.14. NOAA, Flower Garden Banks National Marine Sanctuary. 33.15. NOAA/Florida Keys National Marine Sanctuary/Mike White. 33.16. NOAA/David Burdick. 33.17. NOAA. 33.18. NOAA/David Burdick. 33.19. Adapted from NOAA National Ocean Service. 33.20. OAR, National Undersea Research Program. 33.21. USSL. 33.22. Source Petit et. al, 1999. 33.23. NOAA Office of Ocean Exploration and Research/Art Howard. 33.24. NOAA/NMFS/Allen M. Shimada. 33.25. Meghan Marrero. 33.26. NOAA/NOAA Office of Ocean Exploration and Research/Art Howard. 33.27. NOAA Office of Ocean Exploration and Research/Jeremy Potter. 33.28. Penguin Science. 33.29. NOAA, NCDC, CSIRO. 33.30. NOAA Earth System Research Laboratory. 33.31. USSL, NOAA. 33.32. photos.com. 33.33. NASA, GISS. 33.34. NOAA, Satellite Oceanography and Climatology Division, Laboratory for Satellite Altimetry. 33.35. Glen Schuster. 33.36. USSL. 33.37. Glen Schuster. Page 663 (TE) *Lab Setup*: photos.com. Figures: 33.38. Glen Schuster. 33.39. Glen Schuster. 33.40. NOAA, NWS. 33.41. photos.com. 33.42. NOAA. 33.43. NOAA. 33.44. photos.com, NOAA, Geophysical Fluid Dynamics Laboratory (GFDL). 33.45. NASA, GSFC. 33.46. NOAA, Geophysical Fluid Dynamics Laboratory (GFDL). 33.47. NODC/NOAA. 33.48. USSL. 33.49. USSL. 33.50. NASA. 33.51. NASA's Earth Observatory. 33.52. NOAA Climate Services. 33.53. USSL. 33.54. NOAA Corps/Lieutenant Elizabeth Crapo. 33.55. NOAA. 33.56. NOAA. 33.57. NOAA, National Weather Service (NWS). 33.58. Integrated Ocean Drilling Program's Deep Earth Academy. Page 674 *Study Spotlight*: Integrated Ocean Drilling Program's Deep Earth Academy. Figures: 33.59. NOAA/Jennifer Stock. Pages 676–677: Joseph Stange. Figures: 34.1. photos.com. 34.2. NOAA, NGDC. 34.3. photos.com. 34.4. USSL. 34.5. NOAA, Cordell Bank National Marine Sanctuary, NOAA/Mike Goebel, NOAA/MBNMS/SIMoN/S. Lonhart, NPS. 34.6. USSL. 34.7. NASA. 34.8. Meghan Marrero. 34.9. USSL. 34.10. NOAA. 34.11. NOAA. 34.12. USSL. 34.13. NOAA. 34.14. NOAA. 34.15. NSF/Robyn Waserman. Page 685: *Antarctic Treaty*: www.coolantarctica.com; *Scroll*: photos.com. Figures: 34.16. NSF/Jeff Otten. 34.17. USSL. 34.18. NOAA. 34.19. USSL. Page 687 (TE) *Food Web*: *Arctic Fox*: NOAA;

Euphausiids/Krill: NOAA National Marine Sanctuaries; *Phytoplankton*: NOAA MESA Project; *Duck*: U.S. Fish & Wildlife Service; *Arctic Cod*: NOAA/B. Sheiko; *Bearded Seal*: NOAA; *Squid*: NOAA/NMFS/SEFSC/Andrew David; NOAA's Undersea Research Center: Phantom II ROV/Lance Horn; *Humpback Whale*: NOAA; *Polar Bear*: USGS; *Seabird*: NOAA. Figures: 34.20. NOAA. 34.21. USSL. 34.22. USSL. 34.23. USSL. 34.24. USSL. Page 689 (TE) *Food Web*: *Petrel*: NOAA; *Fish*: NOAA Southwest Fisheries Science Center; *Fur Seals*: NOAA Southwest Fisheries Science Center; *Weddell Seal*: NOAA/Vents, Korea Polar Research Institute (KOPRI); *Sperm Whale*: Hawaiian Islands Humpback Whale National Marine Sanctuary/Pieter A. Folkens; *Penguins*: NOAA; *Elephant Seal*: NMFS/OPR/Dr. Brandon Southall; *Euphausiids/Krill*: NOAA National Marine Sanctuaries; *Phytoplankton*: NOAA MESA Project; *Squid*: NOAA/NMFS/SEFSC/Andrew David; NOAA's Undersea Research Center: Phantom II ROV/Lance Horn; *Copepod*: NOAA/D.Forcucci; *Zooplankton*: South Carolina Department of Natural Resources/NOAA Office of Ocean Exploration: Charleston Bump Expedition 2003/George Sedberry; *Humpback Whale*: NOAA; *Orca*: NOAA/Mike Goebel. Figures: 34.25. NOAA/Mike Goebel. 34.26. USSL. 34.27. USSL. 34.28. USSL. 34.29. USSL. 34.30. NSF/Jon Brack. 34.31. NOAA Arctic Research Office/Dr. Kathy Crane. 34.32. NSF/Adam Jenkins. Appendix B: NIST. Appendix C: NOAA, NGDC. Appendix D: NOAA, Office of National Marine Sanctuaries. Teacher Tip, TE icons, and SE icons: photos.com.